CONTENTS

During 2006 all National Probation Service email addresses will change from gsx to gsi. For a period all gsx emails will be forwarded to the new gsi addresses.

PROBATION SERVICE & PROFESSIONAL ORGANISATIONS

Napo

4 Chivalry Road, London SW11 1HT
020-7223 4887 *fax 020-7223 3503*

e-mail initialsurname@napo.org.uk
www.napo.org.uk

General Secretary: Judy McKnight
Assistant General Secretary (campaign & pr):
Harry Fletcher
Assistant General Secretary (negotiating &
tuo): Jonathan Ledger
Assistant General Secretary (er, training, prof):
Cordell Pillay
Research and Information Officer:
Pete Bowyer (p)
Office Manager: Vacancy
Admin (ICCJ monograph, publications, training):
Jeannie Ah-Fong (p)
Admin (gen sec, neg & st, website): Jenetta
Haley
Admin (resources & reception):
Margaret Pearce
Admin (ags, neg & tuo): Alison Turnbull
Admin (ags, er, pr): Gaenor Kyffin
Admin (ags, cam & pr): Kath Falcon
Admin (membership): Alison Bonner (p)
Admin (nec & officers): Chris McGarry
Admin (reception): Jacqueline Paryag (p)
Admin (finance): Theresa Boorman
Admin (membership): James Carpenter
Chair: Mike McClelland
                    mobile 07788 974839
Vice Chair: Vicky Boroughs
Vice Chair: Mike Weston
Treasurer: Duncan Moss
Vice Chair: (CAFCASS): Sîan Griffiths

Probation Board's Association

83 Victoria Street, London SW1H 0HW
020-3008 7930 *fax 020-3008 7931*

e-mail association@probationboards.co.uk
www.probationboards.co.uk

Chief Executive: Martin Wargent
Employment Manager: Graeme Anderson
Governance Manager: Mike Caldwell
Business Manager: Sarah Gore Langton
Communications & Information Manager:
Christine Leeson
Accountant: Brian Jelley (p)

Office Manager: Liz Hogan
Admin Officer: Agnes Andrade
Admin Officer: Yasmin Jankowski-Doyle
Office Assistant: Helen Ben-Rejeb
Clerical Assistant: Kevin Lowe

National Association of Probation and Bail Hostels

2 New Walk, Totnes, Devon TQ9 5HA
tel (01803) 864781 *fax (01803) 866265*
e-mail: office@napbh.org.uk
www.napbh.org.uk

The national organisation working to support
and promote all Home Office Approved
Premises (formerly probation and bail hostels)
with particular responsibility for the voluntary
managed sector. The Association works in
partnership with other bodies concerned with
residential facilities for offenders and tackling
crime.

General Secretary: Eunice Dunkley
Chair: John Starmer

Association of Black Probation Officers

The Association's definition of Black is a
political one, which emphasises the common
experiences and common determination of
people of African, African-Caribbean and Asian
origin to oppose the effects of racism.

1st Floor, Mitre House, 223/237 Borough High
Street, London SE1 1JD
tel 020-7740 8537 *fax 020-7740 8450*

Chair: Valari Mitchell-Clarke (01509) 212904
Vice Chair: David Brydson 0121-248 6387
Treasurer: Abdallah Nagib-Ali 0118-939 3525
National Co-ordinator: Susan Roye tel 020-7740
8537
Midlands Region Convenor: Marilyn Owens-
Rawle 0116-242 3260
N. Regional Convenor: Hyacinth Gayle 0114-
272 6477
S. Regional Convenor: Natalie Johnson-Stanley
(01252) 324288

National Association of Asian Probation Staff

Encourages and maintains a support group of
members promoting an Asian perspective on
professional issues. Initiates and campaigns for
changes within the CJ System to adjust the
imbalance of disadvantage suffered by all
minority ethnic groups.

National Administrator (to be appointed),
1st Floor, Mitre House, 223/237 Borough High
Street, London SE1 1JD
tel 020-7740 8563/84 *fax 020 7740 8450*

Chair: Shamin Khan 020-740 8584
Vice Chair: Yaser Al-Kilani (01268) 412 241
Treasurer: Yaser Al-Kilani
Membership Secretary: Azra Sharif (01274)
302800
East Midlands co-ordinators: (Leicester)
Sudeep Bone 07840 923516
(Nottingham) Pervez Sadiq 0115-841 5630
S Wales co-ordinator: Melissa Macdonald-
Mohan (01792) 478169
NE co-ordinator: Humayun Shouib (01257)
260 493
SW co-ordinator: to be appointed
NW co-ordinator: Mahamooda Aslam (01204)
387699
Se & SW co-ordinators: Vacancy
(contact Melissa Macdonald for info)
E of England co-ordinator: Faiser Khan (01582)
413172
London co-ordinator: Vacancy
(contact Shamin Khan for info)
Yorks & Humberside co-ordinator: Vacancy
(contact Azra Sharif 01274 302800 for info)
Managers' portfolio: Gurdev Singh 07921
094863

LAGIP for lesbians, gay men, bisexuals and transgendered staff working in probation & family courts

Chair
Helen.Dale@manchester.probation.gsx.gov.uk
Vice Chair Rozanne.Ferber@west-
midlands.probation.gsx.gov.uk
Treasurer Andrea.Crosby-
Josephs@Haringey.gov.uk
Immediate Past Chair
Michael.Lloyd@London.probation.gsx.gov.uk
Michael.Lloyd@hertfordshire.probation.gsx.
gov.uk
Communications Officer
David.Scrivener@derbyshire.probation.gsx.uk
Conference Organiser
Graham.peacock@northumbria.probation.gsx.
gov.uk
Regnl Co-ord Wales & West
Jacquie.Linck@dyfed.powys.probation.gsx.
gov.uk
Regnl Co-ord North East
Libby.Wrighton@west-yorkhire.probation.gsx.
gov.uk
Regnl Co-ord East

Mark.Masterson@Cambridgeshire.probation.
gsx.gov.uk
Regnl Co-ord South-East
Eleanor.Levy@Surrey.probation.gsx.gov.uk
Regnl Co-ord London
Alan.Jarman@London.Probation.gsx.gov.uk

type LAGIP in Lotus Notes for menu of
addresses

Probation Service Christian Fellowship

Open to all Probation, Prison, YOT and
CAFCASS staff, and others working with
offenders and their families. Regular newsletter,
prayer days, local fellowship groups,
conferences, and fellowship weekends.
Affiliated to the Evangelical Alliance.

Contact PSCF, PO Box 783, Croydon CR9 1BT
0870 0127 3091
www.pscf.org.uk
e-mail: enquiries@pscf.org.uk

The Edridge Fund

The Edridge Fund of the National Association
of Probation Officers is a Registered Charity
that gives financial help to those in need. All
members of the service who are members of
Napo, or are eligible to be members of Napo
can benefit, as can retired staff and bereaved
partners and dependants of either of the above.
Each Napo Branch has its own Edridge
Representative. Applications are generally
made through those Representatives and
passed on to the Trustees who sit about 6/7
times a year to consider applications. These
applications have to be based on financial need.
The Secretary of the Fund is:

Richard Martin, The Limes, Lynn Road, Gayton,
King's Lynn, Norfolk PE32 1QJ
(01553) 636570 e-mail edridge@btinternet.com
www.edridgefund.org

IMPACT Probation & Welfare Officers' Branch (Irish Republic)

Probation & Welfare Officers in the Republic
of Ireland are a branch of IMPACT, the Public
Services Trade Union

N.B. When dialling from UK dial 00 353 and
omit first 0 of Irish dialling code

IMPACT, Nerney's Court, Dublin 1
01-817 1512 *fax 01-817 1501*
Asst Gen Secy (working with the branch):

Ray Ryan
e-mail moneill@impact.ie

Branch Officers
Chair: Frank O'Brien, Probation & Welfare
Service , 23 Lawrence Street, Drogheda,
Co Louth
041 980 1580
Vice Chair: David Williamson, Probation &
Welfare Service, Smithfield Chambers,
Smithfield, Dublin 7
01-817 3600
Secretary: Mary O'Sullivan, Probation &
Welfare Service, Smithfield Chambers,
Smithfield, Dublin 7
01-817 3600
Treasurer: Carol Gleeson, Probation & Welfare
Service, Roxborough House, Roxborough Road,
Limerick 061-416 125
PR Officer: Oliver Fallon, Probation & Welfare
Service, Smithfield Chambers, Smithfield,
Dublin 7
01-8173600

Respect

The UK wide membership organisation
promoting best practice amongst statutory and
independent sector projects and individuals
practitioners, trainers and consultants who
work with perpetrators of domestic violence
and their (ex) partners.

1st Floor, Downstream Building, 1 London
Bridge, London SE1 9BG
020-7022 1801 *fax 020-7022 1806*
phone line for perpetrators 0845   122 8609
e-mail info@respect.uk.net www.respect.uk.net

Social Care Councils

The General Social Care Council is the
regulatory body for the social care profession in
England. Similar organisations exist for
Northern Ireland, Scotland, and Wales (see
below). The GSCC was established by
parliament and began on 1.10.01. it issues codes
of practice, registers social care workers and
regulates social work education and training.

England
General Social Care Council, Goldings House,
2 Hay's Lane, London SE1 2HB. 020-7397 5100
fax 020-7397 5101. Information service:
020-7397 5800 *fax 020-7397 5834*
e-mail info@gscc.org.uk   www.gscc.org.uk

Northern Ireland
Northern Ireland Social Care Council, 7th Floor,

Millennium House, Great Victoria Street,
Belfast BT2 7AQ. 028-9041 7600 *fax 028-9041
7601* textphone 02890 239340
e-mail info@niscc.n-i.nhs.uk

Scotland
Scottish Social Care Council: c/o Scottish
Executive, James Craig Walk, Edinburgh
EH1 3BA. 0131-244 1949 *fax 0131-244 3494*
e-mail info-scotland@sscc.uk.com

Wales
Care Council for Wales, South Gate House,
Wood Street, Cardiff
CF1 1EW 029-2022 6257 *fax 029-2038 4764*
e-mail info@ccwales.org.uk
www.ccwales.org.uk

International Social Service of the United Kingdom

International Social Service (ISS) is a voluntary
organisation, staffed by social workers, linking
social services around the world. It exists to
help individuals and families with problems
requiring social work intervention in more than
one country. ISS is used regularly by social
workers and family court welfare officers who
require information and reports from abroad.

If service is required, it is helpful if ISS can be
consulted as early as possible. A duty officer is
available to discuss cases on the telephone and
to estimate the time required to obtain a report.
A referral guide is available on request. ISS
works through its overseas network of branches
and correspondents - thus the service is
normally provided by a national social worker
of the overseas country. A charge is levied for
the service

International Social Service of the UK, Cranmer
House, 39 Brixton Road, London SW9 6DD
020-7735 8941 *fax 020-7582 0696* e-mail
issuk@charity.vfree.com

The National Organisation for Practice Teaching

NOPT is an organisation created to provide
quality practice teaching in social work.
Membership of about 250. Provides members
for several national committees and influences
social work education. Annual, workshop based,
conference plus regional workshops

Administrator: Janet Sewart, 1 Swift Close,
Woodley, Stockport SK6 1JL
0161-430 5218 e-mail janet.sewart@nopt.org

NATIONAL OFFENDER MANAGEMENT SERVICE (NOMS)

(1st Floor Abell House, John Islip Street, London SW1P 4LH)

Director, HQ Functions	Nicolas Sanderson	020-7217 5711
		fax 020-7217 5865
Senior Personal Secretary	Barbara Bartlett	020-7217 5693

MANAGEMENT SUPPORT UNIT
(1st Floor Abell House, John Islip Street, London SW1P 4LH)

Head of Unit	Dave Thorogood	020-7217 5271
Admin Support	Kevin Hampton	020-7217 5866

CHAPLAINCY
(Horseferry House, Dean Ryle Street, London SW1P 2AW)

Chaplain General	William Noblett	020-7217 8997
Personal Secretary	Ann Waterman	020-7217 8201
Policy	Michelle Crerar	020- 7217 0951

CRIMINAL JUSTICE ACT IMPLEMENTATION UNIT
(1st Floor Horseferry House, Dean Ryle Street, London SW1P 2AW)

Head of Unit	Richard Mason	020-7217 0727
Personal Secretary	Ann Saddington	020-7217 0689

CJ Act Sentence Implementation Programme Team

Programme Manager	Brian Cox	020-7217 8200
Programme Office Manager	Adrian Wight	020-7217 8047
Programme Support	Carol Sylvester	020-7217 0708
CJA Communications Advisor	Sue Marsh	020-7217 0658
Community Orders		020-7217 0684

OASys Team
Note: *OASys: Offender Assessment System*
                                     O-DEAT: OASys Data Evaluation and Analysis Team

Head of OASys	Laura Fairweather	020-7217 0680
Personal Secretary	Ann Saddington	020-7217 0689
Personal Secretary	Majorie Baker	020-7217 0700
OASys Implementation Manager	Vacancy	020-7217 8908
OASys & IAPS Software Manager	Carole Davis	020-7217 8561
OASys IT Liaison Manager	Liz Holden	020-7217 0697
OASys Training Manager	Pauline Hill	020-7217 0696
OASys Admin Manager	Maureen Onyejeli	020 7217 0764
OASys Admin Support	Andrew Paternoster	020-7217 8165
OASys Admin Support	Comfort Owusu-Afriyie	020-7217 0691
Head of O-DEAT	Vacancy	020-7217 0699
Senior Research Officer O-DEAT	Philip Howard	020-7217 0698
Senior Research Officer O-DEAT	Michelle Burns	020-7217 8485
Senior Research Officer O-DEAT	Robin Moore	020 7217 0703
Research Officer	Nicola Vallis	020 7217 0656
Research Officer	Vacancy	020 7217 0650

Policy

OASys Policy Development Advisor	Michael Cole	020 7217 5255
OASys Policy Development Officer	Robert Hatch	020 7217 5196
OASys Operation Policy Support Mgr	Andy Munn	020 7217 5025
OASys Operation Policy Support Mgr	Caroline Nowell	020 7217 5825
OASys Operations Manager	Dave Whitfield	020 7217 5825

Custody Plus Project Team

Project Manager	Jackie Seaton	020-7217 8018
Prison Lead	Colin Hay	020 7217 8618
Project Officer	Megan Jones	020-7217 0770
Project Officer	Peter King	020-7217 0678
Project Officer	Adela Kocsprzak	020 7217 8069
Community Orders Project Support	Caroline Ndibe	020-7217 8252
Custodial Sentences Support	Alan Pinel	020 7217 8592
		fax 020-7217 8971

COMMUNITY INTEGRATION UNIT
(2 Marsham Street, London SW1P 4DF)

Head of Unit	Frances Flaxington	020-7035 0213
Senior Personal Secretary	Gráinne Barron	020-7035 0214
National Policy	Patricia Best	020-7035 0023
Regional Policy	Adrian Scott	020-7035 0012
Personal Secretary	Joan Edwards	020-7217 0020
Policy and Programmes Team	Clare Pope	020-8760 1706
Personal Secretary	Anne Read	020-8760 1823
Resettlement Estate Strategy & policy	Dick Weber	020-8774 0236
Personal Secretary	Margaret Farrow	020-8760 1849
(Amp House, Croydon)		

OFFENDER MANAGEMENT UNIT
(Horseferry House, Dean Ryle Street, London SW1P 2AW)

Head of Unit	Chris Johnson	020-7217 0794
Development Manager	Tony Grapes	020-7217 8985
Project Manager	Judith Matthews	020-72178208
Project Manager	Gareth Mercer	020-7217 8499
Administrator	Ola Haruna	020-7217 8607

PUBLIC PROTECTION & LICENSED RELEASE UNIT
[For Public Protection see NPD entry]
(1st Floor Horseferry House, Dean Ryle Street, London SW1P 2AW)

Head of Unit	John Scott	020-7217 0754
Personal Secretary	Anne Gibbons	020-7217 8681

LIFER REVIEW & RECALL SECTION
(1st Floor Abell House, John Islip Street, London SW1P 4LH)

Functions

LRRS is responsible for pre and post release issues on individuals sentenced to Life Imprisonment and Imprisonment for Public Protection (Section 225 of CJA 2003).

Casework teams 1, 2, 4, 5, 6 & 7 are responsible for pre-release cases including, Parole Board reviews, decisions on transfers to open conditions and co-ordinating release on life licence. Team 6 also deal with pre-release cases for all young offender lifers and female lifers. The distribution of casework between these teams is divided up on an alphabetical basis.

Casework team 3 is responsible for all post-release cases including monitoring the progress of life licensees in the community, recall to custody and cancellation of supervision.

The Tariff Team is responsible for implementing transitional provisions in the Criminal Justice Act (CJA) 2003 on tariffs for murder and also deal with general queries on tariff related issues.

Casework Support Team are able to provide policy and general advice on lifer review and recall issues.

Copies of the full LRRS staff list can be obtained by contacting Malcolm Willis on 020-7217 2084

Head of Unit	Alistair McMurdo	020-7217 5181
		fax 020-7217 5865
Out of hours enquiries		**08700 001 585**
Head of Casework Teams 1,2,3	Nikki Penfold	020-7217 5742
		fax 020-7217 5865
Head of Casework Teams 4,5,6,7	Amelia Wright	020-7217 5478
		fax 020-7217 5892
Head of Tariff Team	Tim Morris	020-7217 5701
		fax 020-7217 2143
Team Managers		
Team 1: B, K, Q, R, V, Y	Helen Sayeed	020-7217 5287
		fax 020-7217 5287
Team 2: E, H, L, N, Z	Eileen Drummond	020-7217 5493
		fax 020-7217 1916
Team 3: All post-release cases	Steve Watson	020-7217 5699
		fax 020-7217 5383
Team 4: D, S, T	Lynda Morley	020-7217 5007
		fax 020-2175997
Team 5: A, J, M, U, X	Lisa Burrell	020-7217 5468
		fax 020-72175517
Team 6: All women & young		
Lifers and F, I, O, W	Howard Smith	020-7217 5299
		fax 020-7217 5892
Team 7: C, G, P	Simon Alderman	020-7217 2039
		fax 020-7217 1915
Policy Advisers	Paul Jackson	020-7217 5785
	Vicky Quinn	020-7217 5526
General Enquiries	Mark Ferrigan	020-7217 5583
		fax 020-7217 5865

RELEASE AND RECALL SECTION
Functions

Consider breach reports submitted by the Probation Service in respect of determinate sentence prisoners, subject to licensed supervision and initiate revocation action where appropriate.

Liaise between the Police, Probation Service, Prison Service and the Parole Board to ensure that the recall process is managed effectively.

Consider breach reports in respect of prisoners subject to the Home Detention Curfew scheme and initiate recall action where appropriate.

Represent the Secretary of State at Parole Board oral hearings convened to consider recall decisions.

Consider Parole Board positive recommendations in respect of prisoners serving sentences of 15 years and over.

Consider parole and ERS applications for prisoners subject to deportation and serving a sentence (under the CJA 1991) of 4 years and over for either a sexual or violent offence.

Consider applications for early release on compassionate grounds.

Give advice to Probation Areas on the inclusion of additional licence conditions.

Early Release and Recall Section operate from two different sites:

All ACR and DCR caseworking teams are located on 7th Floor, Amp House, Croydon, CR0 2LX.

All other functions of the Section are carried out in rooms 125-127, 135, & 137 Abell House, John Islip Street, London SW1P 4LH

Head of Unit	Russell A'Court	020-7217 5708
Personal Secretary	Bibi Rodgers	020-7217 5708

Recall requests

All ACR recall requests are dealt with by the Croydon Office (apart from immediate level 3 recalls, these are dealt with by the Public Protection Team in the London office [see below]).

Casework Manager for all ACR Recall Teams

	Jim Watts	020-7217 5226
London		020-8774 0263
Croydon	Alistair Albosh	020-8774 0222
		fax 020-8760 1746

Cases are allocated to staff according to areas within the various regions of England and Wales. If you are enquiring about a particular offender please speak to the appropriate caseworker or a member of their team.

Recall Team 1 responsible for Humberside, London and Yorkshire Probation Regions (Humberside, London, North, South & West Yorkshire Areas)
fax for Breach Notification Reports 020-8774 0268

| EO Casework Managers | Hayley Chalkley | 020-8744 0264 |

Recall Team 2 responsible for North West & South West Probation Regions (Avon & Somerset, Cheshire, Cumbria, Devon & Cornwall, Dorset, Gloucestshire, Greater Manchester, Lancashire, Merseyside, Wiltshire)
fax for Breach Notification Reports 020-8760 1766

| EO Casework Managers | Lynne Thurgood | 020-8774 0261 |

Recall Team 3 responsible for North East, South East, East Midlands Probation Regions (Derbyshire, Durham, Hampshire, Kent, Leicester & Rutland, Lincolnshire, Northamptonshire, Northumbria, Nottinghamshire, Surrey, Sussex, Teesside, Thames Valley)
fax for Breach Notification Reports 020-8760 1746

| EO Casework Managers | Jackie King | 020-8760 1717 |
| | Daniel Bainbridge | 020-8760 1856 |

Recall Team 4 responsible for East of England, Wales & West Midlands Probation Regions (Bedfordshire, Cambridgeshire, Dyfed-Powys, Essex, Gwent, Hertfordshire, Norfolk, North & South Wales, Staffordshire, Suffolk, Warwickshire, West Mercia, West Midlands)
fax for Breach Notification Reports 020-8760 1781

EO Casework Manager	Bradley Campagnac	020-8774 0225
Oral Hearing & Further Reviews	Nuzhat Razvi	020-7217 5067
	Alison Sellers	020-7217 5546

HDC Breach Team (Home Detention Curfew)
All recalls of offenders on HDC

	Shirley Hamilton (p/t)	020-7217 5764
	Gareth Hunter	020-7217 2069
	Conroy Barnett	020-7217 5764
		fax 020-7217 2085

Public Protection Team
All MAPPA level 3 recalls, extended sentence recalls and licence conditions, electronic monitoring and satellite tracking pilot projects recalls and licence conditions, and advice on associated casework and licence conditions.

Team Leader	Lucy Derilo	020-7217 5417
	Laura Gould	020-7217 2063
	Shams Ahmed	020-7217 5205
		fax 020-7217 5223

Queries on Pre-Release casework, including Parole, for Deportees/Licence Conditions

| | James Hough | 020-7217 5276 |
| | | *fax 020-7217 5332* |

VOLUNTARY SECTOR & ASSISTED PRISON VISITS UNIT
(2 Marsham Street, London SW1P 4DF)

| Head of Unit | Jo Gordon | 020-7035 3628 |

EO	Elaine Castle	020-7035 0209
Voluntary Sector Liaison Officer	Carol Buckland	020-7035 0212
HMPS Nat Voluntary Sector Co-ord	Neil Moore	020-7035 0210

Assisted Prison Visits   Alan Jones   0121-626 2208
(APVU Fiveway House, Islington Row, Middleway, Birmingham, B15 1SD)

NOMS, APPLIED PSYCHOLOGY GROUP

310 Cleland House, Page Street, London SW1P 4LN
020 7217 6890 *fax 020-7217 6879*

Head of Unit	Prof Graham Towl	
Personal Secretary	Marie Davies	6890
Deputy head of Unit	Prof David Crighton	
Personal Secretgary	Victoria Bell	6843
Principal Psychologist	Derval Ambrose	6981

DRUG STRATEGY UNIT - Health and Offender Partnerships, NOMS

3rd Floor Abell House, John Islip Street, London SW1P 4LH

Functions
Implementation of the NOMS Drug Strategy; oversight and development of CARATs and treatment policy (and collaboration with Prison Health over clinical services); mandatory and voluntary drug testing policy; supply reduction; research.

Head of Unit	Martin Lee	020-7217-5045
Personal Secretary	Michelle Sandilands	020-7217-2080
Head of Supply Reduction & Testing	Jacqueline Townley	020-7217-5834
Head of Treatment Programme Policy	Cath Pollard	020-7217-5431

Head of Strategic, Aim 5 Liaison
& Ministerial Briefing   Simon George   020-7217-5565

HM PRISON SERVICE – OPERATIONAL DIRECTORATE

7th Floor Abell House, John Islip Street, London SW1P 4LH

Offending Behaviour Programmes Unit

Functions
Provision and development of offending behaviour programmes.

Head of Unit	Trish Wincote	020-7217
5238/5338		
Personal Secretary	Veronica Persaud	020-7217 5238
		fax 020-7217 5871

Sex Offender Treatment Programme (SOTP)

Head of SOTP	Ruth Mann	020-7217 5059
(London)		
		01924-246164
(Wakefield)		
Healthy Relationships Programme	Rebecca Milner	020-7217 5638
Adapted Programmes	Fiona Williams	020-7217 5639
Research Analyst	Vacant	020-7217 5117
		fax 020-72172005

High Intensity Programmes Team

Head of HIP	Gill Attrill	020-7217 5586
Personal Secretary	Rita Bothwick	020-7217 5261
Chromis	Adam Carter	020-72175075
Chromis	Fiona Stuart	020-72175637
CSCP	Vacant	020-7217 5347
		fax 020-7217 5871
DSPD, HRP & SARN	Caroline Schofield	020-7217 2102

Audit and Operational Support

Head of Audit & Operational Support	Adrian Smith	020-7217 5564
Audit and Operational Support	Kevan Dunn-Beeching	020-7217 2149
	Phil Richards	020-7217 2149
	Trevor Swinburne	020-7217 2149
Audit & General Admin Duties	Sarah Lowson	020-7217 5796
Personal Secretary	Rita Bothwick	020-7217 5261
		fax 020-7217 5392

Programmes Development

Head of Programme Development	Jo Day	020-7217 5905
CALM	Janet Creighton	020-7217 2245
Cognitive Skills Booster	Vacancy	020-7217 5660
FOR Programme/Resettlement	David Pidwell	020-7217 5401
Motivation	Judy Faulkner	07968 553882
Evaluation	Rosie Travers	01704 541796
Personal Secretary	Rita Bothwick	020-7217 5261
		fax 020-7217 5392

Training & Support

Head of Training & Support	Sue Porto	020-7217 1888
Training/TM/Supt/Video Monitoring	Peter Dowling	020-7217 5662
	Paul Davies	020-7217 5662
	Tracy Pearson	020-7217 5662
	Kerrie Sherman	020-7217 5662
Training Events Co-odinator	Sharn Kaur	020-7217 5662

Policy/Administration Team

Head	Martin Stephens	020-7217 5921
Policy & Staff	Vacancy	020-7217 5192
Budget Manager	Richard Child	020-7217 5297
Personal Secretary	Veronica Persaud	020-7217 5238
		fax 020-7217 5871

Resettlement/Throughcare Issues

Head of Resettlement/Th'care Issues	Al Reid	020-7217 5119

NATIONAL PROBATION DIRECTORATE

From March/April 2006 phone no's will change when NPD moves to another building. The new address will be: Abell House, John Islip Street, London SW1P 4LH. NPD staff details will be available on the EPIC (Intranet) directory.

Horseferry House, Dean Ryle Street, London SW1P 2AW

The National Directorate exercises on behalf of the Home Secretary all his responsibilities for the probation service in England and Wales. The National Probation Service for England and Wales consists of the National Directorate and 42 local Probation Boards.

The standard way of sending emails to staff is Firstname.Surname@homeoffice.gsi.gov.uk in some instances email addresses may include a number e.g. Firstname.Surname3@homeoffice.gsi.gov.uk it is best to check with the individual.

For any further enquires
tel 020-7217 0659 (NPD automated switchboard)
e-mail NPD.publicenquiry@homeoffice.gsi.gov.uk

Director of Probation's Private Office

Director of Probation	Roger Hill	020-7217 0650
Diary Secretary	Jan Pogmore	020-7217 0737
Private Secretary	Ahmed Azam	020-7217 8656
Assistant Private Secretary	Mike Smith	020-7217 0829
Private Office Administration Officer	Toby Cottrell	020-7217 8445
Information Security & Compliance	Anna Cevidalli	020-7217 8584
Assistant Staff Officer	Nimira Karachiwalla	020-7217 8484
Administration Staff Officer	Shaila Hussain	020-7217 0652
		fax 020-7217 0660

Communications Team

Head of HQ Services	George Barrow	020-7217 8544
Head of Communications	Susan Lord	020-7217 8696
Senior Communications Officer	Tara Hart	020-7217 8409
Senior Communications Officer	Phil McDonough	020-7217 8483
Communications Officer	Joeleen Anderson	020-7217 8510
Administration Officer	Jay Das	020-7217 0653
		fax 020-7217 0823

Business Development Unit

Head of Business Development Unit	David Griffiths	020-7217 0759
Business Development Manager	Sam Latham	020-7217 8118
Business Development Project	David Solomons	020-7217 8320
Business Administration Support	Arlene Munir	020-7217 8316
		fax 020-7217 0660

Offender Management Unit

Head of Unit	Richard Mason	020-7217 0727
Personal Secretary	Ann Saddington	020-7217 0689

The 4 remaining vacancies in the unit will be appointed soon

Criminal Justice Act Implementation Unit & OASys (now part of NOMS)

Head of Unit	Chris Johnson	020-7217 0794
Personal Secretary	Ann Saddington	020-7217 0689

Criminal Justice Act Sentence Implementation Programme Team

Programme Manager	Brian Cox	020-7217 8200
Programme Office Manager	Adrian Wight	020-7217 8047
Programme Support	Carol Sylvester	020-7217 0708
CJA Communications Advisor	Sue Marsh	020-7217 0658

Custody Plus	Megan Jones	020-7217 0770
Custody Plus	Peter King	020-7217 0678
Custody Plus	Adela Kacspzrak	020-7217 8069
Custody Plus Project Manager	Jackie Seaton	020-7217 8018
Project Team Prison Lead	Colin Hay	020-7217 8616
Custody Plus Project Support	Caroline Ndibe	020-7217 8252
Custody Plus Project Support	Alan Pinel	020-7217 8592
		fax 020-7217 0823

Offender Assessment System (OASys) Business Team

Head of OASys	Laura Fairweather	020 7217 0680
PS to Head of OASys	Ann Saddington	020 7217 0689
OASys NPS Operational Manager	Vacancy	020 7217 8908
Personal Secretary	Marjorie Baker	020 7217 0700
OASys Training Manager	Pauline Hill	020 7217 0696
IT Liaison Manager	Liz Holden	020 7217 0697
IT Liaison Manager	Carole Davis	020 7217 0696
OASys HMPS Operational Manager	Dave Whitfield	020 7217 5825
OASys HMPS Operational Support Manager	Andy Munn	020 7217 5825
OASys HMPS Operational Support Manager	Caroline Nowell	020 7217 5825
OASys Policy Development Advisor	Michael Cole	020 7217 5255
OASys Policy Development Advisor	Maureen Onyejeli	020 7217 0764
OASys Policy Development Officer	Robert Hatch	020 7217 5196
OASys Office Manager	Andrew Paternoster	020 7217 0701
OASys Administration Support	Comfort Owusu-Afriyie	020 7217 0691
		fax 020 7217 8971

OASys Data Evaluation & Analysis Team (O-DEAT)

Head of O-DEAT	Vacancy	020 7217 0699
Senior Research Officer	Michelle Burns	020 7217 8485
Senior Research Officer	Phillip Howard	020 7217 0698
Senior Research Officer	Robin Moore	020 7217 0703
Research Officer	Vacancy	020 7217 8056
Research Officer	Vacancy	020 7217 8056
		fax 020 7217 8971

Interventions Unit

| Head of Interventions | Sarah Mann | 020-7217 8432 |
| Personal Secretary | Julie Taylor | 020-7217 8546 |

Community Reintegration Team

Head of Community Reintegration	Meg Blumsom	020-7217 0673
Personal Secretary	Carolyn Gale	020-7217 0686
Programme Implementation Manager	Roger Stevens	020-7217 8283
Programme Implementation Manager	Randel Barrows	020-7217 8323
Programme Implementation Manager	Janet Corcoran	020-7217 8877
Basic Skills	Julie Welch	020-7217 8958
Business Support & Communications Manager	John MacGregor	020-7217 8520
Resettlement Policy Developer	Eldon Ward	020-7217 8992
Policy Advisor	Marcus Smart	020-7217 0766
Development Activities	Seb Falk	020-7217 8448
Events Organiser	Mark Chidwick	020-7217 0681
Events Organiser	Liam Carolan	020-7217 0685
		fax 020-7217 8496

Intensive Interventions Team

| Head of Intensive Interventions | Claire Wiggins | 020-7217 8646 |

Personal Secretary	Carolyn Gale	020-7217 0686
Drug Testing Development Manager	Robin Brennan	020-7217 0916
Secretarial Support	Patrica Merrony	020-7217 8989
Drugs & Alcohol Interventions Manager	Fiona Bauermeister	020-7217 0768
Drug & Alcohol	Robert Stanbury	020-7217 0767
Drug & Alcohol	Richard Lockwood	020-7217 8003
PPO	Peter Pettit	020-7035 0141
Policy Advisor	Edward Griffin	020-7217 0760
		fax 020-7217 8496

Offender Behaviour Programme Team

Head of Offender Behaviour Programme	Vacancy	020-7217
National Prog Implementation Mgr	Sandra Fieldhouse	020-7217 0674
Prog Implementation Training Mgr	Tudor Williams	020-7217 8068
Prog Implementation Mgr	David Skyner	020-7217 8044
Prog Implementation Mgr	Diane Anderson	020-7217 8895
Prog Implementation Mgr	Sue Pearce	020-7217 8081
Software Business Supt Mgr	Liz Calvert	020-7217 8046
Head of Psychology & Evaluation	Danny Clark	020-7217 0675
Principal Psychologist	Joanne Day	020-7217 8999
Senior Psychologist	Karl Williams	020-7217 8991
Psychology Assistant	Nina Marvan	020-7217 0676
Psychologist's Assistant	Sinead Blomfield	020-7217 8813
Psychologist's Assistant	Wendy Smith-Yau	020-7217 8148
Research Officer	Victoria Dawson Wheeler	020-7217 8815
Events Manager	Sophia Akram	020-7217 0803
Events Manager	Ruth Taylor	020-7217 0677
Executive Officer	Lesley Smith	020-7217 8336
Events Organiser	Ali Moghal	020-7217 0679
Training Development Advisor	Eileen Davis	020-7217 8211
Training Development Advisor	Alex Law	020-7217 8211
Training Development Advisor	Emma Myatt	020-7217 8211
Training Development Advisor	Karen Townend	020-7217 8211
Diversity & Women	Christine Okiya	020-7217 0687
		fax 020-7217 0693

Human Resources Unit

| Head of HR Team | Richard Cullen | 020-7217 0731 |
| Snr Personal Secretary to Head of Unit | Ros Tatham | 020-7217 0729 |

Training & Development

Head of Training & Development	Paula Cairney	020-7217 0728
Nat HR Mgr Workforce Planning Info	Helen Smith	020-7217 0738
Asst HR Mgr Workforce Planning Info	Stefan Hendry	020-7217 8556
HR Asst Workforce Planning Info	James Ings	020-7217 8500
Training, Devpt & Events Co-ord	Verna Chung	020-7217 0791
Training, Devpt & Events Co-ord	Hanifa Makda	020-7217 8242
Manager Chiefs/Chairs	Martin Murphy	020-7217 8089
HR Manager	Kelly Collins	020-7217 0741
Project manager	James Cleary	020-7217 8777
Chiefs and Chairs Support	Simon Edwards	020-7217 0740

Policy, Pay & Reward

Head of Policy, Pay & Reward Manager	Iain McIntosh	020-7217 8768
HR Senior Manager	Diane Battershield	020-7217 8661
Health & Safety Manager	Kathryn Ball	020-7217 8954
Health & Safety Assistant Manager	Brenda Pendlebury	020-7217 8736

Policy Development Manager	Sara Pearson	020-7217 8362
Policy Assistant Manager	Kishwar Hyde	020-7217 8589
Policy Assistant	Beverly Warren	020-7217 8343
Adelphi Data Officer	Jason Metsagharun	020-7217 8128
HR Office Manager	Roger Davis	020-7217 0730
HR Recruitment	Adaremi Lamina	020-7217 0790
HR Recruitment	Davinder Rai	020-7217 8803
HR Officer	Vishal Thakrar	020-7217 0788
HR Administration	Stephen Gale	020-7217 0733
		fax 020-7217 0796

Prospects Unit

Programme Director	Lynn Oates	020-7217 0714
National Technical Manager	Mike Kilbane	020-7217 0714
Programme Office Manager	Denis Penna	020-7217 8693
Prospects Prog. Co-ord	Susan Mehmet	020-7217 8572
Property Manager	Ian Sharpe	020-7217 0714
		fax 020-7217 0823

Regions & Performance Management Unit

Head of Unit	Roger McGarva	020-7217 8244
Personal Secretary	Marie Malone	020-7217 0657
Regional Support	Daniel Smith	020-7217 8095

Performance Information & Audit Team

Head of PIA Team	Paris Mikkides	020-7217 8812
Dep Head of PIA Team	Ed Stradling	020-7217 0758
Corporate Risk Manager	Ayodele Kayode	020-7217 8395
Information Manager	Stephen Spurden	01522 580445
Project Co-ordinator	Keith Ward	020 7217 8801
Information Officer	Jeff Endean	020-7217 8261
		fax 020-7217 8986

Delivery and Quality Team

Head Of Delivery and Quality	Christine Lawrie	020-7217 8183
		or 07775 0817513
Enforcement Policy Manager	Helen West	07770 635 303
Delivery and Quality Manager	Kevin Robinson	07717 662 383
Enforcement and Compliance Policy Officer	Andy Frost	07767 770 213
Implementation Manager	Joanne Trevitt	07798 607 891
Implementation Manager	Les Smith	07798 607 828
		fax 020-7217 8986

Equality and Diversity Unit

Head of Diversity	Marg Harris	020 7217 8609
Diversity Manager	Rory Heap	020-7217 8009
Diversity Manager	Olivia Jamison	020-7217 8878
Diversity Administration	Verona Walcott	020-7217 8669
Diversity Administration	Bola Ninalowo	020-7217 8562
		fax 020-7217 8986

Regional Managers
Wales

	Ged Bates	07818 016458
	ged.bates2@homeoffice.gsi.gov.uk	

Wales

	Ian Fox	07818 077250
	ian.fox@south-wales.probation.gsx.gov.uk	

London	Sue Carrie	020-7217 8218
	sue.carrie@homeoffice.gsi.gov.uk	
Yorkshire & Humberside	Vacancy	
East Midlands	Tony Raban	07876 478686
	tony.raban@nottinghamshire.probation.gsx.gov.uk	
East Midlands	Sharon Higson	07770 941745
	sharon.higson@leicestershire.probation.gsx.gov.uk	
North East	Stuart McPhillips	07876 478 687
	stuart.mcphillips@northumbria.probation.gsx.gov.uk	
East of England	Tom McQuillan	07876 478 691
	tom.mcquillan@essex.probation.gsx.gov.uk	
North West	Andrew Underdown	07876 478 685
	andrew.underdown@manchester.probation.gsx.gov.uk	
West Midlands	Colin Pinfold	07770 940505
	colin.pinfold@west-midlands.probation.gsx.gov.uk	
South West	Di Askwith	07876 478 688
	di.askwith@homeoffice.gsi.gov.uk	
South East	Vacancy	

fax 020-7217 8986

Public Protection (now part of Public Protection & Licensed Release Unit, NOMS)

Hd of Public Protection & Licensed Release	John Scott	020-7217 0754
Personal Secretary	Anne Gibbons	020-7217 8681
Deputy Head	Tessa Webb	020-7217 0935
Deputy Head	Gordon Davison	020-7217 8514

MAPPA/Mental Health

Policy Manager (MAPPA)	Tim Bryan	020-7217 0747
Policy Manager (Mental Health)	Chris Potter	020-7217 0692
Support Officer	Jaspreet Bansal	020-7217 8547
Administrator	Vacant	020-7217 8052

Casework Team

Head of Casework	Bettina Crossick	020-7217 0746
Senior Case Manager	Andrew Wills	020-7217 8121
Senior Case Manager	Jackie Wilson	020-7217
Case Manager	Janet Gregory	020-7217 0750
Case Manager (p/t)	Carly Jeffrey	020-7217 0744
Case Worker	Iain Cuthbert	020-7217 0748
Administration Officer	Melissa Thomas (mat leave)	020-7217 0637
Administration Officer	Maria Diez	020-7217 0749

fax 020-7217 0756

Sex Offender Strategy & Programmes

Head of Sex Offender Programmes	David Middleton	020-7217 0672
Programme Manager	Elizabeth Hayes	020-7217 8401
Programme Manager	Janet Cockerham	020-7217 8561
Consultant	Paddy Doyle	020-7217 8561
Support Officer	Lissa McDonald	020-7217 8750

Domestic Abuse, Child Protection, Victims

Policy Manager	Eleanor Marshall	020-7217 0670
Policy Manager	Hilary Collyer	020-7217 8565
Policy Developer	Vacancy	020-7217 0639
Policy Developer	Angela Colyer	020-7217 0702

Support Officer	Archana Patel	020-7217 8031

Supported Witness Section

Head of Section	Malcolm Ayers	0709 238 3541
Support Officer	Daniella Parascandolo	020-7217 8612
		fax 020-7217 0842

Pre & Post Release

Head of Team	Jo Thompson	020-7217 8823
Policy Lead - HMPS	Steve McCarthy	020-7217 5551
Policy Manager	Akile Osman	020-7217 8058
Policy Developer - HMPS	Paul Wright	020-7217 5136
Policy Developer	Vacancy	020-7217 0763
Administrator	Sîan Bachou	020-7217 8576

Approved Premises

Head of Team	Felicity Hawksley	020-7217 0773
Policy Manager	Mike Tennant	020-7217 8226
Policy Manager	Cathy Earlam	020-7217 0824
Policy Developer (p/t)	Carly Jeffrey	020-7217 0744
Administrator	Vacancy	020-7217 0771

Network Support Team

Head of Team/Staff Officer to Head of Unit	Vacancy	020-7217 0752
Support Officer	John Race	020-7217 8573
Administrator	Patricia Christopher	020-7217 8597
Personal Secretary to Head of Unit	Anne Gibbons	020-7217 8681
		fax 020-7217 0799

HER MAJESTY'S INSPECTORATE OF PROBATION

Functions

HM Inspectorate of Probation reports independently to the Home Secretary on the work and performance of the National Probation Service and Youth Offending Teams. HM Inspectorate of Probation's aims are to contribute to improved performance in NPS and YOTs through inspection work; to contribute to policy and service delivery by providing advice and by disseminating good practice; actively to promote race equality and wider diversity issues; and to promote the overall effectiveness of the Criminal Justice Service partly by collaborative work with other Inspectorates.

HM Inspectorate of Probation are based in two locations, in London and Manchester, at the addresses indicated below. London staff are listed together with their extension number. Staff based in Manchester are indicated by 'mcr', and the main Manchester number, as below, should be used for contacting them.

London

2nd Floor, Ashley House, 2 Monck Street, London SW1P 2BQ
General Enquiries 020 7035 2203 *fax 020 7035 2237*
020 7035 + ext

Manchester

6th Floor, Trafford House, Chester Road, Stretford, Manchester M32 0RS
0161-869 1300 YOT Inspections 0161-869 1301 *fax 0161-869 1350*

Staff can be contacted by firstname.surname@homeoffice.gsi.gov.uk
General enquiries to HMIPenquiries@homeoffice.gsi.gov.uk

Staff

HM Chief Inspector of Probation	Andrew Bridges	ext 2200
Personal Secretary	Ann Hurren	ext 2202

Assistant Chief Inspectors

YOT Inspection Programme	Liz Calderbank	mcr
Effective Suprvn Inspection Programme	John Hutchings	ext 2234
Thematic Inspections	Alan MacDonald	mcr
Information & Development	Peter Ramell	ext 2233

Inspectors

	Jane Attwood	mcr
	Helen Boocock	mcr
	Mark Boother	ext 2222
	John Browne	mcr
	Rose Burgess	ext 2213
	Helen Cash	ext 2221
	Ben Clark	ext 2229
	Julie Fox	mcr
	Jude Holland	mcr
	Sally Lester	mcr
	Shirley Magilton	ext 2224
	Ian Menary	mcr
	Joy Neary	mcr
	Nigel Scarff	ext 2217
	Joe Simpson	ext 2219
	Andy Smith	ext 2218
	Ray Wegrzyn	mcr
	Kate White	ext 2216

Full-Time YOT Inspectors

	Steve Glass	mcr
	Mike Mullis	mcr
	Karen McKeown	ext 2223

Practice Assessors

	Jo Bergdahl	ext 2215
	Penny Davies	mcr
	Stephanie Mason	ext 2212
	Nicola Molloy	ext 2227
	Nikki Shave	ext 2210

Inspection Support

Programme Manager	Andy Bonny	mcr
Deputy Programme Manager	Lynn Carroll	mcr
Support Officer	Pippa Bennett	mcr
Support Officer	Beverley Folkes	ext 2209
YOT Support Manager	Grace Dickin	mcr
YOT Inspection Support	Vacancy	mcr
YOT Inspection Support	Natalie Dewsnap	mcr
Inspection Support Officer	Deborah Hood	mcr
Inspection Support Officer	Junior Rhone	mcr
Publications Officer	Zach Rathore	mcr
Proof Reader	Jean Hartington	mcr
Finance Manager	Helen Wright	ext 2203
Information Manager	Kevin Ball	mcr
Asst Information Manager	Vacancy	
Information Enquiries	Paul Cockburn	ext 2207

REGIONAL TRAINING CONSORTIA

1. **East of England Probation Training & Development Consortium**
Crowland House, Withersfield Road
Haverhill, Suffolk CB9 9LA
tel (01440) 705875 *fax (01440) 761399*

   Dermot McCarthy (director)
   Alan Plumb (nvq centre mgr)
   Elizabeth Morgan (devpt mgr)
   Graham Fitchett (regnl trainer)
   Linda Hacon (regnl trainer)
   Nikki Middleton (regnl trainer)
   Janeen Sengendo (regnl trainer)
   Karen Burnell (dips prog mgr)
   Penny Rickman (eff pract mgr)
   Emma Driver (admin)
   Lesley Kibble (admin)
   Karen Naylor (admin)
   Charmian Thompson (admin)

2. **London Probation Area Human Resources Development**
Mitre House, 223-237 Borough High Street, London SE1 1JD
tel 020 7740 8500 *fax 020 7740 8448*
e mail
firstname.surname@london.probation.gsx.gov.uk
   Tim Pagan (hd of hrd)
   Andrew Hillas (hrd mgr, Dips)
   Angela Brown (mgr devpt & assessment centre)
   Mike Jones (hrd mgr effective pract)
   Kay Bixby (hrd mgr admin)
   Susan Carcavella Senior (hrd admin)
   Elizabeth Stuart (hrd admin)
   Graham Wheeler (learning & devpt advr N, Dips)
   Keith Smith (learning & devpt advr S, Dips)
   Krystyna Pilinski (learning & devpt advr E, Dips)
   Vicki Idusohan (learning & devpt advr W, Dips)
   Cicely Sawyer (learning & devpt advr, Dips)

   Delise Anderson (hrd mgr learning & devpt)
   Jan Read (l&d advr, eff pract)
   Andrea Kelly (learning & devpt advr, ld)
   Shula Koch (learning & devpt advr, ld)
   Delphine Duff (eff pract trainer/developer)
   John Edmead (eff pract trainer/developer)

   Michaela Duke (eff pract trainer/developer)
   Judith Granata (eff pract trainer/developer)
   Vacancy (eff pract trainer/developer)
   Vacancy (eff pract trainer/developer)

   Jo Horlock (internal verifier/trainer)
   Brian Morris (learning & devpt advr, nvq centre)
   Nushrat Sayeed-Hussain (learning & devpt advr, nvq centre)
   Cheryl Felgate (learning supt wrkr/trainer)
   Peggy Lynch (learning supt wrkr/trainer)
   Patricia Epie (learning supt wrkr/trainer)
   Vacancy (hrd admin)
   Carole St John-Hadley (hrd admin)
   Rosemary Ayree TEMP (hrd admin)
   Judy Coleman (p, exec asst to hd of hrd)
   Vacancy (learning centre admin)
   David Forbes (devpt off OASys)
   Ray Crews (OASys trainer)

   Externally Funded Posts
   Vacancy (p, learning centre admin)
   Vacancy (pso trainer)
   Vacancy (pso trainer)
   Vacancy (pso trainer)
   Vacancy (pso trainer)
   Vacancy (pso trainer)

3. **North East Probation Training & Development Consortium**
c/o Northumbria Probation Area
Dene House, Durham Road
Low Fell, Gateshead NE9 5AE
tel 0191-491 1693 *fax 0191-491 3726*

   Angus McIntosh (consortium director)
   Mary E Smith (eff pract training mgr)
   Martyn Shakespeare (DipPS mgr)
   Julie Peaden (snr consortium admin)
   Dawn Shacklady (eff pract admin asst)
   Maria Burl (DipPS admin asst)
   e-mail firstname.surname@northumbria.probation.gsx.gov.uk

4. **North West Training Consortium**
Sefton House, 1 Molyneux Way
Old Roan, Liverpool L10 2JA
tel 0151-526 1346 *fax 0151-526 0692*
e-mail firstname.surname@merseyside.probation.gsx.gov.uk

   Lesley Thompson (director)
   Julia Summerfield (rdac mgr)
   Irene Doyle (consortium admin)

   Effective Practice Training Unit
   Lime House, The Green
   Wetherall, Carlisle CA4 8EW

tel (01228) 564638
e-mail firstname.surname@cumbria.
probation.gsx.gov.uk

Jon Lear (ept mgr)
Gillian Anderson (ept admin)

5. **South East Regional Probation Training Consortium**
College House, Woodbridge Road
Guildford, Surrey GU1 4RS
tel (01483) 304963 *fax (01483) 440601*

Avtar Singh (acting director)
Vacancy (nvq centre mgr)
Judy Maughan (DipPS mgr)
Bruce Cunningham (effective pract training mgr)
Carol Morgan (cj devpt mgr)
Jill Tonks (pso devpt mgr)
Peter Hilling (business mgr)
Sandra Stevens (nvq/tpo co-ord)
Jenny Pullen (accredited progs co-ord)
Helen McIntyre (pso co-ord)

6. **South West Training Consortium**
c/o Gloucestershire Probation Area
Bewick House, 1 Denmark Road
Gloucester GL1 3HW
tel (01452) 426733 *fax (01452) 426967*

Martin Smith (director)
Gill Martin (admin)

NVQ Centre
c/o Avon & Somerset Probation Area
St Lawrence Lodge,
37 Chamberlain Street
Wells BA5 2PQ
tel (01749) 683656 *fax (01749) 672169*

Jane McLaughlin (DipPS prog devpt mgr)
mobile 07888 720596
e-mail jgm_mclaughlin@yahoo.co.uk
Geunor Taverner (nvq centre mgr)

mobile 0794 152 3377
e-mail gtaverner@yahoo.com

Helen Spurrell (admin)

Effective Practice Training
c/o Dorset Probation, Wadham House
50 High West Street, Dorchester DT1 1UT
Barry Cooney (eff pract training mgr)
mobile 07845 915083
Wendy Towers (admin)
(01305) 269416

Liz Playle (regional training officer)
mobile 07859 391791
email: liz.playle@devon-
cornwall.probation.gsx.gov.uk

7. **Midlands Consortium**
Stowe Court, Stowe Street
Lichfield , Staffs W13 6AQ
tel (01543) 416776 *fax (01543) 419361*
e-mail firstname.surname@staffordshire.
probation.gsx.gov.uk

Ian Macnair (director),
Ellen Wallace (ops mgr)
Natalie Ryan (eff pract rgnl trg mgr)
Joanna Bell (eff pract trg mgr)
John Richards (eff pract trg mgr)
Dawn Bakewell (office mgr)
Natalie Carroll (pa)
Hannah Barrett (acc progs admin)
Vacancy (acc progs admin)
Jane Cook (finance & clerical off)
Lesley Rawlinson (clerical off)
Beverley Tooth (recep/clerical off)

Programme Unit
Atherstone Probation Office
1 Market Street
Atherstone, Warks CV9 1ET
tel (01827) 713813 *fax (01827) 718677*
e-mail firstname.surname@
warwickshire.probation.gsx.gov.uk

Michelle Walters (learning & devpt mgr qual trg)
Eve Brown (learning & devpt mgr voc awards)
Rob Palmer (trg & devpt off)
Elaine Bewitt (voc awards admin)
Lucy Wheale (qual trg admin)
Sarah Ford (pso admin)

SPO/Lecturers & Pract Devpt Trainers
at various locations
Vacancy (spo/lecturer)
Avril Aust (spo/lecturer)
Mike Octigan (spo/lecturer)
Toni Baptiste (pract devpt trainer)
Kath Beattie (pract devpt trainer)
Sarah Williams (pract devpt trainer)

8. **Yorkshire & Humberside Consortium**
2nd Floor, Devonshire House
38 York Place, Leeds LS1 2ED
tel 0113 244 6044 *fax 0113 245 1394*
e-mail yhpcgen@yhpc.co.uk

Steve Cosgrove (consortium director)
Helen Kirkpatrick (nvq co-ord)
Liz Burgess (dep nvq co-ord)
David Atkinson (eff pract training mgr)
Phil Clare (DipPS progr mgr)
Nicola Woodward (office mgr)
Janet Marchant (admin)

Janette Ridsdale (admin)
Claire Stratton (nvq admin)

9. **Wales Training Consortium**
    Consortium Hyfforddiant Cymru
    4-7 The Broadway, Pontypridd CF37 1BA
    tel (01443) 494337 *fax (01443) 494285*

    Angela Cossins (consortium director)
    Jackie Leggett (hrd mgr)
    Nigel Miller (eff pract training mgr)
    Rob Thomas (qualifications mgr)
    Ceinwen Gwilyn (rto qualifications)
    Sheryn Anthony (rto hrd)
    Vacancy (rto ept)
    Kairen West (office mgr)
    Chris Metcalfe (admin)
    Huw Price (admin)
    Elaine, Cowmeadow (admin)

CIRCLES OF SUPPORT AND ACCOUNTABILITY

Circles of Support and Accountability are a Home Office funded project with three pilot sites. The projects are designed to support, monitor and maintain high risk, high need sex offenders living in our communities. Volunteers are recruited and trained to provide support networks for these men to reduce emotional loneliness and isolation, key factors related to re-offending. Circles of Support and

Accountability work in partnership with Police, Probation and the Prison Service.

1. **Hampshire and Thames Valley Circles**
    (managed by Quaker Peace and Social Witness)
    140a Broadway, Didcot, Oxon OX11 8RJ
    tel (01235) 816050 *fax (01235) 517873*
    circlesqpsw@btconnect.com

    Wilson, Chris (project mgr)
    Saunders, Rebekah (project co-ord)
    Macrae, Ron (circles co-ord)
    Williams, Dominic (circles co-ord)
    Holmes, Anne (office mgr)

2. **Lucy Faithfull Foundation**
    Wolvercote Centre, 46 - 48 East Street
    Epsom, Surrey KT17 1HB
    tel 0870 774 6354 *fax (01372) 847162*
    tlffwol@lucyfaithfull.org

    Sauze, Simon (progrs mgr)
    Parrott, Blair (circles co-ord)

3. **Greater Manchester**
    (managed by Community Chaplaincy)
    Methodist Central Hall
    Oldham Street, Manchester M1 1JT
    tel 01612 362462

    Lorimer, Charlotte (circles co-ord)
    charlotte.lorimer@hmps.gsi.gov.uk
    gmcc@surefish.co.uk

MENTAL HEALTH UNIT

Home Office, 2nd Floor, Fry Building, 2 Marsham Street, London SW1P 4DF
0870 000 1585 or 020-7035 + ext
fax 020-7035-8974/8975/8979 (phone to find appropriate fax)

Cases are allocated to staff according to the first letter of their surname. If you are enquiring about a particular patient please speak, in the first instance, to the appropriate Caseworker. All extensions can be dialled direct by prefacing the number shown with 020-7035 ..... If you have difficulty please ring the Home Office switchboard on 0870 000 1585 and ask for the Mental Health Unit, quoting the patient's surname. This number should also be contacted in cases of emergency outside normal office hours.

Title	Name	ext
Heads of Unit	Elizabeth Moody/ Penny Snow	1478/4974
Secretary	Leni Gayle	1483
Hd of Casewrkng	Nigel Shackleford	1479
Secretary	Valerie Taylor (p)	1481

Title	Name	Casework allocation *(Prison Transfer allocation shown in brackets)*	ext
Caseworkers	Joanne Terry	A	1487
(EO) *also*	Deborah Mortimer	Ba-Bid	1465
responsible for	Harpreet Spall	Bie-Buc	1464
s47 transfer of	Patrick O'Dwyer	Bud-Bz, Sa-Sim	1473
sentenced	Suzanne Bardwell	Ca-Collins J	1456
prisoners	Andy Brook	Collins K-Cz, Rp-Rz, U, V	1457
	Burty Valydon	Da-Dil, N	1454
	Mel Flint	Dim-Dz, E, Q, X, Z	1453
	Stephn Lott	F, Woo-Wz	1485
	Vacancy	Ga-Gav, Hic-Hz	1509
	Claire Ratcliffe	Gaw-Gz	1507
	Pat Dunwell	Ha-Hib	1506
	Vidia Narayan-Beddoes	J, I	1489
	Mike Turner	K, Lm-Lz	1490
	Sylvia Williams	La-Ll, Mosm-Mz	1511
	Christina Clark	Ma – McGi	1513
	Martine Green	McGj-Mosl	1510
	Alison Caldow	O, Y, Williams I-Won	1488
	Fiona Mcghie	Pa-Pri	1502
	Philip Drummond	Prj-Pz, Wa-Williams H	1499
	Christian Secondis	Ra-Ro	1467
	Jane Stearman	Sin-Sul	1468
	Sarah Henderson	Sum-Sz, T	1472
Snr Caseworkers	Greg Nanda	A, F, O, U, Woo-Wz	1468
(HEO) *also*	Lyndel Grover	Ba-Bra, Ra-Ro	1463
responsible for	Kelly Foreman	Brb-Bz, C, Rp-Rz, V	1458
s48 transfer of	Brenda Storey	D, E, Hooe-HZ, N, Q, X, Z	1450
remand prisoners	Lisa Burrell	G, Ha-Hood	1498
	Jessicaa Moorcroft	I, J, K, Lew-Lz, Sum-Sz, Trb-Tz	1493
	Delores Stratton/		
	Geraldine Marsh (p)	La-Lev, M	1514
	Jacqui Woodward-Smith	P, Wa-Won, Y	1504
	Ros Arnold	Sa-Sul, Ta-Tra	1471
Casework Mgrs	Sarah Denvir	A, F, G, O, U, V, Woo-Wz	1496
(Grade 7)	Chris Kemp	Ba-Brov, Ha-Ham, Ra-Ro, T	1475
	Richard Westlake	Brow-Bz, La-Leu, S, Wa-Williams H	1474
	Nick Hearn	C, D, E, N, Q, Rp-Rz, X, Z	1462
	Bernard Bennet-Diver	Han-Hz, I, J, K, Lev-Lz	1494
	Mark Darby	M, P, Williams I-Won, Y	1505
Secretary	Valerie Taylor (p)		1481

DANGEROUS & SEVERE PERSONALITY DISORDER (DSPD) PROGRAMME UNIT

Home Office, 2nd Floor, Fry Building, North East Quarter, 2 Marsham Street, London SW1P 4DF
020-7035 6921
DSPD website www.dspdprogramme.gov.uk
Head of Unit fax 020 7035 6438   General fax 020 7035 7630

The Government made a pledge, in its 2001 manifesto, to deliver 300+ places in high secure hospitals and prisons for the management and treatment of those whose risk of serious offending was linked to a severe disorder of personality.

The Manifesto commitment was met in early October 2005 when the final DSPD pilot unit opened at Broadmoor High Secure Hospital. A total of 304 high secure places are now physically available. HMP Frankland, 80 places, HMP Whitemoor, 84 places, Rampton High Secure Hospital, 70 places and 70 places at Broadmoor High Secure Hospital.

The Programme also includes 5 other pilot projects in appropriate specialist services at medium security and in the community, for offender who have made progress.

We are supporting future decisions about the development of DSPD services by commissioning research and evaluation studies into the effectiveness of the pilot services and their costs, and to deliver a coherent national resource.

Name	Responsibilities	Ext/number
Savas Hadjipavlou	Head of Unit & Programme Mgr	6922
Sue Alexander	Secretary	6919

Service Development Team

Rachael Reynolds	Commissioning Development	6913
John Buckle	High Secure DSPD (prison) Mgr	6918
Sheila Foley	Lead on Women's Services (Health)	020-7655 4061
Jim Halliwell	Construction Advisor (Health)	0113 254 6015
Nick Benefield	Community Progression & Aftercare Mgr (Health)	07899 994875
Theresa Noutch	Communication and Website Mgr	6914
Malcolm Ramsay	Research & Devpt Manager	6901
Samantha Foster	Research & Devpt Project Support	6904
Steven Sizmur	Research & Devpt Project Support	6902
Nicola Vallis	Research & Devpt Project Support	6905
Laura Scurlock	Research & Devpt Project Support	6903

Corporate Support Team

Alan Atkinson	Finance & Corporate Supt Mgr	6910
George Goodwin	Deputy Finance & Corporate Supt Mgr	6907
Debra Jeffrey	Corporate Support Officer	6917
Michael Bechtloff	Corporate Support Officer	6908
Davar Ahmed	Corporate Support Officer	3633
Nahome Aklilu	Corporate Support Officer	6906

RESEARCH, DEVELOPMENT AND STATISTICS DIRECTORATE

Director of Research, Development & Statistics	Paul Wiles	
Senior Personal Secretary	Christina Goodwin	020-7273 2616

Offending & Criminal Justice Group
Horseferry House, Dean Ryle Street, London SW1P 2AW

Assistant Director, RDS	Chloë Chitty	
Personal Secretary	Sue Shelley	020-7217 8838

Functions oversight of all research and statistics relating to criminal justice processing and impact and to improve understanding of persistence and desistance of offending

Criminal Justice System Analysis Programme
Abell House, John Islip Street, London SW1P 4LH

Programme Director	Pat Dowdeswell	
Personal Secretary	Ramona Hoyte	020-7217 5078

Functions statistics relating to the criminal justice process (from arrests, through the courts, to

probation and prison), projections of correctional service workloads, research on the criminal justice process including treatment of victims/witnesses and public confidence.

Criminal Justice System 'What Works' Research Programme
Horseferry House, Dean Ryle Street, London SW1P 2AW

Programme Director	Vacancy
Personal Secretary	Sue Shelley

Functions research relating to 'what works' in the criminal justice process, including research on: sentencing initiatives such as fine enforcement and restorative justice; effectiveness of probation and prison service offending behaviour programmes and community reintegration; research on new technology, such as electronic monitoring: and research on prisons, including drugs programmes.

THE DRUGS STRATEGY DIRECTORATE

Home Office, 50 Queen Anne's Gate, London SW1H 9AT

The Drug Strategy Directorate (DSD) is responsible for coordinating the delivery of the Drug Strategy across Government. This involves working with other key departments including: Department of Health, Department for Education & Skills, Department for Work & Pensions, Foreign & Commonwealth Office, HM Customs & Excise, Office of the Deputy Prime Minister.

DSD's Director is Vic Hogg and his PA, Esther Aryeetey is contactable on 020-7035 0592. All DSD staff are contactable on the Home Office e-mail system which is: firstname.surname@homeoffice.gsi.gov.uk.

At working level, DSD is divided into five units described below.

Drug Interventions Programme
aims to encourage more people into drug treatment via the criminal justice system. It is covers the system from the moment of arrest through to completion of community and custodial sentences.

Head of Unit	Peter Wheelhouse	020-7273 3360
Deputy Department Head	Sal Edmunds	020-7273 3439
Pre-Arrest / Arrest Referral	Anne Taylor	020-7272 4623
Drug Testing	Jo Grinter	020-7273 3669
Management team	Andy Blacksell	020-7273 4007
Throughcare / Aftercare	Shereen Sadiq	020-7273 2277
Legal/ Bail	Peter Grime	020-7273 4132
Young People	Ruth Pope	020-7273 2490
Performance Information Team	Ian Clements	020-7273 2444

Drug Legislation and Enforcement Unit
is responsible for supply (in support of HM Customs & Excise) and the non criminal aspects of Communities Programme.

Head of Unit	Stephen Moore	020-7273 2744
Drugs Inspectorate & Licensing	Alan Macfarlane	020-7217 8582
Drugs Bill	Tony Hall	020-7273 4131
Legislation	Jeremy Sare	020-7273 2994
International	Gabriel Denvir	020-7273 2324
Communities/ Supply/ Crack	Trevor Crook	020-7273 4044
ACMD Secretariat	Stuart Harwood	020-7273 4096

Partnership Performance and Support Unit
is responsible for working through the Government Regional Office Network to bring about visible and sustained improvements in the contribution of local partnerships to the delivery of PSA1 (crime reduction), PSA2 (perception of anti-social behaviour) and PSA4 (drugs).

Head of Unit	Vacancy	020-7035 4867
Regional Performance Team	Diana Sampson	020-7035 5279

Treatment & Young People (Drug) Unit
is responsible for Young People and Treatment targets, as well as for diversity and workforce planning across the entire Drug Strategy.

Head of Unit	Alastair Bridges	020-7273 4653
Head of Prevention Team	Steve Tippell	020-7273 2803
Treatment	Sherife Hasan	020-7273 2149
Young People	Karen Gowler	020-7273 3928
Positive Futures	Neil Watson	020-7273 2892
Blueprint	Ruth Joyce	020-7273 3092
Workforce Planning	Pamela Spalding	020-7273 3326

DSD Secretariat
provides strategy, co-ordination, finance and planning support for wider DSD and to Ministers and colleagues across Government as well as leading on campaigns and on analysis work.

Head of Unit	Judy Youell	020-7035 0589
Strategic Co-ord, Perf & Delivery	Sarah Gawley	020-7035 0582
Finance & Planning	Alastair Thomas	020-7035 0581
Marketing & Campaign Management	Clare Jenning	020-7035 0567
Drug modelling & Analysis	Louise Tinsley	020-7035 0573

Government Office Drug Teams
The nine government offices for the regions each have a drug team responsible for performance management of the National Drug Strategy in their region.

Government Office for the East of England
Eastbrook, Shaftesbury Road, Cambridge, CB2 2DF
tel (01223) 372578
Regional Manager: Matthew Kelly (01223) 372577
Bedfordshire, Cambridgeshire, Essex, Hertfordshire, Norfolk, Suffolk

Government Office for East Midlands
The Belgrave Centre, Stanley Place, Talbot Street, Nottingham NG1 5GG
tel 0115-971 2733
Regional Manager: Lesley Daly 0115-971 2733
Derbyshire Leicestershire Lincolnshire Northamptonshire Nottinghamshire

Government Office for London
Riverwalk House, 157/161 Millbank, London SW1P 4RR
tel 020-7217 3426
Regional Manager: Lucy Dawes 020-7217 3428
Greater London

Government Office for the North East
11th Floor, Wellbar House, Gallowgate, Newcastle upon Tyne NE1 4TD
tel 0191-202 3655
Regional Manager: Susan Peel 0191 202 2223
Cleveland Durham Northumberland Tyne & Wear

Government Office for the North West
17th Floor, Sunley Tower, Piccadilly Plaza, Manchester M1 4BE
tel 0161-952 4116
Regional Manager: Karen Williams 0161 952 4115
Cheshire, Cumbria, Greater Manchester, Lancashire, Merseyside

Government Office for the South East
Bridge House, 1 Walnut Tree Close, Guildford GU1 4GA
tel (01483) 882445

Regional Manager: Clare Marett 01483 882311
Berkshire, Buckinghamshire, East Sussex, Hampshire, Kent, Oxfordshire, Surrey, West Sussex, Isle of Wight

Government Office for the South West
2 Rivergate, Temple Quay, Bristol BS1 6ED
tel 0117-900 3510
Regional Manager: Damaris Le Grand 0117-900 3513
Avon, Cornwall, Devon, Dorset, Gloucestershire, Somerset, Wiltshire, Scilly Isles

Government Office for the West Midlands
2nd Floor, 77 Paradise Circus, Queensway, Birmingham, B1 2DT
tel 0121-212 5131
Regional Manager: Peter Johnson 0121-212 5276
Hereford & Worcester, Shropshire, Staffordshire, Warwickshire, West Midlands

Government Office for Yorkshire & Humber
12th Floor, City House, New Station Street, Leeds LS1 4JD
tel 0113-283 5257
Regional Manager: Mick Chambers 0113-283 5384
Humberside, North Yorkshire, South Yorkshire, West Yorkshire

PRISONS AND PROBATION OMBUDSMAN

Ashley House, 2 Monck Street, London SW1P 2BQ
020-7035 2876 fax 020-7035 2860
e-mail mail@ppo.gsi.gov.uk

Function

To provide independent investigation of complaints from all prisoners, those subject to community penalties and those who have reports written on them by the National Probation Service, who have failed to obtain complete satisfaction through the internal complaints systems of the Prison and Probation Services and to make recommendations to those services to help resolve justified complaints.

To investigate the circumstances of the deaths of prisoners, residents in NPD approved premises and residents of immigration detention accommodation and persons under Immigration Service managed escort.

* staff based in Manchester

Staff

Prisons and Probation Ombudsman	Stephen Shaw	020-7035 2851
Snr Personal Secretary	Jennifer Buck	020-7035 2851
Deputy Ombudsman	Emma Bradley	020-7035 2838
Deputy Ombudsman	Rhian Evans	020-7035 2834
Assistant Ombudsman	Louise Baker	020-7035 2272
Assistant Ombudsman	David Barnes	020-7035 2866
Assistant Ombudsman	Vacancy	020-7035 2875
Assistant Ombudsman	Angela Hickey	020-7035 2873
Assistant Ombudsman	Ali McMurray	020-7035 2869
Assistant Ombudsman	Olivia Morrison-Lyons	020-7035 2870
Assistant Ombudsman	Vacancy	020-7035 2852
Assistant Ombudsman	*Jane Webb	07766 422297
Assistant Ombudsman	Nick Woodhead	020-7035 2865

Assistants'/Dep's Secretary	Janet Jenkins	020-7035 2282
Hd of Probn & Diversity	Marian Morris	020-7035 2881
Information Manager	John Maggi	020-7035 2854
Information Asst	Sandra Bent	020-7035 2868
Office Manager	Geoff Hubbard	020-7035 2855
Admin Officer	Samantha Torrington	020-7035 2885
Investigators	Christina Arsalides	020-7035 2872
	Don Barrell	020-7035 2279
	Stephen Beal	020-7035 2839
	Tamara Bild	020-7035 2941
	David Cameron	020-7035 2831
	Karen Chin	020-7035 2837
	Althea Clarke-Ramsey	020-7035 2858
	Mandi Connor	020-7035 2864
	Lorenzo Delgaudio	020-7035 2832
	Rob Del-Greco	020-7035 2278
	Carol Dowling	020-7035 2842
	Kate Eves	020-7035 2283
	Lisa Flanagan	020-7035 2828
	Kevin Gilzean	020-7035 2726
	Helena Hanson	020-7035 2853
	Michael Hegarty	020-7035 2825
	Ruth Houston	020-7035 2286
	Mark Judd	
	Razna Khatun	020-7035 2829
	Andy King	020-7035 2874
	Madeline Kuevi	020-7035 2886
	Lisa Lambert	020-7035 2882
	Anne Lund	020-7035 2863
	Beverley McKenzie-Gayle	020-7035 2827
	Eileen Mannion	020-7035 2836
	Kirsty Masterton	020-7035 2878
	Wayne Morley	020-7035 2833
	*Gordon Morrison	07968 909601
	Anita Mulinder	020-7035 2879
	Ifeanyi Ochei	020-7035 2862
	Tracey Scheepers	
	Robin Shone	020-7035 2826
	Anna Siraut	020-7035 2859
	Kevin Stroud	020-7035 2883
	Ann Tanner	020-7035 2877
	Dorne Thompson	
	Steve Toyne	020-7035 2867
	Ian Truffet	020-7035 2861
	John Unwin	020-7035 2848
	Thea Walton	020-7035 2835
	Louisa Watkins	020-7035 2821
	*Bryan Woodward	07798 581283
Family Liaison Officers	Abbe Dixon	020-7035 2280
	Lucy Phelan	020-7035 2843
Executive Officer	Jay Mehta	
Admin Officer	Elizabeth Buatsi	020-7035 2741
Admin Assistant (Manchester)	Debbie Hood	0161-869 2300
Transcriber/Typist	Durdana Ahmed	020-7035 2880

Assessment & Implementation Team

Head of Team	Clare Quigley	020-7035 2857
	Carol Martin	020-7035 2873
	Annette Roche	020-7035 2849
	Tracy Wright	020-7035 2856
	Vacancy	020-7035 2887

PAROLE BOARD OF ENGLAND AND WALES

Abell House, John Islip Street, London SW1P 4LH

Chairman	Prof Duncan Nichol
Senior Personal Secretary	Miss L Edwards

Secretariat	
Grade 6, Chief Executive	Ms C Glenn
SEOs	T McCarthy, M Stevens
HEOs	P Boshell, M Longley, V Peters,

Enquiries

Enquiries about Discretionary Conditional Release cases and Discretionary Lifer Panels should be directed to the Parole Board Secretariat

Paper hearings (DCR)	
Pre Panel	020-7217 5512 (A-K)
	020-7217 5387 (L-Z)
Post Panel	020-7217 5222 (A-Z)

Oral hearings (DLP)	020-7217 5340
General Enquiries	020-7217 5314
fax oral hearings	*020-7217 5677*
fax paper hearings pre panel	*020 7217 5108*
fax paper hearings	*020-7217 5488*

THE PRISON HEALTH RESEARCH NETWORK

Hostel 1, Ashworth Hospital, Maghull, Merseyside L31 1HW

The Prison Health Research Network (PHRN) is a Department of Health funded initiative, led jointly by the Universities of Manchester, Southampton and Sheffield, and the Institute of Psychiatry. It comprises a multi-disciplinary team of researchers with strong clinical and research credentials in prison healthcare.

The aim is to develop the infrastructure needed to sustain a programme of research and development, with the intention that prison healthcare systems shall attain equivalence with mainstream provision. Other organisations are actively encouraged to join PHRN and contribute to its work.

PHRN will identify research and development priorities in prison health care, and a programme of research will be encouraged and co-ordinated to address gaps in knowledge and practice.

PHRN will focus on four areas pertinent to prison health research:
Dentistry, Mental Health, Primary care, Substance misuse

In addition to specific projects in these areas, PHRN will work to:

a) establish a network of "best practice" research prisons that offer an open and engaged approach to hosting and participating in health care research.

b) undertake the 'Go Directly To Jail' project, outlining a clear pathway to successfully undertake research in prisons, incorporating considerations such as research quality, ethics and research governance.

c) maintain a website highlighting prison health care research, detailing ongoing work, research findings, funding and training opportunities, and hosting professional chat fora.

d) host an annual national conference and other regional training events.

Contacts
Jane Senior (Research Project Manager)
jane.senior@merseycare.nhs.uk or 0151 471 2351
Dr Jenny Shaw (mental health lead)
jjshaw@dsl.pipex.com or 01772 406614
Dr Martin Tickle (dentistry lead)
martin.tickle@manchester.ac.uk or 0161 275 6610
Dr Mike Farrell (substance misuse lead)
m.farrell@iop.kcl.ac.uk or 0207 740 5701
Prof Bonnie Sibbald (primary care lead)
bonnie.sibbald@manchester.ac.uk or 0161 275 7604

ASSISTED PRISON VISITS SCHEME

Part of the National Offender Management Service in the Home Office

Assisted Prison Visits Unit, PO Box 2152, Birmingham B15 1SD

Customer enquiries 0845 3001423 (10.15 to 11.45 & 14.15 to 15.45, Monday to Friday)
Textphone 0845 3040800 (for people with hearing difficulties)
Application forms 0121-626 2206

Head of Unit, A K Jones 0121-626 2208
Team leaders 0121-626 3700 or 01210626 2772

e-mail: assisted.prison.visits@hmps.gsi.gov.uk
Information available at
www.hmprisonservice.gov.uk

PRISONER LOCATION SERVICE

Part of the National Offender Management Service in the Home Office

Prisoner Location Service, Assisted Prison Visits Unit, PO Box 2152, Birmingham B15 1SD

Prisoner location enquiries should be faxed on 0121-626 3474
Probation enquiries 0121-626 2742 (24 hour answer machine)
Public enquiries 0121-626 2773 (24 hour answer machine)

Head of Unit, A K Jones 0121-626 2208
Team leader 0121-626 3331

e-mail:
prisoner.location.service@hmps.gsi.gov.uk

Information available at
www.hmprisonservice.gov.uk

VICTIM HELPLINE

Part of the National Offender Management Service in the Home Office

NOMS Victim Helpline, Assisted Prison Visits Unit, PO Box 4278, Birmingham B15 1SA

Telephone 08457 585112 Monday to Friday 9am to 4pm (24 hour answer machine at other times)

Head of Unit, A K Jones 0121-626 2208
Team leader 0121-626 3331

Information available at
www.hmprisonservice.gov.uk

CAFCASS – Children and Family Court Advisory & Support Service

Joint Headquarters

1.   **CAFCASS**
     8th Floor, South Quay Plaza
     189 Marsh Wall, London E14 9SH
     tel 020 7510 7000 *fax 020 7510 7001*
     e-mail cafcass@cafcass.gov.uk
     www.cafcass.gov.uk

     Jill Pitkeathley (chairman)
     Anthony Douglas (chief executive)

Regional Offices

2.   **North East Region**
     CAFCASS
     38 Saddler Street
     Durham DH1 3NU
     tel 0191-383 9279 *fax 0191-370 9741*
     e-mail
     durhamcafcass@teesdaleonline.co.uk

     Counties: Northumberland, County Durham, Tyne & Wear, Teeside

     Elizabeth Hall (regnl mgr)
     Hayley Green (business mgr)
     Jill Robinson (regnl co-ord)
     Kirsty Steel (pa)

3.   **Yorkshire and Humberside Region**
     CAFCASS
     1 Park Cross Mews
     Park Cross Street, Leeds LS1 2QS
     tel 0113-394 7474 *fax 0113-247 0929*

Counties: NorthYorkshire, West Yorkshire, South Yorkshire, Humberside

Ann Gladwin (regnl mgr)
Jennifer Howarth (business mgr)
Marie Gray (pa)

4. **North West Region**
CAFCASS
6th Floor, Byrom House
Quay Street, Manchester M3 3JD
tel 0161-830 5720 *fax 0161-835 2246*

Counties: Cumbria, Lancashire, Merseyside, Cheshire, Greater Manchester

Sheena Adam (regnl mgr)
Karen Cairns (business mgr)
Ronnie Lester (regnl co-ord)
Jane Wright (pa)

5. **East Midlands Region**
CAFCASS
St Helen's Street
Derby, Derbyshire DE1 3GY
tel (01332) 866480 *fax (01332) 296284*

Counties: Derbyshire, Nottinghamshire, Lincolnshire, Leicestershire, Northamptonshire

Elizabeth Coe (regnl mgr)
Steve Kerr (business mgr)
Jane Burton (regnl co-ord)
Vicky Timmins (pa)

6. **London Region**
CAFCASS
13th Floor, Archway Tower
2 Junction Road, London N19 5HQ
tel 020 7210 4400 *fax 020 7210 4422*

Counties: All Inner & Greater London Boroughs

Vivien Salisbury (regnl mgr)
Victoria Philipson (regnl mgr)
Alison Wogan (business mgr)
Selina Philips (public)
Lorraine Jannaway (private)
Helena Calixte (pa)

7. **Eastern Region**
CAFCASS
St Mary's House, 90 Victoria Road,
Chelmsford, Essex CM1 1RD
tel (01245) 255660 *fax (01245) 505235*

Counties: Cambridgeshire, Norfolk, Suffolk, Bedfordshire, Hertfordshire, Essex

Alan Critchley (acting regnl mgr)
Sue Lowden (business mgr)
Anna Sheffield (regnl co-ord)
Nicola Blakeborough (pa)

8. **Southern Region**
CAFCASS
1st Floor, Grosvenor House
Basing View, Basingstoke RG21 4HG
tel (01256) 392770 *fax (01256) 392772*

Counties: Buckinghamshire, Oxfordshire, Hampshire

Ruth Chase (regnl mgr)
David Sims (business mgr)
Chris hatman (pa)

9. **South East Region**
CAFCASS
8th Floor, South Quay Plaza
189 Marsh Wall, London E14 9SH
tel 020 7510 7000 *fax 020 7510 7001*

Counties: Berkshire, Surrey, Kent, West Sussex, East Sussex, Isle of Wight

Victoria Phillipson (regnl director)
Richard Lacey (business mgr)
Olga Connery (pa)

10. **West Midlands Region**
CAFCASS
1 Printing House Street
Birmingham B4 6DE
tel 0121-248 6285 *fax 0121-248 6291*
e-mail west.midlands@cafcass.gov.uk

Counties: Staffordshire, Shropshire, Hereford & Worcester, West Midlands, Warwickshire, Coventry, Stoke

Andrew Guymer (regnl mgr)
Angela Dakin (business mgr)
John Roberts (regnl co-ord)
Narelle Rollings (pa)

11. **South West Region**
CAFCASS
6 Mendip House
High Street, Taunton TA1 3SX
tel (01823) 340224 *fax (01823) 323821*

Counties: Gloucestershire, Avon, Wiltshire, Somerset, Cornwall, Devon, Dorset

Suzie Goodman (regnl mgr)
Andrew Dawe (business mgr)
Natalie Pring (regnl co-ord)
Paula Hyde (pa)

Wales

The functions of CAFCASS in Wales are now functions of the Welsh Assembly

TRAINING & CONSULTANCY ORGANISATIONS

Organisations that feel they should be included in this section are invited to contact the Editor. The descriptions included are those of the organisations. The Editor accepts no responsibility for any statements made in this section nor for the violence sometimes inflicted on the English language.

Skills for Justice

Head Office 9 Riverside Court, Don Road, Sheffield S9 2TJ
tel 0114-261 1499

London Office Vigilant House, 120 Wilton Road, London SW1V 1JZ
tel 020-7808 7575

Wales Office 2 Court Road, Bridgend, Mid Glam CF31 1BN
tel (01656) 750 133

Scotland Office 140 Couseway, Edinburgh EH9 1PR
tel 0131-662 5234

Northern Ireland Office 7th Floor, 14 Great Victoria Street, Belfast, BT2 7BA
tel 028-9025 8028

Skills for Care and Development

Skills for Care and Development, the DfES-licensed sector skills council for social care, children and young people, is an alliance of five existing organisations:

Skills for Care, the former Topss England, now dealing with adult social care in England [www.skillsforcare.org.uk]
the Children's Workforce Development Council, also working in England [www.cwdcouncil.org.uk]
the Care Council for Wales [www.ccwales.org.uk]
the Scottish Social Services Council [www.sssc.uk.com]
the Northern Ireland Social Care Council [www.niscc.info].

Skills for Care and Development represents the workforce development interests of some 60,000 employers and 2.5 million workers in the social care and children's workforces of the UK, including development of the national occupational standards for the sector. Each of the partner bodies works closely with government, health and other related sector skills councils.

SSC Administrator, c/o Skills for Care, Albion Court, 5 Albion Place, Leeds LS1 6JL
tel 0113-241 1251 e-mail: sscadmin@skillsforcare.org.uk

MPTC Criminal Justice Training & Consultancy

1 Printing House Street, Birmingham B4 6DE
0121-248 6325 *fax 0121-236 6384*
e-mail info@mptc.org.uk
or on STEPS system @MPTC

Roger Clare (director),
Sally Cherry (asst director)
Louison Ricketts (asst director)

MPTC is a well established not-for-profit training organisation wholly owned by the nine Midlands Probation Areas. It provides training, consultancy, research, mentoring and conferences across the criminal justice sector on an in-house, regional and national basis. It has particular expertise in effective practice, management and organisational development, and training/HR issues. MPTC is a CJNTO endorsed training provider and its directors are CIPD qualified.

ADD Training Ltd

26 Balmoral Crescent, Lodgemoor, Sheffield S10 4NE
07803 930506 e-mail dfhunt@addtraining.co.uk

Provides accredited trainers for the delivery of ETS and Cognitive Booster Programme tutor training, has designed and delivered the nationally recognised training for trainers course. Specialises in the, design and delivery of bespoke training for effective practice of accredited /non accredited programmes and case management (e.g. Socratic method, supervision skills, treatment management). Also provides a personal development training service.

Alan Rousseau Training Ltd

114 Longhurst Lane, Mellor,
Stockport SK6 5PG
tel/fax 0161-449 8789 e-mail
mail@alanrousseautraining.com

An ex-probation service manager, Alan
Rousseau facilitates learning and coaching
services on the themes of project management;
multi-agency collaboration; teamwork; and
personal development. Separately, provides
training in how to work safely with aggression
and violence. Customised services around many
organisational issues can be developed.

Catherine Fuller Training & Development

Cop Castle, Bringsty Common,
Worcs WR6 5UN
(01886) 821403 catherine.fuller@talk21.com

Author of NPD Toolkit of Motivational Skills
and trainer of national trainers. 20 years
experience in criminal justice agencies. Skills
based, interactive training that values diversity,
for offender managers, supervisors ,
administrators, managers and teams. Advanced
motivational skills training for handling conflict,
gaining staff comitment for change and
empowering offenders to go straight.

Child Bereavement Trust

Aston House, High Street, West Wycombe,
Bucks HP14 3AG
(01494) 446648 fax (01494) 440057
info & support line 0845 357 1000

A centre of excellence for improving the care
offered by professionals to grieving families.
The charity provides specialist training and
support for all professionals to improve their
response to bereaved families. Produces
resources and information for children and
families and all the professionals who come into
contact with them in the course of their work

Paul Cooper Consultants Ltd

19 Mossley Hill Road, Mossley Hill,
Liverpool L18 4PT
0151-724 4133 mobile 07734 108 753
e-mail paulcooper@radicalguru.co.uk

Specialises in the application of law to probation
practice and management (compliance,
enforcement, breach, court skills, witness skills,
Human Rights Act, Data Protection and new
legislation). Courses offered also include, PSR
writing skills, Race Crime, Supervision
Planning and Objective Setting and Offender
Management. Also specialises in the application
of law and policy to the work of CAFCASS,
YOTs and Social Work. Offers a comprehensive
programme of management development for
middle managers and customised courses for
senior managers that include organisational
planning, leadership and human resources
consultancy including recruitment and
selection. Accredited with the Open College
Learning Network. Currently offers certificate
courses in 'Effective Practice: Writing Specific
Sentence Reports' & 'Effective Practice:
Understanding Organisational Diversity'.

Delight Training Services Ltd

Hillside Croft, Congleton Edge, Congleton,
Cheshire CW12 3NA
tel (01260) 290 333 fax (01260) 297 333
e-mail admin@delight.co.uk   web
www.delight.co.uk

Currently working across the UK and overseas
on structured offending behaviour programmes
and associated underpinning skills including
groupwork, one to one work, and motivational
interviewing. Able to provide organisational
consultancy on general training delivery and
programme implementation, and facilitate
development of in-house training provision via
generic and programme specific trainer training.
Currently working in prisons, probation, and in
forensic mental health. Areas of work include
general offending, substance misuse related
offending, alcohol and violence, and generic staff
skills development including PSO induction and
development and TPO training. A CJNTO
endorsed training provider.

Equality Works

Shepherdess Walk Buildings, 2 Underwood
Row, London N1 7LQ
020-7251 4939
Manchester Office: The Triangle Business
Centre, Exchange Square, Manchester M4 3TR
0161-838 5860
e-mail info@equalityworks.co.uk
www.equalityworks.co.uk

A consultancy and training company specialising
in integrating equalities into workplace learning
and staff development. The approach is based

on integrating a clear professional analysis of equalities and the way discrimination is embedded in organisations. Currently working with several probation areas, providing services including: core equalities training; recruitment and selection training; performance management training; impact assessment; facilitation; training for mentors of black and Asian offenders; and providing consultancy advice to senior management.

Forensic Psychology Practice Ltd

The Willows Clinic, 417a Birmingham Road, Wylde Green, Sutton Coldfield B72 1AU
0121-377 6276 *fax 0121-377 6027*
e-mail info@forensic psychology.co.uk

Provides forensic and clinical psychology expertise in direct work with clients or in support of statutory and voluntary agencies; advice, support, consultancy and training on all aspects of forensic and clinical psychology; specialist assessment and design and implementation of treatment programmes'. Experienced in developing and running treatment programmes for sex offenders with learning disabilities in both health and criminal justice settings. Provides specialist training in working with sex offenders for practitioners in Probation and NHS settings and acts as consultants to National Probation Service in managing high risk offenders in the community. Experienced in working with mentally disordered offenders and developing risk assessment protocols for private and criminal justice agencies'.

GB Learning Consultancy

3 Basildon Close, Sutton, Surrey SM2 5QJ
0790 661 3081 or 0791 439 7701
e-mail jim@gblearningconsultancy.co.uk or mandy@gblearningconsultancy.co.uk

Specialises in leadership development and consultancy. Has worked with NOMS to develop the Living Leadership Toolkit including open learning materials. Has facilitated leadership workshops and seminars. Consultants have significant experience in the Probation Service and other similar organizations and have developed a leadership assessment tool, the Delta Leadership Profile.

Grey Cell Training Ltd

Cherrybrook, 12 Lakeside, Irthingborough, Northants NN9 5SW
phone & fax (01933) 653845 mobile 07764 199607
e-mail sue@greycelltraining.co.uk
www.greycelltraining.co.uk

Provides strategy consultation and generic training programmes for national and local government customers. Over 90 courses offered, targeted to reflect both the needs of the CJ system and each individual organisation. All grades of staff, covering personal and management development. Particular focus on performance enhancement and improvement through staff motivation. Courses include risk management and assessment, PSO and similar grade core programmes, management development, interviewing skills and report writing, preparation and support, including cognitive behaviour and group skills. All courses compliant with NVQ Levels III and IV in Community Justice. All courses compliant with Home Office circulars and directives. A CNJTO endorsed training provider. Contact Susan Rawden

Groupwork Consultation & Training Ltd

PO Box 363, Southsea, Hants PO4 0YB
phone/fax 02392 750030
e-mail: dave@groupct.demon.co.uk
www.groupct.demon.co.uk

Established in 1987 to provide social groupwork training to groupworkers in the public sector. Probation Services, Social Services, Health Authorities and voluntary organisations. Courses are held in Brighton, London and in-house. They include training in foundation, intermediate and a more advanced level of groupwork. Also short courses e.g. cognitive behavioural, anger management, motivational interviewing and other offending behaviour groups. GCT is a CNJTO endorsed training provider

Grubb Institute

Cloudesley Street, London N1 0HU, 020-7278 8061 *fax 020-7278 0728*
e-mail info@grubb.org.uk www.grubb.org.uk

Works with leaders, managers and professionals on role and institutional transformation, using a

systemic and group relations approach and applied Christian theology. Offers consultancy, development and learning opportunities in one-to-one role consultation, teams and groups, and whole systems. The Institute works across the community in a range of organisations, and has a track record within the criminal justice field.

HealthCV

3 Beckside Gardens, Waterloo, Huddersfield, W Yorks HD5 8RS
(01484) 304800 *fax (01484) 304614*
e-mail info@healthcv.com   www.healthcv.com

Works with probation services providing employee assistance programmes, health risk screening and stress management courses. Also specialises in employee well-being schemes, stress audits, health profiles, ergonomics, risk assessment, dietary analysis, and relaxation techniques. Member of International Stress Management Association (Validated Trainer).

Ignition Creative Learning Ltd

21 Donald Street, Roath, Cardiff CF24 4TJ
tel 0700 394 6217 *fax 029-2045 1823*
e-mail info@ignition-learn.com

Specialised training in forensic motivational interviewing, and active group work skills. Supervision and consultancy of domestic violence group work staff, programme and service design. Training in co-gendered working and domestic violence perpetrator group work.

Linda Gast Training

Somersbourne House, 54 Somers Road, Malvern, Worcs WR14 1JB
tel/fax (01684) 564363
e-mail training@lindagast.co.uk
www.lindagast.co.uk

Has been providing training for probation and criminal justice organisations for over 13 years. Particularly interested in 'people' skills and the development of these through pro-social modelling and a focus on responsivity. Also provides training on a full range of management issues, cutting edge training on work with racially motivated offenders , hate based crime and aspects of race, diversity, staff supervision and team development. Can provide management training accredited by the Institute of Leadership and Management (ILM) to

Diploma and Certificate level. All programmes adapted to meet the needs of commissioners. Also works with other independent trainers.

Link Training

Oldacre House, Court Drive, Shenstone, Lichfield, Staffs WS14 0JG
tel (01543) 481884
e-mail link.training@ppcoaching.co.uk

Link Training is a network of 3 established, independent trainers. All have experience of working in the probation service, helping to develop best practice, and recognise the value to customers of linking their knowledge and skills to deliver quality training. The workshops are focussed around the skills necessary for effective engagement with offenders, the courts, other services providers and meeting the new challenges of NOMS. The practical application of models, research and ideas is encouraged and developed. The workshops will be tailor made to meet the varying skills development requirements of Offender Managers and Supervisors, Key Workers and Case Administrators.

Lucy Faithfull Foundation

Bordesley Hall, The Holloway, Alvechurch, Birmingham B48 7QA
tel (01527) 591922 *fax (01527) 591924*
e-mail referrals@lucyfaithfull.org &
dbarlow@lucyfaithfull.org

A national charity providing specialist assessment and treatment for sexual abusers of children, their families and victims. Provides consultancies and training to social service departments, probation and YOTs. Takes referrals from agencies, courts and solicitors (not from clients directly).

LMT Training and Consultancy

Ellastone House, Maenclochog, Pembrokeshire SA66 7LQ
(01437) 532888 *fax (01437) 532889*
e-mail info@lmt.uk.com

A well established provider of tailor made training, mentoring and consultancy for practitioners and managers working in the crime and disorder arena. Offers effective practice skills development opportunities including offence behavioural and cognition

analysis; pro-social modelling; motivational enhancement; case management; groupwork; diversity; cognitive behavioural methods. Management provision includes all aspects of staff, cultural and transition management and team building. The PATHWAY programme is available for YOTs and other services working with young people.

Marilyn Whibley

Griffins, Grange Road, Leatherhead,
Surrey KT22 7JS
(01372) 279675
e-mail marilynwhibley@aol.com
www.mswconsultancy.co.uk

Has many years experience in the probation service as a practitioner, manager and staff trainer. Now works as a consultant and trainer specialising in stress management and related staff care issues. Provides help and advice in developing policies and procedures and carrying out risk assessments for work related stress to meet statutory health and safety requirements. Also offers training, mentoring and coaching in the areas of management development, presentation skills, assertiveness, training trainers, courtwork, report writing and other areas of probation practice.

New Leaf Training and Counselling – Becky Wright

PO Box 4, Wellington, Somerset TA21 0YU
tel & fax (01823) 660426
e-mail new.leaf@virgin.net
www.newleaf.uk.com

A well established provider of anger and stress management services. Has held a contract with Avon & Somerset Probation Area for many years providing post traumatic stress counselling. Now offers individual counselling and group work for those who have difficulty in managing anger and stress. Individuals can self refer to the service. BACP registered counsellor & UKRC registered independent counsellor.

Noble Openshaw Ltd

Ground Floor, 3 Westminster Court, Hipley Street, Old Woking, Surry GU22 9LG
e-mail admin@noble-openshaw.co.uk or contact Simon Noble on 07766 237312

A management consultancy providing support to senior management teams dealing with day-to-day challenges of change in the service. Work includes managing tendering processes, consulting on & drafting practice standards, the provision of interim management, work with managers and staff to develop and introduce new policies & changes in working practice, business process improvement, project management and evaluation, stakeholder marketing. The company's principal is a former Assistant Chief Officer with more than 10 years experience working at board level in probation, the NHS, the not-for-profit sector and the private sector. Associates include other former probation managers, a serving magistrate, a specialist bid writer, an expert on drink and drug impairment, a specialist on drug and alcohol testing and experts in sex offender and child protection risk assessment.

People Progression - Alison Rudin

7 Sycamore Avenue, Chandlers Ford,
Hants SO53 5RJ
07740 117 495
e-mail arudin@aol.co.uk

A well established provider of practical, tailored training and development solutions for the Probation Service. Specialises in management skills, training, coaching, selection interviewing, presentation skills, group and team building. Also an executive coach and UKRC registered counsellor, providing short-term personal, career or life counselling to individuals.

Peak Performance Coaching

Oldacre House, Court Drive, Shenstone, Lichfield, Staffs WS14 0JG
tel 01543 481884 mobile 07734 053486
Lesley.matile@ppcoaching.co.uk
www.ppcoaching.co.uk

Established 1998, PPC delivers executive coaching and training for those wanting to incorporate coaching skills into their leadership. With over 20 years probation service experience combined with a range of work with customers from the independent and private sectors, PPC offers effective and well-tested resources. PPC has a motivational approach, raising individuals' commitment to change and personal development. Proven experience of facilitating the establishment of coaching cultures, achieving buy-in for change, effective

communication and motivating both practitioners and managers towards excellence. Training packages include bespoke training manuals and a skills-based presentation style.

Strategic People

1 Linnet Walk, Wokingham, Berks RG41 3HE
tel & fax 01189 771159
e-mail marylousvet@strategicpeople.co.uk
www.strategicpeople.co.uk

Focuses on organisational change and activities to achieve successful change including: leadership development, flexible and mobile working, work life balance, planning for mergers and reorganisation, facilitated strategic planning workshops, leadership skills, management skills, team building, effective implementation of performance management and appraisal. Over 15 years experience of working with the probation service, CAFCASS and other public and private sector organisations.

Tavistock Centre for Couple Relationships

The Tavistock Centre, 120 Belsize Lane, London NW3 5BA
020-8938 2353 *fax 020-7435 1080*
tccr@tccr.org.uk   www.tccr.org.uk

Offers training and consultation services in the field of relationships. As well as training directly involved with couples, the Tavistock consult to managers and supervisors who work in agencies involved with family relationships. A course on 'Working with relationship breakdown' is run annually, as is 'Effective Staff Supervision'.

Charlie Watson Staff Development & Training

Mulberry Barn, Main Road, Stanton in Peak, Derbyshire DE4 2LW
tel/fax (01629) 636986 mobile 07739 468351
e-mail charlie.watson@virgin.net

Offers learning and development programmes in the criminal justice, voluntary and higher education sectors concentrating on: Interactional skills, involving engagement and motivation techniques; diversity; management development, including supervision and appraisal; presentation skills; groupwork;

teambuilding; managing conflict; risk and public protection; academic delivery and placement supervision. NVQ assessor and verifier practice training. CJNTO endorsed.

ELECTRONIC MONITORING SERVICES

The Home Office contractors are responsible for the management and enforcement of Home Detention Curfew, Curfew Orders and other applications of electronic monitoring within the criminal justice system of England and Wales.

1. **Serco Home Affairs (Monitoring)**
    Austin House, Stannard Place,
    St Crispins Road, Norwich NR3 1YF
    tel (01603) 428300 fax (01603) 428311

    Terry Harris (contract director)
    Dave Weston (asst director field services)
    Andy Homer (asst director operations supt, agency/customer liaison)
    Colin Flynn (asst director finance & admin)
    Martin Elvin (asst director monitoring centre)

    Serco Home Affairs Monitoring Centre
    PO Box 45, Norwich, Norfolk NR3 1BF

    Monitoring Centre 24 Hours Helplines for all Enquiries
    regarding Electronic Monitoring for HDC, Court Orders,
    Bail, Immigration Monitoring, Tracking, Control Orders,
    Service Delivery Support and Legal Enquiries (office hours).

    London and Eastern
    tel 08080 965124 fax 08700 700321
    West Midlands and Wales
    tel 08080 152369 fax 08700 700321
    Secure e-mail neworders-amendments@pmsl-serco.com.cjsm.net

    Field Regional Manager London & Eastern
    Roop Kalyan (01638) 750449

    Areas Covered
    Bedfordshire, Cambridgeshire, Essex, Hertfordshire,
    London (Metropolitan), Norfolk, Suffolk

Field Service Managers London & Eastern
East Anglia
Natalie Goddard (01638) 750449

North London
Maggie Melvin 0208-364 4756

South London
Kevin Fleary 0208-668 9429

Regional Manager West Midlands & Wales
John Roberts 0121-236 5547

Areas Covered
Dyfed-Powys, Gwent, North Wales, South Wales,
Staffordshire. Warwickshire, West Mercia, West Midlands.

Field Service Managers West Midlands & Wales
North Wales
Derek Mosforth (01743) 465673

West Midlands
Wayne Marshall 0121-236 5547

South Wales
Rob Spear (02920) 491131

2.   **G4S Justice Services Ltd**
PO Box 170, Manchester, M41 7XZ
0161-862 1000 *fax 0161-749 9022/7620*
email: interagency@uk.g4s.com

Paul Moonan (director)
Ian Ridgley (chief operations off)
Claire Sims (interagency director)
Lorna Rose (marketing mgr)
Jane Walsh (service delivery mgr, satellite tracking)

Control Centre
PO Box 170, Manchester, M41 7XZ
0161-862 1200 *fax 0161-749 8358* (24 hours)

Graham Eadie (control centre mgr)
0161-862 1205
Stuart Featherstone (customer relations mgr)
0161 862 1000
Riffat Ramzan (court services mgr)
0161 862 1000
Tracy Annan (snr interagency off)
0113 203 2400

Areas Covered
Cheshire; Cleveland; Durham; Greater Manchester; Lancashire; Merseyside; Northumbria; Derbyshire; Humberside;

Leicestershire; Lincolnshire; North Yorkshire; Northamptonshire; Nottinghamshire; South Yorkshire; West Yorkshire

Graham Shepherd (customer relations mgr, SW)
07899 926 342
Simon Mann (customer relations mg, SE)
07867 647 207
Lesley Lansdowne (court services mgr)
01793 514 646/01753 514 544

Areas Covered
Avon and Somerset; Devon and Cornwall; Dorset; Gloucestershire; Hampshire; Kent; Surrey; Sussex; Thames Valley; Wiltshire

Branch Managers (Operational Issues)
N, S, W Yorks, Humberside
Jeff Sheehan 0113 203 2400

G Manchester, Cheshire
Dee Hampson 0161 864 6270

Lancs, Merseyside, S Cumbria
Phil Wilson 01744 887 120

Durham, Northumbria, Teesside, N Cumbria
Christine Wright 0191 416 9957

East Midlands
Chris Pilkington 0115 924 5855

South East and South West
Mike Wring 01793 514 646/01793 514 544

Offender Management Services (OMS)
A division of G4S Justice Services offering innovative and practical solutions to Criminal Justice agencies involved in the management of offenders in the community.
For further information please contact the OMS Team on 0161 868 2411 or email oms@uk.g4s.com

GLOSSARY OF COMMONLY USED ABBREVIATIONS AND SLANG

The following is a glossary of abbreviations and slang commonly used in the Probation and Prison Services. It is hoped that it will be of use to trainees and others struggling to understand contact records and referral forms. This glossary does not claim to be comprehensive. It has been compiled by the editor from his personal experience and with extra help from Terry Bond, Rod Pickin, Keith Norton and Angela Brown. Abbreviations particularly associated with NVQs, CRAMS or prisons are indicated, but there is obviously some cross over between categories. Any suggestions from colleagues will be gratefully received.

A1	assessor award (nvq)
AA	acceptable absence, Alcoholics Anonymous, alert (flag on CRAMS)
ABH	actual bodily harm (or AOBH)
ACR	automatic conditional release (prison)
ADAs	additional days awarded (internal prison punishment)
AKA	also known as
AOBH	assault occasioning actual bodily harm (or ABH)
APD	approved parole date
APEL	accreditation of prior experience and learning (nvq)
ARD	automatic release date (prison)
ART	aggression reduction training
ASRO	addressing substance related offending (programme)
ASW	approved social worker (mental health)
AU or UA	unacceptable absence
AUR	automatic unconditional release (prison)
bilking	making off without payment
BWNB	bench warrant no bail
Br	breach (of order/licence)
C&G	City & Guilds (nvq)
CAR	cumulative assessment record (nvq)
CALM	controlling anger & learning to manage (programme)
CARATS	counselling, assessment, referral & throughcare services
CJ	community justice (nvq)
CJNTO	community justice national training organisation (nvq)
CM	case manager

CMT/CMU	case management team/unit
CPO	Community Punishment Order (formerly Community Service Order)
CPS	Crown Prosecution Service
CPU	child protection unit
CPRO	Community Punishment & Rehabilitation Order (formerly Combination Order)
CR	child register (flag on CRAMS)
CRAMS	case recording and management system
CRD	conditional release date
CRN	client reference number
CRO	Community Rehabilitation Order (formerly Probation Order)
CSCP	cognitive self change programme
CS	community service
CSO	Community Service Order (now CPO)
CW	child concern (flag on CRAMS)
D32/D33	former assessor awards
DCR	discretionary conditional release (prison)
Deps	depositions (witness statements)
D/H	dwelling house
DIDs	drink impaired drivers (programme)
Dipping	pick pocketing
DipSW	Diploma in Social Work
DLP	Discretionary Lifer Panel (prison)
DNA	did not attend
DO	duty officer
DoB	date of birth
DSS	Department of Social Services
DTTO	Drug Treatment & Testing Order
DV	domestic violence
DWD	drive whilst disqualified
EDR	earliest date of release (prison)
EEM	European excellence model
ETS	enhanced thinking skills (programme)
ETE	education, training and employment
EV	external verifier (nvq)
F2050	code name for main prison file on prisoner
F2052SH	section of F2050 relating to self harm (prison)
F75	progress report on lifer (now obsolete) (prison)
FLED	facility licence eligibility date (in open prisons)
FTA	fail to attend
FTS	fail to surrender (to bail)
FWW	formal/final written warning
GBH	grievous bodily harm

GOAD	good order and discipline (prison)
HDC	home detention curfew (prison)
HDCED	home detention curfew eligibility date (prison)
HO	head office, Home Office
HOC	Home Office circular
HV	home visit
IEP	integrated employability programme
IG54/94	prison service instruction relating to Schedule 1 offenders
IPP	intensive probation programme
IV	internal verifier (nvq)
kiting	issuing dud cheques
LDR	latest date of release (prison)
LED	licence expiry date (prison)
LIDS	local inmate database system (prison computer system)
LSP	life sentence plan (prison)
LSP3E	progress report on lifer (formerly F75) (prison)
MAPPP	multi agency public protection panel
MAPPPA	multi agency public protection panel arrangement
MALRAP	multi agency lifer risk assessment panel (prison)
MDT	mandatory drug test
MOWOP	make off without payment (bilking)
MPSO	Money Payments Supervision Order
NA	next appointment, not applicable
NAI	non accidental injury (to child)
NBW	bench warrant no bail (BWNB)
NEO	no evidence offered
NFA	no fixed abode
No DL	no driving licence
No Ins	no insurance
nonce	(offensive) prison term for sex offender
NPD	non parole date (prison), National Probation Directorate
NS	Home Office National Standards
OASys	offender assessment system
OCR	Oxford, Cambridge, Royal Society (nvq)
OGRS	offender group reconviction score
on the game	Prostitution
on the rule	prisoner segregated under Rule 43 (prison)
OPL	over the prescribed limit (drunk driving)
OV	office visit
Page 16	prison service version of contact sheet
PDA	practice development assessor
PDH	plea and directions hearing
PED	parole eligibility date (prison)

Perp	perpetrator of sexual offence
PH	preliminary hearing (Crown Court)
POA	Public Order Act, Prison Officer's Association
PPU	public protection unit
PSA	petty sessional area
PSD	pre-sentence disclosure
PSI	prison service instruction
PSO	probation service officer, prison service order
PSO 4400	prison service instruction relating to child protection and harassment
PSR	pre-sentence report
RH	high risk (flag on CRAMS)
RMIS	resource management information system
ROTL	release on temporary licence (home leave) (prison)
R & R	reasoning and rehabilitation (programme)
RTO	road traffic offence
Rule 43	prison rule enabling prisoner to request segregation for their own protection
RV	very high risk (flag on CRAMS)
S1	Schedule 1 offender (flag on CRAMS)
Sch 1	offence listed in Schedule 1 1993 Children & Young Persons Act (a sexual or violent assault on a child)
SED	sentence expiry date (prison)
SEU	Sentence Enforcement Unit (Home Office)
SOTP	sex offender treatment programme
SPO	senior probation officer
SSSO	Suspended Sentence Supervision Order
SSR	specific sentence report
TC	telephone call/contact
TDA	take (motor vehicle) and drive away
TICs	offences taken into consideration
TOPs	Targetted Offenders Project
TPO	trainee probation officer
TWOC	take (motor vehicle) without owners consent
UAL	unlawfully at large (prison)
V1	verifier award (nvq)
VDT	voluntary drug test
VLO	victim liaison officer
VOU	victim offender unit
VP	vulnerable prisoner
VS	violence to staff (flag on CRAMS)
Wt no bail	warrant issued not backed for bail
YJ	youth justice
YOT	youth offending team

AVON & SOMERSET PROBATION AREA

Out of hours emergency contact point
Glogan House (01278) 424165

Victim enquiries contact number
0117 930 3732

e-mail Firstname.Surname@avon-somerset.probation.gsx.gov.uk

1. Queensway House
    The Hedges, St George
    Weston-super-Mare
    North Somerset, BS22 7BB
    tel (01934) 528740 *fax (01934) 528797*
    direct dial (01934) 52 + ext

    Board
    Christensen, John (chair)
    Limbrick, Graham (secy) ext 8709
    Berk, Elaine (pa to board) ext 8711

    Chief Officer's Group
    Whitford, Jeanette (co)
    Stewart, Debbie (pa to co) ext 8708
    Hambleton-Ayling, Dean (aco, hr) ext 8718
    Neale, Danielle (aco finance) ext 8705
    Doust, Michelle (pa to D Hambleton-Ayling & D Neale) ext 8707
    Wakefield, Rob (aco) ext 8703
    Cotgrove, Jill (aco) ext 8702
    Wiseman, John (aco) ext 8706
    Roberts, Louise (pa to J Cotgrove, R Wakefield & J Wiseman) ext 8712

    Area Business Managers
    Bristow, Brenda ext 8715
    Kelly, Mel ext 8714
    Pellow, Pat ext 8713

    Business Devpt & Performance
    Morelli, Massimo ext 8747

    Diversity
    Hillier, Graham ext 8731

    Human Resources/Payroll
    Taylor, Alison (hr mgr) ext 8717
    Davies, Anna (hr off) ext 8725
    Jones, Jackie (hr off) ext 8724
    Stuart, Cathy (hr off) ext 8723
    George, Rebecca (asst hr off, recruit) ext 8726
    Matthews, Chris (asst hr off) ext 8728
    Moore, Jenni (asst hr off) ext 8730
    Phull, Gudarshan (asst hr off) ext 8727
    Richards, Anna (acting hr off) ext 8729

Information Technology
Helpdesk 01934 528780

Thompson, Bruce (systems mgr) ext 8781
Asgaraly, Arif ext 8782
Bennett, Lee ext 8790
Carter, Trevor ext 8783
Donelon, John ext 8784
Edwards, Ed ext 8791
Motlow, Ben ext 8787
Shepherd, Scott ext 8788

IT Trainers
Thompson, Shirley ext 8793
Fensom, Pat ext 8792
Hosie, Freda ext 8794
Shepherd, Jane (admin info off) ext 8795

Finance
Clark, Jane (finance mgr) ext 8738
Joyce, Karen (finance mgr) ext 8733
Nutt, Lisa (finance off) ext 8735
Woodward, Lucy (finance off) ext 8737
Welch, Daniel (crossroads proj) ext 8734
Taylor, James (enquiries) ext 8736

Health & Safety
Andrews, Ben (mob 07736 086753) ext 8749

Staff Development
Wilson, Jim (training off) ext 8746
Kent-Probert, Fleur (training off) ext 8745
Harris, Elaine (snr admin off) ext 8744

Victim Liaison Team
Summerhayes, Alex (vlo) ext 8748

Admin
Hall, Tony (office mgr) ext 8741

2. The Old Convent
    35 Pulteney Road **Bath** BA2 4JE
    tel (01225) 460673 *fax (01225) 480404*

    Area Performance Manager
    Hull, Sue

    Offender Mgmnt Assessment Team
    Day, Kevin (middle mgr)
    Brazier, Tony (snr pract)
    Breckenridge, Allyson
    Martin, Deborah
    Middleton-Roberts, Kristy
    Spinney, Jo-Anne
    Summers, Claire
    Wilkinson, Clive
    Gill, Rebecca (pso)
    Love, Di (pso)
    Quinn, Lorraine (pso)
    Silver, Deborah (pso)

Public Protection Team
Torczuk, Ray
Stredder, Lesley

Programmes
Rakoczi, Jenny (middle mgr)
Henry, Olivia
Mountford, Guy (pso)
Pretty, Kelly (pso)

DTTOs/DRRs
Hawken, Sheila
White, Ann

Unpaid Work Unit
Day, Pauline (supvr/placement mgr)
Prior, Martin (supvr/placement mgr)

Trainees
Rymell, Alison (pda)
Larcombe, Laura
Larkin, Dora
Russell, Ruth

Admin
Reed, Liz (office mgr)
Fox, Diane (dep office mgr)

3. **Bridewell Street**
Bristol BS1 2JX
tel 0117-930 3700 *fax 0117-925 5488*
cclo fax 0117-976 3073
direct dial 0117-930 + ext

Victim enquiries contact number
0117-930 3732

Court Team
Hunt, Allason (spo) 3738
Miners, David (spo) 3737
Middleton, Jayne (snr pract) 3735
Cook, Bev (pso) 3756
Yates, Ina (pso) 3757

Breaches Unit
Brown, Diane 3755
Bryant, Carla 3755
Phillips, Beth 3755
Waller, Chris (dep office mgr) 3755

PSR Authors
Birch, Fiona 3745
Brooks, Hayley 3754
Butterly, Andy 3744
Davies, Neal 3747
Fagg, Pat 3748
Fraser, Rosemary 3753
Gledhill, Nicky 3750
Gordon, Caroline 3742
Heather, Alison 3716
Hunter, Jodie 3752
Hutchison, Stuart 3740

Poor, Alex 3739
Thompson, Bridget 3746
Young, Carrie 3747

Offender Mgmnt Assessment Team
Chilcott, Julie (pso) 3700

Public Protection Team
Wise, Mair (apm) 3720
Hodge, Liz (spo) 3721
Cragg, Rachael (snr pract) 3736
Atchison, Jane 3719
Thompson, Steve 3718
Bennett, Phil (police) 3725
Coombes, Alison (police) 3723
Flay, Maurice (police) 3722
Lewis, Tina (police) 3724

Trainees
Watson, Sybil (pda) 3715
Pengelly, Janna (trainee) 3700
Reilly, Deborah (trainee) 3700
Ssali, Sula (trainee)   3727
Wellman, Tom (trainee) 3700

Victim Liaison Team
Abel, Vicky (vlo) 3732
Harvey, Bridgette (vlo) 3732
Stuart, Wendy (vlo) 3732
Edwards, Sarah (dep office mgr) 3732
Smith, Dawn (admin) 3732

Admin
Hudson, Sarah (office mgr courts) 3712
Kelley, Jo (office mgr PPT) 3760
Walters, Diane (dep office mgr) 3708
Witts, Catherine (dep office mgr) 3708

4. **Bristol Crown Court Liaison Office**
Small Street, Bristol BS1 1DA
tel 0117-976 3071/2 *fax 0117-976 3073*

Court & Assessment Team
Comerford, Joanne (pso)

Administration
Taynton, Colin (dom)

5. **Decourcy House**
Upper York Street **Bristol** BS2 8QN
tel 0117-944 7200 *fax 0117-944 7220*

Drug Management Team
admin 0117-944 7215 *fax 0117-942 9285*

Bensted, John (area perf mgr) 7242
Scott, Robin (middle mgr) 07277
Romain, Maria 7248
Walsh, Jonathan 7289
Watkis, Linnett 7254
Fletcher, Linda (pso) 7253
Parker, Lesley (pso) 7254

Scott, Marvre (pso) 7245
Wildish, Kate (pso) 7249
Woodgate, Chris (pso) 7255

Enhanced Community Punishment
Britton, Jeremy (middle mgr) 7275
Wellman, Stuart (qa mgr) 7283
Merchant, Ron (cp res off) 7276
Brass, Mike (cp res asst) 7285
Smith, Troy (supvr/placement off) 7286
Mullins, Kevin (cp supvr) 7284

Crossroads
Billingsley, Jennifer (emplt link off)
Herowych, Tina (emplt link off)

ETE
0117-944 7280
O'Connor, Dan (middle mgr) 7272

Basic Skills/Learning Link Officers
Hawley, Janice (llo) 7266
McMeechan, Adam (llo) 7264
Bricker, Marcia (GSL Co-ordinator) 7283
Dunstan, Nicky (GSL Co-ordinator) 7282

Employment Link Officers
Cain, Paulette 7251
Griffiths, Michaela 7271
Williams, Michael 7273

Offender Mgmnt Assessment Team
0117-944 7250
Harrison, Marilyn (middle mgr) 7292
Hook, Mike (middle mgr) 7284
Hanbridge, Matthew (snr prac) 7236
Bristol, Tiggy 7237
Daly, Clare 7262
Farrelly, Richard 7259
Haines, Liz 7269
Yates, Jenny 7206
Anderson, Hanna (pso) 7268
Boulton, Gemma (pso) 7239
Harewood, Sheila (pso) 7200
Rivers, Nikki (pso) 7261
Martin, Alison (pso) 7231
Campbell, Mary (case mgr) 7278
Griffin, Annie (case mgr) 7281
Merchant, Elaine (case mgr) 7279

Programmes /Groupwork
Perry, Stephanie (middle mgr) 7288
Cormack, Rita (treatment mgr) 7333
van der Eerden, Barbara (treatment mgr) 7235
Calderwood, Islay 7233
Goedhart, Adriana 7229
Harley, David 7243
Hunt, Alice 7221
Reilly, Debra 7232
Sayer, Richard 7222

Banfield, Rose (pso) 7234
Costanza, Francie (pso) 7200
Jennings, Mike (pso) 7224
Potter, Brian (pso) 7200
Thomas, Katherine (pso) 7200
Windle, Debra (pso) 7227
Waller, Barbara (dep office mgr) 7214

Trainees
Trundley, Katy (pda)
Gardner, Pippy (trainee)

Volunteers
Galena, Cherry 7258

Administration
0117-944 7210
Stephens, Debbie (office mgr) 7205
Tye, Sarah (office mgr) 7204

6.   70 Crossways Road
Knowle Park Bristol BS4 2SP
tel 0117-983 0050/316 0680/1
fax 0117-983 0051

Offender Mgmnt Assessment Team
Lane, Keith (middle mgr) 0117-316 0689
Allen, Angie (case mgr) 0117-316 0695
Pengelly, Janna (case mgr) 0117-383 0050
Jenkins, Vaughan (case mgr) 0117-316 0699
Yates, Tony (snr prac) 0117-316 0706
Clark, Colin (pso) 0117
Kenyon, Caroline (pso) 0117-316 0708
Grogan, Jenny (pso) 0117-316 0696
Hayton, Lindsay (pso) 0117-316 0707
Hopgood, Natalie (pso) 0117-316 0697
Wedmore, Rachel (pso) 0117-316 0701
Whitlock, Denise (pso) 0117-316 0700

Public Protection Team
Burnett, Laurence 0117-316 0691

ETE
Pole, Tony 011-316 0684

Unpaid Work Unit
Mulholland, Simon (supvr placement mgr)
Reed, Nick (supvr placement mgr)
Sabin, Shelia (supvr placement mgr)

Trainees
Richards, Matthew 0117-316 0694
Pace, Alex 0117-316 0698
Wray, Nicky 0117-316 0692
Champion, Rob 0117-316 0704

Admin
Beeson, Lesley (office mgr) 0117-316 0688
Reeve, Jacqui (dep office mgr) 0117-316 0703

7. **North Bristol**
Greystoke Avenue, Westbury on Trym
Bristol BS10 6AD
tel 0117-950 9105 *fax 0117-959 1933*

Unpaid Work Unit
Wellman, Stewart (qa mgr) ext 248
Ward, Richard (supvr placement mgr)

Offender Mgmnt Assessment Team
Sanyasi, Marcia (middle mgr)
Rich, Val (snr pract)
Hathaway, David
Moreton, Amanda
Cesenek, Debbie (pso)
Liddiard, Ben (pso)
Meas, Kim (pso)
Rowland, Claire (pso)
Romain, Deane (pso)
Green, Jakki (pso)
Griffin, Annie (pso)

Public Protection Team
O'Connell, Mike
Perry, Roger

PSR Writer
Pasco, Mark
Whittaker, Nina

PSO for Yate
Butler, Jean (pso) (01454) 315945

Trainees
Edwards, Rosie (pda)
Goodhall, Margaret (pda)
Jenner, Sue (pda)

External Funding Business Manager
Thompson, Suzanne

Admin
Reay, Diane (office mgr) ext 239
McLeod, Jamie (dep office mgr)

8. Riverside House, West Quay
Bridgwater Somerset TA6 3HW
tel (01278) 423977 *fax (01278) 453941*
direct dial (01278) 727 + ext

Offender Mgmnt Assessment Team
Spencer, Liz (middle mgr) 118
Grover, Maggie (snr pract) 105
Lewis, Beverley (snr pract) 105
Carver, Adrian 154
Clark, Roger 116
Darbin, Steve 124
Jones, Kevin 130
Tomlinson, Clive 115
Kirby, Anna (pso) 119
Madelin, Chris (pso) 120
Hale, Lyn (pso) 120

Tuke, Mark (pso) 105
Ward, Carly (pso) 123
Sanchez, Paula (pso) 152

Programmes
Cornelius, Simon (apm) 112
Thatcher, Sally (middle mgr) 113
Harper, Sandra 133
Miller, Clare (pso) 155

Public Protection Team
Davis, Paul (middle mgr) 121
Adley, Pat 114
Webster, Robin 137
Price, Carol (pso) 111
Bath, Debbie (police) 145
Dunn, Tracey (police) 142
Fawkes, Gary (police) 143

Unpaid Work Unit
Greenslade, Tracey (upw co-ord) 117
Searle, Alison (qa mgr) 131
Stretch, Sharon (upw administrator) 146
Ernest, Peter (cp supvr) 134
John, Trevor (cp supvr) 128
Wilkinson, Dave (cp supvr) 134

CJIP
fax 01278 434648
Thackerberry, Galena (middle mgr) 140
Jenkins, Caroline 138
Carver, Aileen (pso) 147
Boyce, Alan (tp) 132
Jordon, Miles (sds) 135
Kingsbury, Marian (snr admin off) 139
Locke, Joanne (cjip administrator)
TP & SDS indicate Partner Agencies

Crossroads
Brandt, Peter (middle mgr) 144
Cayley, John (senior admin off) 133
Hampson, Sandra (clerical asst) 247

ETE
Mobsby, Melyan (pso) 125
Hampson, Sandra (clerical asst) 247

INCLUDE
Defazio, Dawn (pso) 127

Trainees
Chin, Mike (pda) 129
Barrie, Collete (trainee) 152
Hector, Katherine (trainee) 152
O'Neal, Maggie (trainee) 152

Business Development Unit
Meadows, Frank (project mgr) 101

Administration
Denslow, Shelley (office mgr) 101
Symons, Sharon (dep office mgr) 103

9. 11 Canon Street
    Taunton TA1 1SN
    tel (01823) 251351 *fax (01823) 321724*
    direct dial (01823) 346 + ext
    Minehead report centre (07974) 109850

    CJIP/CJIT/DIP
    Hextall, Nigel (snr pract)
    Penelhum, Margaret ext 440
    Baker, Jane (pso) ext 404
    David, Rachael (turning pt/cjwrkr) ext 404
    Ford, Linda (turning pt/cjwrkr) ext 404
    Cooper, Sharon (sds/cpn) ext 404

    Crossroads Project
    Danclar-Doody, Dawn ext 431
    Martin, Jenny ext 445

    Community Punishment
    Gardner, Pauline (qa mgr) ext 423
    Booth, Simon (pso) ext 415

    Offender Mgmnt Assessment Team
    Hamilton, Liz (middle mgr) ext 405
    Foy, Tom (snr pract) ext 432
    Lewis, Liz (cro's) ext 437 (also based at
    Minehead)
    Powell, Angie (resmt) ext 402
    Roberts, Paul (psr's) ext 434
    Evans, Mike (psr's) ext 439
    Waugh, Nicky (psr's/res) ext 436
    Radford, Kathy (pso, crown ct)(01823)
    338599
    Rawles, Colette (pso, resmt) ext 403
    Smith, Maxine (pso, crt) ext 408
    Taylor, Claire (pso, crt) ext 404
    Munday, Rachel (pso, cro's) ext 459
    Harman, Roy (case mgr) ext 438

    Programmes
    Boxer, Liz ext 457
    Bradley, Steve (treatment mgr) ext 418
    Cartright, Faith ext 424
    Rosewarne, Pauline ext 420
    Willett , Nicole ext 419
    Capon, Julie (pso) ext 417
    Packman, Heidi (pso) ext 430
    Rexworthy, Frances (pso) ext 417

    Trainees
    Ashton, Richard (pda) ext 435
    Dickins, Andy ext 449
    Higgins, Kerrie ext 456
    Knott, Chris ext 441
    Smith, Chantelle ext 449

    Brooks, Marie ext 449

    Seconded to YOT
    Tomlinson, Jane ext 441

    Administration
    Vacancy (office mgr) ext 425
    Corbett, Rebecca (dep office mgr) ext 426

10. **Taunton Crown Court**
    Shire Hall, Taunton TA1 1EU
    tel (01823) 338599 *fax (01823) 338946*

    Crown Court Administrators
    Radford, Kathy (p, pso)
    Smith, Maxine, (p, pso)

11. St Lawrence Lodge
    37 Chamberlain Street **Wells** BA5 2PQ
    tel (01749) 677779 *fax (01749) 672169*
    direct dial (01749) 683 + ext

    DIP
    Marland, Audrey 654
    Piggott, Jane ext 662

    Unpaid Work
    Higgins, Frank (unit mgr) ext 665
    Bowden, Joe (supvr placement mgr) ext
    666
    Guilford, Wendy (admin) ext 659

    Consortium
    Spurrell, Helen ext 656

    Court
    O'Gorman, Sean ext 656

    Offender Mgmnt Assessment Team
    Friend, Anne (spo) ext 657 (Yeovil)
    Marshall, Brian ext 651
    McCaffrey Mary ext 652
    Ferrero, Marion (pso) ext 252
    Flower, Joan (pso) ext 655
    Poole, John (pso) ext 658

    Turning Point
    Casey, Ursula ext 677

    Trainees
    Knell, Tim (pda) ext 664
    Holgate, Karenza ext 660
    Hall, Andrew ext 663
    Read, Hilary ext 660

    Admin
    Frampton, Lynn (office mgr) ext 657
    Binning, Helen (dep office mgr) ext 675

12. 50 The Boulevard
    Weston-super-Mare BS23 1NF
    tel (01934) 623526 *fax (01934) 621111*

    Community Punishment
    Offender Mgmnt & Assessment Team
    Harris, Andy (middle mgr)
    Rixon, Anna (snr pract)

Hays, John
McBride, Odette
Somerville-Ashby, Helen
Woods, Doug
Coveney, Helen (pso)
Hopton, Natalie (pso)
Stagg, Sarah (pso)

Court & Assessment Team
Berry, John
Tiernan, Joe
Coltham, Joy (pso)

DIP
Miller, Bob
Harris, Elaine (pso)

Programmes
Vale, Alan
Camish, Marilyn (treatment mgr)
Clark, Sarah (pso)
McGreevy, Lisa (pso)

Public Protection Team
Birt, Judy

Admin
Clarke, Annette (office mgr)
Sansom, Tish (dep office mgr)

13. Court Ash House
     Court Ash **Yeovil** BA20 1AG
     tel (01935) 476461 fax *(01935) 475290*
     direct dial (01935) + ext

     Court & Assessment Team
     Glide, Judy (pso) ext 709108

     Unpaid Work
     Ellery, Joy (qa mgr) ext 709112
     Shoemark, Robin (sup/pl.mgr) ext 709119

     CJIP/CJIT/DIP
     Robinson, Shirley ext 476461
     Bushell, Karen (pso) ext 311019
     Lyons, Jon (turning pt) ext 709127
     Ellis, Jo (turning pt) ext 709127
     Gage, Linda (cpn sds) ext 709129
     White, Amanda (cpn sds) ext 709129

     Crossroads
     Cullum, Beth (emplt link off) ext 709118
     White, Deane (emplt link off) ext 709118

     ETE
     Janas, Emily (learning link off) ext 709116

     Offender Mgmnt & Assessment Team
     Friend, Anne (spo) (Wells) ext 709115
     Henderson, Richard (snr pract) ext 709113
     Geraghty, Dominic ext 709111
     Marshall, Brian ext 476461
     Smerdon, Becca ext 709114

Chant, Pete (pso) ext 709121
Cox, Steve (pso) ext 709105
Ferero, Marion (p, pso) ext 709106

Public Protection Team
Adley, Pat (01935) 709110

Project Managers
Heyworth, Elaine ext 709123

Programmes
Jerzykowski, Ernie ext 709124
Lusty, Keith (treatment mgr) ext 709126
Harper, Joe (pso) ext 709126
Smith, Kerren (pso) ext 709125

Trainee
Champeny, Jenny ext 709122

Victims
Abel, Vicki (pso) ext 709100

Admin
Hole, Kate (office mgr) ext 709101
Taylor, Lesley (dep office mgr)

14. **Avon & Somerset Prolific
     OffenderScheme** (ASPOS)
     *email*Firstname.Lastname@avonand
     somerset.police.uk

     New Bridewell Office
     7th Floor, New Bridewell Police Station,
     Bridewell Street, Bristol,BS1 2HQ
     fax 0117 945 5133

     Austin, Rachel (acting area mgr) (07795
     507 409)
     Allum, Jim (spo) 0117-945 5525 (07919
     697720)
     Berry, Kathryn (office mgr) 0117-945 5148
     (07919 017262)
     Carey, Janice 0117-945 5158 (07717
     868211)
     Phillips, Emma 0117-945 5158 (07717
     868211)
     Stewart-Gentle, Angela 0117-945 5166
     (07717 700523)
     Bridal, Deb (pso) 0117-945 5165 (07717
     700526)
     Champagnie, Cynthia (pso) 0117-945 5164
     (07919 628897)
     Clark, Sarah (pso) 0117-945 5160 (07919
     697727)
     Corrick, Rebecca (pso) 0117-945 5168
     (07717 700524)
     Cross, Harriet (pso) 0117-945 5168 (07789
     753 625)
     Francis, Ian (pso) 0117-945 5159 (07919
     017259)
     Hinkins, Stuart (pso) 0117-945 5167
     (07919 017260)

Bath Office
Bath Police Station, Manvers Street
Bath BA1 1JN
fax 01225 842469

Hill, Janette (dep office mgr) 01225 842410
(07919 697717)
Leary, Michaela 01225 842410 (07717
868191)
Northam, Amy (pso) 01225 842522 (07717
700525)

HMP Bristol Office
HMP Bristol, Cambridge Road,
Horfield, Bristol, BS7 8PS
tel 0117-372 3388 *fax 0117-372 3239*

Sherwin, Dave (snr prison off) (07789
753627)
Watkins, Robert (prison off) (07789
753627)
Skeen, Anna (pso)

Staple Hill Office
Staple Hill Police Station, Broad Street,
Staple Hill, Bristol,BS16 5LX
fax 0117-945 4240

Sole, Stuart (snr pract 0117-945 4147
(07789 753628)
Collins, Jill 0117-945 4257 (07919 697712)
Gall, David (pso) 0117-945 4257 (07919
697733)
Smart, Charmaine (pso) 0117-945 4257
(07919 017261)

Taunton Office
Taunton Police Station, Shuttern,
Taunton, TA1 3QA
fax (01823) 363250

Elliott, Jennifer (acting spo) (01823)
363154 (07919 697723)
Montag, Barbara (01823) 363020 (07917
883 847)
Adds, Gillian (pso) (01823) 363020 (07789
753626)

Weston-Super-Mare Office
Weston Police Station,17 Walliscote Road
Weston-Super-Mare, BA23 1UU
fax (01934) 638124

Slack, Dave (01934) 838276 (07717
868221)
Edgell, Kerri (pso) (01934) 638276 (07919
697710)

Yeovil Office
Yeovil Police Station, Horsey Lane
Yeovil, Somerset, BA20 1EA
fax (01935) 402201

Robinson, Shirley (01935) 402249 (07919
697730)
Higginbotham, Coral (pso) (01935) 402249
(07795 316204)

Youth Offending Teams

15. 12 Charlotte Street
     Bath BA1 2NF
     tel (01225) 396966 *fax (01225) 396969*
     Vincent, Sue

16. Kenham House
     Wilder Street **Bristol** BS2 8PD
     tel 0117-903 6480 *fax 0117-903 6481*
     Bowes, Kirsten
     Wood, Becky

17. 48-50 Elm Park
     Filton South Gloucestershire BS34 7PP
     tel (01454) 868558 *fax (01454) 868560*
     Sitron, Jackie

18. 5-7 West End
     Street BA16 0LG
     tel (01458)440820 *fax (01458)449100*
     Jones, Mark
     Tomlinson, Jane

19. 59 Oxford Street
     Weston-super-Mare
     North Somerset BS23 1TR
     tel (01275) 888360 *fax (01275) 888361*
     Shaw, Paul

20. **Reducing Reoffending
     Partnership (South West)**
     The Pithay, Bristol, BS1 2NQ
     tel 0117-945 6754 mobile 07944 663069
     e-mail mark.ellery@rrpsouthwest.org.uk
     Ellery, Mark

Hostels

21. **Ashley House Probation Hostel**
     14 Somerset Street, Kingsdown
     Bristol BS2 8NB
     tel 0117-924 9697 *fax 0117-944 4290*
     Gough, Nick (apm, hostels &
     resettlement)
     Preston, Boyce (mgr)
     Bednall, Matthew (asst mgr)
     Hopkins, Clive (asst mgr)
     Pitman, John (asst mgr)
     Royle, Fiona (asst mgr)
     Whittaker, John (asst mgr)

Wilde, Sally (asst mgr)
Marks, Micky (night supvr)
Morris, Eddy (night supvr)
Rozario, Octavian (night supvr)
Garner, Paul (admin)
Burke, Terry (dep admin)

22. **Bridge House Approved Premises**
78 Filton Road, Bristol BS7 0PD
tel 0117-969 3123 *fax 0117-931 2167*

Preston, Boyce (hostel mgr) (based at 21)
Wallace, Paulette (ops mgr)
Collicott, Lyn (asst mgr)
Goodhind, Ray (asst mgr)
Hesketh, John (asst mgr)
Knill, Lisa (asst mgr)
McEneaney, Bernard (asst mgr)
Rundle, Matt (asst mgr)
Daniels, Ben (night supvr)
Mockridge, Leigh (night supvr)
Gorman, Brendan (office mgr)

23. **6 Brigstocke Road Approved Premises**
Bristol BS2 8UB
tel 0117-942 5851 *fax 0117-944 5945*

Ashby, Richard (mgr) (07718 630663)
Harber, Steven (asst mgr)
Jefferies Julie (asst mgr)
Lake, Catherine (asst mgr)
Orchard, Patrick (asst mgr)
Orchard, Patrick (asst mgr)
Nevin, Arnie (asst mgr)
Richardson, Des (asst mgr)
Warren, Martin (asst mgr)
Bates, Alan (night supvr)
Graham, Jon (night supvr)
Jacobs, Gillian (office mgr)

24. **Glogan House**
59 Taunton Road, Bridgwater TA6 3LP
tel (01278) 424165 *fax (01278) 446054*

Kelly, Phil (op mgr)
Andrews, Wayne (asst mgr)
Foxwell, Tony (asst mgr)
Greenway, Karen (asst mgr)
Murkin, Robert (asst mgr)
Reid, Steve (asst mgr)
Bourton, Bob (night supvr)
McGill, Dave (night supvr)
Brown, Rosie (office mgr)

Institutions

25. H M Prison, Cambridge Road
Horfield **Bristol** BS7 8PS
tel 0117-372 3100 *fax 0117-372 3153*
probn fax 0117-372 3239

Lane, Russell (spo) ext 3297
Trundley, Katy (lifers) ext 3353
Pye, Denise
Bridgmount, Jacqueline (pso)
Broad, Sally (pso)
Bessant, Matthew (bail info)
Rivers, Nikki (pso)
Vacancy
Vacancy
Doran, Anna (pso) ext 3248
Farrell, Nicky (pso, wkshp co-ord) ext 3353
Ayling, Melanie (admin) ext 3239
Clements, Lyn (admin) ext 3239

26. H M Prison **Leyhill**
Wotton-under-Edge, Falfield
Glos GL12 8DB
tel (01454) 264000 *fax (01454) 264001*
direct dial (01454) 26 + ext

Peckham, Zoe (snr pract, lifers) ext 4117
Hothersall, Anna (lifers) ext 4030
Brockbank, Lucy (lifers) ext 4030
Tonkinson, Clare (lifers) ext 4032
Gartner, Kate (lifers) ext 4118
Hancock, Sue (under 4 yrs) ext 4019
Ring, Lisa (over 4 yrs) ext 4036
Smith, Angela (under 4 yrs) ext 4026
Willett, Alison (over 4 yrs) ext 4057
Nash, Carly (pso) ext 4039

27. H M Women's Remand Centre
Eastwood Park Falfield
Wotton-under-edge , Glos GL12 8DB
tel (01454) 382100 *fax (01454) 382101*
sentence management fax (01454) 382092
direct dial (01454) 382 + ext

King, Anne (p, spo) ext 046
Lambert, Pamela (p, spo) ext 046
Garrett, Tina (snr prac) ext 048
Vacancy
Smith, Sean ext 065
Hall, Lesley
Starbuck, Kim (p) ext 127
Sullivan, Gina
Woodward, Sarah (p, admin) ext 127

28. H M Prison & YOI **Ashfield**
Shortwood Road, Pucklechurch
Bristol BS16 0QJ
tel 0117-303 8000 *fax 0117-303 8001*
direct dial 0117-303 + ext

Lane, Sue (snr pract) 8114
Frater, Natasha 8064
Walker, Rob 8064
Coleman, Justin (pso) 8114

29. H M Prison **Cornhill**
     Shepton Mallet BA4 5LU
     tel (01749) 823300 *fax (01749) 823301*

     probn fax (01749) 345256

     Hardman, Howard
     Porter, Richard
     Lauder, Carolyn (pso)
     Fegredo, June
     Smith, Christine (admin)

Local Justice Areas

     2 Bath & Wansdyke
     3-7 Bristol
     11 Mendip
     7 North Avon
     12 North Somerset
     8 Sedgmoor
     13 South Somerset
     9 Taunton Deane & West Somerset

Crown Courts

     4 Bristol
     10 Taunton

BEDFORDSHIRE PROBATION AREA

Victim enquiries contact number
(01234) 358978

e-mail
Firstname.Surname@bedfordshire.probation.sx.
gov.uk

1. **Head Office**
    3 St Peter's Street, Bedford MK40 2PN
    tel (01234) 213541 *fax (01234) 327497*

    Emm, Ben (co)
    Hazeltine, Mike (aco)
    Pace, Lis (aco)
    Powell, Andrew (aco)
    Williams, John (aco)
    Morrison, Audrey (admin services mgr)
    Bolam, Penny (board services off)
    Delves, John (prolific offender impl mgr)
    Harding, Alison (spo, training mgr)
    Doyle, Caroline (training admin)
    Richards, Maggie (public relations)

    Administration
    Gunning, Ros (pa to co)
    Ince, Josie (pa to Lis Pace)
    Jones, Sara (pa to acos & asm)
    Chapple, Belinda (pa to John Williams)

Human Resources
Jennings, Sue (head of hr)
Foinette, Nicole (h.r. advr)
Rowlands, Tracey (h.r. asst)

Performance and Information Unit
Brown, Andrew (performance & info mgr)
Mainwaring, Mick (i.t. mgr)
Martin, Pam (case mgmnt & info devpt off)
Brock, Nigel (network supt off)
Anderson, Yvonne (info service & stats off)
Doyle, Caroline (info asst)

Finance
Robertson, julie (finance mgr/treasurer)
Dunn, Clare (finance off)
Roberts-Cambell, Norma (finance & property admin)

2. **Programmes Unit**
    23-27 Napier Road, Luton LU1 1RF
    tel (01582) 735153 *fax (01582) 451536*

    Programmes
    Wain, Lynda (spo)
    Hooper, Stephen (treatment mgr)
    Smith, Richard (treatment mgr)
    Vacancy (pso)
    Finch, Heidi (pso)
    Flemming, Phillipa (pso)
    Lowther, Maureen (pso)
    Vacancy (pso)
    Henry, Claudette (pso)
    Turney, Darren (pso)
    Victor, Sarah (pso)
    Blake, Kelly (snr sec)

    Healthlink
    Hushie, Liz (nurse)

3. 41 Harpur Street
    Bedford MK40 1LY
    tel (01234) 350401 *fax (01234) 328658*

    Case Management
    Morrison, Roz (spo)
    Burrows, Matthew (spo)
    Alabi, Stella
    Armitage, Lesley
    Cavanagh, Jane
    Chandler, Jo
    Cochrane, Graham
    Cook, Alan
    Cook, Kirstie
    Gould, Dean
    Harris, Dave (popo)
    Holley, Gerald
    Humphries, Victoria
    Khaliq, Ros

Jones, Karen
Maisfield, Susan
Masters, Ruth
Mitchell, Rosemary
Munroe, Val
Teal, Yvonne
Ashton, David (pso)
Baker, Rhiannon (pso)
Dhesi, Balvinder (pso)
Frensham, Julie (pso)
Layne, Clorin (pso)

Drugs Team
Nickels, Kate (snr pract)
Spencer, Vikki
Russell, Carol (pso)
Vacancy (pso)
Theobald, Stuart (pso)
Groom, Fiona (admin)

Trainees
Breakey, Paul (pda/snr pract)
Wale, Richard (pda)
Atterbury, Sarah
Coope, Kirstin
Elmore, Claire
Joynes, Karen
Kansal, Kate
Laing, Liz
Mallard, Elizabeth
Motler, Sarah
Saunders, Rachel
Weller, Victoria

Admin
Blows, Dawn (snr sec)
McCaffrey, Rachel (sec)
Di Salvo, Carina (sec/recep)

Community Service
Gittins, Owen (pso)
Leonard, Joy (pso)
Burraway, Matthew (cs supvr)
Layne, Jacqueline (cs admin)

Programmes
Green, Gabrielle (treatment mgr)
Wildman, Les (treatment mgr)
Gregg, Samantha (psychologist)
Johnston, Andy (pso)
Wilson, Gwen (ete off)

County Victim Contact Service
tel (01234) 358978
de Souza, Chris (spo)
Britton, Joanne (vlo)
De Friend, Janette (vlo)
Desquesnes, Jan (vlo)

Colver, Rachel (sec)

4.   Frank Lord House
72 Chapel Street, **Luton** LU1 5DA
tel (01582) 413172 *fax (01582) 418279*

Case Management
Andrews, Debra (spo)
Beaumont Sue (spo)
Booth, Caroline (spo)
Abbotts, Phil
Akhteer, Yasmin
Bean, Helen
Brown, Jennifer
Cairncross, Sarah (pda/qam)
Edward, Max
Francis-Quinton, Minette
Fraser, Mark
Harrington, Ruth
Haynes, Cheryl
Howard, Tracey
Irving, Helen
Jackson, Gordon
Kirkby, Roz
Miller, Ashley
Mir, Nazia
O'Flaherty, Angela
Price-James, Louise
Robinson, Jenna
Rowe, Ann
Saint, Lisa
Sharples, Linda
Smith, Teresa
Thomas Smith, Julie
Whitehurst, Nicole (popo)

Baptiste, Jenni (pso, popo)
Charlton, Constance (pso)
Connolly, Gail (pso)
Chambers, Colette (pso)
Flavell, Helen (pso)
Foley, Wendy (pso)
Gray, Pam (pso)
McConnachie, Rachel (pso)
Sheldon, Debra (pso)
Wilson, Cyrita (pso)

Trainees
Eaden, Paul (pda/snr pract)
Benzie, Jackie
Briggs, Elizabeth
Brown, Patrick
Harland, Haley
Matthews, Anika
Moonesinghe, Georgina
Moriarty, Elaine
Stiles, Kerry

Administration
Belony, Wendy (snr sec)
Shirran, Andrea (snr sec)

Akhtar, Yasmin (sec)
Donthamsetti, Maddy (sec)
Hughes, Joanne (sec)
Kane, Linda (sec)
Rea, Fiona (sec)
Ross, Julia (sec)
Smith, Ruth (sec)
Taylor, Cenette (sec)
Hill, Jo (receptionist/sec)

Community Service
Delmar, Elaine (mgr)
Barlow, Sherrie (pso)
Bradshaw, Michelle (pso)
Clarke, Stephanie (pso)
Cudjoe, Michael (pso)
Khan, Faiser (pso)
Kanderkore, Julius (pso)
Odd, Stephen (pso)
Stow, Jan (cso)
Whitfield, Alison (supvr)
Wyatt, Richard (supvr)
Caveney, Marian (csu admin)

5. **Luton Youth Offending Team**
    16 Rothsay Road, Luton LU1 1QX
    tel (01582) 547900 *fax (01582) 547901*
    e-mail yot@luton.gov.uk

    Briddon, Anita (head of yo service)
    Paddison, Amanda (dep head of yo service)
    Campbell, Melissa (ops mgr)
    Collins, Dave (snr pract)
    McCarthy, Joanne (yjo)
    Moore, Dawn (yjo)
    Morgan, Nikky (yjo)
    Nixon, Brian (yjo)

    Sorley, Jim (issp co-ord)
    McEvoy, Julie (snr issp officer)
    Scott, Lauretta (snr issp officer)
    Atkinson, Michelle (issp officer)
    Taylor, Emma (issp officer)
    McEvoy, Caroline (issp educn & empl off)

    Pratt, Mikaela (trainee forensic psy)
    Robinson, Steve (police officer)
    O'Neil, Mary (snr educn psychologist)
    Samsuddin, Khadeja (bail supvn off)
    Hulse, Louise (referral order co-ord)
    Green, Jackie (parenting skills co-ord)
    Wright, Cassi (vlo)
    Hutchinson, Troy (snr info mgmnt off)
    Swiecicki, Noreen (admin & finance mgr)
    Griffiths, Katy (admin off)

6. **Bedfordshire Youth Offending Service**
    7 Ashburnham Road **Bedford** MK40 1BX
    tel (01234) 316400 *fax (01234) 349238*

Lucas, Adi (mgr)
McManus, Michelle (po)
Beckford, Sylvia (sw)
Chowdhury, Ashok (sw)
Young, Alison (sw)
Davison, Steve (police)
Phelan, Lucy (ewo)
Ball, Peter (bail supt)

7. **Bedfordshire Youth Offending Service**
    3a Woburn Road **Bedford** MK40 1EG
    tel (01234) 316505 *fax (01234) 316504*

    Thrussel, David (ops mgr)
    Weatherall, Brian (reparations co-ord)
    Kang, Charanjit (parenting co-ord)
    Maule, jo (yisp co-ord)
    Booth, Amanda (locum sw)
    Austin, David (yth wrkr)

8. **Bedfordshire Youth Offending Service**
    39 Oakwood Avenue **Dunstable** LU5 4AS
    tel (01582) 524420 *fax (01582) 424421*

    Anderson, Tony (ops mgr)
    Forde, Audrey (sw)
    Shaw, Martin (police)
    Ward, Catherine (yth & com wrkr)
    Tait, Chris (ewo)
    McNicholls, Dave (probn)
    Williams, Sue (adolescent services co-ord)

Court Services

9. **Magistrates' Court Liaison Office**
    Shire Hall, **Bedford**, MK40 1SQ
    tel (01234) 358402 *fax (01234) 358070*

    Pettengall, Louise (crt supt admin)

10. **Crown Court Liaison Office**
    Luton Crown Court
    7-9 George Street, Luton LU1 2AA
    tel (01582) 452079

    Crown Court Switchboard
    tel (01582) 452846 *fax (01582) 485529*

    Flavell, Helen (pso)
    Khadam, Zahida (sec)

11. **Magistrates' Court Liaison Office**
    The Court House
    Stuart Street, **Luton** LU1 5DL
    tel (01582) 482710 *fax (01582) 457261*

    Davis, Barbara (snr pract)
    Osborn, Audrey (sec)
    Barker, Suzanne (sec)

12. **Guild House** 28b Guildford Street
Luton LU1 2NR
tel (01582) 487808

Berg, Gill (spo)
Dawkins, Carole
Fisher, Val
Mulvie, catherine
Hoyles, Elaine (pso)

Healthlink
Friguin, Clem (snr nurse pract)
Dempsey, Ruth (nurse pract)

Hostels

13. **Luton Hostel**
36-40 Napier Road **Luton** LU1 1RG
tel (01582) 418200 *fax (01582) 737391*

Stott, jonathan (mgr)
Allen, Carol (dep mgr)
Martindale, Victoria (p)
Flavin, Pat (asst warden)
Jordan, Ralph (asst warden)
Morris, John (asst warden)
Wrapson, Nick (asst warden)
Bonsu, Anthony (night waking)
Fox, Dot (night waking)
Inaba, Kesiena (night waking)
Joseph, George (night waking)
Martin, Heather (admin)

14. **Bedford Hostel**
80 Chaucer Road **Bedford** MK40 2AP
tel (01234) 340501 *fax (01234) 351715*

Smith, Ali (mgr)
Nichols, Magdalena (deputy mgr)
Martindale, Victoria (p)
Gibson, Clare (asst warden)
Jones, Allan (asst warden)
Robinson, Maria (asst warden)
Tate, David (asst warden)
Wheatley, Gary (asst warden)
Bijoy, Mathew (night waking)
Conchie, George (night waking)
Dacey, Lynn (night waking)
Nkwocha, Victor (night waking)
Thompson, Jason (night waking)

Institution

15. H M Prison, St Loyes
Bedford, MK40 1HG
tel (01234) 358671 *fax (01234) 273568*

probn fax (01234) 373052
bail info fax (01234) 347268

Hart, Gordon 373058
Lewis, Clare (pso)

Local Justice Areas
3 Bedford & Mid Bedfordshire
4 Luton & South Bedfordshire

Crown Court
10 Luton

CAMBRIDGESHIRE PROBATION AREA

Out of hours emergency contact point
Wesleyan Road Hostel (01733) 551678

Victim enquiries contact number Pamela
Bogusz (01733) 564367

e-mail Firstname.Surname@cambridgeshire.
probation.gsx.gov.uk

1. **Head Office**
1 Brooklands Avenue
Cambridge CB2 2BB
tel (01223) 712345 *fax (01223) 568822*

direct dial (01223) 71+ext

Hughes, John (cpo) ext 2358
Mackett, Chris (acpo) ext 2350
Deller, Andrew (acpo) ext 2369
Clarke, Dot (p, acpo) ext 2352
Ryder, Matthew (acpo) ext 2376
Seaton, Paul (treasurer) ext 2354

1a. **Support Services Unit**
Godwin House, George Street
Huntingdon PE29 3ND
fax (01480) 375731

direct dial (01480) 37+ ext

Hopkinson, Jonathan (staff devpt mgr) ext
5783
Hayden, Alan (staff devpt off) ext 5784
Bale, David (pda) ext 5776
Tighe, Sadie (p, pract devpt assessor) ext
5790
Melrose, Gill (pda)
Minns, Grace (pda) ext 5779
McGregor, Jan (gpwk co-ord) ext 5779
Wemyss, Shona (training admin) ext 5787

Roberts, Mark (acpo, info mgr) ext 5721
Faulkner, Keith (info off) ext 5780
Dockerill, Lorraine (p, info off) ext 5755
Warburton, Diana (info off) ext 5792
Moore, Stephen (info off) ext 5773
Black, Cathy (p, info officer) ext 5791
Clampin, Dawn (p, intranet pubs officer)
ext 5794

Pereira, Chris (perf info officer) ext 5756
Cumberland, Jazz (p, admin clerk) ext 5735
Taylor, Jean (admin services mgr) ext 5775
Lloyd, Linda (cty network supt) ext 5782
Rogers, Flick (cty network supt) ext 5781
Jolly, Karen (p, h&s off) ext 5789

Sedzikowski, Sue (personnel mgr) ext 5707
Stackhouse, Joyce (personnel off) ext 5739
Jackson, Jackie (personnel secy) ext 5788
Springer, Sandra (personnel secy) ext 5788
Young, Mary (office admin) ext 5786
Burridge, Pat (p, admin) ext 5785

1b. **Multi Agency Public Protection Panel**
Cambridgeshire Police HQ
Hinchingbrooke Park,
Huntingdon PE29 6NP
tel (01480) 428013 *fax (01480) 428121*

Ashford, Carol (team mgr)
Jones, Sarah (p, mappa co-ord)
Pollard, Claire (p, mappa co-ord)

2. Warkworth Lodge, Warkworth Street
Cambridge CB1 1EG
tel (01223) 712271 *fax (01223) 712700*

Waghorn, Hannah (pract mgr)
Wallace, David (pract mgr)
Wardell, Linda (pract mgr)
Baker, Geraldine
Bardell, David
Bates, Gemma
Benton, Jacqueline
Beale, Julie
Crowley, Julie
Foreman, Fran
Lowes, Julie
McNamara, Adele
Prosol, Caroline (yot)
Shadbolt, Maureen
Stockford, Ann
Taylor, Amanda

Ashton, Diane (trainee)
Speechley, Rachel (trainee)
Williams, Claire (trainee)

Bowen, Tina (pso)
Colomb, Stella (pso)
Copping, Zoe (pso)
Fieldhouse, Adrian (pso)
Flowerdew, Christopher (pso)
Lightfoot, Cheryl (pso)
Miller, Claire (pso)
Patel, Rajesh (pso)
Robson, Jim (pso)

Savchenko, Rachel (pso)
Stone, Rebecca (pso)
Andrews, Bob (plcmnt mgr, unpaid wk)
de Souza, Jorge (plcmnt mgr, unpaid wk)
King, Tatiana (pso, unpaid wk)
Hayes, Dennis (accom adv wrkr)
Pool, Margaret (victim co-ord)

3. Sessions House, Lynn Road
Ely Cambridge CB6 1DA
tel (01353) 663523 *fax (01353) 669047*

Open Tues & Thurs only
all mail to office 2

4. Old County Buildings
Grammar School Walk
Huntingdon PE18 6LF
tel (01480) 376100 *fax (01480) 376123*

Pease, Adrian (pract mgr)
Tomlin, Laura (pract mgr)
Baillie, Michael
Durose, Jennifer
Donoghue, Dominic
Eshelby, Clare
Goff, Christine
Marsh, Linsey
Seller, Karen
Parker, Marsha
Thwaites, Emma
Wylie, Eileen

Prior, Marie (trainee)
Roberts, Katie (trainee)
Smart Tony (trainee)

Ferrari, Sarah (pso)
Jest, Anna (pso)
King, Michelle (pso)
Ludlam, Marie (pso)
Mawditt, Marilyn (pso)
Taylor, Melanie (pso)
Templar, Ann (pso)

Garratty, Jim (p, plcmnt mgr, unpaid wk)
Mansfield, Keith (p, plcmnt mgr, unpaid wk)
Murphy, Tracy (accom adv wrkr)

Huntingdon Rear Building
Corfield, Helen (team mgr)
Flack, Julia (team mgr) ext 5391
Goffrey, Mark (team mgr) ext 5391
Gooch, Baden (team mgr) ext 5460
Harris, Martin (team mgr) ext 5762
Preston, Jay (team mgr) ext 5772
Walker, Mick (team mgr) ext 5460
Wallis, Stuart (team mgr) ext 5759
Dawkins, Ellwyn (pract mgr) ext 5769

Lewis, Bob (pract mgr)
McAngus, John (pro) ext 5460
Wallis, Lesley (pract mgr) ext 5765
von Rabenau, Elisabeth (pract mgr) ext 5771
Miller, Claire (pso)
Pritchard, Julia (pso)

5.   Castle Lodge, 1 Museum Square
Wisbech PE13 1ES
tel (01945) 461451 *fax (01945) 476350*

Drury, Adrienne (pract mgr)
Brickley, Stephen
Herron, Nicola
Kerr, Sally (p)
Morphus, Becki

Holloway, Stephen (trainee)
Turner, Jayne (trainee)

Garrett, Shaun (pso)
Humphrey, David (pso)
Malloy, Val (p, pso)
Talbot, Sophie (pso)
Stokes, Paula (plcmnt mgr, unpaid wk)

5a.   The Court House
Market Place **March** PE15 9JF
tel (01354) 650677

all mail to office 5

6.   Magistrates Court, Bridge Street
Peterborough PE1 1ED
tel (01733) 564367 *fax (01733) 315758*

Sanderson, Kelly (pract mgr)
Seddon, Graeme (pract mgr)
Breed, Sarah
Drabble, Jacie
Hoche, Anita
Providence, Belinda
Stewart, Malcolm
Stocks, Simone
Strowbridge, David (p, yot)
Szumlicki, Anna
Walton, Claire

Savage, Christopher (trainee)
Smallwoods, Christopher (trainee)
Walker, Christopher (trainee)

Bailey, Maxine (pso)
Bailey, Susan (pso)
Beacham, James (pso)
Bester, Rachel (pso)
Bogusz, Pamela (pso)
Clarke, Lucy (pso)
Buckingham, Louise (pso)
Forte, Monica (pso)

Hanssen, Sue (pso)
Latham, Lynda (pso)
Munir, Mohammed (pso)
Nolan, Gary (pso)
Williams, Christine (pso)
Woods, Paul (pso)

Moore, Fay (accom adv wrkr)
McCoubrey, Derek (emplt)

Crown Court
tel (01733) 352763 *fax (01733) 565284*

Beacham, James (pso)

7.   Gloucester House, 23a London Road
Peterborough PE2 8AP
tel (01733) 348828 *fax (01733) 313765*

Beaumont, Lynn (pract mgr)
Jones, Wendy (pract mgr)
Coleman, Lucy
Curphey, David
Howley, David
Lace, Liz
Morse, Mike (p)

Palmer, Rachel (trainee)
Taylor, Melanie (trainee)

Alderson, Michael (pso)
Austin, Joanne (pso)
Cummings, Lorna (pso)
Follenfant, Rebecca (pso)
Jacques, Caroline (pso)
Lloyd, Scott (pso)
Martin, Rachael (pso)
Neve, Joann (pso)
Smith, Nick (pso)
Spruce, Jenny (pso)
Stanford, Dee (pso)
Woodham, Jackie (pso)

Honeywood, Derrick (unpaid wk pract mgr)
Bird, Betty (plcmnt mgr, unpaid wk)
Browning, Linda (plcmnt mgr, unpaid wk)
Campbell, Anita (p, plcmnt mgr, unpaid wk)
Garratt, Steve (plcmnt mgr, unpaid wk)
Moore, Alan (plcmnt mgr, unpaid wk)
Smith, Susan (p, plcmnt mgr, unpaid wk)

Hostel

8.   Probation and Bail Hostel
5 Wesleyan Road
Peterborough PE1 3RW
tel (01733) 551678 *fax (01733) 345161*

Vacancy (team mgr)
Vacancy (dep mgr)

Henry, Symon (asst warden)
Martin-James, Penny (asst warden)
Jackson, Shane (asst warden)
Jenkins, Brian(pso)
Smith, Steve (pso)
Trower, Adreana (pso)

Institutions

9. H M Prison **Littlehey**
    Perry, Huntingdon, Cambs PE18 0SR
    tel (01480) 333000 *fax (01480) 333001*

    Vacancy (p, team mgr)
    Benn, Colin
    Hill, Anne
    Robinson, Paula
    Sparke, Jackie
    Wood, Phil
    Martin, Donna (p, pso)

10. H M Prison **Whitemoor**
    Longhill Road, March PE15 0AF
    tel (01354) 602350 *fax (01354) 602351*
    direct dial (01354) 602+ext

    Probn clerk ext 616
    Sentence management ext 659
    Domestic visits ext 800
    Special visits ext 472

    Harding, Mike (team mgr) ext 700
    Beech, Garry ext 2691
    Block, Nigel ext 701
    Chapman, Denise ext 467
    Fieldhouse, Nicola ext 796
    Loosley, Suzanne ext 606
    Heighton, Tim (pso) ext 706

11. H M Prison **Peterborough**
    Saville Road, Westfield
    Peterborough PE3 7PD
    tel (01733) 217500 *fax (01733) 217501*

    Aylward, Alison (team mgr)
    Johnson, Richard
    Masterson, Mark
    Toze, John
    Palmer, Barbara (pso)

Local Justice Areas

2 Cambridge
3 East Cambridgeshire
4 Huntingdon
5 Fenland
6, 7 Peterborough

Crown Courts

2 Cambridge
6 Peterborough

CHESHIRE PROBATION AREA

Out of hours emergency contact number
07946 593840

e-mail
Firstname.Surname@cheshire.probation.gsx.
gov.uk

1. **Head Office**
    Beech House, Park West,
    Sealand Road, Chester CH1 4RJ
    tel (01244) 394500 *fax (01244) 394507*

    Collett, Steve (co)
    Davidson, John (aco)
    Evans, Christine (aco)
    Ingram, Keith (aco)
    Link, Sandra (aco)
    Orrell, Marie (aco)

    Communications and Health & Safety
    Gaughran, Liz (corporate services mgr)

    Unpaid Work
    Carruthers, Jim (unpaid work scheme mgr)

    Contracts & Partnerships
    Hulse, Steve (contracts officer)

    County Programmes
    Jones, Sîan (mgr)
    Thornden, Kim (mgr)

    District Managers
    Edwards, Chris
    Gwenlan, Chris

    Diversity
    Theilade, Annemarie (mgr)

    Human Resources & Staff Devpt
    tel (01244) 394503
    Mackenzie, Helen (mgr)

    Finance
    tel (01244) 394502
    Hughes, Derek(mgr)

    Information Services
    tel (01244) 394501
    Vernon, Eileen (mgr)

    Performance & Quality Assurance
    McDermott, Gerry (mgr)
    Smith, Tracy (mgr)

    Public Protection
    Marquez, Ellen-Marie

    Security
    Iremonger, Gordon (mgr)

    Substance Misuse
    Jones, Peter (mgr)

Hewitt, Stephen (pso) (7)
Hughes, Yvonne (pso) (2 & 3)
Meredith, Sandra (pso) (6)
Simpson, Penny (pso) (2)
Taylor, Danielle (pso) (2)

Trainee POs
Collins, Michelle (mgr)

2. Jupiter House, Jupiter Drive
    Chester West Employment Park
    Chester CH1 4QS
    tel (01244) 665100 *fax (01244) 665101*

West Cheshire Offender Mgmnt Unit
Peters, Cherryl (spo)
Quick, John (spo)
Webber, Sue (area admin mgr) (also 3-8)
Biddle, Malveen
Cringle, David
Fairley, Brenda
Finnegan, John
Gray, Nikki
Mordue, George
Moss, David
Orr, Rose
Robertson, Kerry Ann
Robson, Jacqueline
Scott, Christine
Thomas, Lydia
Wall, Helen
Warburton, Helen
Ballard, Caroline (pso)
Burrell, Clare (pso)
Dentith, Karen (pso)
Hammersley, Clare (pso)
Rose, Rachel (pso)

Accommodation Services Unit
tel (01244) 665190 *fax (01244) 665191*

Garner, Liz (mgr) (8)
Bailiff, Patricia (accomm services off)
Raisbeck, Ann (accomm services off)
Robinson, Wendy (accomm services off)

Unpaid Work Unit
Couzens, Denise (treatment mgr) (also 3)
Crawford, Karen (pso)
Lally, Andrea (pso)
Mahar, Dennis (pso)
Shone, Jenny (pso)

Court Services Unit
tel (01244) 665192 *fax (01244) 665193*

Corbett, Catherine (spo)
McDonagh, Christine (spo)
Kernahan, Chris
Sanders, Francis

Anderson, Sue (pso)

Davies, Lisa (pso)
Head, Mavis (pso)
Jenkins, Lee (pso)
Rawlinson-Doyle, Jan (pso)

Percival, Jane (pso) (3)

Boliver, Michael (pso) (4)
Graham, Kim (pso) (4)
Mapson, Frank (pso) (4)
Simpson, Richard (pso) (4)
Summers, Julie Anne (pso) (4)

Hallett, Michelle (pso) (5)
Law, Anne (pso) (5)

Cunliffe, Sally (4)
Rowntree, Rosie (6)
Esegbona, Helen (pso) (6)
Isherwood, Michael (pso) (6)
Telford, Sue (pso) (6)
Woby, Bob (bail info) (6)

Brown, Yasmin (pso) (7)
Rogers, Paula (pso) (7)
Holmes, Bea (pso) (7)

Victim Liaison Unit
tel (01244) 665111 *fax (01244) 665193*

Dyer, Karl (co-ord)
Gibbons, Julie (pso)
Parkinson, Sue (pso)
Stewart, Chris (pso)

3. Marshall Memorial Hall
    Woodford Lane **Winsford** CW7 2JS
    tel (01606) 551166 *fax (01606) 861267*

Offender Management Unit
Butler, Peter (spo)
Webber, Sue (area admin mgr) (also 2, 4-8)
Aspden, Andrea
Entwistle, Ben
Goldthorpe, Heather
Griffiths, Andrew
Keatley, Sarah
Long, Belynda
Pritchard, Carol
Alcock, Angela (pso)
Green, Samantha (pso)
Polshaw, Lee (pso)

Unpaid Work Unit
tel (01606) 593574 *fax (01606) 861267*

Couzens, Denise (treatment mgr) (also 2)
Millington, Grenville (pso)

4. Howard House, 10a Friars Gate
    Warrington WA1 2RW
    tel (01925) 650613 *fax (01925) 445109*

Offender Management Unit
Mayo, Edward (spo)
Neary, Jackie (spo)
Webber, Sue (area admin mgr) (also 2, 3, 5-8)
Catterall, Jane
Esegbona, Clement
Lawlor, Jim
Murphy, Joanne
Palin, Julie
Parkinson, Hilary
Tonkinson, Amanda
Varty, Jan
Whalley, Michael
Wilson, Jessica
Woodruff, John
Gillespie, Jane (pso)
Hamlett, Andrea (pso)
Lowe, Diane (pso)
Maggs, Kathryn (pso)
Merrill, Sarah (pso)
Tickle, Anthony (pso)
White, Kirsty (pso)
Whittle, Elizabeth (pso)

Unpaid Work Unit
tel (01925) 646030 *fax (01925) 654184*

Sloyan, Fiona (treatment mgr)
Astall, Julie (pso)
Johnston, James (pso)
McGregor, Sheila (pso)

5. Norton House, Crown Gate
    Runcorn WA7 2UR
    tel (01928) 713555 *fax (01928) 701985*

Offender Management Unit
Wallace, David (spo)
Webber, Sue (area admin mgr) (also 2-4, 6-8)
Balchin, Susan
Bennett, Diane
Eagles, Jackie
Kneale, Elaine
McIntyre, Kevin
Naylor, Emma
O'Hea, Brendan
Pugh, Karen
Scott, Julie
Verney, Julie
Wyatt, Sue
Bradley, Elizabeth (pso)
Bradshaw, Frank (pso)
Cavallaro, Eileen (pso)
Douglas, Gillian (pso)
McCaskill, Jane (pso)

Basic Skills/ETE
Bennett, Chris (mgr)

Mentor Co-ordination
Maddock, Carolynne (mentor co-ord)

Trainees
Collins, Michelle (mgr) (1)
Blackham, Caroline (practice suprvr)
Pearce, Cynthia (practice suprvr)
Taylor, Karen (practice suprvr)

6. 47 Delamere Street
    Crewe CW1 2JX
    tel (01270) 257781 *fax (01270) 251181*

Offender Management Unit
Scally, Chris (spo)
Smith, Ian (spo)
Webber, Sue (area admin mgr) (also 2-5, 7-8)
Cross, Ricci
Lane, Rebecca
Leebetter, Suzanne
Owen, Mark
Pazio, John
Prendergast, Helen
Stans, Mandy
Thorne, Michael
Waldron, Tracey
Wilkinson, Val
Williams, Nick
Yates, Donna
Collier, Rachel (pso)
Kusair, Pam (pso)
Langton-Flint, Kirsteen (pso)
Tavoulari, Isobel (pso)

Unpaid Work Unit
tel (01270) 256183 *fax (01270) 251181*

Crawford, Ann (treatment mgr) (also 7)
Burgess, Louise (pso)
Hamlett, Elaine (pso)
Scragg, Bill (pso)
Vickers, Wendy (pso)

7. Bradshaw House, 45 Cumberland Street
    Macclesfield SK10 1BY
    tel (01625) 423974 *fax (01625) 421345*

Offender Management Unit
Robertson, Liz (spo) (also at 8)
Webber, Sue (area admin mgr) (also 2-6, 8)
Campbell, Rachel
Duffy, Catherine
Eardley, Yvonne
Hilal, Nadia
May, Ann
Meffin, Marie
Sergeant, David
Woolley, Stephen
Brown, Charlotte (pso)

Corlett, Andrew (pso)
Perez, Sarah (pso)

Unpaid Work Unit
tel (01625) 615650 *fax (01625) 421345*

Crawford, Ann (treatment mgr) (also 6)
Chadwick, Brian (pso)
Gregory, Janet (pso)

8.   6 Parkway
     Wilmslow SK9 1LS
     tel (01625) 530881 *fax (01625) 549353*

Offender Management Unit
Robertson, Liz (also at 7)
Webber, Sue (area admin mgr) (also 2-7)
Bennett, Sue
Walsh, Chris
Lilly, Alan (pso)

9.   **County Programmes Unit**
     Jones, Sîan (mgr) (1)
     Thornden, Kim (mgr) (1)

     Kewley, Stephanie (treatment mgr) (2)
     Croft Eve (treatment mgr) (2)
     Elwin, Nicola (2)
     Aldcroft, Kelly (pso) (2)
     Buckley, Lyndsey (pso) (2)
     Holleran, Steve (pso) (2)
     Ramsdale, Sue (pso) (2)
     Riccio, Marian (pso) (2)
     Roberts, Adele (pso) (2)
     Snow, Heather (pso) (2)

     Baranska, Vanda (treatment mgr) (5)
     Crebbin, Dorothy (5)
     Devenny, Paul (5)
     Humphries, Rachel (5)
     Sykes, Jan (5)
     Thorne, Anna (5)
     Barker, Val (pso) (5)
     Green, Laura (pso) (5)
     Hague, Lyndsey (pso) (5)
     Harvey, Ingrid (pso) (5)
     Hayes, Tracey (pso) (5)
     Maddock, Jane (pso) (5)

     Vacancy (treatment mgr) (6)
     Edgeley, Angela (pso) (6)
     Lewis, Melissa (pso) (6)
     Ratcliffe, Karen (pso)
     Searles, Brenda (pso) (6
     Turner, Debra (pso) (6)

Youth Offending Team

10. The Law Courts,
     Civic Centre **Crewe** CW1 2DT
     tel (01244) 615300

Bootherstone, Kate

11. Byron Centre, Byron Street
     Macclesfield SK11 7QA
     tel (01625) 660500

     Jones, Brian

12. Patten Hall, Winmarleigh Street
     Warrington WA1 1NB
     tel (01925) 634981

     Ashraf, Farah

Hostels

13. **Linden Bank Approved Premises**
     40 London Road
     Elworth Sandbach CW11 3BD
     tel (01270) 759181 *fax (01270) 759579*

     Maskell, Colin (spo) (also 14)
     Day, Julie (dep mgr) (also 14)
     Rowe, Peter (dep mgr) (also 14)
     Halden, Paula (pso)
     Pacheco, Joe (pso)
     Rowsell, John (pso)
     Rozitis, Richard (pso)

14. **Bunbury House Approved Premises**
     Alnwick Drive, Stanney Grange
     Ellesmere Port CH65 9HE
     tel (0151) 357 3551 *fax (0151) 356 2102*

     Maskell, Colin (spo) (also 13)
     Brayshaw, Alana (dep mgr)
     McDonough, Katie (dep mgr) (also 13)
     Rowe, Peter (dep mgr) (also 14)
     Ferguson, Emma (pso)
     Jones, Ian (pso)
     Logan, Matthew (pso)
     Richardson, Colin (pso)

Institutions

15. HM Prison & Young Offender Institution
     Styal Wilmslow SK9 4HR
     tel (01625) 553000 *fax (01625) 553204*

     Meade, Donna (spo)
     Maude, Manjit
     Miklaszewicz, Janina
     O'Rourke, Jackie
     Roscoe, Claire
     Smith, Tom
     Thurlbeck, Gail
     Atkinson, Jan (pso)
     Nuttall, Chris (pso)
     Rogers, Paula (pso)

16. H.M. Prison, Warrington Road
Risley via Warrington WA3 6BP
tel (01925) 733000 *fax (01925) 764103*
probn fax (01925) 766975

Odeka, Fran (spo)
Benbrook, Maureen
Birch, Jean
Bray, Nicholas
Jackson, Helen
Norman, Phil
Pyman, Malcolm
Fox, Charlotte (pso)
Lawlor, Christine (pso)
Pownell, Andrew (pso)

17. H M Young Offender Institution
Thorn Cross Appleton Thorn
Via Warrington WA4 4RI
tel (01925) 605100 *fax (01925) 605101*

Denton, Mike (spo)
Martin, Peter
Clelow, Claire (pso)
Derrig-Vanzie, Cathryn (pso)

Local Justice Areas

2 Chester, Ellesmere Port & Neston
3 Vale Royal
4 Warrington
5 Halton
6 South Cheshire
7 Macclesfield

Crown Courts

2 Chester
2 Knutsford
2 Warrington

CUMBRIA PROBATION AREA

Out of hours emergency contact point
Bowling Green Approved Premises (01228) 340024

e-mail
Firstname.Surname@cumbria.probation.gsx.gov.uk

1. **Head Office**
Lime House, The Green
Wetheral, Carlisle CA4 8EW
tel (01228) 560057 *fax (01228) 561164*

Maiden, Mike (co)
Gadman, Alan (aco interventions)

Hennessy, Annette (aco, offender mngmnt)
Brown, Michelle (aco human res)
Moore, Fiona (secretary, solicitor)
Sait, Sargon (treasurer /aco, finance& resources)
Cleminson, Christine (info mgr)
Martin, Gillian (human res mgr)
Roebuck, Duncan (business process mgr)
Manson, Andrea (h&s off)
Swenson, Adrian (spo)

NW Consortium
Lear, Jan (ettm)
Anderson, Gill (regnl admin etp)

2. 10 Lawson Street
Barrow-in-Furness LA14 2LW
tel (01229) 820870 *fax (01229) 829548*

Green, Caroline (spo offender mngmnt)
Montague, Ted (spo interventions)

Offender Management
Hubbard, Stephen (snr pract)
King, Caroline (snr pract)
Buttery, Rob
Casson, Joanne
Clegg, Julie
Hutt, Robin
Kelly, Trisha
Linton, Pippa
McCormick, Jane
Parks, Ruth
Pervez, Fiona
Sutton, Emma
Reed, Emily (p)
Wilson, Joy
Worsley, Rob
Burdett, Erica (psa)
Carruthers, Brian (psa)
Childs, David (psa)
Keightley, Ian (psa)
Rutter, Maureen (psa)
Wilson, Claire (psa)

Interventions
Huddart, Lynn (qa, unit mgr)
Baker, Stephen (psa)
Birkby, Paul (psa)
Lyon, Bob (psa)
Thorpe, Gary (psa)
Waite, Rebecca (psa)

3. Georgian House, Lowther Street
Carlisle CA3 8DR
tel (01228) 522333 *fax (01228) 552179*

Kimberley, Paul (spo interventions)
Davidson, Chris (spo offender mngmnt)

Offender Management
Irwin, Derek (snr pract)
Buckley, Danielle
Critchlow, Peggy (p)
Doggart, Claire
Downie, Jack
Hobbs, Kim
Kacedan, Alyson (p)
Loy, Helen
McQuillan, Alistair
Maloney, Bill
Maynard, Paul
Murray, Phil
O'Brien, Margaret
Penton, Joanne
Stobart, Linda
Timperon, David
Waugh, Rachel
Wilson, Sue (p)
Stemp, Hayley (psa)
Collingwood, Steven (psa)
Winterton, Annabel (psa)
Walker, Tracey (psa)
Atkins, Rebecca (psa)
Brough, Kathleen (psa)
Grey, Mike (psa)
McNeish, Jean (psa)
Reynolds, Charlotte (psa)
Wilkinson, Rachel (psa)

Interventions
Muller, Karl (unit/qa mgr)
Faith, Alan (psa)
Glaister, Caroline (psa)
Thwaites, Ray (psa)

North West Training Consortium
Byrom, Ruth (pda)

4.   Busher Lodge, 149 Stricklandgate
     Kendal LA9 4RF
     tel (01539) 723126 *fax (01539) 720646*

     Hamilton, Stuart (spo, public protection)
     Dickson, Katrina (mappa registrar)

     Green, Caroline (spo offender mngmnt)
     Montague, Ted (spo interventions)

Offender Management
Carter, Roger
Helliwell, Brian
Robinson, Jane
Teasdale, Bob (psa)

5.   First Floor, Clint Mill
     Cornmarket **Penrith** CA11 7HW
     tel (01768) 864928 *fax (01768) 861929*

Offender Management
Critchlow, Peggy (p)

6.   The Court House, Catherine Street
     Whitehaven CA28 7PA
     tel (01946) 598120 *fax (01946) 598149*

     Craven, Mike (spo offender mngmnt)
     Watson, Richard (spo interventions)

Offender Management
Hodgson, John
Cullen, Marie
Hallam Davies, Steve
Jackson, Barbara
Johnson, Alice
Makin, Stacey (psa)
Scott, Nicholas (psa)
Sewell, Eddie (psa)

Interventions
Arnold, Steve (unit/qa mgr)
Crosby, Fiona

7.   Hall Park, Ramsay Brow
     Workington CA14 4AR
     tel (01900) 604691 *fax (01900) 603572*

     Craven, Mike (spo interventions)
     Watson, Richard (spo assessments)

Offender Management
MacKenzie, Barbara (snr pract)
Albon, Audrey
Barrett, Vivien
Bowker, Pam
Dawson, Robin
Lawson, Sarah (p)
van Lachterop, Jo
Arrowsmith, Noreen (psa)
Chisnall, Lindsey (psa)
Garrett, David (p, psa)
Edwards, Diane (psa)

Interventions
Simpson, John (psa)
Whent, Rebecca (psa)

8.   41 Curzon Street
     Maryport CA15 6LW
     tel (01900) 812467 *fax (01900) 815152*

Interventions
Blythe, Margaret (psa)
Armstrong, George (psa)
Garret, David (p, psa)

Cumbria Youth Offending Team

9.   **North Division**
     5 Brunswick Street, Carlisle CA1 1PB

tel (01228) 607090 *fax (01228) 607094*

Vacancy

10. **West Division**
    67 Wood Street, Maryport CA15 6LD
    tel (01900) 813531 *fax (01900) 812636*

    Bushell, Lindsey

11. **South Division**
    Newbridge House
    Ewan Close, Barrow in Furness LA13 9ED
    tel (01229) 826080 *fax (01229) 824165*

    Hill, Diane

Cumbria Drugs Action Team

12. **North**
    113-117 Botchergate
    Carlisle CA1 1RZ
    tel (01228) 882272

    Kemp, Emily
    Sinclair, Clair

13. **West**
    Addaction, Market Hall
    Workington CA28 7JG
    tel/fax to be announced

    Cardell, Donna
    Dodd, Brenda

14. **South**
    Barrow Probation Office
    10 Lawson Street
    Barrow-in-Furness LA14 2LW
    tel (01229) 820870 *fax (01229) 829548*

    McGowan, Valerie
    Woof, Judy

Hostel

15. **Bowling Green Approved Premises**
    90 Lowther Street, Carlise CA3 8DP
    tel (01228) 522360 *fax (01228) 590967*

    Mears, David (spo warden)
    Miles, Clive (snr pract deputy)

Institution

16. **H M Prison Haverigg**
    Millom LA18 4NA
    tel (01229) 772131 *fax (01229)770011*

    Cooper, Gill (spo)
    Norris, Sue
    Wyatt, Lee
    Nilsson, Deborah (psa)
    O'Brien, Diane (psa)
    Tosh, Jenny (psa)

Local Justice Areas

2 Furness & District
3 Carlisle & District
4 South Lakeland
5 Eden
6 Whitehaven
7 West Allerdale & Keswick

Crown Court

3 Carlisle

DERBYSHIRE PROBATION AREA

Out of hours emergency contact point
Burdett Lodge, (01332) 341324

Victim enquiries contact number:
(01332) 340029

e-mail Firstname.Surname@derbyshire.
probation.gsx.gov.uk

1. **Head Office**
   18 Brunswood Road
   Matlock Bath, Matlock DE4 3PA
   tel (01629) 55422 *fax (01629) 580838*

   tel (01629) 582692
   White, Denise(co)
   Raine, John (chair of board)

   tel (01629) 57692
   Yates, Paul (aco)
   Plang, Rosemary (aco)

   tel (01629) 57691
   Winwin Sein, Sarah (aco)
   Allsop, John (aco)
   O'Sullivan, David (aco)
   Webster, Ian (health & safety mgr)
   Gillham-Hardy, Sandy (personnel mgr)
   Radford, Gary (finance mgr)
   Marshall, Dominic (research & eval off)
   Slade, Michael (info mgr)
   Bissell, Rob (i.t. tech supt mgr, seconded)

1a. **Training Centre**
    1 Institute Lane, Alfreton DE55 7BQ
    tel (01773) 833247 *fax (01773) 831944*

    Cartledge, Isobel (spo training)
    Colegate, Sharon (snr training off)

    Info Systems Training
    tel (01773) 833074
    Burton, Jennifer (snr customer & i.s.
    training supt)
    Smedley, Anna (info systems training off)

1b. Trainee Probation Officer Study Centre
1st Floor, Sitwell House, Sitwell Street off Babington Lane, Derby DE1 2JT
tel (01332) 349539 *fax (01332) 349110*

Bolton, Nicola (pda)
Fisher, Pauline (case admin off)

1c. MAPPP Unit
Derbyshire Constabulary HQ
(Crime Support Dept)
Butterley Hall, Ripley DE5 3RS
tel (01773) 572271 *fax (01773) 572976*

Nuttall, Brian (spo)
Raybould, Verity (case admin off)

2. Derby Crown Court
Derby Combined Court Centre
Morledge, Derby DE1 2XE
tel (01332) 622549 *fax (01332) 622548*

Crown Court Liaison
Smith, Catrin (cclo)
Barnes, Sharon (pso)
Day, Nicola (pso)
Walsh, Carole (pso)

3. 2 Siddals Road
Derby DE1 2PB
tel (01332) 340047 *fax (01332) 340056*

Court's Team
tel (01332) 340018
Dunkley, Charlotte (spo)
Lyness, Fiona (spo)
Buckley, Wendy (breach pso)
Ford, Gillian (breach pso)

Intake Team
Allard, Natalie
Cant, Joseph
Flint, Lesley
Pearne, William
Roots, Susie
Singh, Emma

Core Supervision Team
tel (01332) 340018
Ellicott, David (spo)
Dawkins, Ian
Glanowski, Sarah
Johnson, Claire
Johnson, Sally
Singh, Emma
Purser, Ms Alison
Biddick, Sharon (pso)
Bower, Sarah (pso)
Higgins, Kerry (pso)

Kemp, Kathy (pso)
Mannish, Nanada (pso)
Sansom, Michelle (pso)
Sheldon, Sue (pso)
Smith, Marie (pso)
Stevens, Pete (pso)
Tomlinson, Lisa-Anne (pso)

Enhanced Community Supvn Team
tel (01332) 340047 & 340029
Parker, Sue (spo)
Taylor, Paul (spo)
Aujla, Maninder
Ayodeji, Andrew
Barkley, Alison
Briggs, Jo
Britton, Penny
Coleman, Sheree
Davey, Clare
Egginton, Matthew
Fitch, Adrian
Hannant, Katy
James-Moore, Kathryn
Kelly, Paula
Lewis, Claire
Mandair, Narinder
McCormick, Rosalind
Needham, Carly
Reid, Linda
Schofield, Bob
Robinson-Stanley, Clifton
Farry, Christine (pso)
Glover, Tony (pso)
Mann, Marsha (pso)

Prolific & Priority Offenders
Dosanjh, Michael (spo)
Lawton, Adele
Stretton, Daniel
Ashby, Joanne (pso)
Davie, Karen (pso)

Emplt, Training & Education
Harjit, Sandhu (pso)
Whatton, Pam (pso)

Trainees
Bouse, Martin
Doxey, Gemma
Higgs, Jody
Khalida, Tabasum
Maguire, Helen
Mohmood, Sofena

Admin
Watson, Jane (divnl off mgr)
Anderson, Sara (off mgr)
Malcolm, Robert (info off)

Derby Community Punishment Office
tel (01332) 340053
Burgess, Ms Sheila (divnl cp mgr)
Tallett, Tanya (divnl cp off)
Diedrick, Karlana (cpo)
Hough, Samantha (cpo)
McDonald, David (cpo)
Tibbert, Ms Julie (cpo)
Tutin, Doug (cpo)
Hopkins, Peter (cp supvr)
Ilic, Peter (cp supvr)
Jones, Bob (cp supvr)
Jordan, Denise (cp supvr)
Malcolm, Matthew (cp supvr)
Martin, Susan (cp supvr)
Payne, Keith (cp supvr)
Sandhu, Diljit (cp supvr)

4. The Magistrates' Court, Shire Hall
19 St Mary's Gate **Derby** DE1 3JR
tel (01332) 293081 *fax (01332) 293082*

Southern Derbyshire Magistrates' Court
Francis, Deanna (mclo)
Gordon, Marlene (mclo)
Abbott, Danielle (pso)
Bawley, Victoria (pso)
Dallison, Jane (pso)
Rose, Jean (pso)
Smith, Marie (pso)

5. **Derby Probation Centre**
Willow House, la Willow Row
Derby DE1 3NZ
tel (01332) 346173 *fax (01332) 294011*

Groupwork
tel (01332) 361200
Beardmore, Di (treat mgr)
Smith, Nicola (p)
Kean, Frances
Evans, Sarah (pso)
Fearon, Lynnette (pso)
Hutchinson, Margaret (pso)
Maidstone, Lindsey (pso)
Parveen, Zureena (pso)
Jackson, Ian (pso)
Tracey, Marcus (pso)
Shingler, Trudy (trainee psychologist)

Information
tel (01332) 206042
Lawrence, Neelum (office mgr)
Gillon, Richard (info asst)

Drug Treatment & Testing Orders
tel (01332) 206230
Vassell, Lenford

Bailey, Rebecca
Jagpal, Nimrit
Ashby, Mikki (pso)
Doyle, Kirsty (pso)
Richardson, Lisa (pso)
Tracey, Marcus (pso)
White, Lavina (pso)

Practice Devpt Assessors & Trainees
tel (01332) 346173
Gardner, Martin (pda)
Gell, Lois (pda)

6. 3 Brimington Road
Chesterfield S41 7UG
tel (01246) 276171 *fax (01246) 556505*

Shinfield, Marion (divnl off mgr)
Woolliscroft, Daniel (info off)

Offender Management Teams 1 & 2
Elliott, Gill (spo)
Jackson, Keith
Nudd, Daniella
Poulter, Fiona
Roberts, Sîan
Schreder, Mark
Tugnait, Vanda
Holmes, Phil (pso)
Webster, Mark (pso)

Offender Management Teams 3 & 4
Mason, Glenn (spo) (crts)
Kenny, Danielle
Massey, Mike
Millard, Lynne
Morgan, Jon
Tissington, Miranda
Lawal, Chris (pso)
Starnes, Jeremy (pso)

Prolific & Priority Offenders
Wray, Shelagh (spo)
Agnew, Katherine
Hume, Tracey
Hayre, Jasdeep Singh (pso)
Pepper, Sarah (pso)

Courts
Turner, Phillip
Coupland, Bill (pso)
Palmer, Jason (pso)

Breach Enforcement
Clark, Louise (pso)
Weatherall, Lindsey (pso)

Accommodation
Vacancy

Trainees
Bruty, Emma

Evans, Rebecca
James, Marcus
Manuel, Nicola
Taylor, Gemma

ETE
Hickey, Janet (spo)

Victims
Wray, Shelagh (spo)
Sampson, Adrienne (pso, vlo)

Groupwork
Marjoram, Sandra (spo)
McAteer, Matthew
Gandy, Zephaniah (treatment mgr)
Parry, Chris (treatment mgr)
Heini, Claire (pso)
Monck, Daniel (pso)
Wilcockson, Mark (pso)

DTTO/DRR
Kenny, Paul (spo)
Dymond, Laura
Fitton, Brian
Jackson, Sandy (pso)
Kajla, Mandeep (pso)
McMahon, Richard (pso)

Enhanced Community Punishment
Clay, Stephen (divnl cp mgr)
Rowland, Ms Viv (divnl cpo)
Knight, Mark (cpo)
Ludlam, Craig (cpo)
Morrison, David (cpo)
Freeman, Gaynor (cp placement supvr)
Lennon, Bevin (cp placement supvr)
Smith, Alfred (cp placement supvr)
Gee, Jeff (cp supvr)
Waterfield, Charles (cp supvr)

6a. **Chesterfield Magistrates' Court**
The Court House
Tapton Lane **Chesterfield** S41 7TW
tel (01246) 278340 *fax (01246) 237582*

7.   40/42 Town End
Bolsover S44 6DT
tel (01246) 240404 *fax (01246) 241382*

Offender Management Teams 1 & 2
Rose, Colin (spo)
Birkett, Laraine
Davey, Melanie
Hobson, Tiejha
Markham, Simon
Rawding, Emma
Northedge, June (pso)

Herward, Rebecca (pda)
Hodgson, Robert (pda)

8.   1 Institute Lane **Alfreton** DE55 7BQ
tel (01773) 835536 fax (01773) 831944
weekends only

9.   2d Dale Road
Matlock DE4 3LT
tel (01629) 582148 *fax (01629) 57872*

Offender Management Team
Chapman, Louise
Sloan, Sue
Weston, Jackie (pso)

Wagstaff, Neil (divnl cp mgr)

10. Chesterfield House
24 Hardwick Street **Buxton** SK17 6DH
tel (01298) 25558 *fax (01298) 79132*

Davies, Kate (spo)
Gittins, Jane
Jeanmaire, Liz
Musgrave, Jane
Rogers, Jane
Smith, Ellen
Weston, Jackie
Whitlaw, Clare (trainee)
Cottrell, David (pso, ete)
Glover, Tony (pso)
Lineham, Natalie (pso)
Ashwood, Rebecca (cpo)
Bates, Deborah (cpo)
Buckley, Norman (cp supvr)
Crich, Amanda (cp supvr)
Fox, Joy (cp supvr)

Clitheroe, Pat (divnl off mgr)
Mortimer, Andrew (info off)

10a. 14 Ellison Street
Glossop SK13 8BX
tel (01457) 852546/854652 *fax (01457) 853272*

part time office

Gittins, Jane
Rogers, Jane
Lee, Catherine (p, pso)

11. 34 South Street
Ilkeston DE7 5QJ
tel 0115-930 1123 *fax 0115-930 2503*

Ilkeston Unit 1
Page-Smith, Marion (spo)
Cammack, Jane

Gooch, Daniel
Jones, Corinne
Wilkinson, Jennie
Wharton-Howett, Mark (pso)

Ilkeston Unit 1
MacLennan, Rachel (spo)
Emslie, Ann
Southall, Francine
Stack, Pat
Murphy, Gill (pso)
Smyth, Nicola (pso)

Alfreton Unit 1
Page-Smith, Marion (spo)
Bowden, David
Gibbins, Rebecca
La-Haye, Deanna (p, pso)

Alfreton Unit 2
MacLennan, Rachel (spo)
Hill, Phil
Shankland, Nicola
Martinson, Daryl (pso)

Courts' Team
Sfar-Gandoura, Ms Nina (pso)

ETE Team
Dengate, Cheryl

Prolific & Priority Offenders
Mason, Jacqueline
Rosier, Tim
Wood, Graham (pso)

Enhanced Community Punishment
White, George (spo)

PDAs & Trainees
Penman, Linda (pda)
Wells, Sarah (pda)
Adler, Keren (trainee)
Butler, Melanie (trainee)
Boyer, Sue (trainee)
Sampson, Laura (trainee)
Wallis, Helen (trainee)
Webb, Jonathan (trainee)
Whiteley, Sarah (trainee)

Admin
Nicholson, Barbara (divnl off mgr)

11a. **Community Punishment Office**
Mill Lane, off Greenhill Lane
Riddings DE55 4DB
tel (01773) 605812 *fax (01773) 605347*

Martin, Marjory (divnl cpo)
Sheldon, George (cpo)
Snape, Julia (cpo)
Guy, mark (cp supvr)

Hopkinson, Ken (cp supvr)
Marshall, John (cp supvr)
Meakin, Richard (cp supvr)
Roberts, Melanie (cp supvr)

Seconded Staff

12. **Derby YOT**
2nd Floor, St Peter's House
Gower, Street, Derby DE1 9BR
tel (01332) 256820 *fax (01332) 369297*

Brittain, Mick
Smith, Bubble

13. **Ilkeston YOT**
Kingfisher House, Cotmanhay Road
Ilkeston DE7 8HU
tel 0115-909 8170 *fax 0115-909 8184*

Purewal, Harjit

14. **Chesterfield YOT**
56 Cobden Road, Chesterfield S40 4TD
tel (01246) 347615 *fax (01246) 347651*

Draper, Jeremy

15. **Buxton YOT**
Area Education Office
Kents Bank Road, Buxton SK17 9HR
tel (01298) 308404 *fax (01298) 308411*

Anderson, Lynda

Other Secondments

Midlands Training Assessment & Devpt Consortium
Baptiste, Toni
Ryan, Natalie

Home Office
Connor, Peter (spo)
Bocock, Caroline (spo)

Hostel

16. **Burdett Lodge**
6 Bass Street, Derby DE22 3BR
tel (01332) 341324 *fax (01332) 202089*

Woods, Joe (spo mgr)
Woodhouse, Sharon (bursar)
Bremmer, Carol (hostel off)
Carson, Lynn (hostel off)
Gilligan, Dominic (hostel off)
Green, Julie (hostel off)
Griggs, Alan (hostel off)
Scrivener, David (hostel off)

Wrighte, Shelley (hostel off)
Leek, Rebecca (hostel sup wrkr)
Marshall, Mary (hostel sup wrkr)
Shir Mohammadi Pour, Akba (hostel sup wrkr)
Regan, Rebecca (hostel sup wrkr)
Waheed, Shamshad (p, hostel sup wrkr)
Gordon, Fitzroy (p, hostel sup wrkr)

Institution

17. H M Prison **Sudbury**
     Ashbourne DE6 5HW
     tel (01283) 584000 *fax (01283) 584001*
     probn clerk ext 4074

     Williams, Trevor (spo) ext 4073
     Beck, Ms Laura ext 4100
     Channon, James ext 4097
     Needham, Carly ext 4099
     Gee, Di
     Humphrey, Sheridan
     Neville, Bill ext 4098

18. H M Prison **Foston Hall**
     Foston, Derby DE65 5DN
     tel (01283) 584300 *fax (01283) 584301*

     Maclachlan, Iain (spo) ext 4497
     Gorton, Kate ext 4482
     Morgan, Byron ext 4494
     Edwards, Shaaron (pso, prog tutor)
     Walters, Joanne (pso) ext 4497
     Nuttall, Corinne (pso, resource room)
     Small, Helena (pso remand centre)

Local Justice Areas

6, 7 North East Derbyshire & Dales
3, 4, 5 Southern Derbyshire
9, 10, 11 High Peak

Crown Court

2 Derby

DEVON & CORNWALL PROBATION AREA

Out of hours emergency contact point
Lawson House (01752) 568791

Victim enquiries contact number Exeter
(01392) 421122, Plymouth (01752) 827500,
Torbay (01803) 213535, N Devon (01271)
321681

e-mail firstname.surname@devon-cornwall.probation.gsx.gov.uk

1. **Head Office**
    Queen's House, Little Queen Street
    Exeter EX4 3LJ
    tel (01392) 474100 *fax (01392) 413563*

    McFarlane, Mary Anne (co)
    Smith, Anthony (chair)
    Clewlow, Ian (director of ops)
    Menary, Rob (director of resources)
    Cash, Rosie (divnl business mgr)
    Meaden, Graham (aco, hr)
    Lambert, Maggie (snr hr advisor)
    Addicott, Marie (hr advisor)
    Moss, Duncan (inv off/NAPO Treasr)
    Atherton, Sandra (training off)
    Lamb, Carol (finance mgr/treasurer)
    Luffman, David (financial accountant)
    Lloyd, Lyndsay (financial analyst)
    Felix-Mitchell, Jacquie (pr & comms asst)
    Sussex, Trevor (i.t. systems mgr)
    Cupit, John (info systems off)
    Mandeville Norden, Rebecca (research off)
    Ruffles, Mike (area partnerships mgr)

N & E Division

2. 3/5 Barnfield Road
    Exeter EX1 1RD
    tel (01392) 421122 *fax (01392) 434839*

    Mitchell, Mary (aco)
    Murphy, John (divnl business mgr)
    Perkins, Simon (partnerships & performance mgr)
    Janus-Harris, Colin (spo)
    Fildes, Tim (ETE pathfinder pso)

    Integrated Case Management Team
    Benden, Mark (spo)
    Coker, Charlotte (p, spo)
    Demirci, Tina
    Davis, Mandy
    Johnson, Tig
    Lydon, Shaz
    Rowland, Lyn
    Stockley, Rachel
    Thomas, Vikki
    Thorpe, Brian
    Weeks, Dennis
    Wood, Danielle
    Campbell, Kate (pso)
    Lovell, Gemma (pso)
    Wadsworth, Dan (pso)
    Welland, Sue (pso)

    Courts Advice Desk
    Birchnall, Olive
    Emmen, Peter
    Wilson, Laura (p)

Taylor, Carol (snr legal proceedings off)
Boniwell, Tracey (pso)
Williams, Sarah (pso)

Public Protection
Clapinson, Colin (spo)
Leete, Desiree
Rayfield, Mike
Shaljean, Rosie (vlo)

Remand in Custody
Annison, Keith (spo)
(most of team based at HMP Exeter)

Programmes
Benden, Mark (spo)
Foster, Nikki
Bennett, Neal (prog tutor)
Davis, John (prog tutor)
Munday, Susan (prog tutor)
Stammers, Jackie (p, treatment mgr)
Willett, Rachel (treatment mgr)

Enhanced Community Punishment
tel (01392) 455419
Dan, Sam (scheme mgr)
Davies, Trina (p, case mgr)
Fairweather, Chritine (p, case mgr)
Holland, Darren (case mgr)
Smith, Shirley (case mgr)
Champion, Dawn (p, placement mgr/supvr)
Crockett, Julia (placement mgr/sup)
Hatchek, John (placement mgr/supvr)
Little, John (p, placement mgr/supvr)
May, Alfred (placement mgr/supvr)

Prolific Offender Unit
Banham, Caron
Davies, Diane
Baum, Carole (pso)
Sails, Jacqueline (pso)

Practice Development Unit
Greenslade, Tim (pda)
Hamilton, Mike (pda)
Asker, Jane (trainee)
Bishop, Sasha (trainee)
Brown, Staynton (trainee)
Coleman, Elaine (trainee)
Costello, Anne (trainee)
Fraser, James (trainee)
Keehner, Cindy (trainee)
Pope, Matthew (trainee)
Spiller, Paul (trainee)

3. **East Devon YOT**
Ivybank, 45 St David's Hill
Exeter EX4 4DN
tel (01392) 384933 *fax (01392) 384985*

Caddick, Claire

Haydon, Carol
Kennett, Peter

4. Kingsley House, Castle Street
Barnstaple EX31 1DR
tel (01271) 321681 *fax (01271) 329864*

Integrated Case Management
List, Terry (spo)
Ballam, Sue
Coker, Julian (p)
Dawson, Lesley
Marshall, Barbara
Nugent, Anne
Watts, Sallyanne
Wells, Jenny
Feesey, Sue (pso)
Slade, Wendy (pso)
Thompson, Jo (legal proc off/vlo)

Programmes
Dare, Catherine

Enhanced Community Punishment
Ford, Geraldine (shcme mgr/case mgr)
Ashford, Geraldine (p, case mgr)
Turner-Hewson, Chrissie (case mgr)
Harber, Stephen (placement mgr/supvsr)
Johns, Pauline (placement mgr/supvsr)
Otter, Phil (p, placement mgr/supvsr)
Tomkinson, David (p, placement mgr/supvsr)

N Devon Prolific Offender Unit
Milton, Mark

Practice Development Unit
Raitt, Andrew (pda)
Cummings, Seb (trainee)
Dyer, Bobby (trainee)
Hollingsworth, Nicola (trainee)
Rees, Michelle (trainee)
Williams, Gemma

East Devon Youth Offending Team
Wright, Sara

Plymouth Division

5. St Catherine's House
5 Notte Street, **Plymouth** PL1 2TS
tel (01752) 827500 *fax (01752) 267189*

Nason, Jon (aco)
Williams, Ros (divnl business mgr)
Adams, Barry (health & safety advisor)
Fry, Karen (ETE pathfinder pso)
Peros, Dino (partnerships devt off)
Williams, Bob (volunteer co-ord)
Willson, Greg (basic skills co-ord)
Baines, Carol (ETE pathfinder co-ord)

Integrated Case Management
Geddes, Louise (p, spo)
Lockett, Paul (spo)
Munn, Chris (spo)
Squire, Lynne (spo)
Van Waterschoot, Lucy (spo)
Auty, Angela (p)
Casey, Charlie
Craddock, Frank
Downing, Vanessa
Garvey, Sarah
Gunn, Hilary
Hatfield, Sharon
Hart, Michelle
Heather, Emily
Henderson, Alastair
Hopkins, Lynne
Johnston, Penny (p)
Millin, Geoff (p)
Parks, Rosemarie
Richards, Jane
Ross, Bernadine
Shirley, Ian
Stephenson, Jamie
Stewart, Val
Webb, Georgia
Wood, Hayley (p)
Wooler, Tony (p)
Young, Judith
Amphlett, Kirsten (p, pso)
Bellinger, Sue (pso)
Boulton, Joanna (pso)
Jones, Yvonne (p, pso)
O'Brien, Claire (pso)
Saunders, Janis (p, pso)
Udale, Bridget (pso)
Vaughan, Vanessa (pso)
Whittingham, Pam (p, pso)
Willmott, Beverley (p, pso)
Wilson, Cathie (p, pso)
Measures, Debbie (vlo)

Courts Advice Desk
Lee, David (pso)
Lister, Maggie
Pepperell, Kelly
Thorne, Peter (pso)
Rowe, Dawn (legal proc off)
Wylam, Kelly (legal proc off)

Programmes
Roesner, Sue (spo)
Atkinson, Michael
Edwards, Kristina
Falkingham, Paul (NAPO rep)
Harris, Guy
Lawrance, Nadine (treatment mgr)
O'Callaghan, Diane (treatment mgr)
Solomon, Gail

Tamlyn, Alison (p, treatment mgr)
Toms, Min
Williams, Ceri (prog tutor)

Enhanced Community Punishment
Wakley, Richard (scheme mgr)
Hart, Becky (quality assurance mgr)
Haskell, Norman (case mgr)
Leeming , Val (case mgr)
Tooth, Roger (p, case mgr)
Tricker, Paul (case mgr)
Allen, Sam (placement mgr/supvsr)
Brownlow, John (placement mgr/supvsr)
Cowling, Eddie (placement mgr/supvsr)
Dean, Darren (placement mgr/supvsr)
O'Callaghan, Alan (placement mgr/ supvsr)

Practice Development Unit
Lacey, Hugh (pda)
Wellock, Neil (pda)
Aisbitt, Ian (trainee)
Bishop, Gary (trainee)
Cherrett, Gill (trainee)
Hill, Joanne (trainee)
Gerry, Jayde (trainee)
Lamerton, Mark (trainee)
Letch, Chloe (trainee)
Narin, Jill (trainee)
Studley, Marina (trainee)

Plymouth Prolific Offender Unit
Cannan-Hargrave, Serena
Tarrant, Eleanor (pso)

6.   **Plymouth Youth Offending Team**
     3rd Floor, Midland House
     Notte Street, **Plymouth** PL1 2EJ
     tel (01752) 306999 *fax (01752) 306998*

     Oakes, Naomi

South Devon Division

7.   Thurlow House
     Thurlow Road, **Torquay** TQ1 3EQ
     tel (01803) 213535 *fax (01803) 290871*

     Proctor, Anne (aco)
     Bray, Brydie (spo)
     Hiscox, Kay (divnl business mgr)
     Dubash, Nariman (spo)
     Palmer, Bev (ETE pathfinder pso)

Integrated Case Management
Buddle, Paul
Chapman, Rose
Unwin, Martin
Winter, Debbie (p)
Britton, Colin (pso)
Broaders, Gabriel (pso)
Gerrard, Jan (pso)

Hughes, Chaylla (pso)
Tansley, Susan (p, pso)

Low Risk
Wescott, Paul
Marder, Briony (pso)
Trump, Simon (pso)

Courts Advice Desk
Burgess, Linda
Ferris, Chris
Harris, Sarah
Jones, Amanda
Moore, Polly
Dark, Jacqui (legal proc off)
Randle, Heidi (legal proc off)
King, Rose (pso)
Steer, Cheryl (pso)

Public Protection
Nunn, Melanie (p)
Robinson, Derek (p)
Whiteoak, Anne (pso)
Noble, Val (vlo)

Programmes
Lewis, Maddie (p, treatment mgr)
Swinfen Styles, Marian (p, treatment mgr)
Gaywood, Anthony
Curtis, Sarah (prog tutor)
Hanes, David (prog tutor)
Scattergood, Shirley (prog tutor)

Enhanced Community Punishment
Drennan, Alex (scheme mgr)
Busby, Elaine (p, case mgr)
Waine, Rosemary (case mgr)
Gray, Chris (case mgr)
Bammens, Russell (placement mgr/supvsr)
Eames, Mary (case mgr/placement mgr/sup)
Harding, Linda (quality assurance mgr)
Pitt, Barry (placement mgr/supvsr)
Wickham, Frank (placement mgr/supvsr)

Practice Development Unit
Ross, Louise (pda) (p)
Davis, Simon (trainee)

8. **Commerce House**
    97-101 Abbey Road **Torquay** TQ2 5PJ
    tel (01803) 408510 *fax (01803) 299399*

    Knowles, Veronica (p, spo)
    Roberts, Ruth (partnerships & perf mgr)

Courts Advice Desk
Richards, Mel

DAR/DRR
Jones, Alex

Pattinson, Rachel
Greening, Ken (pso)

DTTOs
Harrison, Lyn
Caulfield, Mike (pso)
Kennedy, Jamie (pso)

S Devon Prolific Offender Unit
Rogers, Andy

9. **Torbay Youth Offending Team**
    Commerce House, 97-101 Abbey Road
    Torquay TQ2 5PJ
    tel (01803) 201655 *fax (01803) 201721*

    Gaubert, Ian

Cornwall Division

10. **Divisional Head Office**
    22 Lemon Street, **Truro** TR1 2LS
    tel (01872) 326262 *fax (01872) 326263*

    Vallis, Peter (aco)
    Jesson, Kathy (divnl business mgr)
    Overend, Mark (aco it)
    Linscott, Cris (knowledge mgt)
    Henry, Stephen (ICT developer)
    Stoddern, James (ICT developer)
    Rose, Luan (ICT training)
    Orchard, Susie (financial analyst)
    Harris, Lucy (hr/as)

11. Tremorvah Wood Lane
    off Mitchell Hill, **Truro** TR1 1HZ
    tel (01872) 261293 *fax (01872) 261311*

    Tucker, John (partnerships & perf mgr)
    Holgate, Max (ETE pathfinder pso)

    Integrated Case Management
    Davies, Jenny
    Element, Jane (peripatetic po)
    Fisher, Carol (p)
    Lewis, Mary
    O'Hagan, Gail (p)
    Thomas, Jo (legal proc off)

Programmes
Wood, Sharon (spo)
Gates, Liz
McDonald, Joe
Coley, Helen (p, treatment mgr)
Bose, Julian (prog tutor)
Miller, Lin (prog tutor)

12. **Cornwall Youth Offending Team**
    Chiltern House, City Road
    Truro TR1 2JL
    tel (01872) 274567 *fax (01872) 242436*

MacDonald, Lorna
Pope, Elaine (pso)

13. Endsleigh House, Roskear
     Camborne TR14 8DN
     tel (01209) 612006 *fax (01209) 612551*

     Mitchell, Deborah (p, spo)
     Whalley, Ian (spo)

     Integrated Case Management
     Bellamy, Jane (p)
     Coad, Lorna
     Godfrey, Trudi
     Leighton, Jenny (p)
     Lowe, Mags
     Southern, Robert
     Williams, Richard
     Berryman, Alison (pso)
     Collier, Maxine (pso)
     Douglas, John (pso)
     Richards, Mike (p, pso)
     Wells, Peter (vlo)

     Public Protection
     Robinson, Helen

     Programmes
     Lawrance, Jo (treatment mgr)

     Enhanced Community Punishment
     Maxwell, Mike (case manager)
     Adams, Robert (placement mgr/spvsr)
     Cotton, Steve (placement mgr/supvsr)
     Mitchell, Ted (placement mgr/supvsr)

     Practice Development Unit
     Haslam, Jane (pda)
     Arrowsmith, Paul (trainee)
     Murdock, Jo (trainee)
     Penhaligon, Sylvia (trainee)
     Rowe, Sarah (trainee)
     Skewes, Nicola (trainee)

14. **W Cornwall Prolific Offender Unit**
     Coach House, Tolvean, West End
     Redruth TR15 2SS
     tel (01209) 881944 *fax (01209) 881919*

     Edwards, Zoe
     Payne, Sara
     Carter, Tim (pso)

15. 1 Guildhall Road
     Penzance TR18 2QJ
     tel (01736) 363934 *fax (01736) 330690*

     Stubbings, Pauline
     Gough, Brendan (pso)

16. 3 Kings Avenue
     St Austell PL25 4TT
     tel (01726) 72654 *fax (01726) 63553*

     Davies, Gareth (spo)
     Mackereth, Sarah (spo)

     Integrated Case Management
     Davies, Linda
     Frazer, Mark
     Malcolm, Sarah (p)
     McConnell, Su (p)
     Thomas, Hannah
     Wilson, Gail
     Bond, Mark (pso)
     Morgan, Dave (pso)
     Watson, Liz (pso)

     Public Protection
     Ciocci, Tony

     Enhanced Community Punishment
     tel (01726) 76282 *fax (01726) 76982*
     Bishop, Sue (scheme mgr)
     Gomersall, Anne Marie (p, case mgr)
     Richards, Geoff (case mgr)
     Rowe, Sandra (case mgr)
     Dronfield, Adrian (placement mgr/supvsr)
     Hill, Steve (placement mgr/supvsr)
     Tonkin, Bob (placement mgr/supvsr)

     Practice Development Unit
     Kirkham, Mary (pda)
     Dane, Lorraine (trainee)
     McGeorge, Penelope (trainee)
     Swann, Mark (trainee)

17. Culverland Road
     Liskeard PL14 6RF
     Resettlement tel (01579) 344299
     Case Management tel (01579) 344299
     fax (01579) 340277

     Flashman, Emma
     Lynch, Gill
     Ryan, Rose (pso)
     Stacey, Sharon (pso)
     Dale, Heather (vlo)

Projects/Secondments

18. **C.A.R.D.**
     14 York Road, Exeter EX4 6BA
     tel (01392) 270279

     Douglas, Paul (spo)

19. **Public Protection Unit**
     Devon & Cornwall Police HQ
     Middlemoor, Exeter EX2 7HQ
     tel (01392) 452865 fax (01392) 452025

email nicola.whiley@devonandcornwall.
pnn.police.uk

Whiley, Nicola (mappa mgr)

Hostels

20. **Lawson House**
    13/14 Paradise Place
    Stoke, **Plymouth** PL1 5QE
    tel (01752) 568791 *fax (01752) 606815*

    Pridmore, Giulia (deputy mgr)
    Bailey, Lisa (asst mgr)
    Bishop, Gerry (asst mgr)
    Foster, Ashley (asst mgr)
    Goodwin, Paul (asst mgr)
    Reeby, Bernard (asst mgr)

21. **Meneghy House**
    East Hill, Tuckingmill
    Camborne TR13 8NQ
    tel (01209) 715050 *fax (01209) 612595*

    Cookson, Andy (hostels mgr)
    Pascoe, Nigel (deputy mgr)
    Aldridge, Kevin (asst mgr)
    Dyer, Dick (asst mgr)
    French, Jenny (asst mgr)
    Hooper, Kay (asst mgr)

Institutions

22. H M Prison **Channings Wood**
    Denbury, Newton Abbot TQ12 6DW
    tel (01803) 814600 *fax (01803) 814601*

    Bown, Gary (spo)
    Clark, Dee
    Durie, David
    Godfrey Dick
    Godfrey, John
    Jones, Chris
    Moore, Bernard
    Turnbull, Adam (p)
    Gue, Kevin (prog co-ord)
    O'Toole, Patrick (prog co-ord)
    Austen, Nicci (pso)

23. H M Prison **Dartmoor**
    Yelverton PL20 6RR
    tel (01822) 892000 fax (01822) 892001

    McGregor, Jamie (spo)
    Arrowsmith-Brown, Tessa (pso)
    Carey, Jack
    Chakrabarti, Santosh (pso)
    Creasy, Pauline (pso)
    Herron, David (p)
    McFarlane, Andy
    McVey, Judy (p)

Mellows, Jenny (pso)
Nicholl, Mark (pso)
Steele, Kate

24. H M Prison **Exeter**
    New North Road
    Exeter EX4 4EX
    tel (01392) 415650 *fax (01392) 415651)*

    Stanley, Paul (spo)
    Savage, Viv
    Burns, Melanie (pso)
    English, Brent (pso)
    Grummett, John (pso)
    Haslam, Carl (pso)

    Remand in Custody
    Alsop, Katherine
    Benbow, Lorriane
    Farrell, David
    Vickers, Janet

Local Justice Areas

    2 Central Devon
    4 North Devon
    5 Plymouth
    7 South Devon
    11 West Cornwall
    12, 15, 16 East Cornwall

Crown Courts

    2 Exeter
    4 Barnstaple
    5 Plymouth
    11 Truro

DORSET PROBATION AREA

Out of hours emergency contact points
Weston Probation Hostel Weymouth (01305) 775742
The Pines Bail & Probation Hostel Bournemouth (01202) 391757

e-mail
Firstname.Surname@dorset.probation.gsx.gov.uk

SPOs are responsible for specialist officers in different offices.

Shown below is a list of teams and SPOs

Offender Mgmnt	(Poole) Carol Miller (7)
Offender Mgmnt	(Bournemouth) Elaine Morgan (8)
Offender Mgmnt	(Bournemouth) Sue Holmes (8)
Offender Mgmnt	(Weymouth) Becky James (4)
Public Protectn	(Bournemouth/ Weymouth) Elana Tessler (8 & 4)
Public Protectn	(Bournemouth) Margaret Harris (8)
Crt & Assessment	(Bournemouth) Mel Gauden (8)
Prbn Cntre – Progrs	(Poole) Alan Yelling (7)
CS	Mike Thomas (6)
IDAP	(Bournemouth) Jennifer Dunlavey (8)

1. **Head Office**
Wadham House, 50 High West Street
Dorchester DT1 1UT
tel (01305) 224786 *fax (01305) 225122*
direct dial (01305)+ext

Copsey, Martin (co) 224669
fax (01305) 224653
Hutchinson, Andy (aco,mgr ops) 224413
fax (01305) 224653
Shackleford, Murray (area mgr, public protectn & p'ships) 224413
Drew, David (finance and supt services mgr) 224670
Curtis, Glo (finance off) 224666
Vacancy (hr mgr) 224787
Southam, Vanessa (hr off) 224918
Kohn, Julian (info & comm off) 224800

2. **Dorchester Probation Office**
Wadham House, 50 High West Street
Dorchester DT1 1UT
tel (01305 224742 *fax (01305)225122*

James, Becky (spo) 224472 (4 & 5)
Corbett, Helen (p) (C&A) 224471
Duxbury, Judy (p) (OM) 224471
Ireland, Duncan (p) (C&A) 224471

3. **CADAS**
28 High West Street
Dorchester DT1 1UP
tel 01305 265635 *fax(01305) 250285*

Webb, Jackie

4. Law Courts, Westwey Road
Weymouth DT4 8SU
tel (01305) 774921 *fax (01305) 780102*
direct dial (01305)+ext

James, Becky (spo) (OM) 752606 (also 5)
Tessler, Elana (spo) (PP) 752622

Offender Management
Goodchild, Mike 752619
Rowe, Christine (p)
Walker, Stephanie 752612
McGown, Sandra (pso) 752618
Payne, Keith (pso) 752614
Quinn, Melanie (pso) 752614
Taylor, Katherine (pso) 752612

Public Protection
Castro, David 752607
Cotgrove, David 752616
Friday, Beryl 752608

Court & Assessment
Goodchild, Mike 752619
Henderson, Cate 752613
Staddon, Linda 752613
Webb, Jackie 752618

Trainees
Pursglove, Melanie
Townley-Walker, Sarah

5. Law Courts, Salisbury Road
Blandford DT11 7DW
tel (01258) 483552/438551 *fax (01258) 483550*
direct dial (01258)+ext

James, Becky (spo) (OM) (also 4)
Moverley, Sarah (OM) 483560

Gauden, Melanie (spo) (C&A) (also 8)
Gaines, Fiona (C&A) 483557
Marland, Penny 483558

Webb, David (spo/trng mgr) 483558
Zakrzewski, Adrian (pda) 483555
Fox, Beth (dev mgr, ete/Cygnet Trng) 483556
Lane, Terri (staff dev off) (Thurs & Fri only) 483558
Sexty, Mavis (Include proj mgr) 483562

Trainees
Dyer, Felicity 483561
Topliss, Oliver 483561

6. **Community Service Office**
Unit 19, Sandford Lane
Wareham BH20 4JH
tel (01929) 556513 *fax (01929) 553756*

Thomas, Mike (spo)
Matthews, Mike (dep mgr/cso)
Openshaw, Heather
Di Canio, Diana (cso)
Carey, Francis (cso)
Doe, Martin (cso)
Hudson, Shellie (cso)
Jones, Janet (cso)
Jones, Julie (cso)
Mason, Tony (cso)
Potts, Trevor (cso)
Richardson, Rosemary (cso)
Smyth, Deirdre (cso)

7. **Poole Office & Probation Centre**
63 Commercial Road, Parkstone
Poole BH14 0JB
tel (01202) 724053 *fax (01202) 724060*
direct dial (01202)+ext

Ridge, Tina (area mgr OM) 724067
[offender mgmnt team, addictions, cs]

Offender Management
Miller, Carol (p, spo) 724001
Brand, Jayne 724058
Jones, Anne 724056
Mathias, Kate 724072
Morgan, Mark 724064
Oliver, Richard 724030
Baker, Nicole (pso) 724073
Goss, Nick (pso) 724071
Hutchings, Juliette (pso) 724066

Public Protection
Chambers, Jan 724068
Rubie, Val 724070

PDA
Reynolds, Diane (p) 728002

Trainees
Adawy, Natalie 724059
Hattam, Natalie 724059
Ritson, Paula 724059

Probation Centre
Yelling, Alan (spo progs/centre mgr)
724051
Simpson, Jackie (p) 724013
Watts, Claire 724016
Dennison, Alex 724015
Cook, Adam 724008
Barr, Estelle (pso) 724007
Crawshaw, Elaine (pso) 724005
Fehr, Sonya (pso) 724065

Garrett, Jillian (pso) 724024
Thorpe, Alan (pso) 724004
McKay, Ian (pso) 724006
O'Connor, Paula (p, pso)

Transport Co-ordinator
Nichols, Colston 724069

ETE Unit
tel (01202) 724098 *fax (01202) 724097*
Fox, Beth (dev mgr) 724002 (see also 5)
Lane, Terri (Skills Dev off) 724098
Bascombe, Rima (ete off/pso) 724098
Keily, Rita (ete off/pso) 724098
Taylor, Wendy (accom off/pso) 724098
Jefford-Horn, Alexia (Opening
the Gates proj off) 7249098
Smith, Paul (emplt sup off – Include proj)

8. 7 Madeira Road
Bournemouth BH1 1QL
tel (01202) 228000 *fax (01202) 228080*
direct dial (01202)+ext

Watkins, Liz (area mgr interventions)
228006

Public Protection
Harris, Margaret (p, spo) 228021
Harris, Elana (spo) 228021
Allsop, Sarah 228059
Evans, Lisa 228012
James, Denice 228054
Newman, Rachael 228013
Price, Martin 228030
Wilson, Sandy 228058
Woolridge, Matthew 228011
McGrath, Della (vlo) 228034

Court & Assessment
Gauden, Mel (spo) 228023
Ennis, Joe 228029
Greaves, Kate 228029
Hussey, Caroline 228029
Psaradelli, Michael 228029
Tarling, Angela 228029
Higgins, Sue (spo) 228053
Stevens, Mel (pso) 228044

Offender Management
Morgan, Elaine (spo) 228036
Cain, Joanna 228032
Dixon, James 228060
Taylor, Anna 228049
Magnum, Nichola (pso) 228048

Holmes, Sue (spo) 228045
Dennison, Mark 228027
Holmes, Debbie 228014
Shepherd, Toni 228028

Billings, Shaun (pso) 228052
Cox, Vanessa (pso) 228050
Reeves, Kelly (pso) 228063

Breach Unit (CAT)
Dark, Nigel (pso, breach off) 228043
Wheeler, Steve (pso, breach off) 228082

PDA
Reynolds, Diane (p) 228039

IDAP
Dunlavey, Jennifer (p, temp spo) 228035

Breach Unit
Dark, Nigel (pso, breach off) 228043
Wheeler, Steve (pso, breach off) 228082

Trainees
tel (01202) 228033
Bell, Stephen
Burgess, Anne
Denton, Kerry
Dickinson, Jasmine
Johnson, Tim
Martin, Alison
Mitchell, Ann
O'Donnell, Jocelyn
Wilkins, Charlotte

9. **Magistrates' Court Liaison Office**
    The Law Courts, Stafford Road
    Bournemouth BH1 1LE
    tel (01202) 291392 (magistrates' admin)
    (01202) 293341 (magistrates' off)
    fax (01202) 789468

10. **Crown Court Liaison Office**
    The Courts of Justice
    Deansleigh Road
    Bournemouth BH7 7DS
    tel (01202) 430565 (admin)
    fax (01202) 430522

11. **Community Alcohol Team**

    c/o Sedman Unit, 16-18 Tower Road
    Boscombe, **Bournemouth** BH1 4LB
    tel (01202) 397003 *fax (01202) 395116*

12. **Dorset Youth Offending Team**
    Southwinds, Cranford Avenue
    Weymouth DT4 7TL
    tel (01305) 760336 *fax (01305) 761423*

13. **Bournemouth & Poole Youth Offending Team**
    5 Hyde Road, Kinson
    Bournemouth BH10 5JJ

tel (01202) 453939 *fax (01202) 453940*

Garland, Sandi
Harcombe, Samantha (p)

Hostels

14. **Weston Probation Hostel**
    2 Westwey Road, **Weymouth** DT4 8SU
    tel (01305) 775742 *fax (01305) 766510*

    Minty, Sharon (spo/mgr)
    Goss, Stephanie (dep mgr)
    Fisher, Carol (asst mgr)
    Hamilton, Ian (asst mgr)
    Koscikiewicz, Martin (asst mgr)
    Mitchell, Tori (asst mgr)
    Woolcock, Sarah (asst mgr)

15. **The Pines Bail & Probation Hostel**
    11 Cecil Road, Boscombe
    Bournemouth BH5 1DU
    tel (01202) 391757 *fax (01202) 391867*

    Minty, Sharon (spo/mgr) (14)
    Morrell, Paul (dep mgr)
    Holmes, Debbie
    Brown, Simon (asst mgr)
    Finch, Kay (asst mgr)
    Pintus, Serena (asst mgr)
    Welch, Susan (asst mgr)
    Yarrington, Alison (asst mgr)

Institutions

16. **HMP Dorchester**
    7 North Square, **Dorchester** DT1 1JD
    tel (01305) 214500 *fax (01305) 214501*
    probn fax (01305) 214607
    direct dial (01305)+ext

    special visits (am only) 214571

    Russell, David (p, spo) 214531
    Dryer, Lorraine (p, pso) 214532
    Gulliford, David (pso) 214534

17. **HMP The Verne**
    Portland DT5 1EQ
    tel (01305) 825000 fax (01305) 825001
    probn fax (01305) 825028
    direct dial (01305)+ext

    Harris, Dee (spo) 825034
    Dolder, John 825037
    Green, Linda 825036
    Woolf, Chris 825038
    Harris, Avril (pso) 825035
    Taylor, Katherine (p, pso) 825041

18. **HM Young Offender Institution**
The Grove, Easton
Portland DT5 1DL
tel (01305) 825600 *fax (01305) 852601*
SPO fax (01305) 825764
direct dial (01305)+ext

Russell, Kay (spo) 825748
Parker, Larry 825838
Stroud, Ann 825677
Butterworth, Sita (pso) 825767
Martin, Alison (pso) 825713
Moger, Barry (pso) 825682

19. **HM YOI Guys Marsh**
Shaftesbury SP7 8AH
tel (01747) 853344 *fax (01747) 850217*
spo fax (01747) 856529
direct dial (01747)+ext

Ward, Martin (spo) 856409
Green, Mark 856531
Hopkins, Trevor 856531
Dixon, Rebecca (pso) 856531
Moon, Donna (pso) 856527
O'Dell, Kirsty (pso) 856532

Local Justice Areas

7, 8, 9, 10 East Dorset
2, 4, 5 West Dorset

Crown Court

10 Bournemouth
2 Dorchester

DURHAM PROBATION AREA

Out of hours emergency contact number
(01642) 826606 or (01642) 456811 (offender
issues c/o Teesside hostels)

Victim enquiries contact number
Dawn Carter (01325) 315444

e-mail Firstname.Surname@durham.probation.
gsx.gov.uk

1. **Head Office**
Forest House
Aykley Heads Business Centre
Durham City DH1 5TS
tel 0191-383 9083 *fax 0191-383 7979*

McPhee Pam (co)
Bruce, Russell (aco)
Hine, Susan (aco)
Carey, Carina (acting aco)

Willoughby, Hazel (aco)
Ibbotson, Margaret (middle mgr)
Vitty, Helen (middle mgr)
Stringwell Margaret (supt staff off)
Wilkinson, Wendy (supt staff off)
Melvin, Kathryn (supt staff off)
Lincoln, Samantha (supt staff comm)
Bartlett, Sandra (supt staff tech)
Craddock, Jonathan (supt staff tech)
Fairgrieve, Simon (supt staff tech)
Hodgson, Joan (supt staff tech)
Horner, Steven (supt staff tech)
Murray, Elizabeth (supt staff tech)
Ward, Mandy (supt staff tech)
Williams, David (supt staff tech)

Public Protection Unit
Creedon, Mike (middle mgr)
Lumley, Mari
O'Sullivan, Claire
Reay, Gillian
Booker, Howard

Seconded
Anderson, Diane (middle mgr)
Ellis, Jayne (h.r. officer) (Teesside)
D'Souza, Nikki (middle mgr)

2. Highfield House, Parliament Street
Consett DH8 5DH
tel (01207) 502821 *fax (01207) 583989*

Community Reintegration
Metherall, Janet (middle mgr)
Byrne, Ben
Cunningham, Martin
Gray, Jane
Taylor, Julieann
Cawson, Sheena (pso)
Buckingham, Jane (pso)
Lawson, Rachel (pso)

Sentence Assessment
Burns, Darryl
Thompson, Sarah
Carney, Liz (pso)
Lopez-Real, Annie (pso)

Accredited Interventions Unit
Guy, Sarah
Watkin, Anna
Boyack, Lisa (pso)
Jobling, Lyndsey (pso)
Moore, Andy (pso)
Thomson, Keith (pso)
Wardman, Alison (pso)

Support Staff
Whiteman, Carole (off co-ord)
Dukes, Margaret (supt staff off

Johnson, Marion (supt staff off)
Wilson, Karen (supt staff off)

3. Oakdale House, Oakdale Terrace
    West Lane **Chester-le-Street** DH3 3DH
    tel 0191-388 7951 *fax 0191-388 1252*

    Community Reintegration
    Thomson, Lynn (middle mgr)
    Johnston, Ian
    Harland, David (pso)
    Hind, Linda (pso)

    Accredited Interventions Unit
    Hounam, Ken (unit mgr)
    Coleman, Paul
    Parker, Fiona (pso)
    Trotter, Jean
    Armstrong, Helen (pso)
    Forster, Norman (pso)
    Harker, Brian (pso)
    McHugh, Maureen (pso)

    Trainees
    Douglas, Stewart (pda)
    Blakey, Sarah
    Ridley, Karen
    Somersall, Paula
    Stewart, Louise
    Willmore, Nichola

    Support Staff
    Vincent, Marie (off co-ord)
    Cox Janice (supt staff off)
    McArthur, Clare (supt staff off)
    Randell, Susan (supt staff off)
    Robinson, James (courier/caretaker)

4. 84 Claypath
    Durham DH1 1RG
    tel 0191-386 1265 *fax 0191-386 4668*

    Community Reintegration
    Askew Sheila (middle mgr)
    Rogers, Gary
    Tyers Jean
    Gray, Eileen (pso)
    Harvey, Connie (pso)

    Sentence Assessment
    Murphy, Anne
    Sanderson, Diana
    Wilson, Louise

    Accredited Interventions Unit
    Buckingham, Howard
    Cooper, Elaine (pso)
    Hamilton, Diane (pso)
    Hancock, Susan (pso)
    North, Saphron (pso)

Russell, Julie (pso)
Smith, James (pso)

Support Staff
Taylor, Sheila (off co-ord)
Appleby, Nicola (supt staff off)
Burnip, Diane (supt staff off)
Murphy Sherida (supt staff off)
Steel, Valerie (supt staff off)

5. **Durham Crown Court**
    Old Elvet, Durham DH1 3HW
    tel 0191-384 8130 *fax 0191-386 2695*

    Howard, Andrew (based at office 4)
    Madgin, Lindy (pso) (based at office 4)

6. Durham House, 60 Yoden Way
    Peterlee SR8 1PS
    tel 0191-586 2480 *fax 0191-586 3442*

    Health & Safety
    Fox, Mavis (middle mgr)

    Community Reintegration
    Storey, Hugh (middle mgr)
    Cadwallader, Steve
    Knox, Amanda
    Robinson, Lisa
    Stoddart, Kathryn
    Thompson, Helen
    Green, Sandra (pso)
    Harland, David Ryan (pso)
    Iverson, Simone (pso)
    Johnson, Eileen (pso)
    Nichols, Melanie (pso)
    O'Neill Fiona (pso)
    Rogers, Sharon (pso)

    Sentence Assessment
    Bagley, John (middle mgr)
    Hodgson, Mel
    Scott, Rachel
    Stead, Brian (pso)

    Accredited Interventions Unit
    Makinson, Margaret (unit mgr)
    Passmore Barbara (middle mgr)
    Anderson, Kay
    O'Keefe, Peter
    Bower, Jeffrey (pso)
    Clarke, Gemma (pso)
    Dobson, Paul (pso)
    Gething, Price (pso)
    Hall, Claire (pso)
    Herrington, Claire (pso)
    Leigh, Fiona (pso)
    Playfor, Duncan (pso)
    Strike, Nigel (pso)

Trainees
Leishman, John (middle mgr)
Douglas, Lynn (pda)
Berry, Steven
Davies, Andrea
Eckert, Dannielle
Francis, Hannah
Greenhaugh, Ian
Griffiths, Charlotte
Longworth, Emma
Richards, Paul
Wong, Po-Ming

Support Staff
Barry, Lin (off co-ord)
Sedgewick, Leila (aiu co-ord)
Riley, Chris (supt staff off)
Newell, Terry (supt staff off)
Richardson, Robert (supt staff off)
Robinson, Denise (supt staff off)
Thompson, Christine (supt staff off)
Waters Sarah (supt staff off)
Wilson, Tony (supt staff off)

7.   9 Corporation Road
    Darlington DL3 6TH
    tel (01325) 486231 *fax (01325) 382760*

Community Reintegration
Thomas, Neil (middle mgr)
Furniss, Paul
Hussain, Akram
Joyce, Ian
Linsley, Kay
McAndrew, Kath
Marr, Anne
Moss, Hayley
Hope, Victoria (pso)
Maddison, George (pso)
Neale, Gay (pso)

Sentence Assessment
Bake, Andrew
Casswell, Glyn
Shah-Stroyan, Naheed
Thompson, Donna
Robertson, Brenda (pso)
Sibert, Maureen (pso)

Accredited Interventions Unit
Leighton, Rhonda (middle mgr)
Crosby, Helen (unit mgr)
Capstick, Anna (middle mgr)
Pearson, Dominic (middle mgr)
Gray, Rosie (psy)
Swift, Hayley (psy)
Byers, Karen
Craig, Jane
Starkie, Erica
Coulson, Anthony (pso)

Begg, Maureen (pso)
Burr, Jean (pso)
Denton, John (pso)
Doswell, Paul (pso)
Edgar, Kevin (pso)
Ferry, Julie (pso)
Hart, Karen (pso)
Henderson, Gavin (pso)
Hood, Jacqui (pso)
Hooper, Mark (pso)
House, Mark (pso)
Johnson, Kelly (pso)
Kelly, Michael (pso)
Lewis, David (pso)
Lochore, Margaret (pso)
Lowery, Mark (pso)
Mahmood, Mursleen (pso)
Merrick, Janet (pso)
Milburn, Susan (pso)
Payne, Hilary (pso)
Porter, Bianca (pso)

Trainees
Place, Shirley (pda)
Hamalainan, Kerry (pda)
Cole, Stephen
Coombs, Laurence
Hill Christine
Hood, Chris
Scarr, Laura
Sygrove, Julie
Walton, Leanne

Volunteers
Kirkbride, Ruth (vol co-ord)

Support Staff
Bruce, Karen (off co-ord)
Raine, Helen (aiu co-ord)
Carletta, Lynne (supt staff off)
McDonald, Carole (supt staff off)
Main, Thomas (supt staff off)
Otto, Carole (supt staff off)
Shaw, Andrea (supt staff off)
Williams, Julie (supt staff off)

8.   Probation Office, Greenwell Road
    Newton Aycliffe DL5 4DH
    tel (01325) 315444 *fax (01325) 329599*

Community Reintegration
Ghosh, Marc (middle mgr)
Cadwallader, Steve
King, Alison
McEvoy, Sopbhan
McEwan, Laura
Docherty, Valerie (pso)
Eland, Maureen (pso)

Hopson, Alison (pso)
Mckenzie, Aidan (pso)
McGuire, Craig (pso)

Sentence Assessment
Brown, Diane
Liivand, Ann
Todd, Jayne
Jordan, Ena (pso)
Waterworth, Marion (pso)

Accredited Interventions Unit
Hunt, Gill (middle mgr)
Helmke, Sandra
Atkinson, Robert (pso)
Bell, John (pso)
Best, David (pso)
Davison, Kenneth (pso)
Geddes, Jonathan (pso)
Jones, Stephen (pso)

Offender Co-ordination Unit
Collins, Helen (middle mgr)
Blackburn, Karen (middle mgr)
Ashworth, Sarah
Bryson, Jean
Brown, Diane
Howard, Joe
Langthorne, Chris
Zacharis, Anna
Carter, Dawn (pso victims)
Proudlock, Susan (pso accom)
Briggs, Maria (case co-ord)
Montgomery Denise (case co-ord)
Popple Nadine (case co-ord)
McMahon, Linda (supt staff off)
Moore, Kenda (supt staff off)

Support Staff
Thompson, Joan (off co-ord)
Meale, Susan (supt staff off)
Nicholson, Jayne (supt staff off)
Palmer, Lynda (supt staff off)
Richardson, Jayne (supt staff off)
Russell, Judith (supt staff off)

9.   Beechburn House, 8 Kensington
     Cockton Hill Road
     Bishop Auckland DL14 6HX
     tel (01388) 602182 *fax (01388) 458403*

Community Reintegration
Albuquerque-Neale, Maria (middle mgr)
Bligh, Carolyn
Clayton, Rob
Timoney, Pearl
Alderton, Julie (pso)
Booth, Ingrid (pso)
Dale, Tracey (pso)

Hardy, Janice (pso)
Humphreys, Anthony (pso)

Accredited Interventions Unit
Walton, Andy (unit mgr)
Sinclair-Day, Julie
Watson, Jane
Allison, Lisa (pso)
Auld, Caroline (pso)
Pears, Derek (pso)
Threscher, Kathryn (pso)
Walton, David (pso)

Sentence Assessment
Auckland, Mary
Hood, Brendan (pso)
Park, Philip (pso)

Support Staff
Currie, Carol (off co-ord)
Coulson, Lynne (supt staff off)
Walton, Patricia (supt staff off)

10. **Co Durham Youth Engagement
     Service
     East Area**
     3rd Floor, Lee House, Yoden Way
     Peterlee SR8 1BB
     tel 0191-518 6302 *fax 0191-518 6328*

     Vacancy

     South Area
     Aycliffe Young People's Centre
     Newton Aycliffe DL5 6JE
     tel (01325) 372808 *fax(01325) 372814*
     Stokeld, Keith

     North Area
     Andill House, North Road
     Catchgate, Stanley
     Co Durham DH9 8UW
     tel (01207) 291400 *fax (01207) 235483*

     Wetherall, Alan

     Darlington Youth Offending Service
     Central House, Gladstone Street
     Darlington DL3 6JX
     tel (01325) 346267 *fax (01325) 346846*

     Hunter, Beryl

Institutions

11. H M Prison, Old Elvet
     Durham DH1 3HU
     tel 0191-386 2621 *fax 0191-386 2524*

     Egglestone David (middle mgr)
     Bell, George
     Irving, Derrick
     Vallente, Claire

Hodgson, Jean
Harrison, Linda
Reid, Colin
Ashley, Mark (pso)
Banham, Stephen (pso)
Cook, Susan (pso)
Duncan, Lynn (pso)
Evans, Harvey (pso)
Gibson, Tracey (pso)
Lopez-Real, Annie (pso)
Mulligan, Mike (pso)
Walls, Angie (pso)

12. H M Prison **Frankland**
Finchale Avenue, Brasside
Durham DH1 5YD
tel 0191-332 3000 fax 0191-332 3001
special visits tel 0191-332 3007

Resettlement admin ext 3260
Discipline ext 3102
Sentence mgmnt ext 3258

Anderson, Keith
Hancock, Derek
Pattison Ian
Penzer, Anne
Copeland, Ena (pso)
Dinsdale, Brian (pso)
Hunter, Fiona (pso)

13. H M Remand Centre **Low Newton**
Brasside, Durham DH1 5SE
tel 0191-376 4000 *fax 0191-376 4001*

Probn clerk ext 298
Discipline ext 308/309

Special visits: switchboard

Cuthbertson, Haley
Hodgson, Jeanette
Paget, Michelle (pso)
Pape, Yvonne (pso)

14. H M Young Offender Institution
Deerbolt Bowes Road
Barnard Castle DL12 9BG
tel (01833) 633200 *fax (01833) 633201*
Resettlement clerk ext 3281
resettlement fax (01833) 633304

Sentence planning officers ext 3258/3306
Discipline ext 3310/3311
Drugs team ext 3366
Special visits ext 3374

Snowball, Sharon
Thomas, Jenny
Ware, Bruce

Local Justice Areas

2, 3, 4, 6 North Durham
7, 8, 9 South Durham

Crown Court

5 Durham

ESSEX PROBATION AREA

**Central Bail Referral telephone number
(01268) 557550**

Out of hours emergency contact point
Basildon Hostel (01268) 557550

Victim enquiries contact number (01268)
412241

e-mail
Firstname.Surname@essex.probation.gsx.gov.uk

1. **Head Office** Cullen Mill
49 Braintree Road, Witham CM8 2DD
tel (01376) 501626 *fax (01376) 501174*
aco's fax (01376) 519955

Archer, Mary (co) ext 244
Ayree, Eric (aco) ext 248
Bamber, Alex (aco) ext 246
Hirst, Gill (aco) ext 303
Johnson-Proctor, Steve (aco) ext 483
Jones, Peter (aco) ext 264
Mangan, Pete (aco) ext 299
Atkinson, Sue (aco human resources) ext
233
Came, Debbie (p, treasurer) ext 251

McCann, Helen (training & staff devpt
mgr) ext 271
Day, Derek (nvq proj mgr) ext 479
Rowlands, Gill (nvq assessor) ext 479

Piccolo, Diana (p, hr mgr) ext 269
Butt, Andrew (h&s) ext 247
Pervez, Neelam (p, diversity) ext 404
Moon, Garry (p, performance) ext 267
Gorrie, Paul (finance) ext 222
Moffat, Colin (supt services mgr) ext 229
Thompson, Bill (info & systems mgr) ext
235
McKay, Lynne (communications officer)
ext 250
Jarvis, Marion (p, pdu mgr) ext 236

Hargrave, Sally (p, spo dtto) ext 265
Haxton, Liz (spo, dtto) ext 265
Ward, Paula (dv co-ord)
Hever, Helen (p, pso, out to wk) ext 236

Woollard, Peter (partnerships) ext 340
Wheeler, Claire (pso ptnrshps) ext 266

2.   Ryegate House, 23 St Peter's Street
Colchester CO1 1HL
tel (01206) 768342 *fax (01206) 768348*

Chapman, Liz (p, spo)
Hepworth, Fay (p, spo)
Juniper, Laurel (p, spo)
Kent, Harry (spo)

Coward, Wendy
Devaux, Dan
Edwards, Sue
Fitzpatrick, John
Gamble, Ray
Garnham, Anne-Marie
Huard, Mike (p)
Kelly, Francis
Kelly, Susan
Lloyd, Steve
McPhillips, Anthony
Meadows, Max
Pearson, Christopher
Pryke, Steven
Robertson, Elmarie
Skinner, Fran
Woulfe, Mick

Ainsworth, Tony (om)
Baldwin, Iris (om)
Bell, Linda (om)
Coker, Steven (om)
Haggerty, Sheila (om)
Leader, Lisa (om)
Litton, Victoria (om)
McQuoid, Lisa (om)
Scott, Heather (om)
Robinson, Sheila (om)
Stokes, Ruth (om)
Whittaker, Jenny (om)
Wright, Sue (om)

Double, Linda (pso)
Richardson, Elana (pso)
Vasquez-Walters, Elisa (p, pso)
Wiltshire, Kathleen (pso)

Programmes
Rodway, Debbie (p, spo)
Ross, David
Mateer, Beau (pso, treatment mgr)
James, Hayley (pso, treatment mgr)
Goddard, Rachel (pso)
Speed, Joanne (pso)

DTTO/DRR
Campbell, Carol (om)
McLaughlin, Jim (om)

Unpaid Work
Mead, David (spo)
Minns, John (qa mgr)

Woodhouse, Karen (supt services mgr)
Barford, Geoff (pda)
Carden, Ellen (women's safety wrkr)
Clarke, Anne (pso basic skills)
Cook, Dorothy (pso accom)

N E Essex Youth Offending Team
tel (01206) 573188
Finch, Martine

3.   4th Floor, Ashby House, Brook Street
Chelmsford CM1 1UH
tel (01245) 287154 *fax (01245) 491321*

Bald, Caroline (spo)
Messam, David (spo)
Perkins, Cheryll (spo)

Arnold, Rhiannon
Auguste, Pauline
Brame, Rachel
Charlton, Douglas
Corbett, Joanne
Hards, Joanne
Mead, Gemma
Smith, Rachael
Stow, Denise
Teather, Carole

Hill, Adele (om)
Howell, Chris (om)
Jones, David (p, om)
Shilan, Jo (om)
Kettle, Alison (om)
Payne, John (om)
Rowe, Susan (om)
Western, John (om)

Aston, Mike (pso)
Bartlett, Sophie (pso)
Clarke, Jeanette, (pso)
Sturch, Tony (pso)

Programmes
Vacancy (mgr)
Boutel, Helen
Bryan, Malcolm (p)
Chatten, Chris
Fairchild, Christine
Fernandez, Sara (treatment mgr)
Griffin, Sarah (pso, treatment mgr)
Saward, Adrian (pso, treatment mgr)
Harris, Kerry (pso)
Rodney, Deyonne (pso)

DTTO/DRR
Sapwell, Steve (om)

Unpaid Work
Vacancy (qa mgr)

Haworth, Vanessa (supt services mgr)
Brun, Heather (pda)
Perrott, Claire (pso accom)
Wardrop, Avril (pso basic skills)

Mid Essex Youth Offending Team
Chelmsford (01245) 358092
Vacancy

4. **Crown Court Liaison Office**
    Crown Court, New Street
    Chelmsford CM1 1EL
    tel (01245) 358833 *fax (01245) 258136*

    Franklin, Arlita (spo, North)
    Parker, Ian (spo, South)
    Cruikshank, Sandra (pso)
    Jackson, Tricia (pso)
    Jarman, Gail (pso)

5. 3rd Floor, Market House, Stone Cross
    Harlow CM20 1BL
    tel (01279) 410692 *fax (01279) 454116*

    Bishop, Neeve (p, spo)
    Butcher, Mick (spo)
    Toper, Sue (spo)

    Brunton, Jason
    Buckland, Sue
    Cornwell, Hazel
    Curtin, Rich
    Francis, Kathryn
    Howes, Cliff (p)
    Hughes, Gerry
    Martin, Nicola
    Mead, Nikki (p)
    Proothi, Savita
    Rapetti, Laura
    Sampson, Carol

    Brown, Jolie (om)
    Franklin, Keri (om)
    Houlahan, Terrence (om)
    Lee, Kim (om)
    Mackenzie, Julia (p, om)
    Scott, Jan (om)
    Turner, Rochelle (om)
    Woulfe, Tim (om)

    Dakin-Smith, Claire (pso)
    Newman, Christian (pso)
    Webster, Dave (pso)

    Programmes
    Stiles, Min (spo)
    Coombes, Paul
    Bennett, Alan (pso)
    Morris, Karen (pso)

DTTO/DRR
Darton, Gemma (om)
Cassidy, Elizabeth (om)
Turnbull, Kathryn (om)

Wallace, Caroline (p, supt services mgr)
Woolf, Denise (p, supt services mgr)
Neill, Lorraine (pda)
Gulrajani, Julie (women's safety wrkr)
Simon, Jennet (pso basic skills)

W Essex Youth Offending Team
Harlow (01279) 427495
Gulliver, Neil

6. Blue Heights, 45 Victoria Avenue
    Southend-on-Sea SS2 6BA
    tel (01702) 337998 *fax (01702) 333630*

    Crown Court enquiries to office 4

    Butlin, Carolyn (spo)
    Gower, Alun (spo)
    Meads, Richard (spo)

    Brenkley, Sam
    Coates, Kim (p)
    Edgar, Linda
    Forward, Jacqui
    Frost, Michelle
    Grant, James
    Hogben, Nick
    Hamilton, Zoe (p)
    Hooper, Terry (p)
    Jess, Michael
    Johnson, Susan (p)
    Ling, Andy
    Lucavetchi, Anne
    Moore, Bruce (p)

    Atkins, Sarah (p, om)
    Brining, Janice (om)
    Carbutt, Carol (om)
    Clarke, Andrea (om)
    Cook, Jacqui (om)
    Dove, Julie (om)
    Hobart, Toni (om)
    Jones, Tony (om)
    Kinder, Keith (om)
    Penton, Kelly (om)
    Penton, Sue (om)
    Pickford, Pauline (om)
    Smith, Tina (om)
    Summerhayes, Lesley (om)
    Vale, Luke (om)
    Williams, Jon (om)

    Chamberlain, Lucy (pso)
    Clarke, Leigh (pso)
    Craske, Pauline (pso)
    Eve, Rebecca (pso)

Programmes
Frost, Russell (p, spo)
Burr, Stephen
Smith, Pat
Childs, Ben (pso)
Merenda, Natalie (p, pso)
Parkes, Ernie (pso)
Tearle, Victoria (pso)

DTTO/DRR
Drummond, Joanne (p, om)
Karby, Leigh (pso)
Taiani, Heidi (pso)

Unpaid Work
Werry, Malcolm (spo)
Owens, Jan (qa mgr)

Sales, Debra (p, supt services mgr)
Lewis, Florence (pda)
Sakai, Barbara (pda)
Scott, Emma (p, pda)
Wood, Dee (women's safety wrkr)
Shuttleworth, Melinda (pso basic skills)
Laurenson-West, Lara (pso accom)

SE Essex Youth Offending Team
tel (01702) 330464
Dent, Julie (p)

7. Carraway House, Durham Road
Laindon **Basildon** SS15 6PH
tel (01268) 412241 *fax (01268) 544241*

Dewitt, Jane (spo)
Linahan, Rosan (spo)
Phillips, Lesley (p, spo)

Al-Kilani, Yaser
Allison, Sue
Culliton, Bob
Gidden, Amy
Hogg, Jenni
Oviatt, Leigh
Prolingheuer, Ecky
Seager, Marija (p)
Somerville, Christine (p)
Rockenbach, Chloe
Williams, Dawn
Wright, Joanne

Beney, Kim (om)
Hanley, Correna (om)
Laycock, Linda (p, om)
Leaworthy, Clare (om)
Lester, Emma (om)
Turner, Diane (p, om)
Price, Sue (om)

Cadzow, Anna (pso)
Gardiner, Claire (pso)
Sheed, Fran (pso)
Waterfield, Kathleen (pso)

Programmes
Routh, Jo (spo)
Dowden, Clive
Spencer, Donna (psychologist)
Davison, Natalie (p, pso, treatment mgr)
McGregor, Tim (pso, treatment mgr)
Mudrovcic, Alison (pso, treatment mgr)
Norman, Stacey (pp, so, treatment mgr)
Baker, Steve (pso)
Ford, Elaine (pso)
Taylor, Jeanette (pso)

DTTO/DRR
Davies, Leann (om)
Nethercoat, Pat (om)
Kalejaiye, Lucinda (pso)

Victim Unit
Philips, Lesley (p, spo)
Clark, Roland (pso)
Levy, Marion (pso)
Anderson, Debbie (pso)

Parratt, Margaret (supt services mgr)
Fallon, Carol (pso, basic skills)
Felice, Paul (pso accom)

7a. **Basildon Crown Court**
The Gore, Basildon SS14 2EU
tel (01268) 458118 *fax (01268) 458116*

Hopkins, Jeanette (pso)

7b. **SW Essex Youth Offending Team**
31 Battleswick, Basildon SS14 3LA
tel (01268) 520612 *fax (01268) 270924*

Colnbrook, Lee

8. Five Wells, West Street
Grays Thurrock RM17 6XR
tel (01375) 382285 *fax (01375) 394715*

Osler, Alex (p, spo)
Parker, Carol (spo)

Baker, Karen (p)
Blaker, Sarah
Budd, Louise
Castle, Katie
Doney, Lisa
Fasulo, Selina
Fletcher, Katherine
Green, Jose (p)
Kay, Michael
Legg, Pat (p)

Redgwell, Tracey
Rossi, Bill

Callender, Claire (om)
Fisher, Marion (om)
Hanser, Helen (om)
Hubbard, Carol (om)
Knight, Stephen (om)
Prosser, Tim (om)
Sadler, Norma (om)

Champ, Jo (pso)
Walters, Neil (pso)

Programmes
Powers, Martin (spo)
Gurnett, Graham (pso, treatment mgr)
Bryant, Jack (pso)
Cherifi, Sindy (pso)
Coleman, Liz (pso)

DTTO/DRR
Hayhow, Tina (om)
Webster, Maggie (om)

Unpaid Work
Watson, Chris (qa mgr)

Ofeke, Ann (supt services mgr)
Roberts, Kim (pda)
Gray, Trevor (pso basic skills)
Rate, Peter (pso accom)

9. **Thurrock Youth Offending Team**
Five Wells, West Street
Grays RM17 6SX
tel (01375) 413900 *fax (01375) 413901*

Kay, Peter (mgr)
Hossack, Roy (team ldr)
Vacancy (po)

Hostel
10. **Basildon Bail Hostel**
1 Felmores, Basildon SS13 1RN
tel (01268) 557550/557600 *fax (01268) 558661*

Goodchild-Allen, Kate (mgr)
Hutchinson, Chris (dep mgr)
Gales, Annette (hostel off)
Gibson, Andrew (hostel off)
Jamieson, Kathy (p, hostel off)
Laycock, Terry (hostel off)
Nestor, Paulette (p, hostel off)
Nichol, Roland (hostel off)
Wood, Anne (p, finance asst)

Institutions
11. H M Young Offender Institution & Prison
Bullwood Hall
High Road, Hockley SS5 4TE
tel (01702) 562800 *fax (01702) 207464*

Ward, Gill (snr pract)
Jones, Barbara (pso)
Kirby Maggie (pso)
Watts, Janice (pso)

12. H M Prison, Springfield Road
Chelmsford CM2 6LQ
tel (01245) 272000 *fax (01245) 272001 probn fax (01245) 272074*

Mozzanica, Louise (spo)
Cranley, Chris
Heywood, Anne
Nicholas, Kate
Bavin, Belinda (om)
Bunyard, Melissa (om)
Gallant, Jane (om)
Redman, Debbie (p, om)

Local Justice Areas
2 North-East Essex
3 Mid-North Essex
5 North-West Essex
6 South-East Essex
7 Mid-South Essex
8 South-West Essex

Crown Courts
7a Basildon
4 Chelmsford
4 Southend

GLOUCESTERSHIRE PROBATION AREA

Out of hours emergency contact point
Ryecroft Hostel (01452) 380268

Victim enquiries contact number (01452) 426330

e-mail
Firstname.Surname@gloucestershire.probation.gsx.gov.uk

1. **Head Office**
Bewick House, 1 Denmark Road
Gloucester GL1 3HW
tel (01452) 426250 *fax (01452) 426239*

Ball, Yvette (co)
Cryer, Naomi (aco)
Holden, Garry (aco)
Oulton, Julia (aco)
Kerr-Rettie, Kathy (staff devpt mgr)
Fogarty, Tim (business syst & info mgr)
Allen, Brian (it officer)
Bircher, Jane (it training officer)
Leese, Ann (hr adviser)
Mills, Caryl (hr adviser)
Maloney, Debra (finance mgr)
Longbotham, Rachel (finance off)
Westhead, Chris (facilities mgr, h&s adviser)

Support Staff
Bendall, Jackie
Eaketts, Judy
Jones, Sue
Murray, Jan
Moss, Elizabeth
Oates, Kath
Richards, Jaqueline
Salcombe, Karen
Taylor, Lesley

East Division

2. County Offices, St George's Road
    Cheltenham GL50 3QF
    tel (01242) 532425 *fax (01242) 532448*

    Public Protection
    Mark Scully (ppt mgr)
    Sedgley, Pat (snr pract)
    Gough, Will
    Knight, Tony
    Vicky Boroughs (victim enquiry)

    Offender Management
    Mead, Gary (om mgr)
    Thomson, Graham (om mgr)
    Smeaton, Christine (service supt mgr)
    Buxton, Sally (snr pract)

    Resettlement Cluster
    Donald, Nick
    Ilsley, Vicky (cmo)

    DRR/PPO Cluster
    Clarke, Anita
    Knott, Jane
    McNeill, Kevin (cmo)

    Offender Management Cluster 1
    Laura Donnelly
    Hallam, Martin (p)
    Havard, Pat (cmo)

    Offender Management Cluster 2
    Dan Hughes

John Cort
Hughes, Joanna (p)
Mills, Lisa (p)
Cudmore, Jean (cmo)
Scullion, John (cmo)

Offender Management Cluster 3
Cox, David (p)
Cowmeadow, Hillary (cmo)
Walker, Lisa (cmo)

Court Cluster
Johnson, Ann (cmo)

Trainees
Mercouris, Paula (pda)
Coulson, Elaine
Day, Vanessa
Hodges, Angela
Waldron, Amanda

Support Staff
Allen, Dave
Brown, Sophie
Edwards, Amanda
Gleed, Sian
Hewitt, Neil
Jonah, Carole
Keeling, Angela
Mason, Wendy
Middlecote, Lesley
Tyler, Joanne
Stanley, Rosamund
White, Lynda

ETE Team
Lear, Margaret (ete off)
Buchanan, Robin (ete wrkr)
Jones, Gillian (ete wrkr)

Support Staff
Bridge, Janet

3. 40a Dyer Street
    Cirencester GL7 2PF
    tel (01285) 652981 *fax (01285) 658835*

    Offender Management
    Spouse, Mike

4. 118 Cainscross Road
    Stroud GL5 4HN
    tel (01452) 760100 *fax (01453) 760107*

    Public Protection
    O'Kelly, Sheelagh

    Offender Management
    Pritchard, Clive
    Williams, Jan
    Leibbrandt, Stephanie (cmo)
    Phelps, Tanya (cmo)

Read, Leanne (cmo)

Wilkinson, Erik (ete mgr)

Support Staff
Ellis, Lisa
Hatherall, Gill
Ward, Sue

West Division

5. Barbican House, 31 Barbican Road
    Gloucester GL1 2JF
    tel (01452) 426300 *fax (01452) 427130*
    Court Fax (01452) 427139

    Offender Management Team
    Maitland-Hudson, John (om mgr)
    McBride, Stephanie (om mgr)
    Herniman, Sally (service supt mgr)
    Rousseau, Pauline (snr pract) (p)
    Taylor, Sue (snr pract)
    Cooper, Andy (snr pract) (p)

    Offender Management Cluster 1
    Cooper, Andrew (p)
    Gibbs, Kate
    Val Powell
    Andrews, Pat (cmo)
    Hanneford, Keith (cmo)
    Palmer, Mavis (cmo)

    Offender Management Cluster 2
    Vacancy
    Sims, Clare
    Rennabach, Rachel (cmo)
    Taylor, Beverley (cmo)

    Offender Management Cluster 3
    Vacancy
    Rea, Mary (p)
    Sheridan, Chris (p)
    Chapple, Andrew (cmo)

    Resettlement Cluster
    Cooper, Lesley
    Sivley, Angela (p)
    Boughton, Angie (cmo)

    DRR/PPO
    Cousins, Terry
    Sheridan, Chris (p)
    Clee, Mark (cmo)

    Court Cluster
    Jones, Barbara
    Tracy, Patrick (cmo)
    Worrall, Sian (cmo)

    Support Staff
    Burcher, Julie
    Butt, Jean
    Edwards, Peter

Harrigan, Margaret
Hill, Kay
Morgan, Deborah
Morris, Clare
Powick, Carolyn
Smith, Val

Trainees
Rousseau, Pauline (pda)
Wilson, Julie (pda)
Clayton, Sharon
Jones, Carolyn
Knight, Peter
Lusty, June
Smith, Kimberley
Walford, Verity

ETE Team
Vacancy (ete wrkr)
Hirst, Veronica (eteo)
Palmer, Kate (p) (ete wrkr)

6. **Coleford Magistrates' Court**
    Gloucester Road **Coleford** GL16 8BL
    tel (01594) 837090 *fax (01594) 837256*

    Offender Management
    Anderson, Bob
    Coombs, Sue
    Smith, Stephen (cmo)

    Support Staff
    Law, Gillian

7. Oakes House, 55-57 London Road
    Gloucester GL1 3HF
    tel (01452) 551200 *fax (01452) 522181*

    Programmes Team
    Baker, Charlie (prog mgr)
    James, Shirley (treat supvr)
    Matchett, Chris (treat supvr)
    Temple, Richard (treat supvr)
    Purcell, Angie (treat supvr)
    Belshaw, Lisa (p)
    Adlard, Stephen (prog wrkr)
    Jones, Karen (prog wrkr)
    Brooks, Sue (prog wrkr)
    Cassidy, John (prog wrkr)
    Fowler, Miranda (prog wrkr)
    Hudson, Julie (prog wrkr)
    Patterson, Chris (prog wrkr)
    Whitney, Vicky (prog wrkr)

    Public Protection
    Mark Scully (ppt mgr)
    Gibbs, Rupert
    Shaw, Mary
    Thandi, Sandeep
    Worsley, Andrew
    Jones, Barbara (victim enquiry)

Support Staff
Baldwin, Julie
Barlow, Kerry
Daws, Monique
McDonald-Bell, Kirsty
Moore, Laura

DIP Team
Yates, Ted (DIP mgr)

8. **Crown Court** Longsmith Street
    Gloucester GL1 2TS
    tel (01452) 426327 *fax (01452) 381292*

    Jones, Barbara

    Support Staff
    Turner, Gill

9. **Community Payback Unit**
    Bewick House, 1 Denmark Road
    Gloucester GL1 3HW
    tel (01452) 426250 *fax (01452) 462639*

    Grant-Jones, Pauline (snr pract)
    Thompson, Allan (snr pract)
    Hanson, Steve (proj off)
    Allan, Daryl (supvsr)
    Green, Ransford (supvsr)
    Greenshields, Jim (supvr)
    Mashta, Hussain (supvsr)
    Scott, Dave (supvsr)
    Smith, Steve (supvsr)
    Tocknell, Richard (supvsr)

    Support Staff
    Brewser, Mandy
    McClay, Eve-Louise

10. **Youth Offending Team**
    48 London Road **Gloucester** GL1 3NZ
    tel (01452) 547540 *fax (014520) 551114*

    Kennedy, Catherine

11. **Gloucestershire Reintegration Service**
    Peter Scott House, 2 Heathville Road
    Gloucester GL1 3DP
    tel (01452) 553584 *fax (01452) 553583*

    Gash, Brian (bus mgr)
    Cooper, Anne (pract mgr)
    Prew, Sue (eteo)
    Fletcher, James (pso)
    Hall, Tracy (pso)

Hostel

12. **Ryecroft Approved Premises**
    78 Ryecroft Street, Tredworth

Gloucester GL1 4LY
tel (01452) 380268 *fax (01452) 302969*

Berry, Dave (hostel mgr)
Dower, Kevin (deputy mgr)
Jukes, Gary (asst mgr)
Merrick, Rachel (asst mgr)
Cottrell, Susan (asst mgr)
Pellant, Christine (asst mgr)
Bees, Harry (hostel sup)
Morgan, Greg (hostel sup)
McGrath, Emma (hostel sup)

Support Staff
Atkins, Christine

Institution

13. HM Prison, Barrack Square
    Gloucester GL1 1JN
    tel (01452) 529551 *fax (01452) 310302*

    Special visits (01452) 308218

    Barrett, Keith (resettlement mgr)
    Kenyon, Judith
    Farr, Derek (pso)
    Gough, Petra (pso)
    Parker, Samantha (pso)
    Wright, Julian (pso)

Local Justice Areas

    2 Cheltenham
    3 Cirencester
    6 Coleford
    5 Gloucester
    4 Stroud

Crown Court

    9 Gloucester

HAMPSHIRE PROBATION AREA

Out of hours contact point
The Grange Probation Hostel 023 9236 3474

Victim enquiries contact number 0845
6040150

e-mail
firstname.surname@hampshire.probation.gsx.
gov.uk

1. **Head Office**
    Friary House, Middle Brook Street
    Winchester SO23 8DQ
    tel (01962) 842202

direct dial (01962) 842 + ext
fax (01962) 865278

Crook, Barrie (co) ext 203
Ashton, Liz (dir offender mgmnt) ext 207
Pearce, Richard (dir perf & planning) ext 210
Whitworth, Anne (dir finance & resources) ext 206
Mitchell, Chris (acting dir ops [interventions]) ext 210
Halliday, Keith (head of personnel & training) ext 208
Carruthers, George (area mgr courts-martial report service & YOT) ext 206
Bahaj, Julia (diversity mgr)
Pudney, Jo (personnel off) ext 202
King, Emma (personnel off) ext 202
Maddocks, Vicky (personnel off) ext 202
Howson, Monica (payroll off) ext 204
Pearce, Mark (personnel asst) ext 202
Hacker, John (info systems officer) ext 202
Turtle, Steve (perf imprvmnt mgr) ext 202
Green, Amelia (devloper analyst) ext 202
Rolley, Rhiannon (perf analyst) ext 202
Maclean, Angus (irt mgr) ext 202
Fenech, Ron (i.t. trainer) ext 202
Collins, Nicki (i.t. tech & supp mgr) ext 202
Higgins, Sarah (i.t. ntwk & sec mgr) ext 202
Jones, Rachael (snr finance off) ext 202
May, Mary (finance off) ext 202
Vacancy (finance off) ext 202
Scott, Barry (finance off) ext 202
Crooks, David (librarian) ext 202
Hatch, Belinda (pa) ext 203
Collings, Rachel (p, pa) ext 208
Gaster, Sue (pa) ext 207
Josling, Sarah (pa) ext 210
Welsh, Chris (pa) ext 206
Townsend-Brown, Angela (office mgr) ext 202

2.   Imperial House, 2 Grosvenor Road
     Aldershot GU11 1DP
     tel (01252) 324288 *fax (01252) 329515*

     Ager, Jacqui (spo) (3, 10)
     Morgan, Catherine (p, spo, mappa) (5, 27)
     Cooper, Tony (resource mgr) (3, 4, 5, 10, 22, 23)
     Cranstone, Michele (asst res mgr) (3,10)
     Barber, Rachael
     Despicht, Kathy
     Dodson, Rachel
     Etherington, Kate
     Loggan, Carol

Phillips, Natasha
Regan, Cliff
Roomes, Mel (drr)
Ward, Maggie
Williams, Nina (p)
Sansom, Carol (ete) (10)
Finch, Jane (pso)
Hocking, Hannah (pso)
Johnson-Stanley, Natalie (pso)
Hesketh, Terry (case mgr)
Wyatt, Leona (case mgr)

3.   25 Normandy Street
     Alton GU34 1DQ
     tel (01420) 84155/88134 *fax (01420) 542375*

     Ager, Jacqui (spo) (2, 10)
     Blanchard, Zara
     Waugh, Suzanne (pso)

4.   The Court House
     West Street **Andover** SP10 1QP
     tel (01264) 364411 *fax (01264) 335457*

     Holmes, Sue (spo) (12, 14, 23)
     Gray, Caroline (spo) (24)
     Appleby, Alan
     Dicker, Richard
     Thomas, Jeremy
     Bendle, Andrea (5, 24)
     Hartley, Ben (pso)
     Gray, Elizabeth (case admin)

5.   Ground Floor, St Clement House
     1-3 Alençon Link **Basingstoke** RG21 7SB
     tel (01256) 464272 *fax (01256) 812374*

     Gardner, Jon (spo)
     Morgan, Catherine (p, spo, mappa) (2, 27)
     Turkington, Robbie (snr pract)
     Alderton, Judith
     Gaster, Rachel
     Griffiths, Ceri
     Heward-Mills, Christina
     Holloway, Mandy
     Mellish, Louise
     Murray, Melissa
     Steed, Julie
     Tomkins, Pete
     Levett, Richard (dv co-ord)
     Hocking, Angela (ppo)
     Boyes, Julie (pso)
     Irving, Pauline (pso)
     Larkins, Toni (pso)
     Palmer, Rebecca (pso)
     Wyeth, les (pso)
     Duff, Tony (breach prosection off)

Hills, Eric (breach prosection off)
Sandhu, Sally (asst resource mgr)

6.   First Floor, St Clement House
1-3 Alençon Link
Basingstoke RG21 7SB
tel (01256) 464272 *fax (01256) 357292*

Programmes
Fry, Chris (spo progs)
Galovics, Maria (spo)
Hardy, Susan (spo progs)
Calver, Sue (prog off)
Cleal, Davinia (prog off)
Davis, Melanie (prog off)
Larkins, Toni (prog off)
Murphy, Peter (prog off)
Saunders, Clare (prog off)
Souter, Lynda (prog off)
George, Amy (psy off)
Kelley, Emma (psy off)
Reeves, Pam (treatment mgr)
Levett, Richard (treatment mgr, idap)
Cadle, Jane (ete off) (4, 24)
Pullen, Kim (progs admin)

7.   3rd Floor, Barclays House
20-24 Upper Market Street
Eastleigh SO50 9FD

Essential Skills & ETE Team
tel 023-8064 7442 *fax 023-8064 7446*

Waldman, Keith (essential skills & ptnrshp mgr)
Cavanagh, Mary (ete mgr)
Cook, Cindy (asst resource mgr)
Leeder, Melanie (offender learning liaison off)
Moore, Diana (offender learning liaison off)
Love, Thea (essential skills admin)
Adams, Christine (essential skills co-ord)

Programmes Team
tel 023-8064 7441 *fax 023-8064 7445*

Vacancy (area mgr) ext 251
Hall, Kirstine (resource mgr) ext 248 (17, 19)
Newman, Mark (sex off prog mgr) ext 254
Tarry, Hammond (sogp treatment mgr)
Weston, Natalie (asst resource mgr)

TV-CSOP
Baker, Sheila (prog off)
Brown, Toni (prog off)
Emery, Jane (prog off)

DRR
Pearce, Melanie (drr prog mgr) ext 249

Central Area & Prisons
Renouf, David (are mgr)

8.   **Training and Health & Safety Unit**
2nd Floor, Barclays House
20-24 Upper Market Street
Eastleigh SO50 9FD
tel 023-8064 7443 *fax 023-8064 7447*

McMullan, Pearl (training & devpt mgr)
Pahil, Paul (training & devpt mgr)
Witt, Margaret (training administrator)
Knowles, Keith (health & safety adviser)
Malt. Lin (h&s training admin asst)
Barrett, Niki (spo, mgr trainee po prog)
Eyers, Eileen (pda)
Jones, Peter (pda)
Roberts, Pam (pda)
Roscoe, Martin (e-OASys co-ord)

9.   20 High Street
Fareham P016 7AF
tel (01329) 235888 *fax (01329) 825023*

Skinner, Corinne (spo)
le Fevre, Anne (snr pract)
Crooks, Avril
Croset, Paula
Earles, Patrick
Haynes, Claire (p)
Herbert, Lorraine (p)
Jones, Alison
Joyce, Jackie
Lester, Gwyneth (p)
Manuel, Rachel
Paradise, Erika
Townsend, Paul
Winkworth, Jane
Burns, Jill (pso)
Chuter, Sam (p, pso)
Evans, Hayley (pso)
Langley, Sue (pso)
Shaw, Kristina (pso)
Pickering, Debbie (p, ete off)
Kemp, Annette (ppo co-ord)
Vacancy (asst resource mgr) (11)

10.   46-48 Victoria Road
Farnborough GU14 7PG
tel (01252) 513020 *fax (01252) 370246*

Ager, Jacqui (spo) (2, 3)
Gallichan, Gail
Skeet, Lorraine
Buckle, Gillian (pso)
Downs, Louise (pso)

11. Elmleigh Road
Havant PO9 2AS
tel 023-9247 3011 *fax 023-9249 8275*

Bridden, David (spo)
Blackwell, Sheila
Carnegie, Joan
Cockeram, David
Crawford, Colin
Devereux, Jan
Hahn, Colin (p)
McDuff, Helen
Wells, Andy (pda)
Wells, Suzanne (ete off)
Lawrence, Nicky (drr)
Leishman, Angela (sogp)
Tiffin, Hannah (sogp)
Duncan, John (pso)
Logan, Sue (pso)
Lonergan, Shane (pso)
McGrath, Sarah (pso)
Allen, Rob (corp devpt & supt mgr) (1)
Shaw, Karen (p, asst resource mgr) (9)

12. West Shore House
West Street **Hythe** SO45 6AA
tel 023-8084 3684 *fax 023-8084 2354*

Holmes, Sue (spo) (4)
Youl, Jonathan
Pearce, Elaine (pso)
Jones, Lesley (ast res mgr)

13. 8 Sea Street, Newport
Isle of Wight PO30 5BN
tel (01983) 523265 *fax (01983) 528994*

Svendsen, Jo-Inge (spo)
Fitch, Sarah (snr pract)
Clarke, George
Dugard-Craig, Barbara
Grimes, John
Lester, Annette
Lidstone, Fiona
Milford, Amy
Mussell, Doug
Pennell, Stephen
Roebuck, Emma
Sanders, Donna
Shardlow, Rob
Thwaites, Natasha
Lewis, Stephen (ete off)
Kelly, Marie (pso drr)
Leighton, Jenny (pso)
Lewis, Amanda (pso)
Newnham, Francis (pso)
Pond, Dawn (pso)
Savege, Vicky (pso ppo)

Yates, Rebecca (pso)
Ward, Ian (cso)
Nelson, Robert (cso)
Campbell, Anne (asst res mgr) (16, 17)

14. Island House, Priestlands Place
Lymington SO41 9GA
tel (01590) 673107/677462 *fax (01590) 671521*

Holmes, Sue (spo) (4)
Smyth, Joan
Black, Tracey (pda)
Black, Janet (pso) (12, 23)
Jones, Lesley (assistant resource mgr) (19, 23)

Unpaid Work (Forest)
tel (01590) 675359 *fax 01590 671521*

Trevor, Emans (cso)

15. **Newforest Magistrates' Court**
The Court House, Pikes Hill
Lyndhurst SO43 7NR
tel (02380) 283189

Somerville, Jenni
Nicholas, Wendy (pso)

16. Portsmouth Probation Office
PO Box 703 **Portsmouth** POI 2WZ
tel 023-9272 8300 *fax 023-9285 1618*

FLOOR 5

Kiely, Dave (area mgr) (13)
Christie, Steve (spo)
Vacancy (spo)
Lightburn, Marilyn (spo)
Stone, Neil (spo)
Davies, Susan (pda)
Smith, Chas (pda)
Goodbody, Tony (resource mgr) (13)
Campbell, Anne (asst res mgr) (js) (13, 17)
Moloney, Mike (asst res mgr) (17)

Court Unit
tel 023-9272 8940 *fax 023-9229 1612*
Tomlinson, Jenny (snr pract)
Joslin, Susan
Meads, Genny
Wilkinson, Caroline
Ball, Jackie (pso)
Forest, Jackie (pso)
Newman, Roger (pso)
Podmore, Anne (pso)

MAPPA
tel 023-9272 8330 *fax 023-9275 5154*
Dillon, Barbara

Hyslop, Alex
Marsh, Rob
Plant, Louise
Vosper, Jo
Welch, Yasmin
White, Libby

Over 25 & Resettlement
tel 023-9272 8360 *fax 023-9285 1618*
Austerberry, Anne
Bizley, Jane
Bowes, Tom
Frampton, Pat
Marshall, Richard
Peckham, Jennifer
Postin, Laura
Arnold, Denise (pso)
Barnard, Dennis (pso)
Gough, Kelly (pso)
Stacey, Lea (pso)

Under 25/PPO/DRR
tel 023-9272 8340 *fax 023-9285 1618*
Burgess, Heather
Foster, Laura
Gray, Rebecca (drr)
Harvey, Matt
Heptner, Nina
Keysell, Ben
Purser, Ellie
Storey, Estelle
Baynham, Myra (pso)
Judd, Peter (pso)
McKeith, Debbie (pso)
Punton, Bridget (pso drr)

FLOOR 6

Unpaid Work (SE Region)
tel 023-9272 8400 *fax 023-928 1183*

Davies, John (area mgr, unpaid wk &
essential skills)
Leigh, Brian (scheme mgr)
Skinner, Alan (qa mgr) (22)
Chambers, Steph (qa mgr) (22)
Richards, Teresa (unpaid wk res mgr) (14,
22, 24)
Dumper, David (case mgr)
Francis, Steve (case mgr)
Greenhalgh, Barrie (case mgr)
Hadden, Karen (case mgr)
Hartman, Jenny (case mgr)
Harris, Jeff (placement mgr)
Hogben, Christine (case mgr)
Ross, Jean (case mgr)
Smith, Penny (case mgr)
Wade, Peter (case mgr)
Pervin, Eddie (ete tutor)
Stedman, Ros (asst resource mgr)

Programmes Unit
tel 023-9272 8470 *fax 023-9282 7841*
Barrett, Sally (spo)
Simpson, Sandra (spo idap)
Heptner, Nina
Keys, Carly
Webb, Dawn
Janvrin, Jane (treatment mgr)
Taggart, Kelly (treatment mgr)
Sherwood, Alex (prog off)
Whitefield, Sarah (prog off)
Bassford, Clair (prog off)
Coomber, Carianne (prog off)
Correa, Helen (prog off)
Dyke, Matthew (prog off)
Morgan, Trevor (prog off)
Tilford, Richard (prog off)
Tripp, Russell (prog off)
White, Sandra (prog off)
Larter, Sharon (pso tutor)
Pendlebury, Alyson (women's safety wrkr)
Vacancy (psy admin)
Adkins, Anna (admin)

17. 52 Isambard Brunel Road
Portsmouth PO1 2BD
tel 023-9283 9800 *fax 023-9287 7340*

Breach
tel 023-9272 8390 *fax 023-9273 5192*
Samways, Lisa
Green, Lisa (pso, bpo)
Richards, Ian (pso, bpo)

ETE
tel 023-9272 8937 *fax 023-9287 7340*
Dewhurst, Janna (ete off)
Reece, Corinne (ete off)
Tatlow, Roy (ete off)

18. 70 London Road
Southampton S015 2AJ
tel 023-8063 5011 *fax 023-8023 1801*

MAPPA Unit
O'Driscoll, Paul (spo)
Barrett, Lin
Cooke, Maggie
Lawrence-Jones, Jill
Markie, Jacqui
May, Simon
Robinson, Jenie
Round, Sarah
Sharma, Aneel
Wensley-Smith, Sonia
Edwards, Paul (pso)
Alden, Sarah (admin)

Bull, Lisa (admin)
Bulpit, Sarah (admin)
Caincross, Leanne (admin)
Evans, Clare (admin)
Selvage, Michelle (admin)
Fovargues, Jax (admin)

Young Adult Offender Team
Cluff, Jeff (spo)
Elcock, Catherine
Hatton, Dean
Vacancy
McDermott, Michelle
Davies, Shona (pso)
Drummond, Paula (pso)
Scurr, Bex (pso)
Skinner, Jo (pso ppo)
Thorndyke, Mel (pso)
Cross, Margaret (admin)
Kitson, Nicola (admin)

Breach Team
Hill, Jo (bpo)
Hall, Leo (bpo)
Farthing, Debbie (admin)
Darlington, Joanne (admin)

Adams, Tracy (asst resource mgr)

19. **Southampton Magistrates' Court**
100 The Avenue, Southampton SO17 0EY
tel 023-8033 6113 *fax 023-8033 6122*

Lewis, Zara (snr pract)
Bridger, Jane
Glew, David
Arnold, Andrea (pso)
Mullen, Lisa (pso)
Swatton, Di (admin)
Widlake, Kris (admin)

20. **Southampton Crown Court**
The Courts of Justice
London Road, Southampton SO15 2AA
tel 023-8023 2642 *fax 023-8023 5929*

Gladwin, Peter (pso)
Nash, Pat (admin)

21. 7 Town Quay House, Town Quay
Southampton SO14 2PT
tel (02380) 831300 *fax (02380) 831333*

Hall, Jackie (area mgr) (18)
Orman, Lin (resource mgr) (18)
Shone, Lynne (asst resource mgr)

**CRO/CPRO Supervision Team &
Resettlement Cluster**
Dunne, Margaret (spo)
Morris, Pete (spo)

Bainbridge, Adam
Brider, Heather
Broughton, Steve
Cato, Len
Charlesworth, Ian
French, Daniella
Hearn, Jenny
Johnson, Don
Rushforth, Rachel
Talbot, Polly
Watt, Sue
Wigg, Simon
Williams, Tina
Pencavel, Katie (drr)
Tarr, Caroline (drr)
Chaloner, Jenny (pso)
Cleeve, Kate (pso)
Goodeve, Jayne (pso)
Kennelly, Gerry (pso)
Morse, Barry (pso)
Evans, Heather (ete)
O'Connor, Lou (ete)

Programmes Unit
Smailes, Alison (spo)
Connell, Soozin (prog off)
Eckersley, Louise (prog off)
Edwards, Julie (prog off)
Hart, Michelle (prog off)
Sitaram, Shashi (prog off)
Thorpe, Val (prog off)
Simkins, Caroline (psychometrics off)

Vacancy (idap treatment mgr)
Hall, Mike (prog off idap)
Kirkpatrick, Sarah (prog off idap)
Levett, Richard (prog off idap)
Vacancy (prog off idap)
Waddington, Sue (prog off idap)
Burton, Mary (women's safety wrkr)

Gatt, Jan (prog admin)
Hoskins, Jan (prog admin)

TV-CSOP Team
Hendricks, Caroline (tv-csop facilitator)
Vince, Russell (tv-csop facilitator)

22. **Unpaid Work Office
(South West Region)**
Old Bank House, 66-68 London Road
Southampton S015 2AJ
tel 023-8033 9992 *fax 023-8023 5778*

James, Nigel (scheme mgr)
Chambers, Steph (qa mgr) (based at 16)
Hansford, Tony (proj mgr)
Crouch, Liz (case mgr)
Emery, Denis (case mgr)

Keites, Hayley (case mgr)
Parker, Bill (case mgr)
Smyth, Patrick (case mgr)
Sutton, Gillian (case mgr)
Robertson, Paula (tutor)
Rutherford, Alison (asst resource mgr) (24)

23. 9 Testwood Lane **Totton**
Southampton SO40 3BT
tel 023-8086 2287 *fax 023-8066 0314*

Holmes, Sue (spo) (4)
Alford, Alison
Costello, Annette
McAllen, Marie
Rynne, Martin
Youl, Jonathan (12)
Black, Janet (pso/ete off) (12, 14)
Jones, Lesley (asst resource mgr) (12, 14)

24. 3rd Floor, Cromwell House
Andover Road **Winchester** SO23 7EZ
tel (01962) 842662 fax (01962) 866228

Beattie, Sarah (area mgr) (2-6, 10, 25)
Wettone, Irene (acting spo) (4)
Gray, Caroline (p, spo) (4, 25)
Boddy, Pat
Dealey, Jill
Edwards, Tamara
Paul, Debbie
Ryder, Zoe
Stainton, Kate
Caswell, Michelle (pso)
Stroud, Sarah (pso)
Gedge, Nikki (case admin)
Penny, Sharon (case admin)

Unpaid Work (North Region)
Winchester (01962) 853699
fax (01962) 866228

Glen, Ray (scheme mgr) (2)
Fisher, Peter (case mgr)
Howell, Steve (case mgr)
Starr, Brian (case mgr)

25. **Winchester Combined Court Centre**
The Law Courts **Winchester** SO23 9EL
tel (01962) 849256 *fax (01962) 870405*

Gray, Caroline (spo) (p, 24)
North, Jo (admin)

26. **HMP Community Mental Health Team**
(Winchester Prison)
8 West End Close, Winchester SO22 5EW
tel (01962) 877664 *fax (01962) 877670*

Vacancy (team ldr) (2, 5)

27. **Victim Contact Unit**
3rd Floor, Cromwell House
Andover Road **Winchester** SO23 7EZ
tel 0845 6040 150 *fax (01962) 844983*

Morgan, Catherine (spo)
Ball, Liz
Turner, Kirsty
Rooney, Debi

Youth Offending Teams

28. **Wessex Youth Offending Team**
85 High Street, Winchester SO23 9AE
tel (01962) 876100 *fax (01962) 876109*

Crocker, Steve (hd of youth offending
svces)
Owen, Mark (perf, info & training mgr)

29. **Wessex YOT (NE & NW)**
180 Culver Road, Basingstoke RG21 3NL
tel (01256) 464034 *fax (01256) 327210*

Humphrey, Jean (area mgr)

30. **Wessex YOT (SE and Portsmouth City)**
Darby House, Skye Close
Cosham, Portsmouth PO6 3LU
tel 023-9237 0013 *fax 023-9220 0374*

Wade, Sue (area mgr)

31. **Wessex YOT
(SW and Southampton City)**
33 Selbourne Avenue
Harefield, Southampton SO18 5DZ
tel 023-8046 3336 *fax 023-8047 0060*

Morse, Sue (area mgr)
Pegler, Barbara (pda)

32. **Wessex YOT (Isle of Wight)**
62 Crocker Street, Newport
Isle of Wight PO30 5DA
tel (01983) 522799 *fax (01983) 523175*

Abbott, Meg (area mgr)

33. **Wessex YOT
Intensive Supervision & Surveillance
Programme**
2nd Floor Ashville House 260-262
Havant Road
Drayton, Portsmouth PO6 1PA
tel 023-9228 3900 *fax 023-9238 1318*

Ballard, Jeff (area mgr)

Hostels

34. **Dickson House Approved Premises**
77 Trinity Street, Fareham PO16 7SL
tel (01329) 234531 *fax (01329) 284523*

McKie, Jennifer (spo)
Binfield, Iris (res services off)
Dobson, Gemma (res services off)
Hawkes, Abi (res services off)
Kitching, Peter (res services off)
Knott, Patricia (night wk supvr)
Wootton, Peter (night wk supvr)
Brockwell, Pam (support services off)
McInally, Teri (res admin support off)

35. **The Grange Approved Premises**
145 Stakes Road, Purbrook PO7 5PL
tel 023-9236 3474 *fax 023-9236 3481*

Vacancy (spo)
Babbington, John (res service off)
Bastable, Jane (res service off)
Connor, Debbie (res service off)
Hopper, Sarah (res services off)
Spencer, Patrick (res service off)
Newman, John (night wk supvr)
Vacancy (night wk supvr)
Mazzetelli, Dianne (support services off)
Robbins, Erin (res admin supt)

36. **Landguard Road Approved Premises**
32 Landguard Road, Shirley
Southampton SO15 5DJ
tel 023-8033 6287 *fax 023-8033 6290*

Sleeman, Sylvia (spo)
Bone, Darren (res services off)
Collins, Paul (res services off)
Fuakye, Priscilla (res services off)
Leeds, Kelly-Ann (res services off)
Pickering, Darren (res services off)
Bell, Justin (night wk supvr)
Felton, Brian (night wk supvr)
Davis, Kate (support services off)
Davidson, Donna (res admin supt)

Institutions

37. H M Prison **Albany**
Newport, Isle of Wight PO30 5RS
tel (01983) 556300 *fax (01983 556332*

Direct dial (01983) 556+ext
Probn Clerk ext 465

Jackson, Chris (spo) ext 467
Vacancy ext 469
Jenkins, Susan (pso) ext 470
Snell, Patricia ext 466
Toovey, Adele ext 462

38. H M Prison **Camp Hill**
Newport, Isle of Wight PO30 5PB
tel (01983) 554600 *fax (01983) 554799*

Direct dial (01983) 55+ext

Caswell, Paul (spo) ext 4696
Vacancy ext 4806
Gagliardini, John ext 4742
Woodham, Sue ext 4697
Vacancy (pso housing) ext 4735
Simon, Pauline (pso housing) ext 4655

39. H M Prison **Parkhurst**
Newport, Isle of Wight PO30 5NX
tel (01983) 554000 *fax (01983) 554001*

Direct dial (01983) 554+ext
Probn Clerk ext 360

King, Andrea (spo) ext 362
Holland, Mary ext 196
Owen, Bryony ext 199
Saunders, Rachel ext 200
Vacancy
Vacancy
Vacancy (p)
Egerton, Karen (p, pso) ext 362
Gladdis, Jayne (pso) ext197
Pimentel, Ana (pso) ext 362

40. H M Prison **Kingston**
122 Milton Road, Portsmouth PO3 6AS
tel 023-9295 3100 *fax 023-9295 3181*

Direct dial 023-92533+ ext

Clist, Terry (spo) ext 217
Coffey, Mike ext 236
Poingdestre, Estelle ext 218
Simpson, Sandra ext 218
Wilkinson, Caroline ext 236

41. H M Prison **Winchester**
Romsey Road, Winchester SO22 5DF
tel (01962) 723000 *fax (01962) 723001*
probn fax (01962) 723008

Direct dial (01962) 723+ext

Vacancy (spo) ext 161
McVeigh, Carole ext 160
Murray, Andrea ext 157
Townsend, Sindi ext 112
Everson, Terry (ete off) ext 077
Damani, Ishret (pso) ext 035
Topping, Graham (pso) ext 159
Vacancy (pso)
Beatson, Jennifer (pso bail info) ext 036
Carter, Judith (pso bail info) ext 036
Thompson, Ian (pso, accom) ext 078

Local Justice Areas

15 New Forest
2, 3 NE Hampshire
4, 5 NW Hampshire
11, 16 SE Hampshire
7, 9 S Hampshire
18 Southampton
13 Isle of Wight

Crown Courts

13 Newport
16 Portsmouth
20 Southampton
25 Winchester

HERTFORDSHIRE PROBATION AREA

Victim enquiries contact number
(01727) 792709

e-mail
Firstname.Surname@hertfordshire.
probation.gsx.gov.uk

1. **Head Office**
    Graham House, Yeoman's House
    Ware Road, Hertford SG13 7HJ
    tel (01992) 504444 *fax (01992) 504544*
    personnel fax (01992) 516902

    Baldwin, Richard (cpo)
    Matthews, Lisa (dir of operations)
    Hughes, John (dir of operations)
    McDougall, Carole (dir of operations)
    Vacancy (dir of resources & admin)
    Ball, Rosie (training mgr)
    Nicki Hulford (p, press & pub)
    Moses, Sandra (h.r. mgr)
    Riccardi, Lisa (service resources mgr)
    Spencer, Lucy (perf improvement mgr)
    Vacancy (h&s officer)

    East Herts Probation Centre
    fax (01992 516900)
    Clarke, David (spo)
    Frayne, John (prog mgr)
    Crawford, Anthony (pda)
    Davies, Gisela (p)
    Dowling, Jackie,
    Foskett, Tina
    Glassock, Jo (p)
    Gordon, Shanti (p)
    Jervis, Andrea
    Kinsey, Ian
    Mackness, Emma

Southgate, Terry
Steigar, Ursula (p)
Weston, Jackie (treament mgr)

Trainees
Swan, Susan
Bucknor, Carlene
Moffat, Jacqueline

PSOs
Dorunay, Ayse (p, gpwk)
Holmes, Min (gpwk)
Williams, Di (gpwk)
Amos, Joanne (gen)
del Toro, Robert (gen)
Davies, Kathleen (gen)
Durrant, Sarah (gen)
McDonald, Cheryl (gen)
Morrell, Zoe (gen)
Winter, Louise (gen)

Community Service
Dickens, Peter (cso)
Johnson, Di (cso)
Vacancy (placement off)

Hook, Doug (com safety mgr)

2. **Mid Herts Probation Centre**
    62-72 Victoria Street
    St Albans AL1 3XH
    tel (01727) 847787 *fax (01727) 792700*

    Keyte, Bernie, Kay (acting spo)
    Leng, Sally (acting spo)
    Jarvis, Phil (regnl sex offndr specialist)
    Baker, Jill (sex offender specialist)
    Shirley, Matthew (sex offender specialist)
    Senverdi, Nalan (sex offender specialist)
    Adams, Katie (p)
    Andersson, Max
    Benson, Claire
    Bond, Nicola
    Clairmonte, Claire
    Fielding, Kay
    Goodall, Anika
    Hollis, Bryony
    Holloway, Tony (pda)
    Judd, Claire
    Ewington, Mark
    McConnell, Elaine
    Mentern Hannah
    Murphy, John
    Ostrowski, Liz
    Rissen, Susan
    Willis, David
    Spencer, Maureen (treatment mgr)

    Trainees
    Bruce, Sarah

Clarke Eccles, Valerie
Hopkins, Alison
Ross, Sarah-Jane
Thompson, Tanya

PSOs
Brown, Stephen (gpwk)
Graham, Rose (gpwk)
Ivey, Linda (gpwk)
Sheedy, June (gpwk)
McGovern, Maureen (dtto)
Nelson, Sally (prolific offender)
Wearne, Ruth (prolific offender)
Cleary, Loredana (women's safety wrkr)

Shults, Peter (police/probn liaison)

Aburrow, Annette (gen)
Agunbide, Adebola (gen)
Berardi, Patrizia (gen)
Borg Wheeler, Fran (gen)
Bouma, Esher (gen)
Harrison, Nicola (gen)
Ling, Darren (gen)
O'Neil, Desmond (gen)
Vacancy (gen)
Parris, Mervyn (gen)
Runham, Jennifer (gen)

Community Service
Hillhouse, Lyne (cso)
Vacancy (cso)
Monery, Peter (placement off)

Victim Unit
tel (01727) 792709 *fax (01727) 792706*

Vacancy (victim devpt mgr)
Hornsèy, Susan (victim contact)
Vacancy (victim contact)

3. **North Herts Probation Centre**
Swingate House, Danestrete
Stevenage SG1 1XB
tel (01438) 747074 *fax (01438) 765206*

Martindale, Clare (spo)
Moore, Marilyn (spo)
Holmes, Alex (prog mgr)
Brooks, Dawn (treament mgr)
Holloway, Tony (pda/staff devpt off)
Cowen, Jon (pda)
Bibi, Majabin
Bolton, May
Downes, Tom
Fawcett, Kelly
Gurr, Lydia
Hagen, Paul
Jones, Victoria
Lawrance, Alison
Moss, Nik (dtto)

Oliver-Blais, Merle
Tooley, Neil
Venters, Catherine

Trainees
Flower, Melanie
Golding, Vikki
Jones, Victoria
Kusevra, Ozen

PSOs
Ebeling-Jones, Cheryl (p, gpwk)
Hintzen, Alison (gpwk)
Mulqueen, Clare (gpwk)
White, Catherine (gpwk)
Cley, Natalie (gen)
Cliffe, Helen (gen)
Cotton, Janette (gen)
Cross, Samantha (gen)
Davis, Linda (gen)
Hood, Alison (gen)
Parker, Heather (gen)
Jarmaine, Cindy (gen)
Johnston, Anne (p, gen)
Meredith, Caitrin (gen)
Pratt, John (gen)
Stickley, Anna (gen)

Community Service
Ross, Hal (spo, cs)
Chaney, Jane (p, cso)
Hayward, Robbie (cso)

Ells, Penelope (service resources mgr)

4. **South & West Herts Probation Centre**
16-22 King Street **Watford** WD1 8BP
tel (01923) 240144 *fax (01923) 699195*

Barnard, Diane (spo)
Mulhair, Fiona (spo)
Cumming, Dennis (pda)
Harvey, Kate (pda)
Johnson, Morris (treatment mgr)
Anderson, Lorraine
Bedward, Leroy
Hughes, Sarah
Hughes, Will
Hylton, Gary
Lawson, Afewu
McNicholas, Katharine (p)
Moss, Elizabeth
Omorogbe, Mark
Penn, Linda
Pinder, Julie
Tiernan, Janet
Urwin, Sue
McClure, Tracey (p)
McFarlane, Julia (p)

Trainees
Boorman, Laura
Harwood, Sara
Wojdyla-St.James, Barbara
Wyper, Fiona

PSOs
Ashard, Laura (p, crt)
Flaherty, Mary (gpwk)
Mullings, Sonia (gpwk)
Warrington, Claire (gpwk)
Woolmer, Paul (gpwk)
Wright, Lex (gpwk)
Allum, Bodrul (gen)
Brooks, Michaela (gen)
Che, Simon (gen)
Gilbride, Aiden (gen)
Ferguson, Sarah (gen)
Isaacs, Susan (gen)
Penn, Rebecca (gen)
Pickard, Wayne (p, gen)
Wilson, Sarah (p, gen)

Community Service
Parkin, Bob (qa mgr)
Egglesfield, John (cso)
Pearson, Tony (cso)
Waite-Gifford, Donna (cso)

Pratt, Diane (service resources mgr)

5. **Crown Court Probation Office**
Bricket Road **St Albans** AL1 3JW
tel (01727) 753290 *fax (01727) 868276*

6. **Youth Offending Team**
S&W, Watford
tel (01923) 229012
Hodgson, James

N Herts, Stevenage
tel (01438) 723113
Jeffery, Peter (p)

S&W, Hemel Hempstead
tel (01442) 388755
Smith, Nicola

E Herts, Hatfield
tel (01707) 897440
Perkins, David

Institution

7. H M Prison **The Mount**
Molyneaux Avenue, Bovingdon
Hemel Hempstead HP3 0NZ
tel (01442) 834363 *fax (01442) 836483*

Kochinky, Manfred (spo)
Maylam, Chris (p)

Webster, Steve
Borg, Michelle (pso)
Church, Julia (pso)
Giles, Anna (pso)

Local Justice Areas
1 East Hertfordshire
2 Central Hertfordshire
3 North Hertfordshire
4 West Hertfordshiore

Crown Court
5 St Albans

HUMBERSIDE
PROBATION AREA

e-mail: Firstname.Surname@humberside.
probation.gsx.gov.uk

1. **Head Office**
21 Flemingate **Beverley**
E Yorks HU17 0NP
tel (01482) 867271 *fax (01482) 864928*

Hemming, Steve (co)
Alexander, Voni (aco)
Razzell, Ian (aco)
Robinson, Janet (aco, hr)
Pettit, Peter (aco, seconded)
Wright, Peter (aco)
Wright, Sheila (aco)
Montgomery, Angela (solicitor)
Siddy, Brian (aco corporate services)
Rhodes, Sharon (personnel mgr)
Goodrick, Steve (contracts mgr)
Scott, Jayne (acting finance mgr)
Lloyd, Matt (perf mgr)
Davidson, Val (ext relations mgr)
Razzell, Gillian (pso mappa)

PPO Unit
Redfern, Kate (spo)
Lee, Stephen
Cunningham, Mo (pso)

1a. **Liberty House,** Liberty Lane
Kingston upon Hull HU1 1RS
tel (01482) 480000 *fax (01482) 480003*

Neal, Mary (diversity mgr)
Ellis, Jean (training mgr)
Walster, John (IT mgr)
Tallant, Chris (spo/nvq co-ord)
Burney, Erica (pda)
Dawson, Pat (pda)
McCartney, Sarah (pda)

2. 4 St Johns Avenue
    Bridlington E Yorks YO16 4NG
    tel (01262) 672512 *fax (01262) 400336*

    Ryan, Sue (spo)
    Edwards, Julie
    Hoar, John
    Priestly, Ray
    Prout, Lisa
    Timperley, Mary
    Ramsden, Rosie
    Wilson, Jennifer
    Boxhall, Lesley (pso)
    Stephenson, Ms Lesley J (pso)
    Wild, Jonathon (pso)
    Wilson, Sally (pso)

3. Greenawn, 1 Airmyn Road
    Goole E Yorks DN14 6XA
    tel (01405) 767177 *fax (01405) 720983*

    Mellor, Adrian (spo)
    Cook, Darren
    Gordon, Les
    Lowden, Peter
    Swales, Liza
    Ware, Ian
    Duncan, Maggie (pso)
    Gawtry, Kerry (pso)
    Throssel, Sara (pso)
    Archer, Kevin (pso)
    Wilson, Sally (pso)

4. Liberty House, Liberty Lane
    Kingston upon Hull HU1 1RS
    tel (01482) 480000 *fax (01482) 480003*

    Offender Management Team
    Neary, Paul (spo)
    Scargill, Vicki (spo)
    Wright, John (spo)
    Armstrong, Rob
    Barmby, Sonia
    Bate, Liz
    Betteridge, Jane (p)
    Birkett, Lynne
    Brookes, Chris
    Burton, Alan
    Carter, Tony (p)
    Hannah,Clare
    Cripps, Rosie
    Draper, Suzanne
    Fishwick, Rachel
    Frank, Joy
    Giffiths, Eleanor
    Giles, Clare
    Girvan, Irene

    Goforth, Kate
    Goldring, Dave (p)
    Hall, Dr Mariam
    Hardy, Rebecca
    Harrison, Catherine
    Harry, Gill (p)
    Heald, Fliss
    Hill, Katrina (p)
    Houghton, Ian
    Kelly, Paul
    Livingston, Katie
    Mitchell, Nick
    Naylor, Leroy
    Parrott, Andrea
    Pick, Rachel
    Porteous, Mandylee
    Robb, Haydn
    Robinson, Lucie
    Simpson, John
    Shaddick, Brian
    Smith, Mark (mappa)
    Stapeley, Joanne
    Taylor, Donna
    Wells Gareth

    Bahn, Steve (pso)
    Clarke, Caroline (pso)
    Collins, Michelle (pso)
    Cross, Jackie (pso)
    Dent, Jane (pso)
    Eyles, Linda (pso)
    Henderson, Julie (p,pso)
    Hickson, Stuart (pso)
    Lee, Diane (p, pso)
    Lupkin, Cynthia (pso)
    McAllister, Carmel (p, pso)
    Mansson, Magnus (pso)
    Marrino, Donna (p, pso)
    Pickering, Lisa (p, pso)
    Procter, Tracey (pso)
    Robinson, Andy (pso)
    Simpson, Karen (pso)
    Styche, Helen (pso)
    Tennison, Leanne (pso)
    Trowell, Paula (pso)
    Watson, Niki (pso)
    White, Steve (pso)
    Wood, Lorraine (pso)

    Higginbottom, Tracey (pso mappa)
    Dent, Pamela (victim support officer)

    Court Services
    Fridlington, Kevan (spo)
    Ware, Ian (spo)
    Flynn, John
    Harwood, Lara (prosecutions officer)
    Wadforth, Neil (prosecutions officer)

Burton, Helen (pso)
Burton, Lisa (pso)
Dhamrait, Neelam (pso)
Green, Sharon (pso)
Jackson, Tracey (p, pso)
Moody, Geoff (pso)
Sleight, Maxine (p, pso)

DTTO/DRR
Atkin, Sarah (spo)
Baker, Glynis
Boyne, Linda
Coles, Stephen
Harrison, Rebecca
Hockney, Garry
Oliver, Anita
Trees, Racheal (p, pso)
Allen, Elaine (pso)
Kirkpatrick, Joe (pso)
Oyston, Sam (pso)

Intensive Change & Control Programme
Baker, Sue (spo)
Hancock, Jane
Kiney, Brighid
Wilkinson, Andrea
Adamson, Liz (pso)
Wilson, Lee (pso)

Interventions Team
Holdcroft, Felix (spo)
Sellors, Rupert (spo)
Brookes, Mike
Hurst, Phil
Sambrook, Mark
Morton, Dave (qa mgr)
Postill, Bill (qa mgr)
Adamson. Liz (pso)
Billam , Lesley (pso)
Collins, Michelle (pso)
Dhamrant, Jazz (pso)
Eyles, Stuart (pso)
Gowland, Paul (pso)
Jubb, Louise (pso)
Kimenia, Kahunyuro (pso)
Merritt, Simon (pso)
Oyston, Sam (pso)
Robins, Steve (pso)
Robinson, Andy (pso)
Rollinson, Sonja (pso)
Simpson, Karen (pso)
Styche, Helen (pso)
Timmings, Dawn (pso)
Walkington, James (pso)
Williams, Gwendoline (pso)
Wright, Ruth (pso)

NVQ/PDA Unit
Burney, Erica (p)
Dawson, Pat
Gibson, Steve
McCartney, Sarah
Parrott, Andrea (p)
Winters, Chris

5. **MAPPA**
    Crime Management Policy Unit
    Humberside Police HQ
    Priory Road, Kingston upon Hull HU5 5SF
    tel (01482) 220248

    Godley, John (spo)

6. **Hull DIT** Suite J
    Conifer Rooms, Shirethorne Centre
    37-43 Prospect Street, Hull HU2 2PR
    tel (01482) 620013 *fax (01482) 210084*

    McNicol, Ian (spo)
    Greenwood, Catherine
    Atkinson, Eve (pso)

7. **Crown Court Liaison Office**
    Hull Combined Courts Centre
    Lowgate, Hull HU1 2EZ
    tel (01482) 585044

8. Queen Street
    Grimsby NE Lincs DN31 1QG
    tel (01472) 357454 *fax (01472) 355572*

    Court Services Team
    Coleman, Sarah (spo)
    Jackson, Robert
    Matson, Mary (prosecution off)
    Taylor, Lynne (prosecution off)

    Offender Management
    Adegbembo, Sally (spo)
    Clarke, Mike (spo)
    Bailey, Becky
    Binns, Alison
    Bolton, Wendy
    Chung, Emma (p)
    Cotterill, Alan
    Cowper, Sophie
    Ford, Jo
    Gillender, Clare
    Harvey, Ruth
    Lynn, Phil
    McGrath, Anne-Marie
    Martin, Julia
    Parnell, Diane
    Rigg, Kerry-Jo
    Sanghera, Peramjit
    Shepherd, John

Smith, Kerry
Sprakes, Marie
Woods, Heather

Blow, Nichola (pso)
Blythin, Lynette (pso)
Corbett, Diane (pso)
Denton, Suzette (pso)
Duffield, Paul (pso)
Fairbank, Martin (pso)
Frith, Linda (pso)
Gunn, Helen (pso)
Harrison, Sonja (pso)
Hookham, Di (pso)
Hoyle, Sarah (pso)
Huxford, Karen (p, pso)
Jackson, Linda (pso)
Riley, Marie (pso)
Rix, Phil (pso)
Stephen, Alan (pso)

Practice Development Assessors
Martland, Arthur
Ratcliffe-Cooper, Enid

DRR/DIP/PPO
Munson, Kate (spo)
Beresford, Robert
Chung, David
Coulton, Alan
Adams, Michelle (pso)
Chadli, Allel (pso)
Fiksen, Victoria (pso)
Glendenning, Dawn (pso)
Jenkins, Rachel (pso)
Kirby, Jihan (pso)
Chowler, Adrian (pso)
Iggo, Amanda (pso)
Suiter, John (pso)
Whittingham, Lisa (pso)

Anti-Violence Project
Clarke, Mike (spo)
Berni, Jane
Evans, Sue (pso)

Interventions
Bingham, Steve (pso)
Blythin, Lynette (pso)
Malpass, Michael (pso)
O'Hanlon, Graeme (pso)
Phillips, Sarah (pso)
Beeson, Ray (pso)
Thorpe, Paul (proj mgr)

Grimsby Crown Court
tel (01472) 357454

9. 1 Park Square
    Scunthorpe N Lincs DN15 6JH
    tel (01724) 861222 *fax (01724) 289343*

Court Services Team
Coleman, Sarah (spo)
Taylor, Rachael
Ellse, Linda (p, pso)
Jarvis, Tina (pso)
Henry, Sue (p, pso)
Stephenson, Tricia (pso)

Offender Management
Evans, Adrian (spo)
Walker, Delyse (spo)
Anderson, Shaun
Bates, Elizabeth
Boyd, Christine
de Souza, Jade
Firth, Rebecca
Green, Jackie
Harding, Keith
Knapton, Jennifer
Rawson, Amanda
Ross, Diane
Smith, Nicola
Thrower, Keith

Benson, Dot (pso)
Chamber, Ravinder (pso)
Cochrane, Halley (pso)
Curtis, Debbie (pso)
Doherty, Carole (pso)
Exton, Zoe (pso)
Joyce, Debbie (pso)
Sivorn, Tony (pso)

DRR
Corkhill, Kirsty (spo)
Bates, Elizabeth (p)
Butterworth, Alison
Hamilton-Rudd, Nicholas (pso)
Jacomb, Donna (pso)
Wright, Lizzie (pso)

DIT
Devine, Jessica

Interventions
Martin, Neill (spo)
Wilson, Ann (qa mgr)
Atherton, Gary (pso)
Cobb, Kevin (pso)
Franklin, Lyndsay (pso)
Harrison, Sonja (pso)
Hartley, Christine (pso)
Howe, Miranda (pso)
Permaine, Erica (pso)
Sivorn, Tony (pso)

10. **Hull Youth Offending Team**
Myton Centre
Porter Street, Hull HU1 2RE
tel (01482) 609991

Stephenson, Kim
Westmoreland, Chris
Harding, Mike (pso)

11. **East Yorkshire YOT**
Council Offices, Main Road
Skirlough, Nr Hull HU11 5HN
tel (01482) 396623

Waudby, Cerie (pso)

Hostels

12. **Probation and Bail Hostel**
41 Queens Road
Kingston upon Hull HU5 2QW
tel (01482) 446284 *fax (01482) 470704*

Beaumont, Celia (spo)
Catterson, Neil (po dep)
Billam, Lynne (pso)
Card, Jean (asst warden)
Dixon, Marilyn (asst warden,
Whiteley, Miss Viv (asst warden)

13. **Scunthorpe Probation and Bail Hostel**
Victoria House, 31 Normanby Road
Scunthorpe DN15 6AS
tel (01724) 289124 *fax (01724) 289126*

Lloyd, Pat (spo)
Hughes, Catherine (po dep warden)
Spindley, Roy (pso)
Adams, John (asst warden)
Hayes, David (asst warden)
Yorke, Karen (asst warden)

Institutions

14. H M Prison **Hull**, Hedon Road
Kingston upon Hull
E Yorks HU9 5LS
tel (01482) 282200 *fax (01482) 282400*

Probn clerk ext 301
Special visits ext 284

Harvatt, Diane (spo)
Zobkin, Ivan (spo)
Cockling, Carl
Galloway Brenda
Garrett, Tony
Jackson, David (p)
Campbell, Tara
Sefton, Wendy
Birt, Chris (pso)

Dee, Rebecca (pso)
Gibson, Claire (pso)
Matthews, Claire (pso)
Rees, Andrew (pso)
Stainforth, Wendy (pso)
Waddy, Rachel (pso)

15. H M Prison, Moor Lane
Full Sutton York YO41 1PS
tel (01759) 475100 *fax (01759) 371206*

Probn clerk ext 028
Parole clerk ext 016
Discipline ext 020/012/016
Sentence mgment ext 152/153/155
Special visits ext 044

Goligher, Marcella (spo) ext 013
Baldwin, Moira
Barnes, Alison
Collins, Susan
Harris, Brian
Kiddle, Jo (p)
MacKenzie, Michelle
Walters-Kelly, Sally
Warner, Ian
Hutchinson, Joe (pso)
O'Donnell, Catherine (pso)
Ward, Jenny (pso)
Wintringham, Wendy (pso)

16. H M Prison
Everthorpe Brough
East Yorkshire HU15 1RB
tel (01430) 426500 *fax (01430) 426501*

Pearson, Rob (spo)
Bissenden, Dave
El Mugadam, Mohammed
Fisher, Amanda
Haynes, David
Akrill, Angela (pso)
Borman, Suzanne (pso)
Guy, Elaine (pso)
Parker, Sebrina (pso)
Rowley, David (pso)
Stride, Gemma (pso)

17. H M Prison **Wolds**
Everthorpe, Brough
East Yorkshire HU15 2JZ
tel (01430) 421588 *fax (01430) 421589*

Grant, Dan (spo)
Elkomi, Gamal
Fraser, Robert
Robinson, Sylvia (pso)
Spaven, Nova (pso)

Local Justice Areas

2 Bridlington
4 Beverley & The Wolds
8 Grimsby & Cleethorpes
3 Goole & Howdenshire
4 Hull & Holderness
9 North Lincolnshire

Crown Courts

7 Kingston upon Hull
8 Great Grimsby

KENT PROBATION AREA

Out of hours emergency contact point
Fleming House (01622 755918)

Victim enquiries contact number
Maidstone (01622) 202120

e-mail:
Firstname.Surname@kent.probation.gsx.gov.uk

Kent has the following specialised posts
(vlo)   victim liaison officer
(probn crt rep)   probation court
                         representative
(dist bus mgr)   district business manager
(bus mgr)   business manager
(cs dev/dep mgr)   CS Development/Deputy
                         Manager
(unit mgr)   Unit Manager
(gpwrkr)   groupworker
(treatment mgr)   Treatment Manager
(cso pcm/qa)   CSO Placement Case
                         Manager/Quality Assurance
(cso pcm/ts)   CSO Placement Case
                         Manager/Tutor Supervisor

1. **Area Office**
    Chaucer House, 25 Knightrider Street
    Maidstone ME15 6ND
    tel (01622) 350820 *fax (01622) 750333*

    James, Hilary (acting co) ext 822
    Verity, Robert (dir public prtctn, perf &
    prisons) ext 828
    Dowie, Alan (dir comm offender mngmnt)
    ext 825
    Last, Lynne (hr dir) ext 829
    Baillieu, Adrian (finance dir) ext 830
    Wilson, Stephen (board secy solicitor) ext
    844
    Clark, Robert (area mgr prison &
    commissioning services mgr) ext 824

Down, Christine (perf & standards mgr)
ext 826
O'Reilly, Maurice (pub prtctn & victims
mgr) ext 827
Collins, Pauline (finance mgr) ext 846
Lampert, Neil (comms mgr) ext 840
McCarthy, Anne (area bus mgr) ext 832
Simpson, Liz (bus mgr/pa to co) ext 833
Davis, Caroline (employee relations mgr)
ext 841
Newberry, Elaine (hr off) ext 843
Morton, Katherine (hr off) ext 857
Harley, Elaine (p, hr asst) ext 842
Phillips, Barbara (p, hr asst) ext 856

Homewood, Brian (h&s off, based at 9)
tel (01795) 423321 *fax (01795) 663240*

2. **Training Unit**
    Chaucer House, 25 Knightrider Street
    Maidstone ME15 6ND
    tel (01622)350820 *fax (01622) 750333*
    e-mail: kpatraining@freezone.co.uk

    James, Nick (spo pract devpt) ext 823
    Doherty, Sean (training mgr) ext 859
    Wilding, Rebecca (p, training admin/co-ord)
    ext 858
    Robson, Nadine (asst training admin)

    Practice Development Assessors
    Bennett, Peter (based at 5)
    Coley, David (based at 7)
    Crabb, Deborah (based at 6)
    Crocker, Alan (p) (based at 10)
    Harris, Sonia (p) (based at11)
    Mackey, Heather (based at 4)
    Martin, Pam (based at 5)
    Peall, Jeanne (based at 11)
    Puce, Eriks (based at 5b)
    Ratledge, Paula (p, based at 10)
    Thorne, Tracy (p, based at 10)

    Community Offender Management
    Dowie, Alan (director) (01622) 350825
    Courts, East Kent, Mid Kent and
    North Kent offender management teams.

3. **Court Services Team**
    Probation Office, Maidstone Crown Court
    The Law Courts, Barker Road
    Maidstone ME16 8EQ
    tel (01622) 202121 *fax (01622) 677312*

    Moers, Helen (admin)
    King, Barney
    Lovell, Christine
    Farrall, Joan (pso)
    Hinsley, Anna (probn crt rep)
    Kelly, Janet (probn crt rep)

Stevens, Julie (probn crt rep)
Wilson, Susan (probn crt rep)

3a. **Canterbury Crown Court**
Liaison Probation Office, The Law Courts
Chaucer Road Canterbury CT1 1ZA
tel (01227) 819299/819301 *fax (01227) 764961*

admin at office 3

Robbins, Janet (po, mag crt)
Lindsay, Brenda (probn crt rep)
Watson, Valerie (probn crt rep)

3b. **Magistrates' Court Staff**

Canterbury tel (01227) 769345
Melrose, Joy (probn crt rep)
Pilcher, Lynne (probn crt rep)

Thanet tel (01843) 228727
Vacancy
Nicolaou, Sophie (probn crt rep)
Stead, Pat (probn crt rep)

South East Kent/Ashford
tel (01303) 852004
all based at South East Kent
Baldwin, Susan (probn crt rep)
Bunn, Sandra (probn crt rep)
Neve, Susan (probn crt rep)
Rickwood, Helen (probn crt rep)
Williams, David (probn crt rep)

Gravesend tel (01474 569546)
Goddard, Julie (probn crt rep)
Low, John (probn crt rep)
Paul, June (probn crt rep)

Maidstone/Sevenoaks
based at Maidstone
tel (01622) 687521
Smith, Angela (probn crt rep)

Tunbridge Wells tel (01892) 559350
Betts, Kim (probn crt rep,)
Taft Morris, Lesley (probn crt rep)

Medway tel (01634) 849284
Samuda, Evonne
Waters, Trevor (probn crt rep)
Ravate, Dawn (probn crt rep)

Swale tel (01795 423321)
Mead, Henry
Blake, David (probn crt rep)
Williams, Mervyn (probn crt rep)

East Kent
Walsh, Cynthia (East Kent district mgr)
Redman, Julia (dist bus mgr)

Spence, Joy (pa/sec to dis mgr)
based at Canterbury (01227) 769345
covering Canterbury, Folkestone, Dover, Ashford and Thanet.

4. **Canterbury Unit**
24 Maynard Road, Wincheap Estate
Canterbury CT1 3RH
tel (01227) 769345 *fax (01227) 764339*

Johnston, Mark (spo)
Ensor, Bobbie (spo prog mgr)
Coleman, Deborah
Cork, Mike
Fitzsimmons, Christopher
Fyles, Susan (sort)
Gillon, Anne (f/t term time)
Hammond, Claire
Hennessy, Penny (p, treatment mgr)
Hollins, Sue (treatment mgr, IDAP)
Robbins, Janet (po, mag crt)
Ryder, Ann
Williams, Sue

Mackey, Heather (pda)
Bassett, Linda (trainee)
Greenhalgh, Julie (trainee)
Morris, Helen (trainee)
Walczak, Rebecca (trainee)

Birkin, Lavinia (p, pso)
Curteis, Michael (pso)
Groves, Val (pso)
Lucas, Liz (p, pso)
Reeves, Tania (pso)

Doherty, Fiona (gpwrkr/treatment mgr)
Holloway, Suzanne (gpwrkr)

5. **Folkestone Unit**
The Law Courts, Castle Hill Avenue
Folkestone CT20 2DH
tel (01303) 851140 fax (01303) 248379/221277

Barry, John (spo)
Tinkler, Phyl (bus mgr)
Atterton, Wendy
Bratton, Jane (p)
Bywater, Elizabeth (sort)
Callister, Andy (p)
Deckard, Richard
Jarvis, Collette
Jones, Claire
Laslett, Jim
Stockle, Anthony

Martin, Pam (pda)
Burton, Laura (trainee)
Goddard, Rebecca (trainee)
Ivory, Tessa (trainee)

Vass, Jane (trainee)

Blackford, Sarah (pso)
Allen, Gillian (pso)
Austen, Louise (pso)
Hayward, Anna (pso)
Mortley, Mark (pso)
Sprinks, Jill (pso)

Cadby, Lynn (vlo)
Newsam, Holly (vlo)

Hyden, Heather (gpwrkr)
Sharpe, Kerry (gpwrkr)

5a. **Dover Unit**
Ground Floor, Maybrook House
York Street **Dover** CT17 9AJ
tel (01303) 244700 *fax (01304) 215561*

Morton, Susie (spo)
Davies, David
Macey, Kathleen
Mitchell, Rebecca
Raeburn, Stephen (p)
Squire, Stephen
Evenden, Colin (pso)
Graham, Robert (pso)
Stabler, Jim (pso)

5b. **Ashford Unit**
Elwick House, Elwick Road
Ashford TN23 1NR
tel (01233) 656500 *fax (01233) 647459*

Edgar, Jeanette (spo)
Boddington, Anita
Sennett, Paul
Moyse, Susan
Udale, Lisa
Williams, Colin

Puce, Eriks (pda)
Akers, Joanne (trainee)
Griffiths, Paul (trainee)
Harvey, Nick (trainee)
Swaffer, Rachel (trainee)
Wright, Stanley (trainee)

Grace, Headley (pso)
Jones, Romi (pso)
Rasmussen, Nichola (p, pso)

6. **Thanet Unit**
38/40 Grosvenor Place
Margate CT9 1UW
tel (01843) 228727 *fax (01843) 291527*

Callingham, Debbie (spo)
Sahagian, Karen (bus mgr)
Borda, Julie

Cesbron, Ben
Coppins, Rachel
Cox, Deborah (p)
Goulbourne, Theresa (sort)
Heaven, Keith
Lane, Anne
Lister, Jane
Rees, Abbie
Townsend, Sîan
Wildman, Jennifer
Williams, Susan-Anne

Crabb, Deborah (pda)
Horsley, Sarah (trainee)
Johnson, Helen (traine)
Lawrence, Carmen (trainee)
Neaves, Michelle (trainee)

Clarke, Terri (vlo)
Brackley, Amanda (pso/vlo)
Cossell, Susan (pso)
Hawksworth, Jeremy (pso)
James, Nina (pso)
Jones, Sara (pso)
Sampson, Jackie (pso)
Scott, Gary (pso)
Smith, Matthew (pso)
Smith, Lorraine (p, pso/treatment mgr)

Mid Kent
Kadir, Tracey (Mid Kent district mgr)
Homewood, Cindy (dist bus mgr)
McGhie, Yvonne (pa sec)
based at Maidstone (01622) 687521
covering Maidstone, Tunbridge Wells, & Swale

7. **Maidstone Unit**
56 College Road, Maidstone ME15 6SJ
tel (01622) 687521 *fax (01622) 661653*

Kenny, Joanne (spo)
Smith, Jan (bus mgr)
Collison, Mark
Goldspring, Joanne (p)
Hook, Heather
King, Patricia
McGuire, Kathy
Moule, Catherine
Mowbray, David
Norman, Joanne
O'Hagan, Melanie (p, treatment mgr)
Robertson, Alison

Coley, David (pda)
Rawlings, Kelly (trainee)
Westcott, Jade (trainee)

Davis, Kevin (pso)
McVeigh, Vanessa (pso)
Marsh, Yvonne (pso)

Robinson, Carol (p, pso)
Vardy, Ashley (pso)
Wall, Delia (pso)

8. **Tunbridge Wells Unit**
    17 Garden Road,
    Tunbridge Wells TN1 2XP
    tel (01892) 559350 *fax (01892) 534728*

    Binning, Suki (spo prog mgr)
    Henderson, Kathryn (p)
    Hogg, Joanna (p)
    Knight, Jane
    Mason, Denise
    Nettleton, Terry
    Reid, Philippa
    Samuels, Sharon
    Wood, Richard

    Lumsden, Nadine (trainee)

    Bainger, Sarah (pso)
    Baker, Alison (pso)
    Town, Heather (pso)
    Westfold, Carly (pso)

9. **Swale Unit**
    *Sittingbourne & Sheerness are
    amalgamated. All admin based at
    Sittingbourne. All phone calls and faxes to
    the Admin at Sittingbourne.*
    Thames House, Roman Square
    Sittingbourne ME10 4BJ
    tel (01795) 423321/2 *fax (01795) 474251*

    46 High Street
    Sheerness ME12 1NL
    fax (01795) 663240

    Penny, Simon (spo)
    Sewell, Anne-Marie (bus mgr)
    Brown, Jane
    Gardner, David (p)
    Kirk, Johanna
    Russell, Ishbel
    Thornton, Brian
    Varker, Annette
    Willis, Sue
    Wood, Andrew

    Bennett, Peter (pda)
    Whittall, Andrea (trainee)
    Williams, Debra (trainee)

    Berry, Karen (p) (vlo)
    Baldock, Jayne (pso)
    Dummott, Karen (p, pso)
    Goodwin, Jayne (pso)
    Jemmett, Trudie (p, pso/dtto)
    Marchant, Clive (pso)

Milner, Jane (pso)
Shaw, Liz (p. pso)

North Kent
Crozier, Sonia (N Kent district mgr)
Robinson, Danny (dist bus mgr)
Roberts, Diane (pa/sec to dist mgr)
based at Medway (01634) 849284
covering Medway/Chatham & Gravesend.

10. **Medway Unit**
    27-35 New Road **Chatham** ME4 4QQ
    tel (01634) 849284 *fax (01634) 812331*

    Hardy, Ruth (spo)
    Morgan, Ian (spo)
    Mason, Toni (bus mgr)
    Campbell, Valerie
    Croft, Colin
    Green, Joseph
    Holness, Anna
    Kimber, Kevin
    MacDonald, Iris
    Mathews, Daphne
    Oliver, Trudie
    Plank, Sally
    Price, Anna
    Thomson, Kelly
    Vecchiolla, Emma
    Willans, Jessica

    Crocker, Alan (pda)
    Ratledge, Paula (p, pda)
    Thorne, Tracy (pda)
    Callar, Brian (trainee)
    Hughes, Pauline (trainee)
    Leek, Katherine (trainee)
    Longley, Lorraine (trainee)
    Smith, Laura (trainee)
    Tupper, Kelly (trainee)
    Waterhouse, Peter (trainee)

    Conelly, Tracey (vlo)
    Baker, Katie (pso)
    Crealock, Carol (gpwkr/treatment mgr)
    Croucher, Lesley (pso)
    Eva, Diane (pso)
    Keable, Angela (pso)
    Silvey, Sonja (p, pso)
    Tremain, Julie (pso)
    West, Sarah (p, pso)
    Wheal, Sarah (p, pso)

11. **Gravesend Unit**
    Joynes House, New Road
    Gravesend DA11 0AT
    tel (01474) 569546 *fax (01474) 335146*

    White, Nick (spo)

Bourke, Paul (spo prog mgr)
Imison, Carol (bus mgr)
Alderson-Rice, Nick
Bleakley, Julie
Bloomfield, Jenny
Campbell, Henry (sort)
Chandler, Peter
Dorrell, Karen
Hooper, Laura
Logan, Susan
Louch, Debbie
Plaiche, Aline
Young, Pamela

Harris, Sonia (p, pda)
Peall, Jeanne (pda)
Hambly, Gemma (trainee)
Morris, James (trainee)
Omoroga, Janet (trainee)
Sanders, Ron (trainee)
Thompson, Allison (trainee)

Cowell, Ernie (vlo)
Gould, Caroline (pso)
Manktelow, Melanie (p, pso)
Povey, Ginny (pso)
Sutherland, Alison (pso)
Vacancy (pso)

Community Punishment & YOTs
Adelsberg, Sarah (county mgr CS & YOS)
based at Faversham (01795) 532587

12. **County Community Service**
     118A West Street
     Faversham, ME13 7UE
     tel (01795) 532587 *fax (01795) 530454*

     Hockley, Rita (cs dev/dep mgr)
     Lee, Carol (admin)

     South East Kent/Canterbury/Thanet
     Canterbury
     Fox, Chris (unit mgr)
     Gregory, Hazel (cso pcm/ts)
     Nicholas, Bill (p) (cso pcm/ts)
     Weaving, David (cso pcm/ts)

     Thanet
     Vacancy (cso pcm/qs)
     Ledley, Graham (cso pcm/ts)
     Vacancy (cso pcm/ts)
     Vacancy (cso pcm/ts)

     Folkestone/Dover/Ashford
     Folkestone
     fax (01303)221277
     Salisbury, Tim (unit mgr) (01233) 656500
     ext 25
     Howes, Winston (cso pcm/qs)
     Foster, Gary (cso pcm/ts)

Mantle, Caroline (cso pcm/ts)

Ashford
Medlock, Pam (cso pcm/qs)
Keeler, Simon (cso pcm/ts)
Wilkinson, Jane (cso pcm/ts)

Mid Kent
Maidstone
Vacancy (unit mgr)
Walmsley, Chris (cso pcm/qs)
Mansfield, Gerry (cso pcm/ts)

Swale
Gradner, Jean (cso pcm/ts)
Whittingham, Sarah (cso pcm/ts)

Tunbridge Wells
Vacancy (unit mgr)
Jenkinson, Linda (cso pcm/qs)
McLaren, Kenneth (cso pcm/ts)

North Kent
Gravesend
Kirby, Kevin (cso pcm/ts)
Legg, Patricia (cso pcm/ts)
Pluck, Steve (cso pcm/ts)
Sharp, Carole (cso pcm/ts)

Medway
Cullen, Stuart (unit mgr)
Reeves, Tim (cso pcm/qs)
Crealock, Nick (cso pcm/ts)
Hayes, Simon (cso pcm/ts)
Mason, Alison (cso pcm/ts)

13. **Youth Offending Teams**

13a. **East Kent**
     Apollo House, Chapel Place
     Ramsgate CT11 9SA
     tel (01843) 587976 *fax (01843) 590009*

     Cox, Martin

13b. Avenue of Remembrance
     Sittingbourne ME10 4DD
     tel (01795) 473333 *fax (01795) 420016*

     Cockell, Richard

13c. **Mid Kent**
     Bishops Terrace, Bishops Way
     Maidstone ME14 1LA
     tel (01622) 691640 *fax (01622) 663928*

     Knight, Kathy

13d. Queen's House, Guildhall Street
     Folkestone CT20 1DX
     tel (01303) 253476 *fax (01303) 224329*

     Vacancy

13e. **West Kent**
Joynes House, New Road
Gravesend DA11 0AT
tel (01474) 544366 *fax (01474) 544569*

Weeks, Barry

13f. Social Services Dept,
Croft House, East Street
Tonbridge TN9 1HP
tel (01732) 362442 *fax (01732) 352733*

Vacancy

13g. **Medway Area**
The Family and Adolescent Centre
67 Balfour Rd **Chatham** ME4 6QU
tel (01634) 818753 *fax (01634) 849660*

Vacancy (pso)
Laws, Jackie (pso)

Public Protection, Performance & Prisons
Verity, Rob (director) (01622) 350828
Public Protection, MAPPPA, Sex Offender Resource Team, victims & Hostel

Performance & Standards
Down, Christine (mgr)
based at 1 (01622) 350826
covering Info Systems, DAT/DTTO, Research & Devpt and Communications

14. **Information Systems Unit (ISU)**
58 College Road **Maidstone** ME15 6SJ
tel (01622) 687521 *fax (01622) 688004*
e-mail is.unit@kent.probation.gsx.gov.uk

Webb, Peter (mgr)
Wickens, Julie (database mgr)
Wright, Julie (it mgr)
Mattison, David (it off)
Wickens, Adam (application devpt)
Burgess, Marcus (syso) based at 11
Cannock, Ali (syso, p) based at 9
Cass, Hazel (syso) based at 10
Sanders, Steven (syso) based at 6
Sellens, Andrew (syso) based at 7
Smith, Rachel (syso) based at 4

DAT & DTTO/DRR
tel (01622) 697102
based at 7
Andrews, Lesley (sub misuse mgr)

Research & Development
Vacancy (performance analyst)
based at 1 (01622)350831
Roberts, Sarah (p, info asst)
based at 7 (01622) 687521

Communications
tel (01622) 350840
based at 1
Lampert, Neil (communications mgr)

Public Protection & Victims
O'Reilly, Maurice (public protection & victims mgr)
based at 1 (01622) 350827
covering Sex Offender Resource Team (SORT), Victim Liaison Services & Fleming Housse Probation & Bail Hostel.

15. **MAPPPA Joint Co-ordination Team**
Kent Police HQ
Sutton Rd **Maidstone** ME15 9BZ
tel (01622) 650459 *fax (01622) 654679*

Gain, Tracy (mapppa co-ord)

16. **Sex Offender Resource Team (SORT)**
58 College Road **Maidstone**, ME15 6SJ
tel (01622) 687521 *fax (01622) 688004*

Remigio, Rebecca (spo, high risk off & prog mgr for TVSOGP)
Tancred, Tinia (forensic psychologist & treatment mgr for TVSOGP)
Maynard, Sarah (p, admin)
Bywater, Elizabeth (SE Kent)(based at 5)
Campbell, Henry (Gravesend) (based at 11)
Croucher, Hazel
Fyles, Susan (based at 4)
Goulbourne, Theresa (based at 6)
Hay, Jenny

17. **Victim Liaison Service**
Probation Office, Maidstone Crown Court
The Law Courts, Barker Road
Maidstone ME16 8EQ
tel (01622) 202120 *fax (01622) 692725*

Rootes, Ros (spo/mgr domestic abuse & vl)
Cadby, Lynn (vlo) (based at 5)
Clarke, Terri (vlo) (based at 6)
Berry, Karen (p, vlo) (based at 9)
Buckle, Tracey (vlo) (based at 10)
Cowell, Ernie (vlo) (based at 11)
Youseman, Janice (p, vlo) (based at 7)

Hostel

18. **Fleming House Probation & Bail Hostel**
32 Tonbridge Road **Maidstone** ME16 8SH
tel (01622) 755918 *fax (01622) 674809*
e-mail unit mail box: Fleming House

Parsons, Andrea (spo)
Wreford, Kevin (dep. mgr)
Pring, Caroline (supt service mgr)
Burlton, Joanne (asst mgr)
Campbell, Glenna (asst mgr)
Curtis, Joanne (asst mgr)
McGrath, Richard (asst mgr)
Smith, David (asst mgr)

Prisons & Commissioning Services
Clark, Robert (mgr)
based at 1 (01622) 350824
covering ETE Team, Basic Skills,
Commissioning Service, and Institutions.

19. 58 College Road
Maidstone ME15 6SJ
tel (01622) 687521 *fax (01622) 688004*
e-mail unit mail box: ETE Team

Emplt, Training & Educn Team (ETE)
Creasey, David (mgr) ext 133
Jefferies, John (p, ete team leader)
Haddon, Sally (p, admin)

Employment Officers
Kane, Sarah (Thanet) (01843) 227479
Burls, Glynis (SE Kent) (01303) 851140
Gardner, Iris (Medway) (01634) 849284
Saxby, Lynn (Canterbury) (01227) 769345

ETE Groupwork Tutors
Langridge, Claire
HMP Rochester/Cookham Wood (01634)
202500

Guided Skills Learning Co-ordinator
Anstee, Alan (Faversham) (01795) 591071

Skills for Life Team
Creasey, David (mgr) ext 133
Mepham, Pamela (devpt mgr)
Scott, James (admin)
Vacancy (tutor)

Partnerships & Mentor Unit/
Commissioning Services
e-mail: kpsvu@hotmail.com

Cohn, Howard (com services mgr)
Greenway, Margaret (co-ord)

Accommodation Unit
Cohn, Howard (com services mgr)
Ford, Malcolm (accom off) (based at
Thanet)
Vacancy (ptnrshps & accom admin)

Drink Drive Rehabilitation Unit
Gibson, Catherine (p, admin)

Institutions

20. HM Young Offender Institution
1 Fort Road **Rochester** ME1 3QS
tel (01634) 803100 fax (01634) 803101

direct dial 80 + ext

Probn clerk (01634) 803273
Discipline (01634) 803211
Special visits (01634) 803237

Gorringe, Radley (spo, head of
resettlement) ext 3120
Kempster, Leanne ext 3299
Peel, Steve ext 3213
Brown, Deborah (pso) ext 3299
Moss, Cheryl (pso) ext 3118

Kent Area Prisons Drug Team
based at Prison Service KSS Area Office
(01634) 673000
Vacancy (area drug strategy co-ord)

21. HM Prison **Standford Hill**
Church Road, Eastchurch
Sheerness ME12 4AA
tel (01795) 884500 *fax (01795) 880041*

Probn clerk ext 298
Discipline ext 309

Smart, George (spo)
Houghton, Lynda ext 278
Tindall, Pam ext 278
Vacancy (pso)
Cordice, Kelley (pso)
Thorpe, Donna (pso) ext 300
Vacancy (pso) ext 300

22. HM Prison, County Road
Maidstone ME14 1UZ
tel (01622) 775300 fax (01622) 775475

Probation clerk 5380

Vacancy (spo) ext 5378
Batchelor, Gillian ext 5379
Emes, Jenny ext 5476
Harte, Mike ext 5477
Vacancy ext 5476
Pabla, Ranjit (pso) ext 5408
Moat, Tina (pso, resettlement) ext 5681
Smedley, Georgina (pso) ext 5408

23. HM Prison & Young Offenders' Institution
East Sutton Park Sutton Valence
Maidstone ME17 3DF
tel (01622) 845000 *fax (01622) 845001*
direct dial (01622) 845 + ext

Probn clerk ext 5030

spo at HMP Cookham Wood
Balsamo, Delaney ext 5036
Kramer, Julie ext 5045
Wood, Melissa (p, pso) ext 5035

24. HM Prison
46 Longport **Canterbury** CT1 1PJ
tel (01227) 862800 *fax (01227) 862801*
probn fax (01227) 862931

direct dial (01227) 862 + ext
e-mail unit mail box: HMP Canterbury

Probn Clerk ext 850
Discipline 853
Legal visits 926

Gray, Colin (spo th'care mgr) ext 849
Moore, William ext 902
Duncan, Lynn (pso) ext 866
Heydon, Margaret (pso) ext 817

25. HM Prison **Blantyre House**
Goudhurst, Cranbrook TN17 2NH
tel (01580) 213200 *fax (01580) 211060*

spo at HMP Maidstone
Harper, Willie ext 251
acancy (pso) ext 250

26. HM Prison **Cookham Wood**
Maidstone Road, Rochester ME1 3LU
tel (01634) 202500 *fax (01634) 202501*
probn fax (01634) 828921
direct dial (01634) 202 + ext
Special visits switchboard

Preston, Helen (spo) ext 544
Ramsey, Marian ext 579
Steyn, Amanda ext 581
Smith, Amanda (pso) ext 584
Wyatt, Kay (pso) ext 586

27. HM Prison **Swaleside**
Brabazon Road, Eastchurch,
Sheerness ME12 4AX
tel (01795) 804100 *fax (01795) 884200*
probn fax (01795) 884128
direct dial (01795) 80+ ext

Probn clerk ext 4128
Discipline ext 4025
Special visits ext 4177

Smart, George (spo) ext 4102
Dold, Gavin ext 4137
Costen, Sheelah ext 4137
Gurr, Michaela ext 4103
Brown, Janet (pso) ext 4233
Ludlow, Jacqueline (pso) ext 4157
Smith, Claire ext 4203/2

28. HM Prison **Elmley**
Church Road, Eastchurch
Isle of Sheppey ME12 4AY
tel (01795) 882000 *fax (01795) 882001*
or phone direct to staff member by
dialing (01795) 88 followed by the ext
number

Resettlement clerks prisoner's surname:
a-d ext 2161
e-k ext 2163
l-q ext 2160
r-z ext 2162
Legal visits (01795) 882327

McGarry, Kevin (spo) ext 2154
Craven, Tim ext 2053
Nicolaides, Michael ext 2074
Walmsley, Tina ext 2065
Allison, Marie (pso) ext 2288
Barber, Sharon (p, pso) ext 2031
Payne, Kelly (pso) ext 2065
Ince, Donna (p, bail info off) ext 2288
bail info tel (01795) 882288
bail info fax (01795) 880140

Local Justice Areas

7, 8, 9 Central Kent
6 Thanet
4 Canterbury & St Augustine
5 Channel
11 North Kent (Dartford)
10 North Kent (Medway)

Crown Courts

3a Canterbury
3 Maidstone

LANCASHIRE
PROBATION AREA

Out of hours emergency contact point:
(01254) 395997

Central Bail Referral no: (01254) 832299

e-mail: Firstname.Surname@lancashire.
probation.gsx.gov.uk

1.   **Head Office**
99-101 Garstang Road
Preston PR1 1LD
tel (01772) 201209 *fax (01772) 884399*

Mathers, Robert (co)
Dearden, Colin (dco)
Mattinson, Louise (treasurer, hd of finance)

Brereton, Chris (aco, h.r.)

Thomas, Janet (aco, offender mngmnt, East District)
Taylor, Louise (aco, offender mngmnt, West District)
Crooks, Phil (aco, offender mngmnt, Central District)
Phillips, Ian (aco, interventions)
Bennett, Andrea (aco, interventions)

Booth, Rob (unpaid work scheme manager)
Allsop, Mark (info service mgr)
Matthews, Anne (communications off)
Milroy, Stephen (senior finance officer)
Ollerton, Julie (district admin mgr, Interventions)
Gildea, Peter (office mgr)
Gill, Emma (probation psychologist)
Bokhari, Amer (equal & diversity liasion off)

2. **Human Resources Team & Staff Development Unit**
    Unit 1, Block B, Albert Edward House
    The Pavilions, Preston PR2 2YB
    tel (01772) 256630 *fax (01772) 208540*

Hall, Susan (hr & training mgr)
Vacancy (hr officer)
Vacancy (hr officer)
Mason, Andrea (hr asst)
Chati, Imran (hr asst, stats & monitoring)

Bannister, Sally (po pract developer)
Holder, Cathy (po pract developer)
Ferguson, Diane (pso pract developer)
Clifton, Jennifer ('what works' trainer)
Bloembergen, Melanie (training off)

Dyer, Rachel (business excellence mgr)
Booth, Lynda (comm re-integration mgr)
Greenwood, Nicola (contracts mgr)
Murray, Nicola (emplt & mentor co-ord)
Padley, Pam (accomodation officer)
Knowles, Cheryl (probn psychologist)
Oakes, Debbie (dist admin mgr, Central District)

Health and Safety
Natalie Corry (h&s advisor)

NW Training Consortium
Regional Devpt & Assessment Centre
Maister, Jane (pda)
Whittaker, Pam (pda, prog co-ord)
Peel, Roger (pda)
Costello, Margaret (RDAC admin off)
Robinson, Elizabeth (admin off)

East District

3. 84 Burnley Road
    Accrington BB5 1AF
    tel (01254) 232516 *fax (01254) 396160*

    Offender Management
    Vacancy (spo)
    Ward, Helen (spo)
    Chiappi, Daniela
    Crawshaw, Christine
    Hopewell, Keith
    Parkinson, Christopher
    Ralph, Clare
    Murphy, Gayle
    Kimberly, Gayle
    Pollard, Jeff
    Fellowes, Nicola (pso)
    Shouib, Kanwal (pso)
    Treitl, Linda (pso)
    Ahmed, Tahir (pso)
    Carlton, Philip (pso)

    Interventions/Unpaid Work
    Bentley, Stephen (placement co-ord)
    Holmes, Vernon (p, proj supvr)
    Keogh, Jack (p, proj supvr)
    Roberts, Paul (proj supvr)
    Pattison, Mark (proj supvr)

    Interventions/Victims
    Brodest, Chris (pso, vlo)

4. 13/15 Wellington Street
    St Johns **Blackburn** BB1 8AF
    tel (01254) 265221 *fax (01254) 697852*

    Offender Management
    Mayren, Scott
    Emmot, Pauline
    McClements, Julia
    Cooper, Steven
    Kett, Alison
    Davies, Mary
    Singleton, Janette
    Jones, Simon
    Stone, Sharon
    Fielding, Ashley
    Scott, Ian
    Endicott, Coleen
    Canning, Helen
    Johnrose, Peter
    Lambert, Jeremy
    Hall, Lynne
    Wilson, John

    Maden, Helen (pso)
    O'Sulivan, Alma (pso)
    Maclaren, Caroline (pso)
    Palmer, Joes (pso)

Desai, Rukshana (pso)
Solkar, Akeela (pso)
Crook, Christine (pso)
Albers, Michelle (pso)
Nyland, Patricia (pso)
Drabble, Jackie (pso)
Waywell, Nicola (pso)

Interventions/Unpaid Work
Whittle, Tracey (pso, skills for life)
Johnson, Cathy (placement co-ord)
Unsworth, Robert (proj supvr)
Howell, Gary (p, proj supvr)
McGuire, Scott (p, proj supvr)
Beck, Andrew (proj supvr)

Trainees
Chadderton, Shiela
Johnson, Emma
Ross, David

5. **Probation Centre**
    55 Preston New Road
    Blackburn BB2 6AY
    tel (01254) 261764 *fax (01254) 53603*

    Interventions/Programmes
    Bedford, Ruth (treatment mgr)
    Bernadette Dowbakin
    Ross, Rod
    Maclaren, Caroline (pso, prog tutor)
    Pollard, Wendy (pso, prog tutor)
    Palmer, Joes (pso, prog tutor)

    Admin
    Mcewan, Linda (office mgr, interventions)

6. Sumner House
    40b Preston New Road
    Blackburn BB2 6AH
    tel (01254) 265221 *fax (01254) 685385*

    Offender Management
    Lee, Paul (spo)
    Munro, Ann (spo)
    Strachan, Ian (spo)
    McCloy, Kirsten (spo)

    Interventions/Unpaid Work
    Baxter, Stephanie (qam)

    Admin
    Galligan, Hazel (dist admin mgr East District)
    Etherington, Beverley (office mgr)

    Information Systems
    Daud, Mohammed (dist info systems off)

    NW Training Consortium
    Morgan, Richard (pda)
    Horrocks, Kath (pda)

Brooker, Martin (pda)

7. **Crown Court**
    Hamerton Street **Burnley** BB11 1XD
    tel (01282) 457443 *fax (01282) 455211*

    Bromley, Shirley (pso)

8. 1st Floor, Stephen House
    Bethesda Street **Burnley** BB11 1QW
    tel (01282) 425854 *fax (01282) 838947*

    Offender Management
    Cahill-Haslam, Katie (spo)
    Lock, Linda (spo)
    Ashraf, Farzana
    Gilmore, Rachel
    McKay, Elizabeth
    Uttley, Catherine
    Ormerod, Anthony
    Murray, Martin
    Pilling, Nick
    Shackleton, Barry
    Shooter, Philippa
    Cridford, Stephen
    Collum, Seamus
    Pollard, Michelle
    Smith, Lynne (pso)
    Armer, Pam (pso)
    Parker, Elaine (pso)
    Tomlinson, Lindsey (pso)
    Mcgrow, Margaret (pso)

    Interventions/Unpaid Work
    Slater, Lorraine (qam)
    Sheikh, Asad (placement co-ord)
    Wilson, Bryan (p, proj supvr)
    Howell, Raymond (p, proj supvr)

    Interventions/Programmes
    Bennett, Fiona (treatment mgr)
    Smith, Ray
    Musker, Heidi
    Harrison, Phillipa (pso, prog tutor)
    Molloy, Daniel (pso, prog tutor)

    Trainees
    Warburton, Natalie
    White, Catherine

    Admin
    Richardson, Pauline (office mgr)

    Brierley, Christine (pso, skills for life)

9. 25 Manchester Road
    Nelson BB9 9YB
    tel (01282) 615155 *fax (01282) 619693*

    Offender Management
    Shinks, Elaine (spo)
    Banks, Bernadette

Ford, Terry
Green, Julie (p, Dordrecht initiative)
Roberts, Marie
Kiernan, Michael (courts)
Wilson, Carlene
Stacey, Emma
Matson, David (courts)
Belfield, Eddie (resettlement)
Drabble, Jackie (pso)
Eatough, Geoffrey (pso)

Interventions/Unpaid Work
Bentley, Richard (placement co-ord)
Penny, Chris (proj supvr)
Krasowski, Carol (proj supvr)

Interventions/Victims
Sullivan, Barry (pso, vlo)

Information Systems
Linda Mulrooney (dist info systems off)

Trainees
Barker, Linda
Powell, Nicholas

10. 1 North Street **Rawtenstall**
Rossendale BB4 7LX
tel (01706) 217577 *fax (01706) 221973*

Offender Management
Farooq, Mohammed (spo, cja impltn mgr)
Willetts, Rachel (spo)
Johnson, Christine
Waide, Walter
Law-Riding, Beverley (pso)

Interventions/Unpaid Work
Lock, Mike (spo, interventions mgr)
Sargaent, Mick (proj supvr)
Blakemore, Stephen (proj supvr)

Central District

11. **The Crown Court**
The Law Courts
Ring Way, Preston PR1 2LL
tel (01772) 832404/5 *fax (01772) 832413*

Robinson, Janet
Buckley, Brian
Fox, Teresa
Calvert, Barbara (pso)
Powell, Shirley (pso)

12. 50 Avenham Street
Preston PR1 3BN
tel (01772) 552700 *fax (01772) 552701*

Offender Management
Byrne-Thompson, Geraldine (spo)
Fisher, Louise (spo)

Kenny, Mick (spo)
Moorhouse, Beverley (spo)
Ainsworth, Susan
Chester, Eve
Fairclough, Emma
Lindow, Bill
McCarthy, John
Ward, Chris
Bewley, Caroline
Da Costa, Louise
Kenyon, Jim
Parr, Pam
Alker, Janet
Boothman, Phil
Fitzgerald, Sharon
Weigh, Steve

Bradley, Janet (pso)
Pollard, Barbara (pso)
Griffiths, Alincia (pso)
Gledhill, Rachel (pso)
Rocks, Helen (pso)
Richardson, Zoe (pso)
Roberts, Graham (pso)
Burke, Louise (pso)
Atkinson, Freda (pso)
Wright, Linda (p, pso)
Lamb, Ben (pso)

Interventions/Unpaid Work
Wilson, Sandra (qa mgr)
O'Hanlon, Sharon (pso, skills for life)
Tune, Linda (placement co-ord)
Nolan, Lynne (placement co-ord)
Harrison, Mike (proj supvr)
Bradshaw, Colin (proj supvr)
Eccles, Paul (proj supvr)

Interventions/Programmes
O'Donnell, Phil (spo, progs mgr)
Wycherley, Sammy (treatment mgr)
Fletcher, Peter (treatment mgr)
Marshall, Alison
Brooks, Patricia
Roberts, Suzanne
Butters, Elizabeth (pso, prog tutor)
Twist, Jonathan (pso, prog tutor)
Baxendale, Caroline (pso, prog tutor)

Trainees
Fowler, Leanne
Rust, Luke
Forster, Maxine
Threlfall, Paul
Qureshi, Fawad

Admin
Foster, Sue (office mgr)

Information Systems
Truswell, Deborah (dist info systems off)

13. Leigh Street
    Chorley PR7 3DJ
    tel (01257) 260493 *fax (01257) 233177*

    Offender Management
    Dann, Joanne (spo)
    Bent, Sarah (spo, temp)
    Barwick, David
    Durkin, Elaine
    Gallagher, David
    Horsefall, Jane
    Horsley, Viv
    Sheridan, Esther
    Warbrick, Kevin
    Staniforth, Gillian
    Crabtree, Michelle (pso)
    Maudsley, Thomas (pso)
    Walsh, Dawn (pso)
    Pace, Lynne (pso)
    Melling, Ruth (pso)
    Jordan, Joanne (pso)

    Interventions/Unpaid Work
    Shouib, Humayun (placement co-ord)
    Williams, Gary (proj supvr)
    Douglas, Paul (proj supvr)

    Trainees
    Lloyd, Tracey

    Admin
    Ramsbotham, Maureen (office mgr)

14. 107 Towngate
    Leyland Preston PR25 2LQ
    tel (01772) 621043 *fax (01772) 435090*

    Offender Management
    Miller, Mark (spo)
    Clegg, Barbara
    Deasha, Greg
    Leach, Marilyn
    McLean, Janice
    Pilkington, Arlene
    Ralley, Stuart
    Roberts, Alyson
    Smith, Elizabeth (pso)
    Westcott, Vivian (pso)

    Interventions/Unpaid Work
    Ingram, Bill (p, qa mgr)
    Mackie, Alexander (placement co-ord)
    Freeman, Bill(cs proj supvr)

    Interventions/Victims
    Wilson, Sarah (pso, victim liaison off)
    Vacancy (pso, victim liaison off)

Information Systems
Daniel Massam (dist info systems off)

15. Probation Office, High Street
    Skelmersdale WN8 8AP
    tel (01695) 720248 *fax (01695) 556579*

    Offender Management:
    Shields, Dorothy (spo)
    Choraffa, Lynne
    Edwards, Jacqueline
    McGuire, Annette
    Shaw, Allan
    Kerrigan, Emmy
    Trout, Adrian
    Holden, Elizabeth (pso)

    Interventions/Unpaid Work
    Roberts, Richard (p, proj supvr)
    Phillips, Kevin (proj supvr)
    Unsworth, Claire (pso, skills for life)

    Equality & Diversity
    Perry, Bobbie (equality & diversity mgr)

    Trainees
    Ashcroft, Janine

West District

16. 384 Talbot Road
    Blackpool FY3 7AT
    tel (01253) 394031 *fax (01253) 305039*

    Offender Management
    Dacre, Michele (spo)
    Patel, Ami (spo)
    Watson, Pauline (spo)
    Poole, Sue (spo)

    Benson, Janene
    Johal, Gurjit
    Naden, Emma
    Sorsky, Lucinda
    Graydon, Lindsey
    Boyle, Wendy
    Harrington, Stephen (tower project)
    Whiteley, Annette (dtto)
    Hamnett, Dawn (dtto)
    Whittaker, Lesley (dtto)
    Dixon, Jacqui (dtto)
    Barrass, Sherry
    Christian, Diana
    Dean, John
    Fish, Lesley

    Greenwood, Chris (pso drug testing)
    Tetlow, Lisa (pso) (dtto)
    Walkden, Zoe (pso, skills for life)
    Gradwell, Rachel (pso dtto)
    Charnley, Ann (pso, tower project)

Anderson, Lauren (pso)
Andrews, Tracy (pso)
Ementon, Helen (pso)
Hardisty, Carole (pso)
Moran, Peter (pso)
Major, Angie (p, pso)
Winterbottom, Barbara (p, pso)

Resettlement & Courts
Aspin, Julie
Cairns, Ralph
Clark, Alistair
Draper, Elaine
Rigg, Judy
Caine, Carol
Robinson, Sarah
Brown, Tanya
Baldwin, Shaun
Brookes, Neal (pso)
Grundy, Karen (pso drug testing)
Chamberlain, Julie (p, pso)
Liversidge, Lesley (p, pso)

Interventions/Unpaid Work
Barlow, Julie (qam)
Brown, Iain, (placement co-ord)
Stansfield, Julie (placement co-ord)
Chambers, Richard (proj supvr)
Weber, George (proj supvr)
Clayton, Peter (p, proj supvr)
Hamer, Colin (proj supvr)
Scanlon, Roger (proj supvr)

Interventions/Victims
Johnson, Debbie (vlo)

Trainees
Whitehouse, Paul
Przybysz, Linda
Heslop, Robert

Admin
O'Neill, Brigid (dist admin mgr, W District)
Cree, Chris (office mgr)

Information Systems
St John-Foti, Diane (dist info systems off)

17. 9 The Esplanade
   Fleetwood FY7 6UW
   tel (01253) 874369/879500 *fax (01253) 776581*
   direct dial (01253) 879+ext

   Offender Management
   Bennet, Nigel (spo) ext 502

   Foster, Jane ext 515
   Bailey, Su ext 501
   Brooks, Karen ext 508
   Gosney, Derek ext 504

Webster, Lisa ext 505
Richardson, Elizabeth ext 512
Waring, John ext 507
Joynes, Nicola ext 517

Connelly, Sharon (pso dtto) ext 506
Nixon, Graham (pso) ext 516

Interventions/Unpaid Work
Greaves, Jane (palcement co-ord) ext 510
Taylor, Richard (cs proj supvr)

Trainees
Morton, Sharon ext 513
Doubleday, Claire

18. 41 West Road
   Lancaster LA1 5NU
   tel (01524) 63537 *fax (01524) 848519*

   Offender Management
   Jolly, Allan (spo)
   Bruno, Maggie
   Carr, Victoria
   Frankland, Roger
   Horsfield, Fiona
   Parkin, Susan
   Ralston, Cath
   Roberts, Alex
   Smith, Anthony
   Thomson, Rebecca
   Quraishi, Fariha
   Thompson, Donna
   Lamba, Manjeet

   Higgs, Cormac (pso)
   Morris, Isabel (pso)
   Thompson, Lisa (pso)
   Wood, Mary (cso)
   Smith, Amber (pso)

   Interventions/Unpaid Work
   Clifton, Val (placement co-ord)
   Green, Barry (proj supvr)
   Blezard, Paul (p, proj supvr)
   Worthing, John (p, proj supvr)

   Trainees
   Jackson, Sarah
   Sherdley, Victoria

   NW Training Consortium
   Johnson, Lisa (pda)

   Admin
   Watson, Jane (office mgr)

19. 2 Kensington Road
   Morecambe LA4 5LX
   tel (01524) 416171 *fax (01524) 832154*

Offender Management
Preston, Roger (spo)
Barrow, Margaret
Clough, Michelle
Prior, Ralph
Robinson, Bryan
Smith, Doug
Johnson, Helen
Levey, Lynne (pso)
Carey, Julia (pso, skills for life)

Trainees
Hall, Rebecca
Mangan, Paul
Rollitt, Steve

Interventions/Victims
Cullen, Larraine (pso, victim liaison off)

20. 2 Avroe Crescent
Blackpool Business Park
Blackpool FY4 2DP
tel (01253) 685050 *fax (01253) 349759*

Interventions/Programmes
O'Donnell, Phil (spo)
Harker, Jane (spo)
Sargaent, Adam (treatment mgr)
Turner, Sonia (treatment mgr)
Young, Rita (treatment mgr)
Gawthrope, Jane (treatment mgr)
Westlund, David
Garner, Alan
Hill, Chris
Johnson, Wendy (po, prog tutor)
Warbrick, Kevin (po, prog tutor)
Nagy, Shiela (po, prog tutor)
Morton, Sharon (po, prog tutor)
Bartley, Michael (po, prog tutor)
Harrison, David (po, prog tutot)
Mchugh, James (po, prog tutor)
Bentley, Glenys (po, prog tutor)
Rees, Sharon (po, prog tutor)
Koowaroo, Natasha (po, prog tutor)
Leeming, Jackie (po, prog tutor)

Nix, Louise (womens safety worker)
Smith, Louise (womens safety worker)

Haworth, Melanie (pso, prog tutor)
Buckley, Shaun (pso, prog tutor)
Suleman, Rehana (pso, prog tutor)
Hill, Doug (pso, prog tutor)

Interventions/Victims
Martin, Geraldine (team manager)

Admin
Ali, Rifat (office mgr, interventions)

Youth Offending Teams
21a. Blake Street
Accrington BB5 1RE
tel (01254) 389456 *fax (01254) 872614*

(inc Hyndburn, Rossendale, Clitheroe, Ribble Valley)
Hartwell, Susan

b. Bank House
44 Wellington Street
St Johns, **Blackburn** BB1 8AF
tel (01254) 299800 *fax (01254) 299801*

Brindle, Neil
Cartwright, Susan

c. Stanley Buildings
1-3 Caunce Street
Blackpool FY1 3DN
tel (01253) 478686 *fax (01253) 478687*

Micallef, Linda
Rickerby, Jane

d. Rokeby Centre, 316 Colne Road
Burnley BB10 1XJ
tel (01282) 456620 *fax (01282) 459706*

Waterworth, John

e. Halliwell House, 15/17 Halliwell Street
Chorley PR7 2AL
tel (01257) 516051 *fax (01257) 516053*

(inc Skelmersdale)
Chershire, Cath

f. 15 North Albert Street
Fleetwood FY7 6DW
tel (01253) 772761 *fax (01253) 771328*

Cayton, Louise

g. 108 St Leonardsgate
Lancaster LA1 1NN
tel (01524) 63458 *fax (01524) 842467*

Loxley, Sarah

h. 143-161 Corporation Street
Preston PR1 2UG
tel (01772) 262047 *fax (01772) 262130*

Richardson, Claire

22. **NSPCC Meadow House Project**
Meadow House, 121 Oxford Street
Preston PR1 3QY
tel (01772) 200765 *fax (01772) 200768*

Clark, Paul (mgr)
Graham, Janet
Hynes, Kevin
Toro, Jacqueline

Hostels

23. **Highfield House Probation Hostel**
Lydia Street, Wood Nook
Accrington BB5 0PX
tel (01254) 395997 *fax (01254) 398536*

Troughton, Dave (mgr)
Drummond, Shona (dep mgr)
Cox, John (asst mgr)
Marsh, Anne (asst mgr)
Mayers, Jane (asst mgr)
Passmore, Ken (asst mgr)
McCarthy, Tony (hostel supvr)
Taylor, Charlene (hostel supvr)
Mclean, Yvette (hostel supvr)
Dean, Deborah (hostel supvr)

24. **Haworth House**
St Peters Street
Blackburn BB2 2HL
tel (01254) 59060 *fax (01254) 672062*

Dewhurst, John (mgr)
Lawson, Amanda (dep mgr)
Hallett, Peter (asst mgr)
Marsden, John (asst mgr)
O'Connor, Alan (asst mgr)
Shingleton, Iain (asst mgr)
Baines, Peter (hostel supvr)
Dennett, Terence (hostel supvr)
Hallett, Heather (hostel supvr)
Marshall, Anthony (hostel supvr)

Institutions

25. H M Prison **Garth**
Ulnes Walton Lane
Leyland, Preston PR26 8NE
tel (01772) 443300 *fax (01772) 443301*

Probn general office ext 3383

Bailey, Graham (spo) ext 3382
Vacancy Draper, John ext 33526
Rosthorn, Lisa
Cookson, Bill (pso)

26. H M Prison **Kirkham**
Preston PR4 2RN
tel (01772) 675400 *fax (01772) 675401*

Probn clerk/special visits ext 5471
Prison admin/temp release enquiries ext
5472

Westrop, Wendy (spo) ext 5669
Hesketh, Phiona ext 5444
Kneale, Christine ext 5671
Walsh, Jane ext 5445
Brewer, Jacquelynne
Leyland, Brian
Greatorex, Pam
Howard, Lesley (pso) ext 5483

Intermittent Custody Project
Hopwood, Peter
Edmondson, Gabrielle (cso)
Webster, Dave (cso)

27. H M Prison
The Castle **Lancaster** LA1 1YJ
tel (01524) 385100 *fax (01524) 385101*
direct dial (01524) 385 + ext

hdc/probn fax (01524) 385233

Probn clerk ext 235
Special visits ext 218
Parole clerk ext 229
A wing ext 240
B wing ext 244
C wing ext 243

Graham, Jed (spo)
Boothman, Barabara (treatment mgr)
Bond, Terry ext 232
Williams, Jo ext 232
Housley, Elizabeth (pso)
Morgan, Donna (pso)
Irwin, Hazel (pso)

28. H M Young Offenders' Institution
Lancaster Farms
Stone Row Head, off Quernmore Road
Lancaster LA1 3QZ
tel (01524) 563450 *fax (01524) 563451*
bail info (01524) 563616
bail info fax (01524) 563520
HDC fax (01524) 842691

Probn admin officer ext 390
Visitor's centre ext 256
Discipline office ext 308
Parole clerk ext 287
Special visits 242

Sunderland, Marcus (spo)
Atkinson, Gwen
Ainsworth, Susan
Edwards, Julie (pso)

Visitors' Centre
Dixon, Pauline (pso)
Brew, Pat (pso)
McClelland, Barbara (pso)

29. H M Prison
     2 Ribbleton Lane **Preston** PR1 5AB
     tel (01772) 444550 *fax (01772) 444551*

     Special visits (01772) 444715
     bail info (01772) 444587
     bail info fax (01772)444553
     reception fax (01772) 444563
     healthcare fax (01772) 444554

     Probn clerk (01772) 444899

     Boydell-Cupitt, Susan (spo)
     Bailey, Lindsey
     Holden, Frank
     Bailey, Jackie (pso)
     Dryden-Bircher, Danielle (pso)
     Ramsden, Joanne (pso)
     Cunliffe, Elizabeth (pso)
     Vacancy (pso)
     Clough, Steven (pso)

30. H M Prison **Wymott**
     Ulnes Walton Lane
     Leyland PR26 8LW
     tel (01772) 444000 *fax (01772) 444001*

     Javed, Anna (Impact seconded probn mgr)

     Thompson, Robin (spo)
     Yates, Louise
     Chadwick, Roy
     Costello, Peter (p)
     Hayman, Vic
     Langley, Ruth
     Simpson, Rosie
     Turner, Christine (treatment mgr)
     Sweeney, Sharon (pso)
     Sweeny, Sharon (Impact seconded pso)
     Gee, Wendy (Impact seconded pso)

Local Justice Areas

     6, 8 Blackburn, Darwen & Ribble Valley
     8, 9, 10 Burnley, Pendle & Rossendale
     11 Chorley
     15, 20 Fylde Coast
     5 Hyndburn
     18, 19, 20 Lancaster
     14 Ormskirk
     13 Preston
     12 South Ribble

Crown Courts

     4 Burnley
     3 Lancaster
     3 Preston

LEICESTERSHIRE & RUTLAND PROBATION AREA

Out of hours contact nos: Kirk Lodge
0116-244 8028, Howard House 0116-254 9059

Victim enquiries contact number
0116-253 6331

Central Hostels referral no: 0116-244 8028
fax 0116-244 8696

e-mail
Firstname.Surname@leicestershire.probation.
gsx.gov.uk

Offices

1. **Head Office**
    2 St John Street, Leicester LE1 3BE
    tel 0116-251 6008 *fax 0116-242 3250*
    direct dial 0116-242+ext
    e-mail LRPA@dial.pipex.com

    Munro, Heather (co) ext 3200
    Findley, Krystyna (aco) ext 3203
    Harnwell, Miriam (aco) ext 3215
    Herbert, Mike (aco) ext 3206
    Hindson, Paul (aco) ext 3205
    Reynolds, Sean (aco) ext 3204
    Worsfold, Trevor (aco) ext 3202
    Bearne, Bob (p, spo area training) ext 3263
    Curran, Martin (spo area training) ext 3261
    Owens-Rawle, Marilyn (po area training)
    ext 3260
    Parle, Greg (po) ext 3262
    Kennedy, Paul (info mgr) ext 3265
    Akers, Linda (personnel) ext 3225
    Rose, Sue (finance) ext 3220
    Stretton, Caroline (finance) ext 3251
    Thomas, Mandy (premises) ext 3221

Offender Management Teams

2. 38 Friar Lane
    Leicester LE1 5RA
    tel 0116-253 6331 *fax 0116-242 4511*

    Leicester 1
    Naylor, Camille, (spo)
    Wynter, Colin (pdm)Coles, Nicola
    Dhokia, Anita
    Doel, Mike Gregory, Mark
    Illston, Suzanne
    Lapidge, Theresa
    Briers, Zoe (pso)
    Drinkwater, Rebecca (pso)
    Griggs, Alex (p, pso)
    Hulbert, Emily (pso)
    Jones, Kim (pso)

McGowan, Caroline (pso)
Sharma, Prembala (pso)

Accom & Supported Housing Team
Tel 0116-242 4585 *fax 0116-253 1463*
Gray, Alan (p, spo)
Mattson, Neil
Gargan, Gillian (p, pso)
Newbrooks, Clare (pso)
Straw, Trisha (p, pso)
Thomas, Suzanne (pso)

City Resettlement Team
Johnston, Lee (pract devpt mgr)
McClymont, Kerstyn (snr psychologist)
Coley, Lenrick
Grieves, Sarah
Holland, Richard
McCarthy, Danielle
Patel, Kusum
Paul, Ellis
Preston, Chloe
Smith, Sarah
Tate-Beasley, Angela
Bhavsar, Anjuna (pso)
Broad, Kim (pso)
Flannagan, Lucy (pso)
Goodman, Hannah (p, pso)
Jackson, Selena (pso)
Niland, Grania (pso)
Okan, Olive (p, pso)
Parmar, Nalini (pso)

3. **Probation Centre**
    2 Cobden Street **Leicester** LE1 2LB
    tel 0116-262 0400 *fax 0116-253 0819*

    Leicester 2
    Jordan, Sue (spo)
    Bellingham, David (pdm)
    Aston, Laura
    Baumber, Luke
    Doughty, Victoria
    Haynes, Michèle (p)
    Hodgins, Ellen
    Holland, Nicola
    Jones, Sîan
    Pearce, Jo (p)
    Clarke, Anthony (pso)
    Ion, James (pso)
    Keysell, Elspeth (pso)
    Manga, Joseph (pso)
    Muskwe, Chester (pso)
    Spicer, Catherine (pso)
    Wilton, Katie (p, pso)

    Leicester 3
    Wale, Carrie (spo)
    Chadwick, Liz (p, pda)

Duckham, Selena
Frazer, Rachel
Hubbard, Joanne
Megennis, Helen
Yates, Paul (p)
Beaumont, Glenn (pso)
Cameron, Natalie (pso)
Foley, Duncan (pso)
McMahon, Rory (pso)
Spencer, Shona (pso)
Thandi, Jin (pso)

4. 27 London Road
    Coalville LE67 3JB
    tel (01530) 836688 *fax (01530) 834136*

    Barber, Pam (p, spo) (8)
    Ball, Margaret
    Evens, Sally
    King, Karen
    Thompson, Sara
    Williams, Sarah
    Barney, Christopher (pso)
    Barney, Fran (p, pso)
    Bonser, Paul (pso)
    Hextall, Sylvia (pso)

5. 35 Station Road
    Hinckley LE10 1AP
    tel (01455) 615645 *fax (01455) 891147*

    Barber, Pam (p, spo) (7)
    Cotterill, Amelia
    Martin, Iain
    Weaver, Lestroy
    Gill, Suki (p, pso)
    Kitching, Suzanne (p, pso)
    Waite, Anthony (pso)
    Wheeler, Helen (pso)

6. 12 Southfield Road
    Loughborough LE11 2UZ
    tel (01509) 212904 *fax (01509) 218954*

    Strong, Grace (p, acting spo/pdm)
    Lake, Nicky (p, pdm)
    Ford, Mark
    Plen, Rene (p)
    Mouland, Janet
    Morfett, Richard
    Oatley, Diane
    Pearce, Alison (p)
    Smith, Jeanne
    Warmington, Christine (p)
    Hallam, Claire (pso)
    Luik, Naomi (pso)
    Neale-Badcock, Stephen (pso)
    Williams, Dawn (pso)
    Woodhouse, Lionel (p, pso)

7. County Council Area Office
    Leicester Road
    Melton Mowbray LE13 0DA
    tel (01664) 410410 *fax (01664) 480042*

    Strong, Grace (p, acting spo/pdm)
    Lake, Nicky (p, pdm)
    Green, Tom
    Price, Arlene (p)
    Vega, Jane (p)
    Ingram, Maxine (pso)
    Metcalfe, Michelle (pso)
    Woodhouse, Lionel (p, pso)
    Wright, Esther (p, pso)

8. 28 Station Road
    Wigston Leicester LE18 2DH
    tel 0116-257 3800 *fax 0116-257 0240*

    Leicester South
    Hulait, Jaspal (spo)
    Fairman, Barbara (p)
    Goodliffe, Andrew
    Jones, Martin (p)
    Kotecha, Rahul
    Leyland, Keeley
    Wiltshire, Jeanette
    Benvenuto, Celine (pso)
    Cross, Lisa-Marie (pso)
    Logalbo Sal (pso)
    Whittam, Linda (p, pso)

9. **MAPPOM** (Multi Agency Prolific &
    Persistent Offender Management)
    39 Millstone Lane, Leicester LE1 5JN
    tel 0116-275 6075 *fax 0116-255 6707*

    Scotson, Tim (strategic mgr)
    Morris, Sam (spo)
    Cousins, Nicola
    Griffiths, Richard (p)
    Langridge, Tony
    Mason, Claire
    Prideaux, Katrina (p)
    Wright, Nicola
    Barney, Fran (p, pso)
    Chippendale, Felicity (pso)
    Foreman, James (pso)
    Geraghty, Michelle (pso)
    Harrison, Emma (p, pso)
    Newton, Neil (pso)
    O'Callaghan, Stephen (p, pso)
    Score, Hazel (p, pso)
    Wellstood-Eason, Vivien (pso)
    Wright, Esther (p, pso)

Interventions

10. **Probation Centre**
    2 Cobden Street **Leicester** LE1 2LB
    tel 0116-262 0400 *fax 0116-253 0819*

    Programme Provision
    Chivers, Andy (spo)
    Lawrence, Diana (treatment mgr)
    Bradley, Stephen (treatment mgr)
    Charlton, David
    Elsmore, Jennifer
    Bradshaw, Sue (psychologist)
    Bottoms, Sarah (pso)
    Brighty, Stacey (pso)
    Bulsara, Hina (pso)
    Cuke, Charlene (pso)
    Edan, Peter (pso)
    Gosling, Paul (pso)
    Hussain, Sajeela (pso)
    Ross-Myring, Laura (pso)
    Saunt, Shelley-Anne (pso)

    Domestic Violence
    Wisniewska, Dreda (p, spo)
    Walworth, John (treatment mgr)
    Kirby, Arlene
    Wain, Stuart
    Heath, Linda (woman's safety wrkr)
    Seniuk, Stefan (pso)

    Sex Offender Unit
    Wisniewska, Dreda (p, spo)
    Scott, Eric (treatment mgr)
    Lawler, Linda
    Modi, Panna (p)
    Smillie, Phil
    Yorke, Tina
    Baguley, Steve (psychologist)

    Skills Devpt Team
    (inc Basic, Key & Pathfinder)
    Doran, Simon (spo)
    Attewell, Andy (pso)
    Bailey, Anne (pso)
    Drewey, Steve (pso)
    Evill, Tony (pso)
    Fegan, Yvonne (p, pso)
    Gamage, Greg (p, pso)
    MacQuillan, Adele (pso)
    Payne, David (pso)
    Spearing, Dirne (p, pso)
    Smith, Kathy (skills devpt co-ord)

    Community Punishment Office
    tel 0116-262 2245
    Marriage, Ghislaine (spo)
    Courtney, Nigel (treatment mgr)
    Li, Joseph (treatment mgr)
    Chenery, Margaret (operational mgr)
    Cave, John (pso)
    Holmes, Richard (pso)

Leatherland, Deanne (pso)
MacQuillan, Andy (pso)
Theobald, Roger (pso)
Turnock, Paula (pso)
Killick, Peter (wkshp mgr)

11. **High Risk Support Workers (SHARP)**
137a Narborough Road,
Leicester LE3 0PB
tel 0116-275 8777 *fax 0116-275 7775*

Crawford, Helena (pso)
Hewitt, Julie (p, pso)
Lockwood-Jones, David (pso)
Walker, Martin (pso)

Hostels

12. **Howard House Hostel**
71 Regent Road, Leicester LE1 6YA
tel 0116-254 9059 *fax 0116-254 0303*

Kirk Lodge
322 London Road, Leicester LE2 2PJ
tel 0116-270 8327 *fax 0116-244 8696*

central referral point
tel 0116-244 8028 *fax 0116-244 8696*
central administration
tel 0116-270 6681 *fax 0116-244 8696*
Zaccarelli, Beverley (admin mgr)

Hostel team members work from either hostel

Jones, Malcolm (spo mgr)
Knowles, Kay (po deputy)
Singh Here, Dalminder (po deputy)
Aouni, Karen (pso)
Bone, Sudeep (pso)
Churchill, Marcella (pso)
Gundry, Kelly (pso)
Jeggo, Steve (pso)
Jones, Sarah (pso)
Lay, Matthew (pso)
Monk, Mary (pso)
Patel, Dipika (pso)

Other Teams

13. 38 Friar Lane, Leicester LE1 5RA
tel 0116-253 6331 *fax 0116-242 4511*

Victim Contact Team
Gray, Alan (p, spo)
Payne, Clare (p)
Whitford, Penny (p)
Acton, Susan (pso)
O'Donnell, Linda (pso)

14. Victoria Buildings
31 Bowling Green Street

Leicester LE1 6AS
tel 0116-285 4444 *fax 0116-285 3425*

Trainee Probation Officer Team
Bearne, Bob (p spo)Flint, Brendon (pda)
Gray, Chrissie (p, pda)
Henry, Jenny (pda)
Robbins, Rena (pda)
Simpson, Chris (pda)

DTTO Team
Warner, Courtney (treatment mgr)
Cousins, Nicola
Dixon, Danielle
Hopkinson, Michael
O'Mahony, Marie
Radford, Jan (p)
Rawle, Paul
Smith, Philippa
Ashby, Elizabeth (pso)
Berridge, Jane (p, pso)
Jones, Mo (p pso)
Kilpatrick, Andy (pso)
Mason, Kerry (pso)
Thoor, Inderjit (pso)
Weaver, Sarah (pso)
Yu, Oscar (pso)

Records Office
(Central Index)
tel 0116-285 3400 *fax 0116-285 3407*
Getliffe, Tony (admin mgr)

14. **Courts Team**
*members of the Courts Team work from the
Magistrates' and Crown Court*

Leicester Crown Court
90 Wellington Street
Leicester LE1 6HG
tel 0116-242 4553 *fax 0116-254 1437*

Leicester Magistrates' Court
Pocklington Walk
Leicester LE1 9BE
tel 0116-255 3799 & 0116-285 3414
fax 0116-255 3805

Scotson, Carolyn (spo)
Houghton, Paul (p)
Kassam, Shiraz
Peeters, Geoff
Piper, David
Pugh, John
Lewis, Philip (pso)
McIntosh, Pam (pso)
Patel, Jaimy (pso)
Reed, Janet (pso)
Rigby, Karen (p, pso)
Savage, John (pso)

Smith, Anita (pso)
Whelan, Claire (pso)

15. **MAPPP Manager**
c/o Leicestershire Constabulary HQ
St John's, Enderby
Leics LE19 2BX
tel 0116-248 5293 *fax 0116-248 5297*

Petrie, Bob (spo)

16. **Youth Offending Teams**
a. Eagle House, 11 Greyfriars
Leicester LE1 5QN
tel 0116-299 5830 *fax 0116-233 6003*

Hughes, Tanya
Newling-Ward, Simon
Summerfield, Kelly
Ducann, Mykel (pso)
Foster, Rachel (pso)
Patel, Jayshree (p, pso)

b. 674 Melton Road
Thurmaston LE4 8BB
tel 0116-260 6000

Thompson, Michelle (p)

c. 4 Druid Street
Hinckley LE10 1QH
tel (01455) 636068 *fax (01455) 613129*

Eldred, Sarah
Dorrington, Samantha (pso)
Walker, Katie (pso)

17. **Criminal Justice Integrated Team**
Castle House, 6-8 Nelson Street
Leicester LE1 7BA
tel 0116-255 3066 *fax 0116-285 4661*
duty desk 0800 7311 118

Scott, Rose (mgr)
Cripps, Ian (spo)
Randon, Melvyn (data mgr)
Disney, Clare (snr casewrkr)
Talbott, Charlotte (snr casewrkr)
Galway, Kayley (p, drug counsellor)
Cave, Joanne (case wrkr)
Champaneria, Ketna (case wrkr)
Duncan, Jude (case wrkr)
Forana, Mara (case wrkr)
Galway, Kayley (drug counsellor)
Hanley, Lianne (case wrkr)
Hawley, Amanda (case wrkr)
Hobster, Mark (case wrkr)
Kaur, Manjit (case wrkr)
Moore, Trish (case wrkr)

O'Callaghan, Joe (case wrkr)
O'Toole, Julie (case wrkr)
Page, Nicola (case wrkr)
Pattni, Sheetal (case wrkr)
Roberts, Paul (case wrkr)
Ruprai, Mandeep (case wrkr)
Tansey, Joanne (case wrkr)
Wan, Sui (case wrkr)
Wren, Alison (case wrkr)
Baxter, Sue (pso)
Breslin, Constance (pso)
Jeanes, Eleanor (pso)

Institutions

18. H M Prison **Ashwell**
Oakham, Rutland LE15 7LF
tel (01572) 884100 *fax (01572) 884101*
direct dial (01572) 88 + ext

Probn clerk/Probn visits ext 4273
Lifer/Parole clerk ext 4215
Discipline ext 4213

Gullick, Andy (p, spo) ext 4271
Brown, Jenny (p) ext 4243
Duncan, Nicky ext 4272
Fish, Mike ext 4274
Ludlam, Melanie (p) ext 4243
Smith, Jeff ext 4274
Bullock, Emma (pso) ext 4216
Cassidy, Jane (p, pso) ext 4243
Clay, Madeleine (pso) ext 4204
Clegg, Ann (pso) ext 4216
Richards, Ben (pso) ext 4275

19. H M Prison **Gartree**
Gallowfield Road
Market Harborough LE16 7RP
tel (01858) 436600 *fax (01858) 436601*

Brotherton, Christine
Costello, Maxine
Lawson, Susan (p)
Marshall, Pete
Panter, Lesley (p)
Robinson, Mandy
Seabrook, Michelle
Stone, Jeff (p)
Wilson, Nicki (p)
Oldham, Esther (pso)
Pipes, Ian
Whiteley, Hannah (pso)

20. H M Prison, 116 Welford Road
Leicester LE2 7AJ
tel 0116-228 3000 *fax 0116-228 3001*

direct dial 0116-228+ext
probn fax 0116-228 3112

Gullick, Andy (p, spo) ext 3036
Cusack, Steve ext 3166
Hallassey, Michael (pso) 3147
McEntaggart, Annette (pso) ext 3059
Mistry, Rebecca (pso) ext 3158
Stevenson, Jill (pso) ext 3158
Winfield, John (probn clerk) ext 3075

21. H M Young Offender Institution
     Glen Parva Saffron Road
     Wigston LE18 4TN
     tel 0116-228 4100 *fax 0116-228 4000*

     Probn clerk ext 4320
     Discipline ext 4392/4291
     Special visits ext 4260

     Pearce, Jan (spo) ext 4336
     Coleman, John ext 4318
     James, Linda ext 4321
     Maxwell, Margaret ext 4317
     Chiavolini, Alessandra (pso)   ext
     4231
     McArdle, Fiona (pso) ext 4285
     Neckles, Julian (pso) ext 4211
     Penney, Kevin (pso)ext 4231
     Wood, Debbie (pso) ext 4286

22. H M Prison **Stocken**
     Stocken Hall Road, Stretton
     Nr Oakham LE15 7RD
     tel (01780) 795100 *fax (01780) 410767*
     direct dial (01780) 48 + ext

     Probn clerk ext 5208/5030

     Collier, Peter (spo) ext 5030
     Evans, Graham ext 5308
     Karby, Christine (p) ext 5308
     Matthews, Annette ext 5309
     Samuel, Pauline ext 5309
     Hunt, Suzanne (pso) ext 5321
     Spence, Becky (pso) ext 5321
     Woolverton, Andy (pso) ext 5321

Local Justice Areas

     2, 3, 10 Leicester
     4 Ashby-de-la-Zouch
     6 Market Bosworth
     7 Loughborough
     8 Melton, Belvoir & Rutland
     9 Market Harborough & Lutterworth

Crown Court

     16 Leicester

LINCOLNSHIRE PROBATION AREA

Out of hours emergency contact point
Wordsworth House (01522) 528520_

Victim enquiries contact number
Lincoln (01522) 510011, Skegness (01754)
763906,
Grantham (01476) 583131

e-mail:
Firstname.Surname@lincolnshire.
probation.gsx.gov.uk

1.   **Head Office**
     7 Lindum Terrace, **Lincoln** LN2 5RP
     tel (01522) 520776 *fax (01522)
     527685/580469*

     Nicholls, Graham (co)
     Adey-Johnson, Peter (aco)
     Gregory, Melanie (aco, hr)
     Lewis, Sally (aco)
     Oliver, Joanne (aco)
     Rushby, Pete (aco, finance/information)
     Burke, Tony (info systems mgr)
     Callery, Beverley (finance mgr)
     Connell, Tony (spo, training & staff devpt)
     Hough, Quin (h&s off)
     Martel, Rachel (communications mgr)
     Starkie, Jayne (p, hr mgr)

2.   8 Corporation Street
     Lincoln LN2 1HN
     tel (01522) 510011 *fax (01522) 514369*

     Hawley, Sarah (spo)
     McMahon, Paul (spo)
     Mountain, Angela (spo)
     Pollard, Simon (spo, offender mgmt)
     Gibbs, Leanne
     Gilbert, Amy
     Griffin, Tammy
     Lillyman, Rebecca
     Melling, Caragh
     Smith, Janet
     Smith, Susan (p)
     Vaughan, Tammy
     Whitelam, Sandra
     Barwise, Steph (pso)
     Collett, Becky (p, pso)
     Dean, Jackie (pso)
     Etoria, Lewis (pso)
     Gostelow, Elaine (pso)
     Jones, Bobbi (pso)
     King, Nigel (pso)
     Lynch, Andrew (pso)

Murphy, Lindsay (vco/pso)
Simpson, Nicci (pso)
Smith, Paul (pso)

High Risk
Norton, Nicole (spo)
Garnett, Hilary
Jackson, Angela (p)
Jones, Angela (p) (9)
Ockleford, Karen (p) (5)
Porter, Angela (7)
Rose, Sue

Pre-Release
Kavanagh, Jo (spo)
McCarthy, Suzanne
Nisbet, Steve
Armstrong, Phil (pso)
Atkinson, Leanne (pso)

Offenders' Healthy Living Project
Chambers, Carol (mgr)

Persistent Offenders
Bennett, Tracey (p) (4)
Middleton, Sue (pso)

Unpaid Work
Goude, Tony (area mgr)
Payne, Chris (quality ass mgr, county)
Byrne, Mick (quality ass mgr)
Merrix, Joanne (p, pso)
Miechowski, Helen (pso)
Wright, Richard (pso)

Programmes
Reed, Sarah (spo) (7b)
Davies, Martin (acting spo) (7b)
Baker, Graham
Walker, Janet
Banks, Janice (pso)
Broughton, Lesley (pso)
Edwards, Fiona (pso)
Harris, Nigel (pso)
Smith, Karen (pso)

Community Sex Offenders' Group
Jackson, Angela (p)
Jones, Angela (p) (9)
Ockleford, Karen (p) (5)
Sylvester, Doreen (p) (16)

Employment, Training and Education
O'Meara, Tricia (mgr)

Training & Staff Devpt Unit
Connell, Tony (spo) (1)
Michelson, Sally (pda) (9)
Plant, Kim (p, pda)
Walker, Ian (pda)
Burdon, Debbie (trainee)(9)
Connelly, Gabi (trainee)

Davies, Mark (trainee)
De Vries, Agaath (trainee)
Goodhand, Nicole (trainee)
Hutchinson, Sandie (trainee) (9)
Izard, Verity (trainee) (9)
Lawson, Amy (trainee) (5)
Morrissey, Matthew (trainee)
Page, Dan (trainee)
Reddish, Michael (trainee)
Reeds, Elaine (trainee) (9)
Sackfield, Helen (trainee)
Stone, Katharine (trainee)
Taylor, Katherine (trainee)

3.   **Lincoln Magistrates' Court Office**
The Courthouse, High Street
Lincoln LN5 7QA
tel (01522) 533352/560063 *fax (01522) 546332*

Oliver, Joanne (spo)
Astill-Dunseith, Rachel (p, crt service off)
Dunkling, Marilynn (crt service off)
French, Jolyon (p, crt service off)
Gostelow, Elaine (crt service off)
Phillips, Martin (crt service off)
Shaw, Maureen (crt service off)

3a.   **Lincoln Crown Court**
The Castle, Castle Hill
Lincoln LN1 3AA
tel (01522) 526767 *fax (01522) 528779*

Staff at office 3

4.   Police Station, Morton Road
Gainsborough DN21 2SY
tel (01427) 612260 *fax (01427) 612975*

Bennett, Tracey (p)
Wood, Janine
Nolan, Linda (p, pso)
Wild, Layla (p, pso)

Courts
Nolan, Linda (p, crt service off)

5.   The Town Hall, North Parade
Skegness PE25 1DA
tel (01754) 763906 *fax (01754) 760202*

Gilbert, Mike (spo) (6, 7)
Miller, Iain (spo) (6, 7)
Kirby, Katie
Peacock, Jean
Sarin, Raish
Draper, Liz (pso)
Hoffman, Kathryn (p, pso)
Hoy, Caroline (p, pso)

Jennings, Nicola (pso)
Williams, Marie (pso)
Nicholls, Alan (p, vco)

High Risk
Norton, Nicole (spo) (2)
Ockleford, Karen (p)

Courts
Delderfield, Richard (crt service off)
Marshall, John (p, crt service off)

6. Police Station, Eastfield Road
    Louth LN11 7AN
    tel (01507) 604427 *fax (01507) 608642*

    Gilbert, Mike (spo) (5, 7)
    Miller, Iain (spo) (5, 7)
    Buxton, Helen
    Roberts, Amy (pso)

7. The Annexe, The County Hall
    Boston PE21 6LX
    tel (01205) 316300 *fax (01205) 316301*

    Gilbert, Mike (spo) (5, 6)
    Miller, Iain (spo) (5, 6)
    Cook, Andrew
    Morris, Andrew
    Roberts, Angie
    Waller, Stacey
    Blackman, Paul (pso)
    Lee, Kathy (pso)
    Lyon, Michelle (pso)
    Weston, Sara (pso)

    Courts
    Downs, Tony (p, crt service off)
    Hartley, Barbara (p, crt service off)

    High Risk
    Norton, Nicole (spo) (2)
    Porter, Angela

    Unpaid Work
    Goude, Tony (acting area mgr) (2)
    Martin, Kristy (qa mgr)
    Cooke, John (pso)
    Day, Jennifer (pso)
    Jutsum, Sue (pso)
    Rate, Rebecca (pso)
    Wattam, Robin (pso)

7a. **Boston Resource Centre**
    Addaction, 70-74 Wide Bargate
    Boston PE21 6RY
    tel (01205) 319920 *fax (01205) 319921*

    Clarke, Alan (pso)

7b. Probation Centre/Programmes
    The Old School, Carlton Road
    Boston PE21 8LN
    tel (01205) 316350 *fax (01205) 316351*

    Davies, Martin (acting spo) (2)
    Reed, Sarah (spo) (2)
    Bhatti, Cherie (pso)
    Clement, Jane (pso)
    Goddard, Lorraine (pso)
    Hancock, Paul (pso)
    Hodgson, John (pso)
    Murray, Wayne (pso)

8. Broadgate House, Westlode Street
    Spalding PE11 2AD
    tel (01775) 722078/767708
    fax (01775) 713936

    Crook David (spo) (9)
    Eveleigh, Carol
    Ogilvie, Esther (pso)
    Stacey, Krystyna (p, pso)

9. Grange House, 46 Union Street
    Grantham NG31 6NZ
    tel (01476) 583131 *fax (01476) 583130*

    Crook, David (spo) (8)
    Briggs, Mel (p)
    Brister, Charlotte
    Leachman, Beccy
    Newborn, Clare
    Smith, Jacqui
    Hamblett, Chris (pso)
    Hobill, Fiona (p, pso)
    Lee, Rebecca (pso)
    Pycock, Janet (pso)
    Smith, Annette (pso)
    Keller, Phil (p, vco)

    Courts
    Blevins, Paul (p, crt service off)
    Patel, Kiran (crt service off)
    Woodhouse, Sandra (p, crt service off)

    High Risk
    Norton, Nicole (spo) (2)
    Briggs, Mel (p)
    Jones, Angela (p)

9a. **Grantham Resource Centre**
    71 High Street, Grantham NG31 6NR
    tel (01476) 512950 *fax (01476) 512951*

    Miller, Barbara
    Leivers, Beverly (p, pso)
    Saunderson, Deborah (p, pso)

10. **Multi Agency Public Protection Panel**
Lincolnshire Police HQ
PO Box 999 **Lincoln** LN5 7PH
tel (01522) 558255 *fax (01522) 558289*

Eyres, Tony (spo)

11. **Youth Offending Service (East)**
Lime House, Foundry Street
Horncastle LN9 6AQ
tel (01522) 554737 *fax (01522) 554731*

Virr, Lesley

12. **Youth Offending Service (South)**
6 St Catherine's Road **Grantham** NG31 6TS
tel (01476) 591522 *fax (01476) 569166*

Gooderson, Steve

13. **Youth Offending Service (West)**
8 The Avenue, Lincoln LN1 1PB
tel (01522) 554550 *fax (01522) 554552*

Loffhagen, Jane

Hostel

14. **Wordsworth House**
205 Yarborough Road **Lincoln** LN1 3NQ
tel (01522) 528520 *fax (01522) 526077*

Laughton, Keith (spo, mgr)
Allnut, Steve (res pso)
Cann, Jean (res pso)
Crisp, Stewart (res pso)
Greasley, Allan (res pso)
Wilson, Bill (pso)
Roberts, Chris (approved premises sup)
Paynter, Malcolm (wkg night care asst)
Smith, Rebecca (wkg night care asst)
Taylor, Roly (wkg night care asst)

Institutions

15. H M Prison, Greetwell Road
Lincoln LN2 4BD
tel (01522) 663000 *fax (01522) 663001*
probn fax (01522) 663177

Probn clerk ext 296/300
Discipline ext 310
Special visits ext 221

Cope, Denise (p, spo)
Byrne, Clare
Evans, Tracey
Smith, Laura (pso)
Wilby, Steve (p, pso)
Thomas, Russell (bail info offr)

16. H M Prison **Morton Hall**
Nr Swinderby LN6 9PS
tel (01522) 666700 *fax (01522) 666775*

Probn direct line (01522) 666730
Parole clerk ext 6706
HDC clerk 6728
Discipline ext 6707
Visits booking line ext 6760

Cooke, Amanda (p, spo) (17)
Birch, Di (pso)
Sylvester, Doreen (intermittent custody)

17. H M Prison **North Sea Camp**
Frieston, Boston PE22 0QX
tel (01205) 769300 *fax (01205) 769301*
probn fax (01205) 760098

Cooke, Amanda (p, spo) (16)
Booth, Chris
Costello, Mike
Steel, Linda (p)
Templeton, Donna (pso)

Local Justice Areas

7 Boston
9, 12 Bourne & Stamford
8 Elloes
4 Gainsborough
9 Grantham
2 Lincoln District
6 Wolds
9, 12 Sleaford
5, 6 Skegness

Crown Court

3a Lincoln

LONDON PROBATION

1 Hammersmith
2 Kensington & Chelsea
3 Westminster
4 Islington
5 City
6 Southwark
7 Lambeth

Note: the details for the London Probation were accurate at the time of going to press but will change during 2006 as the Offender Management Model is implemented.

London Probation has offices in every London borough and is organised on a borough as well as functional basis. The boroughs are managed in four quadrants.

London Postcodes by Borough

Barking & Dagenham
IG11, RM6, RM7 (part), RM8, RM9, RM10

Barnet
N2, N3, N10, N11 (part), N12, N14 (part), N20, N22, NW2, NW4, NW7, NW9, NW11, EN5

Bexley (with Beckenham)
SE2 (part), SE9 (part), SE28 (part), DA1 (part), DA5, DA6, DA7, DA8 (part), DA14, DA15, DA16, DA17 (part), DA18 (part)

Brent
NW6 (part), NW10, HA0, HA9

Bromley
SE20, SE26 (part), BR1 (part), BR2, BR3, BR4 (part), BR5, BR6, BR7, TN16 (part)

Camden
EC1 (part), N7, N19, NW1 (part), NW2 (part), NW3, NW5, NW6 (part), NW8, WC1, WC2 (part)

City of London & Tower Hamlets
EC1 (part), EC2 (part), EC3, EC4, E1, E3, E14

Croydon
SE19, SE25, SW16, CR0, CR2, CR3, CR5, CR6, CR7, CR8

Ealing
W3, W4, W5, W7, W13, UB1, UB2, UB4 (part), UB5, UB6

Enfield
N9, N11 (part), N13, N14 (part), N18, N21, EN1, EN2, EN3, EN4,

Greenwich
SE3, SE7, SE8, SE10, SE18

Hackney
EC1 (part), EC2 (part), E2, E5, E8, E9, N1 (part), N4, N16

Hammersmith & Fulham
SW6, W6, W12, W14

Haringey
N4 (part), N6, N8, N11 (part), N15, N17, N22

Harrow
HA1, HA2, HA3, HA4 (part), HA5, HA7, HA8

Havering
RM1, RM2, RM3, RM4, RM7 (part), RM11, RM12, RM13, RM14

Hillingdon
HA4 (part), HA6, UB3, UB4 (part), UB7, UB8, UB9, UB10

Hounslow
TW3, TW4, TW5, TW6, TW7, TW8, TW9, TW13, TW14

Islington
WC1 (part), EC1 (part), EC2 (part), N1 (part), N4 (part), N5 (part), N7 (part), N16 (part), N19

Kensington & Chelsea
SW1 (part), SW3, SW5, SW7, SW10, W2, W8, W11

Kingston-upon-Thames
SW19, SW20 (part), KT1, KT2, KT3, KT4 (part), KT5, KT9

Lambeth
SE5, SE11, SE21, SE24, SE27, SW2, SW4, SW8, SW9, SW12

Lewisham
SE4, SE6, SE8, SE12, SE13, SE14, SE23, SE26 (part)

Merton
SW17 (part), SW19, SW20, SM4, CR4

Newham
E6, E7, E12, E13, E16

Redbridge & Waltham Forest
E4, E10, E11, E15, E17, E18, IG2, IG3, IG4, IG5, IG6, IG7, IG8, IG10

Richmond-upon-Thames
SW13, SW14, TW1, TW2, TW9, TW10, TW11, TW12

Southwark
SE1, SE5, SE11, SE15, SE16, SE17, SE21 (part), SE22, SE23 (part), SE24 (part), SE26 (part)

Sutton
SM1, SM2, SM3, SM5, SM6

Wandsworth
SW4 (part), SW8 (part), SW11, SW12 (part), SW15, SW16 (part), SW17 (part), SW18, SW19 (part)

Westminster
W1, W2, W9, W10, W11, W12, NW1 (part), WC2 (part)

Abbreviations
lpo   legal proceedings officer
pcso   probation service court officer
crt off   court officer
cro   community resettlement officer
rso   resettlement officer
ama   advanced modern apprenticeship
ISMS   Intensives Supervision and Monitoring Scheme
ICCP   Intensive Control and Change Programme

e-mail Firstname.Surname@london. probation.gsx.gov.uk

1. **Head Office**
    71-73 Great Peter Street
    London SW1P 2BN
    tel 020-7222 5656 (switchboard)
    fax 020-7960 1188 (reception)

    London Probation Board
    Aziz, Suhail (chair) tel 020-7960 1007
    Simon, Toby (secy) tel 020-7960 1161
    tel 020-79601822 *fax 020-7960 1136*

    Chief's Office
    Scott, David (co)
    Grant, Pam (exec asst to co)
    tel 020-7960 1006
    Gavin, Geraldine (chief operations off)
    tel 020-7960 1073
    Mohiuddin, Naseem (exec asst)
    tel 020- 79601140

    Legal
    Brenells, Paul (solicitor)
    Collins, Colenna (exec asst)
    tel 020-7960 1698 *fax 020-7960 1695*

    Directors
    Battye, June (director, London West)
    Spragg, Kelley (exec asst)
    tel 020-7960 1838 *fax 020-7960 1114*

    Responsible for Prisons and boroughs:
    Hammersmith & Fulham and Wandsworth,
    Hounslow and Ealing, Kensington &
    Chelsea and Westminster, Kingston and
    Richmond, Merton and Sutton

Mary McFeely (director, London East & Crown Courts)
Day, Rosanna (exec asst)
tel 020-7960 1120 *fax 020-7960 1114*

Responsible for boroughs: Barking & Dagenham and Havering, Hackney, Newham, Waltham Forest and Redbridge, Tower Hamlets and City

Shackleton, Jill (director, London South)
Kotey, Beverley (exec asst)
tel 020-7960 1140 *fax 020-7960 1114*

Responsible for Substance Misuse and boroughs: Bexley and Bromley, Croydon, Greenwich and Lewisham, Lambeth, Southwark

Jenkin, Malcolm (director, London North & Risk)
Lucas, Emily (exec asst)
tel 020-7960 1653) *fax 020-7960 1114*

Responsible for boroughs: Barnet and Enfield,
Brent, Camden and Islington, Haringey, Hillingdon and Harrow

Harwood, Hilary (director interventions)
Rodwell, Caroline (exec asst)
tel 020-7960 1009 *fax 020-7960 1114*

Responsible for: Approved Premises, Unpaid Work, Accredited Programmes, Domestic Violence & Sex Offender Programmes & Victims Contact

Chitra Karve (director of diversity and equality)
Day, Rosanna (exec asst)
tel 0207960 1120 *fax 020-7960 1114*

Functions: Advice / support to Board and Directors on diversity issues, Partnerships with external stakeholders, Implementation
of Diversity Strategy, Management of Diversity Team, Promote Diversity internally
and externally, Promote the Confidence agenda, and Marketing & Communications

Swash-Wallbank, Pauline (director of finance)
Stinton, Savannah (exec asst)
tel 020-7960 1844

Functions: Finance, Human Resources (Management Policy & Advice, Recruitment
and Selection, Industrial Relations, Terms & Conditions of Employment), Health &

Safety, Estates, Accommodation Services, Audit, Corporate Governance, Legal

Drury, Phil (interim director of HR)
Rodwell, Caroline (exec asst)
tel 020-7960 1009

Functions: Human Resource Management, Human Resource Development, Health and Safety

Moran, Stephen (director of business solutions)
Spragg, Kelley (exec asst)
tel 020-7960 1838 *fax 020-7960 1114*

Functions: Resource Development, Management Information Team, IT Services,
Procurement, Marketing and Communications,
Performance Support Unit

Equality & Diversity
McIntosh, Alethea (aco diversity)
tel 020-7960 1005 *fax 020-7960 1113*

Abernethy, Rosemary (div implt off)
tel 020-7960 1834
Hammond, Nick (div implt off)
tel 020-7960 1821
Joseph, Tess (div implt off, external)
tel 020-7960 1836
Malik, Saima (div implt off, internal)
tel 020-7960 1835
Dixon, Liz
tel 020-7960 1862
Thompson, Ruby (admin)
tel 020-7960 1824

Confidence
Olympic House, 28-42 Clements Road
Ilford, Essex IG1 1BA
tel 020-8514 5353 *fax 020-8478 4450*

Weston, Alan (devpt mgr)
tel 020-8262 6944
mob 07958681839

based at Gt Peter St
Barnes, Albert
tel 020-7960 1864
Hunnisett, Maeve (admin asst)
Asamoah, Audrey (LCJB confidence)
tel 020-7960 1128

Audit & Commissioning
Lee, Geoff (aco, head of audit & commissioning/dep treasurer)
tel 020-7960 1179

Functions: Corporate Governance, Risk Management, Internal and External Audit,

Efficiency and Effectiveness,
Commissioning, contestability,
procurement and resource development,
Facilities, Board link across
Corporate Resources Directorate

Business Solutions
Moran, Stephen (Director of business
solutions)
Spragg, Kelley (exec asst)
tel 020-7960 1838 *fax 020-7960 1114*
Jones, Sian (business mgr)

Marketing & Communications
tel 020-7960 1137 *fax 020-7960 1113*

George, Elizabeth (head of marketing and
communications) ext 1137
Finnegan, Tony (marketing mgr) ext 1654
Smith, Karen (marketing mgr) ext 1015
Alexander, Cornelius (media relations mgr)
ext 1151
Prager, Alison (media relations off) ext
1863
Coles, Brigette (events & admin off) ext
1875

DTTO/DRR & Substance Misuse
based at Mitre House
Darian Mitchell (aco)
Barbara Burns (exec asst)
tel 020-7740 8524

Management Information Team
based at Great Peter Street
Simmonds, Steve (aco mgmnt info)
tel 020-7960 1676 *fax 020-7960 1117*

Performance Support Unit
based at Great Peter Street
Rooms 104 & 105

Anderson, Iain (unit mgr)
tel 020-7960 1667
Adefeso, Titilolami
tel 020-7960 1102
Kenny, Sarah
tel 020-7960 1012
Narnor,Christine
tel 020-7960 1057

Resource Development Unit
based at Great Peter Street
Pick, Tricia (aco)
tel 020-7960 1830
Cooke, Diane (exec asst)
tel 020-7960 1668
Stocker, Fil (devpt mgr)
mobile 0786 048 7735)
Field, Lyn (info off)
O'Brien, Jan (Q&M off)

Technical Services
based at Great Peter Street
Pengelly, Mary (aco technical services)
tel 020-7960 1147 *fax 020-7960 1117*

**Accommodation Services,
Health & Safety, Procurement,
and Key HR Projects**
Piddington, Glen (aco)
tel 020-7960 1065
Kesby, Alan (procurement mgr)
tel 020-7960 1055

Central Support Units
Evans, John (facilities mgmnt co-ord)
tel 020-7960 1063
Engleman, Philip (central supt mgr)
tel 020-7960 1099
Pinto, Neville (central supt mgr)
tel 020-7960 1098

Potter, Ann (central supt mgr)
based at Crosby House
9/13 Elmfield Road
Bromley BR1 1LT
tel 020-8460 6662 *fax 020-8466 1571*

Health & Safety Department
based at Great Peter Street
Ash, Colan (aco head of H&S)
tel 020-7960 1002
Dennett, Nicole (exec asst)
Wade, Brian (H&S advr)
Walton, Ian (H&S advr)
Miller, Beverly (occ health mgr)
based at Crosby House
tel 020-8464 3430

Great Peter Street
71/73 Great Peter Street
London SW1P 2BN
Green, Les (HQ services mgr)
tel 020-7960 1070

Mitre House
223 - 237 Borough High Street, London
SE1 1JD
Moore, Pat (Building mgr)
tel 020-7740 8500 *fax 020-7740 8448*

Human Resources Great Peter Street
Binks, Ian (interim head of hr operations)
Bennet, Nicole (ea)
tel 020-7960 1058

Fassari, Daniel (interventions hr mgr)
ext1832
McFarland, Marriane (north/east hr mgr)
ext1681
Arthur, Janet (south/west hr mgr) ext 1689
Yanis, Tariq (recruitment mgr) ext 1829

Human Resources Development
Mitre House, 223-237 Borough High Street, London SE1 1JD
tel 020-7740 8500

Pagan, Tim (head of hrd) tel 020-7740 8519
Coleman, Judy (exec asst)
tel 020-7740 8534 *fax 020-7740 8448*

Brown, Angela (qual training mgr) ext 8546
Stewart, Julie (qual training mgr) ext 8508
Jones, Mike (effective pract mgr) ext 8533
Thomas, Bernadette (mgmnt devpt mgr) ext 8512
Hillas, Andrew (HR mgr)
Kelly, Andrea (learning & devpt advir) ext 8567

Qualifying Training
Idusohan, Vicki (qual training advr) ext 8543
Pilinski, Krystyna (qual training advr) ext 8545
Sawyer, Cicely (qual training advr) ext 8503
Smith, Keith (qual training advr) ext 8553
Wheeler, Graham (qual training advr) ext 8521

Effective Practice
Honner, Bradley (effective pract advr) ext 8511
Read, Jan (effective pract advr) ext 8455
Morris, Brian (quality assurance advr) ext 8551
Sayeed-Hussain, Nushrat (quality assurance advr) ext 8539

Co-ordinators
Bixby, Kay (hrd co-ord) ext 8506
Johnson, Denise (hrd co-ord) ext 8504
Carcavella, Susan (snr hrd admin) ext 8547

Admin
Stuart, Elizabeth (nvq admin) ext 8507
St John-Hadley, Carole (nvq admin) ext 8538
Phillips, Michelle (hrd admin) tel 020-8771 1542
Ayre, Rosemary (temp hrd admin) ext 8565

Accredited Programmes Training Team
fax 020- 7740 8448
Duff, Delphine (pract trainer/devpr) ext 8558)
Duke, Michaela (pract trainer/devpr) ext 8453

Edmead, John (pract trainer/devpr) ext 8452
Granata, Judith (pract trainer/devpr) ext 8456
Playle, Liz (pract trainer/devpr) ext 8457

OASys Training Team
fax 020- 7740 8448
Forbes, David (OASys mgr/trainer) ext 8542
Borrows, Trisha (OASys trainer) ext 8537
Johnson, Georgette (OASys trainer) ext 8548
O'Connor, Mark (OASys trainer) ext 8452/8563
Chisholm, Kirsty (E-OASys trainer) ext 8563
Brown, Norma (OASys admin) ext 8509
Horlock, Jo (internal verifier) ext 8562

Interventions

Business Managers
Hall, Avrill (South/West)
217 Balham High Road
London SW17 7BP
tel 020-8672 2682

Carron, Sue (North/East)
29/33 Victoria Road
Romford, Essex RM1 2JT
tel (01708) 502224

Volume Programmes
Tuhill, Louise (aco)
based at Great Peter Street
tel 020-7960 1847
Jacobs, Angela (exec asst)
tel 020-7960 1851

Victims, Domestic Violence & Sex Offenders
Jones, Ian (aco)
based at Great Peter Street
tel 020-7960 1852
Jacobs, Angela (exec asst)
tel 020-7960 1851

Unpaid Work
London South/West
Pasquale, Ginny (aco)
based at Great Peter Street
tel 020-960 1845
Harington Hawes, Sarah (exec asst)
tel 020-7960 1850

London North/East
Shaw, Jill (aco)
based at Great Peter Street
tel 020-7960 1054

Harington Hawes, Sarah (exec asst)
tel 020-7960 1850

Approved Premises
Denton, Claude (aco)
based at Great Peter Street
tel 020-7960 1142
Hepburn, Jackie (exec asst)
tel 020-7960 1043

Risk
Hennigan, Linda (aco for risk)
71-73 Great Peter Street
London, SW1P 2BN
tel 020-7960 1104

Mitre House
223-237 Borough High Street
London, SE1 1JD
tel 020-7740 8500

Jackie Owens (spo)
Cameron, Angus (mental health advr)
Jarvis, Lorraine (team admin)

Other Main London Area Offices

Olympic House
28/42 Clements Road, Ilford IG1 1BA
tel 020-8514 5353 *fax 020-8478 4450*

Crosby House
9/13 Elmfield Road, Bromley BR1 1LT
tel 020-8464 3430 *fax 020-8466 1571*

45 High Street
Kingston upon Thames, Surrey. KT1 1LQ
tel 020-8546 0018 *fax 020-8549 7626*

Mitre House
223-237 Borough High Street, London SE1
1JD
tel 020-7740 8500 *fax 020-7740 8448*

LONDON NORTH

Malcolm Jenkin (director)
Amanda Davies & Andrea Goldring (business
mgrs)

Barnet & Enfield
Campbell, Diane (aco)
tel 020-8205 1885
Martin-Ross, Elizabeth (exec asst)
tel 020-8205 1885/1838 *fax 020-8205 5462*

2.   **Hendon Probation Office**
Allied House (1st Floor)
3 Burnt Oak Broadway
Edgware, Middx HA8 5LT
tel 020-8205 2561 *fax 020-8205 5462*

Community Assessment Team
Smith, Kate (spo)

Parr, Roger (spo)
Adelaye, Glyn
Essen, Mick
Gavin, Charlotte
Hind, Richard
McKenna, Kathryn
Mullalley, Clare
Murphy, Anne-Marie
Nunez-Fantie, Marcia
Valmas, Catherine
Yates, Peter
Abbott, Danielle (crt off)
Oduwole, Sonia (crt off)
Simon, Miriam (pso)

Manning, Sheila (hdc off)
Pearce, Mary (hdc off)

Trainees Unit
Headland, Margaret (pda)
Dhillon, Varinder
Hughes, Adele (trainee)
Simons, Sarah (trainee)
Sonnenberg, Jenna (trainee)

McGowan, Angela (office mgr)

Offender Programmes Unit
fax 020-8205 4553

Mary Bailey (spo)
Hignett, Chris (spo)
Borgen, Deborah (treatment mgr)
Alloui, Samantha (treatment mgr)
Cross, Stacy (pso)
Griffiths, Charlotte (pso)
Kershaw, Arlene, (pso)
Modak, Aleem (pso)
O'Donovan, Caroline (pso)
Sommers, Genevieve (pso)

3.   The Old Court House, Windmill Hill
Enfield Middx EN2 6SA
tel 020-8366 6376 *fax 020-8367 1624*

Community Intervention Team
Ferguson, Carl (spo)
Teft, Paul (spo)
Cobbing, Pauline
Davies, Christopher
Fraser-Davies, Irrit
Rice, Scott
Stapleton, Joyce
Stevens, Heather
Cassius, Jeff
Douglas, Paulette (pso)
Ifedoria, Angela (pso)
Trattou, Angela (pso)
Sia, James (ama)

Public Protection Team
Hughes, Anna (spo)
Dervish, Jill
Donkin, Victor
Headey, Sandy
Lonsdale, Dawn

Cordwell, Barbara (crt off)
Reeves, Mercia (crt off)
Sajjad, Barbara (crt off)

Trainees
Forrester, Jennifer (pda)
Beeston, Pippa (trainee)
Hull, Karen (trainee)
Jones, Donna (trainee)
Okendon, Eleanor (trainee)
Smith, Katherine (trainee)
Wallace, Patricia (trainee)

Elias, Mark (snr lpo)
Jones, Ray (lpo)
Waite, Emma (lpo)
Matthews, Harry (dtto)
Regan, Michelle (prog tutor)
Redmond, Lesley (team admin)

4. **Barnet YOT** Colinhurst House
168 Station Road, Hendon NW4 3SP
tel 020-8359 5535 *fax 020-8359 5530*

Yates, Peter

5. **DTTO/DRR** (Barnet and Enfield & Haringey)
71 Lordship Lane, London N17 6RS
tel 020-8808 4522 *fax 020-8885 5946*

Rambarath, Joseph (spo)
Garbutt, Chris
Martin, Marietta (pso)
O'Nwere, Viviene (team admin)

6. **90 Lansdowne Road**
London N17 9XX
tel 020-8808 4849 *fax 020-8365 0981*

Parr, Roger (spo)
David, Christine
Jenkins, Andrew
Karim, Sheik
Lonsdale, Dawn
Valmas, Catherine
White, Denise
Thomas, Richard
McGrowder, Carol (case mgr)
Purryag, Sharmila (case mgr)

Cordwell, Barbara (crt off)
Reeves, Mercia (crt off)
Sajjad, Barbara (crt off)

Forrester, Jennifer (pda)
Odogwu, Rosemary (office mgr)
Clarke, Anastasia (qa mgr

Unpaid WorkUnit
(covers Barnet/Enfield, Haringey, Camden/Islington)
Wells, Mike (spo)
McEvoy, Jean (spo)
Akintokun, Comfort (case mgr)

Brent
Jones, Will (aco)
tel 020-8830 4393 *fax 020-8830 2502*
Martin-Ross, Elizabeth (exec asst)
tel 020-8205 1885/1838

7. 440 High Road
Willesden London NW10 2DW
tel 020-8451 6212 *fax 020-8451 3467*

Public Protection Team
Whyte, Marcia (spo)
Alphonse, Yvonne

Community Assessment Team
Stevenson, Doug (spo)
Johnson, Patricia
Lehane, Gerard
English, Simon (p)
Bruno, Sara (lpo)
Ibbott, Marie (upaid wk supvr)
Smith, Beverley (upaid wk supvr)
Whitten, Catherine (upaid wk supvr)

Community Integration Team
Stevenson, Doug (spo)
Sudds, Allan (p)
Clachar, Caren (pso)
Edwards, Dawn (pso)
Jantjies, Ronel
Kirnig, Zarina
Maguire, Sioban
Maude, Nicola
Muge, Jacqueline (p)

8. 402-408 High Road
Wembley HA9 6AL
tel 020-8903 4921 *fax 020-8795 0472*

Community Assessment Team
Hopwood, Joe (spo)
Redmond, Lesley (office mgr)
Lewinson, Midian (p)
Thomas, Carol
Venter, Yolanda
Viner, Sarah (p)
Petrie, Dominic

Community Integration Team
Hopwood, Joe (spo)

Davies, Felicity (p)
Morris, Lorna (cro)

DTTO/DRR (Brent & Harrow)
McDonald, Linda (p, spo)
Kapadia, Meena (pso)
Davis, Sean (office mgr)

9.   **Seafield Lodge Approved Premises**
     71/73 Shoot Up Hill, London NW2 3PS
     tel 020-8452 4209 *fax 020-8450 2037*

     Ayree, Eric (spo/mgr)
     McLean, Dana (po dep mgr)
     Andrews, Claudette (office mgr)
     Scotland, Debbie (office mgr)
     Callendar, Jennifer (asst mgr)
     Collins, Roy (asst mgr)
     Huggins, Labon (asst mgr)
     Johnson, Vivia (asst mgr)
     Keane, Patricia (asst mgr)
     Lee, Prince (asst mgr)
     Ibe, Bernadette (night asst)
     Soko, Foluso (night asst)
     Fitzgerald, Kathleen (relief wrkr)
     Rose, Leonie (relief wrkr)

10. **Brent YOT**
     1 Craven Park, London NW10 8SX
     tel 020-8965 6020-*fax 020-8961 5181*

     Grant, Valerie

11. **Unpaid Work** Harrow/Uxbridge
     (covers the boroughs of Brent (part),
     Harrow and Hillingdon)
     The Court House, Harefield Road
     Uxbridge, Middx UB8 1PQ
     tel (01895) 231972 *fax (01895) 257972*
     Harrow 020-8427 7246)

     Flynn, Maureen (spo)
     Bone, Jennifer (spo)

     Unpaid WorkOffice
     Wembley *(covers Brent (part))*
     402-408 High Road
     Wembley, Middx HA9 6AL
     tel 020-8903 8551 *fax 020-8795 0472*

     Davis, Sean (office mgr)

Camden & Islington
Ward, Lyla & Felix, Lorna (aco) (js)
Billington, Carol (exec asst)
tel 020-7609 8909

12. **53 Holloway Road**
     London N7 8JD
     tel 020-7609 0913 *fax 020-7700 2553/6936*

Connage-Hamilton, Beverley (office mgr)

13. **Camden House Probation Office**
     199 Arlington Road, London NW1 7HA
     tel 020-7267 9231 *fax 020-7428 8431*

     Scotland, Debbie (office mgr)
     Reynolds, Beverley (snr team admin)
     Charles, Udean (prog tutor)
     James, Marlene (prog tutor)
     Smith, Janet (unpaid wk proj mgr)

14. **Camden Women's Centre**
     199 Arlington Road,
     Camden Town, London NW1 7HA
     tel 020-7267 2646 *fax 020-7284 1967*

     Programmes: Think First, ART and ASRO

     Scotland, Debbie (office mgr)
     Bailey, Mary (p, prog director)
     Borgen, Deborah (p, ART treatment mgr)
     Davies, Anna (prog tutor) - tel 020-7428
     8484
     Bamford, Emma (psychologist)

15. **Camden House Approved Premises**
     199 Arlington Road
     Camden Town, London, NW17HA
     tel 020-7482 4288 *fax 020-7284 3391*

     Hutt, Rob (spo/mgr)
     Atta, Faisal (asst mgr)
     Davies, Vernon (asst mgr)
     Fraser, Janet (asst mgr)
     Madar, Mohammed (asst mgr)
     Mullahy, Susan (asst mgr)
     Pascall, Errol (night off)
     O'Malley, Grace (night asst)
     King, Ernestine (secy)

16. **DTTO/DRR** (Camden, Islington)
     401 St John Street, London EC1V 4RW
     tel 020-7713 8968 *fax 020-7713 8959*

     Dodd, Charles (spo)
     Devlin, John (pso)
     Green, Majella (care mgr)
     Serrano, Titi (snr team admin)
     Stechman, Vivian
     Irish, Janet
     Langton, Julia (pso)

17. Voluntary Approved Premises
     Kelley House
     18-20 Royal College Street
     London NW1 0TH
     tel 020-7388 3945 *fax 020-7383 7211*

     Smith, Susan M (mgr)

18. **Camden YOT**
SSD Centre 3, 115 Wellesley Rd
Gospel Oak, London NW5 4PA
tel 020-7974 6762 *fax 020-7974 1196*

Tilly, Wendy
Davies, Jean (admin)

19. **53 Holloway Road**
London N7 8JD
tel 020-7609 0913 *fax 020-7700 2553/6936*

Goldring, Andrea (business mgr, London
North)

Community Assessment Team
Harris, Phill (spo)
Bertram, Joanne
Blake, Tamara
Hiscock, Lynda
Lanjri, Mohamed
Libby, Alison
McIntosh, Sandra
Millar, Eva
Phillips, Rachel
Pryce, Paul
Williams, Paulette
Gillam, Tony

CAT Camden
McGeown, Mary (spo)
Lewis-Lebailly, Karol
Mitchell, Rebecca
Sydow, Anita
Cordon, Wendy (sessional po)
Blaine, Susan (pso)
Murray, Trevor (pso)
Connolly, Teresa (pso)
Bailey, Stephanie (psco)
Howard, Blanche (psco)
McCalla, Michael (psco)
Sofola, Anthony (psco)
Thomson, Sally (psco)

Kufeji, Jimi (lpo)
Maginley, Yvonne (lpo)

20. **401 St John Street**
London EC1V 4RW
tel 020-7014 9800 *fax 020-7014 9801*

Public Protection Team
Owens, Jackie (spo)
Gollan, Julia
Moir, Elizabeth

Prolific and Priority Offenders Unit
Baker, John (spo)

Islington Community Integration Team
Bodden, Ava
Cumming, Dennis
Evans, Leighton
Ruff, Chris
Thomas, Candy
O'Meara, Theresa

CIT Camden
Bone, Jennifer (spo)
Henry, Susan
Mitchell, Rebecca
Clarke, Nicola
Reid, Douglas
Benka-Davies, Elizabeth

Public Protection Team
McGeehan, Georgina (spo)
Defriend, Nat
Johnson, Neil
Burke, Lorna (ete)

Trainees Unit
McCalman, Barbara (pda)
Henry, Susan (trainee)
Irish, Janet (trainee)
Roberts, Jane (trainee)

Mullens, Hayley (pda)
Day, Karia (trainee)
Hubert, Natalie (trainee)
Hull, Robert (trainee)
O'Flynn, Morgan (trainee)
Sharp, Peter (trainee)

White, Joanne (pda)
Fake, Anna (trainee)
Khan, Saeeda (trainee)
Manning, Kelly (trainee)
Steffen, Shanty (trainee)
Sullivan, Breda (trainee)
Yesufu, Shaka (trainee)

Noone, Mary (snr team admin)

Unpaid Work
*(covers Barnet/Enfield, Haringey,
Camden/Islington)*
based at office 6
tel 020-8808 4849 *fax 020-8365 0981*
Wells, Mike (spo)
McEvoy, Jean (spo)
Akintokun, Comfort (case mgr)

21. Voluntary Approved Premises
Katherine Price Hughes
28 Highbury Grove
London N5 2EA
tel 020-7226 2190 *fax 020-7354 3221*

Owens, Ted (mgr)

22. **Islington YOT**
     27 Dingley Place, London EC1V 8BR
     tel 020-7527 7050 *fax 020-7527 7066*

     Winter, Sarah

Haringey
Walker, Sean (aco & yot and yj)
based at Holloway Road
Billington, Carol (exec asst)
tel 020-7609 8909 *fax 020-8348 9222*

23. **Telfer House**
     Church Road, Highgate, London N6 4QJ
     tel 020-8341 9060 *fax 020-8341 4260*

     Foy, Tony (spo)
     Peazer, Rosie
     Benmore, Joe
     Devlin, Mick
     Everitt-Story, Denise
     Gilbert, Polly
     Gordon, Jean
     Khan, Shamim
     Lunness, Amanda
     Walbank, Sarah (p)
     Williams, Femi
     Wright, Claire
     Manu, Dennis (cro)
     Benwell, Dorithe (pso)
     Humes, Doreen (pso)
     Preston, Fiona (pso)
     Scanlon, Kathy (pso)
     McLaughlin, Emer (pso)
     Martin, Patricia (pso)
     Lawrence, Dionne (pso)

     Burch, Elisabeth (office mgr)

24. **Wood Green Crown Court Team**
     see Courts Section no 158

25. **71 Lordship Lane**
     Tottenham, London N17 6RS
     tel 020-8808 4522 *fax 020-8885 5946*

     Delaney, Monica (spo)
     Tsioupra, Fotini (spo)
     Bonner, Doreen
     Laffan, Kim
     Marsh, Karen
     Pardoe, Jill
     Stevens, Bonny
     Thomas, Jerry
     Walbank, Sarah
     Williams, Petula
     Fadlin, Josie
     Campbell, Dalia (trainee)
     Dottin, Donna (pso)

Fleming-Hodge, Wendy (pso)
Ifedoria, Angela (pso)
Maragh-Olney, Sandra (pso)
Mortimer, Canan (pso)
Ogbuoyne, Maduka (pso)

DTTO/DRR (Barnet and Enfield &
Haringey)
Rambarath, Joseph (spo)
Garbutt, Chris
Matthews, Harry
Williams, David
Martin, Marietta (pso)
Forde, Pat (team admin)
Hall, Nova (team admin)

26. **Haringey YOT**
     476 High Road, Tottenham N17 9JF
     tel 020-8489 1574 *fax 020-8489 1588*

Hillingdon & Harrow
Wright, Hermoine (aco)
based at The Court House, Uxbridge
Manning, Anne (acting exec asst)
Collins, Debbie (exec asst)
(01895) 230035 *fax 01895 271966*

27. **The Court House**
     Harefield Road **Uxbridge** UB8 1PQ
     tel (01895) 231972 *fax (01895) 257972*

     Eugene, Mary (spo)
     Jeffcott, Alison (spo)
     Brett, Kelly
     Burne, Oliver
     Butress, Kim
     Johnson, Steven
     King, Joseph
     Morgan, Trevor
     O'Flaherty, Angela
     Ranger, Paulette
     Tuvey, Mike
     Valero, Brigitte
     Yau, Julie (seconded to yot)
     Gordge, Jackie (pso)
     Henry, Barbara (pso)
     Kenyon, Jeanette (pso)
     Rothwell, Marie (pso)
     Russell, Pauline (pso)
     Ryan, Trish (pso)
     Walkinshaw, Ann (pso)

Trainees Unit
Bellaha, Souad (trainee)
Blowfield, Anna (pso)
Denton, Grace (trainee)
Johnson, Stephen (trainee)
Smith, Ruth (trainee)

28. **Unpaid Work** Harrow/Uxbridge
(covers the boroughs of Brent, Harrow and Hillingdon)
The Court House, Harefield Road
Uxbridge, Middx UB8 1PQ
tel (01895 231972 *fax (01895) 257972*
(Harrow 020-8427 7246)

Flynn, Maureen (spo)
Gibbs, Alton (qa mgr)
Cassidy, Mark (qa mgr)

29. **DTTO/DRR**
(Ealing/Hillingdon/Hounslow)
Lancaster House
Leeland Road, Ealing W13 9HH
tel 020-8566 1122 *fax 020-8567 7900*

Abernethy, Peter (spo)
Barton, Lorna (admin)
Shaw, Francis (pso)

DTTO/DRR (Brent & Harrow)
402/408 High Road
Wembley, Middx HA9 6AL
tel 020-8903 4921 *fax 020-8795 0472*

Davies, Amanda (business mgr, North)
McDonald, Linda (p, spo)
Moore, Brigid
Kapadia, Meena (pso)
Davis, Sean (office mgr)

30. Rosslyn Crescent
Harrow Middx HA1 2SR
tel 020-8427 7246 *fax 020-8424 2101*

Heerah, Marie (spo)
Thakur, Shaila (office mgr)
Adams, Katie
Depass, Rema
Dunbar, Sharon
Francis, Jermaine (seconded to yot)
Gordon, Pat
Laird, Mark
Booker, Sue (pso)
French, Beverley (pso)
Madlani, Kajal (pso)
Marchetti, Louise (pso)
Stephens, Suzanne (pso)

Trainees Unit
Harris, Felix (pda)
Burne, Oliver (trainee)
Logie, Koreen (trainee)
Tiernan, Janet (trainee)
Tuvey, Michael (trainee)
Whiting, Susan (trainee)

31. **Harrow Crown Court**
see Courts Section no 159

LONDON EAST
Mary McFeely (director)
Based at Great Peter Street 020-7222 5656
Cheryl Deane & Maria Oakman (business mgrs)
Based at Olympic House, 020-8262 4215/020-8262 6924

Barking & Dagenham and Havering
Heckroodt, Carina (aco)
based at Olympic House
tel 020-8262 6931
High, Linda (exec asst)
tel 020-8262 6947

32. 4th Floor, **Olympic House**
28/42 Clements Road, Ilford IG1 1BA
tel 020-8514 5353 *fax 020-8478 4450*

Porter, Alan (snr lpo)
tel 020-8262 6911

Gary Atherton (spo multi-agency)
tel 020-8262 6900

33. 1 Regarth Avenue
Romford RM1 1TP
tel (01708) 742453 fax (01708) 753353

Public Protection Team
Kennerson, Shirley (spo)
Ajayi, Grace
Amartey, Amarh
Groce, Leonie
Ronan, Terry (pso)

PPO Team
Okoh, Christopher
Caldwell, Andrew (pso)
Hafeez, Arif (pso)

DTTO/DRR
Grant-Williams, Anita (spo)
Godard, Julie
Baptiste, Cyntra
Gibbons, Stephanie, (pso)

Community Assessment Team
Willemse, Sharifa (spo)
Dajani, Basil
De Goede, Sonja
De Vries, Christa
Smith, Jacquie
Scheepers, Ursula
Smith, Jacquie
Taylor, David

Resettlement
Serugo-Lugo, Sarah (spo)
Downey, Anne (pso)
Lagan, Tracy (pso)

Trainees Unit
Drayton, Felecia (pda)

34. **Barking and Dagenham Magistrates' Court**
Probation Suite, The Courthouse
East Street, Barking IG1 8EW
tel 020-8507 2115 *fax 020-8262 4200*

Akiode, Edward (pso)
Farrell, Chris (pso)

35. **Havering Magistrates' Court**
Probation Suite, The Courthouse
Main Road, Romford RM1 3BH
tel (01708) 502501 *fax (01708) 736533*

Kemp Jackie (pso)
Maiden, Janet (pso)
O'Hallaran, Marcus (pso)

36. **Havering Resource Centre**
29/33 Victoria Road, Romford RM1 2JT
tel (01708) 753555 *fax (01708) 752096*

Community Integration Team
Lucas, Jerome (spo)
Alstrom, Alyson
Benjamin, Debbie
Bergin, Sharon
Howard, Neil
Scott, Elizabeth
Tuitt, Cynthia
Andrew, Susan (pso)
Brown, Linda (pso)
Field, Debbie (pso)
Hawkins, Jo (pso)
Lyall, Zoe, (pso)
Shade, Daniel (pso)

37. **Unpaid Work Office**
29/33 Victoria Road, Romford RM1 2JT
tel (01708) 502203/502204
fax (01708) 752096

Hewitt, Gary (qa mgr)
Padden, Edd (qa mgr)
Smith, Elaine (qa mgr)
Assi Suki (cso)
Dellow, Julie (cso)
Flower, Mark, (cso)
Henderson Barry (cso)
Idowu, Joselyn
Jones, Bryan (cso)
Kendell Paul (cso)
Lindsay, Andrew (cso)
Newman Linda (cso)
Omari, Emma (cso)
Ross, Jenny (cso)

Sherry Anita (cso)
Spence, Kirk (cso)
Wood John (cso)
Jackson, Andrew (snr team admin)

38. **Home Detention Curfew**
4th Floor, Olympic House
28 / 42 Clements Road
Ilford, Essex IG1 1BA
tel 020-8478 8141 *fax 020-8553 8151*

Birthwright, Doreen (pso) ext 6928
Longshaw, Mandy (pso) ext 6928
Khan, Marina (admin) ext 6948

Hackney
Gilbert, Kate (aco)
based at Olympic House
tel 020-7609 8909
Worley, Jill (exec asst)
fax 020-7700 0615

39. **Olympic House**
28/42 Clements Road
Ilford, Essex IG1 1BA
tel 020-8514 5353 *fax 020-8478 4450*

40. **34 Englefield Road**
Hackney, London N1 4EZ
tel 020-7241 9900 *fax 020-7241 9901*

Gardiner, Aveen (spo)

Community Assesment Team
Gardiner, Aveen (spo)
Bradbury, Christine
Di Pino, Miranda
Eldridge, Hannah
Gamanga, Dennis
Harris, Susi
Njie, Florence
Stewart-Fraser, Laverene
Whyte, Denise

Ressetlement Team
Bloice, Thirza (spo)
Gurhan, Tuncay (pso)
John, Nicola (pso)
Rimmell, Ann (pso)
Mark-Kirby, Shirleyann

CJIP
Hill, Kathy,

Krige, Libby (pda)
Hughes, Bonnie (office manager)

41. **Reed House**
1-4 Rectory Road, London N16 7QS
tel 020-7923 4656 *fax 020-7923 4084*

Public Protection Team
Green, Charles (spo)
Roberts, Jane
Stevens, Peter

Community Inetrvention Team
Rose, Anthony (spo)
Lescombe, Anne
McDermott, Shirley-Ann
Bates, Viv
Demisse, Yaregal
Moseley, Yvonne (pso)
Fraser-Kellman, Greta (pso)
Asumadu, Micahel (pso)

PPO Team
Brooks, Noreen
Whitehall-Smith, Steve

DTTO/DRR Team
Howitt, Mike (spo)
Bodden, Ava
Garvey, Judy
Knights, Aloma (pso)
Cooney, Clare (pso)

Drug Abstinence Team
Francis, Jennifer (DIP manager)
Singh, Amrik (pso)

Community Reintergaration Team
Gleeson, Celine
Kocaman, Ahmet (pso Turkish communities)
Odili, Angela (pso)

Whittaker, Anne-Marrie (pda)
Browne, David (office manager)

42. **Hackney YOT**
55 Daubeney Road
Hackney, London E5 0EE
tel 020-8533 7070 *fax 020-8986 7446*

Phillips, Stewart

43. **Unpaid Work Unit**
see office no 50

Newham
Vacancy (aco)
based at Olympic House
Smith, Jenny (exec asst)
tel 020-8262 6917

44. 4th Floor, **Olympic House**
28/42 Clements Road
Ilford, Essex IG1 1BA
tel 020-8514 5353 *fax 020-8478 4450*

45. **Newham**
20 Romford Road, Stratford E15 4BZ

tel 020-8534 5656 *fax 020-8534 8285*

Haastup, Micahel (office mgr)
Tipper Patricia (snr team admin)

DTTO/DRR Team
Taylor, Doreen (spo)
Atherton, Sue
O'Hagan, Marianne
Ogbuonye, Maduka (pso)
Wilfred, Melissa (pso)

Offender Management Team 1
Stableford, Paul (spo)
Bimpson, Linda
Mayes, Soren
Obasuyi, Juliette
Paul, Nick
Whitehead, Michael (pso)
Atkins, Georgina (team admin)
Loughlin, Iris (team admin)
Adeyeye, Fibi (trainee)
Compton, Susan (trainee)
Conteh, Mary (trainee)
Yaqoob, Nazia (trainee)

Offender Management Team 2
Folawiyo, Toyin (spo)
Albertyn, Gerhard
Edwards, Beverley
McCleod, Derek
Onyeaka, Jude
Read, Jenny
Adeogun, Abiola (pso)
Pearce, Lesley (pso)
Catnott, Jacqui (trainee)
Clarke, Alexander (trainee)
Oakley-Hill, Sarah (trainee)
Westwood, Sarah (trainee)

Offender Management Team 3
Norris, Keith (spo)
Akram, Sandra
Clowes, Vicky
DeJager, Vicky
Peart, Paul
Pilgrim, Louise
Shields, Robert
Mthimkulu, Susan (pso)
Skelton, Diane (pso)
Purnell, Sue (team admin)
Deen, Alhan (trainee)
Kerr, Anthony (trainee)
Musa, Suhel (trainee)

46. **Plaistow Police Station**
444 Barking Rd, London E13 8HJ
tel 020-7275 5803 *fax 020-7275 5807*

PPO Team
Taylor, Doreen (spo)
Neimantas Linda
Duffy, Kerry (team admin)

Public Protection Team
Austin, Richard (spo)
Bartlett, Gary
Clifford, Andrea
Curley, Lynda
Illingworth, John
Dennis, Maureen (pso)
Duffy, Kerry (team admin)

47. **Stratford Magistrates' Court**
389-397 High Street
Stratford E15 4SB
tel 020-8522 5000 *fax 020-8534 7356*

    team based at office no 45
    Ashby, Jackie (spo)
    Coupland, Kezia (pso)
    Fitzpatrick, Alan (lpo)
    Stack, Martin (lpo)

48. **Snaresbrook Crown Court**
see Courts Section no 160

49. **Newham YOT**
192 Cumberland Road
Plaistow, London E13 8LT
tel 020-8430 2361 *fax 020-8430 2299*

50. **Unpaid Work Unit**
(covers Newham, Tower Hamlets, Hackney)
15 Belton Road
Forest Gate, London, E7 9PF
tel 020-8472 5412 *fax 020-8471 6673*

    Capy, Janette (office mgr)
    Francis, Vivienne (scheme mgr)
    Flower, Rob (qa mgr)
    O'Kane, Anthony (qa mgr)
    Yarde, Trevor (qa mgr)
    Knox, Malcolm (case mgr)
    Pearce, Colin (workshop mgr)
    Copp, Michael (placement mgr)
    Ali, Sarfraz (case mgr)
    Bryan, Nekeyshia (case mgr)
    Gibson, Tracey (case mgr)
    Hollington, Paul (case mgr)
    Khan, Nabila (case mgr)
    Neary, Joseph (case mgr)
    Njoh, Henry (case mgr)
    Rix, Katherine (case mgr)

51. **Westbourne House Probation & Bail Hostel**
199 Romford Road, Forest Gate E7 9HL

tel 020-8534 0673 *fax 020-8534 8286*

Thomas, Barbara (spo mgr)
Andrews, Claudine (office mgr)
Motundo, Pananka (dep mgr)
Ogwal, Rex (pso)
Akello, Susan (pso)
DeCastro Borba, Zita (asst mgr)
Jaward, Rosamund (asst mgr)
Swift, Ian (asst mgr)
Williams, Billy (asst mgr)
Fashakin, Bunmi (night asst)
Nyekogulu, Samson (night asst)
Smith, Eileen (team admin)

Tower Hamlets & City
Chater, Chris
based at Olympic House
tel 020-8262 6938 *fax 020-8478 4450*

52. **Olympic House**
28-42 Clements Road,
Ilford, Essex IG1 1BA
020-8262 6938 *fax 020-8478 4450*

53. **Valentine House**
Hancock Road
Bow, London E3 3DA
tel 020-8981 5500 *fax 020-8980 8067*

    PPO/DTTO
    covered by Chris Chater (based at Olympic House)
    McNaughton, Vivienne (spo mgr)
    Lloyd, Linda (office mgr)

    PPO
    Webb, Siobhan
    Cullinane, John (pso)
    Rabey, Steve (police)
    Kidd, Rob (police)
    Battle, Mike (housing officer)

    DTTO/DRR
    Metz, Paul
    Carta, Raimondo (pso)
    Collins, Roy (pso)
    Dillon, Kimberley (dip)
    Nolan, Mary (dip)

    Kwapong, Comfort (team admin)

54. **50 Mornington Grove**
Bow, E3 4NS
tel 020-8980 1818 *fax 020-8983 0020*

    Community Assessment Team (Court/PSRs)
    Canning, Becky (spo)
    Chudasama, Darshna

Daley, Shirley (p)
Fitzpatrick, Joanne (p)
Haywood, Sophie
Scully, Joanne
Kwarifa, Vida (lpo)
Llewellyn-Pace, Trefor (lpo)
Audain, Elaine (psco)
Gouldbourne, Corral (psco)
Philbert, Vivian (psco)

Martin, Jan (office mgr)

55. **337 Cambridge Heath Road**
Bethnal Green, London E2 9RD
tel 020-7739 7931 *fax 020-7613 4909*

CIT &Resettlement Team 1
Okine, Mannie (spo)
Page, Maxine
Simela, Aggrey
Appelquist, John
Glenn, Careen (pso)
Alam, Soyful (pso)

Trainees Unit
Stevenson, Tina (pda)

Public Protection Team
Pilgrim, Mary (spo)
Branston, Charlie
Carew, Rose
Taylor, Ruth

CIT &Resettlement Team 2
Lewis, John (spo)
Ogunyankin, Florence
Murray, Brenda
Took, Lesley (pso)
Idowu, Charles (pso)

Programmes
Kirk, Sharon (spo/prog mgr)
Sowoolu, Adetokunbo (treatment mgr)
Hosegood, Claire (prog tutor)
Richards, Zephaniah (prog tutor)
Cives-Enriques, Rosa-Maria (prog tutor)
Davis, Cassandra (pso)

Brooker, Marlene (office mgr)

56. **Central Criminal Court**
see Courts Section no 152

57. **Court of Appeal (Criminal Division)**
see Courts Section no 153

58. **Tower Hamlets YOT**
St Mary's Church Hall
Kit Kat Terrace, Bow
London E3 2SA

tel 020-7364 1142

Athwal, Harninder

59. **Unpaid Work**
See office No 50

Waltham Forest and Redbridge
Hartley, Carol (aco)
based at Olympic House
tel 020-8262 6918
Smith, Jenny (exec asst)
tel 020-8262 6917

60. 4th Floor **Olympic House**
28/42 Clements Road
Ilford, Essex IG1 1BA
tel 020-8514 5353 *fax 020-8478 4450*

Howell-Ives, Nick (spo multi-agency)

Victims Unit
Riley, Brian (spo)
Osula, Linda (vlo)
Jones, Sandra (vlo)
Ahmed, Moulvi (vlo)
Harrison, Sharon (vlo)
Styles, Karen (p, vlo)
Nelson, Tanya (p, vlo)
Goddard, Annete (vlo)
Bailey, Angela (vlo)
Lachman, Helen (p, vlo)
Kodish, Jacquie (snr team admin)

61. **Ilford Probation Centre**
277 High Road, Ilford, Essex IG1 1QQ
tel 020-8478 8500 *fax 020-8478 8518*

Perkins, Emily (vlo)
Carver, Tina (office mgr)
Henton, Sandra (snr team admin)

Community Assessment Team
Turner, Haley (spo)
Johnson, Mike
Robertson, Neil
Mack, Rob
Atkinson, Caroline (crt pso)
Holman, Simone (crt pso)

Community Integration Team
Boyde, Pamela (spo)
Armstrong, Simone
David, Christine
Ekpunobui, Kelly
Francis, Jennifer
Husband, Hazel
Moulvi, Ahmed
Rughooputh, Natasha,
Smith, Nia

Thomas, Penny
Wells, Kim
Adeyeye, Fibi (pso)
Hart, Rob (pso)
Popo, Raimonde (pso)
Ruparell, Padma (pso)
Rush, Carol (pso)
Saund, Kiran, (pso)

PPO/DRR
tel 020-8262 8348 *fax 020-8262 8365*
Francis, Jennifer
Waller, John
Allen, Eve (pso)
Amoonoo, Mary (pso
Brown, David M. (pso)
Cecile, Shirley (pso)
Wharton, Marilyn (pso)
Wogan, Vince

Programmes Unit
fax 020-8553 1972
Osbourne, Soroya (spo)
Gardiner, Judith (trmtnt mgr)
Knight, Deborah (trmtnt mgr)
Rana, Aruna
Farquhar, Claire
Christopher, Lucy
Richards, Zephania
Moses, Gary
Oppon, Julie
Davis, Keith
Adetola, Linda
McFarland, Kathy

Community Sex Offenders Group
fax 020-8553 1972
Rose, Yvonne
Satchell-Day, Lucy (facilitator)
Wilde, Michael (facilitator)
Charles, Dave

**Intergrated Domestic Abuse
Programme**
Linfoot, Rebecca (trmtnt mgr)
Simons, Phillipa
Bertram, Joanne (facilitator)
Maroni, Daniella (facilitator)
Thomas, Candy (facilitator)
Davies, Anna (pso, women's safety)
Roberts, Sandra (pso, women's safety)

62. **1b Farnan Avenue**
Walthamstow, London E17 4TT
tel 020-8531 3311 *fax 020-8531 1319*

Waters, Pat (office mgr)
Browne, Jomo (spo CAT/resettlement)
Cleary, Cyril (lpo)

Walcott, Patsie (lpo)
Bolden, Cheryl (pso)
Foot, Jackie (pso)
Charles, Corrine (resettlement pso)
Enemuwe, David (resettlement pso)

Community Assessment Team
O Ezeigbo, Ronke
Neill, Kathy
Samuel, Priscilla
Sutcliffe, Prue
Vanderputt, Layton
Woodman, Judith

Public Protection Team (PPT)
Drayton, Eddie (spo)
Johnson Michael
Samuel, Priscilla

63. **Unpaid Work Office**
See office No 37

LONDON SOUTH

Jill Shackleton (director)
Betty Foxworthy & Roger Picard (business mgrs)

Bexley and Bromley
Kerr, Adam (aco)
based at Crosby House
Barbara Fathers (exec asst)
tel 020-8464 3430

64. **Crosby House**
9-13 Elmfield Road
Bromley, Kent BR1 1LT
tel 020-8464 3430 fax 020-8466 1571

O'Connor, Lynda (vlo)

65. **Bexley Magistrates' Court**
Norwich Place
Bexleyheath, Kent DA6 7NB
tel 020-8304 5521 *fax 020-8301 5737*

Pearce, Ray (pso)

66. Norwich Place
Bexleyheath Kent DA6 7ND
tel 020-8304 5521 *fax 020-8301 5737*

Glen, Joyce (office mgr)
Tunsley, Barbara (team admin)
Chapman, Alison (team admin)

Community Integration Team
Hannah Mead (spo)
Patsy Tomlin (spo)
Nicholas, Malcolm (p)
Anthony Halls (p)
Beverley Steiner (p)

Jenny Craig (p)
Fisher, Jean (p)
Warnock, Mauricia (p)
Laura Cayton (p)
Graham Edwards (pso)
Martini, Pat (pso)
Farlie, Pam (pso)

PPO Team
Lusk, Ann (spo)
Al Jappy
Nathaniel Arthur
Eaton, Donna (p, team admin)

67. **Bexley YOT**
2 Nuxley Road
Belvedere, Kent DA17 5JF
tel 020-8284 5555 *fax 020-8284 5560*

Eastham, James

68. **DTTO/DRR** (Greenwich and Bexley)
Riverside House, Beresford Street
Woolwich, London SE18 6DH
tel 020-8855 5691 *fax 020-8309 8693*

Catnick-Phillips, Ambrozine (spo)
Thomason, Davey
Olabimpe, Ekeocha
Walker, Rachel
Wadman, Johanna
Patrick, Rebecca (pso)
Clegg, Kathy (snr team admin)
Billen, Leah (team admin)

Offender Management Team
Hutton, Taj (spo)

69. **DRR/PPO**
9/13 Elmfield Road
Bromley, Kent BR1 1LT
tel 020-8464 8433/3430 *fax 020-8466 1571*

John Slaven (spo)
Mike De Waal (p)
Fiona Scott (p)
Deborah Palmer (pso)

70. **Crosby House**
9/13 Elmfield Road
Bromley, Kent BR1 1LT
tel 020-8464 8433/3430 *fax 020-8466 1571*

Central Services
tel 020-8460 6662 *fax 020-8466 1571*

Potter, Ann (central service mgr)
Austen, Ruth (central service officer)
Jeive, Amy (central service officer)

Scriven, Sue (snr systems admin)

Turnbull, Graham (case mgmnt proj mgr)

Criminal Justice Act Implementation
Costello, Peter (aco)

Victims Liaison Unit
tel 020-8466 7630/31 *fax 020-8466 1571*

Bowie, Eleanor
Locket, Ann
Rose, Sarah
Samuels, Wendy
Whitley, Lisa

Public Protection Team
tel 020-8290 6255 *fax 020-8460 9990*

Ian Forsyth (spo)
Barnett, Jane
Batchelder, Marion
Quinette Curran (team admin)

71. **Orpington Office**
6 Church Hill, Orpington, Kent BR6 0HE
tel (01689) 831616 *fax (01689) 875253*

Community Assessment Team
Grandison, Selene (spo)
Roberts, Claire (spo)
Boyes, Jocelyn (p)
Giffin, Lorraine
Harris, Felix
Hay, Eve
Hunter, Maria
Mumford Nana
Tibble, Andrea
Lizzette Ambrose
Sandra Angus (p)
Deborah Palmer (pso)
Louise Britten (pso)
Louise Kesby (pso)
Tinham, Ann (pso)

Trainees Unit
Furner Keith (pda)
Barber Louise (trainee)
Biggs John (trainee)
Hurn Lesa (trainee)
Ryan Martina (trainee)
Whereat Lindsey (trainee)

Admin Team
Richardson, Anne (office mgr)
Milner, Ryder (team admin)
Smith, Freida (team admin)
Smith Valerie (team admin)
Rachael Lloyd (team admin)
Fox, Rita (team admin p/t)
Kennedy, Angie (Receptionist)
Walker, Marilyn (team admin)

72. **Beckenham Approved Premises**
4 Beckenham Road
Beckenham, Kent BR3 4LR
tel 020-8658 3515 *fax 020-8663 6244*

Marshall, Trevor (spo mgr)
Benamaisia, Stephen (po dep)
Blair, Ian (asst mgr)
Evans, Carol (asst mgr)
Fearon, Alma (asst mgr)
Frater, Diana (asst mgr)
Hills, Sue (office mgr)
Mariner, Bob (asst mgr)
Okafor, Polite (asst mgr)
McKenzie, Sharon (night asst)
Welch, John (night asst)
Basten, Gareth (ECP case mgr)
Todd, Maria (ECP case mgr)

73. **Bromley Magistrates Court**
1 London Road
Bromley BR1 1RA
tel 020-8325 4000 *fax 020-8325 4006*
minicom tel 020-8325 6746

Mandy Hoare (pso)
Chin, Lorna (pso)
McIntosh, Norma (pso)

74. **Bromley YOT**
Bromley Civic Centre
Stockwell Close, Bromley BR1 3UH
tel 020-8313 4318 *fax 020-8313 4331*

Eastham, James

75. 6 Beckenham Road
Beckenham Kent BR3 4LR
tel 0208 658 3511 *fax 0208 658 8678*

Community Integration Team
Tomlin, Patsy (spo)
Hardy, Ruth
Jarvest, Fiona (pso)

Domestic Violence Team
Noon, Christine (spo)
(based at 111 Chertsey Cresent, New
Addington)

James, Sally (treatment mgr)
Behr, Andrew
Jahangir, Fozia
Waters, Jill (pso)
Pearce, Debby (pso)
Abrams, Lynne (pso)

Unpaid Work
*(Croydon, Bexley/Bromley and
Greenwich/Lewisham)*
Stainton, Ann (spo)

Gordon, Annette (qa mgr)
Driver, Carol (qa mgr)
House, Peter (qa mgr)
Bishop, Karen (qa mgr)
Johnson, Debbie (qa mgr)
Moheeputh, Raj (qa mgr)

Admin Team
Batchelor, Elaine (office mgr)
Brown, Linda (team admin)
Common, Brenda (team admin)
Gordon, Tina (team admin)

Croydon
Williams, Anne (aco)
based at Church House
Cress, Henry (exec asst)
tel 020-8686 6551

76. **Church House**
Old Palace Road
Croydon, Surrey CR0 1AX
tel 020-8686 6551 *fax 020-8688 4190*

Scott, DeeAnn (office manager)
Kedge, Rob (actg snr team admin)

Offender Management Team
Grindley, Tina (spo)
Nowell, Libby (spo)
Shipley, Di (spo)
Fielder, Vivien
Jacobs, Stanley
Lawrance, Chris
Modikoane, Masisi
Naicker, Nevashni
Oakley, Stefanie
Ofori, Daniel
Patton, Julie
Polius, Yvonne
Samual, Sandra
Stubberfield, Emma
Thompson, Paul
Turner, Trudy
Watts, David
Winters, Sal
Dada, Babatunde (pso)
John, Laverne (pso)
Lunn, Jennifer (pso)
Smith, Charmaine (pso)
Vidale, Zarina (pso)
McVinnie, Jim (hdc)

Public Protection Team
O'Donnell, Teresa (spo)
Choy, Hilary
Hogarth, Claire
Northmore, Helena

PDAs and Trainees
Dix, Angela (pda)
Humfress, Val (pda)
Bajwa, Aman (trainee)
Baptiste, Clarisse (trainee)
Birtwisle, Tim (trainee)
Bishop, Andrew (trainee)
Chapman, Denise (trainee)
Charman, Lisa (trainee)
Flemming, Selina (trainee)
Ifill, Dionne (trainee)
MacLeod, Lynne (trainee)
MacNab, Jonathan (trainee)
Middlewick, Joanne (trainee)
Mithimkulu, Maureen (trainee)
Swift, Sarah (trainee)
Wallace, Michelle (trainee)

Partnerships/Other
Wootton, Dorothy (Red Kite)
Priscott, John (Red Kite)
Knowles, Kim (Learning Skills)
Gayle, Marva (Equinox)

77. **Croydon Crown Court**
see Courts Section no 161

78. **Croydon Magistrates' Court**
Barclay Road, Croydon CR0 3NE
tel 020-8688 0611

Benjamin, Joe (spo)
Nicholls, Eunice (pso)
Norman, Kate (pso)
Smith, Jenn (pso)
Mather, Andy (lpo)
Smith, Nicky (lpo)

79. **DPT** (Croydon DTTO/DRR/PPO)
51 Wandle Road
Croydon, Surrey CR0 1DF
tel 020-8686 4441 *fax 020-8686 4442*

Alice Glaister (spo)
Denman, Sue
Veronica Bryson
Solly, Shalene (pso)
Harris, Charlene (pso)
McClarty, Graham (pso)

Greenwich and Lewisham
LaRose Jones, Lloyd (aco)
based at 39 Greenwich High Road
Sheila Williams (exec asst)
tel 020-8469 1989 (direct line)
fax 020-8469 1994

80. **Riverside House**
Beresford Street

Woolwich, London SE18 6DH
tel 020-8855 5691 *fax 020-8309 8693*

Foxworthy, Betty (business mgr, London South)
Inekuku, Regina (acting office mgr)
Larmond, Valecia (acting snr team admin)
Fagbemi, Wumi (team admin)
Norville, Pat (team admin)
Brinkley, Jacqui (team admin)
McConnell, Pat (team admin)
Emeka, Chinazo (team admin)

Offender Management Team
Hutton Taj (spo)
Bennett, Leisa
Jackson, Serena
Erskine, Eleanor
Scott-Ralphs, Moira
Shereen Wilson (pso)

Elliott Martyn (spo)
Arbourin, Michelle
Bah, Hawah
Howell, Alex
Coston, Sally
Woodley, James
Dennis Aroh (pso)

Public Protection Team
Allman, Sam (spo) (based at 85)
Court, David
Devo, Sue
Feeney, Julie
Harris, Francis

DRR/PPO Team
Catnick-Phillips, Ambrozine (acting spo)
Hasan, Huseyin
Goldsworthy, Kelly
Hewitt, Stacy-Ann
Sey, Kofi (psco)
Clegg, Kathy (snr team admin)
Billen, Leah (team admin)

Trainees Unit
Butler, Jennifer (pda
Denman, Sam (trainee)
Richards, Christina (trainee)
Hampton, Lucy (trainee)
Gerard, Patricia (trainee)
Caney, Jennifer (trainee)
West-Beal, Lisa (trainee)

Harding, Yvonne (pda)
Benamaisia, Grace (trainee)
Duffy, Catherine (trainee)
Oladimeji, Shola (trainee)
Outerson, Ian
Mousbe, Emie (trainee)
Jones, Rachel (trainee)

81. **Greenwich YOT**
Young People's Support Centre
New Haven Gardens
Eltham SE9 6HQ
tel 020-8859 4492 fax 020-8859 2706

Williams, Jennifer (mgr)

82. **Woolwich Magistrates' Court**
Market Street
Woolwich SE18
tel 020-8271 9012/6 *fax*
Thomas, Bobbie (pcso)

83. **Woolwich Crown Court**
see Courts Section no 164

84. **208 Lewisham High Street**
Lewisham, London SE13 6JL
tel 020-8297 7300 *fax 020-8297 7301*

Jones, Junia (office mgr)
Waite, Reta (snr team admin)
Ashton, Maureen (team admin)
Holland, Kath (team admin)
Wilkins, Pat (team admin)
Asher, Ann (team admin)
Skelton, Janet (team admin)
Wilks, Juliet (Recept)
Stevenson, Joanne (team admin)
Stanley, Pat (team admin)

Offender Management Team
Johnstone, Mark (spo)
Ilyas, Sara
MacTaggart, Anne
Gill, Jeffrey
Blackman, Gianna
White, Yvette (pso)
Ajayi, Adenji (pso)
Porter, Cassandra (pso)
Patrick Rebecca (pso)
Smith, Hilary (pso)
Green, Claudia (pso)
Harvey, Angelina (pso)
Riley Talbot, Grace-Ann (pso)

Ashley, Val (acting spo)
Takaindisa, Dorcas
Brereton, Sharon
Exintaris, Ann-Marie
Christmas, Samantha
Adojutelegen, Louise (pso)

Resettlement
Stephen Benamaisia (spo)
Padgett, Derek
Marchetti, Louise
Nembhard, Derek

Hopton, Dennis
Collman, Julie (pso)
Walters, Diane (pso)
Adeyfeya, Kolawole (pso)
Abuwa, Tosan (pso)
Durrant, Val (pso)
Claire Smickler (pso)

PPT
Allman, Sam (spo) (based at 85)
Adjin-Tettey, Thomas
Harris, Angela
Maluleka, Judith
Labon Huggins (pso)

DRR/PPO
Evans, Leighton (spo)
Farrer, Steve
Sibson, Claire
Small, Eugenie
Coleman, Marilyn (pso)
Serrano, Titi (snr team admin)

Trainees
Rouse, Martin (pda)
Bess, Corene (trainee)
Blain, Susanne (trainee)
Burke, Eileen (trainee)
Claydon, Joy (trainee)
Fitzpatrick, Thomas (trainee)
Heavey, Kelly (trainee)
McQuilken, Anne-Marie (trainee)
Terry, Angela (trainee)
Wright, Sophie (trainee)

Programmes
Yarde, Sonia (prog tutor)
Coker, Evelyn (prog tutor)
Donkoh, Beatrice (prog tutor)
Moriarty, Regina (prog tutor)
Sangowawa, Ade (snr team admin)

85. **39 Greenwich High Road**
Greenwich, London SE10 8JL
tel 020-8692 6364 *fax 020-8694 2173*

Lee, Dominick (psco)
Suttle, Brian (psco)
Thomas, Bobbie (psco) (based at 82)
Philip Fawale (lpo)
Natasha Moran (office manager)
Anne Lori (team admin)

Rhone, Avis (support spo)
tel 020-8691 9176
Allman, Sam (ppt spo)
tel 020-8691 6346

86. **Lewisham YOT**
23 Mercia Grove

Lewisham, London SE13 6BJ
tel 020-8314 7474 *fax 020-8314 3177*

McDermott, Ann (mgr)
Rowe, Antoinette

Lambeth
Rance, Sally (aco)
based at Stockwell Rd
Oyekanmi, Margaret (exec asst)
tel 020-7326 7705 *fax 020-7326 7702*

87. **117 Stockwell Road**
Stockwell, London SW9 9TN
tel 020-7326 7700 *fax 020-7326 7701*

Larmond, Valecia (acting office mgr)
Martins, Fay (snr team admin)

Offender Management Teams
Blight, Andrew (spo)
Ansdell, Clare
Baruwa, Nike
Carby, Maisie
Montrose-Francis, Sharon
McLeod-Gayle, Victoria
Moodie, Ike
Taylor, Sarah
Williams, Nicola
Fadoju, Patrick (pso)
Golding, Saffron (pso)
Lawal, Stella (pso)
McAveety, Paul (pso)
Witter, Viviene (pso)

Dalrymple, Melodie (spo)
Beckford, Eric
Donovan, Sian
Jackson, Gary
Kotei, Charles
Layche, Catherine (based at Camberwell Green Mag Crt)
Scarsbrook, Julie
Siderfin, John (based at Camberwell Green Mag Crt)
Stewart, Dawn
Wedge, Patrick
Da Costa, Paul (pso)
Newbold, Erica (pso)
Nicola, Careena (pso)

Spring, Pamela (acting spo)
Blackstock, Samantha (pso) (based at IL Crown Crt)
Crichlow, Chereene (pso)

Trainees Unit
Anderson, Sylvia (pda)
Green, Lesley (trainee)
Idowu, Victoria (trainee)
Jolly, Rachel (trainee)

Keetley, Katie (trainee)
Anna-Kelly Lucy (trainee)
Sabah Sule, (trainee)
Tapa, Ephraim (trainee)
Williams, Prince (trainee)

Jäger, Anette (pda)
Burton, Michelle (trainee)
Farr, Jenty(trainee)
Henderson, Phillip (trainee)
Johnson, Alexandra (trainee)
Jones, Lloyd (trainee)
Spencer, Lucien (trainee)
Sutton, Natasha (trainee)
Williams, Prince (trainee)

DTTO/DRR (Lambeth)
Montgomery, Dave (spo)
Blades, Dene
Onibuje, Kemi
Kukoyi, Sakiru (pso)
Shields, Matt (pso)

PPO Team
Montgomery, Dave (spo)
Marrison, Laura
Gill, Alison (pso)

Programmes Unit
Johnson, Georgia (spo)
Plumley, Jodie (treatment mgr)
Ramsey, Joanne (treatment mgr)
Donkoh, Beatrice
Hendon, Myra
Hopkins, Laura
Kirton, Sandrine
McAveety, Sara
Morgan, Belinda
Murray, Pauline
Turner, Hopeton

88. **Harpenden House**
248-250 Norwood Road
London, SE27 9AJ
tel 020-8766 5700 *fax 020-8766 5746*

Olatunde, Stella (office mgr)

Public Protection Team
Heerah, Marie (spo)
Brosnan, Sean
Clarke, Liz
Monioro, Tarhe
Sutherland, Clive

Offender Management Team
Bristow, Margaret (acting spo)
Baglietto, Sandra
Game, Sam
Gyimah, Raphael
Lynch, Christine

Coleman, Levi (pso)
Garnett, Melanie (pso)
Jarvis, Tracey (pso)
Richards, Marsha (pso)
Sawyer, Kimberley (pso)
Tucker, Jennifer (pso)

Unpaid Work
(covers Lambeth and Southwark)
Wells, Sylvia (spo)
Turner, Lesley (qa mgr)
Parker, Yvonne (qa mgr)
White, Jacqui (qa mgr)
Beverton, Christine
Boreland, Audrey
Boyle, Robert
Deans, Derek
Korley, Floriana
Johnson, Michael (wkshp mgr)
Donaldson, Charlene (case mgr)

Home Detention Curfew Unit
McVinnie, Jim (mgr)
Jones, Alan
Smallbone, Richard
Whitehead, Michael

89. **Lambeth YOT**
1st Floor, 1-9 Acre Lane
London SW2 5SD
tel 020-7926 2557/263 *fax 020-7926 2639*

Symonds, Garath (mgr)
Donohoe, Paula
Small, Yvonne

90. **Tulse Hill Approved Premises**
147 Tulse Hill, London SW2 2QD
tel 020-8671 4086 *fax 020-8671 8546*

Morgan, Rhys (spo mgr)
Harris, Grace (po dep mgr)
Baker, Glen (asst mgr)
Barrett, Adam (asst mgr)
Clayton, Carol (asst mgr)
Dawkins, Jeanette (asst mgr)
Mills, Donna (asst mgr)
Falase, Ade (asst mgr)
Frater, Dexter (night asst)
Walker, Audrey (office mgr)

91. **Voluntary Approved Premises**
Hestia Streatham
298 Leigham Court Road
London SW16 2QP
tel 020-8769 8096 *fax 020-8664 7392*

Clarke Angela (mgr)

Southwark
Sandhu, Kuljit (aco)
tel 020-7740 8522
based at Mitre House
Foard, Gill (exec asst)
tel 020-7740 8526 *fax 020-7740 8447*

92. **Mitre House**
223/237 Borough High Street
London SE1 1JD
tel 020-7740 8500

93. **Inner London Crown Court**
see Courts Section no 156

94. **2 Great Dover Street**
London SE1 4XW
tel 020-7740 8400 *fax 020-7740 8449*

Public Protection Tier 3/4
Reilly, Sigrun (spo)
Edge, Jill
Cluley, Emma
Mulindwa, John
Rollins, Richard
Ashdown, Deirdre
Bascoe, Ingrid
Hegarty, Sally-Anne
Rai, Raveer

General Allocation – Tier 1/3
Hosking, Nigel (spo)
Muir, Jane
Cobley, Anna
Down, Terry
Hay, Marcia (pso)
Pidgeon, Cheryl (pso)

Trainees
Agana, Carol (pda)
Aldridge, Louise (tpo)
Ashley, David (tpo)
Battle, Lorraine (tpo)
Hutchinson, Pauline (tpo)
James, Jermaine (tpo)
Mansaray, Momodu (tpo)

Tofts, Sue (office manager)

95. **2 Kimpton Road**
London SE5 7UW
tel 020-7703 0822 *fax 020-7703 8319*

Court Team
Banton-Douglas, Glasmine (spo)
Ferguson, Alf
Siley, Joan
Myrie, Celeste
Shepherd, Becky
Tickner, Jonathan

Tutt, Carol (pso)
Warren, Carol (pso)
Ivory, Elizabeth (pso)
Campbell, Dawn (pso)
Jacobs, Atasha (lpo)
Wojtczak, Nickolas (lpo)

Resettlement
O'Brien, Gillian (spo)
Wilson, John
Trew, Kim
Obodai, Jacqueline
Babudoh, Alex
Ullah, Symone (rso)
Thomas, Cecilia (rso)
Korley, Floriana (rso)

Trainees
Vacancy (pda)
Harrison, Tom (tpo)
Josling, Anthony (tpo)
Pellatt, Katherine (tpo)
Dyson, George (tpo)
Callum, Gordon (tpo)
Binns, Shareen (tpo)
Hunt, Carlton (tpo)
Lugg, Corin (tpo)
Pryce, Selena (tpo)

DRR/DTTO/PPO
Forbes, Michelle (spo)

DRR/DTTO
Radcliffe, Dan
Riley, Debbie
Dodsworth, Tom (pso)
Opara, Justina (pso)

PPO Unit
Cinamon, Kate
Hamilton, Gemmer (pso)

Ramdheen, Marion (office mgr)

LONDON WEST
June Battye (director)
Beverley Young & Sandra Boyd (business mgrs)

Hammersmith & Fulham and Wandsworth
McKenzie, Yannik (aco)
(based at Balham)

96. **191A Askew Road**
London W12 9AX
tel 020-8811 2000 *fax 020-8811 2001*

Karen Johnson (office mgr)
Askew, Catherine (spo, cat)
Harambee, Sharon (spo drr/ppo)
Farren Niamh (spo ppt)

Felix, Victor

Grihault, Suzy
Hunt, Kathryn
Downton, Debbie
Louison, Trevor
Powrie, Anon
Jones, Sarah
Wall, Daniel
Morris, Daniel
Logie, Koreen
Randall, Francis
Springer, Angela
Balkisoon, Indira (pso)
Bartley, Laurna (pso)
Bradford, Christine (pso)
Davies, Marion (pso)
Lanzer, Susan (pso)

Trainees Unit
Graham, Rosemarie (pda)
Callender, Jennifer (trainee)
Francis, Lawrence (trainee)
Cameron, Laura (trainee)
Malins, Petra (trainee)
Spiers, Daniel (trainee)
Patel, Risha (trainee)
Harvey, Philip (trainee)
Jenkins, Maria (trainee)
Cheke, William (trainee)

Partnership Unit
Brown, Ivor (ete)
Okoro, Grace (partnership, alcohol)
Gardener, Jonathan (ete)
Carmichael, Hannah (housing)
Purbrook, Maureen (skills for life)
Kamara, Abdul (P4E)

Drink Drive Rehabilitation
Miller, Heather (spo)
Ingram, Valerie (course admin)
King, Sean (course admin)

97. **West London Magistrates' Court**
181 Talgarth Road
Hammersmith W6 8DN
tel 020-8700 9351 *fax 020-8700 9494*

Dolan, Janice (pso)
Bastian, Sylvia (psco)
Tobin, Amanda (pso)

Odoemelam, Kingsley (lpo) based at
Marsham Street

98. **Hammersmith & Fulham YOT**
Cobbs Hall, Fulham Palace Road
Fulham, London SW6 6LL
tel 020-8753 6200 *fax 020-8753 6242*

Hosten-McDavid, Norma

99. **217a Balham High Road,**
Balham, London SW17 7BQ
tel 020-8672 2682 *fax 020-8682 3093*

Noone, Mary (office mgr)
Clarke, Sharon (spo, ppt)
Flynn, Paul
Leach, Paul
Saunders, Gavin
Sharpe, Carol
Thompson, Sharon
Taylor, Carol
Lomas, Charlotte (pso)
Parrott, Thelma (pso)
Rhodes-Green, Hellen (pso)
Ryan, Jason (pso)

100. **79 East Hill**
London SW18 2QE
tel 020-8704 0200 *fax 020-8704 0201*

Douglas, Rita (office mgr)
Johnson, Prue (spo drr)
Gulley, Jean (spo)
McMahon, Margaret (spo)
Akanbi, Carol
Barnes, Janet
Hurcum, Charlotte
Isaacs, Ava
Lowe, Tracey
Mann Samantha
Ovenden, Richard
Sone, Mary
Thompson, Errol
Versmesse, Emmanuel
Wyatt, Sue
Healy, Tony (pso)
Thomas, Richard (pso)
Middleton - Stewart, John (lpo)
Pereria, Gerald (cro)
Green, Jodi (psco)

Partnerships
Bryant, Linda (MACA) (based at 99)
Kesby, Louise (D²W) (mon & thurs)
Gayle, Marva (Equinox Worker) (tues &
thurs)
Ejiogu, Kachi (Skills for Life) (thurs)
Erswell, Helen (Safe CDA)
Heywood, Dave (Safe CDA) (tues)

101 **Unpaid Work**
see office no 105

102. **Wandsworth YOT**
177 Blackshaw Road
Tooting, London SW17 0DJ
tel 020-8672 1664/7074 *fax 020-8682 4255*

Cooper, Richard

103. **Voluntary Approved Premises**
Hestia Battersea 9 Cologne Road
London SW11 2AH
tel 020-7223 3006 *fax 020-7924 2156*

Williams, Wyn (mgr)

Hounslow and Ealing
Dunn, Marion (aco)
based at Leeland House
Dickson, Margaret (exec asst)
tel 020-8840 6918 *fax 020-8570 6127*

104. **Leeland House**
Leeland Road, London W13 9HH
tel 020-8840 6464 *fax 020-8579 8165*

Young, Beverley (business mgr, West)
Chana, Satvinder (office mgr)
Moore, Brigid (spo)
Sajero, Rose (spo)
Stevenson, Brian (spo, drr/ppo)
Modrate, Williams (acting spo)
Scullard, Paula (pda)
Moulson, Jackie (pda)
Auld, Surinder (drr)
Burrell, Max (ppo)
De Souza, Julia
Felstead, Cynthia
Jones, Steven
McEvoy, Larry
Mehta, Anisha
Okefuna, Andrea
Ashe, Teresa (pso)
Campbell, Kaesha (pso)
Clements, Sonja (pso drr)
Conhye, Anand (pso, drr)
Elliot, Mark (pso)
Gayle, Lee (pso)
Gill, Kamaljit (pso)
Hoque, Anwar (pso)
James, Leon (pso)
Parris, Floyd (pso)
Sharma, Rekha (pso)

105. **Unpaid Work Office**
(covers the boroughs of Ealing/
Hounslow, Kensington & Chelsea/
Westminster and Hammersmith & Fulham
1st Floor, King's House, The Green
Southall Middx UB2 4QQ
tel 020-8843 1828 *fax 020-8813 9124*

Martin, Heather (acting scheme mgr) ext
8456
Jadunandan, Zairoon (office mgr)
Houslin, Lisa (qa mgr)

Bagot, Michael (qa mgr)
Howell, Frances (team admin)
Klempner, Bridge (proj supvr)
Raja, Kasim (case mgr)

106. **Banklabs House**
41a Cross Lances Road
Hounslow, Middx TW3 2AD
tel 020-8570 0626
fax 020-8814 1238 (PPT,CIT,CRT)
fax 020-8570 1190 (CAT)

Macci, Umehani (office mgr)
Palmer, Steve (spo)
Singh, Amrita (spo)
Ashley, Mark
Bull, Marilyn
Freeman, Anne
Garbett, Cheryl
Hall, Christopher
Joseph, Paulina
Kanana, Mariehana
Long, Louise
McHugh, Claire
Williams, Ann
Williams, Asher
Weale, Briony
Webb, Susan P
Knight, Natasha (pso)
Owen, Sue (pso)
Paul, Samantha (pso)
Knott, David (lpo)

Vassello, David (pda)
Coleman, Sam (trainee)
DoyleMacRae, Cindy (trainee)
Lee, Prince (trainee)
Matharu, Tajinder Singh (trainee)
Nardin, Carolyn (trainee)
Rocio, Deliot (trainee)

107. **Ealing Approved Premises**
2 Corfton Road, London W5 2HS
tel 020-8997 7127 *fax 020-8810 6213*

Holland, Alan (spo mgr)
Royle, Jennifer (po dep mgr)
Lombard, Gayle (office mgr)
Ahmed, Kamron (asst mgr)
Keane, Karen (asst mgr)
East, Lynette (asst mgr)
Pierre, Donovan (asst mgr)
Wilson, Aitch (asst mgr)
Oluade, Christiana (night asst)
Sholagbade, Olu (night asst)

108. **Isleworth Crown Court**
see Court Section no 162

109. **Ealing Magistrates' Court**
Court House, Green Man Lane
Ealing W13 0SD
tel 020-8566 3882

Will Watson
Anwarul Hoque (pso)
Pauline Russell (pso)

110. **Feltham Magistrates' Court**
Hanworth Road
Feltham, Middx TW13 5AF
tel 020-8890 8747 *fax 020-8893 2368*

Batchelor, Kenneth (crt off)
Bew, Bernice (crt off)
Descann, Vijay (crt off)

111. **Hounslow YOT**
Redlees Centre, Redlees Park
Twickenham Road
Isleworth TW7 7EU
tel 020-8847 8000 *fax 020-8847 8001*

Lamont, Eugenia

112. **4 Birkbeck Road**
Acton, London W3 6BE
tel 020-8992 5863 *fax 020-8993 5942*

Bennett, Sonia (office mgr)

Public Protection Team
Russell, Diane (spo)
Barnett, Michelle
Cloete, Richard
Renn, Paul
Sewell, Andy

Kingston and Richmond
Robinson, Sara (aco)
based at 45 High Street
tel 020-8939 4100 *fax 020-8549 8990*

113. 45 High Street
Kingston upon Thames
Surrey KT1 1LQ
tel 020-8546 0018 *fax 020-8549 8990*

Greif, Judith (office mgr)

DRR/PPO
Linkin, Anna (spo)

Community Assessment Team
tel 020-8939 4130 *fax 020-8549 7626*

Jarrett, Jean (spo)
Vacancy (p)
Prevatt, Petra
Hawkins, Joanne
Jones, Lucy

Barlow, Annie (p, pso)
Morris, Sharon (pso)

Pitman, Dafna (spo)
Marshall, Yvette (pda)
Bartlett, Julian
Prevost, Jo (p)
Alli, Beverley (pso)
Apio Achoko, Stella (pso)
Lane, Anne (pso)
Henderson, Grace (pso)
Kooner, Sundeep (pso)
Lovell, Leith (pso)

114. **Kingston Crown Court**
see Courts Section no 163

115. **Kew Approved Premises**
96 North Road, Richmond upon Thames
Surrey TW9 4HQ
tel 020-8876 6303 *fax 020-8876 7402*

Weijman, Hans (spo mgr)
Hill, Jean (po dep mgr)
Omondi, Janet (asst mgr)
Pinna-Nossai, Annarita (asst mgr)
Sexton, Kim (asst mgr)
Woodhouse, Courtney (asst mgr)
Powell-Nelson, Lorraine (asst mgr)
Gordon-Harris, Andrew (night asst)

116. **Kingston YOT**
Eagle Chambers
18 Eden Steet, Kingston
Surrey KT1 1BB
tel 020-8547 6920 *fax 020-8547 6920*

Madanayake, Senaka

117. **Richmond YOT**
Strathmore Centre
65 Strathmore Road
Teddington, Middx TW11 8AU
tel 020-8943 1691 *fax 020-8843 3240*

Merton & Sutton
Brown, Janett (aco)
based at Balham High Road
Lewis, Ingrid (exec asst)
tel 020-8767 5905 *fax 020-8682 4241*

118. **Probation Resource Centre**
Martin Harknett House
27 High Path, Wimbledon SW19 2JI
tel 020-8545 8500 *fax 020-8543 1178*

Domestic Violence Team
Brady, Dermot (spo, prog mgr)
Lindsay, Jane (treatment mgr)

Kankam, Jacqueline (p, prog facilitator)
Ayerst, Caroline (p, prog facilitator)
Francis-Hume, Lucille (women's safety wrkr)
Stevens, Sue (women's safety wrkr)
Osman, Yeliz (women's safety wrkr)
Springer, Jacqueline (women's safety wrkr)

Community Integration Team
Godfrey, Sue (spo)
Bryan, David
Cook, Nicole
Donovan, Paul
Faber, Linda
Fallows, Samantha
McDermott, Jennifer
Hallford, Diane (pso)
Hughes, Rachel (pso)
Lee, Deborah (pso)
Chauhan, Jyoti (trainee)
White, Joanna (tpo trainee)

Unpaid WorkOffice
(covers the boroughs of Merton/Sutton, Richmond/Kingston and Wandsworth)
Spooner, Pam (qa mgr)
Wilkings, Peter (qa mgr)
Eyles, Aviva (case mgr)

Pinkerton, Nina (office mgr)

119. 103 Westmead Road
Sutton SM1 4JD
tel 020-8652 9670 *fax 020-8770 3592*

Public Protection Team
Tuner-Nash, Neil (spo)
Leeming, Bridget
Stanbury, Deborah

Resettlement
Arrindell, Julia (pso)
Mullens, Jemima (pso)

Court & Assessment Team
Corrin, Jane (spo)
Moore, Lissa
Nolan, Gerry
Osbourne, Elizabeth
Sullivan, Tina
Thorne-Jones, Angela
Weatherley, Anne
Whalley, Kate
Wood, Cecelia
McFadden, Philamena (pso)

Austen, Andrew (spo, community devpt)
Dymond, Jan (pda)
Bekusch, Sarah (tpo)
Cornwall, Simon (tpo)
Davy, Natasha (tpo)

Hunt, Andy (tpo)
Keeling, Deena (tpo)
Knox, Karen (tpo)
Nunn, Kim (tpo)
Osbourne, Winsome (tpo)
Spanner, Claire (tpo)
Whitehead, Peter (tpo)

Komey, Adelaide (office mgr)

Westminster, Kensington & Chelsea
Bland, Mike (aco)
based at Dorset Close
tel 020-7563 3610
Erskine, Alex (exec asst)
tel 020-7563 3626

120. **1-5 Dorset Close**
Marylebone, London NW1 5AN
Tel 020-7563 3600 *fax 020-7560 3601*
last year tel 020-7563 3600 fax 020-7560 3601

Community Assessment Teams
Wood, Alistair (spo)
Carson, Tim
Delahunty, John
Penny, Tom
Yacobi, Arik
Hillman, John
Quashie, Sandra

Clarke, Barbara (spo)
Guilfoyle, Mike
Kamara, Max
Khan, Saeeda
Smith, Geoffrey
Udovich, Edna
Walcott, Caroline
Wilson, Terry
Durrans, Elizabeth (sessional psr writer)
Best, Charmaine (pso)
Halsall, Peter (pso)
Tulloch, Tony (pso)

Public Protection Team
Barnish, Mary (spo)
Nash, Katie
Rutterford, Lucy
Stewart, Lorraine

Trainees Unit
Wood, Alistair (spo)
Ragubir, Ansuri (pda)
Lewis, Florence (pda)
Bennett, Lorna (trainee)
Fashungba, Sheri (trainee)
Hughes, Carol (trainee)
Jones, Christopher (trainee)
Matthews, Symon (trainee)

Nwoye, Patricia (trainee)
Tomins, Tracie (trainee)

Mary Barnish (spo)
Akkad, Natalie (trainee)
Achonko, Susan (trainee)
Brown, Keith (trainee)
Gibbs, Florence (trainee)
Ozias, William Bradshaw (trainee)
Taylor, Sarah (trainee)
Moore, Angela (office mgr)

121. **75 Marsham Street**
London SW1P 3DX
tel 020-7222 0331 *fax 020-7233 2807*

Smith, Annell (prog mgr)
Lad, Sunil (treatment mgr)
Brown, Michelle (prog tutor)
Fellowes, Emma (prog tutor)
Ojo, Ina (prog tutor)
Onalaja, Ade (prog tutor)
Robson Santana (prog tutor)

Central London Courts Team
Harrington, Lilly (spo)
Mullen, Ronnie
Linton-Smith, Aidan
Alexander, Daphne (pso)
Allwood, Tim (pso)
Stanberry, Suzanne (pso)
Walsh, June (pso)
Williams, Carmel (pso)
Wood, Janet (pso)
Collier, Karen (office mgr)

Community Integration Team
Roome, Sian (spo)
Alvey, Simon
Gordon, Sylivia
Graham, Emma
Pryce, Paul
Hibbert, Marianne
Senior, Deleita
Lockwood, Katherine (pso)
White, Alex (pso)
Brown, Michelle (pso)

Whitman, Ann (office mgr)

122. **DTTO/DRR**
143 Notting Hill Gate
London W11 3LE
tel 020-7727 9491 *fax 020-7221 4954*

Joels, Jonathan (spo)
Webber, Stuart (ppo)
Reidy, Margaret (pso ppo)

Field, Celia (drr)
Fitzgerald, Ann (drr)

Jones, Liam (pso drr) (cjip)
Taylor, Clive (pso drr)
Whitman, Ann (office mgr)
Basu, Rahul (team admin)

123. **Kensington & Chelsea YOT**
36 Oxford Gardens
London W10 5UG
tel 020-7598 4705 *fax 020-7598 4715*

Hinkley, Bridget

124. **Westminster YOT**
6a Crompton Street
London W2 1ND
tel 020-7641 5422 *fax 020-7641 5311*

Hall, Jannet

125. **Middlesex Guildhall Crown Court**
see Courts Section no 154

APPROVED PREMISES IN LONDON

*Note London Hostels are listed under the
Borough in which they are located*

126. 1st Floor, 71-73 Great Peter Street
London, SW1P 2BN
tel 020-7960 1043 *fax 020-7960 1116*

Denton, Claude (aco)
tel 020-7960 1142
Hepburn, Jackie (exec asst)

*Note: All Approved Premises (Hostels) referrals
are made via the Central Referral Scheme,
including those that are Voluntary Managed.*

127. **Central Referral Scheme**
Mitre House
223-237 Borough High Street
London SE1 1JD
tel 020-7407 7293 *fax 020-7357 7140*

Ray, Jessica (snr rgnl officer/mgr)
Adeyemi, Tunde (referral officer)
Barron, Clive (referral officer)
Skinner, Madeleine (referral officer)
Pearson, John (admin)

UNPAID WORK OFFICES

*Note London Unpaid Work Offices are listed
under the Borough in which they are located*

128. 71-73 Great Peter Street
London SW1P 2BN
Pasquale, Ginny (aco West & South
Quadrants)
Harington Hawes, Sarah (exec asst)

tel 020-7960 1850

Shaw, Jill (aco North & East Quadrants)
Harington Hawes, Sarah (exec asst)
tel 020-7960 1850

Office	Areas covered
Enfield	Barnet/Enfield, Camden/ Islington and Haringey
Forest Gate	Newham, Hackney and Tower Hamlets
Harpenden House	Lambeth and Southwark
Harrow/Uxbridge	Harrow/Hillingdon and Brent
Beckenham	Bromley/Bexley, Croydon, Greenwich/Lewisham
Romford	Redbridge/Waltham Forest and Barking & Dagenham/Havering
Southall	Ealing/Hounslow, Hammersmith & Fulham, Westminster and Kensington & Chelsea
Wimbledon	Merton, Sutton, Richmond & Kingston and Wandsworth

VOLUME PROGRAMMES

Tuhill, Louise (aco)
based at Great Peter Street

129. **Seymour Place C-SOGP/DV Unit**
175 Seymour Place, London W1H 5TP
tel 020-7723 2399 *fax 020-7723 2239*

Norman, Adrian (spo prog mgr)
Cheney, Clare (IDAP facilitator)
Cover, Gwen (treatment mgr)
Riddell, Elizabeth
Biddy, Michelle (women's safety wrkr)

130. **Acton C-SOGP/DVIP Unit**
4 Birkbeck Road
Acton, London W3 6BE
tel 020-8992 5863 *fax 020-8993 5942*

Terry, Mike (spo prog mgr)
Sawyer, Malcolm (treatment mgr)
Yaiche, Susan (treatment mgr)
Ellner, Dawn
Addy, Hilda (admin)

131. **Wimbledon DV Centre**
Martin Harknett House
27 High Path, Wimbledon
London SW19 2JL
tel 020-8545 8500 *fax 020-8543 1178*

Brady, Dermot (spo prog mgr)
Crutch, Tracey (team admin)

132. **'What Works' Unit**
Crosby House
9-13 Elmfield Road
Bromley, Kent BR1 1LT
tel 020-8464 3430 *fax 020-84661571*

Niechcial, Steve (spo progs co-ord)
Treeby, Hilary (exec asst)
Dalrymple, Derek

133. 6 Beckenham Road
Beckenham Kent BR3 4LR
tel 020-8658 3511 *fax 020-8658 8678*

Offender Programmes Team
Osborne, Emma (treatment mgr)
Thomas, Hannah (psychologist)
Portman, Brett (case mgr)
Akin, Yemi (case mgr)
McMillan, Faye (pso)
Sowoolu, Adetokunbo (pso)
Ottewell, Anna (pso)
Onuogu, Ifeoma (pso)
Matthews, Julie (pso)
Mills, David (pso)
Chambers, Sabrina (pso)
Barnes, Danny (proj supvr)
Phipps, Alan (proj supvr)

134. **377 Cambridge Heath Road**
London E2 9RD
tel 020-7739 7931 *fax 020-7729 8600*

McNaughton, Vivienne (spo prog mgr)
Kirk, Sharon (prog mgr)
Mazzone, Georgina (prog admin)

135. **Camden Women's Centre**
199 Arlington Road
Camden, London NW1 7HA
tel 020-7267 2646 *fax 020-7284 1967*

Programmes: Think First, ART and ASRO
Bailey, Mary (prog director) 020-7428 8479
Borgen, Deborah (ART treatment mgr)
Davies, Anna (prog tutor) 020-7428 8484
Bamford, Emma (psychologist) 020-7428 8478
Prendergast, Beverly (admin) 020-7428 8440

136. Leeland House, Leeland Road
Ealing London W13 9HH
tel 020-8 840 6464 *fax 020-8579 7835*

Terry, Mike (spo prog mgr) based at Birkbeck Road
Modrate, William (Bill) (acting spo)

137. **Hendon**
Allied House
3 Burnt Oak Broadway
Edgware, Middx HA8 5LT
tel 020-8205 2561 *fax 020-8205 5462*

Bailey, Mary (spo prog mgr)
Williams, David (spo)
Borgen, Deborah (treatment mgr)
Alloui, Samantha (treatment mgr)
Yapar, Osman (prog tutor)
Vekaria, Jessica (prog tutor)
Taylor, Michele (prog admin)
Radcliffe, Frank (pso)
Forde, Patricia (team admin)

138. **Ilford Probation Centre**
277 High Road
Ilford, Essex IG1 1QQ
tel 020-8478 8500 *fax 020-8553 1972*

Leckey, Mac (spo prog mgr)
Henson, Matthew (treatment mgr)
Gardiner, Judith (treatment mgr)
Rose, Yvonne (treatment mgr)
Christopher, Lucy (prog tutor)
Charles, David
Maroni, Daniela (pso)
Chapman, Ann (office mgr)
Wheal, Tania (prog admin)
Lawson, Rachel (prog admin)

139. **Lewisham**
208 Lewisham High Street
London SE13 6JL
tel 0208 297 7300
fax 0208 297 7304
Leighton, Michelle (treatment mgr)
Agbukor, Humphrey
Bromley, Kim
Hutchinson, Joel
Knight, Deborah
Laisee, Jamie
Nazereth, Lisa
Plumley, Jodie
Reuben, Audrey
Shewry, Jonathan
Simpson, Teresa
Subherwal, Navinder
Watson, Katherine
Whereat, Lindsey
Booker, Richie (prog tutor)
Sangowawa, Ade (prog admin)

140. **75 Marsham Street**
London SW1P 3DX
tel 020-7222 0331 *fax 020-7222 2807*

Dal Pozzo, Magnolia (treatment mgr)
Colk, Kay (prog admin) based at Askew
Road
Darnell, Caroline (prog tutor)
Fogarthy, Cathy (prog admin)

141. **Martin Harknett House**
27 High Path
South Wimbledon
London SW19 2JL
tel 020-8545 8500 *fax 020-8543 1178*

Godfrey, Sue (spo prog mgr)
Onibje, Kemi (treatment mgr)
Almeida, Russell (proj supvr)
Hallford, Dianne (prog admin)

142. **401 St John Street**
London EC1V 4RW
tel 020-7014 9800 *fax 020-7014 9801*

Hignett, Christopher (spo prog mgr)
Ibrahim, Jenny (treatment mgr)
Amin, Nural (treatment mgr) based at
Hendon
Eronfolami, Olaynika (pso)
Taki, Zainab (prog admin)

143. **117 Stockwell Road**
London SW9 9TN
tel 020-7326 7700 *fax 020-7326 7701*

Johnson, Georgia (spo prog mgr)
Ramsey, Joanne (treatment mgr)
Murray, Pauline (prog tutor)
Olaleye, Dolly (prog admin)
Jenkins, Tracy (prog admin)

SUBSTANCE MISUSE

*Note London DTTO/DRR Units are listed under
the Borough in which they are located*

144. Mitre House
223-237 Borough High Street
London SE1 1JD
tel 020-7740 8500 (switchboard)
fax 020-7740 8447

Mitchell, Darian (aco)
tel 020-7740 8564
Burns, Barbara (exec asst)
tel 020-7740 8524

Felix, Lorna (drugs & alcohol devpt mgr)
020-7740 8522
Latimer, Robin (drugs & alcohol devpt
mgr)
020-7740 8518

ETE & HOUSING

145. Partnership Unit, Mitre House
223/237 Borough High Street
London SE1 1JD
tel 020-7740 8530 *fax 020-7740 8447*

Davies, Ilid (aco, ete & housing)
Burns, Barbara (exec asst)
tel 020-7740 8524

ETE/Skills for Life
(based at Great Peter Street)
Austen, Nigel (basic skills mgr)
tel 020-7960 1089

(based at Mitre House)
Heal, Rosanna (ETE devpt mgr)
tel 020-7740 8531
Mensah, Emmanual (emplt pathfinder proj
mgr)

Housing
Keever, Lourdes (housing devpt mg)
mob 079565 08758
Mellish, Paul (housing devpt mgr)
tel 020-7740 8560
Tooth, Amanda (housing devpt mgr)
tel 020-7740 8514
Tully, Martin (housing devpt mgr)
tel 020-7740 8528
Wright, Noah (asst building mgr)

VICTIM/RISK MANAGEMENT

Jones, Ian (aco Victims/Domestic Violence/ Sex
Offenders Programmes)
based at Great Peter Street
tel 020-7960 1852

146. **199 Arlington Road**
London NW1 7HA
tel 020-7428 8474 *fax 020-7428 8431*

Bartram, Diana (spo)
Crane, Susan (p, po vlo)
Dench, Alison (po vlo)
Glennie, Katrina (po vlo)
Shrier, Linda (p, po vlo)
Sielman, Marie (po vlo)
Eadie, Linda (vlo)

147. **Ilford Office**
4th Floor, Olympic House
28/42 Clements Road
Ilford, Essex IG1 1BA
tel 020-8262 6927 *fax 020-8220 2356*

Riley, Brian (spo)
Osula, Linda (vlo)
Joens, Sandra (vlo)
Ahmed, Moulvi (vlo)

Harrison, Sharon (vlo)
Styles, Karen (p, vlo)
Nelson, Tanya (p, vlo)
Goddard, Annete (vlo)
Bailey, Angela (vlo)
Lachman, Helen (p, vlo)
Lyon, Malcolm (vlo)
Andrew-Dzotsi, Lister (trainee)
Chaudhury, Rejaur (trainee)
Catnot, Jackelyn (trainee)
Clarke, Alexander (trainee)
Deen, Alhan (trainee)
Musa, Suhel (trainee)
Ihedioha, Samson (trainee)
Kodish, Jacquie (snr team admin)

148. 4 Birkbeck Road
   Acton Ealing
   London W3 6BE
   tel 020-8993 8613 *fax 020-8992 7408*

   Ijpelaar, Veronica (vlo)
   Watson, Karen (vlo)
   Marin, Elisabetta (vlo)
   Kaur, Sukhvinder (team admin)

149. **Crosby House**
   9/13 Elmfield Road
   Bromley BR1 1LT
   tel 020-8466 7630/7631 *fax 020-8313 1621*

   Pollard, Corinne (IDAP facilitator)
   Porter, Nick (IDAP facilitator)
   Gordon, Alison
   Bowie, Eleanor (vlo)
   Lockett, Anne (vlo)
   Rose, Sarah (vlo)
   Whitely, Lisa (vlo)

150. 45 High St
   Kingston-upon-Thames KT1 1LQ
   tel 020-8939 4119 *fax 020-8549 8990*

   Rooney, Denise (spo)
   Barlow, Annie (p, vlo)
   Harwood, John (vlo)
   Kirk, Belinda (p, vlo)
   Walters, Fiona (vlo)

COURTS & OASys TEAMS

151. 71-73 Great Peter Street
   London, SW1P 2BN
   tel 020-7960 1098
   Hubbard, Louise (aco)
   Hepburn, Jackie (exec asst)

Crown Courts in the London Area	Borough in which Situated
Blackfriars Crown Court	Southwark
Central Criminal Court	City of London
Croydon Crown Court	Croydon
Harrow Crown Court	Harrow
Inner London Crown Court	Southwark
Isleworth Crown Court	Middlesex
Kingston Crown Court	Kingston-upon-Thames
Middlesex Guildhall Crown Court	Westminster
Royal Courts of Justice (Criminal Division, Court of Appeal)	Westminster
Snaresbrook Crown Court	Waltham Forest
Southwark Crown Court	Southwark
Wood Green Crown Court	Haringey
Woolwich Crown Court	Greenwich

152. **Central Criminal Court**
   Old Bailey, London, EC4M 7EH
   tel 020-7248 3277 *fax 020-7236 6692*

   Lakhi, Yasmin (spo)
   Dixon, Kathy
   Hope-Wynne, Tim
   Innis, Cheryl
   Kirwin, Kevin
   Haggett, Sarah
   Moran, Sylvia (office mgr)

153. **Court of Appeal (Criminal Division)**
   Room E303 Royal Courts of Justice
   London WC2A 2LL
   tel 020-7947 6066 *fax 020-7947 6704*

   Gardner, Ken

154. **Middlesex Guildhall Crown Court**
   Broad Sanctuary, Parliament Square
   London SW1P 3BB
   tel 020-7202 0370 *fax 020-7233 2215*

   Ferguson, Kathy (spo)
   Rugen, Oliver
   Edwards, Dave
   Martin, Jill (office mgr)

155. **Southwark Crown Court**
   1 English Grounds, London, SE1 2HU
   tel 020-7403 1045 *fax 020-7403 8602*

   Hearne, Tony (spo)
   Fleming, Rhonda
   Coad, Mick
   Angel, Terry

156. **Inner London Crown Court**
   21 Harper Road, London SE1 6AW
   tel 020-7407 7333 *fax 020-7403 8637*

Mavunga, Peter (spo)
Burkett, Mike
Kedney, Terry (Teresa)
Spring, Pamela
Waterman, Pat
Blackstock, Samantha (pso)
Phillips, Marva (office mgr)

157. **Blackfriars Crown Court**
1-15 Pocock Street, London SE1 OBT
tel 020-7922 5801 fax 020-7401 9138

Connolly, Mike (spo)
Benker, Theresia
Jones, Mechelle
Apatita, Sandra (psco)
Ofoti, Monica (psco)
Regis, Linda (psco)

158. **Wood Green Crown Court Team**
Woodall House, Lordship Lane
Wood Green, London N22 5LF
tel 020-8881 1400 ext 2189/92

Cooke, Pamela (spo)
Fletcher, Charmaine
Charlemagne, Patrick (lpo)
Blower, Pam (acting snr team admin)

159. **Harrow Crown Court**
Hailsham Drive, Harrow
Middx HA1 4TU
tel 020-8424 2294 *fax 020-8424 9346*

Akin, Margaret (spo)
James, Gloria (spo)
Davis, Althea
McDonnell, Patrick
Waite, Emma (lpo)
Moss, Carol (snr team admin)

160. **Snaresbrook Crown Court**
Crown Court, Hollybush Hill
Snaresbrook, E11 1QW
tel 020-8530 7561 *fax 020-8530 1399*

Ashby, Jackie (spo)
Beamish, Edie
Dookit, Prabha
Kilbey, Graham
McMillian, Sean
Stewart, Sonia
Winter, Emma-Jane
Battiwala, Zamed (pso)

161. **Croydon Crown Court**
The Law Courts
Altyre Road, Croydon CR9 5AB
tel 0208-681 5039 *fax 0208-681 6604*

Benjamin, Joe(spo)
Broderick, Ann
Harkins, David (p)
Hunt, Jacky (p)
Raynor, Lindsay (pso)
Banks, Anne (office mgr)

162. **Isleworth Crown Court**
36 Ridgeway Road
Isleworth, Middx. TW7 5LP
tel 020-8380 4500 *fax 020-8758 9650*

Turley, Kevin (spo)
Baker, Janice
Milne, Robert
Watson, Will
Pinto, Wendy (snr team admin)

163. **Kingston Crown Court**
6/8 Penrhyn Road
Kingston upon Thames KT1 2BB
tel 020-8240 2500 *fax 020-8240 2555*

Nelson, Andy (spo)
Fry, Anne (snr team admin)
Byrne, Ellen (p, pso)
Ephson, Elizabeth (psco)

164. **Woolwich Crown Court**
2 Belmarsh Road
London SE28 0EY
tel 020-8312 7000 *fax 020-8317 1605*

Dancer, Mike (spo)
Barton, Sue (office mgr)
Frogatt, Roger
Lewin, Alphonso
Woolstone, Diane

YOUTH & STREET CRIME

165. Mitre House
223/237 Borough High Street
London SE1 1JD
tel 020-7323 7012

Mitchell, Darian (aco)
Responsible for ISMS and ICCP

LOCAL JUSTICE AREAS

*for fines enquiries for all Central and NE Area
Courts plus Camden & Islington, Greenwich
& Lewisham, Woolwich, Lambeth &
Southwark, Tower Bridge, West London and
Wandsworth Magistrates' Courts: Central
Accounting Office 0845 940 0111*

Central Area

City of London LJA
City of London Magistrates' Court

YOUTH COURTS BY REGION

Youth Court	London Borough in which Court is Situated	London Area(s) covered by Youth Court
Acton	Ealing	
Balham	Wandsworth	Wandsworth, Lambeth
Barking	Barking	Barking & Dagenham
Barnet	Barnet	
Bexley	Bexley	
Brent	Brent	
Brentford	Hounslow	
Bromley	Bromley	
Camberwell (Divnl Youth Court)	Southwark	Southwark, Greenwich, Lewisham
Croydon	Croydon	
Enfield	Enfield	
Haringey	Haringey	
Harrow	Harrow	
Havering	Romford	
Kingston	Kingston	
Redbridge	Ilford	
Richmond	Richmond	
Stratford	Newham	
Sutton	Wallington	
Tower Hamlets (sitting at Thames MC)	Tower Hamlets	Tower Hamlets, Hackney, Camden, Islington
Uxbridge	Hillingdon	
Walthamstow	Waltham Forest	
West London (Divnl Youth Court)	Hammersmith	Hammersmith & Fulham, Kensington & Chelsea, Westminster
Wimbledon	Merton	

City of Westminster LJA
Bow Street Magistrates' Court
Horseferry Road Magistrates' Court
Marylebone Magistrates' Court

North East Area

Barking LJA
Barking Magistrates' Court
Hackney & Tower Hamlets LJA
Thames Magistrates' Court
Havering LJA
Havering Magistrates' Court
Newham LJA
Stratford Magistrates' Court
Redbridge LJA
Redbridge Magistrates' Court
Waltham Forest LJA
Waltham Forest Magistrates' Court

North West Area

Barnet LJA
Barnet Magistrates' Court

Hendon Magistrates' Court (closed for rebuilding)
Brent LJA
Brent Magistrates' Court
Camden & Islington LJA
Highbury Corner Magistrates' Court
Enfield LJA
Enfield Magistrates' Court
Haringey LJA
Haringey Magistrates' Court
Harrow LJA
Harrow Magistrates' Court
Hillingdon LJA
Uxbridge Magistrates' Court

South East Area

Bexley LJA
Bexley Magistrates' Court
Bromley LJA
Bromley Magistrates' Court
Croydon LJA
Croydon Magistrates' Court

Greenwich & Lewisham LJA
Greenwich Magistrates' Court
Woolwich Magistrates' Court
Lambeth & Southwark LJA
Camberwell Green Magistrates' Court
Tower Bridge Magistrates' Court
Sutton LJA
Sutton Magistrates' Court

South West Area

Ealing LJA
Ealing Magistrates' Court
Acton Magistrates' Court
Hounslow LJA
Brentford Magistrates' Court
Feltham Magistrates' Court
**Hammersmith & Fulham and
Kensington & Chelsea LJA**
West London Magistrates' Court
Kingston upon Thames LJA
Kingston upon Thames Magistrates' Court
Merton LJA
Wimbledon Magistrates' Court
Richmond upon Thames Magistrates'
Court
Wandsworth LJA
South Western Magistrates' Court

PRISONS

166. **Partnership Unit**
Mitre House
223/237 Borough High Street
London SE1 1JD
tel 020-7740 8500 *fax 020-7740 8447*

Davies, Ilid (aco prisons)
tel 020-7740 8530

Burns, Barbara (exec asst)
tel 020-7740 8524

167. HMP **Brixton**
Jebb Avenue, London SW2 5XF
tel 020-8588 6000 *fax 020-8588 6283*
direct dial 020-8588 + ext

Probation clerk 020-8588 6062
probn fax 020-8588 6342

Howson, Yvette (spo) ext 6201
Hall, Kevin ext 6345
Love, Joy (p) ext 6343
Reed, Thomas ext 6344
Wright, Susan
Barker, Yvonne (bail info off) ext 6017
James, Sue (foreign nationals co-ord) ext
6017

168. HMP **Belmarsh**
Western Way, Thamesmead
Woolwich, London SE28 0EB
tel 020-8331 4400 *fax 020-8331 4401*

fax (probn) 020-8317 8719
Discipline ext 300/301/313

Atkin, Margaret (spo) 020-8331 4600
Norton, Louise 020-8331 4580
Lauchlan, Neil 020-8331 4713
Ashby, Jackie 020-8331 4628
Watchorn, Anne (bail info asst)
Ajayi, Ade (pso)
Vacancy (pso resettlement co-ord)
Vacancy (pso resettlement co-ord)

169. HMP **Holloway**
Parkhurst Road, London N7 0NU
tel 020-7979 4400 *fax 020-7979 4401*

Governor: Willetts, Edd
Head of Resettlement :Brady, Allen

probn fax 020-7979 4763

Professional & Legal Visits
tel 020-7979 4760
probation admin
tel 020-7979 4628/4478

Herson, Karen (spo) 020-7979 4486
Roome, Sîan 020-7979 4630
McLeod, Geraldine 020-7979 4482
Knaggs, Belinda 020-7979 4480
Fairbank, Sally 020-7979 4874
Linton, Donna (pso) 020-7979 4483

170. HMP **Pentonville**
Caledonian Road, London N7 8TT
tel 020-7023 7000 *fax 020-7023 7250*

Tate, Alex (spo) 020-7023 7174
Edwards, Dave 020-7023 7176
Sutton, Oliver 020-7023 7175
Thomas, Lee-Ann 020-7023 7177
Field, Colin 020-7023 7178
Jacob, Ann 020-7023 7317
Anderson, Karen (pso) 020-7023 7179

171. HMP **Wandsworth**
Heathfield Road
London SW18 3HS
tel 020-8588 4000 *fax 020-8588 4001*

probn fax 020-8588 4011
Professional and legal visits
020-8588 4176
Probation admin/duty
020-8588 4229
Probation HDC Clerks
020-8588 4125

Pilgrim, Mary (spo) 020-8588 4300
Milton, Janet 020-8588 4235
Brown, Sonia 020-8588 4235
Nevill, Ralph 020-8588 4233
New, Sue 020-8588 4234
Bhui, Hindpal 020-8588 4094
Hogarth, Claire 020-8588 4233
Benge, Philippa (pso) 020-8588 4237
McMahon, Patricia (bail info asst) 020-8588 4362

172. HMP **Wormwood Scrubs**
Du Cane Road, London W12 0AE
tel 020-8588 3200
fax 020-8588 3201
probn office 020-8588 3238
probn fax 020-8588 3549

Healthcare fax (Suicide alerts) 020-8588 3546
Legal Visits fax 020-8588 3563
(all Legal Visits booked by fax)

Fearnley, Janet (spo) 020-8588 3237
Banse, Amrik 020-8588 3224
Burton, Joss 020-8588 3342
Catling, Sarah 020-8588 3575
Dixon, Kathy 020-8588 3341
Falk, Chloe 020-8588 3575
Harris, Jane 020-8588 3238
Newlyn, Patricia 020-8588 3238
Ward, Emma 020-8588 3240
Farrant, Bryony (pso) 020-8588 3581

173. HMP **Latchmere House**
Church Road, Ham Common
Richmond upon Thames TW10 5HH
tel 020-8588 6650 *fax 020-8588 6698*

Job Club/Probation fax 020-8588 6669

Convisser, Sharon (spo) 020-8588 6711/6665
Beresford, Graham 020-8588 6657
Wilson, Christine (admin) 020-8588 6656

174. HM YOI & Remand Cerntre **Feltham**
Bedfont Road, Feltham
Middlesex TW13 4ND
tel 020-8844 5220 *fax 020-8844 5173*

Hales, Liz (spo) 020-8844 5300
Charles, Dave ext 5314
Wood, Shirley ext 5298
Belham, Charlotte ext 5298
Marshall, Sandra (pso bail info) ext 5234
Ashton, Nina (pso) ext 5234
Wharton, Caro (pso) ext 5512
Cunningham, Serena (pso) ext 5537
Scott, Amy (pso) ext 5455

Penny, Ruth (team admin) ext 5299
Prother, Helen (p, team admin HDC) ext 5236
Brown, Kate (p, team admin HDC) ext 5236

Home Detention Curfew Units

175. **SE Area & SW Area**
292 Camberwell Road
Southwark, London SE5 0DL
tel 020-7701 6640 *fax 020-7708 4384*

McVinnie, Jim (mgr)
Jones, Alan
Smallbone, Richard
Whitehead, Michael
Dada, Esther (temp pso)
Michaels, Annette (temp pso)
Okusu, Jessie (temp pso)

176. **North East Area**
4th Floor, Olympic House
28 / 42 Clements Road
Ilford, Essex IG1 1BA
tel 020-8478 8141 *fax 020-8553 8151*

Mandy Longshaw (pso) ext 6928
Doreen Birthwright (pso) ext 6928
Marina Khan (admin) ext 6948

177. **North West Area**
Allied House (1st Floor)
3 Burnt Oak Broadway
Edgware, Middx HAB 5LT
tel 020-8205 2561 *fax 020-8205 5462*

Dada, Esther (hdc off)
Manning, Sheila (hdc off)
Pearce, Mary (hdc off)

Unions: London Offices

178. Mitre House
223-237 Borough High Street
London, SE1 1JD
tel 020-7740 8500

Association of Black Probation Officers (ABPO)
Roye, Sue (natnl co-ord)
tel 020-7740 8537

NAAPS National Association of Asian Probation Staff
Khan, Shamim (chair)

NAPO National Association of Probation Officers
Carr, Desmond
Cohen, Jack

Unison
Murphy, Joan
West, Lesley
White, Veronica

GMB/SCOOP
Roffey, Derek (branch chair)

GREATER MANCHESTER PROBATION AREA

Out of hours emergency contact point
tel 0161-226 1179

e-mail
Firstname.Surname@manchester.probation.
gsx.gov.uk

1. **Head Office**
   6th floor, Oakland House
   Talbot Road, Manchester M16 0PQ
   tel 0161-872 4802 *fax 0161-872 3483*

   Crawforth, John (co)
   Noah, Chris (dir interventions)
   Hamilton, Roz (dir offender mgmnt)
   Barker, Penny (aco)
   Groves, Nigel (aco)
   Seale, Manjit (aco)
   Bate, Barbara (aco)
   Bristow, Owen (head of i.t.)
   Kelly, Phil (info services mgr)
   Jammeh, Celia (prtnrshps/addtnl funding mgr)
   Jiacoumi, Maria (diversity mgr)

   Jackson, Graham (secy/solicitor)
   Millington, John (treasurer)
   Fury, Donna (hd of pr & comms)
   Thornley, Lucy (head of h.r.)
   McMullen, Julie (pa to co/board clerk)
   Hurley, Karen (housing & resettlement mgr)
   Parris, Helen (librarian/info officer)
   Drake, Sally (offender emplt devpt mgr)
   Brierley, Derek (dist mgr ecp)

2. **Manchester Crown Court**
   Crown Court Buildings, Crown Square
   Manchester M3 3FL
   tel 0161-954 1750/3 *fax 0161-839 3856*

   Minshull Street Crown Court
   Courts of Justice, Minshull Street
   Manchester M1 3FS

tel 0161-954 7654 & 7661/2 *fax 0161-954 7664*

Smith, Celia (spo)
Ali, Salma
Baggoley, Martin
Campbell, Mark
Critchley, David
Edwards, Les
Entwistle, Susan
Goodfellow, Jonathon
Ledder, Jacqueline
Royle, Lynn
Worsley, Andrew
Antrobus, Katie (pso)
Clarke, Fiona (pso)
Dyke, Brenda (pso)
Hodgkinson, Katie (pso)
Hollinworth, April (pso)
Rigby, Emma (pso)

3. **Bolton Crown Court**
   1st floor, Black Horse Street
   off Deansgate, Bolton BL1 1SU
   tel (01204) 372119 *fax (01204) 380963*

4. **Magistrates Court Building**
   Probation Dept, 2nd Floor
   Quay House, Quay Street
   Manchester M3 3JE
   tel 0161-830 2250 *fax 0161-834 3421*

   Keane, Ruth (spo)
   Orr, Cranmer (spo)
   Barnes, Susy
   Bell, Abigail
   Carton, Kathleen
   Cuddy, Louise
   Davies, Howard
   Dutton, Ben
   Entwistle, Karen
   Evans, Maria
   Graham, Peter
   Greenwood, Emily
   Hyland, Julia
   James, Caroline
   Lee-Kilgariff, Mark
   Lundie, Faye
   McNorton, Barry
   Mears, Val
   Nelson, Tania
   Roberts, Priscilla
   Smith, Mary
   Stapleton, Samantha
   Treherne, Nikki

   Bailey, Diana (pso)
   Brownjohn, Julie (pso)

Edwards, Helen (pso)
Evans, June (pso)
Everton, Sue (pso)
Hilton, Louise (pso)
McDermott, Wendy (pso)
Percy, Stephen (pso)
Raggatt, Doris (pso)
Simpson, Pamela (pso)

Bolton

5. St Helena Mill
    St Helena Road, **Bolton** BL1 2JS
    tel (01204) 387699 *fax (01204) 382372*

Brimley, John (district mgr)
Elliott, Nigel (spo)
Hunt, Sean (spo)
Martin, Patricia (spo)
Riley, Kath (spo)

Aslam, Mahmooda
Bannister, Sue
Barnett, Brendan
Butler, Gaynor
Carter, Sue
Clarke, Tracey
Copeland, Susan
Davies, Lynn
Donlan, Mike (tops)
Dunn, Lisa
Eniola, Yinka
France, Janice
Gregory, Alison
Holmes, Zoe
Johnson, Ted
Jones, Karl
Luxton, Suzanne
McDaid, Camille
McGuiness, Samantha
Maddix, Leonie
Maurizi, John
Murphy, Diane
Redfern, Mandy
Rigby, Ben
Scott, Gillian
Sheerin, Karen
Staines, Tracey
Stevenson, Chris
Wake, Rob
Waterhouse, Mandy

Gallagher, Joe (police off)
Ankers, Dave (pso tops)
Bailey, Linda (pso dtto)
Barlow, Jill (pso)
Davies, Ellen (pso)
Downes, Shirley (pso)
Edwards, Chris (pso)

Gardner, Sarah (pso)
Grundy, Joanne (pso)
Hardman, Jim (pso)
Hinchcliffe, Allan (pso)
Holmes, Val (pso)
Hopkinson, Stuart (pso)
Julien, Gordon (pso)
Knight, Phil (pso)
McDonald, Sue (pso)
Moffat, Steve (pso)
Nikrafter, Tish (pso)
Porter, Craig (pso)
Roberts, Nadine (pso)
Sullivan, Jim (pso)
Unsworth, Cathy (pso)
Wateraorth, Kath (pso)
West, Marie (pso)

Unpaid Work
Seddon, Peter (mgr)
Cadwalader, Bob (qa mgr)
Abbott, Bob (cpo)
Hardman, Jim (cpo)
Hunter, Pat (cpo)
Jones, Bill (cpo)
Julien, Gordon (cpo)
Stroud, Anne (cpo)
Sullivan Jim (cpo)
Ahmed, Heather (cps)
Clarke, Bill (cps)
Daley, Paul (cps)
Dixon, Elaine (cps)
Doyle, Julie (cps)
Gayle, Donald (cps)
Heald, Ronald (cps)
Mike, Adolphus (cps)
O'Neal, Phil (cps)
Rothwell, Norman (cps)
Smith, Ken (cps)

Bury & Rochdale

6. Argyle House, Castlecroft Court
    Castlecroft Road **Bury** BL9 0LN
    tel 0161-764 9514 *fax 0161-761 2638*

Burton-Francis, Sheron (spo)
Hulse, Preston (spo)
Charleson, Mags
Deegan, Karen
Fairclough, Justine
Hardacre, Susan
Harrison, Alan
Iqbal, Zahida
Knowles, Leah
McGovern, Gary
Prince, Andy
Riches, Iris

Straughan, Kenrick
Taylor, Sarah
Travis, Simon
Wright, Wayne

Connell, Avis (case mgr)
Davidson, Robert (case mgr)
Egan, Julie (case mgr)
Jones, Francine (case mgr)
Rimmer, Chris (case mgr)
Sherlock, Rachel (case mgr)

7. St Michael's House, Oldham Road
Middleton M24 2LH
tel 0161-643 0826 *fax 0161-643 2414*

Culkin, Pat (dist mgr Bury/Rochdale)
Butterworth, Vance (dist admin mgr)
Hampson, Joan (dist admin mgr)
Henderson, Barbara (mgmnt secy)

Yunus, Mohamed (spo)
Grafton, Fiona
King, Jonathon
Monk, Donna
Murphy, Alison
Robb-Elliott, Mike
Rothwell, Jenny
Ahmed, Sophia (pso)
Ward, Pauline (pso)
Garton, Jack (vlo)
Simpson, Ann (vlo)

DTTO
Litting, Deirdre
Nolan, Judith
Travis, Sue
Yuille, Wendy (clinical team ldr)
Doherty, Patrick (nurse)
McGinn, Phil (nurse)
Bradley, Damien (health wrkr)
Green, Andy (health wrkr)
Howarthm Suzanne (health wrkr)
Birtles, Rod (pso)
Burton, Roy (pso)
Haynes, Mike (pso)
O'Shaugnessy, Lorna (pso)
Squibbs, Emma (pso)

8. 193/195 Drake Street
Rochdale OL11 1EF
tel (01706) 653411 *fax (01706) 713524*

Johnston, Graham (spo)
Perry, Hellen (spo)
Carter, Peter (progs mgr)

Bouhadiba, Nadira
Chadwick, Wendy
Cunningham, Gary

Dale, Margaret
Daybank, Kath
Heyes, Rosemary
Holden, Jeanne
Hoyle, Jayne
Jackson, David
McClintock, Tania
Nabi, Yasmin
Prince, Andrew
Schofield, Jim
Shkandrij, Alex

Briddon, Janine (pso)
Carney, Auriol (pso)
Fletcher, Ray (pso tops)
Kay, Jonathan (pso tops)
McCorriston, Paula (pso)
Sidderley, Colin (pso)
Starkie, Vicki (pso)
Taylor, Milka (pso)

'Think First'
Rochdale/Bury Cluster
Fletcher, Chris (treatment mgr)
Lorimer, Tina (treatment mgr)
Begum, Shazia (pso tutor)
Hay, Gemma (pso tutor)
Yates, Corin (pso tutor)
Smith, Josie (pso tutor)
Farrington, Phyl (pso)

9. **Unpaid Work** 151 Green Lane
Heywood, Lancs OL10 2EW
tel (01706) 620702 *fax (01706) 368951*

Pickering, Yvonne (mgr)
Connor-Crookes, Wendy (cpo)
Dunn, Ray (cpo)
Gawthorpe, Brian (cpo)
Kennell, Elaine (cpo)
Rimmer, Christopher (cpo)
Shaw, Pauline (cso wkshp)
Yates, Steven (cpo)
Bevan, Bob (cps)
Biggs, Roy (cps)
Booth, Lawrence (cps)
Brooks, John (cps)
Caine, Peter (cps)
Connolly, Maria (cps)
Jones, Gerrad (cps)
Kershaw, John (cps)
Lashley, Curtis (cps)
McLaren, N (cps)
Oliver, Bill (cps)
Shaw, Terry (cps)
Walton, Donald (cps)
Wild, Stuart (cps)

Manchester

10. **Manchester City Management Unit**
Victoria Park, Laindon Road
Longsight, Manchester M14 5YJ
tel 0161-224 0231 *fax 0161-248 6953*

Barnes, Richard (dist mgr)
Kyle, Tim (dist mgr)
Bywater, Margaret (dist admin mgr)
Gates, Pam (dist admin mgr)
Shepherd, Andrea (dist admin mgr)
Wild, Andrea (dist admin mgr)
Archer, Carol (acting dist admin mgr)
Bellamy, Claire (spo)
Wood, Nick (spo c&d, prolific offenders)
Jones, Lisa (pso, vlo)
Sharples, Margaret (pso, vlo)

11. 87 Moss Lane West
Moss Side Manchester M15 5PE
tel 0161-226 3515 *fax 0161-232 0649*

Bellamy, Claire (spo)
Charles, Bob (spo)
Coles, Sarah (spo)
Mitchell, Jacqui (spo)
Young, Cheryl (spo)
Bell, Mike
Bryan, Shelley
Casey, Susan
Christopher, Ossie
Cropper, Marilyn
Dalby, Lisa
Diamond, Daniel
Foster, Susan
Horn, Anna
Latham, Helen
Oliver, Lisa-Jo
Reynolds, Tim
Simpson, Craig
Totten, John
Ross, Kirk (pso)

DTTO
Bench, Sue (pso)
Buckley, Bev (pso)
Frain, Rebecca (pso)
Hanley, Paulette (pso)
Hart, Jaki (pso)
Homewood, Chris (pso)
McHenry, David (pso)
Parker, Sharon (pso)
Saunders, Laura (pso)
Taylor, Sue (pso)
Vassell, Janice (pso)
Dallas, Mo (mds)
Hayes, Jimmy (mds)
Kearns, Michael (mds)

Rapley, Andy (mds)
Smith, Claire (mds)
Toothill, Lianne (mds)

'Think First'
Manchester Cluster
Hilton, Paul (treatment mgr)
Stanley, Mark (treatment mgr)
Boyle, Frank (pso)
Clarke, Kim (pso)
Derrett, Kevin (pso)
Goddard, Katie (pso)
Gwilt, Michelle (pso)
Kierney, Luke (pso)
Mather, Helen (pso)
Naylor, Laura (pso)
Quinn, Karen (pso)

12. 20 Humphrey Streeet
Cheetham Hill Manchester M8 7JR
tel 0161-795 1777 *fax 0161-720 6707*

Wright, Louise (spo)
Murphy, Lindsey (spo)
Black, Mike
Donovan, William
Higgins, Jayne
John, Andrea
Keeling, Philip
Lashimba, Desnya
Murphy, Aine
Phillips, Lynne
Raoof, Farha
Saunders, Barry
Seymour, Brian
Wright, Sarah

Coppinger, Jayne (trainee)
Franklin, Kate (trainee)
Jones, Adrian (trainee)
Mansfield, Kirsty (trainee)
Crellin, Julie (cpo)
Giamas, Dawn (pso, basic skills)
Cunningham, Virginia (pso)
Davies, Catherine (pso)
Egan, Kim (pso)
Goodall, Christine (pso)
Oldfield, John (pso)
O'Shaugnessy, Pauline (pso)
Read, Tracey (pso)

13. **Longsight District Centre**
521 Stockport Road
Manchester M12 4NE
tel 0161-248 6273 *fax 0161-248 8679*

Assia, Shah (spo)
Madix, Josie (spo)
Bhamber, Kaldip

Clarke, Margaret (tops)
Freeman, Paul
Grant, Monica
Griffiths, Yvonne
Hill, Raph
Kenyon, Tina
Self, Katherine
Waugh, Sheridan
Wickstead, Lorna
McKeown, Sue (pso)
McLoughlin, Margaret (pso)
Nield, Michelle (pso)
Roth, Julie (pso)
Stevenson, Rebecca (pso tops)

14. **Varley Street**
Miles Platting, Manchester M10 8EE
tel 0161-205 7444 *fax 0161-205 7563*

Mattis, Debbie (spo)
Blair, Del
Coughlan, Patricia
Daye, Kevin
Hill, Raph
Moulsdale, Kerri
Ofori, Michael
Scanlon, Dave
Williams, Hyacinth
Francis, Janet (pso)
Hossner, Angela (pso)
Terrey, Joanne (pso)

15. 258 Brownley Road
Wythenshawe Manchester M22 5EB
tel 0161-436 1919 *fax 0161-498 8304*

Campbell-Miller, Francis (spo)
Kaczynska, nina (spo)
Bernard, Jean
Briggs, Carolyn
Cullinan, Brian
Hawthorne, Elaine
Lambert, Jayne
Nicholls, Carol
Seymour, Brian
Shaheen, Rifat
Ventris, Michael
Walker, George
Wickstead, Lorna

Barker, Sandra (pso tops)
Burney, Karen (pso tops)
Clarke, Hugh (pso)
Daniels, Maxine (pso)
Donnelly, Lorraine (pso)
Germain, Hilary (pso)
Moore, Tim (pso)
Rowe, Harold (pso)
Sanderson, Kirsty (pso)

16. **Unpaid Work**
Victoria Park, Laindon Road
Longsight, Manchester M14 5YJ
tel 0161-224 0231 *fax 0161-248 5378*

Anderson, Paul (mgr)
Cresswell, Adrian (mgr)
Barcoe, Seamus (qa mgr)
Johnson, Carol (qa mgr)
Conway, Tony (placement mgr)
Cooney, Martin (placement mgr)
Dyson, Steve (placement mgr)
Nixon, Ken (placement mgr)
Shorthose, Paul (placement mgr)
Skidmore, Gary (placement mgr)
Asghar, Mohammed (cps)
Cardell, Helen (cps)
Chapman, Brian (cps)
Crolla, Chris (cps)
Francis, Mark (cps)
Holme, Geoff (cps)
Myerscough, John (cps)
Northrop, John (cps)
Phillips, Barry (cps)
Pike, Sue (cps)
Ricketts, Wesley (cps)
Wareing, Alan (cps)
Watters, Tom (cps)
Whitehead, Darren (cps)

17. **Unpaid Work**
Report Centre, 43 Carnarvon Street
Cheetham Hill, Manchester M1 1EZ
tel 0161-839 5032

Oldham

18. 128 Rochdale Road
Oldham OL1 2JG
tel 0161-620 4421 *fax 0161-628 2011*

Cavanagh, Paul (dist mgr)
Ross, Enda (spo)
Rowlands, Dennis (spo)
Saunders, Phil (spo)
Araya, Christian (dist admin mgr)

Ahmed, Islam
Cope, Steve
Fox, Mike
Guerriero, Julian
Grundy, Faith
Hargreaves, William
Hewison, Jim
Hill, Michael
Mullock, Val
Nickson, Alison

O'Grady, Larry
O'Neill, Steve
Paterson, Phillippa
Rogers, Marilyn
Searle, Pat
Smith, Amanda

Burton, Fred (pso)
Buxton, Helen (pso)
Dudderidge, Carl (pso)
Edwardson, Pam (pso)
Jarvis, Squire (pso)
Kershaw, Gill (pso)
Lovell, Polly (pso)
Lloyd, Kelly (pso)
Taylor, Janet (pso)
Warburton, Sheena (pso)
Ward-Hilton, Sandra (pso)
Edge, Margaret (vlo)

19. **Oldham Probation Centre**
64 Bridge Street, Oldham OL1 1ED
tel 0161-620 4421 *fax 0161-628 9970*

Venet, Sally (spo)
Adams, Steve
Davies, Andrea
Hacking, Chris
Heap, John
O'Brien, Maureen
Brookes, David (pso)
Ford, Liz (pso)
Garside, Lisa (pso)
Heliere, Suzanne (pso)
Marsden, Lynn (pso)

'Think First' & ASRO
Oldham/Stockport/Tameside Cluster
Ashworth, Gary (prog mgr)
Sievewright, Shirley (treatment mgr)
Daybank, Ray (pso tutor)
Heywood, Jennifer (pso tutor)
Padkin, Lucy (pso tutor)
Sullivan, Kim (pso tutor)
White, Jane (pso tutor)

Basic Skills
Broli, Kim
Southerton, Ann

Unpaid Work
Finch, Linda (mgr)
Gilliland, Stephen (placement mgr)
Mayers, Paul (placement mgr)
Newton, Teresa (placement mgr)
Rimmer, Derek (placement mgr)
Biggs, Roy (cps)
Lashley, Curtis (cps)
Newton, Doug (cps)

Robinson, Derek (cps)
Rogers, Monica (cps)
Tweedale, Kevin (cps)
Taylor, Sean (unit supvr)

Salford

20. 2 Redwood Street
Pendleton **Salford** M6 6PF
tel 0161-736 6441 *fax 0161-736 6620*

Buckley, Angela (dist mgr)
Connelly, Andrew (spo)
Davis, Paul (spo)
Dransfield, Linda (spo)
Homewood, Roger (spo)
Phillips, Mandy (spo)
Long, Debra (dist admin mgr)

Adam, Jim
Assinder, Claire
Ba Dachha, Simi
Blake, Val
Brearley, Heather
Bullough, Ruth
Cogan, Bev
Chow, Adele
Davies, Stephen
Falokun, Anne-Marie
Fitzpatrick, Sandra
Froggatt, Colin
Glover, Colin
Harding, Elizabeth
Hill, Joanne
Morley, John
Pitts, Joanne
Potts, Darren
Ricketts, Claudia
Sharples, Christine
Thompson, Hilary
Thompson, Neil
Todd, Liane

Awwad, Anne (pso)
Ashton, Chris (pso)
Austin, Harry (pso)
Burke, Claire (pso)
Burrows, Graham (pso)
Busby, Michelle (pso)
Byers, Joanne (pso)
Callaghan, Danny (pso)
Clarke, Joan (pso)
Cooke, Nicola (pso)
Delaney, Janice (pso)
Dormer, Joanne (pso)
Halliwell, Gillian (pso)
Grayson, Joanne (pso)
Griffin, Beth (pso)
King, Zena (pso)

Mayo, Jennifer (pso)
O'Connor, Kim (pso)
Percival, Matthew (pso)
Richardson, Anthony (pso)
Robinson, Karen (pso)
Sackfield, Jayne (pso)
Stroud, Anne (pso)
Thompson, Clare (pso)
Thompson, Simone (pso)
Williams, Pamela (pso)

Programmes/Interventions
Nixon, Dave (prog mgr)
Fraser, Nicola (treatment mgr)
Sweeney, Lynn (treatment mgr)
Arnold, Susan (prog tutor)
Criscov, Emilia (prog tutor)
Carlon, Jo (prog tutor)
Dalton, Lyndsay (prog tutor)
Robinson, Kathryn (prog tutor)
Ryan, Lisa (prog tutor)
Smith, Shelley(prog tutor)

21. **Unpaid Work**
2 Redwood Street, Salford M6 6PF
tel 0161-736 6441 *fax 0161-736 6620*

Anchor, Pam (mgr)
Holden, Terry (qa mgr)
Ellison, Colin (qa mgr)
Barber, Robert (placement mgr)
Gee, Kenneth (placement mgr)
Oakley, Chris (placement mgr)
Percival, Matthew (placement mgr)
Caldwell, Les (cps)
Carter, Roy (cps)
Gilbert, Dennis (cps)
Hazell, Tim (cps)
Rowlands, Gary (cps)
Seddon, Brian (cps)
Sefton, Diane (cps)
Sefton, Paul (cps)
Ward, Angela (cps)

Stockport

22. 19/37 High Street
Stockport SK1 1EG
tel 0161-429 0010 *fax 0161-476 2709*

Meakin, Marion (dist mgr)
Jones, Debra (dist admin mgr)
Nicholls, Steve (spo)
Ross, Jean (spo)

Bunting, David
Coulson, Jim
Finn, Siobhan
Greaves, Stuart

Kennington, Tom
Machin, Mark
Oskooi, Lynne
Penny, Diane
Phillips, Annette
Ritchie, Angela
Saxon, Cheree
Shallcross, Maggie
Tonge, Keith
Wilkinson, John

Bluff, Diane (vlo)
Broadhurst, Zoe (pso)
Coldrick, Paul (pso)
Costello, Annie (pso)
George, Katie (pso)
Higginbotham, Jaine (pso)
Ledger, Jacky (pso)
McCall, Christine (pso)
Roberts, Helen (pso, dtto)

Unpaid Work
Redston, Ron (mgr)
Butterworth, Julie (qa mgr)
Dawson, Judith (placement mgr)
Corlett, Kevin (placement mgr)
Jones, Leslie (placement mgr)
Al-Ghailani, Abdul (cps)
Chadderton, Gary (cps)
Chadwick, Brian (cps)
Frances, David (cps)
Loughlin, Mike (cps)
Macilwraith, Martin (cps)
Tinson, Steve (cps)

Tameside

23. Francis Thompson Drive
off Water Street
Ashton-under-Lyne OL6 7AJ
tel 0161-330 3695 *fax 0161-343 7475*

Johnston, Graham (acting dist mgr)
Olajide, Tunde (dist admin mgr)
Metcalfe, Ian (spo)
Ashworth, Chrissie
Buckley, Elsie
Burton, Shirley
Daniels, Diane
Embleton, Jennie
Sayers, Andrew
Schofield, Ceri
Whitbread, Rebecca

Hackney, Melvyn (pso)
Lingard, Jan (pso)
Marsh, Michael (pso)
Murphy, Julie (pso)
Naum, Michelle (pso)

Unpaid Work
Buckley, Jim (mgr)
Carter, Diane (placement mgr)
Scott, Leroy (placement mgr)
Upton, Carron (placement mgr)
Barcoe, Seamus (cps)
Browne, Joe (cps)
Dixon, Andrew (cps)
Schofield, Martin (cps)
Shurawell, Nina (cps)
Stamper, Peter (cps)
Waite, Delgado (cps)

24.   2 Simpson Street
     Hyde SK14 1BJ
     tel 0161-366 7344 *fax 0161-368 6552*

     Armstrong-Burns, Janet (spo)
     Bulman, Kevin (spo)
     Allen, Fuschia
     Bulmer, Lisa
     Cutts, Brian
     Eastwood, Dave
     Green, Stephen
     Kramer, Jennie
     McCormick, Kirsty
     McKiernan, Bridie
     Plackett, Richard
     Self, Katherine
     Stott, Jenny
     Worrall, Suzanne

     Daley, Sandra (pso)
     Harrison, Oliver (pso)
     Malone, Karen (pso)
     Johnstone, Rose (pso)

24a. **Priority & Prolific Offenders &DRR**
     Tameside DIP, Good Hope Mill
     98 Bentinck Street
     Ashton-under-Lyne OL8 7SS
     tel 0161-343 5622 *fax 0161-343 4754*

     Franklin, Royce (spo)
     Dippnall, Gary (pso)
     Lisle, Adele (pso)
     Coldrick, Paul (pso drr)
     May, Helen (pso drr)

Trafford

25.   Newton Street
     Stretford Manchester M32 8LG
     tel 0161-865 3255 *fax 0161-864 4791*

     Meakin, Marion (dist mgr)
     Cavanagh, Deborah (dist admin mgr)
     Kierc, Lidia (spo)
     Mayo, Eddie (spo)
     Powell, Chris (spo)

Ayodeji, Andrew
Bulman, Laura
Clarke, Matthew
Doody, Olive
Evans, Amanda
Greenstreet, Geoffrey
Gibson, James
Higham, Ria
Lancaster, Dave
McCaughan, Su
McLaughlin, Peter
Mashadi, Fatmia
Robertson, Marianne
Singh, Charan
Sugrue, Laura
Wastell, Liz

Hawkins, Steve (housing)
Barber, Dee (pso)
Hearne, Paul (pso)
Hodgkinson, Katie (pso)
Holmes, Dan (pso)
Mistry, Natalie (pso)
Scott, Amanda (pso)
Thompson, Veronica (pso)
Wilsenham, Nicky (pso)
Wiaktor-Urch, Stasia (pso)
Wright, Sandra (pso)

Unpaid Work
Johnson, Sue (mgr)
Aldred, Dave (placement mgr)
Bennett, John (placement mgr)
Connolly, Caroline (placement mgr)
Murphy, Lance (placement mgr)

Wigan

26.   81 Gloucester Street
     Atherton M29 0JU
     tel (01942) 876889 *fax (01942) 886109*

     Boyd, Christine (dist mgr)
     Martlew, Josie (dist admin mgr)
     King, Clare (spo)
     Pandolfo, Paul (spo)
     Rhoden, Derek (spo)
     Roberts, Andrew (spo)
     Williams, Hyacinth (spo)

     Burke, Michael
     Cole, Frank
     Commissioning, Michael
     Crye, Matthew
     Down, Adele
     Edwards, Mary
     Fletcher, Rebecca
     Heale, Judith
     Heywood, Julian
     Hickey, Joanne

Hollis, Victoria
Hunt, Michael
Hurley, Rachel
Kayley, Maria
Manning, John
Miller, Ann
Morris, Jennifer
Neighbour, Kate
Shaw, Melanie
Shearman, Catherine
Stephenson, Alan
Stokes, Gina
Thompson, Elvis
Walsh, Rachel
Walton, Patricia
Whitehill, Paul
Winn, Anna

Avison, Diane (pso)
Brooks, Jane (pso)
Fenney, Janet (pso)
Goulbourne, Jayne (pso)
Halliwell, Susan (pso)
Harris, Margaret (pso)
Harwood, Susan (pso)
Hopkins, Sarah (pso)
Jones, Elaine (pso)
Kneale-Roby, Kyra (pso)
Little, Dawn (pso)
Lohan, Irene (pso)
Macmillan, Gordon (pso)
McPike, Christine (pso dtto)
Morrison, Sonny (pso)
O'Hara, Janice (pso)
O'Mara, Yvonne (pso)
Phillips, Mike (pso)
Pilkington, Karen (pso)
Price, Lorraine (pso)
Simpson, Heather (pso)
Smith, Claire (pso vlo)
Smith, Heather (pso)
Smith, Michele (pso)
Smith, Paul (pso)
Stock, Ann (pso)
Walmsley, Hayley (pso)
Waring, Kirsty (pso)
West, Tracey (pso)
Bridge, Dennis (treatment mgr)
Willis, Julie (treatment mgr)

27. **Youth Offending Team**
93 Victoria Road
Platt Bridge WN2 5DN
tel (01942) 866507 *fax (01942) 867422*

Foster, Janet

28. **Unpaid Work**
81 Gloucester Street **Atherton** M29 0JU
tel (01942) 876889 *fax (01942) 886109*

Humphries, Malcolm (mgr)
Dodd, Trevor (placement mgr)
Foxwell, Marion (placement mgr)
Oliver, Geoff (placement mgr)
Richardson, Mark (placement mgr)
Barber, Keith (cps)
Carey, Christine (cps)
Emmison, Mike (cps)
Heator, Jean (cps)
Hindley, Edwards (cps)
Souter, Rita (cps)
Roscoe, Denise (cps)
Wilde, Stuart (cps)

Units

29. **Staff Devpt Unit**
Old Town Hall, Bolton Road
Kearsley, Nr. Bolton BL4 8NJ
tel (01204) 863300 *fax (01204) 862940*

Lochead, Caroline (staff devpt admin mgr)
Brown, Joy (pda)
Dunbar, Bev (pda)
Fearon, Aidan (pda)
Hampson, Lesley (pda)
Kerr, Linda (pda)
Marc, Michaela (pda)
McGoffoy, Susan (pda)
Mhar, farzana (pda)
Prokofiev, Anastasia (pda)
Turner, Sue (pda)

30. **12 Minshull Street**
Manchester M1 3FR
tel 0161-237 5173 *fax 0161-228 6745*

Probation Programmes Team
Robinson, Chris (dist mgr)
Mackenzie, Ian (spo)
Gazdecki, David (p, spo)
Aslam, Harris
Bakshi, Nisha
Maddix, Joe
Wilde, Sarah
Dearing, Eric (treatment mgr)
Hay, Gemma (treatment mgr)
Rhodes, Natalie (treatment mgr)
Bailey, Tracey (pso)
Cole, Mark (pso)
Golding, Lorraine (pso)
Jenkins, Rose (pso)
Kerr, Philip (pso)
Macleod, Kerry (pso)
McKenna, Claire (pso)
Morgan, Michael (pso)
Stanley, Tracey (pso)
Walker, Victoria (pso)

31. **MAPPA Support Unit**
c/o Visor Unit
Grey Mare Lane Police Station
Bell Crescent, Beswick
Manchester M11 3BA
tel 0161-856 3636 *fax 0161-856 3685*

Fuller, Clare (spo)
Kenyon, Tina
Mayers, Martin
Rawlinson
Sharples, John
Wood, Jo (forensic psychologist)
Prunnell, Det Sgt Neil (mappa co-ord)

32. **Probn Programmes & Devpt Unit (SORT)** 53 Peel Street
Eccles, Manchester M30 0NG
tel 0161-789 2429 *fax 0161-707 9370*

Taylor, Phil (spo)
Edmundson, Wendy
Graham, Peter
Foster, Susan
Hesford, Karl
Holmes, Deborah
Holton, Janet
O'Keefe, Ian
Ollerton, Lyndsay
Yianni, John

Youth Offending Teams

33 **Bolton YOT**
Le Mans Crescent
Bolton BL1 1SA
tel (01204) 331263 *fax (01204) 331258*

Coleman, Mick (team mgr)

34. **Bury YOT**
Seedfield Resouce Centre
Parkinson Street, Bury BL9 6NY
tel 0161-253 6862

Smyth, Graham (yot mgr)

35. **Manchester YOT**
Grey Mare Lane Police Station
Bell Crescent, Beswick
Manchester M11 3BA
tel 0161-856 3604 *fax 0161-856 3605*

Quinn, Adrian (team mgr)

36. **Manchester North YOT**
7-15 Stilton Drive
Beswick, Manchester M11 3SB
tel 0161-223 0488 *fax 0161-230 8167*

Noble, Lisa (team mgr)

37. **Manchester Central YOT**
Chichester Road
Moss Side, Manchester M15 5PA
tel 0161-226 9714 *fax 0161-226 8477*

Stewart, Carol (team mgr)

38. **Manchester South YOT**
Greenbow Road
Newall Green, Manchester M23 8RE
tel 0161-437 3069 *fax 0161-437 3856*

Brundrett, Mark (team mgr)

39. **Salford YOT**
Enscombe House
10/12 Enscombe Place, Salford M3 6FJ
tel 0161-607 1900 *fax 0161-832 4306*

Healy, Tom (team mgr)

40. **Stockport YOT**
1st Floor, Owl House
59/61 Great Underbank
Stockport SK1 1NE
0161-476 2876 *fax 0161-476 2858*

MacDonald, Kate (team mgr)

41. **Tameside YOT**
Frances Thompson Drive
Ashton under Lyne OL6 7AS
tel 0161-330 3012 *fax 0161-330 3149*

Whittle, John (team mgr)

42. **Trafford YOT**
4th Floor, Arndale House
Stretford Arndale, Chester Road
Stretford M32 9XY
tel 0161-911 8201 *fax 0161-911 8202*

Robinson, Ann (team mgr)

43. **Wigan YOT**
93 Victoria Road
Platt Bride, Wigan WN2 5DN
tel (01942) 776886 *fax (01942) 776856*

Bond, Sharon (team mgr)

Hostels

44. **Hostels Management Unit & Central Admissions Unit**
64 Manley Road, Whalley Range
Manchester M16 8ND
tel 0161-227 1849 *fax 0161 227 9052*

Central Referrals
tel 0161-226 8465 *fax 0161-227 9052*

Cope Angela (dist mgr)
Shaw, Sylvia (spo central admin)
McGartland, John (admin & finance mgr)
Vaughan, Judith (central referral off)

45. **Bradshaw House Approved Premises**
147/151 Walmersley Road
Bury BL9 5DE
tel 0161-761 6419 *fax 0161-763 4353*

Morton, Carol (spo mgr)
Davis, Paul (po deputy)
Colton, Andy (asst mgr)
Davies, Stephen (asst mgr)
Hamer, John (asst mgr)
Schofield, Neil (asst mgr)

46. **St Joseph's Approved Premises**
Miller Street, Patricroft, Eccles
Manchester M30 8PF
tel 0161-789 5337 *fax 0161-707 9085*

Crofts, Roger (spo mgr)
Vacancy (po deputy)
Horton, Mike (asst mgr)
Jeffers, Franklyn (asst mgr)
Kluj, Peter (asst mgr)
Young, Diane (asst mgr)

47. **Withington Road Approved Premises**
172/174 Withington Road
Whalley Range, Manchester M16 8JN
tel 0161-226 1179 *fax 0161-227 9052*

Corstorphine, Bunty (spo mgr)
Hayworth, Ruth (po deputy)
Bailey, George (asst mgr)
Vacancy (asst mgr)
Vacancy (asst mgr)
Reid, Vernon (asst mgr)

48. **Chorlton Approved Premises**
10/12 Oswald Road
Chorlton cum Hardy
Manchester M21 1LH
tel 0161-862 9881 *fax 0161-862 9554*

Williams, Robbie (spo mgr)
Kay, Trevor (po deputy)
Vacancy (asst mgr)
Kirk, Jackie (asst mgr)
Parker, Lisa (asst mgr)
Vacancy (asst mgr)

49. **Hopwood House Approved Premises**
104 Manchester Street
Heywood, Lancs OL10 1DW
tel (01706) 620440 *fax (01706) 625927*

Morton, Carol (spo mgr)
Williams, Carolyn (po deputy)
Bond, Sarah (asst mgr)
Denby, Suzanne (asst mgr)
Jacques, Lynda (asst mgr)
Sykes, Debbi (asst mgr)

50. **Wilton Place Approved Premises**
10/12 Edward Street
Werneth, Oldham OL9 7QW
tel 0161-624 3005 *fax 0161-628 6936*

Chadwick, Wendy (spo mgr)
Vacancy (po deputy)
Appleton, Brian (asst mgr)
Garner, Helen (asst mgr)
Massey, Ed (asst mgr)
Ravey, Ann (asst mgr)

51. **Ascot House Approved Premises**
195 Wellington Road North
Heaton Norris, Stockport SK4 2PB
tel 0161-443 3400 *fax 0161-432 9739*

Williams, Robbie (spo mgr)
MacKenzie, Caroline (po deputy)
Bentley, Jonathan (asst mgr)
Cusick, Nicola (asst mgr)
Gough, Trevor (asst mgr)
Haslam, Alan (asst mgr)

Hostels for Men

Ascot House, Stockport
Bradshaw House, Bury
Chorlton House, Manchester
St Joseph's, Salford (specialist MDO
hostel)
Wilton Place, Oldham
Withington Road, Manchester

Hostel for Women

Hopwood House, Heywood

Institutions

52. H M Prison, Southall Street
Strangeways Manchester M60 9AH
tel 0161-817 5600 *fax 0161-817 5601*

direct dial tel 0161-817+ext
visits tel 0161-817 5656
probn fax 0161-817 5970

HDC admin tel 0161-817 5653

Bramwell, Angela (spo) ext 5742
Connolly, Andy ext 5971
Coulson, Jim ext 5776
Keith, Lynn ext 5743

Mannion, Christine ext 5812
Mattis, Debbie ext 5714
Smith, Rachel ext 5700
Stratton, Sue ext 5776
Taylor, Phil ext 5714
Wilson, Jo ext 5952
Wood, Ethel ext 5743

53. H M Young Offender Institution
Hindley Wigan WN2 5TH
tel (01942) 855000 *fax (01942) 855001*
probn fax (01942) 8855193

Croall, David (spo) 855192
Benjamin, Julie 855280
Carpenter, Miriam 855280
Fletcher, Anne 855281§
Healey, Sandra (pso) 855148
Dunn, Terry (pso) 855281

54. H M Prison **Buckley Hall**
Buckley Hall Road
Rochdale OL12 9DP
tel (01706) 861610 *fax (01706) 711797*

Parole clerk ext 290
Special visits ext 312

Hanley, Anne (spo) 514322
Evans, Marie
Harris, Bernice
Stefani, Sally
Hilton, Mike (pso)
Taylor, Susan (pso)
Ward, Stephen (pso)

55. H M Prison **Forest Bank**
Agecroft Road, Pendlebury
Manchester M27 8FB
tel 0161-925 7000 *fax 0161-925 7001*
direct dial 0161-925+ext
bail info off 0161-925 7000 ext 2018
bail info fax 0161-925 7019
booking visits ext 7029/7030
Healthcare Centre ext 7065
Healthcare Centre fax 0161-925 7055

Macpherson, Sandra (spo) ext 7020
Bryan, Ryan ext 7073
Chambers, Dave ext 7069
Hayworth, Ruth ext 7075
Holmes, Mike ext 7088
Noall, Mark ext 7078
Thom, Linda ext 7071

Local Justice Areas

5 Bolton
6 Bury

20-21 City of Salford
10-14 Manchester
18-19 Oldham
7, 8 Rochdale, Middleton & Heywood
22 Stockport
23, 24 Tameside
25 Trafford
26, 28 Wigan & Leigh

Crown Courts

2 Manchester
3 Bolton

MERSEYSIDE PROBATION AREA

Out of hours emergency contact point tel
0151-920 9201

Victim enquiry's contact number tel 0151-
281 0832 (T H Eastham aco)

e-mail:
Firstname.Surname@merseyside.probation.
gsx.gov.uk

1. **Head Office**
Burlington House, Crosby Road North
Waterloo, Liverpool L22 0PJ
tel 0151-920 9201 *fax 0151-949 0528*

Mellor, Nigel (chair of board)
Stafford, John (co)
Pakula, Mrs Anne (dco)
Sproul-Cran, Ms Kirsten (hd of corporate
services & board secy)
Gotts, Paul (treasurer)
Kenyon, Mrs Lyn (hd of admin services)
Hill, Ms Joanne (hd of h.r. & staff devpt)
Dean, Mrs Ann (snr h.r. adv)
Atherton, Ms Lynne (board clerk/admin
off)
Felton-Aksoy Mrs Kathy (external
relations asst)
Thurston, David (health & safety adv)
Lea, Mrs Katherine (occupational health
adv)
Steele, Ms Rachael (snr research off)

ACO Management Unit
Brown, Ms Sue (aco, gp progs)
Chambers, Steve (aco, community offender
mgmnt divn & crt services)
Eastham, Terry (aco, resettlement
offender mgmnt divn)

Holt, Paul (aco, com punishment & appr premises)
Metherell, Dave (aco, community offender mgmnt divn)
Murray, Peter (aco, community reintegration & info services)
Stelman, Andy (aco, community offender mgmnt divn)
Chudleigh, Claire (aco, gp progs & partnerships)

Partnerships
Halpen, Mrs Helen (admin asst)

2. **Staff Development**
Rainford Hall, Crank Road
St Helens, Merseyside WA11 7RP
tel (01744) 755181 *fax (01744) 454671*

Parr, Mrs Julie (staff devpt mgr)
Powell, Ms Audrey (staff devpt off)
Vacancy ('what works' trainer)
Warren, Mrs Louise ('what works' trainer)

3. **Information, Communications & Technology (Business Devpt Unit)**
1st Floor, State House
22 Dale Street, Liverpool L2 4TR
tel 0151-224 0679 *fax 0151-236 3740*

Steele, Bob (mgr)

ICT Helpdesk
tel 0151-224 0660 *fax 0151 236 3740*

Library
tel 0151-224 0670

Venables, Susan (info off)

4. **Edge Hill Specialist Unit**
13 North View, Edge Hill
Liverpool L7 8TS
tel 0151-281 1245 *fax 0151-281 1246*

Accommodation
Garner, Paul (housing off)
Brennan, Ms Nora (psa)
Edwards, Mr John (psa)
Reddy, Ms Sharon (psa)

Employment Team
Christian, Dave (mgr)
Perry, Ms Jeanette (operations mgr)
Jones, Ms Anne-Marie (operations mgr)

Barlow, Ms Emma (basic skills adv)
Clatworthy, Marguerite (basic skills adv)
Forshaw, Peter (basic skills adv)
Gilbert, Ted (basic skills adv)
Lennard, Ms Jane (basic skills adv)

Baglow, Kenny (psa)
Colohan, Paddy (psa)
Doherty, Tony (psa)
Fletcher, Barry (psa)
Gillies, Miss Roslyn (psa)
McCormack, Mrs Claire (psa)
Watson, Miss Louise (psa)
Adamson, Mrs Helen (psa)

5. **Learning Resource Centre**
63 Argyle Street, Birkenhead
Wirral, Merseyside CH41 6AB
tel 0151-647 2929 *fax 0151-647 2838*

Aubrey, Ms Catherine (snr staff devpt off)
Fright, Peter (tpo prog co-ord)
Beggs, John (pda)
Phillips, Hilton (pda)
Rafferty, Mike (pda)
Vacancy (pda)
Ryde, Miss Louise (pda)
Sweeney, Ms Sue (pda)
Woodruff, Ms Jan (pda)

Community Punishment Division

6. Belle Vale District Centre
Childwall Valley Road, Liverpool L25 2RJ
tel 0151-487 0123 *fax 0151-487 0101*

Knowsley/St Helens
McPaul, Mark (cp scheme mgr) (7, 8, 9, 10)
Kimmance, Ms Pat (qa mgr)
Kavanagh, Miss Jenny (ops mgr)
Allen, Derek (cso)
Dunn, Mrs Karen (cso)
Francis, Ms Lorraine (cso)
Sweeney, Miss Carol (cso)

7. 1b Derby Lane, Old Swan
Liverpool L13 6QA
tel 0151-281 8655 *fax 0151-281 8688*

Liverpool North
Best, Ms Jenny (cp scheme mgr) (6, 8, 9, 10)
Stamper, Miss Lena (qa mgr)
Wright, Noel (qa mgr)
Donoghue, Mr Pat (ops mrs)
Dougan, Bill (cso)
Mathison, Dave (cso)
O'Grady, Mr Stuart (cso)
Torres, Mrs Thelma (cso)

8. South Liverpool Probation Centre
180 Falkner Street, Liverpool L8 7SX
tel 0151-706 6644 *fax 0151-708 5044*

Liverpool South
Best, Ms Jenny (cp scheme mgr) (6, 7, 9, 10)

Phillips, Mrs Jenny (qa mgr)
Sinden, David (ops mgr)
McQuire, Mrs Lesley (cso)
Huthwaite, David (cso)
Losh, Mrs Jackie (cso)
Malvern, Bill (cso)

9. Sefton House, 1 Molyneux Way
    Old Roan, Liverpool L10 2JA
    tel 0151-531 6737 *fax 0151-527 2534*

    Sefton
    McPaul, Mark (scheme mgr) (6, 7, 8, 10)
    Vellacott, Ms Sheila (qa mgr)
    Butterworth, Jack (ops mgr)
    Blythman, Miss Kate (cso)
    Cowley, Brian (cso)
    Morris, Mrs Di (cso)
    Parkinson, Joe (cso)

10. 40 Europa Boulevard
    Birkenhead, Wirral,
    Merseyside CH41 4PE
    tel 0151-666 0400 *fax 0151-666 0402*

    Wirral
    Best, Ms Jenny (cp scheme mgr) (6, 7, 8,
    9)
    Wynn, Paul (qa mgr)
    Frey, Ian (ops mgr)
    Bromley, Rod (cso)
    Loughran, Mrs Julie (cso)
    O'Donnell, Mrs Gill (cso)
    Williams, Miss Joan (cso)

Community Offender Management

11. **Wirral Probation Centre**
    40 Europa Boulevard
    Birkenhead, Wirral CH41 4PE
    tel 0151-666 0400 *fax 0151-666 0401*

    Edwards, Jim (spo)
    Humphreys, Barry (spo)
    Burns, Mrs Julie
    Clow, Miss Jennie
    Hay, Ms Val
    Hunter, Ms Vicky
    Jones, Miss Carla
    Joyce, Brian
    McNiffe, Peter
    Marshall, Mrs Andrea
    Mason, Steve
    Minhas, Amir
    Moore, Mrs Julie
    Nowell, Clayton
    Osbourne, Steve
    Pickstock, Miss Katie
    Snell, George

Tillston, Ms Margaret
Warburton, Miss Hayley
Wigmore, Robert
Williams, Miss Sarah
Hutchinson, Mrs Amy
Worgan, David
Chandler, Mrs Collette (psa)
Haseldon, Mrs Tricia (psa)
Kennedy, Paul (psa)
Murphy, Mrs Angela (psa)
Webb, Mrs Joan (psa)

12. 4 Trinity Road **Bootle**
    Merseyside L20 7BE
    tel 0151-286 5667 *fax 0151-286 6900*

    Dauphin, Colin (spo)
    Hypolite, Mrs Diana (snr pract)
    Beuschlein, Mrs Barbara
    Chambers, Mrs Jenny
    Conroy, Martin
    Haigh, Chris
    Hayes, Malcolm
    Kibbey, Mrs Rosemarie
    McGibbon, David
    Munro, Lee
    O'Hara, Mrs Denise
    Cummins, Miss Pauline (psa)
    Feehan, Ms Sue (psa)
    McQuiggan, Miss Joy (psa)

13. Gordon House, 3-5 Leicester Street
    Southport Merseyside PR9 0ER
    (01704) 534634 *fax (01704) 501845*

    spo at 14
    Seel, David
    Stott, Allan
    Rainford, Ms Jane
    Vacancy (psa)

14. **East Liverpool Probation Centre**
    1b Derby Lane
    Old Swan, Liverpool L13 6QA
    tel 0151-281 8655 *fax 0151-281 8688*

    Barron, Ms Cath (spo)
    Alexandra, Mrs Kat
    Barnes, Roger
    Chesters, Alan
    Cushen, David
    Jones, Mrs Ann
    Jones, Miss Candice
    Kenwright, Ms Kathleen
    Loram, Richard
    Latchford, Mrs Michelle
    Lynch, Mrs Valerie
    Martine, Miss Karen

Moorhead, Justin
O'Grady, Mrs Paula
Rooney, Miss Johanne
Smith, Miss Alison
Bell, Miss Kirsten
Cooke, Mrs Elaine (psa)
Lloyd, Neil (psa)

15. 142/148 Stanley Road
     Kirkdale Liverpool L5 7QQ
     tel 0151-286 6159 *fax 0151-284 7847*

Cameron, Miss Jane (spo)
Manley, Mrs Nanci (spo)
Baker, Miss Fiona
Chadwick, John
Chambers, Ms Clare
Clarkson, David
Eisner, Julian
Howarth, Miss Lisa
Jenkinson, Harry
Jones, Miss Hannah
McClelland, Miss Fiona
Montieth, Miss Tracey
Pennington, Miss Nichola
Riley, James
Sofia, Ms Nikki
Smyth, Mrs Jan
Thomas, Mrs Andrea
Wood, Dave
Buoey, Ms Carol (psa)
Coogan, Steve (psa)
Jones, Mrs Marion (psa)
Oates, Miss Annie (psa)
O'Doherty, Barry (psa)
Williams, Mrs Karen (psa)

16. South Liverpool Probation Centre
     180 Falkner Street, Liverpool L8 7SX
     tel 0151-706 6688 *fax 0151-708 5044*

Liverpool South/Central
Furniss, Peter (spo) (18)
Hughes, Peter (snr pract)
Courtney, Miss Sarah
Dunn, Mrs Sheerie
Forshaw, Mrs Karen
Griffiths, Miss Christina
Lindon-Richey, Mrs Rona
Munro, Mrs Sandy
Pritchard, George
Rolfe, Mrs Katin
Tracey, Mrs Anna
Stevenson, Miss Kerry
Adekanmbi, Mrs Moji (psa)
Kirby, Dave (psa)
Lowe, Mrs Jean (psa)

17. 14 South Parade
     Speke Liverpool L24 2SG
     tel 0151-281 0610 *fax 0151-281 0710*

     spo at 17
Burnell, Ms Wendy
Jones, Geoff
Shaw, Mrs Eileen
Williams, Ms Debbie
Li, Ms Mandy (psa)

18. **South Knowsley Probation Centre**
     597 Princess Drive
     Liverpool L14 9NE
     tel 0151-480 4544 *fax 0151-480 3618*

Dickinson, Ann (spo)
Morris, Mrs Julie (snr pract)
Branford, Miss Patsy
Carroll, Ms June
Degnan, Nigel
Holliday, John
Loyden, Frank
McCully, Simon
Mannion, Mrs Wendy
Nolan, Tony
Williams, Mrs Sarah
Lane, Miss Emma (psa)
Lloyd, Mrs Jan (psa)

19. St Helens Probation Centre
     St Mary's House, 50 Church Street
     St Helens Merseyside WA10 1AP
     tel (01744) 630229 *fax (01744) 606224*

Milnes, Mike (spo)
Collett, Steve
Cox, Mrs Kelly
Disley, Mrs Sarah
Dryhurst, James
Edwards, George
Malone, Miss Zara
Nicholson-Jones, Ms Dianne
O'Neale, Steve
Perkins, Tony
Smee, Mrs Christine
Sweeney, Ms Michelle
Shaw Mrs, Christine (psa)
Wood, Mrs Jean (psa)

Court Services Division

20. **Crown Court**
     PO Box 69, Queen Elizabeth II Law
     Courts,
     Derby Square, Liverpool L69 2NE
     tel 0151-236 5302 *fax 0151-255 0682*

Vacancy (spo)

Collins, Jim
Gowan, Steve
Green, Ms Rosie
O'Grady, Mrs Anne
Orson, Ms Christine
Smith, Mark
Thomas, Mrs Margaret
Cummins, Mrs Susan (psa)
Kirkpatrick, Ms Hilary (psa)
Reil, Miss Sue (psa)
Williams, Mrs Janet (psa)
Wilson, Mrs Ann (psa)

21. **Wirral Probation Centre**
40 Europa Boulevard
Birkenhead, Wirral CH41 4PE
tel 0151-666 0400 *fax 0151-666 0402*

Rutherford, Cec (spo)
Ross, Stephen
McKenzie, Ms Lisa (psa)
Merryweather, Mrs Jacqueline (psa)
Phipps, Mrs Elizabeth (psa)
Purvis, Mrs Wendy (psa)
Surridge, Andrew (psa)

22. **Liverpool Magistrates' Court &
Court Services Liverpool Central**
111 Dale Street, Liverpool L2 2JQ
tel 0151-236 0603 *fax 0151-236 5417*

Hamilton, Richard (spo)
Adams, Mrs Heather
Loughran, Pete
Seddon, Andrew
Arnold, Robert (psa)
Aston, Mrs Barbara (psa)
Carroll, Ms Liz (psa)
Curley, Miss Susan (psa)
Fisher, John (psa)
Grimes, Miss Julie (psa)
Lavin, John (psa)
McLean, Ian (psa)
O'Neill, Mrs Jan (psa)
Pilkington, Mrs Barbara (psa)
Turner, Miss Emma (psa)
Wells, Miss Emma (psa)

23. **South Knowsley Probation Centre**
597 Princess Drive, Liverpool L14 9NE
tel 0151-480 4544 *fax 0151-480 3618*

North, Ms Cherry
Cleary, Francis (psa)
Donovan, Miss Hayley (psa)
Hitch, Mrs Sandra (psa)
Patterson, George (psa)

24. St Helens Probation Centre
St Mary's House, 50 Church Street
St Helens Merseyside WA10 1AP
tel (01744) 630229 *fax (01744) 606224*

spo at 24
Gryzb, Miss Louise (psa)
McCabe, Mrs Sylvia (psa)

25. Gordon House 3-5 Leicester Street
Southport Merseyside PR9 0ER
tel (01704) 534634 *fax (01704) 501845*

Sloman, Roger (spo)
Edward, Mrs Jane
Kelly, Miss Rachel

26. **North Sefton Magistrates' Court**
The Law Courts
Albert Road, Southport PR9 0LJ
tel (01704) 544277 *fax (01704) 545840*

Jones, Pam (psa)
Reilly, Moira (psa)

27. **South Sefton Magistrates' Court**
The Court Building
29 Merton Road, Bootle L20 3BJ
tel 0151-285 6236 *fax 0151-933 8602*

Bright, Mrs Pam (psa)
Dawber, Mrs Jacqueline (psa)
Hilton, Mrs Bernie (psa)

28. 4 Trinity Road
Bootle L20 7BE
tel 0151-286 5667 *fax 0151-286 6900*

spo at 25

**Resettlement Offender Management
Division**

29. Kirkby Probation Centre
Oatlands Road **Kirkby**
Liverpool L32 4UH
tel 0151-547 3160 *fax 0151-547 2244*

Lloyd, Ms Shirley (spo)
Bennett, Tony
Brotherstone, Mrs Cathie
Cleworth, Geoff
Corcoran, Miss Angela
Emecheta, Mrs Frances
Gay, Martin
Heston, Miss Debbie
Kelly, Mrs Julie
McGee, Eddie
Morley, Miss Fiona
Myler, Mrs Sharon (psa)
Nash, Miss Emma (psa)
Rance, Paul (psa)

30. **Liverpool North**
137/139 Breckfield Road
North Anfield, Liverpool L5 4QY
tel 0151-284 4487 *fax 0151-284 8683*

Oluonye, Ms Sandra (spo)
Briggs, Tom
Caton, Barry
Coburn, Miss Kate
Green, Ms Rosie
Keenan, Miss Joy
Macaulay, Bob
McDonald, Mrs Louise
McGrath, Ms Karen
Price, Miss Michelle
Ralph, Miss Renee
Smith, Mark
Basley, Ms Jana (psa)
McQuaid, Miss Claire (psa)

31. **Liverpool South**
South Liverpool Probation Centre
180 Falkner Street, Liverpool L8 7SX
tel 0151-706 6666 *fax 0151-706 6694*

Kayani, Nick (spo)
Blundell, Paul (snr pract)
Craig, Michael
Gowan, Steve
Gill, Miss Helen
Fowlis, Miss Naomi
Jones, Miss Carla
Jameson, Keith
McAnallen, Miss Donna
McIlveen, David
Pond, Mrs Hazel
Price, Graham
Proudlove, Mrs Sarah
Walsh, Mrs Jackie (p)
Webster, Ms Louise
Parkinson, Mrs Julie (psa)
Roberts, Ricky (psa)
Rogers, Miss Sandra (psa)
Smith, Sonsha (psa)

32. **Sefton**
25 Crosby Road South
Waterloo, Liverpool L22 1RG
tel 0151-920 4444 *fax 0151-928 9143*

Rimmer, Don (spo)
Chadwick, Mrs Pat
Clarke, Mrs Ruth
Doherty, Eddie
Maguire, Ms Jan
Mitchell, Ms Janine
Mutch, Ms Jennie

Penn, Mike
Byrne, Mrs Diane (psa)

33. **Wirral**
Wirral Probation Centre
40 Europa Boulevard
Birkenhead, Wirral CH41 4PE
tel 0151-666 0400 *fax 0151-666 0402*

Sherlock, Vin (spo)
Griffiths, Ms Alex
Hamill, Ms Una
Lloyd, Hugh
O'Donnell, Shaun
O'Grady, Ms Anne
O'Mahony, Mrs Cathy
Ross, Ms Bernadette
Stewart, Miss Becky
Fearon, Mrs Ronnie (psa)
McGinty, Mrs Norma (psa)

Group Programmes & Residential Services Division

34. **Drug Testing Pilot**
Wirral Probation Centre
40 Europa Boulevard, Birkenhead
Wirral CH41 4PE
tel 0151-666 0400 *fax 0151-666 0401*

Baird, Allen (spo, mgr)
Farrell, Miss Debbie (psa)
Lynch, Ms Collette (psa)

35. **Merseyside Development Unit**
6/8 Temple Court, Liverpool L2 6PY
tel 0151-229 2000 *fax 0151-236 4265*

Kuyateh, Jeanette (spo)

Domestic Violence
Armstrong, Paul (treatment mgr)
Cooke, Roy (facilitator)
Green, Ms Cindy (facilitator)
Johnson, Norris (facilitator)
Porter, Ms Liz (facilitator)
Waller, Miss Tracey (facilitator)
Higham, Ms Hayley (women's supt wrkr)
Rice, Ms Collette (women's supt wrkr)

Sex Offender Programme
Anderson, Mrs Carol (treatment mgr)
Bellamy, Mrs Mary (facilitator)
Guinness, Mrs Rosie (facilitator)
Johnson, Emma (facilitator)
McCullough, Jim (facilitator)
Oldham, Paul (facilitator)
Stafford, Ms Jill (facilitator)
Watson, Mrs Mary (facilitator)

36. **South Liverpool Probation Centre**
180 Falkner Street, Liverpool L8 7SX
tel 0151-706 6611 *fax 0151-708 9687*

Spencer, Mrs Lesley (spo)

Groupwork Programmes
Andrews, Mike (treatment manager, DIDs)
Davies, Ms Carol (treatment mgr, asro)
Kelly, Mary (treatment mgr, asro)
Mannix, Mrs Nancy (treatment mgr, asro)
Watkins, Doug (treatment mgr, Think First)
Campbell, Ms Christine (psa)
Dauphin, Andre (psa)
Devine, John (psa)
Fuller, Miss Claire (psa)
Gallagher, Mrs Julie (psa)
Halpin, Miss Dawn (psa)
Hughes, Miss Alex (psa)
Hutchinson, Ian (psa)
Jones, Miss Sam (psa)
Lumsden, Ken (psa)
McCarthy, Mrs Jacqui (psa)
McClure, Miss Caroline (psa)
McCoy, Jill (psa)
Maguire, Miss Jeanette (psa)
O'Connor, Miss Claire (psa)
O'Neill, Mrs Jan (psa)
Shaw, Miss Suzanne (psa)
Saxton, Miss Jenny (psa)
Smith, Miss Paul (psa)
Sweatman, Miss Danielle (psa)
Teese, Paul (psa)
Thompson, Angela (psa)
Walsh, Miss Jenny (psa)
Wilkins, Ian (psa)

37. **DTTO Liverpool**
1st Floor, Albion House
30 James Street, Liverpool L2 7PS
tel 0151-255 0330 *fax 0151-255 0440*

Baird, Allen (spo, Sefton, Wirral)
Hamilton, Elaine (spo L'pool, Knowsley, St Helens)
Ashes, Ken
Dunn, Steve
Jones, Hugh (Sefton)
Phillips, Tony (Sefton)
Robinson, Ms Kate
Summerton, Mrs Rhoni
Taylor-Watson, Miss Susan
Connolly, Miss Victoria (psa)
Hypolite, Adissa (psa, Sefton)
Riley, Miss Sandra (psa, Sefton)
Ryan, Miss Jennifer (psa)

38. **DTTO Knowsley/St Helens**
St Helens Probation Centre
St Mary's House, 50 Church Street
St Helens, Merseyside WA10 1AP
tel (01744) 630229 *fax (01744) 606224*

Hamilton, Elaine (spo)
Beesley, Mrs Pat
Curzon, Anna
Markland, Kate
Brownrigg, Mrs Catherine (psa)
Gore, Miss Amanda (psa)
Holland, Mrs Catherine (psa)
Murphy, Miss Carly (psa)

39. **DTTO Wirral**
Arches Initiative, 23 Conway Street
Birkenhead, Wirral CH41 4PE
tel 0151-666 6867 *fax 0151-666 0800*

Baird, Allen (spo)
Evans, Mrs Margaret
Freeman, Miss Susan
Nenna, Paul
Cranney, Miss Emma (psa)
Given, Michael (psa)

Youth Offending Teams

40. **YOT Court Services**
Liverpool Youth Court
Hatton Gardens, Liverpool
tel 0151-233 3382 *fax 0151-236 3263*

Harrison, Mrs Christine (psa)

41. **YOT - Knowsley**
Youth Justice Section
10 Derby Street, Prescot
Liverpool L34 3LG
tel 0151-443 3079 *fax 0151-443 3770*

Hamlin, Ms Janice

42. **YOT - St Helens**
Youth Offending Team
Alexandra House, Borough Road
St Helens WA10 3RN
tel (01744) 677990 *(01744) 677577*

Saleh, Miss Janine

43. **YOT - Liverpool North**
Youth Justice Section
3 Mark Street, Liverpool L5
tel 0151-233 1984 *fax 0151-233 4470*

Daley, Ms Jeanette

44. **YOT - Liverpool Central**
Sefton Grange, Croxteth Drive

Liverpool L17 3AL
tel 0151-233 1912 *fax 0151-233 1915*

Byrne, Paul
Lopez, Ms Donna
Mohammed, Ibrahim
White, Simon

45.   **YOT - Liverpool South**
Youth Justice Section
Liverpool Social Services
89 St Mary's Road, Garston
Liverpool L19 2NL
tel 0151-494 3627 *fax 0151-494 3623*

Vacancy

46.   **YOT - Sefton**
Supervision Assessment/Court Services
Sefton Youth Offending Team
Police Station, Marsh Lane
Liverpool L20 5HJ
tel 0151-285 5127 *fax 0151-934 2779*

Sarkanen, John

47.   **YOT - Wirral**
The Youth Justice Centre
Wirral Social Services
4 Cavendish Road, Birkenhead
Merseyside CH41 8AX
tel 0151-670 5900 *fax 0151-670 5969/8*

Kennedy, Irene
Kinsey, Mrs Becky (psa)

Hostels

48.   **Canning House Probation Hostel**
55 Canning Street, Liverpool L8 7NN
tel 0151-709 4959 *fax 0151-707 0813*

Mahony, Bob (spo, mgr)
Rose, Ms Frances (po, deputy mgr)
Baker, Dave (probn res officer)
Dempsey, Matt (probn res officer)
Freeman, John (probn res officer)
Hobbs, Len (probn res officer)

49.   **Merseybank Hostel**
26 Great Howard Street, Liverpool L3 7HS
tel 0151-255 1183 *fax 0151-236 4464*

Needham, Peter (spo, mgr)
Kennedy, Peter (po, dep mgr)
Hurst, Mrs Sheila (probn res officer)
Morris, Steve (probn res officer)
Roberts, John (probn res officer)
Warren, Gary (probn res officer)
Wright, Gordon (probn res officer)

50.   **Southwood Probation Hostel**
24 Southwood Road, Liverpool L17 7BQ
tel 0151-280 1833 *fax 0151-280 3027*

Aindow, Mrs Gail (spo, mgr)
Smeda, Michael (po dep mgr)
Dunleavy, John (probn res officer)
Gee, Tony (probn res officer)
Lyon, Mrs Ruth (probn res officer)
Rhodes, Paul (probn res officer)

51.   **Adelaide House Probation/Bail Hostel**
115 Edge Lane, Liverpool L7 2PF
tel 0151-263 1290 *fax 0151-260 4205*

Thomas, Ms Pat (mgr)
Edmunds, Miss Gail (dep mgr)

Institutions

52.   H M Prison **Altcourse**
Higher Lane, Fazakerley
Liverpool L9 7LH
tel 0151-522 2000 *fax 0151-522 2121*

Cunliffe, Jack (spo)
Aney, Ms Julie
Jones, Hugh
McKean, Mrs Geraldine
Thomas, Ms Maggie
Taylor, Mrs Kate

53.   H M Prison
Hornby Road **Liverpool** L9 3DF
tel 0151-530 4000 *fax 0151-530 4001*
probn fax 0151-524 1941

Dean, Ms Michelle (spo) ext 4372
Caughey, Ms Debbie
Gough, Ms Lydia
Grunnill, Paul
Holleran, John
Lock, Peter
Milsom, Jim
Morrison, Andy
Rooney, Ms Karen
Smith, David
Williams-Tully, Kevin
Bracegirdle, Miss Clare (psa)
Graham, Nora (psa, 'step on')
Pendleton, Chris (psa)
Smith, Miss Jenny (psa)
Underwood, Miss Shanel (psa)
Sinkinson, Mrs Joan (psa friendly face)

Local Justice Areas

6, 18, 23, 29 Knowsley
7, 8, 14-17, 30, 31 Liverpool

19, 24 St Helens
9, 13, 25, 26, 32 North Sefton
12, 27, 28 South Sefton
10, 11, 21, 33 Wirral

Crown Court

20 Liverpool

NORFOLK PROBATION AREA

Out of hours emergency contact point
John Boag House (01603) 429488

Victim enquiries contact number (01553)
669000 (Jan Kerby)

e-mail
Firstname.Surname@norfolk.probation.gsx.
gov.uk

1. **Head Office**
   4th Floor, St James Yarn Mill
   Whitefriars, Norwich NR3 1SU
   tel (01603) 220100 *fax (01603) 664019*
   direct dial (01603) 220+ext

   Graham, Martin (cpo) ext 105
   Winstanley, Charles (chairman to board) ext 107
   Blackman, Judith (aco) ext 106
   Coker, Pip (aco) ext 108
   Macdonald, Stuart (aco) ext 117
   Wardley, sarah (aco) ext 127
   Rayner, Karen (secy to board) ext 125
   Myhill, James (h.r. mgr) ext 120
   Sendall, Robbie (occup health mgr) ext 128
   Wade, Belinda (finance mgr) ext 109
   Symonds, Robin (it mgr) ext 114
   Kerr, Rowena (diversity mgr) ext 131
   Fitzsimmons, Heather (spo training) ext134
   Wright, Andrew (spo info) ext 123

   MAPPA
   Singleton, Joy (01603) 276321
   Butterworth, David (01603) 276344

   Training
   Gray, Karen (pda)
   tel (01553) 669000
   Payne, Barbara (pda)
   tel (01603) 723200
   Walker, Brian (pda)
   tel (01603) 723200
   Whitehead, Annette (pda)
   tel (01493) 855525
   Winchester Claire (pda)
   tel (01603) 723200

1a. 17 Palace Street
    Norwich NR3 1RT
    tel (01603) 723200 *fax (01603) 614792*
    direct dial (01603) 723+ext

    Programmes Unit
    Hornby, Stephen (prog mgr, idap) ext 203
    Ramshaw, Charles (prog mgr osap, didp, tvp) ext 210
    Hartland, Andy (prog mgr tf, oto, csb) ext 219
    Feeney, Michael (trtmnt mgr idap) ext 229
    Fowler, Mike (trtmnt mgr tvp) ext 211230
    Cooper, Sharon (trtmnt mgr art) ext 228
    Austin, Jo (trtmnt mgr didp) ext 230
    Loome, Alex (trtmnt mgr csb)
    Peaford, Linda (trtmnt mgr oto, think 1st) ext 227
    Payne, Stephen (pso) ext 204

    Interventions
    O'Byrne, Jon (spo) ext 234
    Kirk, Philippa (offender emplt proj mgr)
    Bacon, Helen (pso)

1b. **Substance Misuse Team**
    22-24 Colegate **Norwich** NR3 1BQ
    tel (01603) 877140 *fax (01603) 877145*

    Cuell, Davicd (subst misuse intvntns mgr)
    Day, Alyson (pso)
    Fenn, Sharon (pso)
    Hunt, Philippa (pso)
    Ingram, Stuart (pso pop)
    Millbank, Lyndsey (pso)
    Richards, Matthew (pso)

2. Whitefriars
   Norwich NR3 1TN
   tel (01603) 724000 *fax (01603) 768270*

   Attfield, Clive (spo)
   Butterworth, Liz (spo)
   Cranna, Bob (spo)
   Holt, Caroline (spo)
   Roper, Dan (spo)
   Westmacott, Julie (spo)

   Caton, Margaret
   Connolly, Laura
   Cullingford, Abigail
   Cummins, John
   Dean, Andrew
   Dewsnap, Chris
   Dyde, Sally
   Kennedy, Helen
   Lane, Viv

Mayne, Jean
Orson, Emily
Perlmutter, Anthea
Perrett, Andrew
Pooley, Gill
Ryan, Liz
Whadcoat, Gillian (p)
Young, David

Parr, Jim (asw)
Allison, Charlotte (pso)
Bennett, Pauline (pso)
Blanchard, Victoria (pso)
Bruce, Scott (pso)
Burton, Jim (pso)
Clarke, Valerina (pso)
Cocker, Nicky (pso)
Colbourn, Lynne (pso)
Crockett, Rachel (pso)
Duvall, Jeni (pso)
Forrest, Paula (pso)
Hampson, Nichola (pso)
Hewitt, Kathryn (pso)
Knights, Nicola (pso)
Macdonald, Stacey (pso)
McKay, Mary (pso)
Macleod, Elaine (pso)
Menzies, Liz (pso)
Narducci, Wendy (pso)
Page, Viv (pso)
Pietocha, Mia (pso)
Riley, Nicole (pso)
Toovey, Bryan (pso)
Whitaker, James (pso)
Youngs, Ray (pso)

Crown Court Office
tel (01603) 728268

2a. **68 Bishopgate**
Norwich NR1 4AA
tel (01603) 221600 *fax (01603) 221615*
direct dial (01603) 221 + ext

Griffey, Portia (unpaid wk scheme mgr) ext 628
Murphy, Tracey (area placmnt mgr) ext 605
Kennedy, David (area supvrs mgr) ext 612
Chaplin, Bill (pso) ext 604
Howard, Graham (pso)
Lewis, Phil (pso)
Malone, Robert (pso)
Pyzer, Stphen (pso) ext 608
Williams, John (pso)

Victim Liaison
Burbidge, Kathy (pso) ext 603

3. Rampart Road
Great Yarmouth NR30 1QZ
tel (01493) 855525 *fax (01493) 332769*

East, Paul (spo)
Rainton, Pauline (spo)
Atkins, Tina
Brogan, Rachel
Curl, Tracey
Cook, Maggie (p)
Tricker, Clive
Tricker, Linda
Alfonso, Rosa (pso)
Craske, Sue (pso)
Doherty, Patricia (pso)
Hannant, Linda (pso)
McLean, Annie (pso)
Pack, Rachael (pso)

4. Purfleet Quay
King's Lynn PE30 1HP
tel (01553) 669000 *fax (01553) 776544*

Leaberry, David (spo)
Moulton, Bob (spo)
Barnes, Amanda-Jayne
Bertram, David
Gale, Marie
Hunns, Johanna
Kimmett, Janice
Martin, Terry
Wells, Judith
Allen, Rita (pso)
Arnold, Tracy (pso)
Britton, David (pso)
Bullock, Nathalie (pso)
Carter, Anita (pso)
Garner, Roy (pso)
Harpley, Jenny (pso)
Mainwaring, David (pso)
Scarrott, Brian (pso)
Steward, Kathryn (pso)
Yates, Elizabeth (pso)
Kerby, Jan (vlo)

5. 12/14 Raymond Street
Thetford IP24 2EA
tel (01842) 754071 *fax (01842) 751089*

Greenhalgh, Karen (spo)
Cuthbert, Ann
Hussein, Steve
Racher, Bev
Sweeting, Bill
Wright, Julie
Blackman, Paul (pso)
Bliss, Kim (pso)
Chislett, Joanne (pso)

Kerby, Jan (pso)
Mitchell, Donna (pso)
Riley, Nicola (pso)
Williams, Linzi (pso)

6. 3 Kelvin Place
   Thetford IP24 3RR
   tel (01842) 764591 *fax (01842) 762904*

   Ayris, John (pso)
   Good, Philippa
   Langham, Barry (pso)
   Murphy, Fred (pso)
   Stoodley, Carl (pso)
   Swinger, Adrian (pso)

7. 18 Deneside
   Great Yarmouth NR30 3AX
   tel (01493) 844991 *fax (01493) 332670*

   Burley, Peter (pso)
   Hawkes, Roger (pso)
   McGill, Rosemary (pso)
   McKinnell, Duncan (pso)
   Pamment, Mike (pso)
   Riches, Jason (pso)
   Scully, Eamon (pso)

8. **Youth Offending Team**
   Norwich
   tel (01603) 877500

   Kemsley, Hannah

   Great Yarmouth
   tel (01493) 847400

   Vacancy

   Kings Lynn
   tel (01553) 819400

   Martin, Richard

Hostel

9. **John Boag House**
   1 Drayton Road, Norwich NR3 2DF
   tel (01603) 429488 *fax (01603) 485903*

   Rymer, Julia (spo mgr)
   Medhurst, Ian (po deputy)
   Caron-Mattison, Joe (asst warden)
   Davison, Cathy (asst warden)
   Davison, Stephanie (asst warden)
   Foster, Frank (asst warden)
   Richards, Chris (asst warden)

Institutions

10. H M Prison & YOI
    Knox Road **Norwich** NR1 4LU

tel (01603) 708600 *fax (01603) 708601*
probn fax (01603) 708619

Discipline ext 8791
Probn clerks
Reed, Mike (admin & pub protctn) ext 8803
Moore, Andy (admin & ets) ext 8804

McNelly, John (spo) ext 8802
Wivell, Bill (child & pub protectn) ext 8786
Bayles, Ray (F, G wings, hdc) ext 8752
Dewsnap, Chris (psr writer) ext 8759
Fergusson, Iain (L wing, hdc, health care) ext 8758
Lamond, Charles (pso, A, L, M wings, healthcare)
ext 8878 & 8758
Rutherford, John (pso, child protctn, VPs) ext 8854
Facey, Jenny (pso, F & G wings) ext 8700 & 8758
Baker, Aaron (pso, A, E wings) ext 8854

11. H M Prison **Wayland**
    Griston, Thetford IP25 6RL
    tel (01953) 804100 *fax (01953) 804220*
    direct dial (01953) 858 + ext

    Probn clerk (visits, gen enquiries) ext 073
    Probn typist (sch 1, temp release) ext 071

    Westrop, Jacqueline (spo) ext 072
    Daulby, Dee
    Hardwicke, Dee
    Phillips, David
    Wales, Andy
    Cox, Martin (pso)

Local Justice Areas

2 Norwich
3 Great Yarmouth
2 North Norfolk
5 South Norfolk
5 Central Norfolk
4 West Norfolk

Crown Courts

2 Norwich
4 King's Lynn

NORTHAMPTONSHIRE PROBATION AREA

Central bail referral number
Bridgewood Hostel, tel (01604) 648704

Out of hours emergency contact point
Bridgewood Hostel, tel (01604) 648704

Victims enquiries contact number
tel (01604) 658060 or tel (01536) 526821

e-mail
Firstname.Surname@northamptonshire.
probation.gsx.gov.uk

1. **Head Office**
    Walter Tull House, 43-47 Bridge Street
    Northampton NN1 1NS
    tel (01604) 658000 *fax (01604) 658089*

    Brown, Pete (co)
    Pearse, Roger (aco, hostel, dtto, high risk,
    prog delivery unit, ptnrshps, yot)
    Meylan, Denise, (aco, offender mgmnt
    unit, cp, crts,
    HMYOI Onley, HMP Ryehill, HMP
    W'boro, pre-release)
    King, Helen (aco, treasury & finance,
    facilities)
    Allen, Clare, (aco, h.r, training & develop,
    diversity)
    Horsefield, Judith (temp aco)
    Opong, Baah, (temp aco)

    SMT Unit
    Bedford, Roland (board secy)
    Shepherd, Jean (pa to co)
    Kew, Clare (pa to R Pearse and B Opong)
    Wakelin, Sarah (pa to C Allen and D
    Meylan)
    Vacancy (pa to H King & J Horsefield)
    Robinson, Becky, (proj ass)

    Finance
    Byrne, Cathy (accountant)
    O'Callaghan, Helen (finance off)

    Human Resources Unit
    Wilson, Katie (h.r.mgr)
    Obeng, Abbie (h.r.off)
    Bharadia, Bhavina (h.r. admin)

    Training and Development Unit
    Dunkley, Melissa (unit mgr)
    Vacancy (training & devpt off)
    Whitaker, Sue (diversity off)

    Information Unit
    Walker, Gill (info & it mgr)
    Cornhill, Alan (info systems off)
    Vacancy (it supp off)
    Vacancy (it admin)
    Alland, Mark (performance off)
    Jones, Madie (info off)
    Vacancy (info systems trainer)

2. Walter Tull House, 43-47 Bridge Street
    Northampton NN1 1NS
    tel (01604) 658000 *fax (01604) 658004*

    CJIP
    Fulton, Ian (mgr)
    Carroll, Vince (mentoring co-ordinator)

    Community Punishment
    Garcha, Permjit, (unit mgr)
    Daft, Joh (dep mgr)
    Cookson, Laurie, (pso)
    Griffin, John (pso)
    Newcombe, Bob (pso)
    Paul, Robert (pso)
    Penson, Neil (pso)
    Robinson, Andrew (pso)
    Carrick, Jo (proj sup)
    Clements, Stella (proj sup)

    County Office
    Medley, John (unit mgr)
    Rance, Joan, (health & safety off)

    Court Team
    Pemberton, Andy (unit mgr)
    Bond, Jodi
    Griffiths, Paul
    Jones, Courtney
    Burton, Tracy (pso)
    Leduc, Anglea (pso)
    Lishman, Stevie (pso)
    Osmani, Kimberley (pso)

    DTTO
    Slaven, Louise
    Allen Donald (pso)

    High Risk Unit
    Enfield, Clare (unit mgr)
    Hewitt, Liz (unit mgr mappa)
    Pratt, Joe (deputy mgr)
    Bowers, Anne
    Coleman, Lisa
    Campbell-Fuller, Nadine (psy)
    Johnny Hermiston (prog facilitator)
    Weston, Peter (prog facilitator)
    Grice, Debs (pso)

    Offender Management Unit
    Shorley Cate (unit mgr)
    Hobbs, Jo (dep mgr)
    Clowes, Jess (acting mgr)
    Whelan, Beth (acting dep mgr)
    Convey, Emma
    Crawford, Emma
    Donoghue, Lesley
    Eason, Anne
    Gill, Dave
    Vacancy
    Lestrade, Suzanne
    McAulay, James

McIntosh, Hanif
Martin, Lesley
Lewis, Lawrence
Presbury, Deborah
Thompson, Gary
Walker, Ruth
Woodward, Teresa
Driver, Tracy (pso)
Holmes, Bekke (pso)
James, Paul (pso)
Kiernan, Sandra (pso)
Marlow, Geoff (pso)
Newbold, Andy (pso)
Preskey, Tony (pso)

Partnerships
Kellock, Jim (unit mgr)
Clark, Barbara (ete advisor)

Practice Development
Goodman, Quentin (pda)
Barrett, Sarah (pda)
Biddle, Graeme (pda)
Burgess, Karen (trainee)
Earl, Louise (trainee)
Fielding Lorna (trainee)
Jones, Hannah (trainee)
Morrison, Lindsay (trainee)
Roskell, Sharon (trainee)
Rowell, Lorna (trainee)
Seabrook, Clare (trainee)
Silcott, Chantel (trainee)
Tew Helen (trainee)
Thurland, Vicki (trainee)
Wallace, Noreen (trainee)
Wrighton, Sarah (trainee)

Pre-Release Unit
Nichols, David
Prendiville, Johnny (pso)
Roquecave, Debbie (pso)

Programme Delivery Unit
Bell, Mari (treatment mgr)
Blackshaw, Charlotte (treatment mgr)
Bullock, Sally (pso)
Clement, Danny (pso)
Ettinger, Simone (pso)
Mosdell, Andrew (pso)
Paintin, Gary (pso)

3. 20 Oxford Street
    Wellingborough NN8 4HY
    tel (01933) 303680 *fax (01933) 303699*

Community Punishment
Benford, Kathryn, (pso)
Vacancy (pso)
Lackin, Bill (workshop supvr)

Court Team
Gabriel, Gail
Bartley, Delia (pso)
Winters, Sarah (pso)

DTTO
Vacancy (unit mgr)
Murray, Kirstie (deputy mgr)
Heyworth, Sophie
Cox, Debbie (pso)
Fontana, Caterina (pso)
Salmon, Ginny (pso)

High Risk Team
Robinson, Rebecca

Offender Management Unit
Bayliss Rosie
Beattie, Helen

Practice Development Unit
Freeman, Hayley (trainee)
Jones, Matthew (trainee)

Programme Delivery Unit
Jones, Jackie (treatment mgr)
Clarke, Claire (pso)
Fitch, Jackie (pso)
Gibbons, Paulette (pso)
Westley, Linda (pso)
Wilson, Helen (pso)

4. Edinburgh House, 7 Corporation Street
    Corby NN17 1NG
    tel (01536) 463920 *fax (01536) 406607*

Community Punishment
Tallett, Ben (pso)

Court Team
Bromhall, Chris
Carr, Pat (pso)
Gardner, Chris (pso)
Hector, Jane (pso)

High Risk Unit
Crawford, Thomas
Bennett, Cheryl (pso)

Offender Management Unit
Holmes, Elsa (deputy mgr)
De-st-Aubin, Doug
Jones, Laura
Blackwell, Julian (pso)
Shepherd, Matthew (pso)

Practice Development Unit
Roskell, Sharon (trainee)
Thurland, Vicki (trainee)

Programme Delivery Unit
Adams, Rachel (treatment mgr)
Eden, Rachel (pso)

Geraghty, Amanda (pso)
Harcourt, Diane (pso)
Moyney, Emily (pso)

5. Unit 5, Baron Avenue
    Telford Way Industrial Estate
    Kettering NN16 8UW
    tel (01536) 521740 *fax (01536) 524282*

    Community Punishment
    Abela, Frank
    Carr, Pat (pso)
    Robinson, Lindsey (pso)
    Allen, Simon (proj sup)
    Sutton, Peter (proj sup)
    Cole, Del (workshop sup)

    Court Team
    Vacancy, (pso)

    High Risk Unit
    Lansberry, Denise
    O'Shea, Melanie
    Waters, Marie (pso)

    Offender Management Unit
    Hayat, Zareen, (unit mrg)
    Johnson, Brian
    Hammond, Alison
    Knights, Jackie (pso)
    Steele, Karen (pso)

    Practice Development Unit
    Earl Louise (trainee)

    Pre-Release Unit
    Woodward, Jenny (unit mgr)
    Hegarty, Eamon
    Hicks, Gina (pso)
    Sludden, Patrick (pso)

    Programme Delivery Unit
    Hamson, Chris (unit mgr)

6. **Crown Court**
    85/87 Lady's Lane
    Northampton NN1 3HQ
    tel (01604) 637751 *fax (01604) 603164*

    Inns, Linda (pso)
    Wilson, Anne (pso)

7. **Youth Offending Team South**
    52-53 Billing Road
    Northampton NN1 5DB
    tel (01604) 602400 *fax (01604) 639231*

    Vacancy
    Mangili, Francesca

8. **Youth Offending Team South**
    73 London Road **Kettering** NN15 7PQ
    tel (01536) 533800 *fax (01536) 312240*

    Malivoire, Sarah
    Woolley, Julie

Hostel

9. **Bridgewood House**
    45-48 Lower Meadow Court
    Northampton NN3 8AX
    tel (01604) 648704 *fax (01604) 645722*

    Doran, Paul (unit mrg)
    Pratt, Liz (dep mgr)
    Cantlow, Tracy (probn hostel off)
    Crutchley, Steve (probn hostel off)
    Lloyd-Williams, Debby (probn hostel off)
    Mason, Michelle (probn hostel off)
    Smith, Kerry (probn hostel off)
    Stapleton-Wynn, Lynn (probn hostel off)
    Knight, Bridget (waking nt supvr)
    Waring, Dean (waking nt supvr)
    Vacancy (waking nt supvr)
    Vacancy (waking nt supvr)

Institutions

10. HMP & YOI **Onley**
    Willoughby, Nr Rugby
    Warwickshire CV23 8AP
    tel (01788) 523400 *fax (01788) 523401*

    Langford, Chris (unit mgr) ext 3595
    Cooper, John ext 3584
    Fincham, Mel ext 3546
    Stephens, Chris ext 3651
    Aslett, Peter (pso) ext 3646
    Chaplin, Louise (pso) ext 3512
    Tebutt, Brenice (pso)

11. H M Prison **Wellingborough**
    Millers Park, Doddington Road
    Wellingborough, Northants NN8 2NH
    tel (01933) 232700 *fax (01933) 232847*

    probn clerk ext 2852
    parole clerk ext 2760

    Chantler, Mike (unit mgr) ext 2853
    Brimble, Pat
    Harmston, Edwin ext 2854
    Honour, Mike ext 2851
    Pitt, Vanessa
    Willetts, Janis ext 2846
    Bailey, Yvonne (pso) ext 2850
    Vacancy (pso) ext 2846
    Knights, Jackie (pso) ext 2850
    Vacancy (pso) ext 2846

12. H M Prison **Ryehill**
Onley, Willoughby
Nr Rugby, Warwickshire CV23 8AN
tel (01788) 523300 *fax (01788) 523311*

Baggott, Martin
Maltman, Lesley
Dawn Rose
Vacancy

Local Justice Areas

4 Corby
2 Daventry
5 Kettering
2 Northampton
2 Towcester
3 Wellingborough

Crown Court

6 Northampton

NORTHUMBRIA PROBATION AREA

Out of hours emergency contact no 0191 477 5600

Victim enquiries contact number 0191-261 2541

e-mail Firstname.Surname@northumbria. probation.gsx.gov.uk

1. **Head Office**
Lifton House, Eslington Road
Jesmond, Newcastle upon Tyne NE2 4SP
tel 0191-281 5721 *fax 0191-281 3548*

direct dial 0191-240+ number

Williamson, Pauline (co, chief exec) 7312
Gardiner, David (director of ops) 7309
Fenwick, John (director of finance, i.t. & perf services) 7352
Mackie, Chris (director of business services) 7351
Hall, Nick (dir of people mgmnt & org devpt) 7332
Taylor, Barry (aco perf) 7366
Nesbit, Don (perf devpt mgr) 7362
Holland, Margaret (perf devpt off) 7346
Burns, Liam (asst co, hr & staff devpt) 7333
Dunn, John (financial services mgr) 7326
Smith, Simon (financial services mgr) 7325

McDine, Julie (h.r. mgr) 7379
Houghton, Adrian (h.r. mgr) 7328
Garrick, Rong-Ning (diversity mgr) 7348
Donkin, Julie (contracts & facilities mgr) 7339
Marley, Marie (head office admin mgr) 7368
Wilson, Gillian (business risk mgr) 7304
Stockley, Rod (health & safety) 7331
Ramshaw, Dawn (training & info mgr) 7343
Bone, David (ict mgr)
Pearson, Sue (comms mgr) 7330
Mills, John (offender mgmnt imp mgr) 7327
Barron, Vincent (seconded to NOMS)
Wright, Tony (seconded to GONE)
Dale, Wendy (seconded to GONE)
Taylor, Richard (seconded to HO)
Conway, Malcolm (seconded to DIP, N'land CC)
Hunter, Colin (seconded to St Nicholas Hosp)
Fisher, Pauline (seconded to cjip)
Pooley, Geoff (seconded to cjip)
Parkinson, Gerry (p, seconded to Portsmouth Univ)

2. **Training Centre**
Dene House, Durham Road
Low Fell, Gateshead
Tyne & Wear NE9 5AE
tel 0191-491 1693 *fax 0191-491 3726*

Teasdale, John (area mgr training & staff devpt)
McIntosh, Angus (consortium mgr)
Smith, Mary (consortium training mgr)
McFarlane, Pauline (training & staff devpt off)
Stephenson, Sharon (training & staff devpt off)
Crowther, Lynn (pda)
Harrison, Ken (pda)
Jacques, Denise (pda)
Jackson, Ian (nvq co-ord)

Newcastle

3. **ACO Unit**
6 Lansdowne Terrace **Gosforth**
Newcastle upon Tyne NE3 1HW
tel 0191-213 0611 *fax 0191-213 1361*

Mackintosh, Jane (aco)
Howson, Maxine (admin mgr)

4. 5 Lansdowne Terrace
    Gosforth
    Newcastle upon Tyne NE3 1HW
    tel 0191-213 1888 *fax 0191-213 1393*

    direct dial 0191-2468 + number

    North Team
    McGovern, Mark (spo, mgr) ext 230
    Bowers, Tracy 208
    Brain, Malcolm (p) 219
    Clark, Malcolm 216
    Edison, Elaine 210
    Higgins, Rob 228
    Lowes, Elaine 221
    Masendeke, Sally 218
    Norwood, Tina 212
    Robson, Janice 229
    Williams, Allison 220
    Roberts, Joanne (trainee) 220
    Jones, Clifford (pso) 213
    Mulvenna, Tommy (pso) 211
    Trainor, Pat (pso) 215

5. **Persistent Offenders Team**
    Clifford Street Police Station
    Byker, Newcastle NE6 1EA
    tel 0191-221 8281

    Love, Amanda (p, spo mgr)
    Jaimin, David
    Seebohm, Laura
    Smylie, Elaine (pso)

6. **70-78 St James' Boulevard**
    Newcastle upon Tyne NE1 4BN
    tel 0191-261 9091 *fax 0191-233 0758*

    City Team
    Gavin, Maureen (spo mgr)
    Capper, Elaine
    Cox, Jacqueline
    Elliott, Megan (p)
    Gartland, Elaine
    Mynott, Cynthia
    Ritchie, Heather
    Scott, Mark
    Sharpe, Ian
    Smyth, Sue
    Watson, Nicola
    Lockie, Claire (trainee)
    Butt, Haroon (pso)
    Little, Kiri (pso)
    Wilcox, Chris (pso)

7. 6th Floor **Collingwood House**
    3 Collingwood Street
    Newcastle upon Tyne NE1 1JW
    tel 0191-232 3368 *fax 0191-233 0760*

Court Services Team
Clarkin, Elizabeth (spo mgr) (8, 9)
Ford, Lucy
Lloyd, Philip
Thompson, Kay
Douthwaite, Lynda (pso)
Maxwell, Sandra (pso)
Patterson, Liz (pso)
Smith, Maureen (pso)

8. **Victim Liaison Unit**
    6th Floor, Collingwood House
    3 Collingwood Street
    Newcastle upon Tyne NE1 1JW
    tel 0191-261 2541 *fax 0191-221 1438*

    Clinton, Roy
    Mantey, Jean
    Bruce, Brenda (pso)
    Reid, Gloria (pso)
    Riley, Gillian (pso)

9. **The Law Courts** Quayside
    Newcastle upon Tyne NE1 2LA
    tel 0191-230 1737 *fax 0191-233 0759*

    Davies, John
    Graham, Harry (p)
    Wilsdon, Maureen (p)
    Wood, Janice (pso)

10. **717 West Road**
    Newcastle upon Tyne NE15 7PS
    tel 0191-274 1153 *fax 0191-275 0963*

    West Team
    Francis, Anne (spo mgr)
    Dale, Paul
    Grierson-Smith, Marie
    Key, Helen
    O'Farrell, Paul
    Pyle, Colin
    Rothwell, Diane
    Wilks, Elizabeth (p)
    Binley, Karen (trainee)
    Brough, Anjali (pso)
    Mullen, Angela (pso)

11. 4 Glendale Terrace **Byker**
    Newcastle upon Tyne NE6 1PB
    tel 0191-276 6666 *fax 0191-224 2878*

    East Team
    Ord, Mary (spo mgr)
    Anderson, Shirley
    Cockburn, Fred
    Coxon, Adrian
    Dixon, John (p)
    Hutchinson, Jenny

Ions, Kenneth
Jarvis, Lesley
Pagan-Jones, Nerys
Simpson, Karen
Simpson, Kerry
Stafford, Sandra
Taylor, Christine (p)
Wallace, Joanne
Cardiff, Teresa (pso)
Richardson, Clare (pso)

Trainees
0191-276 9957
McKenna, Maureen (pda)
Miles, Susan (pda)
Shenton, Nicola (trainee)
Smith, Jennifer (trainee)

Northumberland & North Tyneside

12. **ACO Unit**
Former Employment Exchange
South View, Ashington
Northumberland NE63 0RY
tel (01670) 855724 *fax (01670) 854406*

McCartney, Jeff (aco)
Bavidge, Ann (p, admin mgr)
O'Hara, Marcia (p, admin mgr)

13. Former Employment Exchange
South View **Ashington**
Northumberland NE63 0RY
tel (01670) 813053 *fax (01670) 814858*

County Team
Seddon, Amanda (spo mgr)
Campbell, Cathy
Foster, Susan
Lee, Vanessa (p)
Shiells, Jill
Singer, Steve
Tate, Eunike
Wade, Martin
Bewick, Lisa (trainee)
Caush, Natalie (trainee)
Elliott, Neil (trainee)
Bell, Rachel (pso)
Flisher, Eileen (pso)
Khosah, Parmjit (pso)
Middlemass, Lee (pso)
Trainor, Mike (pso)
Warburton, Julie (pso)

14. **Ashington Probation Centre**
South View, Ashington
Northumberland NE63 9AH
tel (01670) 520121 *fax (01670) 816130*

Cornick, Judith (pda)
Gallagher, Paul (pda)
Randall, Barbara (pda)
Randall, Ken (pda)
Marley, Stewart (learning devpt assessor)

15. 27 Bondgate Without
Alnwick Northumberland NE66 1PR
tel (01665) 602242 *fax (01665) 605184*

Evans, Brendan
Slater, Phil

16. 32/34 Richard Stannard House
Bridge Street **Blyth**
Northumberland NE24 2AG
tel (01670) 352441 *fax (01670) 352921*

Turner, Margaret (spo mgr)
Barnes, Matthew
Clarkson, Laura
Dent, Sharon
Gunn, Ann (p)
Hardington, Gary
Lane, Carol
Murphy, Stacey
Smith, Allison
Chilton, Leigh (trainee)
Dodds, Justine (trainee)
Bowler, Howard (pso)
Brown, Josephine (pso)

17. 4 Wentworth Place **Hexham**
Northumberland NE46 1XB
tel (01434) 602499 *fax (01434) 606195*

Ackerman, Sarah
Bennett, Vanessa (p)

18. Lovaine House, 9 Lovaine Terrace
North Shields Tyne and Wear NE29 0HJ
tel 0191-296 2335 *fax 0191-257 6170*

Familton, Bev (spo mgr)
Brannon, Tom
Currie, Ivan
Davidson, Sarah
Doggett, Steven
Dunne, Lennie (p)
Fellows, Debbie
Peacock, Graham
Pollard, Caroline
Price, Deborah
Rudram, Anna
Speed, Warren (p)
Wallwork, Charlie
Nicholson, Tracey (trainee)
Robson, Chantal (trainee)
Ellison, Gladys (pso)

Kelly, Jean (pso)
McBeth, Pam (pso)
Towns, Allan (pso)

19. 13 Warwick Road **Wallsend**
Tyne and Wear NE28 6SE
tel 0191-262 9211 *fax 0191-295 4824*

Downing, Dorothy (spo mgr)
Alexander, Paul
Badhan, Savina
Bates, Annie
Chopra, Sheetal
Jones, Stephanie
Lennox, Mark
Ward, Clare
Brent, Claire (trainee)
Grant, Louise (trainee)
Weatherly, Marcus (trainee)
Wylie, Sarah (trainee)
Beadle, Lorraine (pso)
Beare, Gerry (pso)

20. **MAPPA Unit**
Block 38, Northumbria Police HQ
North Road, Ponteland
Newcastle upon Tyne NE20 0BL
tel (01661) 868077 *fax (01661) 868497*

McLean, Wynne (area mgr, public
protectn)
ext 68286
Albiston, Kath (snr pract, pub protectn)
Connor, Gary (snr pract, pub protectn)
Thompson, Mark (snr pract, pub protectn)

21. **Sexual Behaviour Unit**
14 Pitt Street
Newcastle upon Tyne NE4 5SU
tel 0191-260 2540 *fax 0191-261 1548*

Kennington, Roger

Wearside

22. **ACO Unit**
Warwick Street, Gateshead
Tyne and Wear NE8 1PZ
tel 0191-478 9978 *fax 0191-478 9979*

Sammut-Smith, Ian (area mgr)
Fullard, Lynn (admin mgr)

23. Hylton Road **Pennywell**
Sunderland SR4 8DS
tel 0191-534 5545 *fax 0191-534 2380*

Ferguson, Lawrie (spo mgr)
Bosanko, Kay
Cliff, Marian (p)

Flynn, Tony
James, Heather
Nairne, Finlay
Nolan, Michael
Rafiq, Mohammed
Smith, Clair
Stobbart, Susan
Blevins, Tracy (trainee)
Clydesdale, Kirsty (p, pso)
Greaves, Aly (p, pso)

24. Mainsforth Terrace West
Hendon Sunderland SR2 8JX
tel 0191-514 3093 *fax 0191-565 1625*

Stratford, Mary (spo mgr) (25)
Murray, Alison (persistent offndr team)
Coombe, Jennifer
Locklan, Margaret
Oyolu-Barker, Chin Chin
Smith, Susan
Speight, Lena
Stube, Lori
Sweeting, Tom
Zein-Elabdin, Sara
Brown, Malcolm (pso)
Giles, Julie (p, pso)
Lawther, Sue (p, pso)
Minhas, Virinder (pso)

25. Kings Road **Southwick**
Sunderland SR5 2LS
tel 0191-548 8844 *fax 0191-548 6834*

Bell, Joanne
Dowson, Catherine
Findley, Anne
McQuillan, Steve
Middleton, Linda
Stafford, Keith
Boad, Angela (trainee)
Harrison, Valerie (pso)
Manley, Lynn (pso)
Mooney, Lynn (pso)

26. Old Police Building
Spout Lane **Washington**
Tyne and Wear NE37 2AB
tel 0191-416 8574 *fax 0191-415 7943*

McElderry, Jim (spo mgr) (27)
Grimes, Mike
Gettings, Sarah
Lowerson, Angela
Pridie, Pamela
Murphy, Steven (pda)
Smiles, Simon (pso)

27. 1st Floor, Empire House
Newbottle Street **Houghton-le-Spring**
Tyne and Wear DH4 4AF
tel 0191-584 3109 *fax 0191-584 4919*

Baker, Pam (p)
Cutter, Anne-Marie
Haran, Margaret
James, Heather
Kavanagh, Martin
Pratt, Kathleen
Murphy, Kirsty (pda)
Connor, Stephen (trainee)
Marsh, Charlotte (trainee)
Harrington, Kathryn (trainee)
Vipond, Richard (trainee)
Houghton, Karen (pso)
Richardson, Ian (pso)

South Tyneside & Gateshead

28. **ACO Unit**
Warwick Street, Gateshead
Tyne and Wear NE8 1PZ
tel 0191-478 9978 *fax 0191-478 9979*

Fiddes, Christine (aco)
Falcon, Sheila (admin mgr)

29. Homer Villa, St John's Terrace
Jarrow Tyne and Wear NE32 3BT
tel 0191-489 7767 *fax 0191-483 3961*

Solan, Catherine (spo mgr)
Bell, Andrea
Davison, Olwen
Duggan, Robert
Hill, Linda
Lee, Stephen
Robinson, Kerry
Wilson, Tim (p)
Randall, Ken (pda)
O'Kane, Kathy (trainee)
Turrell, Lorraine (trainee)
Attley, Paul (pso)
Sibbald, Karen (pso)
O'Neill, Maria (pso)

30. Secretan Way, Millbank
South Shields
Tyne and Wear NE33 1HG
tel 0191-455 2294 *fax 0191-427 6919*

Ineson, Lesly (spo mgr)
Atkinson, Jonelle
Blaylock, Johanne
Brookes, Louise
Cunningham, Alita
Dixon, Ian

Hawes, Scott
Hayes, Mary
Jones, Vikki
Norton, Michael
Turner, Melanie
Peggie, Allan (p)
Devlin, Linda (trainee)
Gwilym, Matthew (trainee)
Bevens, Christina (pso)
Byrne, Tonya (pso)
Davison, Susan (pso)
Gibson, Kim (p, pso)
Johnston, Carole (pso)
Morren, Alex (pso)

31. Wesley Court **Blaydon**
Tyne and Wear NE21 5BT
tel 0191-414 5626 *fax 0191-414 7809*

Hull, Mary (spo mgr)
Armstrong, Anne (p)
Franciosi, Heather
Halpin, Aidan
Holcroft, Harma
Jarvis, Rob
Main, Alex
Peaden, Kay (p)
Saddington, Debbie
Taylor, Alison
Davison, Rebecca
Murphy, Steve (pda)
Baker, Mike (trainee)
Breeze, Gareth (trainee)
McKale, Jonathan (trainee)
Bleanch, Graham (pso)
Graham, Lisa (pso)

32. Warwick Street
Gateshead Tyne and Wear NE8 1PZ
tel 0191-478 2451 *fax 0191-478 1197*

Harper, Karin (spo mgr)
Bright, Kelly
Brown, Mandy
Burrows, Gerry
Cockburn, Ben
Codling, Neil
Cox, Julie (p)
Dungait, Lynne
Edwards, Ian
Haberfield, Lee
Hope, Katherine
Jones, Mike
MacQueen, Alastair
Robson, Colin
Truscott, Sylvia
Bell, Catherine (pso)
Hope, Kaye (pso)

McIntosh, Louise (pso)
Sherriff, Amanda (pso)

Programmes & Unpaid Work

33. Lifton House
Eslington Road **Jesmond**
Newcastle upon Tyne NE2 4SP
tel 0191-240 7350 *fax 0191-281 3548*

North, John (aco)

tel 0191-240 7347
Williams, Pat (admin mgr)

Unpaid Work

34. **70-78 St James' Boulevard**
Newcastle upon Tyne NE1 4BN
tel 0191-261 9091 *fax 0191-233 0758*

Coulthard, Gail (uw scheme mgr)
Forster, Maureen (qa mgr)
Simpson, Dawn (qa mgr)
Humphries, James (placement mgr)
Archer, Mark (case mgr)
Baker, Maureen (case mgr)
Harrison, Reg (case mgr)
Hinder, Mick (case mgr)
Lowther, Jimmy (case mgr)
Rice, Vincent (case mgr)
Coxon, Deborah (tutor supvr)
Gray, Gillian (tutor supvr)
Tait, David (tutor supvr)

35. Lovaine House, 9 Lovaine Terrace
North Shields
Tyne and Wear NE29 0HJ
tel 0191-296 2335 *fax 0191-257 6170*

Beadle, Andrew (case mgr)
Aitchison, George (case mgr)

36. 13 Warwick Road
Wallsend Tyne & Wear NE28 6SE
tel 0191-262 9211 *fax 0191-295 4824*

Gordon, Bernard (qa mgr)
Harrington, Jim (case mgr)
Robinson, Jim (case mgr)
Scott, Richard (case mgr)

37. Former Employment Exchange
South View **Ashington**
Northumberland NE63 0RY
tel (01670) 813053 *fax (01670) 814858*

Conlon, Peter (qa mgr)
Burt, Foster (case mgr)
Celino, Frank (p, case mgr)
Holgate, Steve (case mgr)

Paterson, Bill (case mgr)
Robinson, Tony (case mgr)
Hoare, John (tutor supvr)
Lindsay, Alex (tutor supvr)

38. 45 John Street **Sunderland**
Tyne and Wear SR1 1QU
tel 0191-510 2030 *fax 0191-565 7746*

Rees, David (uw scheme mgr)
Cutting, Alan (qa mgr)
O'Neill, Mick (qa mgr)
Ball, John (placement mgr)
Davison, Barry (case mgr)
Elliott, Beverley (case mgr)
O'Neill, Richard (case mgr)
Penty, Barbara (case mgr)
Russell, Mick (case mgr)
Turner, John (case mgr)
Burnett, John (tutor supvr)
Burnett, Karen (tutor supvr)
Stimpson, Mark (tutor supvr)

39. Warwick Street
Gateshead Tyne & Wear NE8 1PZ
tel 0191-478 2451 *fax 0191-478 1197*

Boyne, Stephanie (qa mgr)
Dingwall, Ed (case mgr)
Glendinning, Alan (case mgr)
Redford, Paul (case mgr)
Stimpson, Harry (case mgr)
Fay, Kevin (tutor supvr)
Kirton, Iain (tutor supvr)

40. Secretan Way, Millbank
South Shields Tyne and Wear NE33 1HG
tel 0191-455 2294 *fax 0191-427 6919*

Penfold, Keith (qa mgr)
Coates, George (case mgr)
Harvey, Mike (case mgr)
Williamson, George (case mgr)
Withers, Viv (case mgr)
Hall, Lynsey (tutor supvr)

Groupwork

41. 14 Pitt Street
Newcastle upon Tyne NE4 5SU
tel 0191-261 9515 *fax 0191-261 1548*

Dodds, Maggie (area mgr progs)

NSOG Programme Team
Flynn, Alan (prog mgr)
Gow, Sue
Loxley, Felicity (p)
Murphy, Claire
Strachan, Ian
Ryland, Mark (treatment mgr)

42. YMCA Building, Church Way
    North Shields Tyne & Wear NE29 0AB
    tel 0191-258 6601 *fax 0191-296 2396*

    Hill, Louise (prog mgr)
    Aikman, Debbie
    Bailey, Douglas
    Deary, Katherine (p)
    Dymore, Claire
    Wylie, Karen
    Burns, Christine (pso)
    Gerrard, Jason (pso)
    Reay, Rebecca (pso)
    Sammons, Roger (pso)
    Tobin, Neville (pso)

43. **70-78 St James' Boulevard**
    Newcastle upon Tyne NE1 4BN
    tel 0191-261 9091 *fax 0191-233 0758*

    Walter, Dave (prog mgr)
    Basen, Kerrie
    Brunger, Sheila
    Elliott, Katherine
    Scott, Ian
    Smart, Lindsey
    Talbot, John
    Turner, Daphne
    Hodgson, Kath (pso)
    O'Donnell, Sheree (pso)
    Trembath, Jim (pso)
    Walker, Charlene (pso)

44. 5-8 Cornwallis Street **South Shields**
    Tyne and Wear NE33 1BB
    tel 0191-456 1000 *fax 0191-427 6922*

    McLaren, Cath (prog mgr)
    Amar, Urfan
    Edge, Alan
    Thomas, Ami
    Wilkinson, Judith
    Willan, Kate
    Booth, Cathy (pso)
    Brown, Victoria (pso)
    Dickinson, Kevin (pso)
    Jackson, Suzanne (pso)
    Murray, Hannah (pso)

45. 45 John Street **Sunderland**
    Tyne and Wear SR1 1QU
    tel 0191-510 2030 *fax 0191-565 7746*

    Lamb, Mark (prog mgr)
    Carr, Richard
    Dobell, Stacey
    Heslop, Ian

McLeod, Anita
Walton, Peter
Anagnostopoulou, Mimi (pso)
Falcus, Craig (pso)
McManus, Paula (pso)
McNiven, Helen (pso)
Walker, Joan (pso)

Intensive Supervision

46. Lifton House, Eslington Road
    Jesmond Newcastle upon Tyne NE2 4SP
    tel 0191-281 5721 *fax 0191-281 3548*

    direct dial 0191-240 7+ext

    Knotek, Hana (aco) 376
    Kelly, Liz (area mgr)
    Kingsland, Lory (admin mgr) 373

    Cornwallis Street
    Fiddes, Jeff (partnerships mgr)
    Whitley Bay
    Gilbert, Steve (snr pract)
    Harrison, Tracey (pso)
    South Shields
    Cliff, Andrea (pso)
    Gateshead
    Dinning, Sean (pso)
    Jarrow
    Brickland, David (pso)
    Hendon
    Robertson, Tracey (pso)
    St James Boulevard
    Bateman, Gay (pso)
    Ashington
    Cox, John (pso)

47. **Employment, Training & Education Unit**
    5-8 Cornwallis Street
    South Shields, Tyne & Wear NE33 1BB
    tel 0191-420 6245 *fax 0191-420 2975*

    Ward, Andrea (area mgr ete)
    Davison, Bob (ete off iv)
    Gardiner, Charles (ete off iv)
    Bell, Ashley (ete off)
    Bowmer, Linda (ete off)
    Brook, Eric (ete off)
    Buxton, Jennifer (ete off)
    Elliott, Kerry (ete off)
    Guinsberg, Angela (ete off)
    Penman, Eve (ete off)
    Purvis, Frank (ete off)
    Smith, Anthony (ete off)
    Stephenson, Roger (ete off)
    Taylor, Scott (ete off)

48. **DTTO**
Former Employment Exchange
South View, **Ashington**
Northumberland NE63 0RY
tel (01670) 854867 *fax (01670) 854406*

Booth, Richard (spo, dtto mgr)
Heath, Deborah (spo, dtto mgr)

Blyth
Brabbins, Paul
Knox, Clare (pso)
Gateshead
Campbell, Ged
Miles, Sandra
Simpson, Tom
Carter, Alan (pso)
Cole, Liz (pso)
Gosforth
Reed, Paula
Connor, Rachel (pso)
Colloby, Cheryl (pso)
O'Reilly, Michael (pso)
Jarrow
Allison, Pam
South Shields
Foreman, Siobhan
Southwick
Hardy, Peter
Jones, Victoria
Storey, Fiona
Fearns, Helen (pso)
Key, Gareth (pso)
Thompson, Keith (pso)
YMCA, N Shields
Heron, Bill
Barrett, Michelle (pso)

Youth Offending Teams

49. **Northumberland YOT**
The Riverside Centre
North Seaton Industrial Estate
Ashington, Northumberland NE63 0YB
tel (01670) 852225

Graham, Tanya

50. **N Tyneside YOT**
153 Tynemouth Road
North Shields, Tyne & Wear NE30 1ED
tel 0191-200 6001

Austin, Louise (p)
Fearon, Lee

51. **Newcastle YOT**
Block D, 4th Floor, Jesmond Quadrant
3 Archbold Terrace, Sandyford

Newcastle upon Tyne NE2 1BZ
tel 0191-277 7377

Bridgeman, Nicola
Graham, Helen

52. **Gateshead YOT**
Former Felling Police Station
Sunderland Road, Felling
Gateshead, Tyne & Wear NE10 0NJ
tel 0191-440 0500

Harding, Allison

53. **S Tyneside YOT**
30 Commercial Road
South Shields, Tyne & Wear NE33 1RW
tel 0191-427 2850

Sinclair, Nigel

54. **Wearside YOT**
Lambton House, 145 High Street West
Sunderland, Tyne & Wear SR1 1UW
tel 0191-566 3000

Jamieson, John
Trewick, Robert

Hostels

55. **Cuthbert House Bail Hostel**
Derwentwater Road, Bensham
Gateshead NE8 2SH
tel 0191-478 5355 *fax 0191-490 0674*

Kelly, Jan (area mgr)
Bunney, Crawford (snr pract)
Douglas, Jason (hostel asst)
Hall, Paula (hostel asst)
Hannen, Heidi (hostel asst)

56. **Pennywell House Bail Hostel**
Hylton Road, Pennywell
Sunderland, SR4 8DS
tel 0191-534 1544 *fax 0191-534 1049*

Visram, Ann (snr pract)
Bosher, Shaun (hostel asst)
Murton, Mick (hostel asst)
Whillians, Christine (hostel asst)

57. **Ozanam House Probation Hostel**
79 Dunholme Road
Newcastle upon Tyne NE4 6XD
tel 0191-273 5738 *fax 0191-272 2729*

Gelder, Chris (mgr)
Bell, Geoff (deputy)

58. **St Christopher's House Bail Hostel**
222 Westmorland Road, Cruddas Park
Newcastle upon Tyne NE4 6QX
tel 0191-273 2381 *fax 0191-272 4241*

Yoxall, Gail (mgr)
Oxley, Ann (dep mgr)

Institutions

59. H M Prison **Acklington**
Nr Morpeth
Northumberland NE65 9XF
tel (01670) 762300 *fax (01670) 762301*

Direct dial (01670) 762 + ext

Probn clerk 448/9
SOTP treatment mgr 445
Sentence mgmnt clerk 543
Sentence mgmnt officers 447/453

Marshall, Deborah (aco, sentence mgmnt
& resettlement) 452
Mackin, Phil (acting team mgr) 614
Armstrong, Andrea 449
Cavanagh, Ian 641
Candon, Christine 444
Davidson, Pat 444
Devine, Eileen 617
Foster, Chris 457
Gilmore, Maureen 638
Graham, Brenda 456
Groves, Gene 444
Loughrey, Terry (p) 445
Billington, Tracey (pso) 641
Julian, Cheryl (pso) 352
Reece, Emma (pso) 638
Roberts, Amanda (pso) 453

60. H M Young Offender Institution
Castington Nr Morpeth
Northumberland NE65 9XG
tel (01670) 382100 *fax (01670) 382101*
probn fax (01670) 382034

direct dial (01670) 382+ext

Parole clerk ext 162
HDC clerk ext 033
Discipline ext 113
Special visits ext 018

Gibson, Neil (hd of resettlement) ext 013
Cook, Fred ext 158
Lawrence, Bob
Thompson, Val 116
Wilkinson, Peter 158
Baker, Dawn (pso) 116
Cook, Simone (pso) 158
Hall, Heather (pso) 158

Hamilton, Ann (pso) ext 002
Nattrass, Emma (pso)116
Robson, Helen (pso) 057

61. HM Prison **Frankland**
Finchale Avenue, Brasside
Durham DH1 5YD
0191-332 3000 *fax 0191-332 3001*

Morton, Glynis (resettlement mgr)
Airey, Tony
McGovern, Christine
Wilson, Margaret

Local Justice Areas

15 Alnick
15 Berwick on Tweed
31, 32 Gateshead District
17 Tynedale
24 Houghton-le-Spring
4-11 Newcastle-upon-Tyne
18, 19 North Tyneside
13, 16 South East Northumberland
29, 30 South Tyneside
23, 25 Sunderland

Crown Courts

9 Newcastle upon Tyne

NOTTINGHAMSHIRE PROBATION AREA

Out of hours emergency contact point:
Trent House tel 0115-841 5630

e-mail: Firstname.Surname@nottinghamshire.
probation.gsx.gov.uk

Offices

1. **Head Office**
Marina Road, Castle Marina
Nottingham NG7 1TP
tel 0115-840 6500 *fax 0115-840 6502*
direct dial 0115-840 + ext

Chief Officer Group
fax 0115-840 6453

Geraghty, Jane (co) 6453
Goldstraw, Christine (board chair) 6455
Owen, Derek (board secretary) 6455
Flannery, Sharon (dir of om) 6537
McHugh, Bill (dir of interventions) 6461
Moore, Rob (dir of corp services & bus
devpt) 6519
Lewis, Kirsty (pa) 6462

Goode, Alan (dep dir om South)
0115-845 5220
Hill, Nigel (dep dir om North)
(01623) 460823
Leigh, Julie (dep dir int North)
(01623) 460824
MacLeod, Karen (dep dir seconded,
cjit/dat) 0115-908 2172
Taylor, Mark (dep dir int South)
0115-908 2173
Khalil, Jawaid (asst dir corp services) 6450
Francis, Gill (asst dir ext serv) 6490
Newbold, Shirley (treasurer/fin advr) 6468

Central Administration
general enquiries 6500

Finance & Payroll
Enquiries 6464
Shelton, Barry (mgr) 6467

Human Resources Personnel
enquiries 6483
Gordon, Stuart (mgr) 6485

Staff Development
enquiries 6513
Vacancy (spo) 6508

Management Information & Services
enquiries 6476
Henderson, Derek (mgr) 6478

Facilities & Support
enquiries 6489
Poyzer, Mike (mgr) 6490

Health & Safety
Churchill, Heather (mgr) 6451

Accommodation & Advice Unit
0115-993+ext
Hare Duke, Hilary (mgr) 6520
Mulrenan, Una (mgr) 6524
Williams, Jo (welfare ben adv)

2. **Nottingham City**
206 Derby Road, Nottingham NG7 1NQ
tel 0115-845 5100 *fax 0115-845 5101*

Unit Admin Manager
Towlson, Hilary

City Central
Khan, Abirjan (spo)

Offender Management Unit A
Hyatt-Butt, Tariq
Perkins, Debbie
Wilson, Clare
Longfellow, Rachel (pso)
Viera, Max (pso)

Offender Management Unit B
Conway, Bridget
Hooper, John
Rose, Simon
Smith, Sarah
Dowthwaite, Sîan (pso)
Horton, Samantha (pso)

City North
Burnage, Colin (spo)

Offender Management Unit C
Coyle, Jane
Dyjasek, Marie
Simpson-White, Faye
Goddard, Pat (pso)
Morton, Cemona (pso)
Wilson, Lee (pso)

Offender Management Unit D
Ademulegan, Adewale
Palmer, Vicky
Ramsey, Sally
Slack, Sue
Stoddart, Lorna (pso)

Public Protection
Goode, Linda (spo)

Offender Management Unit A
Cina, Eve
Flewitt, Wendy
Maidens, Karen
Marriott, Paul
Boothe, Carol (pso)

Offender Management Unit B
Boggild, Brenda
Green, Judy
Lowe, Elon
Morris, Lesley
Page, Jason (pso)

Access (ETE) Team
Cooke, Steve (mgr)
Bee, Elaine (ete co-ord)
Jones, Maggie (emplt officer)
Moore, Wendy (emplt officer)
Rothwell, Roger (emplt officer)

PALS Team
Positive Action for Learning
Apiafi, Judi (proj mgr)
Asbury, Carol (devpt wrkr)
Hastings, Lynn (basic skills devpt wrkr)
Archer, Cheryl (assessor)
Fritscher, Deborah (esol tutor)
Brotherhood, Lynda (basic skills tutor)
Glossop, Elaine (basic skills tutor)
Holloway, Anthea (basic skills tutor)
Jenkins, Owain (basic skills tutor)
Weatherall, Rachel (basic skills tutor)

3. **Nottingham City**
    Castle Quay, 9 Castle Boulevard
    Nottingham NG7 1FW
    tel 0115-908 2900 *fax 0115-908 2971*

    Unit Admin Manager
    Stocker, Pat

    City South
    Steele, Carole (spo)

    Offender Management Unit C
    Brown, D
    Hart, Simon
    Murphy, Patrick
    Middleton, Patti
    Easom, Cheryl (pso)
    Mawani, Rukshana (pso)
    Pratt, Leahman (pso)

    Offender Management Unit D
    Clare, Jan
    Green, Pauline
    Hamley, Isabelle
    Kennedy, Wendy
    Koty, Amon
    Gregory, Beverley (pso)
    Roe, Julie (pso)

    City Programmes
    Caesar, Beverley (spo)
    Allen, A (pso)
    Gentle, Kristy (pso)
    Howle, Alison (pso)
    Orton, Ann (pso)
    Romanko, Helen (pso)
    Sansome, Andrea (pso)
    Taylor, Sam (pso)
    Teanby, Gary (pso)

    Victim Contact
    Dhindsa, Hardyal (spo)
    Gerty, Ann
    Raban, Deidre
    Cloughley, Wendy (pso women's supt wrkr)
    Johnson, Cathy (pso)
    O'Dare, Helen (pso)
    Ryan, Marie (pso women's supt wrkr)

    Qualifying Training
    Barber, Di (pda)
    Bernard, Juliette (pda)
    Hooper, John (pda)
    Rawlins, Alison (pda)

    Prolific Offender Unit
    Spencer, Derek (spo)
    Green, Heather (pso)

Jones, Mark (pso)
Horne, Jim (police)
Martin, Colin (police)
Paylor, Nigel (police)

Courts Team
Marley, Tamsin (spo)
Leak, Stewart
Baird, Mary (pso)
Bernasconi, Lorraine (pso)
Brickell, Linda (pso)
Dyer, Maxine (pso)
Hammans, Gloria (pso)
Short, Di (pso)
Spivey, Kaye (pso)
Susiwala, Mosina (pso)
Finnan, Angela (enforcement off)
Hewitt, Jane (enforcement off)

4. Traffic Street
    Nottingham NG2 1NU
    tel 0115-956 0956 *fax 0115-956 0900*

    Unpaid Work Team
    Offender Management Unit 1
    Weaver, Paul
    Allen, Yvonne (pso)

    Offender Management Unit 2
    Jabeen, Saika
    Lewis, Sue (pso)

    Offender Management Unit 3
    Brown, Judith
    Slater, Selina (pso)

    Offender Management Unit 4
    Smith, Adge
    White, Jo (pso)

    Offender Management Unit 5
    Bryson, Bev
    Smillie, Rupert (pso)
    Whittaker, Audrey (pso)

    Offender Management Unit 6
    Stafford, Linda
    Gaddu, Sangeeta (pso)

    Medcalf, Jackie (snr cso)
    Goulder, Andy (cso)
    Guthrie, Mick (cso)
    Henson, Claire (cso)
    Smith, Paul (cso)

    Guided Skills & ETE
    Potts, Sarah (emplt officer)
    Fletcher, Janet (guided skills co-ord)
    Clough, Wendy (NCN tutor)
    Rodgers, Ian (NCN tutor)
    Anderson, Jacqui (pso)

4a. **Magistrates' Court Liaison Office**
Carrington Street, Nottingham NG1 2EE
tel 0115-840 6350 *fax 0115-840 6351*

Marley, Tamsin (spo)

4b. **Crown Court Liaison Unit**
Canal Street, Nottingham NG1 7EJ
tel 0115-910 3540 *fax 0115-958 6135*

Marley, Tamsin (spo)

5. **Substance Misuse Team (City)**
The Ropewalk Nottingham NG 1 5DT.
tel 0115-910 5400 *fax 0115-910 5404*

Singh, Gurdev (spo)
Gatt, Barrie (unit admin mgr)
Butcher, Colin
Carri, John
Faulkner, Dione
Storer, Brian
Marren, Teresa (snr drug wrkr)
Sabat, Sumayya (drug worker)
Smith, Rob (drug worker)
Wilson, Jez (drug wrkr)
Ash, Mark (pso)
McCaffrey, Pauline (pso)
Page, Anna (pso)
Russell, Caroline (pso)
Woods, Zoe (pso)
Rodgers, Ged (ete worker)

6. **Substance Misuse Team (County)**
Titchfield House, 96 Nottingham Road
Mansfield Nottinghamshire NG18 1BP
tel (01623) 488 470 *fax (01623) 488 471*

Holdaway, Susan (spo)
Gatt, Barrie (unit admin mgr)
Allenby, Lisa
Fryer, John
Molloy, Nicola
Williams, Anthony
Mutch, Tracey (snr drug worker)
Freeston, Sonya (drugs wrkr)
Bush, Suzanne (drugs wrkr)
Bano, Raqia (pso)
Hopkinson, Chris (pso)
Hudson, Gill (pso)
Rowlands, Heather (pso)
Osborne, Selina (ete worker)

7. 46 Nottingham Road
Mansfield Notts NG18 1BL
tel (01623) 460 800 *fax (01623) 460 801*

Crookall, Jean (spo)
Hardyal, Dhindsa (spo progs)
McCabe, Michelle (unit admin mgr)

Unpaid Work Team
Boynton, Tim
Etherington, Keith (ecp)
Gardner, Emma
Leak, Stewart
Menhennet, Matthew
Perrell, Caroline (ecp)
Wright, Pete
Copley, Chris (pso)
Harvey, Thea (pso)
Jackson, Gemma (pso)
McCabe, Michelle (pso)
Musgrove, Steve (cso)
Nesbitt, Andrew (cso)
Smith, Paul (cso)

Court Team
Belshaw, Kirsty
Jeffries, Mike
Waddingham, Paul
Dangerfield, Maggie (pso)
Harrison, Lucy (pso)
Nisbet, Cheryl (pso)

Programmes Team
Goulder, Jenni
Turner, Del
Mason, Anna (pso)
Mugglestone, Alison (pso)

PALS/ETE
Hartshorn, Barbara (emplt off)
Osbourne, Seliha (emplt off)
Wallace, Cassie (emplt off)

7a. **Community Supervision & Resettlement**
Sherwood Court, Sherwood Street
Mansfield
tel (01623) 468850 *fax (01623) 468851*

all correspondence to Office 7

Downey, Tony (spo)
Annison, Lesley
Barling, Lisa
Cookson, Lyn
Evans, Rebecca
Hilton, Jane
Maurer, Fergus
Parr, Sarah
Riley, Steve
Rudkin, Carole
Wood, Deborah
Young, Lisa
Ainsworth-Chester, Nicola (pso)
Barrow, Rebecca (pso)
Flint, Anne (pso)
Higgins, Craig (pso)

8. 11 Appleton Gate
    Newark NG24 1JR
    tel (01636) 652 650 *fax (01636) 652 651*

    Hemingwey, Sarah (spo)
    Crossland, Jo (unit admin mgr)
    Barraco, Zola
    Davidson, Jane
    Fothergill, Trevor (ecp)
    Hickinbottom, Alison
    Roworth, Kenneth
    Tutt, Katie
    Vacancy
    Russo, Bob (cso)
    Davidson, Jane (pso)
    Maroulaki, Maria (pso)
    Reilly, Lisa (pso)

9. 11 Newcastle Street,
    Worksop S80 2AS
    tel (01909) 473 424 *fax (01909) 530 082*

    Burton, Julie (spo)
    Taylor, Anita (unit admin mgr)
    Birkett, Lesley
    Ellis, Caroline
    Gray, Helen
    Haith, Andrea
    Leigis, Ed
    Ryer, Nick
    Rayment, Lesley
    White, Rachael
    Walker, Colin (ecp)
    Hall, Debbie (emplt off)
    Allen, Greta (pso)
    Flynn, John (pso)
    Jordan, Janeen (pso)
    Mason, Terry (pso courts)
    Richardson, Jenny (pso)
    Weston, Dave (cso)
    Witts, Philip (pso)

10. **MAPPP Manager & Co-ordinator**
    Public Protection Unit
    CID HQ, Holmes House,
    Ratcliffe Gate Mansfield NG18 2JW
    tel (01623) 483 052 *fax (01623) 483 056*

    Hodgett, Victoria (spo)

11. **Prolific Offender Project**
    Central Police Station
    North Church Street
    Nottingham NG1 4BH
    tel 0115- 844 5985 *fax 0115-844 5989*

    Spencer, Derek (spo)
    Victor, Andy

Barrett, Maxine (pso)
Millard, Maxine (emplt officer)

Central Police Station
Great Central Road **Mansfield** NG18 2HQ
tel (01623) 483092 *fax (01623) 483099*

Spencer, Derek (spo)
Mack, Carolyn
Kinsey, Vanessa (pso)

The Venture Centre
30-34 Watson Road
Worksop S80 2BE
tel (01909) 530213

Bowler, David (pso)
Taylor, Lynne (drugs wrkr)
Smith, Alisdair (drugs wrkr)

12. **Youth Offending Team (City)**
    2 Isabella Street, Nottingham NG1 6AT
    tel 0115-841 3008 fax 0115-841 3009/3010

    Carter, Sheila (po)
    Galea, Yvonne (po)
    Hanford, Karen (po)
    Lockwood, Penny (po)
    Zieba, Helena

13. **Youth Offending Teams**
    (County North) Dale Close
    100 Chesterfield Road South
    Mansfield NG19 7AQ
    tel (01623) 433 433 *fax (01623) 452 145*

    Maurer, Fergus
    Tangen, James

    Ground Floor, Block B,
    65 Northgate, Newark NG24 1HD
    Newark NG24 1HD
    tel (01636) 479929 *fax (01636) 613972*

14. **Youth Offending Team (County South)**
    DBH House, Carlton Square
    Carlton, Nottingham NG4 3BP
    tel 0115-940 8612 *fax 0115-940 8603*

    Duncan, Nathaniel

15. **Drugs Intervention Team**

15a. **Arrest Referral Team**
     Central Police Station
     North Church Street
     Nottingham NG1 4BH
     0115-844 5083 *fax 0115-844 5084*

     Hegarty, Tracey (snr pract)
     Pilgrim, Karen (cj case co-ord)
     Blair, K (cj drugs wrkr)

Hansen, Kirsten (cj drugs wrkr)
Hubbard, C (cj drugs wrkr)
Murphy, C (cj drugs wrkr)
Smith, Bev (cj drugs wrkr)
Stenton, D (cj drugs wrkr)
Taylor, Ben (data mgr)
Smith, Ian (snr admin off)

15b. **Restrictions on Bail Team**
Nottingham Magistrates' Court
tel 0115-955 8142

all correspondence to office 15a

Humphies, Aileen (snr pract) (based at
15a)
Barnes, Wendy (cj drugs wrkr)
Brady, Margaret (cj drugs wrkr)

15c. **Aftercare/Inreach Team**
Top Floor, Waverley Health Centre
105-107 Portland Road
Nottingham NG7 4HE
0115-978 2451 *fax 0115-978 7189*

Cooney, Alison (snr pract)
Butler, Sarah (cj case co-ord)
Davies, Ruth (cj case co-ord)
Dinnall, Audrey (cj case co-ord)
Hagen, Steph (cj case co-ord)
Gardner, Melanie (cj case co-ord)
Remm, Kieron (cj case co-ord)

Hostels

16. **106 Raleigh Street**
Nottingham NG7 4DJ
tel 0115-910 5450 *fax 0115-910 5451*

Walker, Angela (spo)
Rodgers, Tony (dep mgr)
Banjoko, Omari (rsw)
Bennett, Marcus (rsw)
Davies, Dawn (rsw)
Foster, Sharon (rsw)
Goddard, Dawn (rsw)
Harris, Keith (rsw)

17. **5 Astral Grove**
Hucknall, Nottingham NG15 6FY
tel 0115-840 5720 *fax 0115-840 5721*

Balmer, Claire (spo)
Green, Chris (dep mgr)
Pates, Gloria (admin asst)
Amos, Sue (rsw)
MacKenzie, Chris (rsw)
Palmer, Paula (rsw)
O'Brien, Pamela (rsw)
Thornley, Nicola (rsw)

18. **Trent House**
392 Woodborough Road
Nottingham NG3 4JF
tel 0115-841 5630 *fax 0115-841 5631*

Bannister, John (spo)
Feather, Budd (dep mgr)
Hermans, Martien (rsw)
Majid, Naima (rsw)
Sadiq, Pervez (rsw)
Wyer, Lisa (rsw)

19. **Nacro Basford House Accommodation
Project**
40-42 Isandula Road,
Basford, Nottingham NG7 7ES
tel 0115-978 5851 *fax 0115-978 5851*

Johnson, Steve

Institutions

20. HM Prison, Perry Road,
Sherwood **Nottingham** NG5 3AG
tel 0115-872 3000 *fax 0115-872 3005*

Metcalfe, Maggie (spo)
Johnson, Andrew
O'Hare, Samantha
Bal, Sita (pso)
Gregory, Celia (pso)
McLaughlin, Emma (pso)

21. HM Prison **Ranby**
near Retford DN22 8EU
tel (01777) 862000 *fax (01777) 862001*

Smith, Susan (spo)
Mortimer, Sue
Ryer, N
Szulc, Chris
Dent, Verity (pso)
Hardy, Leslie (pso)

22. HM Prison **Whatton**
Nottinghamshire NG13 9FQ
tel (01949) 859 200 *fax (01949) 850 124*

Snowden, Ann (spo)
Boynton, Tim
Downing, Beth
Moss, David
Muller, Matt
Tribe, Sue
Gregory, Samantha (pso)
Firth, Vikki (pso)
Peacock, Lisa (pso)
Strange, Linda (pso)

23. HM Prison **Lowdham Grange**
Lowdham Nottingham NG14 7DA
tel 0115-966 9200 *fax 0115-966 9220*

Saddington, Marion (spo)
Carter, Pam
Johnson, Terry

Local Justice Areas

2, 3, 4, 5 Nottingham
6, 7 Mansfield
9 Worksop & Retford
8 Newark & Southwell

Crown Court

4b Nottingham

STAFFORDSHIRE PROBATION AREA

Out of hours: please note that Staffordshire Police
retain a list of all manager's home telephone numbers.

Victim enquiries contact number:
(01782) 719045 *fax (01782) 799330*

e-mail Firstname.Surname@staffordshire.probation.gsx.gov.uk

1. **Head Office**
University Court
Staffordshire Technology Park
Beaconside, Stafford ST18 0GE
tel (01785) 223416 *fax (01785) 223108*

Mandley, Rob (cpo)
Fieldhouse, Peter (aco offender mngmnt)
Forrester, Sandra (aco interventions)
Lawrence, Muriel (seconded to Value for Money proj)
Jones, Barbara (aco offender mngmnt)
Simpson, Bob (aco finance & resources/treasurer to board)
Clewlow, Linda (financial services mgr)
Bowden, Sandra (personnel services mgr)
Hewitt, Ian (facilities & supt services mgr)

Public Relations
Armour, Wendy (p.r.o.)

Information Services Unit
tel (01785) 231727

Beckwith, John (info services mgr)
Massey, Phil (research off)
Sheehan, Sue (syste /training off)

Parekh, Mohamed (computer services off)
Stanley, James (asst computer services off)

Education, Training & Employment Unit
tel (01785) 231744

Jolley, Mike J (offender emplt & ext resources mgr)
Beddow, Robert (educn off)
Cameron, Beverley (educn off) (at 20)
Vacancy
Harvey, Jeanette (essential skills co-ord, South)

Training & Devpt Unit
tel (01785) 231723

Williams, Sam (spo)
Milnes, Pat(staff devpt off)

Practice Devpt Assessors
tel (01785) 240402 *fax (01785) 240720*

Brereton, Simon (based at 17)
Girling, Leonie (based at 14)
Parkes, Jonathon (based at 18)
Shaw, Judith (based at 18)
Williams, Ruth (based at 18)

Effective Practice Initiative
Trenery, Alison (p, spo)

Business Development Unit
Scott, Peter (business devpt mgr)

Accommodation Officers
at office 23 (Hanley)
tel (01782) 212608 *fax (01782) 208589*
Walton, Bernard (accom off)

at Head Office (based at 1)
tel (01785 231738 *fax (01785 243028)*
Griffiths, Linsey (accom off)

Drug Rehabilitiation Team

2. Eaves Lane **Bucknall**
Stoke-on-Trent ST2 8JY
tel (01782) 261961 *fax (01782) 287459*

Hay, Catherine (spo) (at 1)
Bennett, Judith
Breen, Helen
Stokes, Liz
Stoddart, Neal (pso)
Weaver, Tina (pso)

STOP Substance Misuse Intervention Project
Grant, Dianne (p, proj co-ord (haz))
based at Druglink Tues & Thurs
tel (01782) 287118 *fax (01782) 287539*

3. Caxton House, North Walls
    Stafford ST16 3AD
    tel (01785) 252503 *fax (01785) 252549*

    Molloy, Joy
    Sourbutts, Robert (at 20)
    Beardmore, Paul (pso)
    Davies, Martin (pso)

4. **Tamworth Probation Centre**
    Moor Street, Tamworth B79 7QS
    tel (01827) 302604 *fax (01827) 302649*

    Carpenter, Sheelah
    Woolhouse, John
    Dunkley, Dave (pso)

Drug Abstinence Units

5. **Drug Abstinence Unit**
    25 Park Road **Cannock** WS11 1JN
    tel (01543) 570633 *fax (01543) 577863*

    Catherine Hay (spo) (based at 1)
    Fraser, Geoff (snr proj off)

Programmes Teams

6. Broom Street **Hanley**
    Stoke-on-Trent ST1 2EN
    tel (01782) 283488 *fax (01782) 283661*

    Butler, Chris (spo, progs mgr)
    Sirdefield, Janet (ets treatment mgr)
    Brookes, Jacqui (pso)
    Da Silva, Karel (pso)
    Mayland, Bella (pso)
    Nadin, Kerry (pso)
    Richards, Lisa (pso)
    Singleton, Aaron (pso)
    Smith, Suzi (pso)
    Vernon, Darren (pso)
    Willis, Emma (pso)

    Regional Sex Offender Unit
    Clarke, Dave (mgr)
    Davis, Clive
    Dwight, Ellie
    Gilbride, Sue (p)
    Sgroi, Gerald (p)
    Raven, Mark
    Toohey, Michael
    Broom, Denise

7. Dorrington Drive
    Dorrington Industrial Park
    Common Road, **Stafford** ST16 3DG
    tel (01785) 279951 *fax (01785) 279959*

    Butler, Chris (spo, progs mgr)(based at 6)
    Palin, Rachel (ets treatment mgr)

Wood, Tony (deputy mgr)
Evans, Gavin (pso)
Mottram, Ann (pso)
Welch, Karen (pso)

8. Horninglow Street
    Burton on Trent DE14 1PH
    tel (01283) 565951 *fax (01283) 567978*

    Butler, Chris (spo, progs mgr)(based at 6)
    Gibbs, Louise (dids treatment mgr)
    Bibi, Sophina (pso)
    Torr, Sue (pso)

Courts

9. **Crown & County Court**
    Bethesda Street, Hanley
    Stoke-on-Trent ST1 3BP
    tel (01782) 286831 *fax (01782) 287994*

    Gough, Mick (spo)
    Booth, Jane (p)
    Eckersley, Rod
    Scarratt, Wendy (pso)

    N Staffordshire Magistrates' Court
    tel (01782) 286169 *fax (01782) 287824*

    Gough, Mick (spo)
    all other staff based at office 10

10. **Crown & County Court**
    Victoria Square **Stafford** ST16 2QQ
    tel (01785) 223433 *fax (01785) 224156*

    Gough, Mick (spo) (9)
    Hill, Jeff
    Robins, Jon (p)
    Tyler, Rachel (pso)

11. **N Staffordshire Magistrates' Court**
    Ryecroft
    Newcastle-under-Lyme ST5 2DT
    tel (01782) 286169 *fax (01782) 287824*

    SPO at office 9
    McLoone, Chris (p)
    Ryan, Robert
    Archer, Suzanne (pso)
    Birt, Lynne (pso)
    Franks, Diane (p, pso)
    James-Harford, Tina (p, pso)
    Livesley, Jackie (pso)
    Nixon, Anne Marie (pso)

Area Offices

12. Horninglow Street
    Burton-upon-Trent DE14 1PH
    tel (01283) 564988 *fax (01283) 567978*

Brown, Laura (spo)
Broom, Denise
Burroughs, Tammie
Davidson, Floyd
Garrison, Keith
Grice, Kelly
Lindsay, Rachel
Chown, Nicola
Molloy, Sarah
Saunders, Kim
Brake, Victoria (pso)
Crouch, Zoe (p, pso)
Perry, Anne (p, pso)
Mosedale, Jayne (pso throughcare)

13. 200a Wolverhampton Road
Cannock WS11 1AT
tel (01543) 506112 *fax (01543) 501029*

Darby, Paul (spo)
Amer, Bob
Blakemore, Jill
Charlton, Julie
Corns, Bill
Elliott, Lynne
Flynn, Barry
Francis, Susan
Howieson, Verney (p)
MacFarlane, Alison
Pilling, Stephen
Scott, Simon
Simpson, Nicola
Treble, Lesley
Baines, Herminder (pso)
Burgess, Val (pso)
Hewston, Tarnia (pso)
Perrin, Nicola (pso)

14. Unit 1, Lakeside
Festival Way, Festival Park
Hanley Stoke-on-Trent ST1 5RY
tel (01782) 407900 *fax (01782) 281263*

Staplehurst, Angela (spo)
Adams, Carl
Adderly, Anna
Almond, Bob
Barker, Val
Barlow, Claire
Crabtree, Ruth
Dalgarno, Claire (p)
Dehal, Rupinder (p)
Dunne, Steven
Flannagan, Kate
Hibbs, Lisette
Jones, Richard (at 19)
Kidd, Sharon
MacKinnon, Nicola

Malam, Janine
Mollitt, John
Nixon, Susan
Penton, Emma
Proctor, Wendy
Whittle, Debbie (p)
Brookes, Anne (pso)
O'Leary, Joy (pso)

15. Cross Street
Leek ST13 6BT
tel (01538) 399355 *fax (01538) 399245*

Yarwood, Ellen (spo)
Bentley, Stephanie
Lenton, Jennie (p)
Pointon, Tim
Sproston, Stephanie
Heath, Pam (p, pso)

16. Marlborough Road
Longton ST3 1EJ
tel (01782) 599690 *fax (01782) 598562*

Mountford, John (spo)
Barlow, Angela
Boucher, Shelley
Bratt, Sarah
Cavanagh, Ian
Grindey, Kerry
Heap, Caroline
Hinds, Colin
Holloway, Trevor
Skelton, Ken
Steele, Hayley
Turner, Debra
Watton, Sally
Vacancy (part)
Litherland, Sylvia (pso)
Parker, Rachel (pso)

17. Ryecroft
Newcastle-under-Lyme ST5 2DT
tel (01782) 717074 *fax (01782) 713374*

Mason, John (spo)
Arnold, Catherine
Boyle, John (p)
Cotton-Eyre, Michelle
Garner, Maureen
Groombridge, Andrew
Kent, Helen
Molloy, Saul
Pye, Terry
Steer, Jean
Terry, Lindsey
Whitmore, Andrew
Lowndes, Sandra (pso)
Wheeldon, John (pso)

Victim Liaison Unit
tel (01782) 719045 *fax (01782) 799330*

Cooper, Sally (spo) (at 1)
Alexander, Barbara
Armstrong, Ann (p)

18. South Walls
Stafford ST16 3BL
tel (01785) 223415 *fax (01785) 224159*

Dodgson, Paddy (spo)
Bonser, Jane (p)
Darnbrough, Philip
Hall, Margaret
Lowrence, Nicola
Preston, Andrew
Reynolds, Shona
Robinson, Helen
Vacancy
Viggars, Kelly
Caddick, Janice (p, pso)
Birks, Denise (pso)
Booth, Maggie (pso)

19. Moor Street
Tamworth B79 7QZ
tel (01827) 302600 *fax (01827) 302649*

Jones, Stuart (spo)
Bignell, Janis (p)
Burke, Richard
Coates, Julie
Daubner, Jacqueline
Dunford, Sue
Reynolds, Paula
Styles, Kim
Whitehouse, Katie
Williamson, Jeanette
Collins, Diane (pso)
Hallmark, Sharon (pso)
Maddox, Lynda (pso)

Community Punishment Offices

20. Dorrington Drive
Dorrington Industrial Park
Common Road, **Stafford** ST16 3DG
tel (01785) 228608 *fax (01785) 228708*

Cartlidge, John (cp mgr) (at 1)
Roberts, Peter (qa mgr)
Hartill, Bill (placement mgr)
Lowndes, Chris (placement mgr)
Malone, Oliver (placement mgr)
Vacancy (pso)

21. Broom Street **Hanley**
Stoke-on-Trent ST1 2EN
tel (01782) 213324 *fax (01782) 286265*

Keeling, Neil (qa mgr)
Barker, Tony (placement mgr)
Bromfield, Peter (placement mgr)
Lowndes, Tony (placement mgr)
Pedley, Rebecca (placement mgr)
Wootton, Alan (placement mgr)
Harrison, Gail (p, pso)
Rogers, Emma (p, pso)

22. 200a Wolverhampton Road
Cannock WS11 1AT
tel (01543) 501003 *fax (01543) 501029*

Grice, Julie (pso)

23. Unit 1, Crossfields Industrial Estate
Lichfield WS13 6RJ
tel (01543) 263299 *fax (01543) 419360*

Pearson, Ian (qa mgr)
Bradley, Shirley (placement mgr)
Thorndyke, John (placement mgr)
Harries, Marc (placement mgr)
Lloyd, David (pso)

Specialist Units

24. **Public Protection Unit**
Police Headquarters, Baswich House
Cannock Road, Stafford ST17 0OG
tel (01785) 235170/1 *fax (01785) 235172*

Boult, Chris (unit mgr)

25. **Youth Offending Team**
Ringway House, Bryan Street
Hanley Stoke on Trent ST1 5AJ
tel (01782) 235858 *fax (01782) 235860*

Smith, Jenny
Rutter, Barbara (p, pso)

Seabridge Youth & Community Centre
Newcastle under Lyme
tel (01782) 297615 *fax (01782) 297616*

Downing, Moyra

Anson House, Lammascote Road
Stafford ST16 3TA
tel (01785) 277022 *fax (01785) 277032*

Hayes, Shirley

The Old House
Eastern Avenue **Lichfield**
tel (01543) 512103 *fax (01543) 512100*

Martin, Lisa (issp team mgr)
Lawton, Steve

Staffordshire 163

26. **South Staffordshire**
Mentally Disordered Offenders Team
Marston House, St George's Hospital
Corporation Street, Stafford ST16 3AG
tel (01785) 221306 *fax (01785) 221371*

Robins, Jon (p)

27. **Mentally Disordered Offenders**
Bucknall Hospital
Eaves Lane, Bucknall
Stoke on Trent ST2 8LD
(01782) 275195 ext 2475
fax (01782) 275192

Wilson, Claire (Bettany, Kevin covering
mat leave)

28. **Stoke Prolific Offenders**
Hanley Police Station
Bethesda Street
Hanley, Stoke on Trent ST1 3DR
tel (01785) 233167 *fax (01785) 233106*

Atkins, Jim (spo) (based at 1)
Brough, Gordon
Malam, Janine
Hughes, Kim (pso)

29. **The Chase Prolific Offenders Project**
Stafford Police Station
Eastgate Street, Stafford ST16 2DQ
tel (01785) 234024 *fax (01785) 234028*

Atkins, Jim (spo) (based at 1)
Breeze, Stuart
Grimshaw, Martin
Pilling,Steve

30. **Newcastle & Moorlands Prolific**
Offender Project
(based at Newcastle & Leek Probation
Offices) (15, 17)

Atkins, Jim (spo based at 1)
Flowers, Dave
Rutherford, Philip
Stone, Martin

31. **Trent Valley Prolific Offender Project**
(based at Tamworth Police Station)
Spinning School Lane
Tamworth B79 7AP
tel (01782) 234600 *fax (01785) 234605*

Atkins, Jim (based at 1)
Gilbert, Sylvia
Norris, Lisa

Hostels

32. **Wenger House Probation**
& Bail Hostel
21a Albert Street
Newcastle-under-Lyme ST5 1HJ
tel (01782) 717423 *fax (01782) 714332*

admin (01782) 622683

Hodgkinson, Ian (mgr)
Charlesworth, Margaret (dep mgr)
Graham, Patrick (probn res services off)
Dedic, Michael (probn res services off)
Gordon, John (probn res services off)
Weaver, Peter (probn res services off)

33. **Staitheford House Probation**
& Bail Hostel
14 Lichfield Road, Stafford ST17 4JX
tel (01785) 223417 *fax (01785) 224153*

Cooper, Sally (hostel mgr)
Downing, Sue (dep mgr)
Meara, Heidi (probn res services off)
Butler, David (probn res services off)
Brown, Jayne (probn res services off)
Blakemore, Karen (probn res services off)

34. **Wharflane House Bail Hostel**
34 Rectory Road, Shelton
Stoke on Trent ST1 4PW
tel (01782) 205554 *fax (01782) 205552*

Hartley, Trevor (hostel mgr)
Bettany, Kevin (dep mgr)
Flannagan, Kate (Temp Deputy Manager)
Barber, Robert (probn res services off)
Forrester, June (probn res services off)
Scarratt, Ian (probn res services off)
Walters, Sandra (probn res services off)

Institutions

35. H M Prison, 54 Gaol Road
Stafford ST16 3AW
tel (01785) 773000 *fax (01785)249591*

White, Mark (spo)
Jones, Malcolm
Patterson, Rob (p)
Stockall, Steve

36. H M Prison **Dovegate**
Morton Lane, Uttoxeter ST14 8XR
tel (01283) 829400 *fax (01283)820066*

Large, Malcolm (spo)
Bentley, Robin
Cairns, Esther
Mills, Mike

Wellings, Heather
Williams, Andrew

37. H M Prison **Drake Hall**
Eccleshall, Nr Stafford ST21 6LQ
tel (01785) 774100 fax (01785) 774010

White, Mark (spo)
Cooper, Linda
Fieldhouse, Kath
Gilham, Helen (pso)

38. H M Young Offender Institution
Swinfen Hall 18 The Drive
Swinfen, Nr Lichfield
Staffordshire WS14 9QS
tel (01543) 484000 *fax (01543) 484001*

White, Mark (spo)
Gibbs, Catherine
Harrison, Stephanie
Hibbert, Sharon
Powell, Eleanor

39. H M Prison, New Road
Featherstone Wolverhampton
West Midlands WV10 7PU
tel (01902) 703000 *fax (01902) 703001*

White, Mark (spo)
Esty, Lloyd
Makin, Nick
Withington, Amanda
Vacancy
Young, Lesley (p)
Edwards, Anita (pso)
Nicklin, Victoria (pso)
Salter, James (pso)

Local Justice Areas

13, 18 Central & SW Staffordshire
14, 15, 16, 17 North Staffordshire
12, 19 SE Staffordshire

Crown Courts

9 Stoke-on-Trent
10 Stafford

SUFFOLK PROBATION AREA

Out of hours emergency contact point
The Cottage (01473) 408266

e-mail Firstname.Surname@suffolk.probation.
gsx.gov.uk

1. **Head Office**
Peninsular House, 11-13 Lower Brook
Street, Ipswich IP4 1AQ
tel (01473) 408130 *fax (01473) 408136*

Budd, John (co)
Garside, Martin (aco)
Parker, Kelley (acting aco)
Sharp, Julia (aco)
Pestell, Steve (aco)
Mansell, Carol (spo, training mgr)
Pestell, Sari (spo ptnrshps & basic skills)
Sykes, Tim (mappp mgr)
Jones, Glyn (info mgr)
Patton, Andrew (hd of finance)
Bailey, Siobhan (finance mgr)
Lewis, Gill (h.r. mgr)
Coopooswamy, Ruby (supt services mgr)
Vacancy (health & safety off)

Ipswich Field Team
Palmer, Rob (spo)
McLelland-Brown, Mark (spo)
Barrett, Victoria (spo)
O'Hanlon, Jane (progs mgr)
Aylward, Graeme (ete devpt)
Farrow, Bob (IDAP treatment mgr)
Foy, Rosemary (p, dids)

Abbott, Pat
Barrett, Vicky
Clarke, Pippa
Denny, Kate
Dickson, Sarah
Gladden, Angela
Goddard, Kerry
Hall, Joanna (temp)
Hewitt, Joy
Huggins, Wendy
Jay, Nicky (p)
Joiner, Elise
Lister, Simone
Macdonald, Carolyn
Mendham, Dene (p)
Needham, Marcus
Ofverberg, Julian (p)
Potter, Alison
Stock, Corrina
Pratt, Melvin
Rickatson, Carmel
Rohlfing, Kate (temp)
Sharpe, Don
Stevens, Amber
Winters, Terry

Tweed, Nigel (pract devpt, tvp)
Maddock, Debbie (p, pda)
Green, Mandy (p, pda & nvq assessor)
Maudsley, Richard (nvq assessor)

Baldwin, Claire (trainee)
Bateman, Peter (trainee)
Cawthorn, Sue (trainee)
Foden, Jacqueline (trainee)
Powell, Samantha (trainee)

Black, Jeanette (pso, dtto)
Carney, Louise (pso, crt)
Cossey, Alison (pso)
Crawford, Nicky (pso)
Drew, Michael (pso crt)
Hagon-Smith, Carmen (pso)
John, Shelley (pso, crt)
Lane, Val (pso, crt)
Owen, Eileen (pso)
Parcell, Jayne (pso, basic skills & Princes Trust)
Patel, Haroon (pso, low risk)
Scuffins, Carol (pso)
Thelwell, Tom (pso, low risk, vlo)
Thompson, Liz (pso, crt)

Accredited Programmes
Clarke, Richard (p, treatment mgr)
Ofverberg, Julian (prog mgr)
Marsden, Gillian (pso)
Reid, Heather (p)
Tweed, Nigel (p)
Jasper, James (pso)
Morse, Allwyn (pso)

Unpaid Work Scheme
Vacancy (placement mgr)
Ricketts, Karyn (case mgr)
Stroh, Jim (case mgr)
Wesley, John (case mgr)
Morrison, Kevin (qa mgr)

Peck, Tracy (office mgr)

2. 203 Whapload Road
    Lowestoft NR32 1UL
    tel (01502) 501800 *fax (01502) 525779*

    Comyn, Diane (spo)
    Low, Gordon (spo)
    Alden, Graham
    Brice, Suzanne
    Connor, Elizabeth
    Curtis, Sally
    Everton, Dennis
    Ford, Helen
    Freeman, Catherine (dtto)
    Hannant, Maria (p)
    Hipperson, Sarah
    Larter, Tracy
    Davis, Shayne (progs, yos)

    Curtis, Sally (p, pda)
    Everton, Dennis (p, pda)

Baxter, Kevin (trainee)
Black, Sharon (trainee)
Dunn, Nicola (trainee)
Hawkins, Victoria (trainee)
Kersey, Michaela (trainee)
Moule, Chantelle (trainee)
Stannard, Anne (trainee)

Hannant, Maria (acting treatment mgr)

Ayres, Sylvia (pso)
Chapman-Wright, Ian (pso progs)
Henderson, Craig (pso crt)
Martin, Jon (pso progs)
Newberry, Sue (pso women's safety wrkr)
Paul, Collette (skills for life)
Peck, Nicola (pso)
Elvin, Lucy (pso, progs, skills)
Berry, Christina (pso dtto)

Unpaid Work Scheme
Kelley, Lynn (qa mgr)
Vacancy (placement mgr)
Houseago, Sally (p, placement mgr)
Leer, Colin (case mgr, supvr)
Vacancy (case mgr)

Whyte, Juliet (office mgr)

3. **West Suffolk Probation Centre**
    Dettingen Way
    Bury St. Edmunds IP33 3TU
    tel (01284) 716600 *fax (01284) 716606*

    Fiddy, Anita (spo)
    Joscelyne, David (spo)
    Marshall, Christine (spo)
    Reuben, Cathy (progs treatment mgr)
    Almond, Nick
    Bowman, Anna
    Brinkley, David (p)
    Herbert, Ann
    Hopwood, Andrew
    Lindsell, Issi
    Meiklejohn, Jamie (p)
    O'Hanlon, Barbara
    Phillips, Angela
    Smeeth, Sarah
    Snodgrass, Andrew
    Stainton, Jayne
    Steel, David
    Wood, Janet
    Mitchell, Anne (seconded scars)
    Plumb, Alan (seconded training & devpt)
    White, Colin (seconded yos)

    Beckett, Anna (pso progs)
    Bluett, Marie (pso progs)
    Dorling, Rebecca (pso crt)
    Gaskin-Barber, Aura (pso)

Layzell, Karen (pso)
Lewis, Fran (pso, crt)
Lovick, Liz (p, pso dtto)
Melvin, Peter (pso)
Moye, Pete (p, skills for life)
Prosper, Jeff (pso progs)
Smith, Michael (pso, progs)
Wogan, Chris (pso)

Unpaid Work Scheme
Vacancy (placement mgr)
Hobden, Richard (case mgr)
Phillips, Jim (case mgr)
Puscasu, Ioana (case mgr)
Key, Martyn (qa mgr)

Brinkley, David (p, pda)
Dugdall-Marshall, Ruth (p, pda)
Beales, Sarah (trainee)
Carr, Taryn (trainee)
Maguire, Lee (trainee)
Mills, Jamie (trainee)
Petch, Emma (trainee)

Adkins, Melody (office mgr) (4)

4. 6a Old Market Place
Sudbury CO10 1SZ
tel (01787) 372003 *fax (01787) 883080*

Reporting centre only

Hostels

5. **Lightfoot House**
37 Fuchsia Lane, Ipswich IP4 5AA
tel (01473) 408280 *fax (01473)* 408282

Clements, Paul (spo warden)
Turnbull, Christine (dep mgr)
Breitsprecher, Marie (asst warden)
Last, Paul (asst warden)
Murray, Jim (asst warden)
Pender, Lynda (asst warden)

6. **The Cottage**
795 Old Norwich Road
Ipswich IP1 6LH
tel (01473) 408266 *fax (01473) 408268*

Clements, Paul (spo warden)
Patel, Julie (dep mgr)
Amos, Tony (asst warden)
Ball, Reg (asst warden)
Ramshaw, Steph (asst warden)
Royal, Chris (asst warden)

Institutions

7. H M Prison **Blundeston**
Lowestoft NR32 5BG

tel (01502) 734500 *fax (01502) 734503*
direct dial (01502) 73+ext

Probn clerk ext 4769
Discipline ext 4531
Special visits ext (01502) 734508

Harrison, Susan (p, spo) ext 4768
Pearce, Sandra ext 4580
Moreno, Rene ext 4736
Mitchell, Christine (p, yos)
Hathaway, Taff (pso)
Porter, Suzanne (pso)

8. H M Prison **Highpoint**
Stradishall, Newmarket CB8 9YG
tel (01440) 743100 *fax (01440) 743902*
direct dial (01440) 74+ext

Porter, Stephen (spo) ext 3015
Allister, Jean
Hewitt, Marilyn
Meadows, Karen (p)
Stewart, Annette (p) ext 3081
Tozer, Neil ext 3067
Case, Adrian (pso) ext 3022

9. H M Prison **Edmunds Hill**
Stradishall, Newmarket CB8 9YG
tel (01440) 743500 *fax (01440) 743568*
direct dial (01440) 74+ext

Heath, Richard (spo) ext 3563
Goddard, Lynne ext 3565
Lowe, Rik
Ruffles, Louise (pso)
Salmons, Marie (pso)

10. H M Prison & Young Offender Institution
Hollesley Bay
Hollesley, Woodbridge IP12 3JW
tel (01394) 412400 *fax (01394) 410115*
direct dial (01394) 41+ext

Probn clerk ext 299
Discipline ext 311
Special visits phone unit concerned

Taylor, Barbara (spo) ext 2487
Taylor, Di ext 2603/2704
Maudsley, Richard (p)

Youth Offending Team
Shields, Sue (seconded)

Local Justice Areas

2 SE Suffolk
3 NE Suffolk
4 W Suffolk

Crown Courts

1 Ipswich
1 Bury St Edmunds

SURREY PROBATION AREA

Out of hours emergency contact point
St Catherine's Priory (01483) 571635

Victim enquiries contact number Godalming
(01483) 860191

e-mail Firstname.Surname@surrey.probation.
gsx.gov.uk

abbreviation offender manager: om

1. **Head Office**
    Bridge House, Flambard Way
    Godalming GU7 1JB
    tel (01483) 860191 *fax (01483) 860295*

    Page, Karen (co)
    Pollard, Trish (pa to co)
    Abebrese, Owusu (chairman of board)
    Jolly, Penni (dir supt services)
    Vaughan, Madeleine (p, dir finance)
    Lockhart, Lyn (secretary)
    Jackson, Isobel (area mgr)
    Niechcial, Steve (area mgr)
    Powell, Grace (diversity mgr)
    Little, Ray (public protection mgr)
    Lane, Brenda (corp supt & coms mgr)
    King, Kay (p, personnel mgr)
    Fripp, Clare (p, personnel off)
    Rowley, Julie (p, admin off)
    Russell, Pam (p, personnel admin)
    Adams, Kylie (h.r. admin)
    Stewart, Julie (p, staff devpt mgr) (js)
    Tarrant, Sally (p, staff devpt mgr) (js)
    Layzell, Judith (staff devpt off)
    Whibley, Marilyn (p, staff devpt off)
    Procter, Gemma (training admin)
    Ramsbottom, Jim (cty health & safety off)
    Slee, Chris (principal IT off)
    Edwards, Phil (it off)
    Lawrence, Julie (it off)
    Newman, Richard (it off)
    Barratt, Lee (info off)
    Thomas, Kevin (perf & info off)
    Lewis, Arlene (snr finance off)
    Latton, Leanne (finance analyst)
    Webb, Juliette (p, finance off)
    Windless, Kate (corp supt admin)

    Victim Liaison Team
    Little, Ray (mgr)

    Considine, Mary (vlo)
    Allum, Elaine (p, vlo)
    Bearpark, Una (p, coord)

2. Probation Centre, White Rose Court
    Oriental Road **Woking** GU22 7PJ
    tel (01483) 776262 *fax (01483) 727244*

    Offender Management Team
    Guven, Jenny (mgr)
    Anderson, Daniel (p, snr om)
    Belnavis, Ingrid (p, snr om)
    Strong, Lynne (p, snr om)
    Baker, Emma
    Cannon, Sarah
    Brown Jude
    Eyre, Kate
    Frost, Lisa
    Gallo-Snushall, Emma
    Glover, Debbie
    Kloppers, Mandy
    Jackson, Lisa
    Moffitt, David
    Baillie, Alison (case co-ord)
    Lawlor, Karen (case co-ord)
    Duncombe, Emily (crt liaison off)
    Hafeez, Mohammed (crt liaison off)
    Higgins, Konrad (crt liaison off)
    Dumbrill, Seren (crt co-ord)
    Henry, Katy (centre co-ord)
    Balimuttajjo, Hanat (assessment supt off)
    Allum, Elaine (p, receptionist)
    Mitchell-Jones, Fran (receptionist)
    Sauze, Claire (receptionist)
    Steen, Rebecca (p, receptionist)

    Programmes Team
    Parkinson, Ann (mgr tvsogp/IDAP)
    Porter, Louise (mgr ob)
    Clay, Meme (treat mgr)
    Myers, Fran (p, treat mgr)
    Strong, Lynne (p, treat mgr)
    Briggs, Sue (treat mgr)

    Conaboy, Chris (prog facilitator)
    Smith, Melanie (prog facilitator)
    Morris, Steve (prog facilitator)
    Winstone, Lisa (prog facilitator)
    Reynolds, Emma (IDAP facilitator)
    Swallow, Anne (IDAP facilitator)
    Clague, Kerrie (prog tutor)
    Clark, Claire (prog tutor)

    Biggs, Catherine (prog co-ord)
    Rees, Laureen (prog co-ord)
    Crawford, Karen (women's safety wrkr)

    DTTO/DRR
    Pedrick, Lin (mgr)
    Homyer, Ros (treat mgr)

Crowsley, Louisa (dtto off)
Hall, Carl (dtto off)
Bateman, Lee (dtto off)
Henderson, Clive (subst misuse off)
Hodge, Sue (p, cmo dtto)
Hazlewood, Ellie (cmo dtto)
Howard, Carla (dtto admin)
Merricks, Rachel (dtto admn)

Community Punishment
Whittle, James (dep mgr)
Westwood, Emma (qa mgr)
White, Lucy (cmo)
Woodhatch, Beckie (cmo)
Westwood, Debbie (cmo)
Howard, Malcolm (placement off)
Wright, Peter (placement off)
Ponsford, Chris (placement off)
Sindall, David (placement off)
Bland, Phil (p, proj ldr)
Pilsworth, Linda (p, admin asst)
Pownall, Hayley (admin ass)

3. Probation Centre
    College House, Woodbridge Road
    Guildford GU1 4RS
    tel (01483) 534701 *fax (01483) 453702*

Offender Management Team
Jones, Simon (mgr)
Adams, Mike (snr om)
Higgs, Brian (p snr om)
Blakey, Claire
Butt, Mark
Dennis, Mark (p)
Holt, Anna
Husbands, Joanna
Moore, Margaret
Morrison, Rosina (p)
Raleigh, Matthew
Silvester, Jo
Stone, Alan (p)
Timoney, Alicia
Wainwright, Jo

English, Alison (p, assessment supt off)
Patten, Margaret (p, assessmnt supt off)

Campbell, Rebecca (case co-ord)
Hurlow, Angela (p, case co-ord)
Maiden, Michelle (p, case co-ord)
Pullen, Jenny (p, case co-ord)

Lunnon, Sally (crt co-ord)
Hathaway, Jenny (crt liaison off)
Riordan, Julia (crt liason off)
West, Jan (crt liaison devpt off)

Kendall, Sue (p, receptionist)
Leach, Bernice (receptionist)

Carleton-Gane, Nicola (trainee)
Collins, Becca (trainee)
Greenhow, Nicola (trainee)
Groves, Jo (trainee)
Parsons, Dawn (trainee)
Pringle, Sally (trainee)
Sale, Heather (trainee)
Stoddard, Amy (trainee)
Thomas, Nicola (trainee)
Wardell, Amie (trainee)

Staff Development
Cox, Jacci (p, staff devpt off)
Cornish, Allyson (staff devpt off)

Programmes Team
Potter, Gemma (prog tutor)

DTTO/DRR
Heathcote, Jacqui (dtto/subst misuse off)
Allen, Angela (p, dtto off)
Ferns, Glyn (subst misuse off)
Ibbotson, Claire (cmo, dtto)
Singleton, Debbie (cmo, dtto)

Housing Unit
Lee, Adrian (p, housing off)

4. Probation Centre, Allonby House
    Hatchlands Road **Redhill** RH1 6BN
    tel (01737) 763241 *fax (01737) 765688*

Offender Management Team
McLean, Marion (mgr)
Coltofeanu, Ruth (snr om)
Hurcomb, Martin (snr om)
Armstrong, Jenny
Arzberger, Holly
Barrett, Nicola
Berry, Michelle
Botha, Kate
Clark, Richard
Derbyshire, Gordon
Hooper, Rhian
Jeffries, Victoria
Jones, Sally (p)
Lilley, Kate
Luff, Helen (p)
Sales, Emma
Scourfield, Tracey
Westwood, Jane
Woollett, Chris

Bruton, Olive (assessmnt supt off)
O'Brien, Lin (p, assessmnt supt off)

Brooksbank, Maxine (crt liaison off)
Hooks Caroline (p, crt liaison off)
Hyde, Davina (crt liaison off)
McConnell, Pauline (p, centre co-ord)

Bergin, Kim (p, case co-ord)
Dunne, Caroline (p, receptionist)
Frost, Shelley (p, receptionist)
Tomlinson, Sue (receptionist)

Programmes Team
Hancock, Maryrose (p, prog tutor)

DTTO/DRR
Greenwood, Leah (dtto off)
Irving, Morine (dtto off)
Levy, Eleanor (subst misuse off)
Scoffham, Barbara (cmo dtto)

Community Punishment
Ditzel, Nick (deputy mgr)
Ditzel, Tim (cmo)
Spiller, Susan (cmo)
Sweetman, Julie (cmo)
Rayner, Peter (placement off)
Sanchez, Julia (placement off)
Westgate, Alan (placement off)
White-Doyle, James (placement off)
Joyce, Richard (p, proj leader)

Jeapes, Jan (admin asst)
Stubbings, Valerie (p, admin asst)

5. Probation Centre, Swan House
    Knowle Green **Staines**
    Middlesex TW18 1XR
    tel (01784) 459341 *fax (01784) 449932*

Offender Management Team
Evenden, Roz (mgr)
Ayers, Carol (snr om)
Fletcher, Tamsin (snr om)
Jolly,James (snr om)
Baker, Mel
Burchmore, Lucy
Butler, Jo
Cockburn, Gilyan (p)
Davis, Mike
Lambiotte, David
Line, Jo
Lowes, Ben (p)
Miles, Paul
Millar, Randall
Parsons, Jennifer
Percy, Gayle
Stevenson, Rebecca
Stocker, Cathy (p)
Webb, Carrie
Yeoman, Kevin

Butler, Helen (case co-ord)
Finn, Sarah (case co-ord)

Clarkson, Carol (assessmnt supt off)
Mookherji, Hanna (p, assessmnt supt off)

Addo, Yaa (trainee)
Desai, Paula (trainee)
Jacobsen, Timothy (trainee)

Mason-Thompson, Maria (p, crt liaison off)
Smart, James (crt liaison off)
Jennings, Jenny (crt co-ord)

Pilatowicz, Lisa (p, centre co-ord)
Wolfe, Jacky (receptionist)
Perry, Emma (p, receptionist)

DTTO/DRR
McNuff, Doreen (sub misuse off)
Lewis, Nicki (cmo dtto)
Whiting, Allison (cmo dtto)

Housing Unit
Stocker, Cathy (p, housing off)

6. **The Crown Court**
    Bedford Road, Guildford GU1 4ST
    tel (01483) 568561 *fax (01483) 306724*

    Thomas, Roz (crt off)
    Lane, Lynda (crown crt liaison off)
    Brady, Christine (crown crt liaison off)

7. **Youth Offending Team**
    Churchill House, Mayford Green
    Woking GU22 0PW
    tel (01483) 517000 *fax (01483) 517007*

    Wells, Toby (cty mgr)
    Hibbert, Geoff (mgr west)
    Cameron, Vivienne (yjo)
    Howe, Dawn (yjo)
    Reid, Janice (yjo)

Hostel

8. **St Catherine's Priory**
    Ferry Lane, Portsmouth Road
    Guildford GU2 4EE
    tel (01483) 571635 *fax (01483) 454130*

    Critchlow, Phil (mgr)
    Clark, Brian (deputy mgr)
    Acres, Patrick (cmo, residential)
    Barford, Francesca (cmo, residential)
    Black, Kirsten (p, cmo, residential)
    Doe, Robert (p, cmo, residential)
    Robinson, Kathy (cmo, residential)
    Day, Richard (night supvr)
    Dawson-Marsh, Angela (admin fin off)

Institutions

9. H M Prison **Coldingley**
    Shaftesbury Road
    Bisley, Woking GU24 9EX
    tel (01483) 804300 *fax (01483) 804427*

Parole Clerk ext 4366
Special visits ext 4418

Bazlington, Pepi (th'care mgr) ext 4384
Beadman, Helen (risk, resettlement off)
Hutchins, Lucy (risk, resettlement off)

10. H M Prison **Send**
Ripley Road, Send
Nr Woking GU23 7LJ
tel (01483) 471000 *fax (01483) 471001*

Probn visits ext 3051
Parole clerk ext 3052
Discipline ext 3006

Page, Lesley (th'care mgr) 471062
Braim, Ginny (th'care off)
Carlile, Kate (p, th'care off) 471060
Chapman, John (th'care off) 471058
Matthews, Gerry (p, th'care off) 471060
Allen, Stephanie (th'care supt off)

11. H M Prison **Downview**
High Down Lane
Sutton, Surrey SM2 5PD
tel 020-8929 3300 *fax 020-8929 3301*

Probn clerk ext 389
Discipline ext 299
Special visits ext 285

Teesdale, Mick (mgr) ext 300
Simpkins, Sue (treatment mgr)
Bishop, Carol (th'care off)
Smith, Peter (th'care off)
Woghiren, Sharon (th'care off)
Griggs, Philip (progs off)

12. H M Prison **High Down**
High Down Lane
Sutton, Surrey SM2 5PJ
tel 020-8722 6300 *fax 020-8722 6301*

Probn clerk ext 6617
Custody office ext 6309
Video link ext 6400
Special visits ext 6500

Kenealy-Fox, Denise (resettlement mgr)
ext 6371
Breese, Michelle (th'care off)
Eastham, Liz (th'care off)
Kirk, Valerie (th'care off)
Tester, Roger (th'care off)
Bedborough, Carole (th'care supt off)
Larkin, Anna (th'care supt off)
Morby, Sam (th'care supt off)
Sterry, Gemma (th'care supt off)
Robinson, Brian (resettlement liason off)

13. H M Prison **Bronzefield**
Woodthorpe Road
Ashford, Middx TW15 3JZ
tel (01784) 425690 *fax (01784) 425691*

Paine, Joanne (th'care off)
Bheenick, Melissa (th'care supt off)
Davies, Sian (thr'care off)
Larkins, Georgina (th'care off)
Bheenick, Melissa (th'care supt off)
Sturney, Simeon (th'care supt off)
Wilson, Tracey (th'care supt off)

Local Justice Areas

2 North West Surrey
3 South West Surrey
4 South East Surrey
5 North Surrey

Crown Court

6 Guildford

SUSSEX PROBATION AREA

Out of hours emergency contact point:
(01273) 622300

Victim enquiries contact number: (01273)
810410/1

e-mail Firstname.Surname@sussex.probation.
gsx.gov.uk

1. **Head Office**
185 Dyke Road, Hove
Hove **Brighton** BN3 1TL
tel (01273) 227979 *fax (01273) 227972*

Clark, Brian (co)
Crook, Chris (board chair)
Wells, Steve (board secy)

Berrill, Judith (aco h.r.)
Haines, Ryan (aco Brighton & Hove)
Hayde, Elspeth (aco h.r.)
Hossain, Tareque (aco finance, admin &
facilities)
Rogers, Peter (aco interventions)
Saunders, Andrea (aco E Sussex)
Smart, Nick (aco W Sussex)
Wing, Arthur (aco perf & planning)

Health & Safety
Ferguson, Derek (h&s advr)

Communications
Bridger, Tony (mgr)

Administration and Facilities
Penfold, Imogen (mgr)

Training & Development
Jones, Philip (mgr)
Cummings, Erika (admin)

Human Resources
Attree, Sara (h.r. advr)
Scott, Louise (h.r. co-ord)
Goncalves, Lynda (h.r. advr)
Lucas, Tracy (h.r. advr)
Muir, Julia (h.r. advr)
Pike, Dawn (h.r. admin asst)

Finance
Savage, Lisa (mgr)
Dearn, Teresa (snr finance off)
Chauhan, Sangita (finance off)
Korakin, Laure (finance asst)

I.T.
Kellett, James (i.t. project mgr)
Graham, Jason (i.t. supt off)
Piper, Walter (i.t. system supt off))

Performance & Excellence
Ainscough, Valerie (perf & excellence mgr)
Frost, Nicola (perf analyst)
Gieler, Stefan (perf analyst)
Longman, Joe (info off)

2. 47 Grand Parade
Brighton BN2 9QA
tel (01273) 810300 *fax (01273) 810399*

Accommodation Services Team
Costa, Stephanie (housing co-ord)

Court & Case Management Team
Jones, Allan (spo)
Martin, Claire (spo)
Allcorn, Chris
Brown, Tasha
Gerrard, Wendy
Lee, Adam
Marks, Zoe
Muller, Lynn
Roberts, Emma
Scott, Lisa
Wood, Joanie
Shone, Catherine (breach off)
Bechley, Amber (pso)
Donleavey, Jennifer (pso)
Hall, Olivia (pso)
Hamza, Kaz (pso)
King, Peter (pso)
Lovell, Sarah (pso)
Wisby, Emily (pso)
Wray, Sarah (pso)

Public Protection Team
Cordery, Miriam (spo)
Cairns, Sarah
Cooper, David
Evident, Gary
Franks, David
Gerrard, Jake
Harbane, Jean
Herring, Sharon
Earnshaw, Claire (pso)
King, Peter (pso)

Victims Team
Hutchins, Kevin (scheme mgr)
Lunderstedt, Max (vlo)

Unpaid Work
Knight, Kate (qa mgr)
Batchelor, Kimberley (cp case mgr)
Berry, Stephen (cp case mgr)
Bower-Feek, Veronica (cp case mgr)
Conduct, Emma (cp case mgr)
Jones, Jemma (cp case mgr)
McLean, Janis (cp case mgr)
Moriarty, Matthew (cp case mgr)
Munro, Morag (cp case mgr)
Reed, Chris (cp case mgr)
Timson, Bill (cp case mgr)
Bligh, Sean (cp proj mgr)
Green, Shane (cp proj mgr)
Hopkins, Kate (cp proj mgr)
Mann, Christine (cp proj mgr)

Administration and Facilities
Simpson, Janet (op supt mgr East)
Andrews, Lorraine (admin mgr)
Wood, Karen (admin mgr)

Accredited Programmes
Haynes, Andrea (spo)
Maxwell, Leon (treatment mgr)
Freeborn, Lance (treatment mgr
Vacancy (psychologist)
Charles, Maggie
Cook, Steve
Hughes, Siri
Powley, Dean
Roberts, Val
Attree, Dan (pso)
Davis, Michael (pso)
Donaldson-Njie, Lin (pso)
Nevitt, Helen (pso)
Oko, Steve (pso)
Rowlins, Stephen (pso)
Wileman, Matilda (pso)

DTTO/DRR
Young, Keith (spo)
Donnelly, Sue

Carr, Emily (pso)
Williams, Rachel (pso)

ETE
Tohill, Tracey (area mgr)
Purcell, Suzanne (deputy mgr)
Birch, Hannah (ete/basic skills admin off)
Eason, Cathryn (ete casewrkr)
Glover, Natasha (ete casewrkr)
McBean, Andrew (ete admin)
Spence, Susan (ete admin)
Turnball, Jane (ete casewrkr)
Breary, Andrew (basic skills trainer)
Smuts, John (basic skills tutor)
Williams, Paul (Nacro basic skills ptnrshp mgr)

Persistent OffendersTeam
Airs, Danny (police off)
Armstrong, Jemma (pso)
Light, Jacqui (pso)

PDA Team
Marsh, Christine (pda)
Radcliffe, Claire (pda)
Whitehead, Alison (pda)
Moors, Matthew (pda)
Bradley, Philippa (trainee)
Lang, Joanna (trainee)
Shaw, Robert (trainee)
Smithson, Paul (trainee)
Jones, Paul (trainee)
Hardy, Alison (trainee)
Hanmer, Poppy (trainee)
Eminson, Charlotte (trainee)
Mainwaring, Grant (trainee

2a. **Youth Offending Team
Brighton & Hove**
22 Ship Street **Brighton** BN1 1AD
tel (01273) 296169

Crockett, Peter

3. 8 Market Avenue
Chichester PO19 1YF
tel (01243) 787651 *fax (01243) 781151*

Court and Case Management
Burden, Mark (spo)
Bristow, Candida
Clement, Dee
Fricker, Sue
Leeming, Su
Page, Kerrin
Richards, David
Broadley, Laurien (pso)
Cotton, Carla (pso)
Gough, Amanda (pso)

Lavender, Geoff (pso)
Taylor, Stephen (pso)
Walsh, Teresa (breach off)

PDA
Pointon, Mandy (spo)

Administration and Facilities
Broad, Trudy (admin mgr)

3a. The Old Glassworks
c/o Christian Care Association
St Cyriac's **Chichester** PO19 1AJ
tel (01243 775925)

Blanchflower, Colin (resettlement coordinator)
Hipkiss, Jan (day centre mgr)
Williams, Dominic (outreach worker)

4. Goffs Park House
Old Horsham Road **Crawley**
West Sussex RH11 8PB
tel (01293) 525216 *fax (01293) 525215*

Court and Case Management
Fairbrother, Margaret (spo)
Budden, Claire
Clarke, Lesley
Dowse, Philippa
Lewis, Denise
Bray, Jason
North, Jo
Allen, Kate (pso)
Foreman, Anna (pso)
Lees, Philip (breach off)
Mortimer, Canon (pso)
Nicholas, Harvinder (pso)
Stewart, Neil (pso)

Public Protection Team
Fordham, Colin (spo)
Arnold, Sally
Pearce, Corrine
Wilson, Susan

Victims Team
Heywood, Jennie (vlo)

Community Punishment
Barzdo, Lara (qa mgr)
Bradley, Jan, (cp case mgr)
Frater, Bettine (cp case mgr)
Grant, Roy (cp case mgr)
Jones, Carol (cp case mgr)
Moore, Nick (cp case mgr)
Sweet, David (cp proj mgr)
Ali, Ehsan (cp proj mgr)
Ebulubu, Ralph (cp proj mgr)
Tomlinson, Rachel (cp proj mgr)

Accredited Programmes
Goodchild, Heather
Murray, Ian (pso)
Askey, Sarah (pso)
Barker, Graham (pso)

DTTO
McCullough, Barbara
Muchmore, Holly (pso)

PDA Team
Tierney, Jo (pda)
Weir-Wilson, Maggie (pda)
Bannister, Claire (trainee)
Rogers, Emma (trainee)
Wilson, Jane (trainee)
Wood, Joanne (trainee)
Brown, Jennifer(trainee)
Bruton, Shane (trainee)

ETE
Hill, Michael ete/basic skills casewrkr)
Fairbrother Terri (ete casewrkr)

Persistent Offenders Team
Clay, Andy (police off)

Administration and Facilities
Marman, Gill (admin mgr)

4a. **Youth Offending Team**
190 Three Bridges Road
Crawley RH10 1LN
tel (01293) 643450 *fax (01293) 643472*

Cowley, Paul (spo)
Clark, Gill
Phillipson, Jessica

5. 35 Old Orchard Road
Eastbourne BN21 1DD
tel (01323) 746200 *fax (01323) 640424*

Court and Case Management
Browne, Jane (spo)
Blyghton, Anne
Carey, Louisa
Jauncey, Anna
Painter, Josh
Winch, Caroline
Broom , Brenda (breach off)
Alvey, Alison (pso)
Evers, Rod (pso)
Foreman, Liz (pso)
Fieldhouse, Jill (pso)
Greenstock, Gordon (pso)
Hanson, Terry (pso)
Sinclair, Peter (trainee)
Spiers, Angela (trainee)
Williams, Louise (trainee)

PDA Team
Preston, Peter (trainee)

Public Protection Team
Carr, Susan (spo)
Barnes, Geoff
Jarvis, Fiona
Lightfoot-Ben Richie
Wood, Frank (pso)

ETE
Burgess, Louise (basic skills trainer)
MacDermott, Sandie (ete casewrkr)

Prolific Offenders
Dawson, Natalie (police off)
Lacey, Karen (pso)

DTTO/DRR
Stevens, Tim

Administration and Facilities
Reed, Pat (admin mgr)

6. 1 St Leonards Road
Eastbourne BN21 3UH
tel (01323) 749555 *fax (01323) 738484*

Accredited Programmes Team
Tilbury, Guy
Warner, Johanna
Ncube, Emmanual (pso)
Hellier, Wendy (pso)
Unpaid Work
Richardson, Martin (spo)
Westbrook, Paul (cp case mgr)
Humphreys, Diana (cp case mgr)
Holland, Bernie (cp case mgr)
Barber, Mike (cp proj mgr)
Downs, Nick (cp proj mgr)
Tubbs, Dave (cp proj mgr)

7. Crozier House, 1A Shepherd Street
St Leonards-on-Sea TN38 0ET
tel (01424) 448600 *fax (01424) 448601/2*

Court and Case Management
D'Arcy, Mary (spo)
Alford, Liz
Glover, Sarah
Hamberis, Emma
Hicks, Katy
Platts, Chris
White, Graeme
Tipper, Tracey (breach off)
Farman, Jane (pso)
George, Marian (pso)
Harrod, Lisa (pso)
Jinks, Dean (pso)
Little, Joanne (pso)
Madge, Noelyne (pso)

Matthews, Lorraine (pso)
Rhodes, Lawry (pso)
Willis, Joanne (pso)

PDA Team
Thomson, Clare (pda)
Warrick, Judy (pda)
Whitehead, Alison (pda)
Marsh, Christine (pda)
Adams, Kirsten (trainee)
Cooper, Peter (trainee)
Oakley, Victoria (trainee)
Cuthbertson, Elaine (trainee)
Satchell, David (trainee)
Winthe, Serge (trainee)
Dove, Jo (trainee)

Public Protection Team
Richardson, Martin (spo)
Maxwell, Nicola
Saunders, Rita
Taylor, Malcolm
Goddard, Nicky (pso)
Wells, Anne (pso)

Persistent Offenders Team
Baldwin, Keith (police off)
Connolly, Jenny
Parfitt, Natalie (pso)
White, Graeme (pso)
Wells, Anne (pso)
Howard, Carolyne (admin)
Ritchie, Fay (HARPOS drugs nurse)

Accredited Programmes
Delaney, Mick (pso)
Furlong, Michaela (pso)
Hambling, Phil (pso)
Marshall, Vanessa

Unpaid Work
Price, Julie (qa mgr)
Batchelor, Kimberley (cp case mgr)
Bond, Peter (cp proj mgr)
Harris, Pat (cp case mgr)
Lennie, Gary (cp proj mgr)

DTTO/DRR
Palmer, Chris
Webb, Mick (pso)

ETE
Boden, John (basic skills trainer)
Giles, Tony (ete casewrkr)
Giles, Sue (ete casewrkr)

Administration and Facilities
Stothard, Martha (admin mgr)

7a   **Youth Offending Team**
East Sussex YOT
33 Cambridge Road **Hastings** TN34 1DL

tel (01424) 446396
Newing, Mike

8.   The Law Courts, Hurst Road
Horsham RH12 2DZ
tel (01403) 265445/6 *fax (01403) 272903*

Fagan, Janet
Parker, Mike
Sweeney, Vicky (pso)
Wallis, Karyn (pso)

Administration and Facilities
Marman, Gill (admin mgr)

9.   The Court House
Friars Walk **Lewes** BN7 2PG
tel (01273) 477117 *fax (01273) 483843*

Court and Case Management
Bishop, Yvonne (spo)
Abbott, Jo
Fitzsimmons, Frank
Freeman, Jon
King, Lesley
McStay, Sally
Bramley, Sophie (pso)
Clemson, Gemma (pso)
Thomas, Anne (pso)

PDA Team
Weir-Wilson, Maggie (pda)
Radcliffe, Claire (pda)
Foster, James (trainee)
Tufnell, Athol (trainee)

ETE
Murray Loraine (basic skills trainer)

Administration and Facilities
Picott, Wendy (admin mgr)

10. **Crown Courts**
The Law Courts
High Street **Lewes** BN7 1YB
tel (01273) 487608 *fax (01273) 487610*

Brett, Daphne
Cromarty, Liz (pso)

Administration and Facilities
Picott, Wendy (admin mgr)

Crown Court, Lansdowne Road
Hove BN3 3BN
tel (01273) 778843 *fax (01273) 720532*

Galpin, Phil
Attwater, Sandie (pso)

11. Meadowfield House, East Street
Littlehampton BN17 6AU
tel (01903) 711500 *fax (01903) 711555*

Court and Case Management
Burden, Mark (spo)
Bailey, Marcus
Butler, Michelle
Clift, Suzie
Sanderson, Sam
Darnley, Nadine (pso)
Grenier, Lesley (pso)
Hollington, Abigail (pso)
Trusson, Katie (pso)

Public Protection
Fletcher, Ashley
Mason, Janet
Claw, Katherine (pso)

Unpaid Work
Gear, Beverley (qa mgr)
Carter, Kay (cp case mgr)
Davies, Bridget (cp case mgr)
Goody, Jackie (cp case mgr)
Turner, Andrea (cp case mgr)
Cairns, Rob (cp proj mgr)
Fairbrother, Carl (cp proj mgr)
Unsted, Lesley (cp proj mgr)

ETE
Marshall, Lee (basic skills tutor)
Mott, Debbie (ete casewrkr)

Accredited Programmes
Aycliffe, Glenda
Austen, Amanda (pso)
Burns, Ray (pso)
Miller, Peter (pso)
Mulcahy, Kelly (pso)

DTTO/DRR
Nelmes, Geoff
Field, Sally (pso)

PDA Team
Slatter, Kathryn (pda)
Elphick, Elyse (trainee)
Hope, Shelly (trainee)
Skipworth, Helen (trainee)
Marlow, Penny (trainee)

Administration and Facilities
Porcas, Sarah (op supt mgr West)
Buss, Catherine (admin mgr)

12. **4 Farncombe Road**
Worthing BN11 2BE
tel (01903) 216321 *fax (01903) 204287*

Court and Case Management Team
Pope, Joe (spo)
Denison, Peter
Hoskin, Ros
Oldfield, Rebecca
Pike, Tim

Priestley, Sue (locum)
Richardson, Tiffiny
Shaw, Stacey
Turner, Claire
Walker, Julie
Argent, Heidi (pso)
Benham-Hernetz, David (pso)
Eaton, Barbara (breach off)
Exton, Jackie (pso)
Gowler, Jackie (pso)
Khamlichi, Lanyaa (pso)
McCarthy, Helen (pso)
Mustchin, Suzie (pso)

Public Protection Team
Fletcher, Ashley
Hoskin, Ros
Claw, Catherine (pso)
McCarthy, Helen (pso)

Accredited Programmes
Rogers, Leighe (spo)
Miles, Peter
Ajaegbu, Christiana (pso)
Banks, Jayne (pso)
Leach, Sarah (pso)
Brown, Stephen (apt admin)
Potter, Suzanne (apt admin)

Unpaid Work
Fox, Alex (cp proj mgr)
Heather, Bernie (cp proj mgr)
Valente, Ken (cp proj mgr)

ETE Partnership
Ali, Shazia (basis skills tutor)
Breary, Andrew (basis skills mgr)
Gower, Sandy (ete admin)
Holter, Christine (ete casewrkr)
LeCappelain, Linda (ete casewrkr)
Muir, Eve (ptnrshp mgr)

DTTO/DRR
Chaszczewski, Alex (pso)
Nelmes, Geoff

Persistent Offenders Team
Ford, Steve (police off)
Turner, Claire
Exton, Jacjie (pso)

Accommodation Services Team
Philip, Cathy

PDA Team
Newton, Chris (pda)
Coney, Yve (trainee)
Adams, Jude (trainee)
Brownsey-Joyce Carole (trainee)
Coppard, Cheryl (trainee)

13. Options Project, 24 Grafton Road
   Worthing BN11 4QP
   tel (01903) 204539 *fax (01903) 209416*

Hostel

14. Approved Premises, 162 Marine Parade
   Brighton BN2 1EJ
   tel (01273) 622300 *fax (01273) 623486*

   Shaw, Chris (spo/mgr)
   Loye, Peter (po/deputy mgr)
   Bridges, Melanie (admin)
   Hare, Wendy (bail supt wrkr)
   Bartlett, Heidi (supt wrkr)
   Dury, Min (bail supt wrkr)
   St James, Carrie (supt wrkr)
   Collins, Frank (asst warden)
   Howard, Mark (asst warden)
   McLoughlin, Nessa (asst warden)
   Gonzalez, Juan (night supvr)
   Vacancy (night supvr)

Institution

15. HM Prison Lewes
   Brighton Road **Lewes** BN7 1EA
   tel (01273) 405100 *fax (01273) 405101*
   direct dial (01273) 78 + ext

   Rimmer, Paul (spo)
   Booth, Sally
   Montero, Rosemary
   Youngs, Martyn
   Morrissey, Michael
   Melbert, Cat (pso)
   Bescoby, Steve (th'care off)
   Teare, Andy (bail info)

16. HM Prison **Ford**
   Arundel BN18 0BX
   tel (01903) 663000 *fax (01903) 663001*
   probn (01903) 663195/663186
   probn fax (01903) 663197

   Hoskin, Geoff (spo) 663196
   Payne, Jill 663188
   McRae, Jenny 663187
   Hull, Terry 663199
   Sharples, Henry 663208
   Davey, Charlotte (pso) 663189

Local Justice Areas

   2, 9 Sussex (Central)
   5, 7 Sussex (Eastern)
   3, 11, 12 Sussex (Western)
   5, 8 Sussex (Northern)

Crown Court

   10 Chichester
   10 Lewes

TEESSIDE PROBATION AREA

Out of hours emergency number
(01642) 826606/456811

Victim enquiries contact number (01642)
247438

e-mail Firstname.Surname@teesside.
probation. gsx.gov.uk

1. **Head Office**
   6th Floor, Centre North East
   73-75 Albert Road
   Middlesbrough TS1 2RU
   tel (01642) 230533 *fax (01642) 220083*

   Lumley, Elaine (co)
   Hadfield, Peter (aco, com reintegration)
   Thomas, Brian (aco, cs, 'what works',
   drugs resource team, crts & ecp)
   Saiger, Lucia (aco, hostels, ppu, eem,
   diversity, prisons, mappa)
   Holdhusen, Barbara (aco-hr/secy to probn
   cttee, staff devpt, pract training, diversity)
   Beckett, Tina (service mgr)
   Bolton, Janet (service mgr)
   Burnett, Peter (service mgr)
   Allan, Julie (service mgr)
   Armstrong, Jill (staff devpt mgr)
   Lipthorpe, Denise (HR mgr)
   Petrie, Rod (health & safety off)
   Lorenzen, Roy (it & info mgr)
   Craig, Philip (finance mgr/treasurer, i.t.,
   info/data protection, contracted services)
   Gleeson, Joanne (finance off)
   Parry, Kevin (prolific/priority offenders
   mgr)
   Shakespeare, Martyn (secondment to NE
   Consortium)
   Coyle, Margaret (pa to co)

2. 160 Albert Road
   Middlesbrough TS1 2PZ
   tel (01642) 247438 *fax (01642) 244651*

   Court Liaison
   West, Doug (spo)
   Padgett, Chris (office mgr)
   Devon, Alan
   Hazell, Robin

Nolan, Mike
Bedford, Jane (offender supvr)
Burdon, Joan (offender supvr)
Chapman, Erica (offender supvr)
Craddy, Stuart (offender supvr)
Grey, Stuart (offender supvr)
Michael Russell (offender supvr)
North, Gemma (offender supvr)
Sellers, Joanna (pso, bail information)
Spaven, Tracey (offender supvr)
Storr, Frank (offender supvr)

Public Protection Unit
Townsend, Isobel (spo)
Elliott, Norma (office mgr)
Bennett, Marie
Brown, John
Edgar, Lisa
Horner, Gill
Jones, Jo
Laurence, James
Michie, Jan
Moore, Joanne
Pawson, Julie
Westbrook, Andy
Aldus, Beverly (vlo)
Edgar, Penny (vlo)

Diversion Team
tel (01642) 221358 *fax (01642) 221352*

Hernandez, Frieda

MAPPA
Kendall, Elizabeth (spo/operations mgr)

3.   154 Borough Road
Middlesbrough TS1 2EP
tel (01642) 210717 *fax (01642) 230621*

Reintegration Team
Roy, Rosana (spo)
Brittain, Tracey (temp acting spo)
Grieff, Joan (office mgr)
Barber, Jeremy
Bullen, Carolyn
Carlton, Melanie
Dargue, Darren
Edwards, Juliet
Hewerdine, Lynne
Iverson, Julie
Kunna, David
Martell, Carolyn
Mulpetre, Gemma
Neasham, Laura
Shaw, Jan
Turner, Sarah
Wood, Andrea
Collingwood, Deborah (offender supvr)
McFee, Michelle (offender supvr)

Nunn, Cheryl (offender supvr)
Thomas, Jeff (offender supvr)
Hussain, Liaquet (offender supvr)
Knight, Pam (offender supvr)
Cook, Janet (offender supvr, ete)
Parkin, Pauline (offender supvr, housing supt)

4.   **Teesside Crown Court**
Russell Street, Middlesbrough TS1 2AE
tel (01642) 250469 *fax (01642) 230541*

West, Doug (spo)
Spreadbury, Wendy (office mgr)
Clarke, Caroline (offender supvr)
Lear, Malcolm (offender supvr)
Smith, Joan (offender supvr)

5.   Mowlam House, 1 Oxford Street
South Bank Middlesbrough TS6 6DF
tel (01642) 452346 *fax (01642) 466021*

(note Southbank & Redcar work as one team across two sites)

Community Reintegration
Barnett, Sharon (spo)
Westmoreland, Lynda (office mgr)
Bell, Emma
Berry, Sarah
Hopton, Julie
Suggett, Leigh
Whitehead, Philip
Ashton, Stephen (offender supvr)
Felstead, Carol (offender supvr)

6.   38 Station Road
Redcar TS10 1AG
tel (01642) 494395 *fax (01642) 489424*

(note Southbank & Redcar work as one team across two sites)

Community Reintegration
Barnett, Sharon (spo)
Westmoreland, Lynda (office mgr)
Close, Suzanne
Downing, Jennifer
Morton, Helen
Taylor, Peter
Urban, Lynne
Faye, Jeremy (offender supvr)
Pitt, Allison (offender supvr)
Williams, Linda (ete os)

7.   Advance House, St Mark's Court
Teasdale, Thornaby
Stockton on Tees TS17 6QX
tel (01642) 606111 *fax (01642) 607764*

Community Reintegration
Megan, Sarah (spo)
Bonas, Robin (acting spo)
Garbutt, Jenny (office mgr)
Cotterill, Sarah
Evans, John
Fryett, Russell
Gardner, Gillian
Grainger, Elizabeth
Greener, Lynne
Harburn, Andrea
MacDonald, Andrea
Peel, Debbie
Rabjohns, Tracey
Ransome, Philip
Smart, Claire
Leech, Jennifer (mentor)
Corking, Donna (offender supvr)
Ellison, Laura (offender supvr)
Foster, Alison (offender supvr)
Halasz, Emma (offender supvr, ete)
Turner, Jean (offender supvr)

8. Avenue Road
    Hartlepool TS24 8BL
    tel (01429) 265101 *fax (01429) 231854*

    Community Reintegration
    Wharrick, Julie (spo)
    Ferguson, Barbara (office mgr)
    Cooke, Sally
    Hutchinson, Karen
    Lane, Mike
    Martin, Samantha
    Nicolson, Kay
    Robinson, Sheila
    Stoddart, Steve
    Ul Haq, Ehtesham
    Cains, Pamela (mentor)
    Golden, Claire (offender supvr)
    Kinnersley, Jackie (offender supvr)
    Merritt, Adam (offender supvr)
    Smith, Valerie (offender supvr)
    Vickers, David (offender supvr)

    Court Team
    Borg, Paul (offender supvr)
    I'Anson, Dougie (offender supvr)
    Turnbull, Brian (offender supvr)

    Dordrecht Initiative
    Gill, Barbara (mgr)
    Graham, John
    McShane, Julie (offender supvr, int supvn
    & monitoring)
    Low, Sandra (ppo coord)

9. **'What Works' Programmes
    & Case Management**
    5th Floor, Centre North East
    73-75 Albert Road
    Middlesbrough TS1 2RU
    tel (01642) 225021 *fax (01642) 252215*

    Waddington, Mike (spo)
    Bateman, Jan (dep ops mgr)
    Flanagan, Kath (dep ops mgr)
    Anderson, Jennifer (office mgr)
    Bell, Simon (offender supvr)
    Cotter, Melissa (offender supvr)
    Hall, Andrew (offender supvr)
    Hill, Lesley (offender supvr)
    Mackin, Chris (offender supvr)
    Taylor, Rachel (offender supvr)

10. **'What Works' Programmes
    & Case Management**
    Advance House, St Mark's Court
    Teasdale, Thornaby
    Stockton on Tees TS17 6QX
    tel (01642) 606111 *fax (01642) 607764*

    Gavaghan, Dave (dep ops mgr)
    Johnson, Alan (action team advisor)
    Davies, Bill (prog supt wrkr)
    Ward, Ellen (os, gpwk)
    Brown, Beth (offender supvr)
    Caizley, Alison (offender supvr)
    Horner, Pat (offender supvr)
    Lowe, Sarah (offender supvr)
    McKay, Debbie (offender supvr)

11. **Enhanced Community Punishment**
    Milbank House, 1 Milbank Street
    South Bank, **Middlesbrough** TS6 6DD
    tel (01642) 515315/6 *fax (01642) 290677*

    Portues, Russell (ops mgr)
    Armstrong, Ian (dep ops mgr)
    Smith, Paul (dep ops mgr)
    Wooding, Gordon (dep ops mgr)
    Mantle, Angela (office mgr)
    Alderdice, Jayne (offender supvr)
    Cameron, Mark (offender supvr)
    Cassey, Nicola (offender supvr)
    Charlton, John (offender supvr)
    Coates, Eddie (offender supvr)
    Cooper, Barry (offender supvr)
    Currie, Rob (offender supvr)
    Foggin, Hilary (offender supvr)
    Frostwick, Gemma (offender supvr)
    Gilbey, Alan (offender supvr)
    Hatchwell, Victoria (offender supvr)
    Hey, Anthony (offender supvr)
    Holmes, Jim (offender supvr)

Johnson, Dave (offender supvr)
Jorgensen, Lewis (offender supvr)
Lunn, Michael (offender supvr)
McKenna, Mike (offender supvr)
Millar, David (offender supvr)
Norrie, George (offender supvr)
Paterson, Donald (offender supvr)
Payne, Bob (offender supvr)
Pearce, Peter (offender supvr)
Simmonds, Tony (offender supvr)
Smallwood, Dave (offender supvr)
Smith, Debbie (offender supvr)
Smithyman, Sue (offender supvr)
Turbitt, James (offender supvr)
Vaughan, Brian (offender supvr)
Marson, Louise (offender supvr)
Bacon, Elisabeth (os 'what works')
Garbutt, Claire (os 'what works')
Lawson, Alison (os 'what works')
Raynel, Cora (os 'what works')
Richmond, Kay (os 'what works')
Catton, Bob (prog supt wrkr)
Hunter, Derek (prog supt wrkr)
Nunn, Bob (supvr)

Teesside Interventions Clearing House
Smith, Lynne
Emmerson, Harry (clearing hse off)
Gorbutt, Jane (clearing hse off)

12. **Drug Resource Team**
160 Albert Road
Middlesbrough TS1 2PZ
tel (01642) 247438 *fax (01642) 244651*

Whelan, Viki (ops mgr)
Hill, Susan (office mgr)
Canty, Sue
Pritchard, Nick
Atkinson, Fiona (offender supvr)
Bentley, Michael (offender supvr)
Menzies, Maria (offender supvr)
Smithyman, Angela (offender supvr)

13. **Practitioner Training Unit**
5th Floor, Centre North East
Middlesbrough TS1 2RU
tel (01642) 225021 *fax (01642) 252215*

Nicholson, David (acting spo)
Davy, Virginia (pract devpt assessor)
Dixon, Gill (pract devpt assessor)
Toyne, Margaret (pract devpt assessor)
Whitehead, Tony (pract devpt assessor)

Trainees
Adair, Steven
Almond, Gail
Bailey, Louise
Boyd, Debbie

Brown, Catherine
Clement, Sandra
Day, Joanne
Devitt, Vicky
Ford, Allison
Gaffney, Sarah
Gallagher, Natalie
Hill, Kathryn
Hunter-Clayton, Claire
Hunton, Joanne
Leishman, Martin
Matthews, Barbara
McGee, Keri-Ann
Moore, Louise
Nazir, Shahida
Niijar, Kulwant
O'Brien, Susan
O'Connor, Stella
Rennie, Debbie
Robertson, Ann
Sowerby, Andrea
Ubaka, Anselm
Whitehead, Angela

14. Cowley House
156 Borough Road
Middlesbrough TS1 2EP
tel (01642) 247476 *fax (01642) 248486*

Hall, Maureen (spo/ops mgr, basic skills)
Allan, Jim (offender supvr)
Bell, Sue (offender supvr)
Whitaker, Elaine (offender supvr)
Winn, Nick (pso)

Youth Offending Service

15. **Hartlepool**
The Archive Building
Upper Church Street, Hartlepool TS24
7EQ
tel (01429) 523986 *fax (01429)523971*

Wilkinson, Julie

16. **South Tees**
(Middlesbrough and Redcar)
51a Kings Road
North Ormesby
Middlesbrough TS3 6NH
tel (01642) 501500 *fax (01642) 501800*

Moody, Nikky

17. **Stockton**
76 Brunswick Street
Stockton TS18 1UU
tel (01642) 527597 *fax (01642) 527598*

Robson, Justine

Hostels

18. **Probation Hostel**
13 The Crescent
Linthorpe, Middlesbrough TS5 6SG
tel (01642) 826606 *fax (01642) 829782*

Davis, Glen (dep ops mgr)
White, Sue (office manager)
Davis, Jenny (snr rsw)
Nichol, Paul (snr rsw)
Pearson, Annette (snr rsw)
Nunn, Julie (snr rsw)
Bowers, Emma (rsw)
Dos Santos, Sarah (rsw)
Findlay, Pamela (rsw)
Manning, Karen (rsw)
Menzies, Russell (rsw)
Ayton, Chris (relief rsw)
Crowley, Mark (relief rsw)
Goodchild, Nicola (relief rsw)
Hodge, Rachel (relief rsw)
Johnson, Bob (relief rsw)
Gowing, Doreen (rsw weekends)

19. **Nelson House Probation Hostel**
Middlesbrough Road
Southbank, Middlesbrough TS6 6LZ
tel (01642) 456811 *fax (01642) 468671*

Sam-Drysdale, Sandra (spo)
Gallant, Julie (dep ops mgr)
Watling, Steven (snr rsw)
Bielby, Aisha (rsw)
Heaviside, Jennifer (rsw)
Jackson, Clapham, Deborah (rw)
Moulsher, Philip (rsw)
Stallard, Kay (rsw)
Thompson, Sid (rsw)
Warrior, David (rsw)
Woodhead, Jackaleen (rsw)
Rutland, William (relief rsw)
Sparrow, David (relief rsw)
Welsh, Angela (relief rsw)

Institutions

20. H M Prison **Kirklevington Grange**
Yarm TS15 9PA
tel (01642) 781391 *fax (01642) 790530*

Discipline ext 201
Special visits (via communications office)
ext 230

Hunneysett, Elaine (spo)
Turver, Neil (spo) ext 323
Ford, Dot ext 324
Eddon, Mark (offender supvr)

21. H M Prison **Holme House**
Holme House Road
Stockton on Tees TS18 2QU
tel (01642) 744000 *fax (01642) 744001*
direct dial (01642) 74+extn
probn clerk ext 4327
special visits ext 4280
probn fax (01642) 744264

Eves, Wendy (spo) ext 4030
Keay, Julie ext 4154
Beard, Sylvia ext 4116
Philips, Jo ext 4154
Warrior, Joan ext 4116
Winn, Lesley ext 4116
Creasey, Nat (offender supvr) ext 4337
Moppett, Stephanie (offender supvr, carat)
ext 4317
Turver, Andy (offender supvr) ext 4157

Local Justice Areas

7 Hartlepool
5 Langbaurgh
2-6 Teesside

Crown Court

4 Teesside

THAMES VALLEY

email Firstname.Surname@thames-valley.
probation.gsx.gov.uk

1. **Head Office**
Kingsclere Road, Bicester
Oxon OX26 2QD
tel (01869) 255300 *fax (01869) 255355*

Marshall, Gerry (co)
Beckford, Lorna (p, board chair)
Lawrence-Wilson, Richard (p, secy to
board)
Payne, Clare (p, pa to chair)

Taylor, Riana (dep co & dir of strategy)
Mackenzie, Gaynor (p, dir of hr)
Hudson, Lesley (p, dir of hr)
Vine, Malcolm (dir of finance)
Fishbourne, Ray (dir of ops until 31.03.06)
Tarrant, Fiona (comms mgr)
Payne, Clare (comms off until 31.03.06)
Cooke, Sue (projects supt mgr)
Toner, Michael (spo)

Davies, Ruth (hr mgr)
Singh, Avtar (pract devpt mgr)

Wolfe, Carol (training advr)
Allen, Anne (p, hr advr)
Powell, Jackie (hr advr)
Wook, Sue (hr advr)(mat leave)
Barrett, Sarah (p, hr admin off)
Bates, Heather (p, hr admin asst)
Peck, Jayne (hr mgmnt info off)
Birtles, Lynda (p, hr admin asst)
Francis, Adele (training & devpt service qual co-ord)
Bridges, Michelle (training & devpt admin)
Dean, Vanessa (p, training & devpt event co-ord)
Kempster, Helene (training & devpt event co-ord)
Smith, Esther (p, disability compliance admin)

Widlake, Stephen (health & safety off)

Hardy, Ian (finance mgr)
Harvey, Susie (p, snr finance off)
Unwin, Terri (p, snr finance off/payroll)
Fearn, Vicky (p, snr finance off/payroll)
Chapple, Wendy (finance off)
Roberts, Sonia (finance off)
Durrant, Julia (p, facilities & est off)
Bracewell, Nicki (p, asst facilities & est off)

Fletcher, Karen (pa to co)
Peaper, Hazel (p, pa)
Hobbs, Lesley (p, admin services co-ord)
Emmerson, Kim (recep/admin)

Griffiths, Sue (training & nvq) (based in Reading)
Marshall, David (pda/mentor) (based in Reading)

2. 1-3 Ock Street
Abingdon Oxon OX14 5AL
tel (01235) 535619 *fax (01235) 554511*

Case Management Team
White, Debbie (spo)
Chapman, Margaret
Clark, Susan
Hill, Sarah
Stokes, Paul
Troup, Ian
Welch, Pam
Barry, Abigail (pso tracker link wrkr)
Wendon, Lois (pso)

Training
Claxton, Naomi (pda)
Hudson, Elisabeth (trainee)
Lampton, Vicky (trainee)
Palmer, Corina (trainee)

Administration
Amiri, Julie (admin mgr)

3. 2a Wynne-Jones Centre, Walton Road
Aylesbury Bucks HP21 7RL
tel (01296) 483174 *fax (01296) 415212*

Case Management Team
Drake, Paul (spo)
Elmore, Nicola
Gallagher, Gillian
Goss, Margaret
Greenman, Hilary
Penny, Heather (p)
Pickering, Linda
Shimeld, Irene
Whitaker, Karen
Worthington, Harriet (p)
Cowley, Pauline (pso crt)
Beck, Jacqueline (p, pso crt)
Aburrow, Annette (pso)
Davis, Douglas (pso)
Taylor, Zoe (pso)

Poyner, Hilary (spo)
Butler, Terry (pso tracker link wrkr)

based at Crown Court on (01296) 339770
Throup, Lesley (pso)

Substance Misuse & DTTO Team
Poyner, Hilary (drug services devpt mgr, Bucks)
Errington, Alison (qa mgr)
Tomlin, Eve (subst misuse wrkr)
Jones, Karen (pso)
Mullaney, Louise (pso)

Training
Adams-Rimmer, Jane (p, pda)
Carmichael, Jane (pda)
Fox, Mandy (trainee)
Francis, Annabel (trainee)
Halliwell, Jenni (trainee)
Matthews, Charlotte (trainee)
Merrick, Hilary (trainee)

Community Service
Grimes, Julie (qa mgr)
Hall, Jan (placement/case mgr)
Wright, Paul (placement/case mgr)
Holford, Helena (p, supvr/tutor)
Manwaring, Sara (supvr/tutor)
Spearing, Robert (p, supvr/tutor)
Rogers, Adrienne (csa) (p)

Basic Skills Unit
Simmons, Allister (tutor)

Administration
Ray, Sandra (p, admin mgr)

Information, IT & Research Units
tel (01296) 393925 fax (01296) 398490

Aulton, Michelle (p, perf data mgr) (mat leave)
Gower, Alan (acting perf data mgr)
Barnes, Ian (snr info off)
Mitchell, Sophie (info off)
Spayne, Chris (p, info asst)

Steadman, Julie (IT Systems & projs mgr)
Baker, Ralph (snr it supt off)
Briscoe, Neil (it supt off)
Evershed, Tilly (p, it supt off)
Shergill, Jas (it supt off)
Mafham, Val (it off/training)
Drawe, Lynda (it admin)
Shaw, Clare (team admin)

Smith, Karen (it off, training) (based in Reading)
Simons, Stephen (it admin) (based in Reading)

4. 15 Canada Close, Marley Way
Banbury Oxon OX16 2RT
tel (01295) 268436/7 *fax (01295) 268120*

Hume, Duncan (spo)
Burrell, Anne (p)
McFarlane, Jane
Thorpe, Simon
Yard, Gregory
Bryan, Rachel (pso)
Gwynne, Lucinda (pso)
Ivory, Catrina (pso)
Jarvis-Aitoro, Megan (pso)
Kirtley, Jane (pso tracker link wrkr)
Porter, Ian (p, pso)

Training
Burrell, Anne (p, pda mentor)
Kenna, Karen (p, pda mentor)
Harris, Dawn (trainee)
Hoggins, Michelle (trainee)
Netten, Kate (trainee)
Rogers, Katherine (trainee)
Stapleton, Alison (trainee)

Housing Unit
Rouse, Jane (p, housing advr)

ETE Unit
Aworth, Caroline (ete advr)

Basic Skills Unit
Chilver, Mary (tutor)

Administration
Irving, Deedee (admin mgr)

5. Units 9 & 10 Talisman Business Centre
Talisman Road **Bicester**
Oxon OX26 6HR
tel (01869) 328500 *fax (01869) 328528*

Delves, John (aco, Central & S Bucks)
Power, Janet (aco, cs)
Cowen, Caryl (pa)
fax (01869) 328543 (confidential fax line)

Basic Skills & ETE
Welters, Brian (basic skills & projs mgr)
Evans, Karyn (basic skills co-ord)
Fiander, Liz (p, basic skills qa tutor)
Chapple, Julie (basic skills admin) (mat leave)
Cross, Carol (p, basic skills admin)
Taylor, Karen (basic skills admin)

Martin, Elizabeth (p, ete mgr)
Humphreys, Fran (accred off)
Mayson, Sarah (ete advr)

Community Service
Swift, Erica (cs mgr)
Clarke, Deborah (p, qa mgr)
Goddard, Robert (placement/case mgr)
Ashby, Julie (placement/case mgr)
Henshaw, Gemma (placement/case mgr)
Spargo, Julia (placement/case mgr)
Wood, Michelle (placement/case mgr)
Parker, Lynn (placement/case mgr)
Pittuck, Sue (placement/case mgr)
Bowerman, Mark (supvr/tutor)
James, John (p, supvr/tutor)
McNaboe, Michael (p, supvr/tutor)
Reed, Jennie (p, supvr/tutor)
Keen, David (p, supvr/tutor)
Whiting, Helen (p, supvr/tutor)
Walter, Dudley (storesperson/supvr)

Clayton, Julie (cty cs admin)
Reeves, Emma (p, csa)
Davison, Kerry (p, csa)
Rawding, Kirsty (csa)

Victims Unit
Vigurs, Kilvinder (spo mgr)

Programmes Team
Fraser, Simon (prog mgr)
Martin, Ross (treatment mgr)
Regan, Kate (pso, treatment mgr)
Dobson, Jessie (pso/tutor)
Johnson, Debbie (prog mgr)
Heron, Kath (p, treatment mgr)
Faulkner, Sam (progs tutor)
Weston, Kathryn (progs tutor)
Callow, Jacqueline (pso/tutor)
Sturgess, Stephen (pso/tutor)

Adamczyk, Liz (prog mgr)
Morris, Bernard (progs tutor)
Cockbill, Leona (pso, treatment mgr)
Dainty, Caroline (pso/tutor)

Haxby, Johanna (admin mgr)

Information Unit
Gower, Alan (acting perf data mgr)

Thames Valley Project
tel (01869) 328600 *fax (01869) 328618*

Adamczyk, Liz (prog mgr)
Annetts, Trudi
Guthrie, Lydia (treatment mgr)
Loveday, Marian (prog facilitator)
Ricks, Linda (acting treatment mgr)
Bates, Andrew (principal forensic psy)
(mobile no 07796 948297)
Clarke, Jackie (admin mgr)

6. **Justice Research Consortium**
RJ Project Thames Valley
5 London Road **Bicester**
Oxon OX26 6BU
tel (01869) 369840 *fax (01869) 327097*

Emerson, Geoff (RJ mgr)

7. James Glaisher House
Grenville Place **Bracknell** RG12 1BP
tel (01344) 420446 *fax (01344) 301274*

Chilvers, Jo (aco, E Berks)
Williams, Tracy (p, pa)

Doon, Tracey (spo)
May, Celia
Rooke, Simon
Sutherland, Sarah (p)
Oztemel, Deniz (p)
Kiff, Glenys (pso)
Neate, Vicky (pso)

Substance Misuse & DTTO
Bull, Richard (p)

Training
Bull, Richard (p, pda mentor)
Jarvis, Beckie (trainee)
McGuigan, Stephen (trainee)
Powers, Julia (trainee)
Symons, Karen (trainee)
Williams, Kevin (trainee)

Housing Unit
Rowlands, Cathy (casewk mgr)
Adams, Gill (p, advr)

Basic Skills
Khanum, Naheed (devpt off)

Administration
Cornelius, Freddie (admin mgr)

8. Easton Court, 23a Easton Street
High Wycombe Bucks HP11 1NT
tel (01494) 436421 *fax (01494) 450132*

Case Management
Davies, Jan (spo)
Van Rensburg, Werner (spo)
Algelius, Cecilia
Blowfield, Anna
Brown, Alma
Jenner, Jeannie (p)
Morris, Sally (p)
Sillitoe, Felicity
Smith, Vicki (p)
Taussig, Debbie
Titley, Carol (p)
Bowell, Lynda (pso, crt)
Court, Dennis (pso)
North, Laura (pso)
Wood, Marie (pso)
Derbyshire, Carol (pso tracker link wrkr)

Training
Ross, Marilyn (p, training & nvq)
Ayoub, Abid (trainee)
Chapman, Kate (trainee)
Easton, Candy (trainee)
Lang, Karen (trainee)
Small, Emma (trainee)

Community Service
Coffey, Mike (mgr) (based at 11)
Brown, Karen (placement/case mgr)
Evans, Julie (placement/case mgr)
Hopping, Eleanor (placement/case mgr)
Pinner, Karenlynn (placement/case mgr)
Strivens, Jonathan (supvr/tutor)
Barkes, Liz (p, csa)

Basic Skills, ETE & Housing Units
Richardson, Jo (ete advr)
Massaquoi, Mustapha (housing advr)

Administration
Deeks, Avril (admin mgr)

9. Bridge Road
Maidenhead SL6 8PB
tel (01628) 770858 *fax (01628) 788675*

Substance Misuse and DTTO Team
Sceeny, Wendy (drug services devpt mgr, Berks)
Blakesley, Clive
Powell, Vivian (p)
Clarke, Frank (subst misuse wrkr)
Gray, Lesley (pso, rob co-ord)

Guthrie, James (pso)
Johnson, Linda (pso)
Mallowan, Toby (pso)
Mallowan, Nicola (pso, rob co-ord)
Stevens, Alan (pso)
Wright, Cara (p, pso)

10. Magistrates' Courts
301 Silbury Boulevard, Witan Gate East
Milton Keynes MK9 2YH
tel (01908) 679734 *fax (01908) 230050*

Ball, Brenda (aco)
Hazell, Paulette (p, pa)

Case Management
Cook, Pauline (spo)
St Amour, Paul (spo)
Butt, Denise (spo)
Cann, Nicola (p)
Carter-Philpott, Amanda (p)
Crate-Lionel, Patrick
Harris, Ann (p)
Marais, Herman
Kidd-White, Melanie
Lynch, James
Myers, Rebecca
Newall, Jo (p)
Passant, Rebecca
Rogers, Carol
Sylvester, Alison
Watt, Karen
Walker, Vivien
Juned, Ali (pso)
Vickery, Sally (pso crt)
Martin, Viv (pso)
O'Brien, Phil (pso)
Patterson, Sandra (pso, crt)
Stafford, Ruth (pso)
Stratfold, Deborah (p, pso)
Jones, Sarah (pso tracker link wrkr)

Basic Skills, ETE & Housing Units
Stewart, Lorraine (tutor)
Aworth, Caroline (ete advr)
Ford, Mellissa (ete adv wrkr)
Williams, Paul (housing needs & partnership mgr)
Oldfield, Amanda (housing advr)
May, Hayley (housing admin)

Training
Priseman, Nigel (trainee)
Ridgway, Arlene (trainee)
Sexton, Lesley (trainee)
Spencer, Johnson (trainee)
Stebbens, Jo (trainee)

Substance Misuse & DTTO Team
Butt, Denise (drug services devpt mgr)

Jones, Allan
Anstey, Susan (pso)
Duke, Vincent (pso)

Programmes Team
Lindsay, Mary (p, tutor)
Allen, Christina (progs tutor)
Christie, Dod (pso/tutor)
Holyhead, Lydia (pso/tutor)
Morse, Sharon (p, pso/tutor)
Stubbs, Christine (pso/tutor)
Smith, Eileen (pso/tutor, women's safety wrkr)
Shah, Neeta (pso/tutor)

Administration
Strain, Jane (admin mgr)

11. 20 Market Square
Stony Stratford
Milton Keynes MK11 1BE
tel (01908) 564812 *fax (01908) 262846*

Community Service
Coffey, Mike (mgr)
Ayers, Paula (qa mgr)
Barber, Philippa (placement/case mgr)
Melisi, Hannah (placement/case mgr)
Spurrier, Sean (placement/case mgr)
Brown, Israel (supvr/tutor)
Ayers, Terry (p, supvr/tutor)
Douglas, Judan (p, supvr/tutor)
Grover, Terry (p, supvr/tutor)
Jones, Lee (p, supvr/tutor)
Lant, Tracey (supvr/tutor)
Read, Trevor (supvr/tutor)
Studniarz, Beverley (cty cs admin)
Jones, Jane (csa)
Eveling, Jennifer (p, csa)
O'Callaghan, Glynis (p, csa)

12. Mill Lane
Newbury RG14 5QS
tel (01635) 43535 *fax (01635) 42103*

Reilly, Sheila (spo) (based at 18)
Aldridge, Richard
Quigley, Sandy (p)
Randle, Gillian (p)
Tyson, Peter
Baron, Sally (p, pso)
Moore, Niki (pso)
Worthington, Frank (p, pso)

Substance Misuse
Smith, Paul
Loomes, Hazel (p, pso)

Training
Graham, Debbie (trainee)

Harris, Carol (trainee)
Robinson, Rowena (trainee)

Administration
Lawes, Carole (p, admin mgr)

13. Albion House
Littlegate Street **Oxford** OX1 1JN
tel (01865) 240750 *fax (01865) 240780*

Oxford Magistrates' Court Office
tel (01865) 202039 *fax (01865) 200078*

McCartney Graham (aco, Oxon)
Ferguson, Jeanette (p, pa)

Smith, Greg (spo)
Czajewski, Steve (spo)
Ciotti, Megan (p)
Emberson, Gill
Hearn, Lorraine (p)
Lee, Tim (p)
Mepham, Vicky
Morrison, Donald
Payne, Giles
Aitkins, Russell (pso)
Baldauf-Clark, Beatrix (p, pso crt)
Crossley, Adrian (pso crt)
Gannon, Sophia (pso, crt)
Jefford, Michelle (pso)
Moores, Derek (pso, crt)
Phillips, Caroline (pso)
Quinlan, Beryl (pso, crt)

Programmes Team
Jolly, Ruth (p, pso tutor)

Training
Lampton, Victoria (trainee)
McConnell, Elena (trainee)
Webb, Esther (trainee)
West, Sarah (trainee)
Wilson, Pat (trainee)

Basic Skills, ETE & Housing Units
Hughes, Avril (p, tutor)
Haline, Aziz (p, tutor, also covers 17)
Campbell, Lynne (p, ete advr) (mat leave)
Kelly-Ward, Pauline (housing advr) (mat leave)

Substance Misuse & DTTO Team
King, Linda (drug services devpt mgr)
Weetman, Ros (qa mgr)
Waterston, Rob
Godin, Janet (subst misuse wrkr)
Merivale, Nicola (subst misuse wrkr)
Ainsworth, Carole (pso)
Parveselli, Caroline (p, pso)

Administration
Britten, Sandra (admin mgr)

14. Temple Cottage
164 Oxford Road **Cowley** Oxford OX4 2LA
tel (01865) 775482 *fax (01865) 770311*

McIntyre, Shuna (p, spo)
Hedge, John (p, spo)
Banks, David
Everatt, Lou
Haigh, Alex (p)
Hogg, Jo
Medley, Stephanie
Miller, Stephen
Pritchard, Vicky
McCalmon, Colin (pso)
Turner, Sheila (pso)
Doolan, Mike (pso tracker link wrkr)

Housing Unit
Thomas, Elizabeth (p, housing advr)
Watson, Karen (housing advr)

Training
Smith, Sheila (pda, mentor)

Administration
Tohill, Phyllis (admin mgr)

15. The Old Shire Hall
The Forbury **Reading** RG1 3EH
tel 0118-967 4430 *fax 0118-967 4431*

Reading Crown Court Team
Holland, Sarah (spo)
Crisp, Linda (pso, crt)
Mead, Linda (p, pso, crt)
Whyte, Peter (pso, crt)

16. 18a Castle Street
Reading RG1 7SD
tel 0118-958 6141 *fax 0118-958 6119*

Reading Magistrates' Court Team
Holland, Sarah (spo) (based at 15)
Martin, Sarah (p)
Oliver, David (p)
Warwick, Leah (p)
Bhatti, Jasvir (pso crt off)
Heath, Jim (pso crt off)
O'Neill, Michael (pso crt off)
Taylor, Eileen (pso crt off)

Victims Unit
Vigurs, Kilvinder (spo) (based at 5)
De Jongh, Caroline
Honeysett, Clare
Smith, Vicki (p)
Churchill, Emma (pso)
Harvey, Kaylee (pso)
Spilsted, Helen (pso)
Spalding, Emma (p, co-ord)
Smith, Erika (women's safety wrkr)

Community Service
Mondaye, Andrew (mgr)
Medhurst, Elizabeth (qa mgr)
Whiston, Lisa (qa mgr)
Andrews, Catherine (placement/case mgr)
Croxford, Nicholas (placement/case mgr)
Ewins, Aileen (placement/case mgr)
Duncan, Laura (placement/case mgr)
Fidler, Anna (placement/case mgr)
Leader, Frances (placement/case mgr)
Hodder, Elizabeth (placement/case mgr)
Webb, Rebecca (placement/case mgr)
Wells, Liz (placement/case mgr)
Corton, Robert (supvr/tutor)
Dickinson, Leila (supvr/tutor)
Dickinson, Richard (supvr/tutor)
Ensor, Jane (p, supvr/tutor)
Finan, Mick (supvr/tutor)
Fox, Ted (p, supvr/tutor)
Harrison, Nicola (supvr/tutor)
Mathias, Maria (p, supvr/tutor)
Mullett, Graham (p, supvr/tutor)
Richardson, Andrew (p, supvr/tutor)
Stamp, Maria (p, supvr/tutor)
Wilkinson, Sharon (cty cs admin)
Addison, Helen (p, csa)
Tarte-Booth, Christine (p, csa compliance)
Wallis, Ethel (csa)
Williams, Alex (p, csa)
Hill, Karen (p, admin)
Kinch, Heather (admin)

17. Crown House, Crown Street
    Reading RG1 2SE
    tel 0118-956 0466 *fax 0118-962 0301*

    Gillbard, Paul (aco, W Berks)
    Browne, Carol (p, pa)

    Evans, Grant (spo)
    Williams, Kevin (spo)
    Britton, Jo
    Cawdell, Mark
    Ennis, John
    Hyder, Ruth Farrall (p)
    Hanfling, Juliet (p)
    Innes, Nicola (m/l)
    Kasozimusoke, Sozzie
    McKendrick, Gisella
    Porteous, Laura
    Sandum, Shelley
    Stephens, Beryl (p)
    Tagoe, Gina
    Titcomb, Fiona
    Walden, Amy
    Wilkinson, Emma
    Jenkinson, Jan (pso)
    McDonald, Linda (pso)

Morris, Delia (pso)
Naidoo, Sharon (pso)
Hewstone, Peter (pso tracker link)
Lataweic, Tomasz (pso tracker link)

Substance Misuse
Amahwe, Gabriel (drug services devpt mgr W Berks)
Gothard, Ann
Evans, Lisa (pso)
Hendrick, Maria (pso)
Lutaaya, Anthony (pso)
Porter, Jane (p, pso)

Training
Greenwood, Judy (p, pda)
Boyd, Gillian (trainee)
Cannell, Sabina (trainee)
Cox, Sarah (trainee)
Rees, Maryanne (trainee)
Stubbs, Erin (trainee)

Basic Skills, ETE & Housing Units
Welters, Brian (basic skills & projects mgr) (based at 5)
Owoo, Christiana (pso basic skills) (also covers 7 & 19)
Wakeling, Alison (ete advr)
Phillips, Madeleine (p, ete advr)
Stoddart, Gary (housing advr)

Programmes Team
tel 0118-939 3525
Acteson, Doreen (treatment mgr)
Harvey, Julian (treatment mgr)
O'Kelly, Catherine (p, treatment mgr)
Mayston, Greg (tutor)
Nagib-Ali, Abdalla (tutor)
Rowlands, Jon (tutor)
Akinshegun, Nzinga (pso/tutor)
Cooney, Jennifer (pso/tutor)
Hunt, Martin (pso/tutor)
Mendy, David (p, pso/tutor)
Odain, Lloyd (pso/tutor)
Porter, Jane (p, pso/tutor)
Stanley, Beth (pso/tutor)
Victor, Sarah (pso/tutor)

Administration
Brincat, Jackie (p) (admin mgr)

18. Revelstoke House, Chalvey Park
    Slough SL1 2HF
    tel (01753) 537516 *fax (01753) 552169*

    Courts Team
    De Silva, Maureen (p, pso, crt)
    Deepak, Bobby (p, pso, crt)
    Newton, Mary (pso, crt)
    Margetson, Carolyn (p, pso, crt)

Case Management Team
Kuerberuwa, Norma (spo)
Billington, Kerry
Carty, Ingrid
Gherendi, Ioan
MacInnes, Caroline
Oakes, Helen
Oke, Manny
Pickthall, Brian
Collins, Sarah (pso)
Isabelle, Stephen (pso)
Martin, Rebecca (pso)

Fisher, Claire (spo)
Azad, Usha (m/l)
Bourget, Robbie
Dunn, Christine (p)
Henstridge, Jennie
Nair, Renuka
Stewart, Alan
Isabelle, Eddy (pso)
Olley, Georgina (pso)
McMullan, Jane (pso tracker link wrkr)
Parash, Varda (p, pso)
Sellick, Charlie (pso)

Training
Foxell, Oliver (trainee)
Le-Gendre, Kelita (trainee)
Smith, Mark (trainee)
Thornton, Hayley (trainee)

Basic Skills & ETE
Sherwood, Darlene (bs tutor)
Kenny, Michael (ete advr)

Housing Unit
Cann, Frances (adv wkr)

Administration
Hamilton, Val (admin mgr)

Secondments

19. **South East Region Training Consortium**
College House, Woodbridge Road
Guildford, Surrey GU1 4RS
tel (01483) 304963 *fax (01483) 440601*

Cunningham, Bruce (devpt mgr)
Morgan, Carol (p, cj awards mgr)

20. **Youth Offending Teams**
2nd Floor, Crown House
193 Cowley Road **Oxford** OX4 1UT
tel (01865) 721212 *fax (01865) 246614*

Reading & Wokingham
34-36 Crown Street, Reading RG1 2SE
tel 0118-939 0420 *fax 0118-939 0935*

West Berkshire (Newbury)
Youth Offending Team
20 Mill Lane, Newbury RG14 5QS
tel (01635) 264800 *fax (01635) 264801*

Slough
Partnership House, Chalvey Park
Slough, Berks SL1 2HT
tel (01753) 522702 *fax (01753) 572355*

Russell, Chris (pso)

21. **Project Iris**
St Aldates Police Station
Oxford OX1 1SZ
(01865) 266022 *fax (01865) 266035*

Nelson, Sarah

Hostels

22. Probation Hostel
112 Abingdon Road **Oxford** OX1 4PY
tel (01865) 248842 *fax (01865) 794680*
Mobile 07836 235707

Perry, Sheila (spo mgr)
Trotman, Rick (po deputy)
Barrett, Laura (asst warden)
Elliott, Marion (asst warden)
Hall, Christine (asst warden)
Macfadyen, Andrew (asst warden)
White, Alan (asst warden)
Edgeley, Sue (hostel admin)

23. Bail Hostel
Clark's House Clark's Row
Oxford OX1 1RE
tel (01865) 248841 *fax (01865) 790756*
Mobile 07836 637934

Simpson, Simon (spo mgr)
Richardson, Kay (p, po deputy)
Tartakover, Julie (p, po deputy)
Arundell, Heidi (asst warden)
Gardner, Jeanne (asst warden)
Harris, Paul (asst warden)
Stuart, Mark (asst warden)
Ward, Kieran (asst warden)
Fuller, Stanford (night care asst)
Brown, Vincent (night care asst)
Blacker, Sam (p, hostel admin)
Robinson, Mark (p, hostel admin)

24. **Manor Lodge Hostel**
8 Straight Road, Old Windsor SL4 2RL
tel (01753) 868807 *fax (01753) 620466*

closed until 1.4.2006

Buck, Jackie (po deputy)

Cooper, Ian (asst warden)
Gayton, Pat (asst warden)
Lauri, Vicki (asst warden)
Tajima, Shula (asst warden)
Lang, Anne (hostel admin)

25. Probation & Bail Hostel
     1 Haddon, Great Holm
     Milton Keynes MK8 9AL
     tel (01908) 569511 *fax (01908) 265949*

     Radford, Anne (spo mgr)
     Perry, Anna (po deputy)
     Buck, Jackie (po deputy)
     Blackman, Elaine (asst warden)
     Henriques, Jackie (asst warden)
     Hogan, Priscilla (p, asst warden)
     Jones, Alan (asst warden)
     Norman, Alan (p, asst warden)
     Parker, Natalie (asst warden)
     Riley, Joanna (p, asst warden)
     Pearson, Stephen (night care asst)
     Young, Sam (night care asst)
     Price, Ann (team admin)

26. **St Leonard's Hostel**
     2 Southcote Road, Reading RG30 2AA
     tel 0118-957 3171 *fax 0118-956 0677*

     Bradley, Felicity (p, spo mgr)
     Davis, Geoff (po deputy)
     Jones, Kate (asst warden)
     Khaleel, Clement (asst warden)
     Mabey, Dianne (asst warden)
     Ryan, Susan (asst warden)
     Williams, Terri (asst warden)
     Parkes, Margo (admin)

Voluntary Hostel

27. **Elizabeth Fry Hostel**
     6 Coley Avenue, Reading RG1 6LQ
     tel 0118-957 2385 *fax 0118-951 0340*

     Kebby, Shirley (mgr)
     Oke, Caroline (dep mgr)
     President, Liz (drugs co-ord)
     Appiah, Frederick (proj wrker)
     Gainford, Louise (proj wrker)
     Gregory, Nadine (proj wrker)
     Green, Sophie (proj wrkr)
     Soley, Joanne (proj wrker)
     Yapp, Anita (proj wrker)
     Lammas, Jan (admin)

Institutions

28. HM YOI, Bierton Road
     Aylesbury Bucks HP20 1EN

tel (01296) 444000 *fax (01296) 444001*

Bell, Lyn (Charlie)
Lewis, Nick (p)
Oke, Manny
Phillips, Dave
Thorpe, Rodney
Fox, Amy (pso)
Ody, Bill (pso)
Robins, Hannah (pso)
Hull, Anthea (probn clerk)

29. HMP **Bullingdon**
     P O Box 50, Bicester , Oxon OX25 1WD
     tel (01869) 353100 *fax (01869) 353101*

     Jameson, Pat (spo)
     Brown, Kit (p)
     Eastwood, John
     Lebeanya, Uche
     Powell, Richard
     Wheatley, Dorothy (p)
     Winter, Kay
     Aslam, Tahira (pso resettlement)
     Juggins, Tracy (pso public prtctn)
     Howard, Dawn (pso hdc)
     Bloomfield, Ian (probn clerk)

     Bail Information Unit
     fax (01869) 353171

     Lewis, Christine (pso)

30. HMP **Grendon**
     Grendon Underwood
     Aylesbury, Bucks HP18 0TL
     tel (01296) 443000 *fax (01296) 443001*

     Walls, David (spo)
     Powell, Lesley
     Whymark, Gay
     Bossom, Leia (pso)
     Griffith, Cassandra (pso)
     Harrison, Mia (pso)
     Malone, Cindy (pso)
     Shippen, Jane (pso)
     Leach, Carolyn (probn clerk)

31. HM Remand Centre
     Forbury Road **Reading** RG1 3HY
     tel 0118-908 5000 *fax 0118-908 5004*

     Cowan, Sally
     Yapp, Liam (custody to work)
     Curtis, Rebecca (pso asessment &
     resettlement)
     Goodliffe, Joy (pso)
     Ibironke, Yenzile (pso)
     Cole, Jeannette (p, pso bail info)

32. HMP **Spring Hill**
Grendon Underwood
Aylesbury, Bucks HP18 0TH
tel (01296) 443000 *fax (01296) 443002*

Foster, Karen (spo)
Anthony, Rosemary
Carr, Diane
Cohen, Stan
Cooper, Bridget
Gateley, Margaret (p)
Colton, Lee (pso)
Nash, Therese (probn clerk)

Housing Advice
Parsloe, Laura (p, housing advr)

33. HMP **Woodhill**
Tattenhoe Street
Milton Keynes, Bucks MK4 4DA
tel (01908) 722000 *fax (01908) 722001*

Litchfield, Theresa (ets resettlement mgr)
Webb, Alan
Davis, Sharon (pso)
Kew, Debbie (pso)
Patidar, Prity (pso resettlement)
Staff-Lonie, Sue (pso)
Tate-Williams, Gill (pso resettlement)
Wilkins, Matthew (pso resettlement)
Worsfold, Barbara (pso)

34. HM YOI **Huntercombe**
Huntercombe Place
Nuffield, Henley on Thames RG9 5SB
tel (01491) 643100 *fax (01491) 643101*

Foot, Lyn (p)

Local Justice Areas
3 Central Buckinghamshire
2 Southern Oxfordshire
10 Milton Keynes
13, 14 Oxford
16, 17 Reading
18 East Berkshire
12 West Berkshire
4, 5 Northern Oxfordshire
9 Wycombe & Beaconsfield

Crown Courts
3 Aylesbury
13 Oxford
15 Reading

WARWICKSHIRE PROBATION AREA

Out of hours emergency contact point
Kenilworth Road Hostel (01926) 339331
Victim enquiries contact number tel 0845
1202325 *fax 0845 1202326*
e-mail Firstname.Surname@warwickshire.
probation.gsx.gov.uk

1. **Head Office**
2 Swan Street
Warwick CV34 4BJ
tel (01926) 405800 *fax (01926) 403183*

Stafford, Liz (co) 405850
I'Anson, Cathy (pa) 405843

Johnson, Pat (aco) 405812
Henshall, Christie (pa) 405807

Lacey, Wes (aco) 405813
Newbold, Sue (pa, training admin) 405811

Insley, Anne-Marie (finance mgr) 405841
Surtees, Carol (staff devpt mgr) 405818
Henshaw, Ian (ptnrshp projs mgr) 405817
Caswell, Heather (hr mgr) 405808
Borrows, Trish (effective pract mgr)
405828
Frampton, Lesley (area mgr, progs) 405871
Goodyear, Kevin (info manager) 405823
Sharp, Jim (accred prog treatment mgr)
405827
Rogers, Sue (basic skills co-ord) 405831
Dragutinovic, Ivica (pso progs)
Sweatman, Matthew (pso progs)
Thomas, Adam (pso progs)
Smith, Darren (progs admin)

Trainees
*trainees are based in various offices
contact via Carol Surtees (01926) 405818*

Second Year
Ball, Beverley
Burnett, Christopher
Furnival, Monika
Grant, Richard
Hamilton, Natalie
Kent, Stephen
Snelson, Catherine

First Year
Dow, Katherine
Fox, Natalie
Jones, Andrew
Ward, Rianne

Crown Court Unit
fax (01926) 405801

Burt, Christine (pso) 405845
Furnivall, Pam (pso) 405824
Farquhar, Angela (admin) 405840
Worton, Lynn (admin) 405840

1a. **Victim Contact Unit**
(part of Victim & Witness Information
Partnership)
93-95 Bedford Street
Leamington Spa CV32 5BB
tel 0845 1202325 *fax 0845 1202326*

Kalm, Indi (pso) (01926) 680254
Campbell, Charlotte (temp pso) (01926)
680254
Wetton, Helen (admin) (01926) 680253

2. 1 Euston Square
Leamington Spa CV32 4NB
tel (01926) 331860 *fax (01926) 887808*

McGovern, Donald (area probn mgr)
Lawson, Neil (snr practitioner)
Elfain, Lynne (snr pract)
Jones, Eira (snr pract)
Abram, Paula
Basi, Kiran
Cory, Nick
Donnelly, Jim
Finn, Thomasina
McConville, Patrick
Macleod, Ros
Moore, Tara
Turner, Polly
Adams, Dave (qa mgr, cp)
Kingston, Linda (pso, personal adv)
Sandhu, Manny (pso, personal adv)
Duffy, Peter (pso)
Gallagher, Victoria (pso)
Jackson, Heather (pso)
Marsella, Lyn (pso)
O'Sullivan, William (pso)
Simons, Sharon (pso)

3. Grove Road
Stratford-upon-Avon CV37 6QR
tel (01789) 299520/267032 *fax (01789)*
298264

Ghafoor, Mehmeena
Lewis, Wendy
Mannion, Danny
Sullivan, Karen
Caudell, Edna (sao)

4. The Courthouse, Newbold Road
Rugby CV21 2LH
tel (01788) 534900 *fax (01788) 547576*

Noon, Nina (temp spo)
Chappell, Sharon (spo)
Chambers, Rosey
Cook, Val
Farthing, Mark
Ghaiwal, Kanwal
Hurley, Michael
Kelly, Hazel
Peaston, Jolie
Sahota, Kiran
Kenny, Julia (pso progs)
Bullock, Sarah (pso)
Hewitt, Joanne (pso)
Hiron, Yvonne (pso)
Eaves, Craig (cpo)
Gallagher, Anne (cpo)

5. Warwickshire Justice Centre
Vicarage Street **Nuneaton** CV11 4JU
tel (02476) 483140 *fax (02476) 482806*

Bains, Peter (area probn mgr)
Guru, Sam (snr pract)
Measom, Jack (snr pract)
Parmar, Deena (snr pract)
Ademetun, Ade
Birchall, Daphne
Burns, Roy
Chapman, Sarah
Crunkhorn, Sue
Curtis, Suzanne
Davies, Janice
Doughty-Lee, Niki
Gilbert, Beverley
Goodman, Carol
Jones, Lisa
Kiggell, Jackie
Kockelbergh, Marion
Ramswell, Amy
Taylor, Viv
van der Molen, Jenny
Weclawek, Mark
Wood, Kelly
Coles, Helen (treatment mgr, progs)
Oldham, Nicola (pso progs)
Price, Simon (pso progs)
Devine, Catherine (pso)
Dewis, Hayley (pso)
Goodall, Nigel (pso)
Howe, Faith (pso)
Patten, Sharon (pso)
Lewis, Linda (sao)

Gravenor, Frank (unpaid wk mgr)
Mawby, Chris (qa mgr)
Fowler, Des (cpo)
Dalman, Martyn (cpo)

Warwickshire Youth Offending Team

6. Stirling House
    12 Hamilton Terrace, Holly Walk
    Leamington Spa CV32 4LY
    tel (01926) 736200 *fax (01926) 736201*

    Johnson, Diane (hd of yo services)
    Weatherall, Brian (yot pract)

7. Newton Hall
    Lower Hillmorton Road
    Rugby CV21 3TU
    tel (01788) 331256 *fax (01926) 476900*

Drug Action Resettlement Team

    Chambers, Diane (pso) (Leamington)
    Stewart, Margaret (pso) (Nuneaton)

Community Punishment Unit

8. **Warwick Workshop**
    Montague Road, Warwick CV34 5LL
    tel (01926) 413448 *fax (01926) 411265*

    Baxter, Sue (cpo)
    Griffin, Velma (cpo)
    Norman, Abigail (cpo)
    Smith, Les (cpo)

Hostels

9. **33 Kenilworth Road**
    Leamington Spa CV32 6JG
    tel (01926) 339331 *fax (01926) 312518*

    Baxendale, Nadine (area probn mgr)
    Hanks, Rosemarie (deputy mgr)
    Vacancy (asst warden)
    Godfrey, Leroy (asst warden)
    Kavanagh, Maxine (asst warden)
    Kettyle, Heather (asst warden)
    Wallis, Julia (asst warden)

10. **McIntyre House**
    125 Edward Street, Nuneaton CV11 5RD
    tel 024 7638 2889 *fax 024 7635 3982*

    Evans, Bev (mgr)
    Tamlyn, Carole (dep mgr)
    Barlow, James (asst warden)
    Hodges, Matthew (asst warden)
    Pickard, Rosanna (asst warden)
    Power, Joy (asst warden)
    Wallis, Steve (asst warden)

Local Justice Area

    2-6 Warwickshire

Crown Court

    1 Warwick

WEST MERCIA PROBATION AREA
Herefordshire, Shropshire, Worcestershire, Telford & Wrekin

Out of hours emergency contact point:
Braley House (01905) 723975

e-mail Firstname.Surname@west-mercia.
probation.gsx.gov.uk

1. **Head Office**
    Stourbank House
    90 Mill Street **Kidderminster**
    Worcs DY11 6XA
    tel (01562) 748375 *fax (01562) 748407*

    Chantler, David (co)
    Bradbury, Patricia (board chair)
    Allen, Helen (aco offender interventions &
    devpt)
    Brewerton, Tony (aco planning & perf)
    Masters, Julie (aco offender mngmnt)
    Jones, Sandra (aco h.r.)
    Baker, Paul (area mgr interventions)
    Simmonds, Karen (exec asst to co)
    Fisher, Vicki (snr admin off)
    Bell, Jackie (p.r. off)
    Sharples, Jennifer (pa to S Jones)
    Gleeson, Leanora (pa to H Allen)
    Wilks, Gemma (pa to T Brewerton)
    Johnstone, Kirsty (pa to P Bradbury)
    Peters, Sarah (pa to J Masters)

    Bury, Shirley (finance mgr)
    Champken, Tina (dep finance mgr)
    Preston, David (commissioning mgr)
    Fraser, Shelley (contracts off)
    Smith, Linda (i.c.t. mgr)
    Lewis, Darren (systems mgr)
    Everrett, Jo (database admin & proj supt)
    Jones, Jeff (info mgr)

    Connect
    Brewerton, Anthony (regnl proj dir)
    Chantler, Sue (ops mgr)
    Vacancy (snr info off)
    Wilks, Gemma (proj supt)

1a. **Connect Information Unit**
    Unit 7, 1-4 Windsor Court
    Clive Road Redditch, B97 4BT
    tel (01527) 67805 *fax (01527) 592486*

Close, Emily (info off)
Honor, Christie (info off)
Callow, Sue (info off)
Elmes, Rob (info off)
Bennett, Katherine (info supt off)
O'Sullivan, Angela (info supt asst)
Hitchins, Julie (info supt asst)

Connect Project Co-ordinators
(work from home)
Aston, Heather (spo) mobile 07968 397825
Smith, Ruth (spo) mobile 07976 530901
Thompson, Chris (spo) mobile 07793 977324

Connect Project Workers
based at the following prisons
Blakenhurst (20)
Brockhill (18)
Hewell Grange (19)
The Dana (17)
Stoke Heath (16)
Drake Hall (Staffordshire)
Glen Parva (Leicestershire & Rutland)
Birmingham (West Midlands)
Brinsford (West Midlands)

1b. **Training & Development Suite**
36 Leswell Street,
Kidderminster DY10 1RP
tel (01562) 66150 *fax (01562) 825899*

Fuller, Catherine (training mgr)
Vose, Derek (training off)

Area Wide

2. **Accredited Programmes (South)**
3-4 Shaw Street **Worcester** WR1 3QQ
tel (01905) 723591 *fax (01905) 724833*

Farebrother, Jim (spo mgr)
Foster, Andy (treatment mgr, did)
Taylor, Audrey (treatment mgr, osap)
Wilks, Helen (treatment mgr, ets)
Davenne, John
Morris, Lin
Stevens, Dave
Ball, Kathryn (pso)
Jarvis, Sharon (pso)
Meese, Sharon (pso)
Morgan-Chadwick, Leanne (pso)
Moule, Kate (pso)
Stewart, Jayne (pso)
Bearcroft, Gill (location mgr)

3. **Accredited Programmes (North)**
Courtside House, Telford Square
Malinsgate **Telford** TF3 4EQ

tel (01952) 299366 *fax (01952) 200896*

Law, Tom (spo mgr)
Briscoe, Mark (treatment mgr)
Hankinson, Ian (treatment mgr)
Willetts, Diane (treatment mgr)
Heywood, Sue (pda)
Morris, Emma
Armstrong, Guy (pso)
de Vos, Les (pso)
McCarthy, Sarah (pso)
Newcombe, Gillian (pso)
Abbs, Anita (team admin)
Vacancy (team admin asst)
Broome, Anne (commissioning)

Hereford
Chilton, Barbara (pso)
Davey, Amanda (pso)
Merchant, Phillip (pso)

Shrewsbury
Clarke, Janet (pso)
Norfolk, Gael (pso)
Rennie, Gemma (pso)
White, Ashleigh (pso)

Telford Division

4. Telford Square
Malinsgate **Telford** TF3 4HX
tel (01952) 214100 *fax (01952) 214111*

Davies, Glyn (dist team mgr)
Southwell, Debra (dist team mgr)
Breen, Jan (ecp mgr)
Vacancy (qa mgr)
Adams, Sheila
Bennett, Sally
Collin, Chris
Cope, Ron
Cotton, Louise
Danesi, Rosa
Grant, Desmond
Kwarteng, Michelle
Larkin, Dave
Nellist, Nicola
Smith, Alan
Timmins, Jenna
Vaughan, Lucy
Wheeler, Clare

Nelson, Laura (crt duty off)
Bond, Kelly (pso)
Morrow, Ann (pso)
Cox, Lesley (pso victim supt)
Hughes, Chris (pso enforcement)

Gorse, Derek (cpo)
Horobin, Colin (cpo)
Richardson, Wendy (cpo)

Murray, Phil (cpo)

Watts, Jim (trainee)
Wright, Karen (trainee)

DRR
Challenger, Paul (pso)
Herd, Clare (drug wrkr)
Hood, Della (drug wrkr)

Gittins, Amanda (location mgr)
Bird, Bev (team admin)

Telford Magistrates' Court
tel/fax (01952) 210074

New Shropshire Division
Shrewsbury, Ludlow, Market Drayton
Oswestry, Whitchurch

5. 135 Abbey Foregate
    Shrewsbury SY2 6AS
    tel (01743) 231525 *fax (01743) 244914*

    Hatfield, Michele (area mgr)
    Gaffney, Jane (dist team mgr)
    Warren, John (dist team mgr)
    Roberts, Anne (risk mgr)
    Kelly, Doug (cp unit mgr)
    Bench, Rosalind (p)
    Buckley, Carol
    Busk, Bob
    Chilton, Lis
    Goodban, Diana
    Harvey, Carrie
    Jeffries, Sandra
    Kaleta, Angyla
    Law, Margaret (p)
    Morgan, David
    Proctor, Anne
    Ruffell, Clare (p)
    Smith, Susan (p)

    Dean, Ruth (pso)
    Clarke, Janet (progs)
    Rennie, Gemma (progs)
    White, Ashleigh (progs)
    Hinde, Christopher (pso)
    Norfolk, Gael (progs)
    Price, Bev (pso)
    Smith, Susan M (pso)
    Edwards, Sally (offender learning mgr)
    Johnson, Colin (enforcement off)
    Warner, Brant (skills for life co-ord)

    Coleman, Annita (cpo)
    Heskey, Richard (cpo)
    McIntyre, Don (cpo)
    Smith, Paula (cpo)
    Telford, Dawn (cpo)

DRR
Pennal, Jesse
Obertelli, Joanne
Wilson, Fiona
Pearce, Anna (pso)
Aston, Phil (drug wrkr)
Groves, David (drug wrkr)

Felton, Helen (trainee)
Owen, Lynne (trainee)
Pearce, Wendy (trainee)

Konkel, Carolyn (location mgr)
Hatton, Margaret (team admin)

5a. **Crown Court Probation Office**
     The Law Courts, Shirehall
     Abbey Foregate **Shrewsbury** SY2 6LU
     tel (01743) 252934 *fax (01743) 252936*

     Marshall-Clarke, Vincent

Herefordshire Division

6.   Gaol Street
     Hereford HR1 2HU
     tel (01432) 272521 *fax (01432) 350408*

     Pimpernell, Pam (area mgr)
     Barnes, Chris (dist team mgr)
     Stephenson, Jenny (dist team mgr)
     Douglas, Sandra (risk mgr)
     Powell, John (risk mgr)
     Anderson, Kathleen (unit mgr)
     Beard, Richard
     Bennett, David
     Brandon-White, Chris
     Clarke, Lloyd
     Daly, Maggie
     Denning, Andrew
     Mills, Sue
     Rees, Mandy
     Rees, Sharon
     Wildig, Sarah

     Cassidy, Moira (pso)
     Chilton, Barbara (pso)
     Dovey, Amanda (pso)
     Greig, Denns (pso)
     Morgan, Louise (pso)
     Morris, Sarah (pso)
     Simson, Kate (pso)
     Swan, Jane (pso)
     Wainwright, Urszula (pso)
     Wilkinson, Mike (pso)
     Guy, Ginny (enforcement officer)
     Petts, Susannah (vlo)

     Lewis, Jane (location mgr)
     Angell, Susan (team admin)

North Worcestershire Division

7.   1-4 Windsor Court
     Clive Road **Redditch**
     Worcestershire B97 4BT
     tel (01527) 585152 *fax (01527) 596459*

     Currie, Tom (area mgr)
     Ashworth, Julie (dist team mgr)
     Jenkins, Neil (snr pract, risk mgr)
     Aston, Jeff (pda)
     Morgan, Jane (com devpt off)
     Chaudhry, Aftab
     Chung, Dawnn
     Fowler, Claire
     Fraser, Margaret
     Hammes, Anthony
     McLean, Paula
     Mellor, Ruth
     Middleton, Penny
     Ramsay, Sheena
     Sherrard, Tony
     Slater, Neil

     Atkins, Sara (hd pso cp)
     Bovington, Sara (pso cp)
     Reeves, Catherine (cp h&s off)

     Heighway, Lee (pso)
     Potter, Julia (pso)
     Prince, Lis (pso)
     Allen, Karen (pso crts)

     Batsford, Louis (trainee)
     Pawsey, Ruth (trainee)
     Tolley, Stephen (trainee)

     Bawler, Tim (location mgr)

8.   Stourbank House, 90 Mill Street
     Kidderminster
     Worcestershire DY11 6XE
     tel (01562) 820071 *fax (01562) 862425*

     Currie, Tom (area mgr)
     Lee, Martin (dist team mgr)
     Sinclair, Margaret (snr pract, risk mgr)
     Greenwood, Richard
     Johnson, Adam
     Mamos, Lynn
     Nicholls, Jacquie
     Turner, Rob

     Atkins, Sara (hd pso cp)
     Gibbons, Jenny (pso cp)
     Webster, Trevor (pso cp)

     Allen, Karen (pso crts)
     Bassrall, Laura (pso)
     Loane, Liz (pso)
     Thomson, Kirsty (pso)
     Prince, Lis

     Mowbray, Nicola (vlo)
     Bawler, Tim (location mgr) (based at 7)

South Worcestershire Division

9.   3-4 Shaw Street
     Worcester WR1 3QQ
     tel (01905) 723591 *fax (01905)
     20516/29057*

     Currie, Tom (area mgr)
     Haywood, Jonathan (dist team mgr)
     Smith, Liz (dist team mgr)
     Skelton, Dave (dist team mgr)
     Grove, John (risk mgr)

     Crump, Carol
     Da Silva, Claira
     Fields, Alistair
     Gill, Janet
     Guest, Kerry
     Gurney, Dan
     Haycock, Natasha
     Koser, Razwana
     Lloyd, Val
     Marshall, Rachel
     Parsons, Kate
     Purewal, Davs
     Rimoncelli, Polly
     Sampson, Marita
     Secrett, Rebecca
     Sheath, Jan
     Thurston, Anna
     Tooke, Susannah
     Walters, Stephen
     Webb, Young
     Young, Tania

     Burrell, Ann (pso crt)
     Ellerington, Ray (pso crt)
     Frindi, Maureen (pso supvn)
     Leeuwangh, Jon (enforcement)
     McDonald, Dee (pso supvn)
     Schwab, Richard (pso crt)
     Sirman, Catherine (pso supvn)

     Windows-Yule, Ian (cp unit mgr)
     Thomas, Jason (qa mgr)
     Bacon, Stephen (cpo)
     Charles, Kim (cpo)
     Hampton, Ian (cpo)
     Rushton, Doug (cpo)
     Southall, Keith (cpo)
     Willis, Pete (cpo)

     Bramford, Kate (pda)
     Smith, Ursula (pda)
     Chambers, Lucy (trainee)
     Gualano, Marco (trainee)
     Matthews-Jones, Nigel (trainee)

Newton, Tony (trainee)
Payne, Elizabeth (trainee)
Rosoman, Richard (trainee)

DRR
Harris, Emma
Hodgkins, Sue (pso)

Bettison, Jan (location mgr)

Worcester Crown Court
tel (01905) 723594

10. **Acclaim Project**
Youth Support Services
Suite 1, Quilgold House
Hampton Lovett Industrial Estate
Droitwich, Worcs WR9 0QH
tel (01905) 799690 *fax (01905) 799692*

Williams, Jane (proj mgr)

Hereford/Worcester
Emmett, Beckie (area case mgr)
Bennett, Jeannie (acclaim off)
Bevan, Lyn (acclaim off)
Swann, Karen (acclaim off)

Telford/Shropshire
1 Dawley Road
Telford, Shropshire TF1 2HW
tel (01952) 257467 *fax (01952) 246113*

Baynton, Glen (area case mgr)
Aldridge, Tina (acclaim off)
Grantham, Debs (acclaim off)
McGlue, Suzanne (acclaim off)

Youth Offending Services

11. c/o Smallwood Health Centre
Church Green West
Redditch B97 4DJ
tel (01527) 593645

12. 24 Victoria Road
Wellington **Telford** TF1 1LG
tel (01952) 257477

13. Tolladine Road
Worcester WR4 9NB
tel (01905) 732200

Hostels

14. **Braley House Approved Premises**
89 Ombersley Road
Worcester WR3 7BT
tel (01905) 723975 *fax (01905) 617687*

Bentley, Mike (hostel mgr)
Baynton, Jenny (po dep)

Crouch, Carole (asst warden)
Coleman, Neil (asst warden)
Kaur, Ranjit (asst warden)
Khan, Nadim (asst warden)
Smith, Jason (asst warden)

15. **Iris House Voluntary Hostel**
68 Bath Road
Worcester WR5 3EW
tel (01905) 353884

Institutions

16. HM YOI **Stoke Heath**
Market Drayton TF9 2JL
tel (01630) 636000 *fax (01630) 636001*
probn fax (01630) 636263

Holland, Glyn (spo)
Adams, Carol
Barrow, Marie
Cummings, John
Noble, Helen
Stokes, Katie

17. H M Prison **The Dana**
Shrewsbury SY1 2HR
tel (01743) 273000 *fax (01743) 273001*
probn fax (01743) 273003

Ritson, Catherine (p, spo) ext 3054
Isaacs, Tricia ext 3054
Jones, Jo ext 3053

18. H M Prison **Brockhill**
Redditch B97 6RD
tel (01527) 552650 *fax (01527) 552651*
probn tel (01527) 552821/552656
probn fax (01527) 552651

Davis, Hyacinth (spo)
Harding, Emma
Bishop, Mandi
Griffiths, Samantha (pso connect)
(01527) 552975

19. H M Prison **Hewell Grange**
Hewell Lane, Redditch B97 6QQ
tel (01527) 552000 *fax (01527) 552001*
probn dept (01527) 552207

Hill, Eddie

20. H M Prison **Blakenhurst**
Hewell Lane, Redditch B97 6QS
tel (01527) 400500 *fax (01527) 400501*

Williams, Pete (acting spo)
Akhtar, Azeem
Carroll, Andrew

Darlow, Teresa
Matthews, Kim
Mesonde, Kabel
Firman, Kathryn (pso)
Taylor, Christine (pso)

21. **H M Prison Long Lartin**
South Littleton, Evesham WR11 3TZ
tel (01386) 835100 *fax (01386) 835101*

Wain, John (spo)
Concannon, Ignatius
Cox, Jane
Wildig, Sarah
Fergus, Paul
Weston, Mike (pso)

Local Justice Areas

5 Drayton
7 Bromsgrove & Redditch
6 Herefordshire
5 South Shropshire
5 Oswestry
8 Kidderminster
5 Shrewsbury
9 South Worcestershire
4 Telford & Bridgnorth

Crown Courts

6 Hereford
5a Shrewsbury
9 Worcester

WEST MIDLANDS PROBATION AREA

Victim enquiries contact number
tel 0121-248 6100

e-mail Firstname.Surname@west-midlands.
probation.gsx.gov.uk

1. **Head Office**
1 Victoria Square, Birmingham B1 1BD
tel 0121-248 6666 *fax 0121-248 6667*

Thompson, Hilary (cpo)
Mallabone, Teresa (dir of operations)
Holland, Catherine (dir of people & perf)
Steer, Richard (secretary/solicitor)
Nelson, Andy (dir of finance & facilities)
Hartley, Linda (aco perf, planning & info)
Nyoka, Joshua (personnel mgr)
Leigh-Hanson, Veronica (hd of personnel)
Kerslake, Mike (qual imp mgr)
Madders, Michael (aco i.t. services)

Daly, William (aco business supt)
Whitehouse, David (aco finance)
Vacancy (planning mgr)
Flaxman, James (perf & systems info mgr)
Allcott, Ros (area admin devpt mgr)
Mitchell, Rita (risk mgr)
Sawbridge, Judith (info & comms mgr)

2. **King Edward House**
5th Floor, 135A New Street,
Birmingham B2 4QJ
tel 0121-248 2700 *fax 0121-248 2701*

Equality & Diversity Unit
Hanley, Susan (aco equal & diversity)
Kelly, Tony (e&d off)
Sharma, Ushma (e&d off)
Whelan, Paula (e&d off)
Harris, Keith (race, equal & devpt off)

Assistant Chief Officers Unit
Hanley, Sue (aco diversity & victims)
Fenby, John (aco offender mgmnt, West of
County & approved premises)
Green, Richard (aco services to crts,
EOASYS, expedited breach & deaths
under supervision)
Gill, Stephen (aco interventions)
Byford, Nigel (aco risk & resettlement,
mental mealth)
Appleby, Neil (aco
ptnrshps/commissioning, basic skills,
DTTO/DRR)
Wall, Chris (aco offender mgmnt,
Birmingham.

Effective Practice
Garton, Kashmir (spo)

Partnerships and Interventions Unit
Vann, Barbara (admin mgr)
Chopourian, Gemma (ptnrshps monitoring
off)
Haywood, Sue (dtto/drr comissioning off)
Shelton, Paul (basic skills commissioning
& supporting people officer)
Connelly, Jane (dist mgr ptnrshps &
interventions)
Hudson, Sue (spo)

Basic Skills
Appleby, Neil (aco)
Connelly, Jane (dist mgr)

ETE Unit
Vacancy (spo, ete mgr)
Vacancy (mentoring co-ord)
Hendley, Sara (basic skills co-ord)
Carr, Caroline (skills for life co-ord
Birmingham)

Evans-Healey, Annice (skills for life co-ord
Coventry)
Vacancy (skills for life co-ord West of
County)

at Chelmsley Wood 0121-770 9090
Gaughan, John (pso)
at Coventry (02476) 630555
Arnold, Peter (pso)
Vacancy (pso)
at Dudley (01384) 455351
Harris, Shelley (pso)
at Greencoat House 0121-248 5705
McGowan, Yvonne (pso)
at Hamstead Rd 0121-248 6500
Ali, Iftika (pso)
at Harborne 0121-248 6230
Cook, Steve (pso)
at Lower Essex St 0121-248 6400
Braithwaite, Kevin (pso)
Thomspon, Shahara (ete pso)
Henry, Jackie (pso)
at Perry Barr 0121-248 6348
Leslie, Tracey (pso)
at Rolfe St 0121-565 4411
Smith, Richard (pso)
at Saltley 0121-248 6150
Vacancy (pso)
at Stonnall Road Hostel (01922) 459574
Mclarnon, Nonnie (pso all hostels)
at Walsall (01922) 721341
Gainer, Martin (pso)
at Wolverhampton (01902) 576000
Stevens, Chris (pso)
at Wolverhampton (01902) 351518
Whitehouse, Lesley (pso)

3. **Area Victim Liaison Unit**
at 52 Newton Street Birmingham B4 6NF
tel 0121-248 6100 *fax 0121-248 6101*

Beckford, Audrey (spo)
Astley, Denise
Collier, Catherine
Madeley, Helen
Keeley, Patrick
Fitzmaurice, Tracey (pso)
Nembhardt, Osbourne (pso)

at 70 Little Park Street Coventry CV1 2UR
tel 024-7655 3268 *fax 024-7663 1531*

Tudor, Barbara (victim liaison devpt off)
Meir, Janice
Patton, Brian (pso)

at Union Street, Horseley Fields
Wolverhampton WV1 3JS
tel (01902) 576001 *fax (01902) 455180*

Steventon, Jason
West, Jacque (pso)

Dudley Districts

4. **District Management Unit**
Suite 5, Trafalgar House,
47-49 King Street, Dudley DY2 8PS
tel (01384) 326020 *fax (01384) 326021*

Thompson, Viv (dist mgr)
Brown, Steve (admin mgr)

5. 44 New Road **Stourbridge** DY8 1PA
tel (01384) 440682 *fax (01384) 441354*

Tier 3/Tier 4 Team
Dunbar, Janet (spo)
Dee, John
Ingram, Sandra
Langstone, Diane
Leith, Richard
Long, Jennifer
Mantle, Nick
Page, Saundra
Storer, Jim
Taylor, Barbara
Vickers, June
Baker, Sonia (pso)
Farrar, Susan (pso)

6. The Court House, The Inhedge
Dudley DY1 1RR
tel (01384) 455351 *fax (01384) 235680*

Tier 3
Yeap, Christine (spo)
Bishop, Claire
Chohan, Sharnjit
Knight, Susan
Mann, Caroline
Reid, Karen
Tarinor, Timothy
Whittam, Jayne
Dee, Elaine (pso)
Garcha, Daive (pso)

Tier 1/2
Watson, Janet (spo)
Amni, Angela
Williams, Gerry
Zihni, Jenny
Brown, Shirley (pso)
Dixon, Christian (pso)
Jones, Chris (pso)
Round, Deborah (pso)

ETE
Harris, Shelley (pso)

at office 4
Stearn, Steve
Cookson, Geoff (pso)
Mullett, Alan (pso)

7. Laurel Lane **Halesowen** B63 3DA
tel 0121-550 1496 *fax 0121-585 5582*

PPO
Burnham, Dolores (spo)
Walker, Stephen
Cox, Ira (pso)
Fearon, Davis (pso)

DRR/DTTO
Burnham, Dolores (spo)
Platt, Andy
Clancy, Kirsty (pso)
Taylor, Jessica (pso)
Vacancy (pso)

Courts and Allocation
Griffiths, Ray (spo)

Halesowen Magistrates' Court Office
tel 0121-550 1496 *fax 0121-585 5582*
Brecknell, Davina
Barrett, Ann Marie (pso)
Darlington, Daphne (pso)
Cooper, Roger (pso)
Hawley, Anne (pso)
Mukwamba, Michael (pso)

Dudley Magistrates' Court Office
tel (01384) 455351 *fax (01384) 235680*
Fitzgerald, Kevin
Bishop, Claire
Jordan, Oliver (pso)
Spiteri, Paula (pso)

8. **Dudley Youth Offending Team**
Brindley House, Hall Street, Dudley DY2 7DT
tel (01384) 813060 fax 1(01384) 813270

Driscoll, Steve
Higgit, Gary

Sandwell District

9. 14-16 New Street
West Bromwich B70 7PN
0121-533 5400 *fax 0121-533 4501*

Royal, Pat (dist mgr)
Brown, Steve (admin mger)
Sutton, Sandra (ete co-ord West of Area)

Tier 4
Coxall, Mary (spo)
Barrington, Karyn
Bibi, Shaida

Goldie, Joanne
Kaur, Rajinder
Price, John
Pritchard, Andy
Rai, Ravinder
Stokes, Elaine
Vaughan-Phillips, Louise
Radford, Edwina (pso)
Sarai, Kulvinder (pso)
Whale, Paul (pso)

Tier 3
Thompson, Jacky (spo)
Chand, Gheeta
Dillon, Claire
Edwards, Alyson
Forrest, Sean
Francis, Vanessa
Hampton, Jane
Johnson, Lemwell
Rai, Harmail
Samria, Daljit
Grant, Sheena (pso)
Greenhill, Diane (pso)

Interventions
Ellis, Phillip J (spo)
Fowler, Graham (treatment mgr)
Burton, Carol (treatment mgr)
Brigue, Rekha
Geach, Mary (po trainer)
Williams, Liinos
Eaton, Andrew (pso)
James, Jane (pso)
Saddler, Stephen (pso)

DRR/DTTO
Ellis, Phillip J (spo)
Brigue, Rekha
Williams, Morene
Leather, Debbie (pso)
Lee, Alison (pso)
Nelson, Sharon (pso)
Wheeler, Monica (pso)

ETE
Smith, Richard (pso)

Tier1/2
Gould, Ian (spo)
Cookson, David
Fowler, Louise
Glean, Janice
Hulston, Deborah
Rees, Sarah
Ali, Asif (pso)
Hubbold, Melissa (pso)
Riley, Paul (pso)
Williams, Charles (pso)

Courts and Allocation
Kaur-Pahal, Rashpal (spo)
Facer, Rebecca (pso DIP)

Warley Magistrates' Court Office
tel 0121-533 3427 *fax 0121-525 6751*
Kaye, Peter
Badhen, Asha
McGhee, James
Bloice, Lawrence (pso)
Mervyn Jackie (pso)

West Bromwich Magistrates' Court Office
tel 0121-525 5381 *fax 0121-525 6751*
Littlehales, Sue
Nott, Laura
Proud, Nikki
Sidaway, Yvonne
Alexander, Marion (pso)
Balu, Amarjit (pso)
Smith, Karen (pso)

10. **Sandwell Youth Offending Team**
SGS House, Johns Lane, Off Tipton Road,
Tividale, Oldbury B69 3HX
tel 0121-557 8804 *fax 0121-521 0991*

Crawford-Brown, Junior
Hogan, Marie

Coventry District

11. 70 Little Park Street
Coventry CV1 2UR
tel 024-7663 0555 *fax 024-7663 1531*

Pymm, Lesley (dist mgr)
Chapman, Janette (admin mgr)

Coventry Courts & Allocation Team
fax 024-7655 3393

Fawcett, Karen (spo)
Caine, Louise
Harris, Faith
Nugent, Denis
Robertson, Helen
Purdy, Lynn
Allder, Heather (pso)
Lee, Jennifer (pso)
Mellor Jackie (pso)
Rollason, Karen(pso)

Coventry Tier 4
Killeen, Chris (spo)
Bevan, Shelley
Dade,Emma
Green, Bev
Heath, Alison
Jones, Raymond

McCarthy, Sinead
Thorpe, Elaine
Wibberley, Steve
Lake, Justine (pso)
Wright, Rosie (pso)

Coventry Tier3
Treacy, Laura (spo)
Fleming, Sandra
Gill, Ranjit
Holten, Nöelle
James, Emma
Laidler, Karen
Norton, Deborah
Odenbreit, Louise
O'Neill, Jim
Randhawa, Harbinder
Riley, Jenny
Rose, Samantha
Smith, Ian
Windridge, Kelly
Flemons, Kirstie (pso)
Groves, Rose (pso)
Lea, Darren (pso)
Miller, Cath (pso)

Coventry Programmes
Toor, Haramandeep (spo)
Appleton, Jane
Briffa, Claire
Baker, Kirsty
Ford, David
Knights, Kelly
Heath, Peter (pso)
Poole, Maureen (pso)

Coventry DRR
fax 02476 630378
Toor, Haramandeep (spo)
Gheent, Harvi
Gill, Ciara (pso)
Rudd, Charlie(pso)
Skinner, Joanne (pso)

ETE
Evans-Healey, Annice (ETE co-ord)
Arnold,Peter (pso)

12. Bishop Street, Coventry CV1 1HU
tel 024-7655 5638 *fax 024-7655 0192*

Coventry Tiers 1 & 2
O'Donoghue, Deirdre (spo)
Almquist, Debbie
Ferron, Lynne (pso)
Gardner, Chris (pso)
Johnson, Barbara (pso)
Kane, Lorraine (pso)
Lee, Mark (pso)

13. **Coventry Youth Offending Team**
Ground Floor, Christchurch House
Greyfriars, Lane, Coventry CV1 2GY
tel 024-7683 1414 *fax 024-7683 1400*

Cosser, Mike
Knights, Kellie
Taylor, Wayne
Whitehurst, John

Solihull District

14. The Old Post Office, Bosworth Drive
Chelmsley Wood
Birmingham B37 5EX
tel 0121-770 9090 *fax 0121-779 6528*

Chand, Sarah (dist mgr)
Chapman, Janette (admin mgr) (based at 12)

Solihull Tier 4
Cooke,Natasha (spo)
Buckley, Jane
McCauley, Chris
Richards, Sandra
Young, Therese
Chapman,Sarah (pso)

Solihull Tier 3
Aziz, Naheed (spo)
Brown, Kathleen
Canning, Michael
Fitzer, Zelda
Gissey, Sharon
Hackett, Nina
Herbert, Carole
Holt, Helen
Littleford, Ceri
O'Donoghue, Claire
Smith, Claire
Ward, Jenny
Holmes, Carly (pso)

Solihull Tiers 1 & 2
Murphy, Majella
Ellis, Sophie (pso)
Nutting, Marie (pso)

Solihull DRR
Allder, Marian (spo)
Leach, Margaret
Connolly, Bill (pso)
Foster, Maria (pso)

ETE
Gaughan, John (pso)

15. **Solihull Magistrates' Court Team**
Homer Road, Solihull B91 3RD
tel 0121-711 7331 *fax 0121-711 7050*

Coldrick, Ralph
Hilyer, Rob
Worley, Nick
Atkins, Jenny (pso)
Lambden, Anne (pso)
Fitzsimmons, Elaine (pso)
Murland, Richard (pso)
Reeve, Max (pso)

16. **Solihull Youth Offending Team**
Keeper's Lodge, Chelmsley Road
Chelmsley Wood, Birmingham B37 7RS
tel 0121-779 1750 *fax 0121-779 1755*

Green, Claire

Wolverhampton District

17. Prue Earle House
Union Street, Horseley Fields
Wolverhampton WV1 3JS
tel (01902) 576000 *fax (01902) 455180*

District Management Unit
Pejatta, Jas (dist mgr)
Ainsbury, Robert (admin mgr)

Tier 4
Ashby, Ted (spo)
Batham, Angie
Charmling, Swaroop
Easthope, Norma
Halawin, Kath
Robinson, Angela (dtto)
Sharman, Dave
Wallace, Claire
Wilson, Jean
Chahal, Rajinder (pso dtto)
Phipps, Sally (pso dtto)
Russell, Claire (pso dtto)
Thompson, Gemma (pso dtto)

Tier 3 East
Patel, Lalita (spo)
Tracey, Danny (snr pract)
Brittle, Emma
Chumber, Amrit
Cooper, Heather
Fincher, Jenny
Male, Anita
Meredith, Nina
Pschenyckyj, Denise
Teale, Ian
Turner, Stuart
Dee Jill (pso)
Rees, Jennie (pso)
Stevens, Chris (pso basic skills)
Wilson, Lisa (pso)

Tier 3 West
Whinya, Pascal (spo)
Chamberlain, Sarah
Cooper, Judith
Dannatt, Sarah
Garrett, Elizabeth
Mail, Stephanie
Wilkins, Ian
Blow, Adrian (pso)
Browne, Philippa (pso)

Tier 1/2
Hird Maria (spo)
Anand, Vijay
Martin, Val
Parmar-Poynter, Bhavna
Thackwray, Michelle
Uppal, Pinder
Garrett, Joan (pso)
Lockley, Sheila (pso)
Ramzan, Mohammed (pso)
Williams, Odette (pso)
Vacancy (pso)

Enforcement and Allocation Unit
tel (01902) 576000 *fax (01902) 576010*

Nash, Tim (spo)
Clark, Tracey
Bennett, Faye (pso)
Goodman, Danielle (pso)
Norton, Denise (pso)

18. **Wolverhampton Programmes Unit**
Minerva Wharf, Horseley Fiels
Wolverhampton WV1 3LX
tel (01902) 576008 *fax (01902) 576010*

Hird, Maria (spo)
Berry, Jo
Marsh, David
Phillips, Eva
Richardson, Eva

19. **Wolverhampton Magistrates' Court**
Law Courts, North Street,
Wolverhampton WV1 1RA
tel (01902) 711499 *fax (01902) 772361*

Nash, Tim (spo)
Aston, Jenny
Denny, Nicola
Emmanuel, Jennifer
Tatton, Tracey
Lloyd, Frances
Rawlings, Jim
Waterhouse, Sam
Dyke, Marjorie (pso)
McManus, Sally (pso)

Rusoon, Janet (pso)
Turley, Lucy (pso)

20. **Wolverhampton Crown Court**
Pipers Row, Wolverahmpton WV1 3LQ
tel (01902) 481108/9 *fax (01902) 713355*

Nash, Tim (spo)
Boydon, Jo
Bryan, Elaine
Chopra, Kulwinder
Davis, Hortense
Gerrard, Joyce
Geal, Elizabeth (pso)
Nash, Kate (pso)

21. **Wolverhampton Youth Offending Team**
c/o Social Services Department
Beckminster Houses, Birches Barn Road
Wolverhampton WV3 7BJ
tel (01902) 553722 *fax (01902) 553733*

Nash, Sally (YOS mgr)
Payne, Cecilia (spo)
Jones, Barry
Osbourne, Annette
McBean, Angela (pso)
Winstone, Diane (pso)
Clarke, Tracey (pso)

Walsall District

22. Walsall Probation Complex
Midland Road **Walsall** WS1 3QE
tel (01922) 721341 *fax (01922) 725616*

District Management Unit
Brown-Richards, Pat (dist mgr)
Ainsbury, Robert (admin mgr)

Tier 4
Brownswood, Andrew (spo)
Ball, Pamela
Branwood, Dave
Duffy, Patrick
Head, Nigel
Holden, Angela
Holsey, John
Jones, Adrian
McGovern, Kathy
Morgan, Claradell
Patel, Shanta
Vose, Janet
Johns, Valerie (pso)
Preedy, Karen (pso)
Gainer, Martin (pso walpop)

Tier 3 Offender Management
Blake, Sonia (spo)
Thawait, Pratima (snr pract)

Ainslie, Sam
Arrowsmith, Ben
Billingham, Ruth
Brookes, Angie
Corbett, Victoria
Fiero, Roma
Garland, Sharon
Jordan, Carla
Kelsey, Hayley
Linton, Hazelle
Martin, Clive
Spence, Audrey
Walker, Glenford
Ball, David (pso)
Kaur, Bilwinder (pso)
Lowe, Vanessa (pso)
Skellern, Yvonne (pso)

Tier 3 Interventions
Coyle, John (spo)
Cunningham, Julian
Edwards, Jamie-Ann
Henderson, Victoria
Ball, Sarah (pso dtto)
Brown, Damien (pso dtto)
Evans, Yvonne (pso dtto)
Garrow, June (pso)
Jackson, Charles (pso)
Morris, Mike (pso)
Nash, Karen (pso dtto)

Tier 1/2
Russell, Pete (spo)
Hamkalo, Michelle
Roberts, Becky
Sagar, Vid
Austins, Alan (pso)
Bull, Martin (pso)
Cayrol, Sylviane (pso)
Goode, Debbie (pso)
Panesar, Paramjit (pso)

Walsall/Aldridge Magistrates' Court
Vacancy (spo)
Dean, Rachel
Dhillon, Surrinder
McLeish, Gillian
Mills, Pamela
Neville, Chris
Osmond, Andy
Carolan, Bernie (pso)
Dhani, Hasmukh (pso)
Ford, Lesley (pso)
Malone, Angela (pso)
Richards, Marjorie (pso)
Tarajia, Zaynab (pso)

Enforcement & Allocation
tel (01922) 724637

23. **Youth Offending Team**
Blakenhall Village Centre, Thames Road
Blakenhall, Walsall WS3 1LZ
tel (01922) 714966 *fax (01922) 492462*

Russell, Pete (spo)
Jacques, Janet
Robertson, Les

Birmingham District

24. **Birmingham ACO & Admin Unit**
5th Floor, King Edward House
135A New Street, Birmingham. B2 4QJ
tel 0121-248 2700 *fax 0121-248 2701*

Wall, Chris (aco Birmingham & Coventry)
Elphick, Bronwen (dist mgr)
Lomas, Simon (dist mgr)
McNulty, Adrian (dist mgr)
Mitchell, Tessa (dist mgr)
Kaur, Christine (admin mgr)
Walton, Neil (admin mgr)

25. **Victoria Law Courts**
PO Box 4081, Corporation Street
Birmingham B4 6QU
tel 0121-248 6080
crt info fax 0121-248 6081
crt liason fax 0121-248 6096

Henderson, Jane (spo)
Burt, Tania
Dooley, Phil
Edwards, Althea
Edwards, Cheryl-Ann
Flynn, Val
Greensill,Carole
Hewitt, Christine
Jakhu, Sodhi Ram
Mulowoza, Christine
Murphy, Brian
Penney, Kevin
Samrai, Dalwinder
Davenport, Jeanette (trainee)
Thompson, Sally (trainee)
Wilkinson, Sally (trainee)
Allen,Julie (pso)
Booth, Samantha (pso)
Isaac, Karen (pso)
Shillingford, Angela (pso)
Skinner, Leeza (pso)
Young, Mary (pso)
Brown, Adele (pso)
Williams, Martin (pso)
Rich, Brian (pso)

Drug Intervention Programme
tel 0121-248 1283 *fax 0121-248 1276*

Kelly, Tony

Sutton, Sandra (bus mgr)
Clarke, Cynthia (pso)
Da-Costa, Lisa (pso)
Ubhi, Nav (pso)
Spence, Christopher (pso)

26. **Queen Elizabeth II Law Courts**
1 Newton Street, Birmingham B4 7NA
tel 0121-248 0099 *fax 0121-248 0045*

Sutton Coldfield Magistrates' Court
The Court House, Lichfield Road
Sutton Coldfield, Birmingham B74 2NS
tel 0121-354 3715 *fax 0121-355 8984*

Crown Court Team
& Sutton Court Team
Hughes, Phillip (spo)
Jones, Martin (based at Mags Crt)
Astley, Denise
Durbin, Ray
Miller, Dick
Wilson, Mick
Gaddu, Diamond (trainee)
Rollason, Juliette (pso)
Buttler, Anika (pso)
Grundy, Victoria (pso)
Wilks Larmon, Karen (pso)

Peripatetic Team
Matile, Miles
Eason, Marie
Belboda Queeley, Claudine

27. **11-15 Lower Essex Street**
Birmingham B5 6SN
tel 0121-248 6460 *fax 0121-248 6461*

Homeless Offenders
Resettlement Unit
Briscoe, John (spo)
Bailey, Rema
Cooner, Sanjit
Carman, Stephen
Dhillon, Kulvinder
Reynolds, Gillian
Sandu, Jagit
Whitehouse, Lynne
Braithwaite, Kevin (pso)

28. **Saltley Programmes Unit**
12 High Street, Saltley
Birmingham B8 1JR
tel 0121-248 6184 *fax 0121-248 6151*

Rogers, Marj (spo)
Ballard, Claire
Simms, Arlene
Anderson, Patricia (pso)
Richards, Laurie (pso)

29. **Perry Barr Programmes Unit**
76 Walsall Road, Perry Barr
Birmingham B42 1SF
tel 0121-248 6387 *fax 0121-248 6341*

Jackson, Judith (spo)
Beard, Helen
Brydson, Davlin
Campion, Sally (pso)
Smith, Joyce (pso)

30. 12 High Street
Saltley Birmingham B8 1JR
tel 0121-248 6150 *fax 0121-248 6151*

Tier 3/4
Vassallo, Carmella (spo)
Blackman, Gwyllym
Dickenson, Nicole
Eason, George
Hoo, Marcus
Meikle, Caron
Minto, Sharon
Myers, Paul
Myerscough, Karen
Pasha, Naveed
Perkins, Colin
Philippedes, Toni
Woods, Pat
Bebbington, Christine (pso)
Chambers, Kalvin (pso)

Tier 3
Mitchell, Tessa (spo)
Mullis, Dave (spo)
Raphael, Melissa (spo)
Astley, Deborah
Cansfield, Karen
Heslop, Mike
Jordan, Patricia
King, Maria
Mohammed, Rahim
Morris, David
Myers, Erica
Overthrow, Karen
Poland, Mickey
Slater, Malcolm
Seadon, Sally
McPherson, Stuart (pso)
Watts, Leonard (pso)

DTTO
Vacancy
Barnett, Patricia (pso)
Pitt, Dean (pso)
Stuart, Kevin (pso)

31. Greencoat House, 259 Stratford Road
Sparkbrook Birmingham B11 1QS
tel 0121-248 5611 *fax 0121-248 5613*

Tier 3/4
Mayers, Julie (spo)
Alden, Andy
Jan, Araf
Lam, Angela
Martin, Bryan
Phillips, David
Pope, Caroline
Rees, David
Walsh, Leisa
Webster, Jenny
Williamson, Zoe
Baker, Joanne (trainee)
Beardmore, Rennie (pso)
Hedderick, Bev (pso)

Tier 3
Smith, Paul (spo)
Dowse, Elizabeth
Felton, Stuart
Hyman, Joy
Islam, Mohammed
Keeley, Patrick
King, Maria
Lidell, Catherine
Milinkovic, Victor
Rehman, Rafia
Rhoden, Sonia
Mohammed, Weddad (trainee)
Thurman, Bernadette (trainee)
Brown, Vanessa (pso)
Perkins, Eve (pso)
Jordan, Althea (pso)
Millard, Adrianna (pso)

32. 826 Bristol Road **Selly Oak**
Birmingham B29 6NA
tel 0121-248 6680 *fax 0121-248 6681*

Tier 3/4
Elphick, Bronwen (spo)
Anderson, Dawn
Brown, Carolyn
Francis, Aaron
Harragan, Candy
Knowles, Ann
Kyne, Chris
Morgan, Gail
Morton, Jon
Tyler, Annie
Watkins, Laurence
Peynado, Fenton
Nott, Elaine (pso)
Rowley, Glenda (pso)
Woolley, Malcolm (pso)

33. **18-28 Lower Essex Street**
Birmingham B5 6SN
tel 0121-248 6400 *fax 0121-248 6401*

Tier 1/2
Taylor, Owen (spo)
Kyle, Susanna
Turner, Hilary
Gallagher, Nicola
Baker, Barbara
Lindo, Elizabeth
Kennedy, Jennifer
Bailey, Eileen
Abanikanda, Tunde (pso)
Chaplin, Eileen (pso)
Crawford, Jean (pso)
Gray, Diane (pso)
Kelley, Linda (pso)
Rollins, Gina (pso)
Sheard, Mary (pso)
Walker, Jackie (pso)

DTTO
Altaf, Samina
Edgar, Karen
Browne, Bev (pso)
Gordon, Pat (pso)
Habib, Saima (pso)
Spillane, Kelly (pso)

34. 76 Walsall Road
Perry Barr Birmingham B42 1SF
tel 0121-248 6340 *fax 0121-248 6341*

Tier 3
Grant, Cassell (spo)
Akram, Safraz
Baker, Joanne
Dannat, Sarah
Green, Janet
Powell, Wayne
Thompson, Jacque
Hazeley-Jones, Christopher
Abrams, Pat
Stevenson, Fiona
Dillon, Jenniofer
Dodd, Claire
Ward, Rosaleen (trainee)
Oakley, Pat (trainee)
Twist, John (trainee)
Bassan, Ravinder (pso)
Taylor, Vanessa (pso)

DTTO
Kaur, Inderbir
Clarke, Ann (pso)
Vacancy (pso)
Mills, Olive (pso)

35. Stuart Court, 73/75 Station Road
Erdington Birmingham B23 6UG
tel 0121-248 5600 *fax 0121-248 5605*

Tier 3/4
Morris, Paulette (spo)
Connelly, Fiona
Ditchburn, Margaret
Hunt, Emma
Smith, Keith
Thompson, Angela
Mohammed, Sohail (pso)
Shaw, Bart (pso)

36. 326/328 Hamstead Road
Handsworth Birmingham B20 2RA
tel 0121-248 6500 *fax 0121-248 6501*

Tier 3/4
Gleadall, Vikki (spo)
Bourne, Andrew
Clarke, Tracey
James, Maria
Marchant, Mel
Millington, Sonia
Green, Ben (pso)
Wells, Angela (pso)
Scoular, Stuart (pso)
Ford, Noel (pso)

37. 4 Albany Road
Harborne Birmingham B17 9JX
tel 0121-248 6230 *fax 0121-248 6231*

Tier 3
Purewal, Manjinder (spo)
Fergus, Mike (spo)
Aziz, Zanfar
Blake, Sarah
Dickman, Susan
Frati, Catherine
Hanley, Richard
Sewell, Jean
Wookey, Stephen
Chapasuka, Judith (pso)
Fuller, Mandie (pso)
Johns, Sue (pso)

38. Greencoat House Programmes Unit
259 Stratford Road
Sparkbrook Birmingham B11 1QS
tel 0121-248 5611 *fax 0121-248 5613*

Jackson, Judith (spo)
Afzal, Kaiser (treatment mgr)
Lynch, Leeanna
Marshall, Rebecca
Moulton, Patricia (pso)
Wilson, Deniese (pso)
Wilson, Deniese (pso)

39. **Birmingham Youth Offending Service**

39a. **Youth Offending Service Head Office**
18 Gravelly Hill North

Erdington, Birmingham B23 6BQ
tel 0121-464 0600 *fax 0121-464 0609*

Batchelor, Sharon

39b. **Youth Offending Service (North)**
Pype Hayes Hall, Pype Haye Park
Pype Hayes, Birmingham B24 0HG
tel 0121-303 0252 *fax 0121-464 0921*

Cain, Claudia
Jones, Sezal

39c. **Youth Offending Service (South)**
Halescroft Square, off Shenley Hill
Halescroft, Birmingham B31 1HD
tel 0121-476 5111 *fax 0121-411 2198*

Heath, Jeanette (admin asst)
Bonas, Leon (trainee)

778 Bristol Road South
off Shenley Hill, Selly Oak
Birmingham B31 1HD
tel 0121-248 8216

Southall, Joanne (trainee)

39d. **Youth Offending Service (East)**
15 Commons Lane, Washwood Heath
Birmingham B3 2US
tel 0121-464 7719 *fax 0121-464 6261*

Coleman, Angela
Parkes, Sarah

39e. **Youth Offending Service (West)**
115 All Saints Street
Hockley, Birmingham B18 7RJ
tel 0121-464 8484 *fax 0121-464 7575*

Golby, Chris
Hazell, Liz

39f. **Youth Offending Service (Central)**
157-159 St Lukes Road, Highgate
Deritend, Birmingham B5 4DA
tel 0121-464 1827 *fax 0121-464 1826*

Parchment, Lorna
Williams, Martin (pso)

39g. **Youth Offending Service (B'ham Youth Court)**
c/o 52 Newton Street
Birmingham B4 6NF
tel 0121-233 3600 *fax 0121-236 0828*

James, Donna
Pattison, Laure (trainee)
Moss, Gwyneth (admin asst)

40. **DTTO**
18-28 Lower Essex Street, Birmingham
B5 6SN
tel 0121-248 6400 *fax 0121-248 6401*

Edgar, Karen (treatment mgr)
Williams, Paul
Altaf, Samina
Kaur, Indebir
Gordon, Pat (pso)
Habib, Samina (pso)
Rimmel, Emma (pso)
Badesha, Jas (pso)
Browne, Bev (pso)
Spillane, Kerry (pso)
Barnett, Pat (pso)
Pitt, Kevin (pso)
Stuart, Dean (pso)

41. **52 Newton Street**
Birmingham B4 6NF
tel 0121-248 6136 *fax 0121-248 6135*

Supporting People Unit
Vacancy (spo)

Unpaid Work Division

42. 5th Floor, King Edward House
135a New Street **Birmingham** B2 4QJ
tel 0121-248 2700 *fax 0121-248 2702*

Gill, Stephen (aco)
Brown, Len (dist mgr)
Hall, Kobina (dist mgr)
Tolley, Pat (admin mgr)
Huckerby, Keith (health & safety off)

43. 67/8 Rolfe Street
Smethwick B66 2AL
tel 0121-565 4411 *fax 0121-555 5717*

Unpaid Work Unit
Dyson, Peter (unit mgr)
Brown, Barry (imp mgr)
Loft, Lesley (qa mgr)
Showell, Leonard (pso)
Hewitt, Alan (pso)
Reeve, Adam (pso)

44. 162 Halesowen Road
Netherton **Dudley** DY2 9TS
tel (01384) 456482 *fax (01384) 457441*

Unpaid Work Unit
Mills, John (unit mgr)
Busby, Marinda (pso)
Woolridge, John (pso)

45. Bishop Street
Coventry CV1 1HU
tel 024-7625 8485 *fax 024-7663 0183*

Unpaid Work Unit
Daly, Marcella (unit mgr)
Breen, Gabrielle (pso)
Jackson, Trevor (pso)
Farmer, Terry (qa mgr)
Boland, Patrick (pso)

46. Minerva Wharf, Horseley Fields
Wolverhampton WV1 3LX
tel (01902) 351518 *fax (01902) 452496*

Unpaid Work Unit
Kennedy, Yvonne (unit mgr)
Coley, Trevor (qa mgr)
Hill, Karen (pso)
Portsmouth, Brian (pso)
Hardy, Neil (pso)

47. Walsall Probation Complex
Midlands Road **Walsall** WS1 3QE
tel (01922) 720661 *fax (01922) 723080*

Unpaid Work Unit
Mulligan, Emma (unit mgr)
Brown, Roger (qa mgr)
Bissell, Andrew (pso)
Gibney, Audrey (pso)
Leslie, Tracey (pso)

48. United Friendly House
76 Walsall Road
Perry Barr Birmingham B42 1SF
tel 0121-248 6348 *fax 0121-248 6324*
Unpaid Work Unit
Choudhury, Sheku (unit mgr)
Barlow, Lynne (qa mgr)
Heath, Lisa (pso)
Bhopal, Varinder (pso)
Stokes, Tony (pso)

49. 826 Bristol Road
Selly Oak Birmingham B29 6NA
tel 0121-248 6700 *fax 0121-248 6710*

Unpaid Work Unit
Walker, Steve (unit mgr)
Balfour, Richard (pso)
Hawkins, Craig (qa mgr)
Glanfield, Roger (pso)
Walker, Lionel (pso)

50. 18-28 Lower Essex Street
Birmingham B5 6SN
tel 0121-248 6420 *fax 0121-248 6452*

Unpaid Work Unit Workshop
Meacham, Robert (wkshp mgr)
Gee, Alan (wkshp mgr)

51. **11-15 Lower Essex Street**
Birmingham B5 6SN
tel 0121-248 6334 *fax 0121-248 6109*

(covering Saltley, Chelmsley Wood & Sparkbrook)

Unpaid Work Unit
Smith, Penny (unit mgr)
Walton, Martin (unit mgr)
James, Will (qa mgr)
Al-Moghraby, Mazen (pso)
Barnacle, Sharon (pso)
Guinan, John (pso)
McLaughlin, Eddie (pso)
Mohamed, Khalik (pso)
Thompson, Shahara (pso)

Human Resources Division

52. **Training Unit**
826 Bristol Road
Selly Oak Birmingham B29 6NA
tel 0121-248 6720 *fax 0121-248 6721*

Armstrong, Kim (h.r. admin)
Bailey, Claudette (hd of training & staff devpt)
West, Kim (pre-qualifying mgr)
Hockin, Trevor (spo, trainer)
Octigan, Mike (spo, joint appt with De Montford University)
Dunkley, Rose (acting dep pre-qualifying mgr)
Vacancy (business supt training mgr)
Vacancy (admin staff trainer)
Vacancy (pract developer)
Vacancy (pract developer)
Vacancy ('What Works' trainer)
Vacancy ('What Works' trainer)

Practice Development Assessors
Allison, Una (based at Saltley)
Altaf, Azhar (based at Sparkbrook)
Caesar, Yvette (based at Handsworth)
Chaudhry, Geet (based at Selly Oak)
Glennie, Karin (based at Chemlsley Wood)
Hughes, Marilyn (based at Wolverhampton)
Hunter, Eileen (based at Coventry)
Jester, Katie (based at Selly Oak)
Kuffa, Tony (based at Smethwick)
McCarthy, Terry (based at Coventry)
McConnell, Kate (based at Walsall)
Mair, Patsy (based at Handsworth)
Palmer, Caroline (based at Sparkbrook)

Richmond, Rita (based at Harborne)
Wilson, Kath (based at Wolverhampton)

Regional Sex Offender Unit

53. King Edward House, 5th Floor
135A New Street
Birmingham B2 4QJ
tel 0121248 2700 *fax 0121-2482701*

Farmer, Mark (regnl mgr)
Vann, Barbara (admin mgr)

In West Midlands Area

54. **Sex Offender Unit**
826 Bristol Road
Selly Oak Birmingham B29 6NA
tel 0121-248 6760 *fax 0121-248 6761*

Clarke, Dave (spo/prog mgr)
Barzdo, Veronica (treatment mgr)
Chary, Eve
Davies, Steve
Edwards, Richard
Gibbs, Caroline
Gray, Deborah
Houston, Sally
James, Rachel
Price, Meryl
Twist, Lorraine
Joslyn, Jean (Based at Telford)
Ring, Lindsey (psychologist)

In Staffordshire Area

55. **Regional Sex Offender Unit**
Stafford Programmes Unit, Dorrington Drive
Dorrington Industrial Park
Common Road, Stafford ST16 3DG
tel (01785) 279951 *fax (01785) 279959*

Davis, Clive (acting spo/prog mgr)
Dwight, Ellie (treatment mgr)
Sgroi, Gerald
Gilbride, Sue
Raven, Mark
Toohey, Michael
Broom, Denise

In West Mercia Area

56. **Regional Sex Offender Unit**
Courtside House
Telford Square, Malinsgate
Telford TF3 4EQ
tel 01952 299366 *fax (01952) 200896*

Davis, Clive (acting spo/prog mgr based at 56)

Willetts, Diane (treatment mgr)
Joslyn, Jane

57. **Regional Sex Offender Unit**
135 Abbey Foregate
Shrewsbury SY2 6AS
tel 01743 231525 *fax (01743) 244914*

Diana Goodban

58. **Regional Sex Offender Unit**
3-4 Shaw Street
Worcester WR1 3QQ
tel 01905 723591 *fax (01905) 724833*

Jo Lovelock
Maggie Stephenson

Residential Services Division

59. 11-15 Lower Essex Street
Birmingham B5 6SN
tel 0121-248 2828 *fax 0121-248 6490*

Short, Mike (acting dist mgr)
Morgan, Ms Chloris (admin mgr)

Hostels

60. **Bilston Probation & Bail Hostel**
23 Wellington Road
Bilston, Wolverhampton WV14 6AH
tel (01902) 497688 *fax (01902) 498150*

Gill, Andy (spo mgr)
Clarke, Mandy (po dep)

61. **Carpenter House Probation & Bail Hostel**
33 Portland Road, Edgbaston
Birmingham B16 9HS
tel 0121-454 0394 *fax 0121-454 7379*

Vacancy (spo mgr)
Joseph, Drayton (po deputy/acting spo mger)

62. **Crowley House Probation & Bail Hostel** *(for women)*
31 Weoley Park Road, Selly Oak
Birmingham B29 6QY
tel 0121-472 7111 *fax 0121-415 4072*

Moran, Lynne (spo mgr)
Francis, Ireca (po deputy)

63. **Elliott House Probation & Bail Hostel**
(for mentally disordered offenders only)
96 Edgbaston Road, Moseley
Birmingham B12 9QA
tel 0121-440 2657 *fax 0121-446 6818*

Baker, Jeff (spo mgr)
Ward, Marie (po deputy)

64. **Welford House Probation & Bail Hostel**
31 Trinity Road, Aston
Birmingham B6 6AJ
tel 0121-523 4401 *fax 0121-515 1355*

Murdoch, Mike (spo mgr)
Lowe-Thompson, Yvonne (po deputy)

65. **Stonnall Road Probation & Bail Hostel**
85 Stonnall Road
Aldridge, Walsall WS9 8JZ
tel (01922) 459574 *fax (01922) 455373*

Gill, Andy (spo mgr)
Jones, Roderick (po deputy)

66. **Sycamore Lodge Bail Hostel**
Clay Lane, Langley
Oldbury B69 4TH
tel 0121-552 9930 *fax 0121-544 6994*

Norford, Hermon (spo mgr)
Mitchell, Carol (po deputy)

Institutions

67. H M Prison, Winson Green Road
Birmingham B18 4AS
tel 0121-345 2500 *fax 0121-345 2501*
hdc fax 0121-554 7793

Parole clerk ext 2579
Special visits ext 2565

Ashley, Wendy ext 2412
Fellowes, Richard ext 2423
Marsh, Robert (hdc) ext 2503
Moss, Alison ext 2669
Ormsby, Janet ext 2413
Tarry, Marion ext 2356
Byron-Scott, Sharlene (pso) ext 2527
Jenoure, Jean (pso) ext 2527

68. H M YOI & Remand Centre **Brinsford**
New Road, Featherstone
Wolverhampton WV10 7PY
tel (01902) 532450 *fax (01902) 532451*
Special visits tel (01902) 532605

Teden, Helen (spo) ext 2524
Farrar, Maggie ext 2526
John, Alan ext 2528
Hunter, Colin ext 2525
Shotton, Julie ext 2567
Padley, Jayne (pso, bail info) ext 2571

Pratley, Jacqueline (pso) ext 2461
Tabberer, Phil (pso, bail info) ext 2571

Local Justice Areas

22 Walsall & Aldridge
25-38 Birmingham
11 Coventry District
5, 6 Dudley
14 Solihull
5, 6 Stourbridge and Halesowen
34, 35 Sutton Coldfield
9 Warley
9 West Bromwich
17 Wolverhampton

Crown Courts

26 Birmingham
11 Coventry
20 Wolverhampton

WILTSHIRE PROBATION AREA

Victim enquiries contact number:
(01225) 763401

e-mail Firstname.Surname@wiltshire.
probation.gsx.gov.uk

1. **Head Office**
    Rothermere, Bythesea Road
    Trowbridge BA14 8JQ
    tel (01225) 781950 *fax (01225) 781969*
    Direct dial (01225) + number

    Fulbrook, Diana (co) 781960
    Lumb, Steve (p, treasurer)
    Munday, Mal (aco spec serv) 781956
    Strike, Martyn (aco int) 781957
    Elliott, Julie (hr mgr) 781966
    Turnbull, Heather (hr off) 781965
    Quinney, Gemma (hr asst)
    Davis, Sue (finance mgr) 781967
    Pearce, Alan (finance off) 781968
    Mullerworth, Debbie (staff devpt mgr) 781963
    Gage, Emma (staff devpt asst) 781955
    Higgins, Barrie (area mgr IT) 781952
    Watson, Sean (systems admin) 781953
    Green, Hilary (pa to aco) 781959
    Murray, Tracy (pa to aco) 781958
    Tawn, Janet (pa to co) 781962

2. 2 Prospect Place
    Trowbridge BA14 8QA
    tel (01225) 763041 *fax (01225) 775667*

    Bristow, Kath (area mgr, rural)
    Wootten, Lynn (snr pract)
    Franklin, Veronica (ext srvcs mgr)
    Barnfather, Gemma
    Parmenter, James
    Sexton, Laura
    Stirling, Kathie (p)
    Carter, John (pso)
    Holmes, Kathryn (pso)
    Gillam, Lyn (vlo)
    Murray, Andrew (pda)
    Bath, Chris (trainee)
    Kelley, Tom (trainee)
    Owen, Gwyneth (trainee)
    Rhodes, Emma (trainee)
    Wilkinson, Rhona (conf admin)
    Heydon, Carolyn (p, admin off)
    Reeves, Sara (p, admin off)
    Thornton, Karen (admin off)
    Hungerford, Lesley (info/data officer)
    Knight, Philip (ext svcs off)
    Jackson, Sue (Include case wrkr)
    Gerrish, Ray (accom pso)

    Programmes Team
    Bennett, Mark
    Clarke, Simon
    Amoroso, Richard (pso)
    Arnold, Christopher (pso)
    Mason, Sara (pso)
    Frost, Simon (pso)

    Community Service Office
    Trowbridge (01225) 753508

    Thornton, Mrs Teresa (snr cso)
    Bird, Dale (cso)
    Brown, Joanne (cso)
    Fryer, John (p, css)
    Line, Mette (p, css)
    Milford, Rosemary (css)
    Morrison, Stuart (p, css)
    Mutch, Gordon (p, css)
    Snell, Norman (css)

3. 51-52 Parkfields
    Chippenham SN15 1NX
    tel (01249) 656836 *fax (01249) 445497*

    Phillips, Jan (snr pract)
    Clifford, Maggie
    Harrop, Jon
    Millington, Sally
    Owen, Karen
    Scott, Penny

Budd, David (pso)
Bramwell, Catherine (pso)
Iason, Pauline (pso)
Jackson, Terry (pso)
Love, Sandi (p, pso)
Lancashire, Cheryl (snr admin off)
Easden, Vivien (conf admin)
Wilkinson, Rhona (conf admin)
Scoble, Karen (admin off)

4.   The Boulter Centre
     Avon Approach **Salisbury** SP1 3SL
     tel (01722) 327716 *fax (01722) 339557*

Harris, Diana (area mgr, eff pract)
Dillon, Monica (snr pract)
Flynn, Lisa (snr pract)
Ryan, Tony (facilities/H&S mgr)
Cavanagh, Siobhan
Frost, Joanna
McBain, Kerry
O'Shaughnessy, Debbie (p)
Taylor, Ann (p)
Taylor, Michael
Woodward, Sybil (p)
Worth, Margaret
Crocker, John (pso)
Knight, Georgina (pso)
Picton, Doreen (p, pso accomm)
James, Avril (pso)
O'Pray, Andy (pda)
Brown, Steph (trainee)
Davies, Cheryle (trainee)
Jay, Tina (trainee)
Macken, Gemma (trainee)
Williams, Liz (trainee)
McKenzie, Ray (snr admin off)
Regan, Sarah (conf admin)
Adlam, Joanna (admin off)
Bevilacqua, Elisa (admin off)
Collinson, Pam (admin off)
Mansbridge, Emily (p, admin off)

Community Service Office
Salisbury (01722) 320897

Uphill, Amanda (cso)
Cawood, David (p, css)
Gibbins, Alan (peripatetic css)
Porter, Ian (p, css)

5.   Mary Floyd House, 15 Milton Road
     Swindon SN1 5JE
     tel (01793) 536612 *fax (01793) 541110*

Murray, Amanda (off mngmt int mgr)
Andrade, Pat (area mgr)
Weedon, Tom (snr pract)
Davis, Caroline (snr pract)

Chapman, Kate
Davies, Albertine
Duffy, Andrea
Derbyshire, Wayne
Forrester, Julianna
Glasscoo, Stephanie
Gray, Jean
Kennedy, Angela
Light, Rachel
Maull, Gerald
Morris, Janine
Stephens, Tanith
Winter-Smith, Siobhan
Barnett, Phillip (pso)
Clydesdale, Geraldine (pso, accomm)
Coombs, Laura (pso)
Dudman, Jennifer (pso)
Fuller, Lester (pso)
Higgins, Sara (pso)
Howard, Joanne (pso)
Hurford, Richard (p, pso)
James, Michelle (pso)
Jerram, Kirsty (pso)
Matsushima, Carol (p, vlo)
Melvin, Joanna (pso)
O'Hara, John (pso)
Pipe, Janine (pso)
Read, Dan (pso)
Wilson, Cheryl (pso)
Winning, Dawn (vlo)

Parker, Eileen (area mgr, admin eff pract)
Bird, Kelly (conf admin)
Vacancy (conf admin)
Bryant, Lynn (p, admin off)
Dipierro, Alicia (admin off)
Drudy, Anne (p, admin off)
Edmonds, Pat (p, admin off)
Fardon, Howard (info/data off)
Grace, Carol (admin off)
Greenslade, Julie (admin off)
Truman, Claire (admin off)

6.   1-2 Commercial Road
     Swindon SN1 5NF
     tel (01793) 534259 *fax (01793) 496468*

Programmes Team
Crallan, Katherine (area mgr, progs/dtto
 ·p/t)
Kuzyk, Tricia (area mgr, dro's/dtto p/t)
Jones, Rhiannon (p, snr pract, dtto)
Brazier Andrea (p, snr pract, dtto)
Fry, Chris (treatment supvr)
Henry, Marilyn (p, treatment supvr)
Hurcom, Maureen (treatment supvr)
Gooden, Eleanor
Welsh, Clare

Mack, Leanne (pso)
Webb, Peter (pso)
Taylor, Maxine (forensic psychologist)
Headon, Sheila (snr admin off)
McMullan, Carol (conf admin)
Dempster, Chloe (admin off)
Fortune, Evelyn (admin off)
Smith, Julie (admin off)
Woodward, Hilary (admin off)

Community Service Office
Swindon (01793) 534259/496622

Coleshill, Joe (area mgr cs)
vacancy (snr cso)
Simpson, Tracey (cso)
Soane, Melanie (cso)
Stonehouse, Ann (cso)
Garratt, Marilyn (p, css)
Holland, John (css)
Newcombe, Ernie (peripatetic css)
O'Connor, Christine (css)

Training
Beddis, Anna (pda)
Adams, Trish (trainee)
Bamford, James (trainee)
Hall, Louise (trainee)
Hellier, Emma (trainee)
Ross, Emma (trainee)
White, Emma (trainee)

7. **Youth Offending Team**
    The Limes, 21 Green Road
    Upper Stratton **Swindon** SN2 6JA
    tel (01793) 823153 *fax (01793) 820578*

    Scarle, Jane
    Holmes, Ann

7a. The Martins, 56a Spa Road
    Melksham SN12 7NY
    tel (01225) 793616 *fax (01225) 793556*

    Vacancy (yjo)

7b. 1st Floor, Salisbury Activity
    CentreWilton Road
    Salisbury SP2 7GX
    tel (01722) 341644 *fax (01722) 341655*

    Jackson, Liz (pso yot)

8. **MAPPA & DIPS Co-ordination**
    Wiltshire Constabulary HQ
    London Road, **Devizes** SN10 2DN
    tel (01380) 734001

    Hemming, Alan (mappa co-ordinator) ext
    2398
    Perry, Jon (dip/ppo mgr)

Institution

9. HM Prison **Erlestoke**
    Devizes SN10 5TU
    tel (01380) 814250 *fax (01380) 818663*

    Minch, Ms Alison (spo) 814436
    Glassock, Karen 814437
    Cope, Simon

Local Justice Areas

    2 NW Wiltshire
    3, 4 SE Wiltshire
    5 Swindon

Crown Courts

    4 Salisbury
    5 Swindon

NORTH YORKSHIRE PROBATION AREA

Out of hours emergency contact point
Southview App Premises (01904) 780358

e-mail firstname.surname@north-yorkshire.
probation.gsx.gov.uk

1. **Head Office**
    Thurstan House, 6 Standard Way
    Northallerton DL6 2XQ
    tel (01609) 778644 *fax (01609) 778321*

    Brown, Roz (co)
    Burns, Walter (aco corporate governance)
    Marginson, Lynda (aco offender mgmnt)
    Cullen, Amanda (aco, h.r.)
    Sheard, Jon (treasurer, p)
    Ryan, Mike (aco interventions)
    Seed, Kevin (organisational devpt mgr)
    Porteus, Richard (senior finance off, p)
    Lucas, Chris (finance asst)
    Foster, Clare (admin asst finance, p)
    Widmer, Jacqui (pa to co)
    Johnson, Sheila (snr secy, offender mgmnt)
    Williams, Lorraine (snr secy, corp
    governance & chair)
    Minns, Tracy (p, snr secretary, hr)
    McClelland, Shirley (p, snr secretary, hr)
    Vacancy (snr secy, interventions)
    Taylor, Justine (personnel & training mgr)
    Bateson, Julie (personnel officer)
    Topping, Diane (p, personnel assistant)

2. Essex Lodge, 16 South Parade
    Northallerton DL7 8SG
    tel (01609) 772271 *fax (01609) 772931*

Offender Management
Calam, Toni
Dutton, Gregg (pso)
Major, Beverley (snr secretary)
Becky Croser (receptionist/admin, p)

START
Radcliffe, Susan
Wilkes, Sue
Minchin, Alison

Interventions
Hird, Charlotte
Yeo, Laura

Human Resources
Charters, Gillian (trainee)
Elsworth, Clare (trainee)

3.   5/7 Haywra Crescent
      Harrogate HG1 5BG
      tel (01423) 566764 *fax (01423) 565790*

Offender Management
Burns, Fran (spo)
Halliwell, Jason
Pearson, Clare
Piedot, Vivienne
Sanders, Karen
van der Gucht, Sheila
Eastwood, Tony (pso)
Elias, Annie (pso)
Waters, Joyce (snr secretary)
Cryer, Maureen (ca)
Murray, Sarah (ca)
Oddy, Caroline (ca)
Pike, Marcella (ca)

START
Hunt, Rebecca (pract mgr)
Gallagher, Margaret
Jones, Wilma
Bown, Jonet (pso, p)
Costello Liz (pso)
McKenner, Karen (office mgr)

Interventions
Gibson, Mark (pract mgr)
Almond, Tracy (pract mgr)
Charis, Amanda
Pearson, Clare
Walker, Katrina
Wright, Laura-Jane
Bolton, Rebecca (pso)
Rushton, Liz (pso)
Terry, Peter (cso)
Brown, John (css)
Coles, Mick (css)
Smith, Ian (css)
Turner, Alvin (css)
York, Judy (css)

Human Resources
Kirk, Paul (pract manager)
Clayden, Sarah (trainee)
Kicks, Emma (trainee)

3a.   The Court House
       Bunkers Hill, **Skipton** BD23 1HU
       tel (01756) 794797 *fax (01756) 798614*

Offender Management
Smith, Ann (ca)

4.   12 Falsgrave Road
       Scarborough YO12 5AT
       tel (01723) 366341 *fax (01723) 501932*

Offender Management
Watkins, Elaine (spo offender mgmnt)
O'Brien, Vikki (p, pract mgr)
Whiteley, Nigel (pract mgr)
Gaddass, Sarah
McBurney, Don
Maughan, Stephen
Taylor, Richinda
Williams, Diane
Connor, Faye (pso)
Harper, Mal (pso)
Naylor, Deborah (cso)
Lukehurst, Beryl (office manager)
Boyle, Diane (snr secretary)
Austwick, Wendy (ca)
Campion, Janice (ca)
Carter, Melanie (ca)
Foster, Margaret (ca)
Gemma Sly, (ca)
Groves, Margaret (ca)
Pain, Stella (ca)

START
Ansell, Gillian (pract mgr)
Davidson, Malcolm
Hutchinson, Ian
Rose, Linda
Ruth, Paul
Wray, Lesley
Littlewood, David (pso)
Young, Irene (ca)

Interventions
Holmes, Geoff (pract mgr)
Cockerham, Janet (pract mgr)
Burke, Alan (pract mgr)
Barber, Ian
Pattison, Yvonne
Pentland, Heather
Bowman, Rachel (pso)
Broadbent, Sarah (pso)
Moseley, Susan (pso)
Reeve, Phil (pso)

Willan, Paul (pso)
Walker, Dave (pso)
Lumsdon, Sarah (ca)

Human Resources
Whiteley, Nigel (pract mgr)
Flinton, Matthew (trainee)
Sellers, Svetlana (trainee)
Struthers, Jennifer (trainee)
Day, Malcolm (info systems asst)

5. 108 Lowther Street
    York YO31 7WD
    tel (01904) 526000 *fax (01904) 526001*

    Offender Management
    Stokell, Pauline (spo risk & pub protectn)

    START
    Griffiths, Gina (pract mgr)
    Weatherstone, Paul (pract mgr)
    Drury, Michelle
    Daley, Michelle
    Hamilton, Elaine
    Hardy, Felicity
    Hilton, Wendy
    Lewis, Chris
    Shelley, Susan
    Spadone, Dominic
    Wright, David
    Moss, Andrew (pso)
    Wace, Carol (pso)
    Westwood, Marie (pso)

    Offender Management
    Chatters, Sandra (spo offender mgmnt)
    Littler, Jon
    Pavlovic, Michael
    McKnight, Marilyn (pso)
    Morley, June (pso)
    Watson, Andrew (pso)
    Wilkinson, Maria (pso)
    Chipper, Sara (office mgr)
    Thorley, Gela (snr sec)
    Franks, Joyce (p, ca)
    Hall, Helen (ca)
    Jacques, Barbara (ca)
    Jaques, Eileen (ca)
    Lloyd, Sue (ca)
    Riddiford, Liz (ca)
    Shepherd, Jean (ca)
    Thompson, Pat (ca)
    Rawcliffe, Maria (ca)

    Interventions
    Atkin, Joanne (p, spo)
    Wilkinson, Pauline (pract mgr)
    Gray, Edward (cpo)
    Cusworth, Sarah (pso)

Langford, Lyn (pso)
Sullivan, John (pso)
Wilton, Christine (pso)
Whittaker, Ian (pso)
Gray, Edward (cso)
Kamara, Ros (cso)
Bell, Rachel (css)
Bickerdike, Noel (css)
Couttie, David (css)
Craft, Stephen (css)
Glew, Debbie (css)
Heron, David (css)
Smith, Brian (css)
Stewart, Laurie (p, css)

Human Resources
Davies, Penny (pm, seconded to HMIP)
Drury, Michelle
McGrath, Annie
Wright, Howard
Bushby, Emma (trainee)
Entwhistle, Gemma (trainee)
Nicholson, Lucy (trainee)
Harker, Steve (info services asst)

6. Pavilion 2000 (P2K), Amy Johnson Way
    Clifton Moor **York** YO3 4XT
    tel (01904) 698920 *fax (01904) 698929*

    Interventions
    Atkin, Joanna (acting spo ecp)
    Corney, Bev (spo start team)
    Hart, Peter (spo offender management)
    Knowles, Liz (spo ecp & basic skills)
    Martin, Jonathan (spo accred progs + iccp)
    Wilkes, Paddy (spo, subst misuse mgr)

    Human Resources
    Richards, Mark (info services mgr)
    Brown, Garvey (h&s officer)
    Clement, Emma (public relations mgr)
    Neale, Marie (diversity manager)
    Moule, Kay (training officer)
    Richardson, Dianne (p, office mgr)
    Freeman, Paula(snr secretary)
    Gill, Jenny (p, snr secretary)
    North, Angelique (snr secretary)

7. **York Crown Court**
    The Castle, York YO1 9WZ
    tel (01904) 651021 *fax (01904) 652397*

    Cooper, Kath (p, cclo)
    Shelley, Susan (p, cclo)
    Franks, Joyce (p, snr secretary)

8. Union Lane
    Selby YO8 4AU
    tel (01757) 707241 *fax (01757) 213911*

Morley, June (pso)
Anderson, Josephine (ca)

Offender Management
Powell, Ann (practice mgr)
Brogan-Hewitt, Gemma
Smith, Leo
Cowood, Sheradan (pso)
Duncan, Lynne (pso)
Rowbotton, Joanne (pso)

9. **CRI** (Crime Reduction Iniatives)
6 Peckitt Street, York YO1 9SF
tel (01904) 675040 *fax (01904) 521108*

Youth Offending Teams

10. **N Yorkshire Youth Offending Team**
Delta House, 12B North Park Road
Harrogate HG1 5PG
tel (01423) 522880 *fax (01423) 522949*

Johnson, Louise (team leader)
Hughes, Mark
Walker, Iain

11. **N Yorkshire Youth Offending Team**
Third Floor, Pavilion House
Pavilion Square
Scarborough YO11 2JN
tel (01723) 341367 *fax (01723) 361368*

Diver, Stephen

12. City of York Council
1st Floor, George Hudson Street
York YO1 6ZE
tel (01904) 554565 *fax (01904) 554566*

O'Neil, Pamela

Hostel

13. **Southview Approved Premises**
Southview, 18 Boroughbridge Road
York YO26 5RU
tel (01904) 780358 *fax (01904) 780475*

Lomas, Neil (spo)
Ripley, Ann-Marie (pract manager)
Dawson, David
Bagueley, Sylvia (pso)
Holmes, Catherine (pso)
Lawson, John (pso)
Nicholson, Judith (pso)
Atkin, Christina (night support wrkr)
Davies, Lyn (night support wrkr)
Gray, George (night support wrkr)
Nolan, Andy (night support wrkr)
Bosworth, Sue (p, snr sec)

Institutions

14. **HM YOI**
East Road, **Northallerton** DL6 1NW
tel (01609) 785100 *fax (01609) 785102*

HDC Clerk (01609) 785209
Sentence Planning Clerk (01609) 785143
probation fax (01609) 785102

Capes, Wendy, (pract mgr)
Fisher, Daniela (pso)
Wilkinson, Kirstie (pso)

15. **HM Prison Askham Grange**
Askham Richard, York YO23 3PT
tel (01904) 772000 *fax (01904) 772001*
probation fax (01904) 772003

Scarrott, Rosie
Shey, Anne (pso)
Berry, Shirley (ca)

Local Justice Areas

3 Harrogate
2 Northallerton & Richmond
4 Scarborough
8 Selby
3a Skipton
5, 6 York

Crown Court

7 York

SOUTH YORKSHIRE PROBATION AREA

Central bail referral no: 0114-278 0075
fax 0114-278 8520

Out of hours emergency contact point
Norfolk Park Hostel 0114-275 3054

Victim enquiries contact number
0114-276 7276

e-mail Firstname.Surname@south-yorkshire.
probation.gsx.gov.uk

1. **Head Office**
45 Division Street, Sheffield S1 4GE
tel 0114-276 6911
fax (co) 0114-275 2868
fax (reception) 0114-276 1967

Harker, Heather (co)
Harrison, Shirley (chair of board)
Fox, Julian (secretary to the committee)

Kerslake, Brian (director of finance/partnerships)
McMullan, Paul (director of operations)
Brown, Rosemary (aco hr)
Wright, Marion (aco)
Thomas David (aco performance)
Tarr Jack (pr mgr)
Scott Shelley (aco)
McGuiness, Craig (h&s off)
Jackson, Bob (hr mgr)
Murray Liz (spo)

Practive Development Unit
tel 0114-276 6911 *fax 0114-272 5293*

Chu, Sam (forensic psychologist)
Dyson, Mike (spo, training mgr)
Beatson, Max (spo, public protection mgr)
Swinden, David (spo, employment market services manager)
Mcnerney, Phil (spo, strategic implementation manager)
Brown, Janice (training co-ord)
Williams, Barbara (spo, devpt mgr, local co-ord trainees)

2. 3 West Bar **Sheffield** S3 8PJ
    tel 0114-272 6477 *fax 0114-278 1892*

Jones Graham (dvnl mgr)

Community Rehabilitation Team
Holdsworth, Adrian (spo)
Clarke, Dean (spo)
Colleyshaw, Julie (spo)
Small, John (spo)

Afzal, Taira
Betts, Melissa
Brennan, Andrea
Brown, Thomas
Bufton, Sally (p)
Burt, Michelle
Came, Suzanne (p)
Drabble, Phillip
Finneran, Sarah
Gayle, Hyacinth
George, Samantha
Gilmour, Claire
Harley, Bryan
Hermiston, Paul
Hermiston, Sue
Jackson, Mel
Johnson, Susan
Jones, Paula
Keeton, Jane
Lecutier, Louise (p)
Maton, Daniel
Mellor, Soyna
Penney, Sally-Anne

Price, Sharon
Robson, Sheila
Samuels, Kay (p)
Scott, Samantha (p)
Simpson, Rachel
Shaw, Ruth
Stocks, Christine (p)
Taylor, Nick
Wake, Sarah
Walker, Rebecca
Woodhouse, Joan
Windith, Adele

Davies, Jackie (pso)
Herron, Janine (pso)
Horbury, John (pso)
O'Neil, Isobelle (pso)
Samuels, Milton (pso)
Toft, Andrew (pso)

Practice Development Assessment Unit
Lubienski, May (pda)
Wells, Emma (p, pda)
Critchlow, Deborah (trainee)
Hadley, Helen (trainee)
Elverson, Timothy (trainee)
Storey, Ruth (trainee)

Resettlement Team
Reading, Neil (spo)
Broadhead, Julian
Ingham, Rachel
Johnson, David
Jones, Karen
Kenny, Helen
Kerr, Laura
Lockington, James
Moreland, Greg
Moss, Susan
Parkin, Maxine
Smith, Andrew
Stoddart, Barbara
Sullivan, Jeremy
Titus, Karen
Keyworth, Tony (pso)
Knowles, Alex (pso)
McDonnell, Coleen (pso)
Morgan, Ann (pso)

Court Team
Self, Mark (spo)

Magistates' Court
Antcliffe, Cynthia (pso)
Barber, Sheila (pso)
Bartle, Karen (pso)
Bayliff, Laura (pso)
Bunting, Katherine (pso)

Everett, Sue (pso)
Gill, Linda (pso)
Knebel, Beth (pso)
Milner, Sarah (pso)
Pressley, Melaine (pso)
Rhodes, Stephen (pso)
Roe, Margaret (pso)
Seaman, Susan (pso)
Smith, Cherrylene (pso)
Williams, Mark (pso)

2a. **Crown Court**
50 West Bar, Sheffield
tel 0114-270 1060 *fax 0114-275 9816*

all post to office 2

Victim Unit
tel 0114-276 7276 *fax 0114-276 8356*

Smith, Jacky (spo) (based at 1)
Denton, Margaret (vco)
Olivant, Wendy (vco) (based at 15)
Pickup, Eileen (vco) (based at 2)
Brook, Anne (vco) (based at 11)
Maw, Claire (admin support)

3. 8 Eastern Avenue **Sheffield** S2 2FY
tel 0114-241 6097 *fax 0114-239 4675*

Jackson, Ian (spo)
Bostock, Graham (pso, accom)

DTTO
Gregory, Sharon
Hogan, Katy
Mylotte, Martin
Edwards, Angela
Edmunds, Katy (pso)
McEvoy, Declan (pso)
Neville, Helen (pso)

Prolific Offenders Project
Tully, Marianne
Hurst, David (pso)

4. 7 St Peter's Close **Sheffield** S1 2EJ
tel 0114-228 8555 *fax 0114-228 8500*

Youth Offending Team
Manifold, Garry
Shann, Christine
Galton, Jill (pso)

5. 269 Pitsmoor Road **Sheffield** S3 9AS
tel 0114-272 5058 *fax 0114-275 4997*

Community Punishment Unit
Connelly, John (spo)
Daughtry, Emma
Gordon, Colin

Palmer, Gillian
Shorthouse, Richard
Renshaw, Ann (cs operations mgr)
Akpaka, Berthrand (pso)
Beresford, John (pso)
Clayton, Francine (pso)
Jackson, Rachel (pso)
MacDonald, Gwen (pso)
Mosley, Jenny (pso)
Slack, Philip (pso)
Crookes, Joan (css)
Grubb, David (css)
Hunter Kevin (css)
Layhe, Mary (p, css)
Matthewman, G (p, css)
Large, Harry (css)
Rhodes, Irene (p, css)
Somerset, Michael (css)
Tomlinson, Ian (css)
White, R (css)
Spowage, Judith (pso)
Walton, Christine (pso)

6. **Practice Development Unit**
365 Southey Green Road
Sheffield S5 7QE
tel 0114-231 0754 *fax 0114-285 5063*

Not permanently staffed
Enquiries to office 1

7. Court House
Churchfields **Barnsley** S70 2HW
tel (01226) 243331 *fax (01226) 294908*
divnl mgr fax (01226) 295080

Forbes-Williams, Paulette (dvnl mgr)

Court Team
Montgomary, Avril (spo)
Chambers, Tracy (pso)
McDermid, Charlie (pso)
Morton, Darren (pso)
Stanley, Eileen (pso)

Resettlement Team
Pawson-Morris, Ray (spo)
Bright, Hannah
England, Sara (p)
Macbeth, Ian
Prolific Offenders Project
Ibbotson, Bryan
Delamore, Sue
Taylor, Helen
Langer, Stella (pso)

DTTO/DRR
Harper, Clare
Otter, Roy

Peacock, Jane
Coniston, Diane (pso)
Hodgkinson, Michael (pso)

8. 6 Victoria Road
    Barnsley S70 2BB
    tel (01226) 283411 *fax (01226) 287441*

    Community Rehabilitation Team
    Kime, Sheena (spo)
    Birkbeck, Barbara
    Couldwell, Amber
    Dyson, Rita
    Ellis, Mark
    Errington, Dawn
    Firth, Emma
    Ibbotson-Devine, Kerry
    Jones, Samantha
    Holdsworth, Suzanne
    Horridge, Pete
    Heeley, Rachel
    Kenny, Elanor
    Middleton, Emma
    Pollard, Rod
    Rose, Samantha
    Richards, Christine
    Scott, Alison
    Shaw, Josephine
    Swift, Andrea
    Turner, Emma
    Wheeler, Jill
    Wilson, Kelly

    Supervision Support Team
    Andersson, Pamela (spo)
    Allsopp, Sarah (p)
    Kennedy, Sarah
    Edwards, Barbara (pso)
    Emerson, Jason (pso)
    George (Rock), Julie (pso)
    Goodale, Graham (pso)
    McNeil, Emma (pso)
    Padgett, Rosemary (pso)
    Richardson, Neil (pso)
    Whyke, Larry (pso)

    Community Punishment Unit
    Avison, Jacqueline (spo)
    Beckford-Peart, Marjorie
    Birkbeck, John
    Edwards, Lynda
    Dixon, Philip (cs operations mgr)
    Morrisroe, Simon (pso)
    Sanders, Martin (pso)
    Tindall, Liz (pso)
    Steele, Betty (pso)
    Cullumbine, Lynn (css)
    Lean, Philip (css)

Varley, Andrew (css)
Smith, Russell (css)
Hodgson, Stanley (css)

**Practice Development
Assessment Unit**
Edwards, Linda (p, pda)
Holdsworth, Suzanne (pda)

8a. **Youth Offending Team**
    Phase 1-2, County Way
    Barnsley S70 2DT
    tel (01226) 774986 *fax (01226) 774968*

    Slimon, Dave

9. The Law Courts
    College Road **Doncaster** DN1 3HU
    tel (01302) 366585 *fax (01302) 320853*

    Court Team
    Kendall, Pauline (spo)
    Barends, David (pso)
    Curtis, Sally (pso)
    Dix, Cathryn (pso)
    Green, Joanne (pso)
    Meades, Louise (pso)
    Siddons, Christine (pso)
    Weerdmester, Maia (pso)
    Wilkinson, Melanie (pso)
    Willerton, Clair (pso)
    Wilson, Sharon (pso)

    Drug Treatment Pilot
    Skinner, Noreen (pso)
    Steen, John (pso)

10. **Community Punishment Unit**
    Yarborough Terrace
    Bentley, Doncaster DN5 9TH
    tel (01302) 787758 *fax (01302) 390865*

    Platt-Hopkin, Gill (spo)
    Fitzwater, Sarah
    Foster, Jayne
    Lupton, Clare
    Steve, Shaw (cs operations mgr)
    Keye, Christy (pso)
    Crookes, Win (pso)
    Doyle, Brenda (pso)
    Mcmaster, Valerie (pso)
    Murdoch, Scott (pso)
    Aimson, John (css)
    Barks, Terry (css)
    Dutchak, Pete (css)
    Gant, Chris (css)
    Heath, Bob (css)
    Henry, Roy (css)
    Illingworth, Peter (css)

Lockie, Patrica (css)
Sigfussion, Anthony (css)
Wilson, Paul (css)

11. Bennetthorpe, 34 Bennetthorpe
Doncaster DN2 6AD
tel (01302) 730099 *fax (01302) 730220*
divnl mgr/dsu fax (01302) 730720

Hannant, Jan (divnl mgr)

Resettlement Team
Mansaram, Ray (spo)
McHale, Anne
Mombershora, Davie
Musgrave, Rita
Peat, Sarah
Satchwell, Dorothy
Wheatcroft, Sally
Allison, Tracey (pso)
Thomas, Janice (pso)

Community Rehabilitation Team
Clarke, Monica (spo)
Porter, Jennifer (p, spo)

Badcoe, Liz
Brewitt, Helen
Breen, Deborah
Eagle, Sally
Harris, Clare
Hornsby, Helen
Holland, Lindsey
Howkins, Sally
James, Jane
Jenkinson, Paul
Latibeaudiere, June
Lawrence, Aimee
Potter, Helen
Popple, Teressa
Richards, Donna
Shaw, Lorna
Thornberry, Helen
Townsend, Mark
Tyson, Carla
Walker, Lorriane
Wilson, Kerry
Williams, Elizabeth

Allison, Tracey (pso)
Hirst, Richard (pso)
Honey, Greame (pso)
Jackson, Sharron (pso)
Porritt, Pat (pso)
Prince, Gemma (pso)

Supervision Unit
Turgoosee, Josie (spo)
Page, Paulette (spo)
Eagle, Sally

Norris, Deborah
Hill, Jayne (pso)
Thomas, Pat (pso)
Johnson, Imelda (pso accom)

Practice Devpt Assessment Unit
Rejaie, Kaveh (pda)
Reeves, Sheila (pda)
Anderson, Laura (trainee)
Glass, William (trainee)
Hodgson, Sarah (trainee)
Hubber, Tacita (trainee)
Nawaz, Nasarah (trainee)
Weston, Robert (trainee)
Wormley, Zoe (trainee)

DTTO/DRR
Poulson, Amy (spo)
Broadbent, Tony (p)
Ellis, Paul
Maille, Doug
David, Sharon (pso)
Davidson, Jacqeline (pso)
Elkington, Zoe (pso)
Houghton, Michelle (pso)

Drug Testing Team (DAOs/DARs)
Tottie, John (pso)

Prolific Offender Project
Toole Alison (pso)
Vause, Pat (pso)
Head, Colin (cpn)
Hicking, Garry (police officer)

Victim Liaison
Askew, Sarah (p, pso)
Brooke, Anne (pso)

12. **Doncaster Drug Team**
The Garage, 37 Thorne Road
Doncaster DN1 2EZ
tel (01302) 730956 *fax (01302) 361453*

Broadbent, Tony (p)

12a. **Thorne Office**
Middlebrook Lane, Thorne DN8 5DR
Probation Office tel (01405) 812738
Youth at Risk (01405) 741707 (phone/fax)
Remedi (01405) 818866 (phone/fax)

13. **Youth Offending Team**
Rosemead Centre, May Avenue
Balby Doncaster DN4 9AE
tel (01302) 736100 *fax (01302) 736103*

Eyre, Peter (01302) 736108
Moss, Samantha (01302) 736123
Cocker, Glynn (pso) (01302) 736108

14. **Magistrates' Court**
The Statutes, PO Box 15
Rotherham S60 1YW
tel (01709) 361321 *fax (01709) 370172*

Hayes, Kay (pso)
Land, Judy (pso)
Rhodes, Janet (pso)

15. 12 Main Street **Rotherham** S60 1AJ
tel (01709) 376761 *fax (01709) 838715*

Holmes, Ruth (divnl mgr, Rotherham)
Vernon, Glyn (spo)
Buckley, Ellen (spo)
Welch, Simon (spo)
Lee, Malcolm (spo)

Ayub, Shaqoor
Brennan, Lenday
Broadhead, Melanie
Carrington, Diane
Clark, Francesca
Crookes, Fraser
Cureton-Fletcher, Debbie
Deen, Shaheen
Davitt, Rachel
Ducker, Andy
Ford, Liz (p)
Harris, Naomi
Hoole, Paul
Machin, Helen
Mclaughlin, Marie
Newsum-Brown, Anthony
Norton, Julia
Ogden, David
Phillips, Staffel
Pullan, Stuart
Ullah, Ali
Saville, Jane (p)
Tweedle, Claire

Dutton, Toni (pso)
Foster, Julie (pso)
Heeds, Charlotte (pso)
Lester, Kevan (pso)
O'Neill, Mark
Nicholls, Angie
Patterson, Clare (pso)
Pullar, Derv (pso)
St Pierre, Sarah (pso)
Smith, Hannah
Wainwright, Janette (p, pso)
Watson, Margaret (pso)
Wragg, Karen (pso)
Yeardley, Gloria (pso)

Practice Devpt Assessment Unit
Doherty, Anthony (pda)

Ford, Liz (pda)
Oates, Danies (trainee)
Henry, Tamar (trainee)
McCuish, Linda (trainee)
Ayub, Shaqoor (trainee)
Carrington, Diane (trainee)
Morris, Lisa (trainee)
Pass, Claire (trainee)

Community Punishment Unit
Gregory, Ian (spo)
Taylor, Jill (p)
Walker, Steve (cs operations mgr)
Bargh, Alan (pso)
Clarke, Lesley (pso)
Gordon, Martin (pso)
Henry, Christina (pso)
Fallowfield, Ron (css)
Hancock, Stuart (css)
Lumwai, John (css)
Staves, Glyn (css)
Thacker, Gillian (css)
Woodthorpe, Derek (css)

16. **Groupwork Programmes Unit**
Masborough Street **Rotherham** S60 1HW
tel (01709) 561533 *fax (01709) 550952*

Turvey, Maryke (div mgr group progs unit)
Seiles, Sarah (div admin mgr)
Gooch, Janet (spo)
Johnston, Fiona (spo)
West, Kathryn (spo)

Cosgrove, Caroline
Edge, Philip
Ellis, Rhys
Glover, Lynda
Hurst, Jane
Nowell, Pete
Pratley, Mary (p)
Suddaby, Jane
Walton, Frank

Adams, Laura (p, pso)
Castleton, Tracey (pso)
Grocott, Wayne (pso)
Hammett, Mandy (pso)
Hutchinson, Gerladine (pso)
Macpherson, Niki (pso)
Miller, Fiona (pso)
Narracott, Katherine (pso)
Parker, Tracey (pso)
Parry, Stephen (pso)
Pavitt, Emily (pso)
Robinson, Libby (pso)
Uzodinma, Liisa (pso)
Wales, Steve (pso)
Wilkinson, Emma (pso)

16a. **Youth Offender's Scheme**
4/6 Moogate Road, Rotherham S60 2EN
tel (01709) 516999 *fax (01709) 836584*

Charnley, Anne
Glentworth, John

POP Team
Burnett, Ian
Rimmer, Julia (pso)
Smith, Russ (police constable)

DTTO
Murphy, Lynda (pso)

Approved Premises (Hostels)

Central bail referral number
tel 0114-278 0075 *fax 0114-278 8520*
Taylor, Stephanie (central referrals off)

17. **Hostel Administrative Support**
tel (01709) 361001 *fax (01709) 835496*

Abbott, Penny (dvnl mgr) (at office 19)
Kerr, Janet (dvnl mgr)

18. **Norfolk Park Hostel**
100-108 Norfolk Park Road
Sheffield S2 2RU
tel 0114-272 1950 *fax 0114-275 3054*

Fletcher, Andy (spo)
Middleton, Karen (po, dep mgr)
Hodgkinson, Faye (hostel wkr)
Halpin, Sheron (hostel wkr)
Worthy, Linda (hostel wkr)

19. **Rookwood Hostel**
Doncaster Road, Rotherham S65 1NN
tel (01709) 361001 *fax (01709) 835496*

Sinclair, Andrew (spo)
Cartlidge, Jenny (hostel dep)
Bannister, Graham (bursar)
Andrews, Diane (hostel wkr)
Bennett, Delroy (hostel wkr)
Berry, Tracy (hostel wkr)
Page, Robert (hostel wkr)
Abbott, Penny (dvnl admin mgr)

20. **Town Moor Bail Hostel**
38/40 Christchurch Road
Doncaster DN1 2QL
tel (01302) 739127 *fax (01302) 761920*

Niven, Chris (spo)
Cox, Joan (hostel dep)
Bourne, Rod (hostel wkr)
Faulkner, Brian (hostel wkr)
Machin, Pam (hostel wkr)

Institutions

21. H M Prison & YOI **Doncaster**
Marsh Gate, Doncaster DN5 8UX
tel (01302) 760870 *fax (01302) 760851*

Discipline (edr enquiries) ext 308
Discipline (discharge) ext 265
Special visits (01302) 342413

Probn direct dial (01302) 763+ext
Probn clerk ext 203
Houseblock 1 probn ext 287
Houseblock 2 probn ext 290
Houseblock 3 probn ext 291
Bail info ext 293
Bail info fax (01302) 368034

Eastwood, Mick (p, spo) ext 288
Aspden, Paul
Dallas, William
Gasper, John
Marsh, Martin
Petersen, Lynn
Turner, Pat
Cokeham, Michelle (pso)
Milne, Pamela (pso),
Wright, Patrica (pso)
Lindsay, Meave (temp sec)

22. H M Prison **Lindholme**
Bawtry Road, Hatfield Woodhouse
Doncaster DN7 6EE
tel (01302) 524700 *fax (01302) 848750*

Cotterell, Rob, (spo)
Lee, Easter
Mackenzie, Phillip
Mockford, Mark
Thomposn, Carol
Millington, Gill (pso)
Revill, Debbie (pso)
Torn, Shelley (pso)
Whitworth, Jean (pso)
Willerton, Clair (pso)
Winstanley, Jacqueline (pso)

23. H M Prison & YOI **Moorland (Closed)**
Bawtry Road, Hatfield Woodhouse
Doncaster DN7 6BW
tel (01302) 523000 *fax (01302) 523001*

Probn clerk ext 3108

Odusanya, Julie (spo)
Base, Mandy
Cruickshank, Tim
Harrison, Janet
Marley, Sean
Morgan, Gaynor

24. **HM Prison & YOI Moorland (Open)**
Thorne Road Hatfield
Doncaster DN7 6EL
tel (01405) 746500 *fax (01405) 746501*

Skelding, Steve
Greaves, Rita (pso)
Pearson, Samantha (pso)
Phipps, Serena (pso)

Local Justice Areas

2-5 Sheffield
14-16 Rotherham
7, 8 Barnsley
10-12 Doncaster

Crown Courts

2a Sheffield
9 Doncaster

WEST YORKSHIRE PROBATION AREA

Out of hours emergency contact point
Elm Bank Hostel (01274) 851551

e-mail Firstname.surname@west-yorkshire.
probation.gsx.gov.uk

1. **Head Office**
Cliff Hill House
Sandy Walk, Wakefield WF1 2DJ
tel (01924) 885300 *fax (01924) 885395*

Hall, Sue (chief officer)

Offender Management
Siddall, Mark (dir om)
Ball, Kevin (area mgr om)
Mills, Liz (devpt mgr)
Pilling, Kay (devpt mgr)

Interventions
Myatt, Maxine (dir int)
Culkin, Maggie (aco ete & unpaid work)
Voakes, Rob (aco resettlement & programmes)
Whitehead, Gini (aco accommodation & health)
Avetoom, Melanie (support people cross authorities co-ord)
Cannon, Louise (ete devpt mgr)
Fagg, Caterina (devpt & prog mgr)
vacancy (devpt & prog mgr)
Gray, Bronwen (bs devpt off)
Hart, Peter (housing services mgr)

Mackowski, Antonia (emp liaison off)
Steed, Mary (bs devpt mgr)
Wallace, Julie (ete devpt mgr)

Human Resources
Brandwood, Ian (director h.r.)
Brereton, David (training & devpt mgr)
Fisher, Alison (local area co-ord)
Geeson, Roger (internal verifier)
Hudson, Jeni (local area co-ord)
Mason, Barbara (personnel mgr)
Singh, Rajinder (area mgr diversity & devpt)

Finance Section
King, Jayne (director finance)
Bland, Karen (financial accountant)
Brace, Denise (payroll & expenses)
Goznik, Denise (policy mgr – finance/estates)
Mason, Louise (management accountant)
Scally, Colette (admin mgr head office)
Sheard, Jonathan (dep director finance)

Legal/Health & Safety Section
Thorpe, Nigel J, (secretary)
Bond, Bob (h&s off)
Johnston, Peter (breach & contracts area mgr)

Information Services
Brown, Imogen (aco info services)
Burgess, Steve (library info mgr)
Kitson, Margaret (info systems proj mgr
Manktelow, John (it systems mgr)
Robinson, Dave (technical networks proj mgr)
Thornton, Janet (perf info mgr)
Turner, Russell (research mgr)

Communications
Grazin, Elaine (comms & p.r. mgr)
Culkin, John (comms & p.r. officer)

Bradford District

2. **Fraternal House**
45 Cheapside **Bradford** BD1 4HP
tel (01274) 703700 *fax (01274) 703701*

Moloney, Neil (aco)
Macpherson, Stuart (area mgr)
Ali, Abid, (dist admin mgr)

Programmes Team
tel (01274) 703720 *fax (01274) 703721*
Bardsley, Jane (spo)
Ambler, Margaret (team mgr)
Fitzmaurice, Steve (pract mgr)
Elsom, Joanne
Lynch, Jacqueline

Bates, John (pso)
Day, Helen (pso)
Dunne, Susan (pso)
Forber, Gillian (pso)
Lloyd, Rachel (pso)
McCullough, Sanda (pso)
Naheed, Farzana (pso)
Richardson, Carolyn (pso)
Thackray, Andy (pso)
Wickham, Ralph (pso)

CP/CPRO Team
tel (01274) 703760 *fax (01274) 703761*

Brett, Marion (dist cp mgr)
Bryan, Jim (spo)
Hall, Brian (pract mgr)
Wallis, Clare (pract mgr)
Gill, Becky
Hunter, Gillian
Lamb, Jacqueline
Miller, Lorraine
Prior, Eleanor
Wells, Libby
Ali, Shaista (cso)
Bashir, Mohammed (cso)
Brooks, Gillian (pso)
Cole, Helen (cso)
Hainsworth, Jonathan (pso)
Horsman, Karl (pso)
Milczanowski, Richard (cso)
Mistry, Narendra (cso)
Morley, David (cso)
Gerald Raper (cso)
Rozee, Andrew (cso)
Stansfield, Rebecca (pso)
Akbar, Sima (css)
Armstead, Jean (css)
Bailey, David (css)
Blakeley, Carol (css)
Caton, Andrew (css)
Cazan, Sorin (css)
Finney, David (css)
Hussain, Abid (css)
Hussain, Razeena (css)
Nash, Michael (css)
Netherwood, Stuart (css)
Oldroyd, James (css)
Selby, Richard (css)
Simmonds, Sean (css)
Smith, Michael (css)
Sultan, Mohammed (css)

3. **The City Courts**
    P O Box 6 **Bradford** BD1 1LB
    tel (01274) 704500 *fax (01274)*
    721010/704501
    Ridley, Alison (pda)

CRO Team
Cooper, Mike (acting spo)
Wilson, Margaret (spo)
Bradley, Laura (pract mgr)
Anjum, Zahida
Ball, Clare
Beech, James
Bilney, Jo-Anne
Bowe, Stephen
Burke, Maureen
Gregory, Jill
Khan, Saieka
Lewis, Denis
McNulty, Bernard
Mallows, Glynis
Mahmood, Shahid
Mansfield, Richard
Martinus, Justine
Richards, Gemma
Richardson, Naomi
Ross, Helen
Small, Seb
Stringfellow, Rachael
MacCafferty, Laura (pso)
Myers, David (pso)
Pollard, Leanne (pso)
Rowe, Donna (pso)
Karim, Zenab (pso)
Ward, Michael (pso)
Woolley, Alison (pso)

Resettlement Team
Ali, Sajid (spo)
Moore, Colin (acting spo)
Moody, Linda (pract mgr)
Ali, Momasar
Brennan, Deborah
Burden, Simone
Cooper, Sarah
Corrie, Kate
Crossley, Shaun
Doyle, Mary
Hanley, Michelle
Ibrahim, Shahid
Khan, Hikmat
Lynch, Bill
Medd, Catherine
Mullinder, Lynne
Sharif, Azra
Suggett, Angela
Thompson, Michelle
Wilson, Gail
Burran, Eileen (pso)
Chalk, Emily (pso)
Cowgill, Judy (pso)
Henry, Ruth (pso)
Khan, Ferzana (pso)

Martinus, Justine (pso)
Parker, Christopher (pso)
Shackleton, Alyson (pso)

Drugs Intervention Programme
Firth, Dannie (pso)

Combined Court Team
Bonfield, Jacqui (spo)
Bell, Nowell
Miller, Michael
Nelson, Marva
Plunkett, Michael
Clarke, Christine (pso)
Fox, Helen (pso)
Grant, Jasmine (pso)
Hardy, Margaret (pso)
Harris, Claire (pso)
Hirst, Dorota (pso)
Lock, Harriet (pso)
Page, Richard (pso)
Simpson, Diane (pso)
Wensley, Susan (pso)

Bradford Victim Services &
Public Protection Unit
Sheikh, Bushra (spo)
Prescott, John (pract mgr)
Armitage, Mark (pso)
Khan, Alia (pso)
Tilbury, Carol (pso)

4.　1st Floor, Manor Building
2-4 Manor Row **Bradford** BD1 4NL
tel (01274) 302800

DTTO/DRR Team
Roberts, Terry (spo)
Alam, Sajid
Akrigg, Donna
Atkin, Sarah
Davidson, Karen
Green, Gareth
Armitage, Kenny (pso)
Armitage, Nigel (pso)
Caine, Heidi (pso)
Khan, Sadaqat (pso)

5.　**The Law Courts**
Exchange Square
Drake Street **Bradford** BD1 1JZ
tel (01274) 742140 *fax (01274) 726394*

Crown Court Team
Bonfield, Jacqui (spo)
Plunkett, Michael
Harris, Claire (pso)
Wensley, Susan (pso)

6.　11/19 Cavendish Street
Keighley BD21 3RB
tel (01535) 662771/2 *fax (01535) 611346*

Austwick, Martin (spo)
Lawson, Sue (pda)
Barraclough, Linda
Guy, Jacqueline
Terrington, Christina
Timlin, Carol
Watson, Sally
Croker, Simon (pso)
Eloi, Jules (pso)
Thackray, Andy (pso)
Thorp, Julie (pso)

Leeds West District

7.　**Waterloo House**
58 Wellington Street **Leeds** LS1 2EE
tel 0113-243 0601 *fax 0113-399 5374*
fax 0113-234 4057 Dist
admin/ACO/DAM/Public Protection

Smallridge, Maggie (aco Leeds West)
Halloran, Anne (district admin mgr)

Practice Devpt Assessors
Doherty, Eugene
McLeish, David
Schlaberg, Yvonne

Programmes Team
fax 0113-399 5223
Maud, Graham (spo)
Tate, Karen (spo)
Ashford, Rita (pract mgr)
Lowton, Mark (pract mgr)
Vare, Tracey (pract mgr)
Fontenay, Nathalie
Horne, Kathy
John, Gareth
McAuslane, Jenny
Osman, Paul
Scott, Jamie (p)
Tebbutt, Russell
Walker, Karen (p)
Bhogal, Iqbal (pso)
Gerrard-Ehrlich, Mel (pso)
Hinds, Dominy (pso)
Lacy, John (pso)
Lenski, Rosemary (pso)
Lewis, Angela (pso)
Ludewig, Emma (pso)
Morrill (pso)
Mountain, Gail (p) (pso)
Rowe, Jayne (pso)
Sellars, Ashley (pso)
Swan, Jane (pso)
Wrighton, Libby (p, pso)

DTTO/DRR Team
fax 0113-399 5370
Johnson, Imogen (spo)
Addlestone, Debbie (pract mgr)
Ali, Nazia
Cockerill, Tanya
Lawless, Tim
Musgrave, Eme
Nagy, Teréz
Peace, Melanie
Bircumshaw, Pam (pso)
Mann, Ranjit (pso)
Mountain, Gail (p) (pso)
Scott, Margaret (pso)

CRO Team 1 *fax 0113-399 5381*
Ashton, Julie (spo)
Nolan, Karen (pract mgr)
Clarke, Sarah
Crombie, Julie
Hymas, Steve
Judd, Marcus
McDonnell, Simon
McBride, Eimear
Neech, Jenni
Kilbane, Angela (pso)
McPhail, Ian (pso)

CRO Team 2
Vacancy (spo)
Nolan, Karen (pract mgr)
Cheyne, Beccy
Hartley, David
Neave, Zoe
Prior, Clare
Sadler, Fiona
Scroop, Ellen
Tedstill, Lisa
Tibbetts, Phillippa
Wells, Owen (p)
Cassar, Georgia (pso)
Sheikh, Aaliya (pso)
Sewell, Earl (pso)
Wilkins, Steph (pso)

Resettlement Team 1 *fax 0113-399 5380*
Jarvis, Sarah (acting spo, pract mgr)
Beardsall, Paula
Coupland, Claire
Glazier, Tamsin
Green, Andy
Horsfall, Ruth
MacDonald, Andrew
Plant, Carol
Welton, Sarah
Willcock, Karen
Wilson, Kerry

Baz, Shameem (pso)
Botwood, David (pso)
Conway, Martin (pso)
Mooney Revell, Gail (pso)

Resettlement Team 2
Clark, Debbie (spo)
Andrew, Beth
Firth, Cassy
Hooson, Chris
Hooson, Cindy (p)
Swain, Mark
Gray, Charlotte (pso)

8.   **Magistrates' Court**
28 Westgate, Leeds LS1 3AP
tel 0113-399 5440 *fax 0113-245 0967*

Ellis, Robert (spo)
Everett, Maggie
Jarosz, Josie
Pickering, Gerry
Smitheram, Christine
Charnley-Richards, Elizabeth (pso)
Dinsdale, Rod (pso)
Eggleston, Mark (pso)
Haywood, Merle (pso)
Hunt, Trevor (pso)
Lloyd, Rozanne (pso)
Sowerby, Catherine (pso)
Walker, Norah (pso)
Whelan, Kim (pso)

9.   **Drug Intervention Project (DIP)**
Millgarth Police Station
Millgarth Street, Leeds LS2 7HX
tel 0113-241 3133 *fax 0113-241 3140*

Hawley, Nick (pract mgr)
Croft, Dee (pso)
Love, Mark (pso)
Silver, Andrea (pso)
Sorhaindo, Evans (pso)

Leeds East District

10.   **379 York Road**
Leeds LS9 6TA
tel 0113-285 0300 *fax 0113-285 0301*

Chandler, Andrew (aco Leeds East)
Evans, Steve (dist admin mgr)

Practice Devpt Assessors
De Angelis, Maria
Dewey, Cris

CRO Team 1
fax 0113 2850364
Melaugh, John (p, spo)
Teasey, Mark (p, pract mgr)

Miller, Gail
Smith, Sarah
van Rossum, Henk
Westerman, Yvette
Bygrave, Joanne (pso)
Cameron-Collins, Maura (pso)
Murgatroyd, Peter (pso)

CRO Team 2
Pickering, John (spo)
Teasey, Mark (p, pract mgr)
Hannant, Andrew
Hudson, Karen
McCluskey, Ian
Sattar, Musrat
Woodrow, Michelle
Gunn, Sorrell (pso)
Kilbride, Gary (pso)
Munir, Samaina (pso)
Nunns, Helen (pso)
Sinclair, Jim (pso)
Wrighton, Libby (pso)

CP/CPRO Team
CP/CPRO fax 0113-285 0377
CS fax 0113 285 0302
Button, Sue (spo)
Dugdale, Ian (spo)
Milner, Christine (district cs mgr)
Parrish, Diane (pract mgr)
Roach, Walter (pract mgr)
Clarke, David
Deen, Val
McGlinchey, Richard
Meek, Sarah
Roberts, Trish
Taylor, Lucy
Robinson, Joanne
Underwood, Ria
Walker, Karen (p)
Watkins, Rachael
Wiseman, Alison

Ali-khan, Ansar (cso)
Brown John (cso)
Matharu, Jagdish (cso)
Nunns, Helen (cso)
Walker, Jonathan (cso)
Walker, Lorraine (cso)
Watts, Ian (cso)

Bellwood, Irene (pso)
Burns, Carol (pso)
Mills, Rachel (pso)
Pollard, Daniel (pso)
Saunderson, Helen (pso)
Scott, Alison (pso)
Seavers, Heidi (pso)
Summan, Mukhtiar (pso)

Wales, Sharon (pso)

Armitstead, David (css)
Ashton, Rose (css)
Davies, Hugh (css)
Gata-aura, Satpal (css)
Godsell, Gail (css)
Hayward, Pamela (css)
Jeffers, Shammin (css)
Jowett, Angela (css)
Mahmood, Arshad (css)
Manning, Raymond (css)
Osahn, Balwinder (css)
Rai, Sukbinder Kaur (css)
Robson, Neil (css)
Sheridan, Paul (css)
Turner, Philip (css)
Watson, Lynne (css)
Watson, Roy (css)
Wolstenholme, Christine (css)

Resettlement Team 1
fax 0113 285 0392
Lanfranchi, Maximillian (spo)
Garry, Rachel (pract mgr)
Baxter Crisp, Karen
Brotton, Richard
Burgess, David
Dixon, Fiona
Mair, Sarah
Thompson, Hannah
Quinn, Carol
Wilson, Alison
Birkumshaw, Edwin (pso)
Cruse, Ann (pso)
Khan, Zaq (pso)

Resettlement Team 2
Neal, Elise (spo)
Hutchinson, Tanya (pract mgr)
Booth, Sue
Burrows, Ray
Crute, Emma
Folker, Dawn
Halstead, Diane
Hooson, Mick
Hussain, Zaffar
Lynch, Rosanna
Marston, Jack
Munden, Angharad
Spink, Ben
Bell, Gillian (pso)
Evans, Maureen (pso)
Packer, Anne (pso)

**Leeds Victim Services &
Public Protection Unit**
tel 0113-285 0308 *fax 0113-285 0373*

Turner, Peter(spo)
Wood, Avril (pract mgr)
Baker, Debra (pso)
Coates, Glynnis (pso)
Henshaw, Karen (pso)
Pitchford, Angela (pso)
Ryder, Susan (pso)

11. **Combined Court Team**
Crown Court
1 Oxford Row, Leeds LS1 3BE
tel 0113-243 1107 *fax 0113-234 1952*

Melaugh, John (p, spo)
Phillips, Leroy
Rodney, Brian
Underwood, William
Gordon, Carole (pso)
Eaglen, Joanne (pso)
Jeffers, Joan (pso)
Palmer, Hilary (pso)

Calderdale District

12. Probation Centre, 173A Spring Hall Lane
Halifax HX1 4JG
tel (01422) 340211 *fax (01422) 320998*

Scott, Joan (aco)
Hall, Vicky (dist admin mgr)
Nelson, Richard (unison shop steward)

Practice Devpt Assessors
Booker, Tracey
Gallagher, Tony

Resettlement Team
Charlesworth, Susan (spo)
Devenport, Bill (pract mgr)
Cartwright, Judith
Gardner, Pauline
Kerr, Richard
Radicke, Maria
Jennison, Margaret (pso)
Khan, Quaiser (pso)

Programmes Team
Branton, Chris (spo)
Bennett, Barbara (pract mgr)
Long, Jim
Ryan, Mary
Atkinson, Christine (prog tutor)
Clarkson, David (prog tutor)
Dalgleish, Marie (prog tutor)
Hay, Angela (prog tutor)
Rank, Zoe (prog tutor)
Vikse, Hilary (prog tutor)

Court Team
Hillas, Deryck (spo)
Rudderforth, Jeff

Friessner-Day, Shayne (pso)
Lister, Georgina (pso)
Thomson, Jessica (pso)

DTTO Team
Hillas, Deryck (spo)
Lester, Liz
Nowell, Fran
Nicholl, Helen (pso)

CRO Team
Wright, Cath (spo)
Devenport, Bill (pract mgr)
Cameron, Charlotte
Foster, Susan
Goodsell, Eve
Griffith, Gail
Hamid, Sobia
Holdsworth, Charlotte
Ogden, Tracy
Pierre-Madigan, John
Vaicekauskas, Kestutis
Chapman, Gary (pso)
Gromitt, Joanne (pso)
Kite, Alison (pso)
Woods, Anja (pso)

CP/CPRO Team
Hines, Janine (spo)
Bonham, Nicola
Chambers, Lynn
Daniels, Gerry
Coe, Diana (pso)
Pedley, Mike (pso)
Ranson, Anna (pso)
Roberts, Vicky (pso)
Walker, Craig (pso)
Ahmed, Jamil (css)
Gannon, Glyn (css)
Gilmartin, Susan (css)
Hutton, Malcolm (css)
Kavanagh, Karen (css)
Morley, Susan (css)
Ramsden, Peter (css)

Victim Services and Public Protection Unit
Armitage, Mark (pso)
Wood, Janet (pso)

Kirklees District

13. Broadway House, Crackenedge Lane
Dewsbury WF13 1PU
tel (01924) 464171/3 *fax (01924) 453279*
aco (01924) 454900 *fax (01924) 454404*

Johnson, Diana (aco)
Dawson, Stephanie (dist admin mgr)

Practice Development Assessor
Bray, Sheila

CRO Team
Trevitt, Joanne (spo)
Higgins, Paula (p, pract mgr)
Anforth, Pat
Buch, Nina
Burkinshaw, Clare
Hanson, Phil
Dean, Mary-Rose
Roberts, Jean
Roberts, Jude
Shaw, Martin
Canning, Steven (pso)
Gardner, Sandra (pso)
Perrot, Matthew (pso)

Court Team
Bramley, Liz (p, spo)
Todd, Sue (pract mgr)
Cartledge, Brian
Town, David
Wallace, Mona
Butterworth, Adele (pso)
Lees, Sharon (pso)
Mulla, Nasim (pso)
Newsome, Melanie (pso)
Sheard, Ruth (pso)
Stones, David (pso)

DTTO/DRR Team
fax (01924) 485676
Bramley, Liz (p, spo)
Todd, Susan (p, pract mgr)
Parker, Beverley
Shaw, Martin
Sheeky, Emma
Slawinski, Diane
Wise, David
Moore, Julie (pso)
Oldroyd, Philip (pso
Ray, Leanne (pso)

Resettlement Team
fax (01924) 460382
Ward, Marianne (spo)
Higgins, Paula (p, pract mgr)
Hattersley, Patricia
Kellett, Helen
Khan, Afzal
Lowe, Michelle
Watson, Kate
Wilmot, Denise
Spenceley, Karen (pso)
Sumner, Nicola (pso)

14. 21 St John's Road
Huddersfield HD1 5BW

tel (01484) 826100 *fax (01484) 422218*

Practice Devpt Assessor
Evans, Dave

CRO Team
fax (01484) 826197
Lee, Gavin (spo)
Barnes, Irena (p, pract mgr)
Cooke, Nadine
Edmondson, Alison
Lenihan, Kelly
Lawrence, Penny
Martin, Emma
Ridgway, Lorraine
Scott, Debbie
Swanson, Gaynor
Bohanna, Glenn (pso)
Fox, Margaret, (pso)
Hussain, Shabaz (pso)
Sykes, Karen (pso)

Resettlement Team
fax (01484) 826198
Burns, Janine (spo)
Barnes, Irena (p, pract mgr)
Bentley, Alison
Cooper, Ian
Daley, Lorna
Morris-Augustine, Jolene
Simpson, Jacqui
Haider, Halima (pso)
Martin, Graham (pso)
Williams, Rebecca (pso)

CP/CPRO Team
fax (01484) 826177
Parker, Lisa (spo)
Walker, Mandy (pract mgr)
Barrett, Elaine
Fenby, Neil
Gardner, Susan
Gimblett, Rachel
Haines, Louise
Mason, Emily
Willis, Sheila
Belbin. Veronica (cso)
Charlesworth, Ben (cso)
Daniel, Karen (cso)
Ellis, Belinda (cso)
Hemingway, Helena (cso)
McNamara, Eva (cso)
Pedley, Janine (temp cso)
Radcliffe, Nicola (pso)
Sykes, Tracey (pso)

Bartholomew, William (css)
Bohanna, Paul, (css)
Pedley, Janine (css)

Davies, John (css)
Frankland, Gordon (css)
Frisby, Andrew (css)
Hewitt, Jean (css)
Smith, Jean (css)

15. 5 Albion Street
     Dewsbury WF13 2AJ
     tel (01924) 457744 *fax (01924) 458564*

     Programmes Team
     McAvoy, Jackie (spo)
     Barber, Jean (pract mgr)
     Bassett, Sharon (acting pract mgr)
     Crabtree, Dawn
     Shater, Suzanne
     Wright, Chris
     Akbar, Zahir (pso)
     Armitage, Sally (pso)
     Belly, Andy (pso)
     Gillon, Emma (pso)
     Hartley, Sarah (pso)
     Woods, Martin (pso)

Wakefield District

16. 20/30 Lawefield Lane
     Wakefield WF2 8SP
     tel (01924) 361156 *fax (01924) 291178*
     aco (01924) 885425 *fax (01924) 332551*

     Loney, Kathy (aco)
     Jones, Margaret (dist admin mgr)
     Pitchford, Bill (pract devpt assessor)

     Court Team
     Todd, Viv (spo)
     Doran, Diane
     Borrill, Stephen (pso)
     Evans, Steve (pso)
     France, Martin (pso)
     Rainforth, Paul (pso)

     CRO Team
     Maxwell, Chris (spo)
     Reid, David (p, pract mgr)
     Cadamarteri, Sharon
     Hunt, Lauren
     Maguire, Clare
     White, Martin
     Wood, Susan
     Appleyard, Tracey (pso)
     Gavins, Chrine (pso)
     Middleton, Kathryn (pso)

     Resettlement Team
     Sweeting, Chris (spo)
     David Reid, (p, pract mgr)
     Bacon, Alex
     Barker, Katherine

Brereton, Liz
Brown, Phil
Munro, Donald
Parker, Catherine
Nightingale-Clark, Lorraine (pso)

Programmes Team
Millinship, Gerald (spo)
Kelly, Angela (pract mgr)
Brown, Claire (prog tutor)
Duggan, Sharna (prog tutor)
Evdokiou, Katy (prog tutor)
Flynn, Paula (prog tutor)
Henry, Sarah (prog tutor)
Jones, Peter (prog tutor)
Just, Simon (prog tutor)
Neto-Claringbold, Ana (prog tutor)
Ridge, Gemma (prog tutor)
Todd, Andrew (prog tutor)
Warwick, Leanne (prog tutor)

Wakefield & Kirklees Victim Services and Public Protection Unit
tel (01924) 332550 *fax (01924) 332551*

Parsisson, George (spo)
Brook, Margaret (pract mgr)
Jenkinson, Suzy (pso)
Kerry, Ruth (pso)
Palmer, Gail (pso)

CP/CPRO Team
tel (01924) 885420 *fax (01924) 885520*

Kyle, Jerry (spo)
Oliver, Maureen (pract mgr)
Bonner, Jo
Hussain, Wajid
McCullough, Julia
Nolan, Steve
Smith, Ronnie
Johnson, Lynn (cso)
Khan, Ghohar (cso)
Steele, Deborah (pso)
Thorpe, Wendy (pso)
Turner, Maria (cso)
Wardle, Sue (pso)
Barry, William (css)
Cramm, Eric (css)
Grason, David (css)
Hargreaves, Julie (css)
Kirrane, Mark (css)
McNichol, Laraine (css)
Wales, Granville (css)
Ward, Andrew (css)

17. Harropwell Lane
     Pontefract WF8 1QY
     tel (01977) 791357 *fax (01977) 602041*

Practice Development Assessor
Godley, Simon

CRO Team
Lawton, Mary (spo)
Clark, Carol (p, pract mgr)
Bergin, Susan
Dickinson-Ramsden, Issy
Heslop, Lynne
Lynch, Timothy (p)
Payne, Phil
Shields, Kathrine (p)
Johnson, Don (pso)
Soerensen, Susanne (pso)

Resettlement Team
Sweeting, Christopher (spo)
Clark, Carol (p, pract mgr)
Brettell, James
Green, Jackie
Jordan, Cathy
Schofield, Bill
Spence, Robert
Young, Michelle
Knowles, Christine (pso)

18. Grosvenor House
     8-20 Union Street **Wakefield** WF1 3AE
     tel (01924) 784999 *fax (01924) 781405*

     DTTO/DRR Team
     Todd, Viv (p, spo)
     Goodchild, Jennifer (pract mgr)
     Brown, Voirrey
     Jones, Lynn
     Smith, Miles
     Snell, Natalie
     Walker, Lindsey
     Charles, Shirley (pso)
     Jones, Stephen (pso)

Youth Offending Teams

19. Bank House, 41 Bank Street
     Bradford BD1 1RD
     tel (01274) 436060 *fax (01274) 436061*
     e-mail Firstname.Surname@bradford.
     gov.uk

     Szweda, Bozena
     Waterworth, Michelle
     Haworth, Leanne (pso)

20. **Leeds North**
     The District Centre, Town Street
     Chapel Allerton Leeds LS7 4NB
     tel 0113-214 5663 *fax 0113-214 5684*

     Olwyn Watt

21. **Leeds West**
     Hough Lane Centre
     Hough Lane, Bramley
     Leeds LS13 3RD
     tel 0113-395 0101 *fax 0113-395 0102*

     Metcalf, Lucy

22. **Leeds East**
     Halton Moor Centre
     Neville Road, Leeds LS15 0NW
     tel 0113-214 1369 *fax 0113-214 1377*

     Hannant, Ian
     Meek, Sarah

23. **Leeds South**
     38 Sweet Street, Holbeck
     Leeds LS11 9DB
     tel 0113-214 5300 *fax 0113-214 5299*

     Afzal, Nazir
     Folker, Dawn

24. **Intensive Supervision &
     Surveillance Programme**
     47 Marshall Street, Holbeck
     Leeds LS11 9RZ
     tel 0113-214 1514 *fax 0113-214 1517*

25. 3 Trinity Place
     Halifax HX1 2BD
     tel (01422) 368279 *fax (01422) 368483*

     Baxendale, Carole
     Kubala, Henryk

26. 1st Floor, Somerset Buildings
     Church Street **Huddersfield** HD1 1DD
     tel (01484) 226263 *fax (01484) 226919*

     Smith, Richard
     Tock, Heather

27. 5 West Parade
     Wakefield WF1 1LT
     tel (01924) 304155 *fax (01924) 304156*

     Mohans, Eammon

**Residential, Accommodation &
Partnership Unit**

28. **Holbeck House Probation & Bail
     Hostel**
     Springwell View, Springwell Road
     Leeds LS12 1BS
     tel 0113-245 4220 *fax 0113-245 4910*

     James, Peter (mgr)
     Blanc, Johny (dep mgr)

Shephard, Leigh (res off)
Young, Grace (res off)
Bennett, Dawn (asst res off)
Hall, Monica (asst res off)
Kennedy, Carl, (asst res off)
Masood, Umair (pso)

29. **Elm Bank Hostel**
59 Bradford Road
Cleckheaton BD19 3LW
tel (01274) 851551 *fax (01274) 851079*

Haddrick, David (mgr)
Thompson, John (dep mgr)
Binns, Joanne (res off)
Dalawar, Ifzal (res off)
Elliott, Marsha (res off)
Ingram, Kimberley (res off)
French, Dawn, (asst res off)
Ramsden, Devon, (asst res off)
Richardson, William (asst res off)
Higson, Trudie (admin off)

30. **Albion Street Hostel**
30 Albion Street, Dewsbury WF13 2AJ
tel (01924) 452020 *fax (01924) 455670*

Brown, Ralph (mgr)
Cox, Paula (dep mgr)
Elliott, Stuart (res off)
Evans, Andrew (res off)
Lee, Julia (res off)
Smith, Stuart (res off)
Brown, Donnavon (asst res off)
Hirst, Alison (admin off)
Lumb, John, (asst res off)
Lynch, Alistair, (asst res off)

31. **Westgate Hostel**
188-198 Westgate, Wakefield WF2 9RF
tel (01924) 203730 *fax (01924) 203731*

Vacancy (mgr)
Hickman, James (res off)
Phillips, Amanda (res off)
Sharrock, Julie (res off)
Atkinson, Natalia (asst res off)
Bretherick, Sarah (asst res off)
Chester, Chantelle (asst res off)
Eggleton, Matt (asst res off)
Grocott, Wayne (asst res off)
Moss, Sarah (asst res off)
Napier, Ron (asst res off)
Parvez, Ghazal (asst res off)
Wendel, Nicola (asst res off)

Voluntary Approved Hostels

32. **Cardigan House**
84 Cardigan Road, Leeds LS6 3BJ
tel 0113-275 2860 *fax 0113-274 5175*

Barker, Tim (mgr)
Morris, Mike (dep mgr)

33. **St John's Hostel**
259/263 Hyde Park Road
Leeds LS6 1AG
tel 0113-275 5702 *fax 0113-230 5230*

Berry, Tony (mgr)
Miller, Lynn (dep mgr)

34. **Ripon House**
63 Clarendon Road, Leeds LS2 9NZ
tel 0113-245 5488 *fax 0113-242 3675*

Pickin, Rod (mgr)
Hadcroft, Marie, (dep mgr)

Institutions

35 HM Prison **Wealstun**
Thorp Arch, Boston Spa
Wetherby LS23 7AZ
tel (01937) 848500 *fax (01937) 848501*
probn fax (01937) 848766
Probn clerk (01937) 848568
Parole clerk (01937) 848555
Movements (01937) 848835
Probn Admin (01937) 848676

Brand, Dave (spo)
Stadward, Chris (spo) 848600
Bucksun, Margaret (open)
Harrison, Carol (closed) X4699
Jeffers, Lennie (closed) X4666
Hayes, Rick (open) X4675
Acornley, Nicola (pso) X4800
Berry, Michael (pso) X4529
Coulthard, Penelope (pso) X4800
Fell, Theresa (pso) X4641
Forster, Karen (pso)X4529
Holmes, Rebecca (pso)X4529
Sheppard, Sally (pso) X4778

36. HM Prison **Armley**
Leeds LS12 2TJ
tel 0113-203 2600 *fax 0113-203 2601*

probn admin ext 2644
probn fax 0113-203 2870

Ralcewicz, Elizabeth (spo) 2657
Dersley, Ian 2647
Iqbal, Tahir 2615
Klaus, Judith 2686

Razaq, Mohammed 2641
Bradley, Clair (pso) 2626
Ehrlich, Sergio (pso) 2689
Moore, Fiona (pso) 2668
Reynold, Graham (pso) 2649

Bail Information
ext 2648
Bail info fax 0113-2032869

Stansfield, Bernie (pso) 2640

37. HM Prison, Love Lane
Wakefield WF2 9AG
tel (01924) 246000 *fax (01924) 2462799*

Probn clerk ext 6485
Parole clerk ext 6071
Special visits ext 6250

Brearton, Julie (spo) ext 6362
Foster, Sara
Hanby, Pamela
Hirons, David
Johnson, Anne
Langton, Cris

38. HM Women's Prison
New Hall Dial Wood
Flockton, Wakefield WF4 4AX
tel (01924) 844200 *fax (01924) 844201*
probn fax (01924) 844248

Probn clerk ext 4298
Discipline ext 4308/9
Sentence planning ext 4234
HDC clerk ext 4479
Special visits ext 4394

Carless, Susan (spo)
Forrest, Janet
Hirst, Penelope
Redhouse, Liz
Flynn, Jacqueline (pso)
Denniss, Maria (pso)
Ratcliffe, Janette (pso)

Local Justice Areas

2-4 Bradford
6 Keighley
7, 9 Leeds
12 Calderdale
13, 15 Batley & Dewsbury
14 Huddersfield
16 Wakefield
17 Pontefract

Crown Courts

5 Bradford
11 Leeds

DYFED-POWYS PROBATION AREA
GWASANAETH PRAWF DYFED-POWYS

e-mail Firstname.Surname@dyfed-powys.probation.gsx.gov.uk

1. **Head Office**
Llangunnor Road, Carmarthen SA31 2PD
tel (01267) 221567 *fax (01267) 221566*

Morgan, Caroline R (co)
Rutter, Frances (acpo)
Pearce, Jan E S (aco)
Davies, Geoffrey L (aco, hd of h.r.)
Wheatley, Lynn (area mgr offender mngmnt)
Thomas, Elizabeth ('what works' mgr)
Fisher, Kevin (cjdip mgr)
John, Jackie (snr co pa)
James, Catrin (pa to aco)
Richards, Mair (admin to cjdip mgr)
Watson, Susan (pa to aco)
Warwick, Susan (admin to 'what wks' mgr & area mgr offender mngmnt)
Johns, Helen (training mgr)
Bundock, Sarah (h.r. off)
James, Tracey (h.r. off)
Pritchard, Wayne (ict systems mgr)
Bale, Shirley (snr ict off)
Glasson, Steve (snr ict off)
Williams, Neil (snr ict off)
Ladbrook, Martin (ict asst)
Cadd, Theresa (iaps in-putter)
Davies, Arfon (snr finance off)
Maguire, Karen (snr finance off)
Griffiths, Alison (p, snr finance off, transport)
Nash, Teresa (p, finance admin)
Wright, Peter (finance admin)

2. Court Building, 7 Glamorgan Street
Brecon LD3 7DS
tel (01874) 614150 *fax (01874) 610602*

Corbett, Jeremy (acpo)
Davies, Anita (pa to aco)

3. 7a & 7b Water Street
Carmarthen SA31 1PY
tel (01267) 222299 *fax (01267) 222164*

Dyfed Central
Wakelam, Ruth (divnl mgr)
Phillips, Heather (cpo, qa mgr)
Elliott, Helen (treatment mgr)
Coleridge, Tom

Davies, Catherine
Holton, Doreen (p)
Jarvis, Tara
Jones, Jayne
Lloyd, Ben
Morgan, Debbie

Bibby, Thomas (trainee)
Hunter, Katie (trainee)
Parker, Claire (trainee)
Worth, Tracey (trainee)

Burd, Judith (pso)
Inglesant, Bob (pso)
John, Gaye (pso)
Rees-Thomas, Michelle (pso)
Foster, Michael (vlo)

Saunders, Sian (divnl admin)
Davis, April (p, divnl secy)
Evans, Jane (divnl secy)
Hodge, Iris (p, divnl secy)
Millar, Rhyla (p, victim liaison admin &
divnl secy)

4. Lloyd Street
    Llanelli SA15 2UP
    tel (01554) 773736 *fax (01554) 758491*

    Dyfed East
    Hussey, Alan (divnl mgr)
    Churchill, Janet (snr pract, risk)
    Hoyles, Lee (snr pract, drr)
    Grant, Desmond (treatment mgr)
    Adams, Gill (p, yot)
    Brenton, Liz (p)
    Creed, Martyn
    Edwards, Christine
    Harries, Davinia
    Hiscocks, Karen
    Jones, David
    King, Peter
    Ripley, Carol (p, yot)
    Rosser, Mandy

    Brennan, Jacqueline (trainee)
    Guest, Naomi (trainee)
    Harris, Nicola (trainee)
    Jackson, Rachel (trainee)
    James, Angela (trainee)
    Waygood, Laura (trainee)
    Wilford, Huw (trainee)

    Jenkins, Tim (cpo)
    John, Clive (cpo)

    Bouleghlimat, Janet (pso)
    Harries, Christine (pso)
    Stone, Terry (pso)
    Vacancy (pso)
    Waters, Sîan (pso)

Harries, Janet (divnl admin)
Thomas, Janet (p, divnl secy)
Standfield, Will (divnl secy)
Davies, Gloria (divnl secy)
Lomax, Linda (p, divnl secy)
Samuel, Barbara (divnl secy)
Ransome, Harriet (p, cwcs admin)

5. 14 High Street
    Haverfordwest SA61 1DA
    tel (01437) 762013 *fax (01437) 765423*

    Dyfed West
    Houton, Janet (divnl mgr)
    Caveille, Loraine (snr pract, drr)
    Linck, Jacquie (treatment mgr)
    Bennett, Mike
    Birks, Sandra
    Brosnan, Mark
    Chappill, Frank (p, yot)
    Davies, Nicola
    Davis, Steven
    Horner, Jim
    Thomas, Sarah

    Moore, Alistair (trainee)
    Sheehan, Matthew (trainee)

    Quinnell, Diane (cpo)
    Owen, Bob (cpo)

    Giacci, Blanche (pso)
    Gibbs, Lynn (pso)
    James, John (pso)
    Stacey, Kevin (pso)

    Lewis, Trish (divnl admin)
    Phillips, Julia (divnl secy)
    Kidd, Margaret (operational admin)
    Llewellyn, Sandra (divnl secy)
    Thomas, Ann (p, divnl secy)

6. 23 Grays Inn Road
    Aberystwyth SY23 1DE
    tel (01970) 636460 *fax (01970) 624713*

    Dyfed North
    Alman, Mark (divnl mgr)
    Ayriss, Debbie (p, pda)
    Llewellyn, Sera (p, pda)
    Williams, Hugh (snr pract)
    Davies, Bob
    Griffith, Gwyn
    Jones, Gary (p, yot)
    Staite, Aine
    Whittaker, Jane (p)

    Critchley, Ros (trainee)
    Edwards, Samantha (trainee)
    Weinzweig, Nicole (trainee)

Smith, Clive (cpo)

Davies, Ruth (pso)
Griffiths Sharon (pso)
McDouall, Laura (pso)
Matthews, Dawn (pso)

Price, Jane (divnl admin)
Lindsay, Helen (divnl secy)
Owers, Pat (p, divnl secy)
Sillars, Rose (p, divnl secy)

7. Court Building
    7 Glamorgan Street **Brecon** LD3 7DS
    tel (01874) 614150 *fax (01874) 610602*

    South Powys
    Powis, Kathy (divnl mgr)
    Daniel, Darren (cwcs mgr)
    Burdett, Andrea (p)
    Gregory, Janet (p)
    Livesley, Julia
    Williams, Helen
    Wooldridge, Jonathan (p, yot)

    Vacancy (cpo case mgr)
    Dodds, Maureen (cpo)

    Price, Philip (p, pso)
    Pelonero, Trieva (pso)
    Scott, Jenny (pso)
    Smith, Fay (pso)
    Taylor, Helena (pso)
    Watts, Mel (pso)

    Williams, Margaret (divnl admin)
    Leakey, Gillian (divnl secy)
    Evans, Clare (p, divnl admin)

    Offender Employment & Housing Unit
    Carter, Charlie (devpt mgr)

8. Straight Lines House
    New Road **Newtown** SY16 1BB
    tel (01686) 611900 *fax (01686) 611901*

    North Powys
    Williams, Yvonne (divnl mgr)
    Arrowsmith, Stevie (treatment mgr)
    Ennis, Juliet
    Simpson, Laura
    Mooney, Nicola
    Wooldridge, Jonathan (p, yot)

    Cookson, Trish (trainee)
    Greig, Dennis (trainee)

    Hickman, Tracey (cpo)

    Brown, Anna Marie (pso)
    Randle, Brian (p, pso)
    Webb, Alex (pso)

Harvey, Laura (divnl admin)
Roberts, Nicola (p, divnl secy)
Robinson, Jennifer (divnl secy)

Youth Offending Teams

9. **Pembrokeshire YOT**
    Customer Services Centre
    Argyle Street
    Pembroke Dock SA72 6HL
    tel (01437) 776036/8 *fax (01646) 684563*

    Chappill, Frank (p)

10. **Carmarthenshire YOT**
    1 West End, Llanelli
    Carmarthenshire SA15 3DN
    tel (01554) 740120 *fax (01554) 740122*

    Adams, Gill (p)
    Ripley, Carol (p)

11. **Mid Wales & Ceredigion YOT**
    25 Market Street, Newtown SY16 2PD
    tel (01686) 617670 *fax(01676) 617681*

    Jones, Gary (p)
    Wooldridge, Jon (p)

Local Justice Areas

3 Carmarthen
6 Ceredigion
7 De Brycheiniog
8 De Maldwyn
4 Dinefwr
4 Llanelli
5 North Pembrokeshire
7 Radnorshire & N Brecknock
5 South Pembrokeshire
8 Welshpool

Crown Court

3 Carmarthen
3 Haverfordwest
8 Welshpool

GWENT PROBATION AREA
GWASANAETH PRAWF GWENT

e-mail
Firstname.Surname@gwent.probation.gsx.gov.uk

1. **Head Office**
    Cwmbran House, 3rd Floor
    Mamhilad Park Estate
    Pontypool NP4 0XD
    tel (01495) 762462 *fax (01495) 762461*

direct dial (01495) 74+ext

Coates, Jane (co) 5702
Langdon, Chris (aco) 5704
Blease, Adrian (aco) 5703
Gotley, Adam (aco) 5705
Seymour, Carolyn (aco) 5706
Coombes, Mark (hr mgr) 5713
Turner, Karen (team mgr, staff devpt tm) 5712
Jones, Neil (team mgr, finance & estates tm) 5714
Jones, Simon (team mgr, business tm) 5711
Ryan, Mary (pa to co) 5707
Cole, Rose (pa to aco's) 5710
Holland, Susie (pa to aco's) 5709
Caple, Michelle (board admin off) 5708
Fisher, Bärbel (admin off, hr) 5717
Patrick, Andrea (admin off, hr) 5741
Phillips, Cherryl (admin off, office services) 5701
Howells, Helen (fin off)
Hamilton, Jo (admin off, finance) 5720
Clarke, Tony (info mgr, systems) 5721
Edwards, Gail (info off, systems) 5722
Butler, Tomos (info off, systems) 5723
Howells, Zoe (info off, data)
Tapp, Gemma (info off, perf)
Davies, Anthony (info off, perf) 5724
Humphreys, Gaynor (admin off, comms/training) 5718
Oram, Dawn (snr clerical off) 5719

2.   50 Bethcar Street
      Ebbw Vale NP23 6HG
      tel (01495) 309799) *fax (01495 306997)*
      direct dial (01495) 35+ext

Ebbw Vale Team
Fields, David (team mgr) 6468
Goulding, David 6477
Lloyd, Rhiannon 6477
McPherson, Robin 6466
Pizey, Sarah 6474
Powell, Claire 6476
Rance, Nichola 6467
Williams, David 6471
Affleck, Robert (pso) 6466
Hughes, Suzanne (pso)
Thomas, Iwan (pso) 6481
Williams, Timothy (pso)

Staff Development Team
Vowden, Nicole (pract teacher) 6469

High Risk of Harm Team
Holloway, David 6472

Prolific Offenders Team
Strange, Jeffrey 6480

ETE Team
Davies, Andrew (pso) 6473

Drug Rehabilitation Team
Birchmore, Alan (01495) 356480
Palmer, Jason (pso) (01495) 356480

Trainees
Feiken, Leeanna 6465
Davies, Non 6479
Hood, Maree 6478
Rees-Jones, Julian 6479
Skinner, Michelle 6463
Stonelake, Neil 6463
Tetley, Nicholas 6478
Wan, Lisa 6465

3.   Probation Office
      Park Road **Bargoed** CF81 8SP
      tel (01443) 875575 *fax (01443) 831114*
      direct dial (01443) 87 + ext

Rhymney Valley Team 1
Walters, Sharon (team mgr) 3824
Boulter, Paul 3819
Davies, Helen 3825
Davies, Linda 3820
Jones, Kristina 3811
Lavelle, Kate 3812
Partridge, Chris 3809
Sheppard, David 3807
Thomas, Sian 3816
Alexander, Sharon (pso)
Daniel, Peter (pso) 3814
Dixon, Grace (pso) 3810
Taylor, Rachel (pso) 3815

Rhymney Valley Team 3
Richley, Linda (team mgr) 3823
Nilsen Tony 3818
Coles, Linda (pso) 3826

Staff Development Team
Lewis, Margaret (pract teacher) 3822

High Risk of Harm Team
Gillard, Karen 3817

Prolific Offenders Team
Dunne, Michael 3813

ETE Team
Palmer, Rosa (pso) 3808

Trainees
Dacey, Ian
Ellis-Hall, Karen
Irish, Sarah-Jayne
Nash, Katie

O'Connell, Siobhan 3806
Robinson, Sinead 3806
Thomas, Sian Louise

4. Mountain Road
    Caerphilly CF83 1ZA
    tel (02920) 885 861 *fax (02920) 865929*

    Rhymney Valley Team 2
    Packham, Jill (team mgr)
    Dunley, Karen
    Shaw, Linda
    Warke, Clifford
    Jones, beth (pso)
    Price, Katie (pso)
    Solomons, Gloria (pso)

    Rhymney Valley Team 3
    Hamed, Janine
    Thomas, Elizabeth
    Vallely, Gillian
    Powell, Nadine (pso)
    Timothy, Sarah (pso)
    Turner, Vicky (pso)
    Williams, Katie (pso)

    ETE Team
    Walsh, Johanna (pso)

    Youth Offending Team
    tel (01495) 235623
    Rees, Stephen
    Brunt, Peter (pso)

5. **Accredited Programmes Centre**
    The Highway, Croesyceiliog
    Cwmbran NP44 2HF
    tel (01633) 877716 *fax (01633) 867251*
    direct dial (01633) 83 + ext

    Accredited Programmes Team
    Spacey, Nigel (team mgr) 5935
    Bowkett, Stephen (treatment mgr) 5932
    Curtis, Sherrie (treatment mgr) 5931
    Callow, Leah (pso) 5933
    Davies, Frank (pso) 5936
    Rees, Abbie (pso) 5934
    Thomas, Fiona (pso) 5934
    Vaughan, Karen (pso) 5937
    Warry, John (pso) 5933
    Yapp, Rhiannon (pso) 5936

6. Torfaen House, Station Road
    Sebastopol, **Pontypool** NP4 5ES
    tel (01495) 755221 *fax (01495) 763233*
    direct dial (01495) 74 + ext

    East Gwent Team
    Owen, Peter (team mgr) 5005
    Corkhill, Sarah 5033

Harrison, Susan 5031
Jones, Leigh 5018
Pearson, Ann 5006
Smith, Bernard 5035
Thorpe, Keiron 5021
Hughes, Natalie (pso)
Jenkins, Jason (pso) 5034
Milton, Lisa (pso) 5015
Sellick-Brown, Ann (pso) 5020
Walters-Moore, Andrew (pso) 5036
Wilcox, Sarah (pso) 5038
Young, Mark (pso) 5017

Staff Development Team
Sullivan, Jane (pract teacher) 5022

High Risk of Harm Team
Andrews, Christine (team mgr) 5011
Mason, Heather 5032
Jenkins, Helen (pso) 5031
Trotman, Rhonwen (mappa registrar) 5037

ETE Team
Goodall, Lianne (pso) 5012

Youth Offending Team
tel (01495) 768300
Gourlay, Alison

Trainees
Baker, Carol 5023
Collier, Rowena
Flage, Leeanne
Haskins, Lee 5025
Howse, Sarah
Maynard, Lucilla 5024
Sarwar, Zaheen
Wright, Hannah

7. 19/20 Gold Tops
    Newport NP20 4UG
    tel (01633) 213221 *fax (01633) 221568*

    Newport Team 1
    Vernon, Claire (team mgr)
    Burr, Rodney
    Evans, Lisa
    Richards, Kelly
    Rowlands, Heather
    Davies, Laura (pso)
    Gabica, Zoe (pso)
    Ivens, Luke (pso)

    Newport Team 2
    Gillo, Deborah (team mgr)
    Evans, Michael
    Asher, Kate
    Llewellyn-Rowe, Janet
    Clarke, Tony (pso)
    Moore, Kate (pso)

Newport Team 3
Watkins, Catherine (team mgr)
McCormack, Caroline
Porter, Rick
Hatfield, Catherine
Johns, Kirsty
Thorne, Stephen
McGuire, Eleanor (pso)
Williams, Nicola (pso)

Newport Team 4
Edwards, Sarah (team mgr)
Powell, Kate (team mgr)
Blandford, Rebecca
Wadcock, Michael
Beck, Ruth (pso)
Brass, Erin (pso)
Edwards, Sharon (pso)
Lewis, Frances (pso)
Lloyd, Susan (pso)
Owen, Peter (pso)
Smith, Rebecca (pso)
Williams, Brian (pso)

High Risk of Harm Team
Morris, Lucy
Webb, Ellen

Prolific Offenders Team
Davies, Alan (team mgr, POT)

Youth Offending Team
tel (01633) 292900
Davies, Kirsty

8.   27 Argyle Street
Newport NP20 5NE
tel (01633) 822007 *fax (01633) 820839*

Community Punishment Team
King, Mike (team mgr)
Brown, Joanne (pso)
Bynon, Julie (pso)
Gibbon, Louise (pso)
Price, Marilyn (pso)
Walker, Sharon (pso)
Whittington, Fiona (pso)
Bidgood, David (snr cp off)
Ritchie, Grant (snr cp off)
Axenderrie, Paul (cp off)
Mogford, Michael (cp off)
Morgan, Robin (cp off)
Sims, James (cp off)
Wilks, Roger (cp off)

9.   **Drug Rehabilitation Team**
The Annexe
Rear of Pentonville Magistrates' Court

Newport NP20 5XQ
tel (01633) 840298 *fax (01633) 840334*
direct dial (01633) 84 + ext

Reed, Gail (team mgr) 0296
Ayres, Rob 0295
Collins, Katherine 0294
Gittoes, Catherine 0290
Gough, Louise 01495 228829
Pearn, Vernon 0292
Pudge, Lindsey 0301
Bullock, Donna (pso) 01495 228829
Davies, Kerry (pso) 0301
Dicks, Samantha (pso) 0294
Stone, Emma (pso) 0297
Wells, Andrew (pso) 0293

10.   **Pentonville Office**
Pentonville Magistrates' Court Building
Newport NP20 5HZ
tel (01633) 841249 (ete) (01633) 841256
(Nwpt team)
fax (01633)841278
direct dial (01633) 84 + ext

ETE Team
Bell, Doreen (team mgr) 1255
Cresswell, Sarah (pso) 1261

Newport Teams
Howe, Emma (nt 4) 1275
Mukhtar, Kauser (nt 2) 1275
Peckham, Tracey (nt 3) 1272
Phillips, Emma (nt 4) 1271

Prolific Offender Team
Nicholls, Robert 1253
Thomas-Owen, Mandy 1258

Institutions

11.   H M Prison
47 Maryport Street **Usk** NP15 1XP
tel (01291) 671600 *fax (01291) 673800*

Harry, Robert (team mgr)
Allford, Michelle-Marie
Case, Lesley
Thomas, Siobhan (pso)

12.   H M Young Offender Institution
Prescoed Coed-y-Paen
Nr Pontypool NP4 0TB
tel (01291) 675000 *fax (01291) 672197*

Bird, Jayne
Halligan, Jean
Tew, Stephanie (pso)

Local Justice Areas
2, 3, 4 NW Gwent
6, 7 SE Gwent

Crown Court
7 Newport

Staff on Secondment
A'Hearne, Jim
Dunne, Jill (dv proj) (based at 4) (02920) 885861
Law, Alex (based at 10) (01633) 841262

NORTH WALES PROBATION AREA (Counties of Anglesey, Denbighshire, Flintshire, Wrexham, Gwynedd, Conwy) GWASANAETH PRAWF GOGLEDD CYMRU (Siroedd Ynys Mon, Ddinbych, Fflint, Wrecsam, Gwynedd, Conwy)

Out of hours emergency contact point
Ty Newydd Hostel (01248) 370529
Plas y Wern Hostel (01978) 821202

Victim enquiries contact number
(01492) 875083/876961

e-mail Firstname.Surname@north-wales.probation.gsx.gov.uk

NB North Wales Probation Area is undergoing a major organisational re-structure . With effect from 1st February 2006 the personal contact details shown below may have changed.

Offices

1. **Head Office**
Alexandra House, Abergele Road
Colwyn Bay LL29 9YF
tel (01492) 513413 *fax (01492)513373*

Moore, Carol R (co)
Ray, Stephen G (aco)
Driver, Matthew (aco)
Murphy, Ray (aco, perf & planning)
Barton, Kit (aco, resources)
Livingston, Wulf (subst misuse area mgr)
Lloyd, Geraint (admin & financial services off)
Pickering, Steve (info support)
Roberts, Simon (perf info off)

Cresswell, Ruth (personnel mgr),
Parsons, Kelly (cjb, Comms off)

2. Llys Garth, Garth Road
Bangor Gwynedd LL57 2RT
tel (01248) 370217 *fax (01248) 372422*

Evans, Jane (spo)(crt & com supvn west)
Roberts, Alona (admin asst)

Court & Community Supervision West
Riou, Jill (snr pract)
Jones, Delyth
Griffith, Hannah
Smith Katherine
Williams, Sharon
Whatling, Mike (snr pso)
Williams, Sîan (atm)
Wright, June (pso)
Phillips, Liz (pso)
Burton, Maxine (p, pso)

DTTO Team
Richards, Steve
Williams, Emma
Roberts-Price, Lynne(pso)

Enhanced Community Punishment
Hughes, Ken (cs unit mgr)
Pritchard, Vivien (cso)
Adshead, Carole
Healy, Diane (pso)
Chamberlain, John (p,css)
Jones, Robert (css)
Thomas, Dave (css)
Thomas, Bob (p, css)
Wilding, Bob (css)
Hughes, Beth (ca)

3. 14 Market Street
Caernarfon Gwynedd LL55 1RT
tel (01286) 674346 *fax (01286) 672668*

Owen, Llew (p, spo, resettlement west)
Griffiths, Mrs. Mimma (admin asst)

Resettlement, West
Sims, Georgina (snr pract)
Middleton, Sue
Farrer, Susie
Thomas, Catrin
Rees, Awen
MacDonald, Fergie (snr pso)
Owen, Cathy (snr pso)
Edwards, Karen (pso)
Roberts, Matt (pso)

4. Lombard Street, Dolgellau
Dolgellau Gwynedd LL40 1HA
tel (01341) 422476 *fax (01341) 422703*

Cumming-Watt, Karen (p,ca)
Harrison, Mrs. Marian (p, pso)
Jones, Geraint (css)

5.   18 Augusta Street,
Llandudno LL30 2AD
tel (01492) 875083/876961 *fax (01492) 872034*

Barton, Gaynor (spo, resettlement central)
Marsh, Ms Sue (admin asst)

Resettlement Central
Jones, Andy (snr pract)
Lowe, Sheila (snr pract)
Blackwell, Lis
Clark, Carolyn
Ifans, Elenid
Owen, Tracey
Roberts, Sue
Williams, Paul
Wilson, Adrian
Haggett, Carol (trainee forensic psychologist)
Tyrer, Catherine (spso)
Thomas, Rachel (pso)
McKeavaney, Siobhan (pso, snr vlo)
Owen-Rees, Nia (pso, vlo)
Walker, Caroline (pso,vlo)

ECP Central
Knowles, Richard (css)

6.   13 Princes Drive
Colwyn Bay LL29 8HT
tel (01492) 530600/532692 *fax (01492) 532283*

Staff Training & Development
Adlam, Doris (spo)
Webb, Rob (admin asst)

Amirech, Mohammed (pda)
Laing, Angharad (p, pda)
Parry, Trish (pda)
Dance, Sheila (staff devpt & nvq co-ord)
Aristeidou, Cristina (trainee)
Byfield Jones, Anna (trainee)
Clark, Jonathan (trainee)
Croft, Katherine (trainee)
Davies, Dewi (trainee)
Evans, Llinos (trainee)
Griffith, Gerallt (trainee)
Hardwick, Pippa (trainee)
Hughes, Elin (trainee)
Hooley, Emily (trainee)
Jones, Gillian (trainee)
Jones, Llinos (trainee)
Kidd, Gareth (trainee)

Maggs, Christopher (trainee)
Mooney, Claire (trainee)
Murphy, Michael (trainee)
Partington, Michelle (trainee)
Peters, Llyr (trainee)
Preece, Llinos (trainee)
Reid, Jane (trainee)
Walkley, Julia (trainee)
Williams, Lynne (trainee)

all trainees may be contacted through the Staff Training & Devpt Unit

All Wales Training Consortium
Gwilym, Ceinwen (snr pract, internal verifier)

Enhanced Community Punishment
Hughes, Liz (cs area mgr)
Gush, Lynn (admin asst)

7.   Epworth Lodge, Brighton Road
Rhyl Denbighshire LL18 3HF
tel (01745) 344521 *fax (01745) 356137*

Catton, Tessa (spo, crt & com supvn central)
Richardson, Judy (admin asst)

Crt & Community Supervision Central
Owen, Lucie (snr pract)
Dhaliwal, Jaspal
Donnelly, Paul
McAlley, Ian
Phillips, Len
Rattigan, Sylvia
Swinden, Liz
Burton, Maxine (p, pso)
New, Tony (pso)
Roberts, Eirian (pso)
Roberts, Jan (atm)
Shelbourne, Jane
Valentine, Richard (pso)

Substance Misuse Team
McIntyre, Karen

ECP Central
Thomas, Graham (cs unit mgr)
Hooson, Sîan
Burton,Maxine (pso)
Fletcher, Louise (pso)
Wright, John (cso)
Kitchen, Linda (ca)
Jones, David (css)
Parry, Paul,(css)

8.   Unit 6, Acorn Business Centre
Flint Flintshire CH6 5YN
tel 01352 792140 *fax (01352 792141)*

Roberts, Mike (spo, resettlement east)
Garvey, Margaret (admin asst)

Resettlement East
Evans, Tracey (p)
Hughes, Sharon
Lord, Christine
Ryan, Jane (p)
Williams, Judith
Shepherd, Natasha (pso)

Court & Community Supervision East
Boycott, Angela
Green, Dave
Hayward, Jane
Jones, Ceri (pso)
Wynn, Mair (pso)

9. Ellice Way, Wrexham Technology Park
Wrexham LL13 7YX
tel (01978) 346200 *fax (01978) 346206*

Dyment, Joy (spo, crt & com supvn east)
Vacancy (admin asst)
Towers, Viv (admin asst)

Court & Community Supervision East
Hands, Angela (snr pract)
Aitken, Jackie (snr pract)
Oats, Lis (snr pract)
Almark, Nigel
Griffiths, Ceri
Humphries, Kathleen
Jones, Llinos
Jones, Rhian (p)
McKenzie, Kirstin
Thornburn, Anna
Roberts, Pamela (snr pso)
Connah, Andrew (pso)
Mitchell, Emma (p, pso)
Sedgwick, Eddie (pso)

Resettlement East
Henery, Jill (snr pract)
Carrison, Janet
Foulkes, Jenny
Brett, Emma
Jones, James
Price, David
Taylor, Joanne
Seward, Derek
Stein, Pat (snr pso)

ECP East
tel (01978) 346207

Davies, Chris (csum)
Evans, Charlie (csum)
Lloyd, Dave (cso)
Baines, Kathleen (p, css)
Clapham, Mike (css)

Gaughran, Eamonn (css)
Heath, Tony css)
Mooney, Claire (pso)
Poyner, Mike (css)
Purton, Richard (pso)
Richards, Sharon (p,css)
Wynne, Allan (css)
Rafique, Mohammed (css)
Wilson, Rob (p, css)
Ellis, Paula (admin asst)

9a. 21 Grosvenor Road
Wrexham LL11 1BT
tel (01978) 366941 *fax (01978) 366945*

Substance Misuse Team
Goodwin, Phil (temp snr pract)
Davidson, Ian
Jones, Caren
Pawulska, Jacqui
Webster, Frances
Davies, Patrick (pso)
Davies, Teresa (pso)
Griffiths, Myfanwy (pso)
Owen, Elain (pso)
Jones, Helen (ca)

10. **Youth Offending Teams**
6th Floor, County Hall
Mold Flintshire CW7 5BD
tel (01352) 702603 *fax (01352) 750601*

Woolford, Ffion (pso)
Woodward, Paul (css)

Swyddfa Menai
Glan y Mor, Felinheli
Bangor LL56 4RQ
tel (01248) 679183 *fax (01248) 679180*

Hughes, Fred

3rd Floor Kelso House
13 Grosvenor Road
Wrexham LL11 1BS
tel (01978) 267404 *fax (01978) 267401*

Connolly James (pso)
Evans Gabriella (pso)

68 Conway Road
Colwyn Bay LL29 7LD
tel (01492) 523500 *fax (01492) 523555*

Parry, Glynne

11. **Crown Courts**
Mold Crown Court
Law Courts, Civic Centre

Mold CH7 1AE
tel & fax (01352) 751649

Carrison, Janet (cclo)
Ellis, Phil (H&S advisor)

Caernarfon Crown Court
Shire Hall Street
Castle Ditch
Caernarfon LL55 2AY
tel (01286) 675717 *fax (01286) 675717*

MacDonald, Fergie (spso, cclo)

Hostels

12. **Plas y Wern**
Ruabon, Nr Wrexham LL14 6RN
tel (01978) 814949 *fax (01978) 810435*

Higgins, Chris (spo, warden)
Evans, Edwyn
Evans, Luke (pso)
Hughes, Donna (pso)
Higgins, Gareth (rso)
Quinn, Michael (pso)
Le Brun, Sian (rso)
Scott-Melville (rso)
West, Lewis (rso)
Stewart, Chris (admin asst)

13. **Ty Newydd**
Llandygai Road
Bangor, Gwynedd LL57 4HP
tel (01248) 370529 *fax (01248) 371204*

Ellis, Dafydd (spo, warden)
Jones, Rhys
Sawicz, Philip
Pugh, Richard (pso)
Cleary, Patrick (pso)
Jones, Tina (pso)
Mead Damon (rso)
Shone Norman (rso)
Williams Emyr (rso)
Cox, Karen (admin asst)

Petty Sessional Areas

2 Anglesey/Ynys Mon
5, 6 Conwy
7 Denbighshire
8 Flintshire
2, 3, 4 Gwynedd
9 Wrexham Maelor

Crown Courts

11 Caernarfon
11 Mold

SOUTH WALES PROBATION AREA
GWASANAETH PRAWF DE CYMRU

Out of hours emergency contact numbers
Mandeville House Approved Premises
029-2039 4592
Tony Richards (aco) 01792 232448
Janet Chaplin (aco) 07889 486994
Granville Brunt (aco) 07968 172796
Liz Rijnberger (aco) 07810 854237
Julia Attwell (aco) 07810 854229

e-mail Firstname.Surname@south-wales.probation.gov.uk

1. **Head Office**
Tremains House, Tremains Road
Bridgend CF31 1TZ
tel (01656) 674747 *fax (01656) 674799*
direct dial: (01656) 67 + ext

Lankshear, Ian (co) ext 4800
Egan, Paul (director of corp serv) ext 4802
Cossins, Angela (director of operations) ext 4801
Potter, Mark (director of finance) ext 4803
Singh, Suckvindar (diversity mgr) ext 4796
Postans, Saranne (communications mgr) ext 4818
James, Russell (admin serv mgr) ext 4794
Viant, Gwenllian (sec/pa to co) ext 4798

Business Devpt Unit
Ace, Christine (aco) ext 4790
Attwell, Julia (aco, perf & info, Bridgend) ext 4771
Chaplin, Janet (aco) ext 4820
Blower, Dawn (area mgr) ext 4831
Donoghue, Nicola (area mgr) ext 4833
Jones, Bobbie (area mgr) ext 4830
Barrow, Ian (area mgr) ext 4832
Thomas, Sarah (research off) ext 4814
Farthing, Sue (exel asst) ext 4775
Smith, Jayne (admin) ext 4789

Human Resources Unit
Ferris, Cathryn (hr mgr) ext 4715
Pring, Maxine (principal hr asst) ext 4777
Atkinson, Jessica (snr hr asst) ext 4781
Birkenshaw, Jacqueline (hr asst) ext 4778
Light, Sheena (hr asst) ext 4779
Riddiford, Collette (hr asst) ext 4780
Breese, Ruth (hr asst) ext 4780

Staff Training & Devpt Unit
Moss, Pamela (staff devpt & training mgr) ext 4759

Bickerton, Ian (comm just trainng devt off) ext 4758
O'Kelly, Frances (comm just trainng devt off) ext 4766
Olson, Carl (crams training off) ext 4755
Morgan, Leah (nvq training & supt off) ext 4757
Lewis, Sian (training off/admin) ext 4756

Information Unit
West, Sheila (info mgr) ext 4748
Jones, Phillip W, (sen analyst) 4746
Lamprey, Margaret (analyst) ext 4750
Thomas, Irene (analyst) ext 4751
Keattch, Sue (analyst) ext 4753
Mohammed, Shamim (analyst) ext 4752
Curtis, Simon (info off) ext 4743
Arnold, Michael (info off) ext 4750

Finance Unit
Dixon, Janis (fin mgr) 4774
MacDonald, John (principal fin off) ext 4775
Arnott, Aneurin (principal fin off) ext 4776
Fowler, Ian (fin off) ext 4782
Mordecai, Kim (fin off) ext 4785
Rees, Lindsey (fin off) 4783
Cooke, Lee (fin off) ext 4784

Property/Facilities Unit
Burridge, Gareth (mgr) ext 4786
Kembery, Tracey (asst) ext 4787

IT Services Unit
Ford, Mike (mgr) ext 4768
Rees, Lisa (helpdesk mgr) ext 4761
Dalling, Stephen (snr it serv supp) ext 4763
Head, Andrew (it serv suppt) ext 4760
Hewitt, Christopher (it serv suppt) ext 4762
Pritchard, Leon (it admin asst) ext 4765

Health and Safety Unit
Johns, Chris (h&s adv) ext 4823

Trainee PO Scheme
Jenkins, Robert (mgr) ext 4822
Allen, Mike (pda) ext 5086
Evans, Robert (pda) ext 5137
Jones, Jessica (pda) ext 5135
Lyons, Amanda (pda) ext 5135

tel (01685) 728910
Cowan, Pat (pda)

tel (01792) 478182
Bouleghlimat, Abdel-Aziz (pda)
Edwards, Jeanne (pda)
Parker, Alis (pda)
Morgan, Ian (prac teach)

Cardiff & Vale of Glamorgan District
2.   33 Westgate Street
     Cardiff CF10 1JE
     tel 029 2023 2999 *fax 029-2023 0384*
     direct dial 02920 78 + ext

Brunt, Granville (aco) ext 5007
Bradbury, Susan (p, exec asst) ext 5003
Meakin, Tracey (p, exec asst) ext 5003
Summers-Atkins , Keri (business svcs co-ord) ext 5005
Jarvis, Barbara (pract teach) ext 5137
Morris, Claire (basic skills coordinator) ext 5126
Hourihan, Joanne (psychologist) ext 4219

Offender Mgmnt, High/Very High Risk
Clatworthy, Nicola (mgr) ext 5001
Atherton, Moira ext 5106
Bailey, Ken ext 5107
Davies, Gavin ext 5114
James, Debbie ext 5065
Mulligan, Diarmuid ext 5113
Vacancy ext 5112
Richardson, Denise ext 5116
Taylor, Phil ext 5111
Williams, Jo ext 5110

Victim Liaison
Watts, Amanda (pso) 5017
Wilce, Andrew (pso) 5019
Williams, Amanda (pso) 5018

Offender Mgmnt, Medium/Low Risk
Pallister, Sheila (mgr) ext 5006
Evans, Eirian (mgr) (p) ext 4990
Kirk, Tony (mgr) ext 5122
Brown, Lyndsey ext 5135
Chandler, Rachael ext 5108
Gibbons, Kathleen ext 5102
Hair, Anne ext 5109
Halsey, James ext 5130
Heaton-Jones, Saul ext 5065
Hughes, Lowri ext 5120
Hygate, Zoe ext 5102
Kasmani, Shenaz ext 5129
Mulligan, Zelda ext 5091
Morris, Graham ext 5084
Nicholson, Rachael ext 5130
Price, Sally ext 5091
Short,Cherry ext 5102
Stevens, Ellen ext 5091
Wareham, Robert ext 5130
Williams, Lisa ext 5091
Williams, Simone ext 5091
Willis, Sue ext 5107

Vacancy (pso) ext 5068

Vacancy (pso) ext 5083
Clinton, Lisa (pso) ext 5098
Evans, Bernice (pso) ext 5098
Gapper, Rhian (pso) ext 5073
Jones, Bethan (pso) ext 5073
Maidment, Sean (pso) ext 5076
Olding, Karen (pso) ext 5077
Walsh, Timothy (pso) ext 5118
Bowdery, Joanne (pso) ext 5118
Pearson, Maria (pso) ext 5133
Townsend, Lawrence (pso) ext 5076
Williams, Lucy (pso) ext 5169
Hazzard, Karl (p, pso) 4992

Interventions - Programmes
Purchase, Sue (mgr) ext 5070
David, Gerry (treatment supvr) ext 5136
Vacancy ext 5136
Vacancy ext 5139
Martin, Anne ext 5085
Baker, Byron (pso) ext 5097
Evans, Sara (pso) ext 5097
Ewing, Sashika (pso) ext 5124
Vowles, Gus (pso) ext 5140
Wareham, Karen (pso) ext 4329
McTair, Grace (pso) ext 5125
Williams, Sarah (trmt monitor) ext 5095
McNally, Aileen (pso) ext 5127
Whitcombe, Victoria ext 5127

Offender Mgmnt, Court Services
Shellens, Peter (mgr) (based at 4) ext 5050
Barker, Les ext 5058
Beck, Sandra ext 5164
Vacancy ext 5061
Vacancy ext 5062
Hearnden, Alex ext 5022
Smith, Len ext 5058
Williams, Jane ext 5062

DTTO/DRR Unit
Hughes, Gwyneth (mgr, dtto/iccp) ext 5010
Foulner, Jane ext 5067
Smith, Jeremy ext 5093
Vacancy ext 5067
Stockley, Pru (drug awareness) ext 5101
Vacancy (pso) ext 5097
Floyd, Nicola (pso) ext 4209
Thomas, Mike (pso) ext 4209

Offender Accomm/Emplt Resources Unit
Hale, Gareth (mgr) ext 5041
Guise, Anne ext 5027
Smithson, Mandy ext 5028
Wilkinson, Chris ext 5026
Mayne, Ruth (pso) ext 5025
Neale, Andrea (pso) ext 5072

3. **Interventions - Unpaid Work**
2a Lewis Street, Canton
Cardiff CF10 8JX
tel 029 2023 2999 *fax 029-2066 7870*
direct dial 029-2078 +ext

Warner, Helen (mgr)
James, Bryan (based at 2) ext 5121
Martin, Philip (qa mgr) ext 5029
Watkins, Hywel (p, qa mgr) ext 5031
Aston, Ted (cso)
Bendell, Mike (cso) ext 5030
Arthur, Stephen (cso) ext 5035
Edmunds, Nicola (cso) ext 5034
Preece, Alastair (cso) ext 5037
Jones, Dennis (cso) ext 5039
Sullivan, Steve (cso) ext 5035
Taylor, Yvonne (cso) ext 5030

Powell, Richard (cs supvr)
Bowen, William (cs supvsr)
Jefferies, Nigel (cs supvsr)
Jones, Kim (cs supvsr)
McTair, Kelly (cs supvsr)
Maidment, Liam (cs supvsr)
Hurley, Paul (cs supvsr)
Cummings, Mark (cs supvsr)
Powell, Stephen (cs supvsr)
Steer, Gerard (cs supvsr)
Thomas, Alan (cs supvsr)
Westcott, Gwynne (cs supvsr)
Zeigler, Simon (cs supvsr)
(all cs supvsr ext 5040)

4. **Cardiff Crown Court**
Cathays Park, Cardiff CF10 3NL
tel 029-2035 8460 *fax 029-2034 5705*
direct dial 029-2035 + ext

Shellens, Peter (mgr) ext
Dent, Sian ext 8897
Smith, Len ext 8893
Nicholas, Colin ext 8896
Smythe, Anne ext 8891
Williams, Joan ext 8898
Davies, Maxine (pso) ext 8895
Franklin, Anna (pso) ext 8895
Hathaway, Rebecca (pso) ext 8894
Meredith, Lacey (pso) ext 8894

5. **Cardiff Magistrates' Court**
Fitzalan Place, Cardiff CF24 1RZ
tel 029-2035 8460 *fax 029-2049 8587*
direct dial 029-2035 + ext

Somerville, Martin (mgr) ext 8463
Stone, Neil (mgr)
Alecock, Tricia (pso) ext 8462
Drew, Ian (pso) ext 8468
Vacancy (pso) ext 5044

Jones, Gill (pso) ext 8461
Norman, Julie (pso) ext 8462

Vale of Glamorgan Magistrates Court
Thompson Street, Barry CF63 4SX
tel 01446 729964 fax 01446 734180

Shellens, Peter (mgr) (based at 4)
Dent, Siân
James, Debbie
Williams, Tara
Holmes, Louise (pso)
Moyle, Gaynor (pso)

Merthyr Tydfil & Rhondda Cynon Taff District

6. 4-7 The Broadway
   Pontypridd CF37 1BA
   tel (01443) 494200 *fax (01443) 494284*
   direct dial (01443) 49+ext

   Rijnenberg, Liz (aco) ext 4272
   Sartin, Joanne (sec/pa) ext 4245
   Young, Alison (bus serv co-ord) ext 4247
   Hughes, Mike (pract teach) ext 4209

   Offender Mgmnt, Medium/Low Risk
   James, Beverly (mgr) ext 4233
   Cain, Dominic
   Crane, Alison ext 4210
   Harris, Robert ext 4208
   Hodders, Alice
   James, Heulwen
   Johnson, Emma ext 4213
   Morgan, Charlotte ext 4211
   Neville, Dean
   Andrews, Angela (pso) ext 4205
   Bennett, Suzanne (pso) ext 4208
   Davies, Siân (pso) ext 4205
   Davies, Judith (pso) ext 4236
   Cornwall, Sarah (pso) ext 4207
   Elston, Diane (pso) ext 4204
   Jones, Ceri (pso) ext 4203
   Williams, Siwan (pso) ext 4212

   Offender Mgmnt, High/Very High Risk
   Higgins, Bernard (mgr) (based at 7)
   Bebb, David ext 4276
   Boswell, Sarah ext 4270
   Eynon, John ext 4237
   Griffiths, Caroline ext 4206
   Jones, Karen (p) ext 4240
   Richards, Emma (p) ext 4241
   Roberts, Stephen ext 4268
   Sabor, Monika ext 4266

   Interventions - Programmes
   Hooper, Nicola (mgr) ext 4260
   Hegarty, Patricia ext 4259
   Bartlett, Judy (pso) ext 4260

Evans, Simon (pso) ext 4260
Gerrard, David (pso) ext 4260
Haines, Beth (pso) ext 4260
Hunt, Emma (pso) ext 4260

Offender Mgmnt, Court Services
Evans, Lynn (mgr) (based at 7)
Bedwell, Marcus ext 4241
Cox, Joanne (pso) ext 4234
Manley, Sarah (pso) ext 4235

Intensive Supervision Unit
Richards, Emma (mgr) ext 4232
Cowan, Pippa ext 4238
Hughes, Mike ext 4239
McKenzie, Lynne (pso) ext 4232
Thomas, Denise (pso) ext 4234

Interventions - Unpaid Work
Girton, Tracey (mgr) (based at 7)
Hughes, John (cso) ext 4228
Holder, Mike (cso) ext ext 4231
Robertson, Allan(cso) ext 4229
Bailyes, Andrew (cs supvsr)
Zeigler, Simon (cs supvsr)
Jones, Simon (cs supvsr)
Holland, Phillip (cs supvsr)
Williams, Gareth (cs supvsr)
Wright, Dennis (cs supvsr)

7. Oldway House, Castle Street
   Merthyr Tydfil CF47 8UJ
   tel (01685) 728900 *fax (01685) 728921*
   direct dial (01685) 72 + ext

   Rijnenberg, Liz (aco) (based at 6)
   Richards, Keith (pract teach) ext 8934

   Offender Mgmnt, Medium/Low Risk
   Mahoney, Martin (mgr) ext 8929
   Billingsley, Lee ext 8918
   Jones, Emma ext 8954
   Davies, Natalie, (pso) ext 8928
   James, Claire (pso) ext 8919
   Price, Alison (pso) ext 8917
   Thomas, Nicola (pso) ext 8917

   Offender Mgmnt, High/Very High Risk
   Higgins, Bernard (mgr) ext 8912
   Bush, Andrew ext 8915
   Lewis, Catrin ext 8914
   Yarrow, Julie ext 8916

   Offender Mgmnt, Court Services
   Evans, Lynn (mgr) ext 8912
   Haselhurst, Laura ext 8945
   Simpson, Patricia (p) ext 8926
   Beaumont, Patricia ext 8933
   Anderson, Janice (pso) ext 8923
   Evans, Paula (pso) ext 8925
   Owen, Bernadette (pso) 8932

Bailey, Johnathan (pso) 8923
Williams, Andrea (pso) ext 8931

Intensive Supervision Unit
Vacancy (mgr) (based at 6)
Thomas, Nicola (pso) ext 8913

Interventions - Programmes
Hooper, Nicola (mgr) (based at 6)
Norgrove, Ross (treatment mgr)
Bartlett, Judy (pso) ext 8905
Lafferty, Bridget (pso) ext 8932
Coleman, Phil (pso) ext 8906

Interventions - Unpaid Work
Girton, Tracey (mgr) ext 8947
Collins, Terry (qa mgr) ext 8929
Watkins, Hywel (p) ext 8920
Jones Fred (cso) ext 8908
Shemwell, Karen (cso) ext 8920
Holland, Phil (cs supvr)
Vacancy (cs supvsr)
Vacancy (cs supvr)
Powell, Gareth (cs supvr)
Richards, Ryan (cs supvr)
Hughes, Suzanne (cs supvr)
Jones, Simon (cs supvr)

Victim Liaison
Kirby, Alison (pso) ext 8913
Roberts, Margaret (pso) ext 8922

Bridgend District

8.   Tremains House
     Tremains Road **Bridgend** CF31 1TZ
     tel (01656) 674747 *fax (01656) 674702*
     direct dial(01656) 67 + ext

Attwell, Julia (aco) ext 4771
Jury, Caren (pract teach) ext 4733

Offender Mgmnt, High/Very High Risk
McAllister, Wil (mgr) ext 4719
Antrobus, Emma ext 4730
Carley, Michael ext 4837
Jackson, Jackie ext 4724
Porter, Michelle ext 4730
Rees, Paul ext 4708
Thomas, Sianelen ext 4700
Walton, Helen ext 4722
Wanklyn, Delyth ext 4723
Wybron, Stephanie ext 4735

Offender Mgmnt, Court Services
Harley, Christine (mgr) ext 4726
Allen, Graham ext 4720
Burridge, Lynne
Galvin, Suzanne (pso) ext
Hatherly, Colin (pso) ext
Hyde, Megan (pso) ext 4727

John, Pen (pso) ext 4728
Jones, Anna (pso) ext 4728
Nye, Kelly (pso) ext 4811
Richards, Leanne (pso) ext 4730
Thomas, Natalie (pso) ext 4730
Thomas, Lindsey (pso) ext 4839
Yip, Deborah (pso) (p) ext 4839

Interventions - Programmes
Harley, Christine (mgr) ext 4826
Caffrey, Emma (pso) ext 4707
Jones, Lisa (pso) ext 4707
Lewis, Joanna (pso) ext 4705
Perriam, Helen (pso) (p) ext 4825
Bagnall, Helen (pso) ext 4708
Roche, Anne (pso) ext 4706

Interventions - Unpaid Work
Durgan, Roger (mgr) (based at 9)
Vacancy (p) ext
Vacancy (cso) ext 4704
Francis, Yvonne (cso) ext 4703
Davies, Paul (cs supvr) ext 4701
Halliday, Brian (cs supvr) ext 4701
Hogg, Phillip (cs supvr) ext 4701
Payek, Christopher (cs supvr) ext 4701
Stephens, Melissa (cs supvr) ext 4701

Swansea & Neath Port Talbot District

9.   West Glamorgan House
     23 Orchard Street **Swansea** SA1 1BN
     tel (01792) 645505 *fax (01792) 478132*
     direct dial (01792) 47 + ext

Richards, Anthony (aco) ext 9322
Percival, Beverley (bus svcs co-ord) ext 9300

Offender Mgmnt, Medium/Low Risk
Parry, Adele (mgr) ext 8155
Davies, Wynne ext 8169
Evans, Heather ext 8107
Hunt, Bill ext 9326
Jones, David ext 8103
Miles, Nicholas ext 8159
Protheroe, Tammy, ext 8103
Rowlands, Emma ext 8184
Smythe, Hugh ext 8172
Tanner, Rachael ext 8119
Young, Marie ext 9395
Young, Joanne ext 8103
Budge, Steve (pso) ext 8168
Evans, Wendy (pso) ext 8164
Grimes, Sarah (pso) ext 8164
Jones, Jayne (pso) ext 9333
Mobbs, Susan (pso) ext 8153
Reece, Karan (pso) ext 8123
Richardson, Darren (pso) ext 9394
Vesuviano, Philip (pso) ext 8169

Offender Mgmnt, Medium/Low Risk
Meredith, Roger (mgr) ext 8177
Banner, Helen ext 8113
Barker, Cliff ext
Guite, Cerys ext 8113
Long, Peter ext 8114
Mason, Deanne ext 8115
Rees, Bernie ext 9317
Roberts, Colette ext 8111
Sheridan, Paula ext 9320
Codling, Jenny (pso) ext 9314
Frudd, Andrew (pso) ext 8109
Jones, Gillian (pso) ext 8106
Sparks, Ian (pso) ext 9339
McClure, Irene (pso) ext 8173

Offender Mgmnt, High/Very High Risk
Colbeck, David (mgr) ext 9323
Costigan, Rachel ext 9326
Goodman, Gail ext 9328
Hughes, David ext 9331
James, Paul ext 9329
Lewis, Audra ext 8121
Osuji, Ian ext 9301
Rees, Julie ext 9303
Tyler, Sue ext 9327
Stringer, Sue ext 9328

Interventions - Programmes
Turner , Monica (mgr) ext 9348
Jones, Ray (treatment mgr) ext 9356
Parry, Helen ext 9358
Vacancy (pso, trmt monitor) ext 9357
Thomas, Sharon ext 9351
Adams, Lynne (pso) ext 9360
Davies, Dorian (pso) ext 9349
Jones, Ian (pso) ext 9350
Lewis, Hannah (pso) ext 9349
Frame, Susan (pso)
Slee, Laura (pso) ext 9359
Thomas, Chantal (pso) ext ext 9359

Offender Mgmnt, Court Services
Maynard, David (mgr) ext 9324
Beckers, Helen ext 9317
Francis, Anne ext 9316
Glennie, Wendy ext 9319
Vacancy ext 9337
Jones, Graham ext 9336
Vacancy ext 9315
McDonald, Edna ext 9318
Rabaiotti, Ella ext 9321
Thorne, Alicia ext 9320
Evans, Sheila (pso) ext 9328
Hale, Phil (pso) ext 9338
Kovacs, Tine (pso) ext 9339
Lewis, Libby (pso) ext 9328
Poiner, Bev (pso) ext 9343
Steadman, Joanne (pso) ext 9338

Thomas, Jane (pso) ext 9342
Williams, Kerry (pso) ext 9340
Wolsey, Joanne (pso) ext 9396

Intensive Supervision Unit
Roberts, Collette (mgr) ext 8177
Walsh, Jed ext 8136
Hyett, Wendy ext 9393
Oscowitz, Debbie ext 8131
Davies, Ian (pso) 8153

Victim Liaison
Sculluion, Rachel (pso) ext 9333
Kircough, Anne (pso) ext 9334
Lewis, Joanna (pso) ext 9335

Interventions - Unpaid Work
Durgan, Roger (mgr) ext 8193
Davies, Peter ext 8192
Nantel, Caroline ext 8134
Fraser, Tony (qual ass mgr) ext 8198
Meadowcroft, Sarah (cso) 8121
Jenkins, Eifion (cso) ext 8133
Llewellyn, Einir (cso) ext 8129
Lewis, Helen (cso)
Matthews Fred (cso) ext 8127
Fox, Melanie (pso) ext 8192
Morse-Jones, Simon (cso) ext 8192
Stock, Nathan (cs supvr)
Evans, Alwyn (cs supvr)
Griffiths, Nigel (cs supvr)
Morgan, Andrew (cs supvr)
Stephens, Melissa (cs supvr)
Seabright, Chris (cs supvr)
Uzzell, Laurence (cs supvr)
Williams, Noel (cs supvr)

Hughes, Alison (perf admin) 8186
Bolton, Alison (prog admin) ext 9352

10. **Swansea Crown Court**
St Helens Road, Swansea SA1 4PF
tel (01792) 461381 *fax (01792) 457783*

Maynard, David (mgr) (based at 8)
Richards, Claire (pso)
Richards, Susan (pso)
Stokes, Trisha (pso)

11. **Youth Offending Teams**

Bridgend Youth Offending Team
Tremains House, Tremains Road
Bridgend CF31 1TZ
tel (01656) 657243 *fax (01656) 648218*

Maddocks, Goodman

Cardiff Youth Offending Team
Penhill, The Rise, Cardiff CF11 9PR
tel 029 2056 0839 *fax 029-2057 8746*

Fairie, Sonia
Waite, Leny

Merthyr Tydfil Youth Offending Team
Merthyr CBC Youth Justice, 47-48
Pontmorlais Centre,
Merthyr Tydfil CF47 8UN
tel (01685) 389304 *fax (01685) 359726*

Lewis, Stephanie

Neath Port Talbot Youth Offending Team
Cramic Way, Port Talbot SA13 1RU
tel (01639) 885050 *fax (01639) 882809*

Hinder, Vic

Rhondda Youth Offending Team
Unit 2, Fairway Court, Tonteg Road
Treforst Industrial Estate, Pontypridd
CF37 5UA
tel (01443) 827300 *fax (01443) 827301*

Davies, Cheryl
Morgan, Charlotte
O'Brien, Michael (pso)

Swansea Youth Offending Team
Llwyncelyn Campus
Cockett Road, Cockett
Swansea SA2 0SJ
tel (01792) 522800 *fax (01792) 522805*

Hoare, Philip (snr pract)
James, Jackie

Vale Youth Offending Team
91 Salisbury Road, Barry
Vale of Glamorgan CF62 6PD
tel (01446) 745820 *fax (01446) 739549*

Crombie, Moyra
Watkins, Leon

12. **Intensive Supervision - DRR Offices**

Bridgend DRR/DTTO
38a Caroline Street
Bridgend CF31 1DO
tel (01656) 769009 *fax (01656) 647402*

Roberts, Collette (mgr)
Apreda, Claire
Rowlands, Eleri
Jenkins, Kate
Brown, Reg (pso)

Cardiff DRR/DTTO
57/59 St Mary Street
Cardiff CF10 1FE
tel 029-2022 7327 *fax 029-2037 6252*

Hughes, Gwyneth (mgr)

Suggett, Hannah
Sheppard, Anita
Lucking, Bethan
Thomas, Michael (pso)
Wools, Emma (pso)
Pearce-Cundle, Donna (pso)
Jones, Eirwen (admin off)

Pontypridd DRR/DTTO
4-7 The Broadway
Pontypridd CF37 1BA
tel (01443) 494200 *fax (01443) 494284*

Fisher-Sharp, Tracey (pso)
Howells, Cliff (pso)

Swansea DRR/DTTO
West Glamorgan House, 23 Orchard Street
Swansea SA1 1BN
tel (01792) 645505

Roberts, Collette (mgr) (based at 9)
O'Malley, Chris
Dyer, Charlotte
Ganz, Lisa (pso)
Lee, Peter (pso)

12a. **S Wales Area MAPPA Unit**
Public Protection Bureau
Police HQ, Cowbridge Road
Bridgend CF31 3SU
tel (01656) 306043/48 *fax (01656) 303464*

Rees, Nigel (co-ord)
Francis, Kate (admin)

Hostels
Ace, Christine (aco) (based at 1)

13. **Mandeville House Bail Hostel**
9 Lewis Street, Canton
Cardiff CF10 8JY
tel 029 2039 4592 & 029-2023 2999 ext 4530
fax 029-2023 3857

Merriman, John (team mgr)
Barnes-Ceeney, Kevin (dep mgr)
Driscoll, Janice (app prem serv off)
Vacancy (app prem serv off)
Lundbech, Dave (app prem serv off)
Barrett, Nicola (app prem serv off)
Vacancy (app prem serv off)
Batten , Edgar (waking night supvr)
Vacancy (waking night supvr)
Miles, Kay (admin)

14. **Quay House Probation Hostel**
The Strand, Swanea SA1 2AW
tel (01792) 641259 *fax (01792) 641268*

Protheroe, Anne (team mgr)

John, Chris (dep mgr)
Howells, Simon (app prem serv off)
Jones, Alan (app prem serv off)
Vacancy (app prem serv off)
Oakley, Angela (app prem serv off)
Williams, Nigel (app prem serv off)
Edwards, Alan (waking night supvr)
Jones, William (waking night supvr)
Bevan, Helen (admin)

Institutions
Chaplin, Janet (aco) (based at 1)

15. HM Prison
Knox Road, **Cardiff** CF24 1UG
tel 029-2043 3100 *fax 029-2043 3318*

Gibbins, Chantal (mgr)
Evans, Leighton
Bicknell, Helen
Edwards, Meinir
Evans, Margaret (pso)
Davies, Siobhan (pso)
Vacancy (pso)
Wanty, Simon (pso)

16. HM Prison **Parc**
Heol Hopcyn John, Bridgend CF35 6AR
tel (01656) 300200 *fax (01656) 300201*

Smith Rachel (mgr)
Bray, Anthony
Edwards, Huw
Fenuik, Jan
Williams, Emma
Vacancy (pso)
Francis, Sean (pso)
Thomas, Nicola (pso)
Wadlow, Maxine (pso)
Wybron, Nicola (pso)

17. HM Prison
Oystermouth Road **Swansea** SA1 3SR
tel (01792) 464030 *fax (01792) 632979*

Lewis, Jill (mgr)
Howells, Wynford
Thomas, Donna
Edwards, Suzanne (pso)
Evans, Vivian (pso)
Alexander, Leslie (pso)
Powell, Andrew (pso)

Secondments

Williams, Tudor (aco) seconded to NPD
Zammit, Ingrid (team mgr) seconded to NOMS
Smith, Earl (team mgr) seconded to Welsh Assembly

Pickles, Janet (po) seconded to Womens Safety Unit Cardiff
Routledge, Steve (exec off) seconded to LCJB

Petty Sessional Areas

2 Cardiff
6 Cynon Valley
7 Merthyr Tydfil
6 Miskin
8 Newcastle & Ogmore
9 Neath Port Talbot
9 Swansea County
2 Vale of Glamorgan

Crown Courts

4 Cardiff
7 Merthyr Tydfil
10 Swansea

NORTHERN IRELAND

Northern Ireland Office
Criminal Justice Services Division
Massey House, Stoney Road
Belfast BT4 3SX
tel 028-9052 7348

The NIO is the sponsoring Department for the Probation Board for Northern Ireland. Criminal Justices Services Division develops and supports the legislative and policy environment in which PBNI operates. In conjunction with the Department's Financial Services Division, CSJD ensures that the Board carries out its activities within the overall policy and resources framework set by the Secretary of State; and adheres to the requirements and procedures attaching to its expenditure of public money.

Statistics and Research Branch
Massey House, Stoney Road
Belfast BT4 3SX
tel 028-9052 7534

The Branch supplies professional statistical and research advice and services to the Northern Ireland Office. It also disseminates statistical and research information via requests from parliament, academia, official publications and the public in general.

Northern Ireland Prison Service
Dundonald House, Upper Newtownards Road
Belfast BT4 3SU
tel 028-9052 2922

The NI Prison Service is responsible for policy on all aspects of the treatment of prisoners in Northern Ireland. It provides that part of the Probation Board for Northern Ireland budget relating to probation staff who work within prison establishments. In addition it administers the Boards of Visitors and Visiting Committee, which oversee the running of prisons on behalf of the public. It has responsibility for pre-release Home Leave Schemes including the Compassionate Temporary Release Scheme, Home Leave at Christmas and the Home Visits Scheme. It has responsibility for the management of all casework relating to life sentence prisoners, including that relating to review and release through the preparation and submission of dossiers to the Life Sentence Review Commissioners.

Criminal Justice Inspection, Northern Ireland
14 Great Victoria Street, Belfast BT2 7BA
Under the Justice (Northern Ireland) Act 2002, the new Criminal Justice Inspectorate took over from the Social Services Inspectorate responsibility for inspection of the Probation Board for Northern Ireland. CJI is responsible for inspecting all the criminal justice agencies in Northern Ireland, except for Courts.

Chief Inspector
Kit Chivers 028-9025 8001

Deputy Chief Inspector
Brendan McGuigan 028-9025 8002

Inspector
Tom McGonigle, 028-9025 8003

e-mail firstname.surname@cjini.gov.uk

PROBATION BOARD FOR NORTHERN IRELAND

Emergency out of hours contact point:
028-9066 1629

e-mail firstname.surname@pbni.org.uk

1. **Head Office**
    80/90 North Street, Belfast BT1 1LD
    tel 028-9026 2400 *fax 028-9026 2470*

    Rooney, Noel (chief executive)
    McCaughey, Brian (dir of operations)
    van der Merwe, David (dir corp services)
    Doran, Paul (aco)

Hamill, Hugh (aco)
Kelly, Graham (aco)
Lamont, Ms Cheryl (aco)
Rooke, Andrew(aco)
Moss, Peter (secy to the board)
Hill, Frank (hr mgr)
McCrory, Miss Gayle (training mgr)
McCutcheon, Brian (it mgr)
Bailie, Ms Rosemary (mgr)
Maginnis, Mrs Lisa (pr/communications)

Information Services Team
tel 028-9026 2468 *fax 028-9026 2470*

McRoberts, Mrs Claire (p, mgr)
Ferguson, Philip (sp loc)
Reid, Maurice
Willighan, Stephen

Assessment Unit
tel 028-9026 2400 *fax 028-9026 2472*

O'Hare Miss Rita (mgr)
Lappin, Ms Jane (p, mgr)
Bartlett, Ms Patricia
Calvin, Mrs Marilyn (p)
Carville, Ms Carol
Conlon, John
Cumming, Miss Mary (p)
Gillespie, Mrs Barbara
MacNeill, Eoin
McKelvey, Miss Claire
Matthews, Jim
Murphy, Ms Christine
O'Neill, Mrs Oonagh (p)
O'Shea, Ms Johanna
Reynolds, Ms Aisling
Richardson, Mrs Eileen
Robinson-McDonald, Mrs Rosaleen
Smith, Ms Helen
Jordan, Robert (pso)
Milburn, Mrs Rhonda (pso)
Mottram, Ronald (pso)
McIlveen, Paul (pso)
Nawaz, Mrs Eileen (pso)

Psychology Department
tel 028-9026 2408 *fax 028-9026 2472*
O'Hare, Ms Geraldine (principal psych)
Jordan, Robin (trainee forensic psych)

1a **Training Unit**
Unit 5, Antrim Technology Park
Belfast Road, Antrim BT41 1QS
tel 028-9446 5421 *fax 028-9446 3935*

Cavan, Mrs Mary (p)
Christie, Ms Patricia (p)
Hill, Kieran
Maguire, Ms Catherine (p)

McGibbon, Gareth
Rainey, Mrs Lindsay (p)

2. **330 Ormeau Road**
Belfast BT7 2GE
tel 028-9064 7156 *fax 028-9064 1409*

McCusker, Paul (mgr 8,9,9a)
Greer, Bill
Lenzi, Ms Shauneen
Malone, Mrs Caitriona (p)
McClinton, Ms Janet (p)
McMahon, Fergal
Vaughan, Ms Fiona

3. Unit 4, Wallace Studios
27 Wallace Avenue
Lisburn BT27 4AE
tel 028 9267 4211 *fax 028-9260 4018*

Best, Mrs Pat (p, mgr, training)
McAllister, Mrs Eileen (mgr, risk)
Coogan, Ms Nicola
McCann, Kevin

4. **306 Antrim Road**
Belfast BT15 5AB
tel 028-9075 7631 *fax 028-9074 3983*

McKenna, Jane (area mgr)
McAuley, Ms Nicola
McGlade, Ian
McKee, Ms Mary (isu)
Mills, Rory
Mooney, Angela
Ramsey, Ms Angela
Watson, Ms Sarah
Potts, Gordon (pso)

5. **93-107 Shankill Road**
Belfast BT13 1FD
tel 028-9032 1141 *fax 028-9031 3334*

contact Office 4

6. Glenshane House
202a Andersonstown Road
Belfast BT11 9EB
tel 028-9060 2988 *fax 028-9061 9313*

Grant, Ms Deirdre
McKenna, Miss Gloria
Paterson, Ms Carolyn (youth justice)
Maitland, Michael (pso)

7. **270-272 Falls Road**
Belfast BT12 6AL
tel 028-9023 1763 *fax 028-9032 6280*

Arthur, Mrs Liz (mgr) (3,6)
Gately Ms Madonna

Johnston, Ms Emma
McKee, Ms Briege
Rutledge, Ms Alison
Quail, Ms Moira (acting po)

8. **297 Newtownards Road**
Belfast BT4 1AG
tel 028-9073 9445 *fax 028-9046 0119*

Doran, Ms Andrea
Dougan, Mrs Carol
McKee, Chris
Nethercott, Ray (pso)
Watters, Ms Eilis (pso)

9. 15 Castle Street
Newtownards BT23 3PA
tel 028-9181 7778 *fax 028-9181 8905*

Breen, Mrs Siobhan
Ritchie, Jim (isu)
Wylie, David

10. 2 Church Street
Downpatrick BT30 6EJ
tel 028-4461 4061 *fax 028-4461 2506*

reporting centre only

11. 12 Lodge Road
Coleraine BT52 1NB
tel 028-7035 3141 *fax 028-7035 2442*

Doherty, Terry (mgr, multi agency
procedures for assessment & management
of sex offenders [masram])
Archibald, Ms Julie
Holmes, Ms Paula
Lees, Ray
Meenan, Paul (p)
Turner, Ms Seanagh
Mooney, Mrs Bernadette (pso)
Nelis, Liam (p, pso)
Quigley, Mrs Marlyn (pso)
Walsh, Seamus (pso)

12. The Bridge House, 106 Bridge Street
Ballymena BT43 5EP
tel 028-2565 2549 *fax 028-2565 5523*

Smyth, Miss Julie (mgr) (11)
Rodgers, Ms Brigie (proj mgr)
Curran, Ms Lisa
Wiseman, Paul
Wilson, Mrs Dorothy
Grace, Vincent (pso)
McMullan, Mrs Joanne (pso)
Nelis, Liam (p, pso)
Walsh, Seamus (pso)
Wilkinson, Stephen (pso)

13. 8 Crawford Square
     Londonderry BT48 7HR
     tel 028-7126 4774 *fax 028-7126 7374*

     O'Kane, John (mgr) (14)
     Clifford, Miss Briege
     Devlin, Ms Anne
     Dorsett, Ms Caroline
     Higgins, Michael
     Lennox, Ms Julie
     Nash, Miss Martina
     O'Hagan, John

14. 7 Limavady Road
     Londonderry BT47 1JU
     tel 028-7134 6701 *fax 028-7134 1034*

     Archibald, Ms Selina
     Barr, Mrs Nicola
     Dunlop, Raymond
     McGuire, Miss Leah
     Monaghan, Ms Siobhan
     Wetherall, Miss Kathleen
     Ferguson, Liam (pso)
     Kelly, Mrs Donna (pso)
     Nightingale, Tim (p, pso)

15. 38 Fountain Street
     Antrim BT41 4BB
     tel 028-9442 8475 *fax 028-9446 9123*

     Graham, Ms Joan (mgr) (16, 17, 18)
     Dyer, Paddy
     McClintock, Ms Liz
     McMillan, Mrs Pauline
     Ralph, Chris
     Teacy, Ms Andrea
     Rainey, Stuart (pso)

16. Tower House, 33-35 High Street
     Carrickfergus BT38 7AN
     tel 028-9336 2088 *fax 028-9336 3049*

     Parry, John
     Winnington, Michael

17. 41 Point Street
     Larne BT40 1HU
     tel 028-2827 9231 *fax 028-2827 5990*

     Hobson, Mrs Bronwyn
     Hamill, Mrs Sheila (pso)

18. 123 Doagh Road
     Newtownabbey BT37 9QP
     tel 028-9085 4123 *fax 028-9086 4158*

     contact Carrickfergus office

19. 1d Monaghan Street
     Newry BT35 6BB
     tel 028-3026 3955 *fax 028-3026 9548*

     Hamilton, Stephen
     Lamb, Mrs Linda (p)
     Nelson, Miss Paula

20. McGredy Buildings, 31-33 High Street
     Portadown BT62 1HY
     tel 028-3833 3301 *fax 028-3839 4334*

     Thompson, Paul (mgr) (19, 25)
     Ferguson, Philip (sp loc)
     McEvoy, Niall
     Quigley, John
     Smyth, Ms Stephanie
     McCreery, David (pso)
     Murray, Ms Tracey (trainee forensic psych)

21. 11A High Street
     Omagh BT78 1BA
     tel 028-8224 6051 *fax 028-8224 8437*

     Devlin, Paul (mgr) (22, 23, 24)
     Brady, Mrs Julie
     Carty, Ms Selina
     Doran, Mrs Mary (p)
     Montgomery, Harry
     McKelvey, Ms Ruth (p)
     McLaughlin, Terry
     McCrory, Thomas (pso)

22. 14 Dublin Road, Cathcart Square
     Enniskillen BT74 6HH
     tel 028-6632 4383 *fax 028-6632 5988*

     Connolly, Gary
     Cunningham, Ms Julie
     Flynn, Mrs Susan
     McKeever, Mrs Patricia
     Montgomery, Harry

23. 58 Loy Street
     Cookstown BT80 8PE
     tel 028-8676 1211 *fax 028-8676 6276*

     Feeney, Ms Geraldine
     Quigg, Ms Martina

24. 30 Northland Row
     Dungannon BT71 6AP
     tel 028-8772 2866 *fax 028-8775 2318*

     Johnston, Ms Jo-anne
     McCann, Dermot
     Devlin, Fiona (pso)
     Powell, Gary (pso)

25. 25 College Street
Armagh BT61 9BT
tel 028-3752 5243 *fax 028-3752 8530*

Grant, Mrs Michelle
Montgomery, Miss Gillian
Wylie, Mrs Margaret
Abernethy, Ms Jayne (pso)
Donaldson, Victor (pso)
Doran, Miss Nicola (pso)
Hanna, Ms Elizabeth (pso)
Hazlett, Miss Louise (pso)

26. **40-44 Great Patrick Street**
Belfast BT1 2LT
tel 028-9033 3332 *fax 028-9043 8990*

Programme Delivery Unit
Leckey, Mrs Roisin (p, mgr)
Cubillo, Bill
Cummings, Kyle
Hopkins, Mrs Shirley (p)
McCourt, Miss Eileen
Tracey, Damien
Woods, Mrs Geraldine (p)
McWilliams, Ms Jacqueline
Johnston, David (pso)
Nicholl, Ms Irene (pso)
Scroggie, Mrs Shauna (pso)
Shields, Miss Claire (pso)
McClenaghan, Joe (probn comm off)

Prison Link Team
tel 028-9028 4848 *fax 028-9059 2959*
Darnbrook, Alan (po mgr, lifer
resettlement)
Keenan, Mrs Bernie (family wrkr)

27. **Alderwood House (Integrated
Supervision Unit)**
Hydebank Wood, Purdysburn Road
Belfast BT8 7SL
tel 028-9064 4953 *fax 028-9064 1435*

Muldoon, Ms Roisin (mgr)
Owens, Mrs Val (mgr)
Armstrong, Miss Nichola
Boyle, Thomas
McCarthy, Vincent
McSherry, Mrs Tina
O'Loughlin, Ms Kathryn
Simpson, Ms Simone
McVeigh, Ms Josie (pco)

28. **Ramoan Centre**
The Old Rectory, 11 Novally Road
Ballycastle, Co Antrim BT54 6HB
tel 028-2076 2835 *fax 028-2076 9698*

29. **Impact (Inclusive Model of
Partnership Against Car Theft)**
Sally Gardens Community Centre
Sally Gardens Lane
Belle Steele Road
Poleglass, Belfast BT17 0PB
tel 028-9062 7321 *fax 028-9062 9428*

Millar, Paul (operations mgr) seconded
Gadd, Tim (pso Impact)
Gray, Miss Laura (pso Impact)
McKenna, Ms Lorraine (temp pso)
Picard, Miss Maya (temp pso)
Watson, Gary (pso)

30. **Victim Information Scheme**
Office 40, Imperial Buildings
High Street, Belfast
tel 028 9032 1972 *fax 028 9032 1973*

Hunter, Mrs Christine (p spo mgr)
McCaughey, Miss Mary

31. **PROTECT N&S**
*(Probation reducing offending
through enhanced co-operation &
training North and South)*
Unit 4 Wallace Studios
27 Wallace Avenue
Lisburn BT27 4AE
tel 028 9264 1268 fax 028 9262 7812

Moore, Jimmy (spo, team ldr/proj co-ord)

32. **Youth Justice Team**
330 Ormeau Road, Belfast, BT7 2GE
tel 028 9031 3162 *fax 028 9023 5297*

Bourke, John (mgr)
Cahir, Seamus
Mullan, Ms Brigeen
Nelson, Ms Kathy
Weatherup, Miss Laura

Institutions

33. Welfare Unit
H M Prison **Magilligan**
Co Londonderry BT49 0LR
tel 028-7775 0434/5 *fax 028-7775 0312*

Shiels, Mrs Marlene (mgr)
Canning, Ms Donna
Cunningham, Mrs Bernie
McConomy, Martin
McWilliams, Ms Gil
O'Donnell, Noel
Pegg, Ms Jackie
Quigley, Michael

34. Welfare Unit
    Hydebank Wood
    Hospital Road, Belfast BT8 8NA
    tel 028-9049 1015 *fax 028-9064 2868*

    O'Neill, Mrs Jean (p, mgr)
    Ball, Mrs Rosemary (p)
    Bell, Mrs Lesley (p)
    Burns, Michael
    Shaw, Stephen
    Taylor, Mrs Siobhan (p)
    Weir, Mrs Stephanie (p)

35. Welfare Unit
    HM Prison **Maghaberry**
    17 Old Road, Upper Ballinderry
    Lisburn BT28 2PT
    tel 028-9261 2665 *fax 028-9261 9976*

    Connolly, Mike (mgr)
    Barry, Mrs Patricia
    Brush, Ms Jacqueline
    Haslett, Ms Andrea
    Nicholson, Mark
    O'Neill, Mrs Noreen (p)
    Rooke, Mrs Genivene
    Sheppard, Paul
    Sloan, Ms Allison

On Secondment

    Davies, Chris (mgr)
    Dempsey, Colin
    Maguire, Ms Catherine (p)
    Moore, Mrs Donna
    Murphy, Ms Deirdre
    Roberson, Ms Brigid

On career break

    Brannigan, Miss Oonagh
    Sands, Miss Caroline (p)

REPUBLIC OF IRELAND PROBATION & WELFARE SERVICE
Seirbhís Phromhaidh agus Leasa

Abbreviations
appwo Assistant Principal Probation & Welfare
Officer
spwo Senior Probation & Welfare Officer
where no letters appear after a name, that
person is a Probation & Welfare Officer

Dialing from UK 00 (international code) 353
(country code) and omit the first 0 of the local
code (so, for example, for the Headquarters dial
00 353 1 817 3600)

1. **Headquarters**
    Smithfield Chambers
    Smithfield, Dublin 7
    tel 01 817 3600 *fax 01 872 2737*

    Donnellan, Michael (director)
    Connolly, Anna (appwo)
    Cotter, Anthony (appwo)
    Dack, Brian (appwo)
    Dooley, Marie (appwo)
    Geiran, Vivian (appwo)
    Kennedy, Ciaran, (appwo)
    McNally, Gerry (appwo)
    O'Donovan, David (appwo)
    Vella, Suzanne (appwo)
    O'Hare, Maeve (spwo)
    Willliamson, David (spwo)

    Cawley, Leona (admin)
    Commins, Pat (admin)
    Fay, Margaret (admin)
    Grimes, Carmel (admin)
    Healy, Fran (admin)
    Irwin, Paula (admin)
    Jordan, Karen (admin)
    Jordan, Lisa (admin)
    Kelly, Sarah (admin)
    O'Doherty, Fiona (admin)
    Sweeney, William (admin)

    Brennan, Natasha (i.t.)
    Cummins, Yvonne (i.t.)
    Hennessy, Shane (i.t.)
    O'Keeffe, Karen (i.t.)
    Rodgers Noreen (i.t.)

    Benson, Gerry (spwo)
    Fallon, Oliver
    Gates, Paul
    Groome, Tommy
    Kelly, Frankie
    O'Sullivan, Mary

    Macken, Nuala (spwo)
    Kavanagh, Elaine
    Murphy, Dave
    O'Byrne, Ambrose
    Quinn, Kerry
    Ryan, Cathy

    Doyle, Una (spwo)
    Bailey, Daragh
    Burke, Brigetta
    Clarke, Susan
    Nagle, Susan
    O'Reilly, Elaine

Santry, Brian (spwo)
Balfe, John
Commins, Susan
Hickey, Bernadette
Moss, Brian
McCarthy, Elizabeth
O'Connell, Valerie
O'Sullivan, Cathal

Linnane, Paul (spwo)
Connolly, Aine
Glynn, David
Kelly, Lorraine
O'Dwyer, Geraldine

Cronin, Rosemary (spwo)
McDermott, Michelle
Stretton-Kelly, Eadaoin

Jennings, Pat (spwo)
Henley, Karen
Wason, Laura
Treacy, Patricia (admin)
Shields, Susan

Carlin, Tony (spwo)
Curtis, Victoria
Dowling, Sorcha
Mulpeter, Maria
Pickles, Rob
Timoney, Lena

2.   Second Floor Office Block
     Donaghmede Shopping Centre
     Grange Road **Donaghmede** Dublin 13
     tel 01 816 6800 *fax 01 816 6801*

Leetch, Judith (spwo)
Corrigan, John
Dooley, Niamh
Keane, Linda
McCarthy, Justin
McNally, Maggie
Purcell, Denise
Lawlor, Therese (admin)
Moore, Karen (admin)

Ailish Glennon (spwo)
Brennan, Claire
Fisher, Sean
Keogh, Valerie
O'Toole, Ann-Marie

3.   Unit 3, Parnell Business Centre
     24 Parnell Street Dublin 1
     tel 01 814 6760 *fax 01 814 6762*

Gibbons, Maria (spwo)
Connell, Brian
Jones, Steve
Kelly, Paula

Loughrey, Sile
McNamara, Suzanne
Murphy, Elaine
Smith, Eimear
Brady, Margaret (admin)

4.   Poppintree Mall
     Finglas Dublin 11
     tel 01 864 4011 *fax 01 864 3416*

Hanna, Emer (spwo)
Condon, Johanna
Devine, Corina
Foley, Elizabeth
Morris, Aine
Moylan, Breda
Trant, Aidan
Lawlor, Breda (admin)
Smith, Brenda (admin)

5.   Le Fanu Road,
     Ballyfermot Dublin 10
     tel 01 623 3621 *fax 01 323 3737*

O'Connor, Ciara (spwo)
Carolan, Patricia
Kearney, Ian
Nichol, Derek
Ryan, Mary
Connaughton, Linda (admin)

6.   Mark's Lane, Neilstown Road
     Clondalkin Dublin 22
     tel 01 623 6230 *fax 01 623 6236*

Brooks, Veronica
Canty, Lena
Cowzer, Elaine
Devine, Andrea
Keane, Ann Marie
Aughney, Brenda (admin)
Gibson, Marguerite (admin)

7.   390-396 Clonard Road,
     Crumlin Dublin 12
     tel 01 492 5625 *fax 01 492 5631*

Rynn, Anna (appwo)
McGagh, Mary (spwo)
Kavanagh, Siobhan
Lavin, Dermot
McCabe, Paddy
Trainor, Mary
Doyle, Maria (admin)

Foley, Tony (spwo)
Bentley, Philip
Buckley, Hilary
Kane, Tara

McGinley, Gabrielle
O'Brien, Maria
Rock, Mark
Callery, Dot (admin)

Staff Development Unit
Fernee, Ursula (spwo)
Geiran, Elaine

8. Westpark **Tallaght**
    Dublin 24
    tel 01 462 3033 *fax 01 462 3767*

    Horgan, Brian (spwo)
    Alvey, Jan
    Charles, Anita
    Dalton, Neville
    Downey, Pauline
    Farrell, Eileen
    McMahon, Kathryn
    O'Reilly, Dorothy
    Ward, Liz (admin)

9. Foundation House
    Northumberland Avenue
    Dun Laoghaire Co. Dublin
    tel 01 230 1860 *fax 01 230 1870*

    Wilson, Mark (spwo)
    Corcoran, Catherine
    Darragh, Sandra
    Donnelly, Declan
    King, Jim
    Morahan, Marion
    O'Doherty, Ann
    Needham, Mavis
    Twomey, Anne
    Johnson, Elizabeth (admin)

Prisons Region 1

10. **Arbour Hill Prison**
    Arbour Hill, Dublin 7
    tel 01 671 9519 *fax 01 671 9565*

    Clark, Nick
    Murphy, Andrew

11. **Cloverhill Remand Prison**
    Cloverhill Road,
    Clondalkin, Dublin 22
    tel 01 630 4680 *fax 01 630 4580*

    O'Sullivan, Donal (spwo)
    Gilmore, Irene

12. **Cloverhill Courthouse**
    Cloverhill Road,
    Clondalkin, Dublin 22
    tel 01 630 4942

O'Farrell, Ann
Richardson, Michelle
Joyce, Phyllis (admin)

13. **Wheatfield Place of Detention**
    Cloverhill, Dublin 22
    tel 01 626 0021 fax 01 623 7439

    Reade, Anne (spwo)
    Cahill-Hughes, Sharon
    Christie, Irene
    Cowzer, Elaine
    Phibbs, Tracey
    O'Neill, Jenny (admin)

Prisons Regions 2

14. **Mountjoy Prison**
    North Circular Road, Dublin 7
    tel 01 806 2834 *fax 01 830 2712*

    O'Brien McNamara, Joan (spwo)
    Algottson-Gallagher, Anna
    Farry, Néasan
    Kelly, Janice
    Monks, Ethna
    O'Sullivan, Sarah

    Moore, Mary (spwo)
    Anderson, Lisa
    Broderick, Geraldine
    Duffy, Paul
    Zagibova, Danica
    Reid, Pauline (admin)

    O'Donoghue, Liz (spwo)
    Doyle, Barbara
    McFadden, Neil
    O'Neill, Martina

15. **St Patrick's Institution**
    North Circular Road, Dublin 7
    tel 01 806 2941 *fax 01 830 1261*

    Kelly, James (spwo)
    Connor, Siobhan
    Lillis, Rachel
    Matthews, Deirdre
    Milne, Sarah
    Kenny, Renee (admin)

16. **Oberstown Special School**
    Lusk, Co. Dublin
    tel 01 843 8600 *fax 01 843 8619*

    Campbell, Fiona

17. **Trinity House School**
    Lusk, Co. Dublin
    tel 01 843 7811 *fax 01 843 8932*

    Kearney, Lisa

Mid West Region

18. The Crescent, Ballymahon Road
    Athlone Co. Westmeath
    tel 090 648 3500 *fax 090 647 5843*

    Kilcommins, John (dppwo)
    Murray, David (spwo)
    Byrne Fallon, Collette
    Gavin, Alma
    Tansey, Liam
    Carney, Mary (admin)
    Ward, Enda (admin)

19. Mill House, Friar's Mill Road,
    Mullingar Co. Westmeath.
    tel 044 35666 *fax 044 35663*

    Hartley, Moya
    Ryder, Tom

20. Government Buildings
    Shannon Lodge
    Carrick on Shannon
    Co. Leitrim
    tel 078 20966 *fax 078 21230*

    Murray, Aine

21. **Midlands Prison**
    Dublin Road,
    Portlaoise, Co. Laois
    tel 0502 72210 *fax 0502 72209*

    Coakley, Deirdre (spwo)
    Doyle, Alan
    Duke, Eileen
    Kenny, Dave
    Hanlon, Joy
    Heffernan-Price, Majella
    Leonard, Sinead
    Delahunt, Claire (admin)

22. Government Buildings
    Abbeyleix Road,
    Portlaoise Co. Laois
    tel 0502 244644 *fax 0502 60218*

    McGlynn, Rex (spwo)
    Boyle, Jennifer
    Cuddy, Pat
    Cummins, Mary
    Fahy, Caroline
    Scully, Agnes
    Walshe, Ann
    Mannion, Carmel (admin)

23. Abbey Arch
    8 Upper Abbeygate Street
    Galway Co. Galway.

    tel 091 565375 *fax 091 567286*

    Prendergast, Margaret (spwo)
    Egan, Pat
    Ganly, Sheila
    Halpin, Mary
    Halpin, Una
    Mannion, John
    Mulligan, Noirin
    Quinlan, Sheila
    Hannon, Claire (admin)
    O'Grady, Marion (admin)

    Staff Development
    Boylan, John

24. Harristown House, Harristown,
    Castlerea Co. Roscommon
    tel 094 962 1400 *fax 094 962 1440*

    Quinlan, Judy

Northern Region

25. Government Buildings
    Cranmore Road,
    Sligo Co. Sligo.
    tel 071 914 5203 *fax 071 914 4840*

    Devine, Josephine (spwo)
    Halligan, Colin
    Leahy, Denise
    Myles, Bridget
    Meehan Eileen (admin)

26. 1st Floor, 3 Castle Street,
    Sligo
    tel 071 914 1616 *fax 071 914 9937*

    Cooney, Paula (appwo)
    Dellar, Val (admin)

27. De la Salle Arcade
    Castlebar Co. Mayo
    tel 094 902 1511 *fax 094 902 4961*

    Dunne, Colm (spwo)
    Brett, Maeve
    Morrin, Helena
    Sheppard, Sue
    Tallon, Miriam
    Duffy, Siobhan (admin)

28. **Castlerea Prison**
    Harristown, Castlerea,
    Co. Mayo.
    tel/fax 094 962 5277

    Connolly, Kieran

29. 48-50 Lower Main Street
    Letterkenny Co. Donegal
    tel 074 912 5264 *fax 074 912 6008*

    Coughlan, Tim
    Duke, Anne
    Friel, Breda

30. Loughan House
    Blacklion Co. Cavan
    tel/fax 072 53026

    Kelly, Tracey

31. 23, St. Laurence's Street
    Drogheda Co. Louth
    tel 041 980 1580 *fax 041 980 1583*

    Donnelly, Carmel (spwo)
    Brennan, Mary
    Lennox, Yvonne
    McCourt, Caroline
    O'Brien, Frank
    Roche, Melanie
    Roche, Mette
    McHugh, Martina (admin)

32. Government Offices, Millenium Centre
    Dundalk Co. Louth
    tel 042 933 2163 *fax 042 933 2501*

    McDonald, Mary (spwo)
    Diamond, Mary
    Gervin, Alice
    Faulkner, Monica
    Murphy, Margaret
    Quigley, Sheena
    Jordan, Ita (admin)
    McKeever, Sinead (admin)

South Eastern Region

33. 3 Catherine Street,
    Waterford Co. Waterford.
    tel 051 872548 *fax 051 878238*

    Moriarty, Sean (appwo)
    Goode, Mary (spwo, staff devpt)
    Keen, Jane (spwo)
    Bourke, Andrea
    Gaden, Rosemarie
    Kennedy, Sharon
    Mitchell, Patrick
    Murphy, Mary T.
    O'Brien, Thomas
    Mansfield, Patricia (admin)
    Tobin, Margaret (admin)

34. Government Buildings
    Anne Street, **Wexford**

Co. Wexford.
tel 053 42076 *fax 053 23565*

Weir, Michelle (spwo)
Corcoran, Anna Mai
Duffy, Christine
Long, Carol (admin)
Waters-Kehoe, Margaret (admin)

35. Over Extra Vision
    Wexford Road,
    Arklow Co. Wicklow.
    tel 0402 21066 *fax 042 91114*

    Gurrin, Catherine
    Halpenny, Seamus
    Cullen, Anne-Marie (admin)

36. Shelton Abbey
    Arklow Co. Wicklow
    tel 0402 32912 *fax 0402 39924*

    Doyle, Catherine

37. Harbour House, The Quay
    Clonmel Co. Tipperary
    tel 052 23880 *fax 052 25874*

    Murphy, John (spwo)
    Aylward, Mary
    Cooney, John
    Leahy, Deirdre
    Lynam, Elizabeth
    O'Connor, Jacqueline
    O'Dwyer, Niamh
    Lyons, Mandy (admin)

38. Teach an Chuinne
    Parnell Street **Thurles**
    Co. Tipperary.
    tel 0504 24772 *fax 0504 24605*

    Hughes, Ina

39. Quinn House,
    Mill Lane, **Carlow**
    Co. Carlow.
    tel 059 913 5186 *fax 059 913 5194*

    Kavanagh, Billy (spwo)
    Brown, Carolyn
    Costigan, Marita
    Young, Dolores
    McGagh, Aisling (admin)

40. Government Offices
    Hebron Road, **Kilkenny**
    Co. Kilkenny
    tel 056 776 5201 *fax 056 776 4156*

    Redmond, Helen (spwo)

Brennan, Maura
Devereaux, Della
Lacey, Joan
Walsh, Geraldine
O'Sullivan, Moyra (admin)

Southern Region

41. 54 South Mall
    Cork Co. Cork
    tel 021 427 0726 *fax 021 427 5722*

    Boyle, Terry (appwo)
    Gill, Catherine (spwo)
    Busteed, Eleanor
    Gallahue, Elizabeth
    Kelleher, Roseanne
    Lynch, Dympna
    Lynch, Frank
    O'Leary, Paula
    Steffens, Ton

    McCarthy, Vanessa (spwo)
    Desmond, Thomas
    Dunne, Richard
    Fox, Rosemary
    O'Brien, Joe
    O'Farrell, Timothy
    Ryan, Eoin

    Cowan, Marie (admin)
    Desmond, Maria (admin)
    Kelleher, Laura (admin)
    O'Brien, Margaret (admin)

42. Grattan House
    Grattan Street **Cork** Co. Cork
    tel 021 427 2396 *fax 021 427 2404*

    Corcoran, John (spwo)
    Coughlan, Tony
    Coveney, Eugene
    Moriarty, Theresa
    O'Riordan, Jennifer (admin)

43. Robert Scott House,
    St. Patrick's Quay **Cork**
    tel 021 450 5591 *fax 021 450 5594*

    O'Connell, Dermot (spwo)
    Cashman, Siobhan
    Lawton, Jerry

44. **Cork Prison**
    Rathmore Road
    Cork, Co. Cork
    tel/fax 021 450 3277

    Campbell, Susan
    McAuley, Robert
    O'Connell, Sinead

Berkery, Madeline (admin)

45. Ashe Street,
    Tralee Co. Kerry
    tel 066 712 2666 *fax 066 712 1764*

    Shanahan, Richard (spwo)
    Brassil, Nora
    Hickey, Patrick
    Keane, Siobhan
    Moore, Michele
    O'Connor, Hannah (admin)

46. Church Street **Newcastlewest**
    Co. Limerick
    tel 069 66288 *fax 069-66331*

    Keane, Norma (spwo)
    Brosnahan, John
    Griffin, Gerry
    Holly, Eileen
    McNulty, Brian
    O'Donnell, Helena
    Tierney, Catherine
    Quigley, Gerard (admin)
    Minogue, Anne (admin)
    Dwane, Mary (admin)

47. **Limerick Prison**
    Mulgrave Street
    Limerick, Co. Limerick
    tel 061 294718 *fax 061 419812*

    Cahill, Frank
    Hurley, Donal

48. 1 Abbey Arcade
    Ennis Co. Clare
    tel/fax 065 684 0682

    Coughlan, Hedvig
    King, Mary
    Mohan, Sadie

CHANNEL ISLANDS, ISLE OF MAN, AND THE COURTS-MARTIAL REPORT SERVICE

The Channel Islands and the Isle of Man are separate jurisdictions. Community Orders are not formally transferable to or from them. Special procedures exist for the transfer of post custodial Licences. Contact should be made with the relevant Service before any offender moves to the Channel Islands or the Isle of Man.

GUERNSEY PROBATION SERVICE

1-5 Court Row
St Peter Port, Guernsey GY1 2PD
tel (01481) 724337 *fax (01481) 710545*
e-mail probation@gov.gg

Guilbert, Anna (cpo)
Harvey, Greg (snr pract)
Crisp, Stuart (snr pract)
Le Cheminant, Kerry (prison)
Greening, Gemma
Jennings, Cathy
Ozanne, Carol
Richmond, Isobel
Speers, David
Lowe, Vanessa (admin mgr)

Victim enquiries to Anna Guilbert (cpo)

ISLE OF MAN PROBATION SERVICE

2nd/3rd Floors, Prospect House
27-29 Prospect Hill
Douglas, Isle of Man IM1 1ET
tel (01624) 687323/24 *fax (01624) 687333*

Sellick David B L (cpo)
Ingram, Pat (pract mgr)
Griffin, Simon (dir of service)
Cubbon, Dawn (mgr of monitoring &
financial services)
Deverau, Anne (pa to cpo)
Quayle, Eddie (admin)
Dooley, Anne (admin)

Wildman, Frank (drug & alc team) (07624)
488514
Bass, John (prison) (01624) 621306 ext 232
East, John
Erani, Hilary
Ledger, Ian
Stott, Elaine
Robertson, John
Creer, Matthew (victim/offender reparation
off)
Vacancy (cso)

Hunter, Gillian (family crt welfare)
Wheeler, Mark (family crt welfare)

Christian, Louise (secy)
Britain-Jones, Elizabeth (secy)

JERSEY PROBATION SERVICE

PO Box 656, 1 Lempriere Street
St Helier JE4 8YT
tel (01534) 833933 *fax (01534) 833944*
e-mail initial.surname@gov.je
www.gov.je

Heath, Brian (cpo)
Cutland, Michael (acpo)
Cooley, Jenny (office mgr)
Miles, Helen (p, research & info mgr)
Urquhart, Janette (team ldr)
Brown, Susan
Tobler Joanne (mat leave cover till May
2006)
Carré, Marilyn (marilyn.carre@gov.je)
Houiellebecq, Kevin
Ibbotson, David
Ormesher, Adelaide
Pike, Chay
Saralis, Mark (crt liaison/subst misuse)
Taylor, Robert
Trott, David

Elliott, Natalie (trainee) (mat leave till
May 2006)
Christmas, Jane (p, psa)
da Silva, Sergio (p, psa)
Machon, Barbara (psa)
Rose, Chantelle (p, psa restorative justice)

Bouchard, Angela (p, case mgmnt asst)
Castledine, Alisha (p, case mgmnt asst)
Child-Villiers, Norah (case mgmnt asst)
Gosselin, Gillian (p, case mgmnt asst)
Lagadu, Tina (p, case mgmnt asst)
Banks, Shaun (p, cs mgr)
Allix, Nicky (p, asst cso)
Le Marrec, Andy (asst cso)
Corson, Anne (p, cs supvr)
Doolan, Ali (p, cs supvr)
Langlois, Kerrie (p, cs supvr)
Najib, Ghazi (p, cs supvr)
Pallett, Denis (p, cs supvr)
Perry, Michael (p, cs supvr)

THE COURTS-MARTIAL REPORT SERVICE

formerly known as the Army Probation Service

Courts-Martial Report Service (CMRS)
Building 183, Room 3
Trenchard Lines, Upavon, Pewsey
Wilts SN9 6BE
tel (01980) 618050/618101/618065
fax (01980) 618048

Carruthers, George (mgr)
Clawley, Tracey (office mgr)
Williamson, Lisa (admin officer)
Dyke, Carol (admin officer)

CMRS Germany Office
Direct dial from UK 0049 524184
3827/3828
fax 0049 524184 3815

Entwistle, Steve
Stewart, Mark

In Germany HQ CMRS have responsibility for the following:
British Forces Germany
British Forces Low Countries
Civilian employees working for the Army and RAF, and dependants

SCOTTISH EXECUTIVE JUSTICE DEPARTMENT

Community Justice Services
For the purposes of delivering Community Justice Services, Scottish Local Authorities are grouped into eight groupings, three unitary authorities and three island councils:

1. Aberdeen City, Aberdeenshire, Highland, Moray

2. Clackmannanshire, Falkirk, Stirling

3. Edinburgh City, East Lothian, West Lothian, Midlothian, Scottish Borders

4. Dundee City, Angus, Perth & Kinross

5. E Ayrshire, N Ayrshire, S Ayrshire

6. North Lanarkshire, South Lanarkshire

7. Renfrewshire, E Renfrewshire, Inverclyde

8. W Dunbartonshire, E Dunbartonshire, Argyle & Bute

9. Fife

10. Dumfries & Galloway

11. Glasgow

12. Orkney, Shetlands, Western Isles

Community Justice Services Division

Room GW-03, St Andrew's House, Regent Road, Edinburgh EH1 3DG
tel 0131-244 + ext *fax 0131-244 3548*
e-mail @scotland.gov.uk

Hd of Division, Elizabeth Carmichael, ext 5434
A3/PS, Fiona Cowan, ext 4236

Branch 1
a. General policy on criminal justice social work services.
b. Funding of local authorities and voluntary organisations for offender services.
c. Policy on offender accommodation.
d. Policy in respect of probation, community service orders, supervised attendance orders and social enquiry reports.
e. Offender service casework in area groups 2, 3, 7 and 12.
f. Policy on enhanced probation, deferred sentences, DTTOs, arrest referral.
g. Offender service casework in area groups 1, 5 and 10 & 11.
h. Policy on women offenders, bail, diversion, and residential placements and youth crime.
i. Offender service casework in area groups 4, 6, 8 & 9.

Functions	Grade	Name	Ext
a-i	C1	Brian Cole	5438
a, c, f, g, h, i	B2	Gareth Brown	4233
a, b, d, e	B2	Maurice Williams	4539
a, b, d,e	B1	Alan Cockburn	5435
a, f, g, h	B1	Alison Kerr	3549
a, h, i	B1	Vacancy	5356
b, e, g, i	A4	Carol McKegney (p)	4349
Admin supt	A1	Laura Alexander (p)	4234
	A1	Jade Finlayson	4273
enquiry point			**4349**
			fax 3548

Branch 2
a. Restriction of liberty orders and policy on electronic monitoring.
b. Expert panel on sex offending – follow up.
c. Drug courts.
d. Custodial sentences – social work interests including throughcare and aftercare.
e. Supervised release orders and extended sentences.
f. Mentally disordered offenders – social work interest.
g. Clerical support.

Function	Grade	Name	Ext
a-f	B3	Sharon Grant	3514
a	B2	Jackie Knox	3662
a-f	B1	Bobby McLernan	4259
a, b	B1	Bruce Sutherland	5476
a-f	B2	Christine Thomson	4250
a-f	A3	Andrew Piggott	4235
g	A1	Jade Finlayson	4273
enquiry point			**4235**
			fax 3548

Branch 3
a. Policy on effective practice.
b. Accreditation.
c. Risk Assessment and training.

Function	Grade	Name	Ext
a, b. c	Prof		
		Adviser Jackie Deas	6975
a, b, c	B1	Anna Graham	4258
admin supt	A1	Jade Finlayson	4273
enquiry point			**4258**
			fax 3548

Social Work Inspection Agency: Criminal Justice Team

Ladywell House, Ladywell Road, Corstorphine
EH12 7TF

The Social Work Inspection Agency undertakes
the following functions:
Inspection, review and reporting across social
work and social care services.
Sectoral and aspect evaluations of social work
and social care services.
Commissions from the Scottish Ministers,
relevant Departments of the Scottish Executive
and other bodies.
Provision of professional advice to Scottish
Ministers and others.

Depute Chief Inspector
Alistair Gaw   0131-244 3526
alistair.gaw@swia.gov.uk

Personal Secretary
Margaret McDavid   0131-244 5418

Inspectors

John Waterhouse   0131-244 5449
john.waterhouse@swia.gov.uk

Irene Scullion   0131-244 2753
irene.scullion@swia.gov.uk

Clare Wilson   0131-244 5494
clare.wilson@swia.gsi.gov.uk

Willie Paxton   0131-244 5491
willie.paxton@swia.gsi.gov.uk

PAROLE AND LIFE SENTENCE REVIEW DIVISION

2nd Floor West, St Andrews House, Regent
Road, Edinburgh EH1 3DG
0131-244 8524/8530 *fax 0131-244 8794*

Functions: administration of parole, life

sentence and early release, children in custody

Staff
Head of Division: Mrs Jane Richardson
Branch heads: Mrs L MacDonald, Mrs A Sharp
& Mr J T Hislop

PAROLE BOARD FOR SCOTLAND

Saughton House, Broomhouse Drive,
Edinburgh EH11 3XD
0131-244 8373 *fax 0131-244 6974*

Secretary to the Board: H P Boyle
General enquiries: 0131-244 8373

ABERDEEN CITY COUNCIL

Central Bail Referral telephone no:
Kirstin Parkes (ssw, team 1) (01224) 765000
John Connon (ssw, team 1) (01224) 765000

Emergency out of hours contact point
(01224) 693936

e-mail oohs@socialwork.aberdeen.net.uk

Central Services

1.   St Nicholas House
      Broad Street **Aberdeen** AB10 1BY
      tel (01224) 522110 *fax (01224) 523195*

      Smith Stan (hd of social services policy,
      community services, social work)
      e-mail ssmith@aberdeencity.gov.uk

1a.   AECC, Balgownie 1
      Conference Way, Bridge of Don
      Aberdeen AB23 8AQ
      tel (01224) 814510 *fax (01224) 648256*

      Tumelty, Dave (hd of service (health &
      care)
      neighbourhood services (north))
      e-mail DTumelty@aberdeencity.gov.uk

1b.   Neighbourhood Services (North)
      Criminal Justice Social Work
      Exchequer House, 3 Exchequer Row
      Aberdeen AB11 2BW
      tel (01224) 765000 *fax (01224) 576109*

      Bell, George (team mgr cj)
      e-mail gbell@aberdeencity.gov.uk

      Balme, Jane (research/info officer)

Specialist Criminal Justice Teams

2. Exchequer House, 3 Exchequer Row
Aberdeen AB11 2BW
tel (01224) 765000 *fax (01224) 576109*

   Team 1
   (level 1 probn, crt services, sao, diversion)
   John Connon (ssw)
   Parkes, Kirstin (ssw)
   Atkins, Laura (temp sw)
   Brownlie, Linda (sw)
   Delaney, Elaine (p, sw)
   Fogg, Noreen (sw)
   Fullerton, Mick (sw)
   Lorimer, Leanne (sw)
   McAllister, Anne (p, sw)
   McCubbin, Lyn (temp sw)
   Pullar, Judith (sw)
   Rutherford, Jean (p, sw)
   Sandison, Steve (sw)
   Smith, Edwina (p, sw)
   Strachan, Norma (p, sw)
   Trew, Carrie (sw)
   Young, Nicola (sw)
   Mearns, Kathleen (p, sao)
   Rennie, Margaret (p, sao)

   Team 2
   (level 2 & 3 probn)
   Rennie, Kate (ssw)
   Simpson, Lesley (ssw)
   Buchanan, Neil (sw)
   Cameron, Claire (sw)
   Edgar, Jackie (sw)
   Fox, Sue (p, sw)
   Fyffe, Karaina (p, sw)
   Logan, Alistair (sw)
   McLean, Lyndsey (temp sw)
   McCloy, Marion (sw)
   Michel-Stephen, Tina (temp sw)
   Roach, Philip (sw)
   Sellens, Diane (temp sw)
   Shepherd, Mike (sw)
   Stoker, Ross (temp sw)

   Team 3
   (throughcare)
   Youngson, Nicola (ssw)
   Bryce, Vivienne (sw)
   Evans, Lorna (sw)
   Gillan, Gillian (sw)
   MacDonald, Gus (sw)
   Reid, Fiona (sw)
   Robertson, Marianne (sw)
   Vacancy (p, sw)
   Vacancy (sw)
   Campbell, Karen (comm supt wrkr)
   Will, David (comm supt wrkr)

3. **Drug Treatment & Testing Orders**
   137 Gallowgate, Aberdeen AB25 5BU
   tel (01224) 267100 *fax (01224) 645473*

   Murray, Lorna (team ldr)
   Greig, Karen (sw)
   Halford, Vina (sw)
   Ure, Amanda (sw)
   Donald, Abbey (subst misuse nurse)
   Vacancy (subst misuse nurse)
   Russell, Ann (subst misuse nurse)
   Greg, Natalie (subst misuse wrkr)
   Watt, Gillian (subst misuse wrkr)
   Wylie, Brenda (subst misuse wrkr)

Community Service

4. 11 Willowdale Place
   Aberdeen AB24 3AQ
   tel (01224) 624317 *fax (01224) 626544*

   Community Service Resource Team
   Murray, Joan (mgr)
   Paterson, Neil (projects officer)
   Finnie, Pam (order supving off)
   Freeman, Derek (order supving off)
   Murdoch, Colin (order supving off)
   Waite, David (p, order supving off)
   Peacock, Carol (personal placement off)

Probation Hostel

5. **St Fitticks House**
   36 Crombie Road, Torry
   Aberdeen AB1 3QQ
   tel (01224) 877910 *fax (01224) 894303*

   (males & females aged 18+)
   Dawson, Gary (unit mgr)

Penal Establishment

6. Social Work Unit
   HM Prison, Craiginches
   Aberdeen AB9 2HN
   tel (01224) 238315 *fax (01224) 238343*

   Williamson, Sheena (ssw)
   Hendry, Christine (sw)
   Vacancy (sw)

Health Services

7. Social Work Department
   Royal Cornhill Hospital
   Cornhill Road, Aberdeen AB9 2ZH
   tel (01224) 663131

   Elliot, Sue (sw, forensic unit ext 57415)

Independent Sector

8. **APEX Scotland**
    St Martin's House, 181 Union Street
    Aberdeen AB11 6BB
    tel (01224) 840430 *fax (01224) 840431*

    supervised attendance orders, employment
    Bruce, Jane (snr trainer)

8a. **Victim Support (Scotland)**
    32 Upperkirkgate
    Aberdeen AB10 1BA
    phone & fax (01224) 622478

    Sharp, Wendy (area co-ord)
    Scott, Mary (co-ord)
    Russell, Sandra (co-ord)

8b. **SACRO**
    110 Crown Street, Aberdeen AB11 6HJ
    tel (01224) 560550

    Proe, Mike (snr mgr ops North)
    Simpson, Mark (service mgr)

Courts

Aberdeen Sheriff Court
City of Aberdeen District Court

ABERDEENSHIRE COUNCIL

1. Woodhill House
    Westburn Road
    Aberdeen AB16 5GB
    tel (01224) 664991 *fax (01224) 664888*

    Mackenzie, Colin (director of sw & housing)

2. 53 Windmill Street
    Peterhead AB42 1UE
    tel (01779) 477333 *fax (01779) 474961*

    English, Philip (sw mgr responsible for cj)
    Witts, David (info & research officer)

3. **Joint Sex Offender Project**
    88 King Street **Peterhead** AB42 1HH
    tel (01779) 490904 *fax (01779) 474961*

    Watson, Sheena (ssw)
    Abraham, Brian (sw)
    Gibson, Fiona (sw)
    Matthews, Rory (sw)
    Stuart, Gaynor (sw)
    Murphy, Jayne (sw)
    Selkirk, Deirdre (sw)

Vacant (p, sw)
McIntosh, Margaret (admin)

4. **Addictions Team**
    88 King Street **Peterhead** AB42 1HH
    tel (01779) 490904 *fax (01779) 476435*

    Dickson, Stewart (ssw)
    MacDonald, Kathy (sw)
    Mulvey, Kim (sw)
    Ogilvie, Claire (sw)
    Meade, Dorothy (sw)
    McIntosh, Margaret (admin)

5. **Community Service**
    56 Cameron Street **Stonehaven** AB39 2HE
    tel (01569) 767553 *fax (01569) 767906*

    Westland, Fiona (ssw)
    Holtes, Morag (proj. off.)
    Birse, Kim (admin)

6. **Supervised Attendance Orders**
    53 Windmill Street **Peterhead** AB42 1UE
    tel (01779) 477333 *fax (01779) 474961*

    Black, Celia (proj. off.)

Aberdeenshire North Team

7. 88 King Street
    Peterhead AB42 1HH
    tel (01779) 490904 *fax (01779) 476435*

    Munro, John (team manager)
    McIntosh, Margaret (admin)

8. 53 Windmill Street
    Peterhead AB42 1UE
    tel (01779) 477333 *fax (01779) 474961*

    Black, Celia (sw)
    Connon, Susan (sw)
    Innes, Corinne (sw)
    Mason, Barbara (sw)
    Dowding, Margaret (admin)

9. Winston House
    39 Castle Street
    Banff AB45 1FQ
    tel (01261) 812001 *fax (01261) 813474*

    Cambridge, Megan (sw)
    Bailey, Amanda (admin)

10. 14 Saltoun Square
    Fraserburgh AB43 9DA
    tel (01346) 513281 *fax (01346) 516885*

    Henderson, Angie (sw)

Smith, Sarah (sw)
Walsh, Joe (sw)
Cowie, Anne (admin)

11. 25 Gordon Street
     Huntly AB54 5EQ
     tel (01466) 794488 *fax (01466) 794624*

     Biggs, Peter (p, sw)

Aberdeenshire South Team

12. 56 Cameron Street
     Stonehaven AB39 2HE
     tel (01569) 767553 *fax (01569) 767906*

     Westland, Fiona (team manager)
     Rhodes, Jayne (sw)
     Urquhart, Pam (p, sw)
     Wood, John (p, sw)
     Birse, Kim (admin)
     Christie, Gillian (admin)

13. 25 Station Road
     Ellon AB41 9AA
     tel (01358) 720033 *fax (01358) 723639*

     Addison, Liz (sw)

14. 93 High Street
     Inverurie AB51 3AB
     tel (01467) 625555 *fax (01467) 625010*

     Clark, Michele (sw)
     Rhodes, Susan (p, sw)
     Hay, Lorna (admin)

Penal Establishment

15. Social Work Unit
     HMP Prison
     Invernettie **Peterhead** AB42 6YY
     tel (01779) 473315 *fax (01779) 471269*

     Gibson, Eileen (team manager)
     McDonnell, Kim (sw)
     Millar, Agnes (sw)
     Mottram, Evelyn (sw)
     Vacant (sw)
     Guild, Joan (admin)

Courts

     Banff Sheriff Court
     Peterhead Sheriff Court
     Stonehaven Sheriff Court
     Aberdeenshire District Court at Banff
     Aberdeenshire District Court at Inverurie
     Aberdeenshire District Court at Peterhead
     Aberdeenshire District Court at Stonehaven

ANGUS COUNCIL

Emergency out of hours contact point
(01382) 436430

1. Social Work Headquarters
    County Buildings
    Forfar Angus DD8 3WS
    tel (01307) 461460 *fax (01307) 473366*

    Peat, Robert (director of social work & health)

1a. Social Work Department
    Ravenswood, New Road
    Forfar Angus DD8 2AF
    tel (01307) 462405 *fax (01307) 461261*

    McIntosh, Gordon (head of operations, children's services & criminal justice services)

2. Criminal Justice Services Office
    9 Fergus Square **Arbroath** DD11 3DG
    tel (01241) 871161 *fax (01241) 431898*

    Hodgkinson, Mark (service mgr)
    Gaffney, Mark (ssw)
    Spicker, Dominique (ssw)
    Watt, Dave (ssw)
    Smith, Valerie (research/i.t. officer)
    Barrer, Lynn (sw)
    Beierlein, Jackie (sw)
    Calvert, Elizabeth (sw)
    Cherrington, Isobel (sw)
    Ferrier, Emma (sw)
    Fyfe, John (sw)
    Gall, Stuart (sw)
    Hendry, Alison (sw)
    Lorimer, Vicki (sw)
    McPherson, Tracy (sw)
    Nicolson, Don (sw)
    Smith, Colin (sw)
    Bancroft, Paul (cja)
    Burness, Fiona (cja)
    Catherall, Philip (cja)
    Herron, Wendy (cja)
    Millar, Avril (cja)
    Richards, Lynn (cja)
    Wilson, Lesley (cja)
    Dickson, Fiona (admin asst)

Penal Establishment

3. Social Work Unit
    HM Prison **Noranside**
    Fern, by Forfar, Angus DD8 3QY
    tel (01356) 650217

    Rennie, Diane (sw)

Michie, Joy (sw)
Mollison, Henry (sw)

Courts

Arbroath Sheriff Court
Forfar Sheriff Court
Angus District Court at Arbroath
Angus District Court at Brechin
Angus District Court at Forfar

ARGYLL & BUTE COUNCIL

1. Argyll & Bute Council
    Dept of Community Services
    13a East King Street
    Helensburgh G84 7QQ
    tel (01436) 677187 *fax (01436) 677195*

    Filshie, Alex (criminal justice mgr)

2. 16 Church Street
    Dunoon PA23 8BG
    tel (01369) 707829 *fax (01369) 703641*

    Criminal Justice Team
    Community Service Office
    Dunoon Sherif Court Social Work Unit
    Kelsall, Pat (ssw)

3. **Criminal Justice Services &**
    Community Service Office
    Soroba Road **Oban** PA34 4JA
    tel (01631) 563068 *fax (01631) 566724*

    all CJ services for Oban & Lorn areas

4. **District Headquarters**
    Dalriada House, Lochnell Street
    Lochgilphead PA31 8ST
    tel (01546) 602177 *fax (01546) 606589*

    tel (01546) 604538
    Green, Kirsteen (planning & eval off)

5. Criminal Justice Service
    Municipal Buildings, Station Road
    Dumbarton G82 1QA
    tel (01389) 738484 *fax (01389) 738480*

    for CJ Services for Helensburgh and
    Lomond

6. Social Work Department
    Old Quay Head **Campbeltown** PA28 6ED
    tel (01586) 552659 *fax (01586) 554912*

    CSO & CJ Services for Campbeltown and
    Kintyre Peninsula

Belton, Jon (island ssw for Mull, Islay, Coll,
Tiree, Rothesay)

7. Social Work Department
    Union Streeet
    Rothesay, Island of Bute PA20 0HD
    tel (01700) 501300 *fax (01700) 505408*

    all CJ Services for the Island of Bute

8. Social Work Department
    Breadalbane Street
    Tobermory Island of Mull PA75 6NZ
    tel (01688) 302216 *fax (01688) 302089*

    all CJ enquiries to Office 3

9. Social Work Department
    Kilarrow House
    Bowmore Island of Islay PA43 7LH
    tel (01496) 301350 *fax (01496) 810457*

Courts

Cambletown Sheriff Court
Dunoon Sheriff Court
Oban Sheriff Court
Rothesay Sheriff Court
Argyll & Bute District Court at Bowmore
Argyll & Bute District Court at
Campbeltown
Argyll & Bute District Court at Dunoon
Argyll & Bute District Court at
Lochgilphead
Argyll & Bute District Court at Oban
Argyll & Bute District Court at Rothesay

CLACKMANNANSHIRE COUNCIL

e-mail yrobson@clacks.gov.uk

1. Services to People - Social Services
    Lime Tree House, Castle Street
    Alloa FK10 1EX
    tel (01259) 452371 *fax (01259) 452400*

    McGeoch, Gerry (hd of childcare, pre-fives
    & cjs)
    gmcgeoch@clacks.gov.uk
    Nolan, Francis (secy)

2. Unit 6, Alloa Trading Estate
    Bruce Street, **Alloa** FK10 1RX
    tel (01259) 721069 *fax (01259) 723998*

    Robson, Yvonne (service mgr, c.j. services)
    yrobson@clacks.gov.uk

Criminal Justice Team
Smillie, Alistair (team mgr)
asmillie@clacks.gov.uk

Buchanan, June (ssw)
Aien, Alison (sw)
Conoboy, Catherine (sw)
Duncan, Shona (p, sw)
Jones, Chris (sw)
McCourt, Michele (sw)
McVeigh, Janet (p, sw)
Miller, Anne (sw)
Pearson, Pauline (sw)
Bowen, Gail (sw asst)
Cant, Anne (sw asst)
Jarvie, Katrina (sw asst)

Community Service Team
Gibson, Ruth (cso)
Binnie, Chris (wk supvr)
Drysdale, Ken (wk supvr)
Lumsden, Irene (wk supvr)

Admin
Aitken, Gillian
Coyle, Tricia
McDougall, Marilyn
Reid, Anne
Williamson, Julie

3.   Social Work Unit
     HM Prison & YOI **Glenochil**
     King O' Muirs Road
     Tullibody FK10 3AD
     phone & fax (01259) 767315

     Banyard, Libby (team mgr)
     Libby.Banyard@sps.gov.uk
     Collin, Eleanor (sw)
     Craig, Alison (sw)
     Dickson, Hazel (sw)
     Graham, Amanda (sw)
     Patterson, Caroline (sw)

     Admin
     Fox, Susan
     Noblett, Susan
     O'Donnell, Ann

Courts

     Alloa Sheriff Court
     Clackmannanshire District Court at Alloa

COMHAIRLE NAN EILEAN SIAR WESTERN ISLES COUNCIL

Out of hours contact: (01851) 701702

e-mail imacaulay@cne-siar.gov.uk
margaret.macleod@cne-siar.gov.uk

1.   Social Work Department Headquarters
     Council Offices
     Sandwick Road **Stornoway**
     Isle of Lewis HS1 2BW
     tel (01851) 703773 *fax (01851) 709532*

     Smith, Malcolm (director of sw)
     Macaulay, Iain (depute director of sw)
     Macleod, Margaret (cj services mgr)
     MacDonald, Maggie (cj sw)

Courts

     Lochmaddy Sheriff Court
     Stornoway Sheriff Court
     Western Isles District Court at Stornoway

DUMFRIES & GALLOWAY COUNCIL

Out of hours contact no 01387 260000

e mail AllanMo@dumgal.gov.uk

1.   Education and Community Services
     Woodbank, Edinburgh Road
     Dumfries DG1 1NW
     tel (01387 260417) fax (01387 260453)

     Smith, B (chief social work officer)

2   Criminal Justice Social Work
     39 Lewis Street
     Stranraer DG9 7AD
     (01776) 706167 *fax (01776) 706884*

     Monteforte, A (service mgr, cj social work)

Criminal Justice Social Work East

3.   79 Buccleuch Street
     Dumfries DG1 2AB
     tel (01387) 262409 *fax (01387) 267964*

     Glynn, J (team mgr)
     Kerr, A (admin mgr)
     Lockerbie, N (business info & research off)
     Walkerdine, S (sw)
     McNaught, A (sw)
     Fortune, P (sw asst)
     Smeaton, E (cso)

Mulholland, R (cso)
Stenhouse, N (cso)
Clark, C (snr clerical asst)
Macpherson, C (snr clerical asst)

4.   52A/B Buccleuch Street
Dumfries DG1 2AP
tel (01387) 262409 *fax (01387) 262431*

Monteforte, A (service mgr, cj)
Sturgeon, J (team mgr)
Davies, R (team mgr dtto)
Knipe, C (snr practitioner-sex offenders)
Beattie, D (prison liaison officer)
Fitzpatrick, E (sw dtto)
Hall, J (sw throughcare)
Hannah, J (sw)
McCarron, A (sw)
McMeikan, E (sw)
Muir, T (sw)
Oscroft, G (sw)
Whitfield, L (sw)
Wilson, I (sw)
Wuerffel, V (sw)
Dudgeon, W (swa dtto)
Cottle, L (snr clerical asst)
Herd, L (snr clerical asst)
Thomson, M (snr clerical asst)

5.   Community Service
8 King Street
Dumfries DG2 9AN
tel (01387) 248495 fax (01387) 248495

operational depot only

East - Annandale and Eskdale Area

6.   2 Bank Street
Annan DG12 6AA
tel (01461) 203411 *fax (01461) 205964*

Glynn, J (team mgr) (based at 3)
Mackay, Mrs F (sw)
Laverty, G (sw)
Hall, J (sw throughcare) (based at 4)
Mulholland, R (cso) (based at 3)

7.   Council Offices
Dryfe Road **Lockerbie** DG11 2AP
tel (01576) 203040 *fax (01576) 204411*

contact office

Stewartry/Throughcare/Prison

8.   Claverhouse
117 High Street, **Kirkcudbright** DG6 4JG
tel (01557) 332538 *fax (01557) 332537*

McKenzie, R (team mgr)

Unsworth, J (sw)
Vacancy (sw)
Hall, J (sw throughcare) (based at 4)
Stead, J (sw throughcare) (based at 9)
Hamilton, B (cso)
Ferries, A (snr clerical asst)

West

9.   39 Lewis Street
Stranraer DG9 7AD
tel (01776) 706167 *fax (01776) 706884*

McCallum, A (team mgr)
Halliday, G (sw)
Olsen, J (sw)
Vacancy (sw)
Walsh, P (sw-dtto)
Stead, J (sw throughcare)
Douglas, D (cso)
Vacancy (swa)
Findlay-Dean, R (prison liaison officer)
Dodds, A (snr clerical asst)
Loudon, M (snr clerical asst)

10.   Penninghame Centre
Auchendoon Road
Newton Stewart DG8 6HD
tel (01671) 403933 *fax (01671) 403017*

contact office 8

Penal Establishment

11.   HM Prison **Dumfries**
Terregles Street, Dumfries DG2 9AX
tel (01387) 261218 *fax (01387) 264144*

Farrier, J (sw)
Vacancy (sw)

Courts

Dumfries Sheriff Court
Kirkcudbright Sheriff Court
Stranraer Sheriff Court
Dumfries & Galloway District Court at
Annan
Dumfries & Galloway District Court at
Dumfries
Dumfries & Galloway District Court at
Lockerbie
Dumfries & Galloway District Court at
Stranraer

DUNDEE CITY COUNCIL

Out of hours contact no: (01382) 436430
fax (01382) 436435

1. Friarfield House
   Barrack Street **Dundee** DD1 1PQ
   tel (01382) 435001 *fax (01382) 435032*

   direct dial (01382) 453 + ext

   Jane Martin (hd of cj service) ext 5017
   Adam, Lorraine (secy) ext 5059
   Wood, Gordon (service mgr, criminal justice) ext 5046
   Lloyd Glynn (service mgr, criminal justice) ext 1420
   Lewis, Jill (ptnrshp devpt mgr) ext 5061
   Mellor, Charlaine (snr admin offier, criminal justice) ext 5058
   Naeem, Shahida (planning officer) ext 5084
   Thomson, Nan (p, info asst) ext 5084

   Team 1 (Probation)
   Jane Fenton (ssw) ext 5087
   Davies, Jenni (sw) ext 5514
   Delaney, Fiona (sw) ext 5515
   Moira Dobson (sw) ext 5516
   Sinclair Rose (sw) ext
   Reid, David (sw) ext 5057
   Titterington, Eric (sw) ext 5074
   Garrigan, Helen (cj asst crt) ext 2188

   Team 2 (Probation)
   Ramsay, Jacky (ssw) ext 5004
   Dow, Ashley (sw) ext 5513
   Duncan, Susan (sw) ext 5005
   Howard, Terry (sw, diversion off) ext 5050
   McLean, Susan (sw) ext 5048
   McLeish, Kelly (sw) ext 5076
   Wallace-King, Gwen (sw) ext 5060
   Vaughan, Ewan (sw) ext 5031

   Community Service/APEX
   Patterson, Grant (ssw) ext 5015
   Brewster Lesley (scja) ext 5008
   Dunnett, Janette (cj asst) ext 5089
   Leadbetter, Michelle (cj asst) ext 5002
   Kalsi, Pam (cj asst) ext 5035
   Massie, Donna (cj asst) ext 5049
   Murray, Gillian (cj asst) ext 5044
   North, Joyce (cj asst) ext 5091
   Brown, Jenny (eda) ext 5062

   APEX Employability
   Sneddon Julie (team leader) ext 5026
   Rule, Liz (eda)
   Mortimer Val (Link Worker) ext 5020
   Rowe, Debbie (admin) ext 5085

   Tay Project
   Millar, Anna (ssw) ext 5054
   McDonald, Teresa (sw) ext 5037
   Paton, Lisa (sw) ext 5075
   Smith, Ron (sw,) ext 5018

Rae, Kathryn (sw) ext 5019
Milne, Janice (cj asst) ext 5068

DTTO
Mitchell, Dave (ssw) ext 5051
Barrow, Trisha (sw) ext 5029
Bruce, Nicole (sw) ext 5091
Littlejohn, Sandra (sw) ext 5056
McIlravey, Pauline (sw) ext 5021
Banks, Shona (nurse) ext 5072
Craig, Jamie (nurse) ext 5055
Harley, Pauline (nurse) ext 5047
Lindsay, Stuart (nurse) ext 5078

2. **Groupwork Team**
   Flaxmill House
   67 King Street, Dundee DD1 2JY
   tel (01382) 431400 *fax (01382) 431431*

   Team Three
   Micheal O'Rourke (ssw) ext 1433
   Carnegie, Maureen (sw) ext 1415
   Greene, Brenda (sw) ext 1414
   Hill, Alyson (sw) ext 1408
   Hinnrichs, Jill (sw) ext 1411
   Hutt, Elizabeth (sw) ext 1413
   Swingler, Carol (sw) ext 1412

   Team Four
   Lindsay, Stephen (ssw) ext 1418
   Blair, Rosie (sw) ext 1407
   Campbell, Lesley (sw) ext 1403
   Duff, Iain (sw) ext 1404
   Kettles, Joyce (sw) ext 1406
   Scott, Rachel (sw) ext 1409
   Walker, Debbie (sw) ext 1405

3. **East Port House**
   65 King Street, Dundee DD4 1JY
   tel (01382) 431441 *fax (01382) 435286*

   Kidd, Jessie (mgr) ext 1442
   Hendry, Mike (depute mgr) ext 1451

Courts

   Dundee Sheriff Court
   City of Dundee District Court

EAST AYRSHIRE COUNCIL

1. Social Work Headquarters
   John Dickie Street
   Kilmarnock KA1 1BY
   tel (01563) 576907/2 & 576969
   fax (01563) 576654 & 576644

   Donnelly, Jackie (exec head of sw)

Kelly, Sally-Ann (snr mgr, children, families & cj)
Mackinnon, Fiona (service mgr cj & youth justice)

2. Social Work Department
43/49 John Finnie Street
Kilmarnock KA1 1BL
tel (01563) 539888 *fax (01563) 538055*

Fitzpatrick, Eugene (team mgr, cj)
Watson, Evelyn (team mgr, youth justice)

Community Service Team
(01563) 539809
Turner, Ian (cso)

3. Social Work Department
Barrhill Road
Cumnock KA18 1PG
tel (01290) 428372 *fax (01290)* 428380

McRoberts, Grace (team mgr, cj)

4. Ayrshire Change Project
Social Work Department
24B Grange Street
Kilmarnock KA1 2AR
tel (01563) 529211 *fax (01563) 574854*

Vacancy (project leader)

5. **Courts**
MacAdam House
34 Charlotte Street, Ayr KA7 1EA
tel (01292) 289749

SSW covering Courts
Hall, Drew (ssw crts)

Penal Establishment

6. Social Work Unit
HM Prison, Mauchline Road
Kilmarnock KA1 5JH
tel (01563) 548851 *fax (01563) 548869*

Miller, Morvan (team mgr, prison & throughcare service)

Courts

Ayr Sheriff Court
Kilmarnock Sheriff Court
E Ayrshire District Court at Kilmarnock
E Ayrshire District Court at Cumnock

EAST DUNBARTONSHIRE COUNCIL

Out of hours standby service: Freephone 0800 811505

1. Communities Headquarters
Tom Johnstone House
Kirkintilloch G66 4TJ
tel 0141-578 8000 *fax 0141-578 8470*

Bruce, Sue (chief exec)
Anderson, David (corp director - community)

2. **Criminal Justice Unit**
Unit 23, Fraser House
Whitegates **Kirkintilloch** G66 3BQ
tel 0141-578 0100 *fax 0141-578 0101*

Fleming, John (acting service mgr)
Vacancy (team leader)

Offender Services
Lynch, Tracy (sw)
Cranston, Morven (sw)
Worrall, Helen (sw)
Kennedy, Kirsty (sw)

Community Service & Supervised Attendance
Sutherland, Neil (cso)
Nixon, Joseph (cs asst)
Dickson, William (cs supr)
Coyne, Martin (cs supvr)
Karpinski, Noel (cj asst)

Administration Section
Vacancy (admin asst)
Vacancy (clerical off)
Young, Lynn (clerical off)

Penal Establishment

3. Social Work Unit
HM Prison **Lowmoss**
Crosshill Road, Bishopbriggs
Glasgow G62 2QB
tel 0141-762 4848 *fax 0141-772 6903*

Ure, Ian (sw)

Court

E Dunbartonshire District Court at Kirkintilloch
E Dunbartonshire District Court at Milngavie

EAST LOTHIAN COUNCIL

Out of hours contact: emergency social work service: freephone 0800 731 6969

e-mail jramsay@eastlothian.gov.uk

1. Dept of Social Work & Housing
    9-11 Lodge Street
    Haddington EH41 3DX
    tel (01620) 825393 *fax (01620) 824295*

    Vacancy (director of sw & housing)
    Cochran, Jan (hd of comm supt)

2. **Criminal Justice Team**
    6-8 Lodge Street **Haddington**
    East Lothian EH41 3DX
    tel (01620) 826600 *fax (01620) 826345*

    Ramsay, Jane (service mgr)
    Kaminski, P (team ldr)
    Coates, G (ssw youth justice)
    Barbour, Carolyn (sw)
    Dodson, Janet (sw)
    Doyle, Maureen (sw throughcare)
    Dudley, Susan (sw)
    Harvey, Stephen (sw)
    Steel, Audrey (sw th'care)
    Horne, Iain (sw)

    Love, R (cs mgr)
    Vacancy (cs asst)
    Kevan, Neil (cs asst)
    McAlpine, O (cs asst)

    Vacancy (service support)
    Holm, J (service support)

Courts

Haddington Sheriff Court
E Lothian District Court at Haddington

EAST RENFREWSHIRE COUNCIL

Out of hours contact no: 0800 811 505

e-mail letusknow@eastrenfrewshire.gov.uk

1. East Renfrewshire Council Headquarters
    Eastwood Park, Rouken Glen Road
    Giffnock G46 6UG
    tel 0141-577 3839 *fax 0141-577 3846*

    Hunter, George (dDirector of sw)
    Baxter, Safaa (head of operations)

2. St Andrew's House
    113 Cross Arthurlie Street
    Barrhead G78 1EE
    tel 0141-577 3357 *fax 0141-577 3762*

    Aitken, Doris (cj servive mgr)

3. 211 Main Street
    Barrhead Glasgow G78 1XE
    tel 0141-577 8337 *fax 0141-577 8342*

    Criminal Justice Team
    Hinds, Jonathan (team mgr)
    Craig, Dawn (snr sw pract)
    Bain, Andrea (sw)
    Stevenson, Terry (sw)
    Gaff, Les (peripatetic sw)
    O'Donovan, Roberta (peripatetic sw)
    Downie, Eddie (cj assistant)
    Kerr, Peter (cs supvr)
    Bell, Shona (admin asst)
    McQuade, Anne Marie (admin asst)

4. **Forensic Community Mental Health Team**
    Blythswood House
    Fulbar Lane, Renfrew PA4 8YX
    tel 0141-314 9216/7 *fax 0141-314-9214*

    Hendry, Shona (team ldr)
    Bonini, Marina (sw)
    McFarlane, Andy (sw)
    Taylor, Mel (sw)
    McIntosh, Pauline (medical secretary)
    Lauder, Rhona (medical secretary)

5. **Drug Treatment and Testing Order Project**
    St Andrew's House
    113 Cross Arthurlie Street
    Barrhead G78 1EE
    tel 0141-577 8442 *fax 0141-577 3762*

    Buntrock, Christine (team ldr)
    Cunningham, Neil (sw)
    Soper, Helen (sw)
    Murray, Patricia (sw)
    Gallagher , Rita (addiction wrkr)
    Rush, Wendy (addiction wrkr)
    Strachan, Paula (addiction wrkr)
    Barnes, Dr Rosalind (doctor)
    Nelis, Michael (snr addiction nurse)
    Stocks, Diane (addiction nurse)
    Taylor, James (snr clerical asst)
    McGettigan, Kerry (clerical asst)

Court

E Renfrewshire District Court at Giffnock

CITY OF EDINBURGH COUNCIL

Out of hours contact: emergency social work service: freephone 0800 731 6969

1. Social Work Headquarters
   Shrubhill House, Shrub Place
   Edinburgh EH7 4PD
   tel 0131-554 4301 *fax 0131-554 0838*

   Gabbitas, Peter, (director)
   MacAulay, Duncan, (general mgr)
   Brace, Sue (hd of strategic planning & commissioning)
   Boyle, Monica, (hd of quality and resources)

   Criminal Justice Services
   tel 0131-553-8212 *fax 0131-554-0838*
   Lancashire, Ron (criminal justice services mgr)
   Millar, Don (asst criminal justice services mgr)
   Tyson, John (asst criminal justice services mgr)

Court Liaison Services

2. **Edinburgh**
   (District, Sheriff and High Courts)
   21 Market Street
   Edinburgh EH1 1BL
   tel 0131-469 3408/9 *fax 0131-469 3410*

District Criminal Justice Practice Teams

3. **Edinburgh North East**
   9-11 Giles Street
   Edinburgh EH6 6DJ
   tel 0131-553 3835 *fax 0131-553 6540*

   Robertson, Harry (practice team mgr)

4. **Edinburgh South East**
   40 Captain's Road
   Edinburgh EH17 8HN
   tel 0131-529 5300 *fax 0131-529 5384*

   Stewart, Ian (practice team mgr)

5. **Edinburgh North West**
   34 Muirhouse Crescent
   Edinburgh EH4 4QL
   tel 0131-343 1991 *fax 0131-315 2172*

   Gray, Marian (practice team mgr)

6. **Edinburgh South West**
   5 Murrayburn Gate
   Edinburgh EH14 2SS

tel 0131-442 4131 *fax 0131-442 4842*

Brewer, Margaret (acting practice team mgr)

7. **Central Criminal Justice Services**
   21 Market Street **Edinburgh** EH1 1BL
   tel 0131-469 3408/9 *fax 0131-469 3410*

   Fraser, Rona (practice team mgr)

   Services include: bail info and assessment, diversion from prosecution, resettlement team, domestic violence probation project and:

   Crane Services (supported accommodation facility)
   24 Broughton Place, Edinburgh EH1 3RT
   tel 0131-556 9969 *fax 0131-558 1809*

   Fraser, Dorothy (mgr)

   Drug Treatment & Testing Orders
   29-31 Alva Street
   Edinburgh EH2 4PS
   tel 0131-225-7788 *fax 225-9039*

   Lawrie, Valerie (mgr)

Penal Establishment

8. Social Work Unit
   HM Prison, 33 Stenhouse Road
   Edinburgh EH11 3LN
   tel 0131-444 3080 *fax 0131-444 3036*

   Youngson, Graeme (practice team mgr)

Courts

Edinburgh Sheriff Court
City of Edinburgh District Court

FALKIRK COUNCIL

1. Social Work Headquarters
   Brockville, Hope Street **Falkirk** FK1 5RW
   tel (01324) 506400 *fax (01324) 506401*

   Birks, Janet (director of housing & social work)
   Anderson, Margaret (head of children, families &cj)

   Criminal Justice Service
   tel (01324) 506464 *fax (01324) 506465*

   Stirrat, Sharon (service mgr)
   Duncan, Robin (research, training & info off)

Probation & Throughcare Team
Burgess, Nick (team mgr)
Parnell, Anne Marie (snr wrkr)
Aitken, Claire (sw)
Andrews, Carol (sw)
Boslem, Mary (sw)
Brown, Donna (sw)
Vacancy (sw)
Brodie, Andrew (sw)
Duffy, Sarah (sw)
Goodwin, Anne-Marie (sw)
Kent, Gill (sw)
Marshall, Kay (sw)
McCartney, Lynn (sw)
Melvin, Shirley (sw)
O'Neill, Colin (sw)
Rhodie, Michelle (sw asst)
Goodwin, Nicola (sw asst)

Community Service & Supervised Attendance Team
Howard, Fred (sw)
Hamilton, Mary (snr wrkr)
Deeley, Gillian (sw asst)
Cooper, Dave (cs/sao)
Brockie, Clem (cs/sao)

Administration
Cartwright, Sandra

2. **Connect Youth Justice Service**
Unit 1, St John's Sawmill
Etna Road **Falkirk** FK2 9EG
tel (01324) 501060 *fax (01324) 501061*

Vacancy (team mgr)
Brown, Bill (sw)
Tait, Lee (sw)
Vacancy (sw)
Hughes, Caroline(snr wrkr)
McColl, Peter (proj wrkr)
Davies, Alan (com educn wrkr)
Stevenson, Fiona (snr nurse prctnr)
Hutton, Carolanne (subst wrkr)

Voluntary Organisation

3. **SACRO**
Groupwork Service
Restorative Justice Service
Accommodation Service
22 Meeks Road **Falkirk** FK2 7ET
tel (01324) 627824 *fax (01324) 622006*

Richley, Tim (service mgr)
Conway, Bill (snr wrkr, rest. just.)
McSherry, Mark (service team ldr, gpwk)
Norman, Ian (service team ldr, accom)

Penal Establishment

4. Social Work Unit
HM YOI **Polmont**
Redding Road, Brightons
Falkirk FK2 0AB
tel (01324) 711708 *fax (01324) 722297*

Whyte, Jackie (team mgr)
Connolly, Kristine (snr wrkr)
Berry, Ruth (sw)
Brady, Sîan (sw)
Chalmers, Jill (sw)
Irvine, Anne (sw)
Walker, Natalie (sw)
Wilson, Jim (sw)
Brown, Susan (snr clerical)
Archibald, Kathleen (clerical asst)

Courts

Falkirk Sheriff Court
Falkirk District Court

FIFE COUNCIL

Out of hours contact (01592 414000)

1. **Social Work Headquarters**
Fife House, Glenrothes
Fife KY7 5LT
tel (01592) 414141 *fax (01592 413044)*

Moore, Stephen (head of social work)
Miller, Michelle (snr manager)
Peat, Doreen (service mgr) (based at 2)

Administration & Support Services
Rodger, Angus (planning & perf off) (based at 2)

2. **Court Service Team**
21 St Catherine Street, Cupar KY15 4TA
tel (01334) 412015 *fax (01334) 412034*

Peat, Doreen (service mgr)
Lawson, Mary (secretarial supt)

Young, John (team leader)
Arthur, Jane (sw)
Longmuir, Patricia (sw)
Nairn, Sandra (sw)
Nicholson, Alex (sw)
Reid, Aileen (sw)
Russell, Dan (sw)
Donaldson, Tracey (cja)
Mott, Ibby (cja)

Robson, Angela (cja)
Paterson, Carol (team ldr admin)
Fairfoul, Lynda (admin supt)

Sheriff Court Social Work Services

3. **Dunfermline Sheriff Court**
   Carnegie Drive, Dunfermline KY12 7HJ
   tel (01383) 312950 *fax (01383) 312951*

   Arthur, Jane (sw)
   Hutt, Stephanie (admin supt)

4. **Kirkcaldy Sheriff Court**
   Whytescauseway KY1 1XQ
   tel (01592) 412375 *fax (01592) 412378*

   Nicholson, Alex (sw)
   Brown, Carrie (admin supt)

5. **Cupar Sheriff Court**
   21 St Catherine Street, Cupar KY15 4TA
   tel (01334) 412015 *fax (01334) 412034*

   Nairn, Sandra (sw)
   Fairfoul, Lynda (admin supt)

6. **Bail Officer**
   96 Wellesley Road, Buckhaven KY8 1HT
   tel (01592) 414488 *fax (01592) 414482*

   Callaghan, John (bail officer)
   Green, Ralph (cja)

Community Service by Offenders Scheme

7. **Main Office**
   21 St Catherine Street
   Cupar KY15 4TA
   tel (01334) 412015 *fax (01334) 412034*

   Smith, Margaret (projs off)
   Mitchell, Kerry (admin supt)

8. **Buckhaven Base**
   96 Wellesley Road, Buckhaven KY8 1HT
   tel (01592) 414488 *fax (01592) 414482*

   McMurchie, Charlie (team leader)
   Anderson, Shelley (cja)
   Barclay, Jackie (cja)
   Bernard, Caroline (cja)
   Gilmour, Laura (cja)
   Jamieson, Sharon (cja)
   Lister, Lorraine (cja)
   McGowan, Audrey (cja)
   Melville, Archie (cja)
   Pattie, Cheryl (admin supt)

9. **Dunfermline Base**
   Rannoch House, 2 Comely Park

Dunfermline KY12 7HU
tel (01383) 312131 *fax (01383) 312134*

Bayne, Alison (cja)
Gallo, Joan (cja)
Gordon, Emma (cja)
Horsburgh, Audrey (cja)
Lister, Lorraine (cja)
Dunn, Mandy (admin supt)

Services to Kirkcaldy Court District

10. **Report Writing Team**
    Wemyssfield, East Fergus Place
    Kirkcaldy KY1 1XT
    tel (01592) 412424 *fax (01592) 412321*

    MacArthur, Stuart (team leader)
    Harris, Rowan (sw)
    Hopton, Yvonne (sw)
    Kinnell, Beth (sw)
    Lucas, Richard (sw)
    Nicholson, Karen (sw)
    Reddick, Ailsa (sw)
    Sneddon, Karen (sw)
    Wedge, Angela (sw)
    Cook, Rebecca (admin supt)
    McGuire, Bernadette (admin supt)

11. **Probation Supervision Team (East)**
    a. 96 Wellesley Road
        Buckhaven KY8 1HT
        tel (01592) 414488 *fax (01592) 414482*

        Pullar, Arlon (team leader)
        Rattray, Fiona (ssw)
        Ferrol, Jean (sw)
        Francis, Gordon (sw)
        Green, Angela (sw)
        Halliday, Myer (sw)
        Mitchell, Gill (sw)
        Brawley, Bryan (cja)
        Roy, Kelly (cja)
        Christensen, Brenda (admin supt)

    b. 390 South Street
        Glenrothes KY7 5NL
        tel (01592) 415252 *fax (01592) 415278*

        Bell, David (sw)
        Dewar, Mary (sw)
        Lynch, Irene (sw)
        Mullen, Heather (sw)
        McPherson, Julie (admin supt)

Services to Dunfermline Court District

12. **Probation Supervision Team (West)**
    Rannoch House, 2 Comely Park
    Dunfermline KY12 7HU

tel (01383) 312131 *fax (01383) 312134*

Myers, Ray (team leader)
Brown, Karen (sw)
Chalmers, Moyra (sw)
Gifford, Beverley (sw)
Grubb, Melanie (sw)
Hinton, Karen (sw)
Nicol, Elspeth (sw)
Ramage, Maureen (sw)
Brawley, Brian (cja)
Wade, Carol (admin asst)

13. **Young Offender Strategy Team**
11 Boston Road, Glenrothes KY6 2RE
tel (01592) 416708 *fax (01592) 416582*

Kinnear, Bill (team leader)
Baker, Paul (sw)
Barclay, Derek (sw)
Slater, Stuart (sw)
Turner, Phyllis (sw)
Ritchie, Matthew (cja)
Smith, Gayle (admin supt)

14. **Report Writing Team**
Rannoch House, 2 Comely Park
Dunfermline KY12 7HU
tel (01383) 312131 *fax (01383) 312134*

McArthur, Stuart (team ldr)
Hinton, Karen (sw)
Innes, Mike (sw)
Matthews, Maureen (sw)
Munton, Richard (sw)
Rushford, Kelly (admin supt)

Community Protection Team

15a. **Dunfermline Base**
Rannoch House, 2 Comely Park
Dunfermline KY12 7HU
tel (01383) 312131 *fax (01383) 312134*

Kinnear, Bill (team leader)
Hood, Christina (sw)
Ross, Suzanne (sw)
O'Brien, Georgina (admin supt)

b. **Kirkcaldy Base**
Broomlea, 1 Swan Road
Kirkcaldy KY1 1UZ
tel (01592) 417966 *fax (01592) 412139*

Clark, Kevin (sw)
Ricketts, Maggie (sw)
McGuinness, Odette (cja)
Somerville, Sharon (admin supt)

Drug Court Supvn & Treatment Team

16. 7a East Fergus Place
Kirkcaldy KY1 1XT
tel (01592) 4 11563 *fax (01592 412172*

Thom, Martin (team ldr)
Dewar, Gillian (ssw)
Collins, Margaret (sw)
Ealand, Chris (sw)
Hall, Katie (sw)
Kay, Gill (sw)
McGovern, Tom (sw)
Mudie, Kath (sw)
Yule, John (sw)

Smith, Evelyn (addiction wrkr)
Bell, Donna (addiction wrkr)
Craig, David (addiction wrkr)
Emerson, Sara (addiction wrkr)
Henderson, Linda (addiction wrkr)
Turner, Tracey (addiction wrkr)

Murray, April (cja)
Serbie, Carol (cja)
Stewart, Karin (cja)

NHS
Henderson, Ann (team leader)
Hughes, Dr Bob
Pitt, Ingrid (senior nurse)
Baker, Steve (nurse)
Burt, Wilma (nurse)
Collins, Lynne (nurse)
Cowie, Dave (nurse)
Henry, Derek (nurse)
Horstmann, Kerry (nurse)
McKenzie, Kevin (nurse)
Waterman, Alan (nurse)
Herd, Ashley (ca)
King, Dawn (ca)
McLean, Jenny (ca)
Pettigrew, Anne (ca)

17. **Throughcare Team**

a. Dunfermline Base
Rannoch House, 2 Comely Park
Dunfermline KY12 7HU
tel (01383) 312131 *fax (01383) 312134*

Haywood, Phil (sw)
Lee, Helen (sw)
McPake, Joanne (sw)
Rodger, Maureen (sw)
Keenan, Dawn (cja)
Simpson, Craig (cja)
Simpson, Kay (admin supt)

b.   Buckhaven Base
     96 Wellesley Road, Buckhaven KY8 1HT
     tel (01592) 414488 *fax (01592) 414482*

     Fernee, Pat (ssw)
     Fraser, David (sw)
     Holton, Ann (sw)
     Rose, Susan (sw)
     Simpson, Angela (sw)
     Gilmour, Charlene (cja)
     Kinnell, David (cja)
     Barrett, Marie (admin supt)

Courts

     Cupar Sheriff Court
     Dunfermline Sheriff Court
     Kirkaldy Sheriff Court
     Fife District Court at Cupar
     Fife District Court atDunfermline
     Fife District Court atKirkaldy

GLASGOW CITY COUNCIL

1.   Social Work Headquarters
     3rd Floor, Nye Bevan House
     20 India Street, **Glasgow** G2 4PF
     tel 0141-287 8700 *fax 0141-287 8840*

     Comley, D J (director of social work services)

1a. **Criminal Justice Unit**
     Centenary House, 100 Morrison Street
     Glasgow G5 8LN
     tel 0141-420 5500 *fax 0141-420 5760/5957*

     direct dial 0141-420 + number

     McQuillan, Raymund (head of service cj)
     5754
     Sexton, J (principal officer, cj) 5867
     Doherty, L (ops mgr) 5889
     Smith, C (ops mgr) 5699
     Dunbar, F (research officer, cj) 0141-287
     8748
     O'Donnell, J (resource wrkr, cj) 5903
     Vacancy (snr training officer, cj)

2.   **West Area CJ Team**
     Mercat House, 31 Hecla Square
     Glasgow G15 8NH
     tel 0141-276 4320 *fax 0141-276 4331*

     Kerr, S (operations manager, children &
     families/cj services)
     Edgely, Lynsey (pract team ldr cj)
     Campbell, Susan (pract team ldr cj)

3.   **North West Area CJ Team**
     Unit 8b The Quadrangle
     59 Ruchill Street, Glasgow G20 9PY

tel 0141-287 6300 *fax 0141-287 6267*

     Hanley, M (operations mgr, children
     & families/cj services)
     MacPhail, M (pract team ldr cj)
     Friel R (pract team ldr cj)

4.   **North East Area CJ Team**
     6 Buchanan Street, Baillieston
     Glasgow G69 6DY
     tel 0141-276 4100 *fax 0141-276 4135*

     McKendrick, S (operations manager,
     children & families/cj services)
     Anderson, I (pract team ldr cj)
     Strong, G (pract team ldr cj)

5.   **North Area CJ Team**
     7 Closeburn Street
     Possil Park, Glasgow G22 5JZ
     tel 0141-276 4560 *fax 0141-276 4555*

     Simpson, E (operations mgr, children
     & families/cj services)
     Bradley, E (pract team ldr cj)
     Munro, J, (pract team ldr cj)
     McDonald, A (pract team ldr cj)
     Brittain, J (pract team ldr cj)

6.   **Homeless Persons Team**
     118 Osbourne Street
     Glasgow G1 5QH
     tel 0141-276 4800 *fax 0141-276 4801*

     Jim Littlejohn (operations mgr)
     Quinn, J (pract team ldrcj)
     McShane, T (pract team ldrcj)

7.   **East Area CJ Team**
     The Newlands Centre
     871 Springfield Road
     Glasgow G31 4HZ
     tel 0141-565 0230 *fax 0141-565 0164*

     Robb, L (operations mgr, children
     & families/cj services)
     Stewart, W (pract team ldr cj)
     McLaughlin, L (pract team ldr cj)
     McLaughlin, S (pract team ldr cj)
     Milne, B (pract team ldr cj)

8.   **South & South East Area CJ Team**
     187 Old Rutherglen Road
     Glasgow G5 0RE
     tel 0141-420 8012 *fax 0141-420 8004*

     Purdie, L (operations mgr, children
     & families/cj services)
     Mair, B (pract team ldr cj)
     Johnstone, Y (pract team ldr cj)
     Vacancy (pract team ldr cj)

9. **South West Area CJ Team**
1 Merryland Street, Glasgow G51 2QG
tel 0141-276-6430 *fax 0141-276-6512*

George, S (operations mgr,children &
families/cj services)
Kyle, E (pract team ldr cj)
McCullough, J (pract team ldr cj)

10. **Greater Pollok Area CJ Team**
130 Langton Road, Glasgow G53 5DD
tel 0141-276 2960 *fax 0141-276 2914*

Dyball, K (operations mgr, children &
families/cj services)
Sneddon, D (pract team ldr cj)
Hollywood, L (pract team ldr cj)

11. Centenary House, 100 Morrison Street
Glasgow G5 8LN
fax 0141-420 5760

Access Project (Mental Health)
tel 0141-420 5508

Narloch, A (project leader)

Probation Resource Unit
tel 0141-420 5943
Kyle, Liz (pract team ldr)

Clyde Quay Project (Sex Offenders)
tel 0141-420 5868
Brown, A (pract team ldr))

12. **DTTO/Drug Court Team**
80 Norfolk Street, Glasgow G5 9EJ
tel 0141-274 6000 *fax 0141-274 6069*

Hendry, Paul (pract team ldr)
Coyle, Martin (pract team ldr)

13. **Prison Throughcare Team**
80 Norfolk Street, Glasgow G5 9EJ
tel 0141-274 6000 *fax 0141-274 6069*

Ashworth, Mary (pract team ldr)
Kirk, Colin (pract team ldr)
Bell, D (pract team ldr)
Rodden, L (pract team ldr)

Community Service Orders
*CS assessment/supervision now located at
relevant area CJ Team*

14. Community Service (Industry) Team
Centenary House, 100 Morrison Street
Glasgow G5 8LN
tel 0141-420 5805 *fax 0141-420 5957*

McCann, P (CS organiser)

Courts
15. **Glasgow Sheriff Court**
1 Carlton Place, Glasgow G5 9DA
tel 0141-429 8888 *fax 0141-418 5244*

Social Work Unit
tel 0141-429 6830 *fax 0141-420 1703*

Fyfe, R (ops mgr)
Walker, Kylie (pract team ldr)
Ross, C, (pract team ldr)

15a. **Glasgow Sheriff Court**
Social Work Unit, 80 Norfolk Street
Glasgow G5 9EJ
tel 0141 274 600 *fax 0141 276 6088*

Vacancy (pract team ldr)

16. **Stipendiary/District Court**
21 St Andrews Street, Glasgow G1 5PW
tel 0141-227 5401 *fax 0141-552 7895*

Social Work Unit
68 Turnbull Street, Glasgow G1 5PW
tel 0141- 552 1671 *fax 0141-552 5422*

17. **Glasgow High Court**
1 Mart Street, Glasgow G1 5NA
tel 0141-559 4526

Social Work Unit
tel 0141-559 4529 fax 0141-559 4528

Walker, Kylie (sw)

18. **Supervised Attendance Orders**
80 Norfolk Street, Glasgow G5 9EJ
tel 0141-274 6000 *fax 0141-274 6088*

19. **Bail Services**
80 Norfolk Street, Glasgow G5 9EJ
tel 0141-274 6000 *fax 0141-274 6088*

Gravina, Helen (pract team ldr)

Voluntary Organisations
20. **Glasgow Partnership Project**
(NCH/APEX Scotland/Glasgow City
Council)
Intensive Supervision Project
Floor 2, 94 Hope Street
Glasgow G2 6PH
tel 0141-248 7749 *fax 0141-243 2483*

21. **Car Crimes Project**
Floor 2, 94 Hope Street
Glasgow G2 6PH
tel 0141-248 7749 *fax 0141-243 2483*

22. **SACRO** (inc supported accommodation)
93 Hope Street, Glasgow G2 6LD
tel 0141-248 1763 *fax 0141 248 1686*

23. **Glasgow Council on Alcohol**
7th Floor, Newton House
457 Sauchiehall Street, Glasgow G2 3LG
tel 0141-353 1800 *fax 0141-353 1030-*

24. **Victim Support (Glasgow)**
131-141 Saltmarket, Glasgow G1 5LF
tel 0141-553 2415 *fax 0141-553 2405*

25. **Victim Support (West of Scotland)**
10 Jocelyn Square, Glasgow G1 5JU
tel 0141-553 1726 *fax 0141-552 3316*

26. **Probation Hostels**
(Church of Scotland Board of Social
Responsibility)
Dick Stewart Hostel
2 Westercraigs, Glasgow G31 2HZ
tel 0141-554 0212

    Dick Stewart Hostel
    40 Circus Drive, Glasgow G31 2JE
    tel 0141-554 0277 *fax 0141-554 6646*

27. **Talbot Association**
Govanhill Project, 75 Coplaw Street
Glasgow G42 7JG
tel 0141-433 9223 *fax 0141-433 9255*

28. **APEX (Scotland)**
6th Floor, 94 Hope Street
Glasgow G2 6PH
tel 0141-248 4537 *fax 0141-248 4542*

29. **218 Time Out** (Turning Point)
218 Bath Street
Glasgow G2 4HW
tel 0141-331 6200

30. **Phoenix House** (DTTO)
Unit 4b, Templeton Business Centre
62 Templeton Street
Glasgow G40 1DA
tel 0141-551 0703 *fax 0141-556 1374*

Penal Establishment

31. HM Prison **Barlinnie**
Lee Avenue, Glasgow G33 2QX
tel 0141-770 2000 *fax 0141-770 9448*

    Social Work Unit
    tel 0141-770 2123 *fax 0141-770 9808*

    Reid Tom (ops mgr)

Bryce, H (pract team ldr)
Tolmie, B (pract team ldr)

Courts

Glasgow & Strathkelvin Sheriff Court
City of Glasgow District Court

THE HIGHLAND COUNCIL

Out of hours contact no: 08457 697284

1. The Highland Council Headquarters
Glenurquhart Road, Inverness IV3 5NX
tel (01463) 702874 *fax (01463) 702855*

    Dempster, Ms Harriet (director of social
    work)
    Palin, Fiona (head of operations, cj and
    central services)

1a. **Social Work Headquarters**
Kinmylies Building
Leachkin Road **Inverness** IV3 8NN
tel (01463) 703456 *fax (01463) 713237*

    Maybee, James (principal off, cj)
    Nicholls, Pat (admin asst, cjs/central
    services)

Criminal Justice Services

2. **Inverness Area**
Carsegate House, Glendoe Terrace
Inverness IV3 8ED
tel (01463) 724022

    Paulin, Jeremy (team mgr, South)
    Graham, Helen (sw)
    Fletcher, Luisa (sw)
    Knott, Naomi (sw)
    MacRae, Margo (sw)
    MacKenzie, Eileen (sw)
    Young, Anne (sw)
    Murdoch, Sara (crts)
    Fraser, Claire (ca/typist)
    Shankland, Sandra (ca/typist)

3. **Ross and Cromarty**
Criminal Justice Service
Station Road **Dingwall** IV15 9JX
tel (01349) 865600

    Rainnie, William (team mgr, North)
    Barr, Bob (sw)
    Forbes, Bill (sw)
    Langley, Ruth (p, sw)
    Morrison, Gail (p, sw)
    Easton, Denise (ca/typist)

4a. **Lochaber**
Unit 4B1, Blar Mhor Industrial Estate
Caol **Fort William** PH33 7NG
tel (01397) 704668

McDermott, Pauleen (ssw)
MacDonald, Andrew (sw)
MacDonald, Lynne (ca/typist)

4b. **Skye**
Social Work Area Office
Top Floor, Tigh na Drochaid
Bridge Road **Portree**
Isle of Skye IV50 9ER
tel (01478) 612943

MacKinnon, Mary (p, sw)
MacPherson, Ann (ca/typist)

5a. **Caithness and Sutherland**
Unit 27b, Airport Industrial Estate
Wick KW1 4QS
tel (01955) 603161

Rainnie, Bill (team mgr, North)
MacConnachie, Neil (sw)
Booth, Gillian (sw)
Scott, Emma (ca/typist)

5b. Social Work Area Office
Olsen House, Main Street
Golspie KW10 6RA
tel (01408) 634040

Langley, Ruth (p, sw)
MacRae, Diane (ca/typist)

Substance Misuse & Structured Deferred Sentence

6. The Old Schoolhouse
196 Culduthel Road **Inverness** IV2 4BH
tel (01463) 716324

Millar, Lynn (ssw)
Lowe, Linda (sw)
Murray, Isobel (p, sw)
Redmond, Susie (sw)
Murray, Lisa (cpn)
Cascarino, Marie (ca/typist)
MacKenzie, Lisa (p, ca/typist)

Community Service, Supervised Attendance & CRO

7. 196 Culduthel Road
Inverness IV2 4BH
tel (01463) 242511

Boyd, David (cso)
MacLennan, Peter (proj off)

MacRae, Ian (asst cso)
Mitchell, Alan (ca/typist)

Community Service, Supervised Attendance

7a. Unit 5
River Wynd Teaninich Industrial Estate
Alness Ross-shire IV17 0PE
tel (01349) 884118

Oag, Alistair (cso)
Currie, Alistair (proj off)
Terry, Jeanne (ca/typist)

7b. Unit 4B2, Blar Mhor Industrial Estate
Caol, Fort William PH33 7NG
tel (01397) 704668

MacDonald, Andrew (cso)

7c. Unit 27b, Airport Industrial Estate
Wick KW1 4QS
tel (01955) 603161

Brass, Rodney (cso)

Voluntary Projects

8. **APEX (Employment Guidance)**
17 Lotland Street
Inverness IV1 1ST
phone & fax (01463) 717033

McDonald, Alistair (unit mgr)
Tripp, Helen (team ldr)

9. **NCH (Intensive Probation)**
2nd Floor, 46 Church Street
Inverness IV1 1EH
tel (01463) 717227 *fax (01463) 236335*

Mawby, Mike (mgr)
Cameron, Michael (proj co-ord)

10. **SACRO (Supported Accomodation)**
Ballantyne House, Academy Street
Inverness IV1 1LU
tel (01463) 716325 *fax (01463) 716326*

Vacancy (mgr)
Bissett, David (proj wrkr)

Bail Beds
Jeremy Paulin, (team mgr, South)
(01463) 724048

11. Huntly House, 1-3 Huntly Place
Inverness IV3 8HA
tel (01463) 234123

Campbell, Alex (officer in charge)

12. **Venture Trust**
Applecross, Strathcanon IV54 8ND
tel (01520) 744332 *fax (01520) 744306*

Barton, Greg (mgr)

Penal Establishment

13. HM Prison, Porterfield
Inverness IV2 3HH
tel (01463) 223489 *fax (01463) 236595*

Bill Rainnie, (team mgr, North)
(01349) 865600

McIvor, Alec (sw)
Isobel Murray (psw)
Fraser, Stephanie (p, ca/typist)

Addictions Team
tel (01463) 229014 *fax (01463) 229066*

Aburrow, Agnes (sw)
Fraser, Stephanie (p, ca/typist)

Courts

Dingwall Sheriff Court
Dornoch Sheriff Court
Fort William Sheriff Court
Inverness Sheriff Court
Portree Sheriff Court
Tain Sheriff Court
Wick Sheriff Court
Highland District Court at Dingwall
Highland District Court at Dornoch
Highland District Court at Fort William
Highland District Court at Kingussie
Highland District Court at Nairn
Highland District Court at Portree
Highland District Court at Tain
Highland District Court at Wick

INVERCLYDE COUNCIL

e-mail firstname.surname@inverclyde.gov.uk

1. Social Work and Housing Services
Dalrymple House
195 Dalrymple Street
Greenock PA15 1LD
tel (01475) 714000 *fax (01475) 714060*

Murphy, Robert (head of sw service)

Criminal Justice Services

2. **Court Liaison/Fieldwork**
2nd Floor Right, 99 Dalrymple Street
Greenock PA15 1HU

tel (01475) 714500 *fax (01475) 714515*

Gowans, Rab (service mgr)
Bradley, John (ssw)
Howard, Audrey (ssw)

3. **Greenock Sheriff Court**
Social Work Office
1 Nelson Street, Greenock PA15 1TR
tel (01475) 785321 *fax (01475) 785194*

4. **Community Service**
Unit 6, Kingston Business Park
Port Glasgow PA14 5DR
tel (01475) 715791 *fax (01475) 715794*

Clark, Anne (cs org)

5. **NCH Gap Project**
9 Terrace Road, Greenock PA15 1DJ
phone & fax (01475) 727363

and

NCH Intensive Probation Unit
Inverclyde/NCH Integrated Team
7 Duncan Street
Greenock PA15 4JT
tel (01475) 723044 *fax (01475) 723045*

Vacancy (mgr)

6. **Supervised Attendance Order Scheme**
Unit 6, Kingston Business Park
Port Glasgow PA14 5DR
tel (01475) 715791 *fax (01475) 715794*

Darroch, George (sup att off)

Penal Establishments

7. Social Work Unit
HM Prison **Greenock**
Gateside, Greenock PA16 9AH
tel (01475) 883323 *fax (01475) 883335*

Miller, Ann (ssw)

Courts

Greenock Sheriff Court
Inverclyde District Court at Greenock

MIDLOTHIAN COUNCIL

Out of hours contact: emergency social work
service: freephone 0800 731 6969

e-mail enquiries@midlothian.gov.uk

1. Social Work
Fairfield House, 8 Lothian Road

Dalkeith EH22 3ZH
tel 0131-270 7500 *fax 0131-271 3624*

2. **Criminal Justice Team**
    Dalkeith Social Work Centre
    11 St Andrew Street **Dalkeith**
    Midlothian EH22 1AL
    tel 0131-271 3860 *fax 0131-660 6792*

    Neil, I (service mgr)
    e-mail ian.neil@midlothian.gov.uk
    Kelly, J (team leader)
    Sinclair, J (team ldr/throughcare wrkr)
    Anderson, M (cso)
    Borowski, M (sw)
    Vacancy (sw)
    Pemble, I (sw)
    McKenzie, I (sw)
    Varndell, D (sw)
    Brady, J (cs asst)
    Hicks, B (cs asst)
    Kerr, D (cs asst)

Court

Midlothian District Court at Penicuik

THE MORAY COUNCIL

Out of hours contact no: 08457 565656

Community Services Department

1. Council Office
    High Street **Elgin** IV30 1BX
    tel (01343) 543451 *fax (01343) 540183*

    Riddell, Sandy (director of community
    services)
    Sullivan, John (head of children, families &
    cj services)

2. Criminal Justice Team
    9 North Guildry Street
    Elgin IV30 1JR
    tel (01343) 557200 *fax (01343) 557201*

    Dempsie, Blair (operations manager)
    Keys, Miranda (team mgr) (js)
    Carter, Tish (team mgr) (js)
    Anderson, Peter (sw)
    Dufficy, Fran (sw)
    Jack, Esther (sw)
    Meade, Dorothy (sw)
    Reid, Ron (sw)
    Terry, Liz (p, sw)
    Westmacott, Jane (sw)

Other Social Work Teams

3. 1 Gordon Street
    Elgin IV30 1JQ
    tel (01343) 557222 *fax (01343) 541125*

    Moray Central Child Care Team
    Rizza, Graeme (team manager)

    Moray North Childcare Team
    Harkins, Gerry (team manager)

4. **Moray West Child Care Team**
    Auchernack House, High Street
    Forres IV36 1DX
    tel (01309) 694000 *fax (01309) 694001*

    Cotter, Mark (team manager)

5. **Moray East Child Care Team**
    13 Cluny Square **Buckie** AB56 1AH
    tel (01542) 837200 *fax (01542) 837201*

    Gordon, Jennifer (team mgr)
    Leitch, Robert (sw criminal justice)

Courts

Elgin Sheriff Court
Moray District Court at Elgin

NORTH AYRSHIRE COUNCIL

1. Social Services
    Elliott House, Redburn Industrial Estate
    Kilwinning Road **Irvine** KA12 8TB
    tel (01294) 317700 *fax (01294) 317701*

    Docherty, Bernadette M (corporate
    director - social services)
    Paterson, Sandra (hd of service , children
    & families & cj)

2. **Criminal Justice Services**
    157 New Street **Stevenston** KA20 3HL
    tel (01294) 463924 *fax (01294) 471283*

    McCrae, James (principal off, cj services)
    Weaver A (team ldr cj services)

3. **Criminal Justice Services**
    60 Bank Street, **Irvine** KA12 0LP
    tel (01294) 273110 *fax (01294) 278795*

    Hamilton, J (team ldr cj services)

4. **Criminal Justice Resource Unit**
    Community Service Order Scheme
    Supervised Attendance Order Scheme
    Block 4, Unit 2, Moorpark Place Industrial
    Estate
    Stevenston KA20 3JT
    tel 01294) 608900 *fax (01294) 608897*

    Mooney, J (team ldr cj services)

5. **Criminal Justice Services**
    1 Glebe Street **Stevenston** KA20 3EN
    tel (01294) 475800 *fax (01294) 475810*

    Supporting People Team
    Corcoran, K (proj ldr cj services)

6. **DTTO (Ayrshire CJ Services
    Social Work Partnership)**
    11 Bank Street **Irvine** KA12 0LJ
    tel (01294) 311595 *fax (01294) 273870*

    Kane, T (team ldr cj services)

Court

N Ayrshire District Court at Irvine

NORTH LANARKSHIRE COUNCIL

1. Social Work Department
    Scott House, 73/77 Merry Street
    Motherwell ML1 1JE
    tel (01698) 332000 *fax (01698) 332095*

    Dickie, Jim (director of sw)
    Fegan, Mary (head of sw services)

    Taylor, Susan (mgr, children & families &
    criminal justice)
    Scullion, Jim (service mgr criminal justice)
    Cringles, Lillian (co-ord, criminal justice)
    Gardner, Keith (snr cj officer, high risk
    offenders)
    Vacancy (resource wrkr, justice)
    McAuley, Iain (co-ord, youth justice)
    Vacancy, (young people at risk)

2. Social Work Department
    Coats House, Gartlea Road
    Airdrie ML6 6JA
    tel (01236) 757000

    Airdrie Area Team
    Smith, Owen (ssw, cj)

3. Carron House
    Town Centre, Cumbernauld G67 1DP
    tel (01236) 784000

    Cumbernauld Area Team
    Ranachan, Gerry (ssw, cj)

4. 8 Emma Jay Road
    Bellshill ML4 1HX
    tel (01698) 346666

    Bellshill Area Team
    O'Neill, Terri (ssw, cj)

5. 122 Bank Street
    Coatbridge ML5 1ET
    tel (01236) 622100

    Coatbridge Area Team
    Mitchell, Anthea (ssw, cj)

6. Kings Centre
    King Street
    Wishaw ML2 8BS
    tel (01698) 348200

    Wishaw Area Team
    Juttlay, Rajinder (ssw, cj)

7. Scott House, 73/77 Merry Street
    Motherwell ML1 1JE
    tel (01698) 332100

    Motherwell Area Team
    Nicol, Karen (ssw, cj)

    Throughcare
    tel (01698) 346881
    Bell, Liz (ssw)

    Admin
    tel (01698) 346899
    Winkler, Moira

8. **Restorative Justice**
    2 Hunter Street,
    Bellshill ML4 1RN
    tel (01698) 346873

    Hughes, Maureen (co-ord)
    MacDougall, Denham (ssw)

Penal Establishment

9. Social Work Unit
    HM Prison **Shotts**
    Newmill, Canthill Road
    Shotts ML7 4LE
    tel (01501) 824100

    Mary Reilly (ssw)

Courts

Airdrie Sheriff Court
N Lanarkshire District Court at Coatbridge
N Lanarkshire District Court at
Cumbernauld
N Lanarkshire District Court at
Motherwell

ORKNEY ISLANDS COUNCIL

Out of hours emergency contact: via Balfour
Hospital, Kirkwall (01856) 888000

e-mail jon.humphreys@orkney.gov.uk

1. Department of Community Social Services
    School Place **Kirkwall** KW15 1NY
    tel (01856) 873535

    Garland, Harry (director of community
    social services)
    McKinlay, Sandra (asst director,
    community care)
    Williams, Adrian (asst director, children &
    families, criminal justice)
    Morrison, Gillian (hd of strategic services)

2. **Criminal Justice Section**
    Council Offices, School Place
    Kirkwall KW15 1NY
    tel (01856) 873535 *fax (01856) 886453*

    Humphreys, Jon (service mgr)
    Sinclair, Caroline (sw seconded)
    Larmouth, John (sw)
    Hall, Lindsay (cso)
    Neish, Aileen (clerical asst)
    Wards, Tracy (clerical asst)

Court

Kirkwall Sheriff Court

PERTH & KINROSS COUNCIL

1. Criminal Justice Service
    Education & Children's Services
    Perth & Kinross Council
    Pullar House, 35 Kinnoull Street
    Perth PH1 5GD
    tel (01738) 476200 *fax (01738) 476210*

    Clark, Joyce (lead officer, children's
    services & criminal justice services)
    Gilruth, John (service manager, criminal

and youth justice services)
Paton, Mary (snr admin asst)(js)
Patterson, Gillian (snr admin asst)(js)
tel (01738) 476360/476363
e-mail Mpaton@pkc.gov.uk or
GTPatterson@pkc.gov.uk

2. Criminal Justice Service
    Unit 45, St Martin's House North
    King Edward Street **Perth** PH1 5UT
    tel (01738) 444244 *fax (01738) 444250*

    Newton, John (improvement manager)
    Jorna, Kerstin (research & info officer, cj
    services)

Courts & Community Team
Nisbet, Elizabeth (ssw)
Brewer, Jeff (sw)
Egan, Susan (sw)
Fairlie, Alison (sw)
Gavin, Anne (sw)
Thomson, Robert (sw)
Duncan, Brenda (cj asst)
Edwards, Paul (cj asst)
Horne, Albert (cj asst)
McGregor, Shona (cj asst)
Moran, Audrey (cj asst)

Probation & Throughcare Team
Warren, Alasdair (ssw)
Beck, Eddie (sw)
Duncan, Robbie (sw)
Fraser, Gordon (sw)
Greig, Alexis (sw)
Mortimer, Derek (sw)
Penman, Shirley (sw)
Morgan, Christine (cj asst)
Pow, Barbara (cj asst)

Youth Justice Team
Chappell, Alexis (ssw)
Dickson, Alan (sw)
Garland, Tracy (sw)
McClymont, Alastair (social care officer)
Rodgers, Wayne (social care officer)

Admin Support
Campbell, Shelley (admin asst)
Bryant, Jacqueline
Dobie, June
Gowans, Susan
Kelly, Jeri

3. **Community Service Workshop**
    Glover Street **Perth** PH2 0JD
    tel (01738) 445793

    Johnston, Ken (cj asst, cso)
    Spark, John (cs supvr)
    Given, William (cs supvr)

4. Social Work Unit
    H M Prison, 3 Edinburgh Road
    Perth PH2 8AT
    tel (01738) 626883 *fax (01738) 625964*

    Rogerson, Nicola (ssw)
    Cassidy, Susan (sw)
    Geddes, Richard (sw)
    MacDonald, Flora (sw)
    McIntosh, Heather (sw)
    Judge, Carey (admin support)

5. Social Work Unit
    HM Prison **Friarton**
    Perth PH2 8DW
    tel (01738) 625885 *fax (01738) 630544*

    Vacant (sw)
    Vacant (sw)
    Wilkie, Sonya (admin support)

6. Social Work Unit
    HM Prison **Castle Huntly**
    Longforgan, By Dundee
    tel (01382) 319333 *fax (01382) 360510*

    Brown, Christina (ssw)
    Banks, Pamela (sw)
    Lewis, Ann (sw)
    McIntyre, Becky (sw)

Courts

    Perth Sheriff Court
    Perth & Kinross District Court

RENFREWSHIRE COUNCIL

1. Social Work Headquarters
    4th Floor, North Building
    Cotton Street **Paisley** PA1 1TZ
    tel 0141-842 5957 *fax 0141-842 5144*

    Crawford, David (director of sw)
    MacLeod, Peter (head of operations)
    Mclachan, Patricia (temp head of strategy
    & devpt)

    Criminal Justice Section
    tel 0141-842 5130 *fax 0141-842-4144*
    Hawthorn, Dorothy (principal officer, cj)
    Connolly, Mike (joint co-ord, cj)

2. **Community Service Team**
    62 Espedair Street, Paisley PA2 6RW
    tel 0141-840 1001 *fax 0141-849 0715*

    West, David (ssw)

McCallum, Joe (cso)
Hendry, George (cso)
Paterson, Willie (cso)
Stewart, Mary (cso)
Skouse, John (csa)

3. **Community Alternatives Unit**
    20 Backsneddon Street
    Paisley PA3 2DF
    tel 0141-842 3020 *fax 0141-842 1078*

    Kelly, Julie (ssw)
    Broderick, Anne (sw)
    Vacancy (sw)
    Boylan, John (sw asst)

4. St James Street
    Paisley PA3 2HW
    tel 0141-889 0617 *fax 0141-848 9348*

    Paisley Sheriff Court
    Maloney, Liz (ssw)
    Pitt, Gordon (sw)
    Steele, Caroline (sw, bail off)
    Vacancy (diversion off)

    Supervised Attendance Order Team
    Crichton, John (ssw, sao)
    Jefrrey, Elizabeth (resource officer)

5. **Johnstone Area Team**
    Floorsburn House, Floors Street
    Johnstone PA5 8TL
    tel (01505) 342300 *fax (01505) 342380*

    Haggerty, Jim (area mgr)
    Allan, Linda (ssw)
    Buchan, Anne (sw)
    Graham, James (sw)
    McEwan, James (sw)
    Seager, Mandy (sw)

6. **Paisley Area Team**
    Kelvin House, River Cart Walk
    Paisley PA1 1YS
    tel 0141-842 5151 *fax 0141-842 4136*

    Torrens, Jacqueline (area mgr)
    Carmichael, Caroline (asst mgr)
    Kelly, Julie (ssw)
    McCrae, Jackie (ssw)
    Cloherty, Tom (sw)
    Jamieson, Paula (sw)
    Lockhart, Robert (sw)
    Grant, Scott (sw)
    McNamara, William (sw)
    Matheson, Cathy (sw)
    Earl, Joyce (sw)
    Wright, Irene (sw)

7. **Renfrew Area Team**
6-8 Manse Street, Renfrew PA4 8QH
tel 0141-886 5784 *fax 0141-886 8340*

Trainer, John (area mgr)
Allan, Linda (ssw)
Bryce, Sandy (sw)
McAleer, Alice (sw)

8. **Renfrew Drug Service**
10 St James Street, Paisley PA3 2HT
tel 0141-889 1223 *fax 0141-848 9776*

Boyle, Ailsa (project leader)
Hamilton, David (snr project wrkr)
Fitzpatrick, Elaine (acting snr project wrkr)
Bogle, Susan (young persons wrkr)
Smith, Jim (young persons wrkr)
Stuart, Caroline (family devpt wrkr)
Findlay, Michael (dual diagnosis wrkr)
Adams, Joan (gp outreach wrkr)

Health Board Trust Personnel
Ferguson, Mandy (clinical nurse mgr)
Perry, Angela (snr nurse)
Shields, Connie (snr nurse)
Sommerville, Kate (snr nurse)
Forrest, Jane (snr nurse)
McArthur, Shirley (snr nurse)
McLellan, Elaine, (harm reduction nurse)
McCrae, Kirstine (harm reduction nurse)
Parkinson, Margaret (nurse specialist, dual diagnosis)

9. **Renfrew Council on Alcohol**
Mirren House, Backsneddon Street
Paisley PA3 2AF
tel 0141-887 0880 *fax 0141-887 8063*

Crawford, Dr Alec (director)
Irvine, Philip (proj leader, young people/offenders)
Dooley, Gina (proj leader alcohol advise)
Docherty, Brian (proj leader support accommodation)

10. **Pathways Partnership Project**
Kelvin House, River Cart Walk
Paisley PA1 1YS
tel 0141-842 4113/4188 *fax 0141-842 4132*

Scott, Allison (proj leader, ssw)
Clabby, Jim (sw)
Strachan, Fiona (sw)
Vacancy (sw)
Vacancy (sw)
Mair, Jackie (sw)

11. **Youth Justice Team**
6 Glasgow Road
Paisley PA1 3QA
tel 0141-583 2040 *fax 0141-583 2002*

Emerson, Brian (proj mgr)
Vacancy (proj wrkr)
Lesley, Gillian (proj wrkr)

Courts

Paisley Sheriff Court
Renfrewshire District Court at Paisley

SCOTTISH BORDERS COUNCIL

1. Social Work Headquarters
Newton St Boswells
Melrose TD6 0SA
tel (01835) 825080 *fax (01835) 825081*

Lowe, Andrew (director of sw)
Hawkes, Chris (group mgr, criminal justice)

2. Criminal Justice Team, Social Work
13/14 Paton Street **Galashiels** TD1 3AT
tel (01896) 661400 *fax (01896) 661401*

Keates, Dorothy (ssw crt/probn)
Parker, Ralph (ssw cs/sao/dtto)
Cousin, Marilyn (sw)
Grant, Brian (sw)
Hinsley, Judy (sw)
McConchie, Geraldine (sw)
Robertson, Toni (sw)
Sobek, Anne (sw)
Wood, Liz (supervised attendance officer)
McDonald, Kathryn (cj off)
Birse, Billy (cj off/cs/sao)
Pretsel, Richard (cj off/cs/sao)
Matthews, Angela (cj off)
Scott, Eirin (admin asst)

3. **DTTO/CSO/SAO Office**
Unit 6, Linglie Mill
Level Crossing Road
Selkirk TD7 5EQ
tel/fax to be announced

Courts

Duns Sheriff Court
Jedburgh Sheriff Court
Peebles Sheriff Court
Selkirk Sheriff Court
Scottish Borders District Court at Duns

Scottish Borders District Court at Jedburgh
Scottish Borders District Court at Peebles
Scottish Borders District Court at Selkirk

SHETLAND ISLANDS COUNCIL

Out of hours contact: duty social worker
(01595) 695611

e-mail firstname.surname@sic.shetland.gov.uk

www.shetland.gov.uk

1. Department of Community Services
    Social Work Department
    91-93 St Olaf Street
    Lerwick Shetland ZE1 0ES
    tel (01595) 744400 *fax (01595) 744460*

    Doughty, Brian (interim head of service)

    Criminal Justice Social Work Unit
    tel (01595) 744446 *fax (01595) 744445*

    Morgan, Denise (criminal justice services
    mgr)
    McKay, Shirley (p, sw)
    Morton, Fiona (sw)
    Prittie, Francis (sw)
    Alderman, Andy (cs supvr)
    Gilfillan, Frank (cs supvr)
    Halcrow, Julie (cj asst)

Court

Lerwick Sheriff Court

SOUTH AYRSHIRE COUNCIL

e-mail jim.hunter@south-ayrshire.gov.uk

1. Social Work Headquarters
    Holmston House, Holmston Road
    Ayr KA7 3BA
    tel (01292) 262111 *fax (01292) 270065*

    Watson, N (acting head of sw)
    Hunter, Jim (criminal justice mgr)

2. **Criminal Justice Team**
    MacAdam House
    34 Charlotte Street, Ayr KA7 1EA
    tel (01292) 289749 *fax (01292) 260065*

    Court Services, Fieldwork Services
    CS Scheme, Administration
    Gilmour, A (ssw)

Brannan, T (ssw)
Hall D (ssw crts)

3. **Supervised Attendance Team**
    Wellington House
    25 Wellington Square, Ayr KA7 1EZ
    tel (01292) 264493 *fax (01292) 290837*

    Thompson, J (sao off)

Courts

Ayr Sheriff Court
S Ayrshire District Court at Ayr
S Ayrshire District Court at Girvan

SOUTH LANARKSHIRE COUNCIL

1. Social Work Headquarters
    Criminal Justice Services
    Council Offices, Almada Street
    Hamilton ML3 0AA
    tel (01698) 453700 *fax (01698) 453784*

    Cameron, Sandy (exec director social work
    resources)

    Brackenridge, Mairi (Head of Justice
    Services)
    (01698) 453715
    Cowden, Iain (ops mgr, cj/social work)
    (01698) 453918
    McGregor, Hugh (cj services mgr)
    (01698) 307543

Area Teams

2. **East Kilbride Local Office**
    1st Floor, Civic Centre
    Andrew Street, East Kilbride G74 1AD
    tel (01355) 807000 *fax (01355) 264458*

    Finnegan, Hilary (team leader)

3. **Rutherglen & Cambuslang Local
    Office**
    380 King Street
    Rutherglen G73 1DQ
    tel 0141-613 5000 *fax 0141-613 5075*

    James McInnes (ssw)

4. **Blantyre Local Office**
    45 John Street, Blantyre G72 0JG
    tel (01698) 527400 *fax (01698) 527428*

    Johnson, Hazel (team leader)

5. **Hamilton Local Office**
Brandongate, 1 Leechlee Road
Hamilton ML3 0XB
tel (01698) 455400 *fax (0698) 283257*

McTaggart, Ranald (ssw)

6. **Clydesdale Local Office**
Council Offices, South Vennel
Lanark ML11 7JT
tel (01555) 673000 *fax (01555) 661678*

McKendrick, Alf (ssw)

7. **Larkhall Local Office**
6 Claude Street, Larkhall ML9 2BU
tel (01698) 884656 *fax (01698) 307504*

Gorman, Tina (ssw)

8. **Blantyre Local Office**
45 John Street, Blantyre G72 0JG
tel (01698) 527484/527467/527408
fax (01698) 417428

Hazel Johnson (cj team leader)

9. **Community Service Workshop**
2/3a Third Road
High Blantyre Industrial Estate
High Blantyre GT2 0UP
tel (01698) 452030 *fax (01698)*

Allan English (team leader)

Court Units

10. **Hamilton Sheriff Court**
Beckford Street, Hamilton ML3 6AA
tel (01698) 282957

Social Work Court Unit
101 Almada Street
Hamilton ML3 0EX
tel (01698) 452050 *fax (01698) 457427*

Gorman, Tina (ssw)

11. **Lanark Sheriff Court**
Hope Street
Lanark ML11 7NQ
tel (01555) 661531

Social Work Unit
Council Offices, South Vennel
Lanark ML11 7JT
tel (01555) 673000 *fax (01555) 673401*

DTTO

12. High Patrick Street
Hamilton

tel (01698) 452800 *fax (01698) 452831*

Santosh, Dade (team ldr)

Youth Justice Team

13. Calder House, Bardykes Road
Blantyre G72 9UJ
tel (01698) 527230 *fax (01698) 527210*

McAllister, Marion (yj co-ord)

Courts

S Lanarkshire District Court at E Kilbride
S Lanarkshire District Court at Rutherglen

STIRLING COUNCIL

Out of hours contact: emergency duty team
(01786) 470500

1. Criminal Justice Services
Wolfcraig, 1 Dumbarton Road
Stirling FK8 2LQ
tel (01786) 463812 *fax (01786) 443850*

Criminal Justice Service
Pinkman, Anne (head of cj services)
Parkinson, Tim (pract mgr)

Probation, Court & Throughcare Team
Ginly, Helen (team ldr)
Richardson, Marie (team ldr)
Haney, John (snr pract)
McCormick, Jim (snr pract)
Hill, Janice (sw)
Sanchez, Alexandra (sw)
Walls, Alison (sw)
Whyte, Stephanie (sw)
Wilson, Jimmy (sw)
Kay, Linda (crt sw)
Provan, Gemma (cj off)
Shillington, Aileen (cj off)

**Community Service & Supervised
Attendance Orders**
Clark, Sarah (cj off)
Gilmour, Norman (cj off)

2. Forth Valley Criminal Justice Drug
Services
Drummond House, Wellgreen Place
Stirling FK8 2EG
tel (01786) 443900 *fax (01786) 443901*

Grassom, Michael (team mgr)

DTTO Team
Aland, Margaret (snr pract)
Cassells, Irene (charge nurse)
Blair, Calum (sw asst)

Fast Track Team
Snell, Susan (charge nurse)
Grieve, Alistair (charge nurse)
Neary, Denise (charge nurse)
Mackie, Dot (snr pract)

Penal Establishment

3. Social Work Unit
    HM Institution **Cornton Vale**
    Cornton Road, Stirling FK9 5NY
    tel (01786) 832591 *fax (01786) 833597*

    Corvi, Elaine (team ldr)
    Thomas, Janet (team ldr)
    Haggart, Lesley-Anne (snr pract)
    Edgington, Jane (sw)
    Murray, Ian (sw)
    Stewart, Michael (sw)

Courts

Stirling Sheriff Court
Stirling District Court

WEST DUNBARTONSHIRE COUNCIL

Out of hours contact no: 0800 811 505

1. Social Work Services Dept
    Council Offices, Garshake Road
    Dumbarton G82 3PU
    tel (01389) 737599 *fax (01389) 737513*

    Clark, William (acting director of sw services)

2. Social Work Services Dept
    Criminal Justice Services
    Municipal Buildings, Station Road
    Dumbarton G82 1QA
    tel (01389) 738484 *fax (01389) 738480*

    McQuillan, Raymund (partnership mgr)

    Assessment Team
    Steven, Craig (ssw)

    Supervision Team
    Dady, Philip (ssw)

    Throughcare Team
    Livingstone, Maureen (ssw)

Community Service
Vacant

DTTO
Firth, Norman (ssw)

Courts

Dumbarton Sheriff Court
W Dunbartonshire District Court at Dumbarton
W Dunbartonshire District Court at Clydebank

WEST LOTHIAN COUNCIL

Out of hours contact no: (01506) 777401

e-mail David.Rowbotham@westlothian.gov.uk (non-secure)

David.Rowbotham@westlothian.gsx.gov.uk (secure)

1. Social Policy
    Strathbrock Partnership Centre
    189a West Main Street
    Broxburn EH52 5LH
    tel (01506) 777000 *fax (01506) 771827*

    Blair, Grahame (head of social policy)

    Criminal Justice Services
    Rowbotham, David (criminal justice mgr)

2. Lomond House, Beveridge Square
    Livingston EH54 6QF
    tel (01506) 775900 *fax (01506) 775925*

    Court & Assessment Team
    Streater, Paul (team mgr)
    Creighton, John (snr pract)
    Foster, Lynne (snr pract)
    Hogg, Edith (snr pract)
    Gilchrist, Jim (snr pract)
    Kenny, Ada (snr pract)

    Monitoring & Supervision Team
    Ward, Tim (team mgr)
    Conacher, Moira (snr pract)
    Ferguson, Linda (snr pract)
    Paterson, Norma (snr pract)
    Probka, Linda (snr pract)
    Weir, Anne (snr pract)
    Carter, Kevin (sw)
    Glumoff, Simo (sw)
    Morton, Andrew (sw)
    Paxton, Chris (sw)
    Wilkinson, Anna (sw)

Community Work Order Team
Streater, Paul (team mgr)
Hughson, Brian (cwo off)
Young, David (cwo off)
Millar, Lesley (cwo asst)
Moore, Joanne (cwo asst)

Drug Treatment & Testing Orders Team
Oghene, Gillian (team mgr)
Oxley, Sharon (sw)
Pritchard, Geoff (proj wkr)
Simpson, Dr Richard
Napier, Alayne (nurse)
Vacancy (nurse)

Courts

Linlithgow Sheriff Court
Livingston Sheriff Court
W Lothian District Court at Livingston

Nacro

NATIONAL HELPLINES

Resettlement Plus Helpline
For information and advice to ex-offenders, their families and people working with them
tel 020-7840 6464 *fax 020-7735 4666*
Freephone 0800 0181 259 for ex-offenders, their family and friends only
e-mail helpline@nacro.org.uk

e-mail *(unless otherwise stated)*
firstname.lastname@nacro.org.uk

Head Office
169 Clapham Road, London SW9 0PU
tel 020-7582 6500 fax 020-7735 4666
Nacro is registered as a charity no. 226171

websites
corporate: www.nacro.org.uk
mental health:
www.nacromentalhealth.org.uk
resettlement: www.resettlement.info
safer society magazine:
www.safersociety.org.uk

CENTRAL SERVICES

Board of Directors
Paul Cavadino (chief exec)
tel 020-7840 6418 *fax 020-7840 6449/6736*
e-mail ceo@nacro.org.uk

Vacancy (chief operating off)
Val Todd (dir h.r.)
Jackie Worrall (dir community & cj)

Craig Harris (dir educn & emplt)
567a Barlow Moor Road, Chorlton-cum-Hardy, Manchester M21 8AE
tel 0161-860 7444 *fax 0161-860 7555*

Tim Bell (dir housing)
16 Vivian Road, Sherwood Rise, Nottingham NG5 1AF
tel 0115-985 7744 *fax 0115-962 8949*

Communications
Melior Whitear (natnl coms mgr)
tel 020-7840 6460 *fax 020-7840 6444*
e-mail communications@nacro.org.uk

Anne Richardson (events)
tel 020-7840 6466
e-mail events@nacro.org.uk

Rachael Quilton (media relations mgr)
tel 020-7840 6497
e-mail media@nacro.org.uk

Jon Collins (policy advr & *Safer Society* editor)
tel 020-7840 6448

Cynthia Sutherland (publication sales)
tel 020-7840 6427
e-mail publications@nacro.org.uk

Corporate Affairs
Beverley Manderson (hd of corp affairs)
tel 020-7840 6751
Denise Sanderson (corporate devpt mgr h.r.)
tel 020-7840 6750

Finance & Resources Directorate
Vacancy (chief operating off)
Alan Carr (acting dir)
tel 020-7840 6758

Finance
tel 020-7582 6500 *fax 020-7840 6440*
Edward Annang (educn & emplt)
Elroy Harry (housing)
Warren Hillier (other directorates)
Ellen Blenkinsop (payments)
Delia Geraghty (receipts)

IT
tel 020-7840 6401 *fax 020-7840 6720*
Robert Grant (hd of i.t.)
e-mail helpdesk@nacro.org.uk

Internal Audit
tel 020-7840 6472 *or* 07870 275337
Toni West

Health and Safety
29 Welbeck Road, Byker Village
Newcastle-upon-Tyne NE6 2HU
tel 0191-265 7571 *fax 0191-275 9418*
e-mail nacrohands@btconnect.com
Mick Ormsby

Property and Insurance
Challenge House, 148-150 High Street
Aston, Birmingham B6 4US
tel 0121-250 5250 *fax 0121-359 6528*
Rocco Zitola

Fundraising
tel 020-7840 6430/6498 *fax 020-7840 6449*
e-mail fundraising@ nacro.org.uk
Pete Aldridge (mgr)

Human Resources Directorate
Val Todd (director)
tel 020-7582 6500 *fax 020-7840 6414*
e-mail hr@nacro.org.uk

George Moody (general enquiries)

Head of Equality Strategy
PO Box 142

Fishponds, Bristol BS16 7WG
tel/fax 0117-910 4990

Kulbir Shergill

Sports Development
Football
1 Hastings Street, Derby DE23 6QQ
tel 07815 858497 *or* (01322) 273703
Ian Hands

Other sports activities
567a Barlow Moor Road, Chorlton-cum-Hardy
Manchester M21 8AE
tel 0161-860 7444 *fax 0161-860 7555*
Sarah Kaler

Volunteer Development
70 Earl Street, Sheffield S1 4PU
tel 0114-275 3160 or 07973 270109
fax 0114-272 4103
Rachel Jones

Youth Project Development
Challenge House, 148-150 High Street
Aston, Birmingham B6 4US
tel 0121-250 5232 *or* 07802 944620
fax 0121-359 6528
Chris Dare (co-ord)

OPERATIONAL DIRECTORATE STRUCTURES

Community & Criminal Justice
Jackie Worrall (director)

at Head Office
Ann Tighe (asst dir, services)
tel 020-7840 6434 *fax 020-7840 6420*
Jackie Lowthian (natnl resettlement mgr)
tel 01924 893621 or 07968 477984
Corrinne Seymour (asst dir, resettlement off)
tel 07976 715270
e-mail cseymour@nacro014.easynet.co.uk

Chris Stanley (hd of crime reduction policy)
tel 020-7840 6435

567a Barlow Moor Road
Chorlton-cum-Hardy
Manchester M21 8AE
tel 0161-860 7444 *fax 0161-860 7555*
e-mail kevin.wong@ukonline.co.uk
Kevin Wong (asst dir, business devpt)

Sue Thomas (Nacro Cymru youth offending unit)
tel 07968 315072
e-mail sue@sbthomas.freeserve.co.uk

Education and Employment
Craig Harris (director)

Assistant Directors
11 Tan Bank, Wellington
Telford TF1 1HJ
tel (01952) 243689 *fax (01952) 245445*
Ian Threlfall

30 Broad Street, Seaford BN25 1ND
tel (01323) 894034 fax (01323) 894395
Ellen Cuerva

Services Publications & Info Unit
at Head Office
tel 020-7840 6458/6455 *fax 020-7735 4666*
or 0113-239 2604
e-mail spiu@nacro.org.uk
Selina Corkery
Kathryn Quinton

Quality Team
Bath House, Bath Street
Walsall WS1 3DB
tel (01922) 625060 fax (01922) 625101
Christopher Ward (nat qual mgr)

Criminal Justice Agencies Liaison
Keartons Office, Room 1
Market Place, Alston, Cumbria CA9 3SL
tel (01434) 382386 or 07768 631187
e-mail ian.sorrell@virgin.net
Ian Sorrell

Staff Development
1st Floor Office, Forest Road
New Ollerton, Newark NG22 9PL
tel (01623) 861879
Chele Lawrence

National Management Information Manager
5 Bridge Street, Wisbech PE13 1AF
tel (01945) 587898
Linda Goult

Divisional Offices

East Anglia
5 Bridge Street, Wisbech PE13 1AF
tel (01945) 587898 *fax (01945) 582670*
Susan Crampton (divnl mgr)

Greater London
Unit 16, The Windsor Centre
Windsor Grove, West Norwood
London SE27 9NT
tel 020-8761 6242 *fax 020-8761 1825*
e-mail nctlambethyt@aol.com
Sam Sykes (divnl mgr)

Midlands
Apollo House, Rounds Green Road
Oldbury B69 2DF
tel 0121-552 9589 *fax 0121-552 1786*
Brian Kynaston (divnl mgr)

North West
2nd Floor, Russell Buildings School Lane
Liverpool L1 3BT
tel 0151-707 8368 *fax 0151-707 1344*
e-mail vall.metcalf@virgin.net
Val Metcalf (divnl mgr)

Prisons and Resettlement (Midlands)
Challenge House, 148-150 High Street
Aston, Birmingham B6 4US
tel 0121-250 5231 *fax 0121-523 9865*
e-mail
helen.stevenson@nacro016.easynet.co.uk
Helen Stevenson (divnl mgr)

South
at Head Office
tel 020-7840 6492 *fax 020-7735 4666*
Nigel Good (divnl mgr)

Tees Valley/Tyne & Wear
Hutchinson Street
Stockton-on-Tees TS18 1RW
tel (01642) 615554 *fax (01642) 611050*
e-mail brian.rowcroft@hotmail.com
Brian Rowcroft (divnl mgr)

Wales – Nacro Cymru
63 High Street, Bangor LL57 1NR
tel (01248) 354602 *fax (01248) 353400*
e-mail nacrocymru.
northwalesnct@tesco.net
Anne Newhall (divnl mgr)

Yorkshire and Humberside
70 Earl Street, Sheffield S1 4PY
tel 0114-272 2319 *fax 0114-275 1503*
Eileen Lamb (divnl mgr)

Housing
Tim Bell (director)

Performance & Planning
1 Hastings Street
Normanton, Derby DE23 6QQ
tel (01332) 272414 *fax (01332) 273810*
Helen O'Connor (asst dir perf & planning)

Property and Development
567a Barlow Moor Road
Chorlton-cum-Hardy
Manchester M21 8AE
tel 0161-860 7444 *fax 0161-860 7555*
Dave McCarthy (asst dir)
John Scarborough (property devpt mgr)

Resettlement, North
16 Vivian Avenue, Sherwood Rise
Nottingham NG5 1AF
tel 0115-962 8943 *fax 0115-962 8948*
Paul Phillips (asst dir)
Linda Soars (area mgr, Midlands)

567a Barlow Moor Road
Manchester M21 8AE
tel 0161-860 7444 *fax 0161-860 7555*
Marie Hurley (nat training mgr, North)
Patsy Davis (area mgr, G Manchester)

12 Melville Street, Lincoln LN5 7HW
tel (01522) 525383 *fax (01522) 870178*
Sara Jones (area mgr, Lincs)

1 Trinity Square, Llandudno LL30 2PY
tel (01492) 860437 *fax (01492) 878703*
Vincent Murtagh (area mgr, N Wales)

Unit F68, Parliament Business Park
Commerce Way, Liverpool L8 7BA
tel 0151-708 7064 *fax 0151-707 9917*
Susan Shaw (area mgr, Cheshire, Lancs &
Merseyside)

Resettlement, South
2nd floor, Chelmer House
11-21 Springfield Road,
Chelmsford CM2 6JE
tel (01245) 606010 *fax (01245) 606011*
John Lowery (asst dir)
Helen Payne (nat training mgr, South)
Brendan O'Mahony (area mgr, Essex &
Herts)

Southbank House, Black Prince Road
London SE1 7SJ
tel 020-7463 2225 *fax 020-7463 2226*
Joe Hellawell (area mgr London)

SERVICES FOR ORGANISATIONS AND PARTNERSHIPS

Crime Reduction Directorate Services
Ann Tighe (asst dir, services)
Sophie Haines (divnl mgr)
07977 936989
via Head Office

77 Spencer Avenue, Earlsdon
Coventry CV5 6NQ
tel 07976 712077
Pete Gill (divisional mgr)

Mental Health

**General enquiries & consultancy
services**
at Head Office
tel 020-7582 6500 *fax 020-7735 4666*

e-mail mentalhealth@nacro.org.uk
Lucy Smith

Consultancy services in the South West
Barton Hill Settlement, 43 Ducie Road
Barton Hill, Bristol BS5 0AX
tel 0117-935 0404
Dave Spurgeon

Prison and Resettlement Service

Regional Teams

National Resettlement Manager
Jackie Lowthian
tel (01924) 893621 or 07968 477984
e-mail jlowthian@ukonline.co.uk

General enquiries and mail to
Challenge House, 148-150 High Street
Aston, Birmingham B6 4US
tel 0121-250 5235 *fax 0121-359 6528*
e-mail plu@nacro.org.uk

Midlands
Angela Hughes (regnl resettlement mgr)
tel 0121-250 5235 or 07976 715359

South West, Thames Valley and Wales
Judith Ford (regnl resettlement mgr)
tel 01299 269218 or 07976 711987
e-mail judith.ford@nacro079.easynet.co.uk

Lynn Punter (race issues adv off)
tel 01305 257356 or 07866 594806
e-mail lynn@ punter55.freeserve.co.uk

North
Sue Howes (regnl resettlement mgr)
tel 01924 339154 or 07967 177890
e-mail sue@howes16.fsnet.co.uk

London, South East and Eastern
Sally Wentworth James (regnl resettlement mgr)
tel 07714 099155

National Services

Resettlement Communications Service
(consisting of EASI and Resettlement *Plus* Helpline)
at Head Office
tel 020-7840 6432 *fax 020-7735 4666*
Mervyn Barrett

EASI (Easily Accessible Service Information database for probation services)
tel 020-7840 6461

e-mail easi@nacro.org.uk

Resettlement Plus helpline
tel 020-7840 6464
e-mail helpline@nacro.org.uk

Prisons Link Unit
(resettlement training for prison staff)
Challenge House, 148-150 High Street
Aston, Birmingham B6 4US
tel 0121-250 5235 *fax 0121-359 6528*
e-mail plu@nacro.org.uk
Liz Shorthouse

PS Plus Housing Advice Team
tel 07966 773385
e-mail patwright@aol.com
Pat Wright

Resettlement Website
www.resettlement.info
Corinne Seymour

Race and Criminal Justice

at Head Office
General Enquiries
tel 020-7840 6456 *fax 020-7840 6728*
e-mail raceunit@nacro.org.uk

Consultancy Services
tel 020-7840 6457
James Riches

Research Services
tel 07773 343984
Neena Samota

Training Services
tel 07976 711989 *fax 0151-707 8073*
e-mail Nacro10@dircon.co.uk
Abi Pointing

Youth Crime

General Enquiries
at Head Office
tel 020-7840 6439/6443 *fax 020-7840 6420*
e-mail youthcrime@nacro.org.uk

Nacro Cymru Youth Offending Unit
e-mail sue@sbthomas.freeserve.co.uk
Sue Thomas

SERVICES FOR INDIVIDUALS AND COMMUNITIES

Bangor

Nacro Cymru Housing in North Wales
Contact via Llandudno office

Nacro Cymru Educn & Emplt Services in N Wales
63 High Street, Bangor LL57 1NR
tel (01248) 354602 *fax (01248) 353400*
e-mail anne.newhall@nacro.org.uk

Nacro Youth Choices
117 High Street, Bangor LL57 1NT
tel/fax (01248) 354667

Barnsley

Nacro Barnsley New Deal Unit
4 Churchfield Court, Barnsley S70 2JT
tel (01226) 321388 *fax (01226) 241336*
e-mail sharon.dennis@nacro.org.uk

Nacro Grimethorpe Training Centre
The Old Library, Elizabeth Street
Barnsley S72 7HZ
tel (01226) 780961 *fax (01226) 711483*
e-mail e2egrimethorpe@hotmail.com

Barrow-in-Furness

Nacro Barrow Youth Inclusion Project
Burlington House, Michaelson Road
Barrow-in-Furness LA14 2RJ
tel & fax (01229) 871420
e-mail sue-barrowyip@copperstream.co.uk

Basildon

Nacro Housing in Essex
Contact via Chelmsford office

Bedford

Nacro Educn & Emplt Services in E Anglia & Nacro Score Project
Block B, Rogers Court
Cauldwell Street, Bedford MK42 9AD
tel (01234) 344058 *fax (01234) 354484*
e-mail ruth@nacrobeds.org.uk
e-mail paul@nacrobeds.org.uk (Score Project)

Birmingham

Nacro Educn & Emplt Services in Birmingham
Northside Centre, 330 Hospital Street
Newtown, Birmingham B19 2NJ
tel 0121-554 6342 *fax 0121-523 9865*

Southside Centre, 113 Griffinsbrook Lane
Bournville, Birmingham B30 1QN
tel 0121-477 5863 *fax 0121-477 5862*

e-mail info.birmingham@nacro.org.uk

Nacro Housing in Birmingham Prisons & Resettlement (Midlands)
Challenge House, 148-150 High Street
Aston, Birmingham B6 4US
housing
tel 0121-359 8070 *fax 0121-523 9865*
e-mail surinder.kapur@nacro.org.uk
prisons & resettlement
tel 0121-250 5231 *fax 0121-359 6528*
e-mail
helen.stevenson@nacro016.easynet.co.uk

Blackburn

Nacro Time Out Project
10 Richmond Terrace, Blackburn BB1 7BB
tel (01254) 679828
fax (01254) 675706
e-mail timeout000@btclick.com

Nacro Educn & Emplt Services in Lancashire
Units 3 and 4, Walker Street
Blackburn BB1 1BG
Tel/fax (01254) 695653
e-mail blackburnlifeskills@yahoo.co.uk

Blackpool

Nacro Housing in Lancashire
1st Floor, 19 Caunce Street
Blackpool FY1 3DT
tel (01253) 625204 *fax (01253) 620458*
e-mail paula.rutherford2@uk2.net

Bolton

Nacro Educn & Emplt Services in Lancashire
Ruth Street, off St George's Road
Bolton BL1 2QA
tel (01204) 381656 *fax (01204) 559952*
e-mail catherine.kenny-ramos@nacro.org.uk

Boston

Lincolnshire Youth Activity Project
Fydell House, South Square
Boston PE21 6HU
tel & fax (01205) 359664
e-mail nacrotheatreco@yahoo.co.uk

Nacro Housing in Boston
34 Middlecott Close, Boston PE21 7RD
tel (01205) 310718 *fax (01205) 367966*
e-mail nacro.boston@virgin.net

Bradford

Nacro Bradford
(Intensive Supervision & Surveillance Prog.
resettlement & aftercare prog, volunteer prog)
Bank House, 41 Bank Street
Bradford BD1 1RD
tel (01274) 436060 *fax (01274) 436061*
e-mail jim.brady@bradford.gov.uk

Braintree

Nacro Braintree Community Sports Project
c/o Braintree District Council
Causeway House, Braintree CM7 9HB
tel (01376) 552525 ext 2323
fax (01376) 557726
e-mail brewa@braintree.gov.uk

Nacro Housing in Essex
(Trinity House)
Contact via Chelmsford office

Brighton

Nacro Educn & Emplt Services Sussex
Unit D5, Enterprise Point
Melbourne Street, Brighton BN2 3LH
tel (01273) 704010 *fax (01273) 704028*
e-mail nacro.sussex@nacro.org.uk

Burnley

Nacro Youth Inclusion Project
2-4 Venice Avenue, Burnley BB11 5JX
tel (01282) 455457 *fax (01282) 455458*
e-mail caroline.porter@nacro.org.uk

Burton-on-Trent

Nacro Educn & Emplt Services in Staffordshire
4 Hawkins Lane
Burton-on-Trent DE14 1PT
tel/fax (01283) 546727

Bury

Nacro Educn & Emplt Services in Lancashire
Unit 3, Birch Business Park
Todd Street, Bury BL9 5BQ
tel/fax 0161-763 5566
e-mail nacro.bury@btconnect.com

Carlisle

Nacro Extra-Time Football Project
c/o Culture, Leisure & Sport Services

Carlisle City Council
Civic Centre, Carlisle CA3 8QG
tel (01228) 817371 or 07790 013779
e-mail tracyga@carlisle.gov.uk

Chatham

Nacro Educn & Emplt Services in Kent
Newbridge House, 18 New Road Avenue
Chatham ME4 6BA
tel (01634) 818305 *fax (01634) 812727*
e-mail bridgid.parr@nacro.org.uk

Chelmsford

Nacro Housing in Essex and Hertfordshire
2nd Floor, Chelmer House
Springfield Road, Chelmsford CM2 6JE
tel (01245) 606010 *fax (01245) 606011*
e-mail jackie.leno@nacro.org.uk

Nacro Chelmsford Sport in the Community Project
Melbourne Park Athletics Centre
Salerno Way, Chelmsford CM1 2EH
tel (01245) 263688 *fax (01245) 491851*
e-mail nick.emery@nacro.org.uk

Chester

Nacro Housing in Merseyside
2 Handels Court, Northgate Street
Chester CH1 2HT
tel (01244) 318555 *fax (01244) 318858*
e-mail nacro99@btopenworld.com

Nacro Milestones Housing Project
16 Canalside, Chester CH1 3LH
tel (01244) 318232/340794 *fax (01244) 314009*

Clacton-on-Sea

Nacro Educn & Emplt Services in E Anglia
102 Oxford Road,
Clacton-on-Sea CO15 3BH
tel (01255) 431877 *fax (01255) 224129*
e-mail donna@nacroessex.org.uk

Nacro Housing in Essex
Contact via Chelmsford office

Colchester

Nacro Housing in Essex
Contact via Chelmsford office

Colwyn Bay

Nacro Cymru Youth Choices
21 Abergele Road, Colwyn Bay LL29 7XS
tel/fax (01492) 534674

Nacro Cymru DAWN
35-37 Princes Drive, Colwyn Bay LL29
8PD
tel (01492) 523690 *fax (01492) 523691*

Nacro Cymru Housing in N Wales
Contact via Llandudno office

Corby

Nacro Corby Sports Project
c/o Corby Volunteer & Community
Services
The TA Building, Elizabeth Street
Corby NN17 1PN
tel/fax (01536) 206079

Coventry

Nacro Housing in Coventry
Rooms 13/14, 1st Floor, Koco Building
Arches Industrial Estate
Spon End, Coventry CV1 3JQ
tel 024-76 715113 *fax 024-76 711693*
e-mail ian.dawson@nacro.org.uk

Darlington

**Nacro Educn & Emplt Services
Tees Valley**
12 Wooler Street, Darlington DL1 1RQ
tel (01325) 282934 *fax (01325) 465771*
e-mail nacro_durham@hotmail.com

John Street, Darlington DL1 1GD
tel (01325) 245587 *fax (01325) 242599*
e-mail val_work@hotmail.com

Denbigh

Nacro Cymru Housing in N Wales
Contact via Llandudno office

Derby

Nacro Housing in Derby
1 Hastings Street, Normanton
Derby DE23 6QQ
tel (01332) 273703 *fax (01332) 273910*
e-mail dale.nicholson@nacro.org.uk

Nacro Osmaston Family Project
28-30 Varley Street
Allenton, Derby DE24 8DE
tel (01332) 384414 *fax (01332) 203679*
e-mail
osmaston.family.project@ukonline.co.uk

Epping

**Nacro and Epping Forest Community
Sport & Leisure Project**
Epping Forest College, Loughton Hall
Borders Lane, Loughton IG10 3SA
tel 020-8502 4778
e-mail louise.cross@nacro.org.uk

Nacro Housing in Essex
Contact via Harlow office

Gainsborough

Nacro Housing in Lincolnshire
Contact via Lincoln office

Grantham

Nacro Housing in Lincolnshire
35 Westgate, Grantham NG31 6LY
tel (01476) 578503 *fax (01476) 592935*

Great Yarmouth

Nacro Great Yarmouth YAP
c/o Electra House, 32 Southtown Road
Great Yarmouth NR31 0DU
tel/fax (01493) 650979
e-mail wypdp@aol.com

Harlow

Nacro Housing in Essex & Herts
Shield House, Elizabeth Way
The Pinnacles, Harlow CM19 5AR
tel (01279) 443303 *fax (01279) 443304*
e-mail christine.mckie@nacro.org.uk

Hartlepool

**Nacro Educn & Emplt Services in Tees
Valley**
Unit 2, Hartlepool Workshops
Usworth Road, Hartlepool TS25 1PD
tel (01429) 863335 *fax (01429) 860960*
e-mail o.davis@talk21.com

Harwich

Nacro Housing in Essex & Herts
Contact via Harlow office

Holyhead

Nacro Cymru Housing in N Wales
Contact via Bangor office

Huntingdon

**Nacro Educn & Emplt Services
in E Anglia**
Orchard House, 1 Orchard Lane

Huntingdon PE28 3QT
tel (01480) 377045 *fax (01480) 356063*
e-mail carol.marlow@nacro.org.uk

Ipswich

**Nacro Educn & Emplt Services in E
Anglia
& E Anglia Prison Resettlement Team**
247 Felixstowe Road, Ipswich 1P3 9BN
tel (01473) 729230 *fax (01473) 729216*
educn & emplt e-mail
julie@nacrosuffolk.org.uk
prison resettlement
ann@nacrosuffolk.org.uk

Leeds

**Nacro Educn & Emplt Services
in Leeds**
Valley Mills Trading Estate, 334
Meanwood Road
Meanwood, Leeds LS7 2JF
tel 0113-239 2674 *fax 0113-237 9499*
e-mail leedsnct@nacro.org.uk

**Nacro Middleton Youth Inclusion
Programme
& Neighbourhood Support Fund
Project**
c/o Middleton Skills Centre
110 Middleton Park Avenue
Middleton, Leeds LS10 4HY
tel 0113-271 8671 *fax 0113-270 7659*
e-mail raquelgreenwood@btconnect.com

Leicester

Nacro Braunstone Sports Project
Braunstone Community Association
Units 3 & 4, Forest Business Park
Oswin Road, Braunstone, Leics LE3 1HR
tel (08701) 706940 *fax (08701) 706999*
e-mail dean.tams@braunstone.com

Lincoln

Nacro Housing in Lincolnshire
12 Melville Street, Lincoln LN5 7HW
tel (01522) 525383 *fax (01522) 870178*
e-mail sara.jones@ nacro.org.uk

Liverpool

**Nacro Housing in Cheshire, Lancs
& Merseyside**
Unit F68, Parliament Business Park
Commerce Way, Liverpool L8 7BA
tel 0151-708 7064 *fax 0151-707 9917*
e-mail susan.shaw@nacro.org.uk

Nacro Housing in Merseyside
Stopover House, 10 Croxteth Road
Liverpool L8 3SG
tel 0151-728 9339 *fax 0151-726 0822*
e-mail sheilahowardstopover@tiscali.co.uk

**Nacro Kensington Youth Inclusion
Project, Junior YIP**
201 Kensington, Liverpool L7 2RF
tel 0151-260 3768 *fax 0151-260 4322*
e-mail kensingtonyip@btconnect.com

**Nacro Educn & Emplt Services in
Merseyside**
5th Floor, Russell Buildings
School Lane, Liverpool L1 3BT
tel 0151-707 7744 *fax 0151-707 7747*

Nacro Liverpool Youth Sport Project
c/o Liverpool Sports Action Zone
Job Bank, 4 Tunnel Road
Liverpool L7 6QD
tel 0151-233 6142 *fax 0151-233 6144*
e-mail rhiannon.brown@liverpool.gov.uk

Nacro MOVES Project – Bootle
Venture House, 2 Bridge Road
Litherland, Liverpool L21 6PQ
tel 0151-928 9993 *fax 0151-928 9299*
e-mail movesproject@fiscali.co.uk

Llandudno

Nacro Cymru Housing in N Wales
1 Trinity Square, Llandudno LL30 2PY
tel (01492) 860437 *fax (01492) 878703*

Llangefni

Nacro Cymru Youth Choices
1 Glanhwfa Road, Llangefni LL77 7EN
tel/fax (01248) 750732

London

Nacro Creekside Foyer
(The Learning Centre &
Lewisham/Greenwich YAU)
14 Stowage, London SE8 3ED
Foyer
tel 020-8694 8143 *fax 020-8694 8162*
Learning centre and YAU
tel 020-8469 3366 *fax 020-8469 2233*
e-mail creeksidelc@yahoo.co.uk

**Nacro Educn & Emplt Services in S
London**
1st Floor, 230-234 Brixton Road
London SW9 6AH
tel 020-7738 4355 *fax 020-7738 4359*
e-mail nctlambeth@aol.com

Unit 16, The Windsor Centre
Windsor Grove, West Norwood
London SE27 9NT
tel 020-8761 6242 *fax 020-8761 1825*
e-mail nctlambethyt@aol.com

Golden Arrow House
237a Queenstown Road
Battersea, London SW8 3NP
tel 020-7978 3000 *fax 020-7978 3001*
e-mail john.johnson@nacro.org.uk

Nacro Housing in London
159 Clapham Road, London SW9 0PU
tel 020-7840 6480 *fax 020-7840 6481*
e-mail london.housing@nacro.org.uk

**Nacro Inner London ISSP
and Community Remand Project**
c/o Southwark YOT, 1 Bradenham Close
Walworth, London SE17 2QA
tel 020-7525 0949 *fax 020-7525 7876*

Nacro Restorative Justice Project
c/o Hackney YOT, 55 Daubeney Road
London E5 0EE
tel 020-8533 7070 ext 260
fax 020-8986 7446
e-mail vocskath@hotmail.com

**Nacro Resettlement Info & Advice
Service**
C Wing, HM Prison Brixton
PO Box 369, Jebb Avenue
London SW2 5XF
tel 020-8588 6032/6078
e-mail joyce.headley@hmps.gsi.gov.uk

**Nacro Wandsworth Community Sports
Project**
c/o Battersea Youth & Sports Project
Hope Street, London SW11 2DA
tel 07950 923258

Loughton

Nacro Housing in Essex & Herts
Contact via Harlow office

Luton

**Nacro Educn & Emplt Services
in E Anglia**
Contact via Bedford office

Nacro Luton YAP
Sarum Road, Luton LU3 2RA
tel (01582) 507204 *fax (01582) 507152*
e-mail ruth@nacrobeds.org.uk

Nacro Turnaround YIP
Manor Family Resource Centre

Chase Street, Luton LU1 3QZ
tel/fax (01582) 481623
e-mail projectturnaround@fsmail.net

Macclesfield

Nacro Steps Project
c/o Macclesfield Police Station
Brunswick Street, Macclesfield SK10 1HQ
tel (01244) 613481 *fax (01244) 614473*
e-mail lesley.price@cheshire.pnn.police.uk

Maldon

Nacro Housing in Essex
Contact via Chelmsford office

Manchester

Nacro Discus
(YIP Families Support Project, Duke of
Edinburgh Award)
The Ridgeway Centre
7-15 Stilton Drive, Manchester M11 3SB
tel 0161-223 3568 *fax 0161-230 8167*
e-mail discusproject@nacro.org.uk

**Nacro E Manchester Sport in the
Community Project**
The Ridgeway Centre
7-15 Stilton Drive, Manchester M11 3SB
tel 0161-230 6749
e-mail roythickett@yahoo.com

Nacro Housing in G Manchester
567a Barlow Moor Road
Chorlton-cum-Hardy,
Manchester M21 8AE
tel 0161-860 7444 *fax 0161-860 7555*
e-mail joanne.mack@nacro.org.uk

Middlesbrough

**Nacro Educn & Emplt Services in Tees
Valley**
123 Marton Road,
Middlesbrough TS1 2DU
tel (01642) 223551 *fax (01642) 254244*
e-mail nacroboro@talk21.com

**Nacro Educn & Emplt Services in Tees
Valley
(Making Headway) & Court Help
Desk, Prison
& Community Resettlement Project**
230a Grange Road,
Middlesbrough TS1 2AQ
tel (01642) 252386 *fax (01642) 242700*
e-mail makingheadway@hotmail.com
e-mail nacroresettlement@yahoo.co.uk

Newark

Nacro Housing in Nottinghamshire
Newark and Sherwood District Foyer
Elmhurst, 42/44 Lombard Street
Newark NG24 1XP
tel (01636) 702639 *fax (01636) 679538*
e-mail mianp@ ncha.org.uk

Newcastle upon Tyne

**Nacro Educn & Emplt Services
in Newcastle**
29 Welbeck Road, Byker
Newcastle-upon-Tyne NE6 2HU
tel 0191-265 8164 *fax 0191-224 1400*
e-mail newcastle@nacro.org.uk

**Nacro Tyne & Wear YAP
& Community Football Project**
29 Welbeck Road, Byker
Newcastle-upon-Tyne NE6 2HU
tel 0191-265 8164 *fax 0191-224 1400*
e-mail srtorre@hotmail.com

Newport

**Nacro Cymru Educn & Emplt Services
in S Wales**
Bridge Chambers, 1 Godfrey Road
Newport NP20 4NX
tel (01633) 213434 *fax (01633) 213435*
e-mail southwalesnct@ nacro.org.uk

Norwich

Nacro Norwich YAP & Football Project
Bessemer House, Bessemer Road
Norwich NR4 6DQ
tel (01603) 665124 *fax (01603) 660075*
e-mail nigel@ nacronorfolk.co.uk

Nacro Families at Bowthorpe Project
7-8 Waldegrove, Bowthorpe
Norwich NR5 9AW
tel (01603) 747471 *fax (01603) 746901*

Nottingham

**Nacro Services & Nacro Housing
in Nottinghamshire**
16 Vivian Avenue, Sherwood Rise
Nottingham NG5 1AF
tel 0115-985 7744 *fax 0115-962 8948*
e-mail nikki.proudfoot@nacro.org.uk

**Nacro Nottingham Mediation Service
and S Notts Personal Adviser Service**
25 Vivian Avenue, Sherwood Rise
Nottingham NG5 1AF

tel 0115-962 0035 *fax 0115-985 7397*
e-mail nottinghammediation@
hotmail.com
personal adviser
e-mail dawn.smith@nacro.org.uk

Nacro Nottingham YAP, Junior YIP
Aspley Youth Club, Melbourne Park
Melbourne Road, Aspley
Nottingham NG8 5HL
tel 0115-942 2837/4555
fax 0115-942 2837
e-mail nacro@btinternet.com

Nacro Parent Point
Queensbury Baptist Church
Queensbury Street, Basford, Nottingham
NG8 9DG
tel 0115-978 4778 fax *0115-942 4779*

Oldham

Nacro Sport Project
Centre for Professional Development
Fitton Hill, Rosary Road,
Oldham OL8 2QE
tel 0161-911 3052 *fax 0161-911 3664*
e-mail stephen.lee@oldham.gov.uk

Ollerton

**Nacro Housing in Nottinghamshire
& N Notts Personal Adviser Service**
First Floor Office, Forest Road
New Ollerton, Newark NG22 9PL
tel (01623) 863699 *fax (01623) 861649*
e-mail rob.wass@nacro.org.uk

Peterborough

**Nacro Educn & Emplt Services
in E Anglia & YAP**
16 Lincoln Road, Peterborough PE1 2RL
tel (01733) 561596 *fax (01733) 344401*
e-mail (e&e) balwinder.gill@ nacro.org.uk
e-mail (yap) carina.greenaway@
nacro.org.uk

Poole

**Nacro Educn & Emplt Services in
Dorset
& Bournemouth Football Project**
The Lion Works, 543 Wallisdown Road
Poole BH12 5AD
tel (01202) 539966 *fax (01202) 539986*
e-mail (e&e) tom.lund@nacro.org.uk
e-mail (ftball) dominic.weir@nacro.org.uk

Portland

Nacro Milestones Resettlement Project
Grenville Wing, HM YOI Portland
Grove Road, Easton, Portland DT5 1DL
tel (01305) 825694/5
e-mail johnbayley@hmps.gsi.gov.uk

Retford

Bassetlaw Footballing Chance
Bassetlaw Sports Development Unit
17b The Square, Retford DN22 6DB
tel (01777) 713889 *fax (01909) 534529*
e-mail sarah.green@bassetlaw.gov.uk

Nacro Housing Floating Support in Notts
Contact via Ollerton office

Rhyl

Nacro Cymru Housing in N Wales
Contact via Llandudno housing office

Nacro Cymru DAWN
St Helen's Place, off High Street,
Rhyl LL18 1UH
tel/fax (01745) 342585

Roydon

Nacro Housing in Essex
contact via Harlow Office

St Helens

Nacro St Helens YIP
2 Tickle Avenue, Parr, St Helens WA9 1RZ
tel/fax (01744) 677795
e-mail alexthompson@sthelens.gov.uk

Nacro St Helens Alternative Motor Project
Parr Stocks Fire Station
Parr, St Helens WA9 2LN
tel/fax (01744) 28265
e-mail gillwebster@sthelens.gov.uk

Salford

Nacro Salford Sports Project
c/o YOT, 10-12 Encombe Place
Salford M3 6FJ
tel 0161-607 1930 or 07775 591778
e-mail phillip.fitton@salford.gov.uk

Sandwell

Nacro Educn & Emplt Services in the Black Country
Marriott House, West Cross Shopping

Centre
Oldbury Road, Smethwick B66 1JG
tel 0121-558 1902 *fax 0121-558 6909*
e-mail nacrosandwell@hotmail.com

Apollo House, Rounds Green Road
Oldbury B69 2DF
tel 0121-552 9589 *fax 0121-552 1786*

Nacro Housing in Birmingham & the Black Country
Contact via Birmingham office

Sheffield

Nacro Father Figures
c/o Sheffield Family Services Unit
88/90 Upper Hanover Street
Sheffield S3 7RQ
tel 0114-249 5981 *fax 0114-249 5997*

Nacro Educn & Emplt Services in Yorks & Humberside & Kick Off (Football) Project
70 Earl Street, Sheffield S1 4PY
tel 0114-272 2319 *fax 0114-272 4103*
e-mail sheffieldtraining@nacro.org.uk
e-mail sheffield.kickoff@nacro.org.uk

Shotton

Nacro CymruYouth Choices
72 Chester Road West, Shotton CH5 1BZ
tel/fax (01244) 812643
e-mail flintshirenacro@hotmail.co.uk

Shrewsbury

Nacro Educn & Emplt Services in Shropshire
10 Shoplatch, Shrewsbury SY1 1HL
tel (01743) 364582 *fax (01743) 235063*

Skegness

Nacro Housing in Lincolnshire
Contact via Lincoln office

Southend

Nacro Housing in Essex
Contact via Chelmsford office

Staines

Nacro Educn & Emplt Services in Surrey
1st Floor Offices, 11-17 Kingston Road
Staines TW18 4QX
tel (01784) 492192 *fax (01784) 492101*
e-mail christina.williams@nacro.org.uk

Stevenage

Nacro Housing in Essex and Herts
14-16 High Street, Old Stevenage
Stevenage SG1 3EJ
tel (01438) 313132 *fax (01438) 313134*

Stockton on Tees

Nacro Educn & Emplt Services in Tees Valley
Hutchinson Street
Stockton-on-Tees TS18 1RW
tel (01642) 615554 *fax (01642) 611050*
e-mail nacrotv@hotmail.com

Stoke-on-Trent

Nacro Educn & Emplt Services in Staffordshire
2-4 Howards Place, Shelton
Stoke-on-Trent ST1 4NQ
tel (01782) 272525 *fax (01782) 279017*

Rutland Road, Longton, Stoke-on-Trent
ST3 1EH
tel/fax (01782) 332 699

Tamworth

Nacro Educn & Emplt Services in Staffordshire
59-60 Church Street, Tamworth B79 7DF
tel (01827) 56420 *fax (01827) 51587*
e-mail staffordshirenct@nacro.org.uk

Telford

Nacro Educn & Emplt Services in Shropshire
11 Tan Bank, Wellington, Telford TF1 1HJ
tel (01952) 243689 *fax (01952) 245445*
e-mail mike.bainbridge@nacro.org.uk

Nacro MOVES Project
20 Russell Square, Madeley,
Telford TF7 5ES
tel/fax (01952) 272348
e-mail moves.madeley@ukonline.co.uk

Thetford

Nacro Youth Activities Project
c/o Peddars Way Housing Association
56 York Way, Thetford IP24 1EJ
tel/fax (01842) 755281
e-mail ben@nacronorfolk.org.uk

Thurrock

Nacro Housing in Essex & Herts
Contact via Chelmsford office

Wakefield

Nacro Wakefield & Knottingley Junior YIP
The Gas Light, Lower Warren Gate
Wakefield WF1 1SA
tel (01924) 378399 *fax (01924) 378388*
e mail jo.froggatt@nacro.org.uk

Walsall

Nacro Educn & Emplt Services in the Black Country
Positive Futures (Football) Project
Bath House, Bath Street,
Walsall WS1 3DB
tel (01922) 625060 *fax (01922) 625101*
e-mail (e&e) nacro_walsall@yahoo.co.uk
e-mail (ftball) katejakeways@yahoo.co.uk

Waltham Abbey

Nacro Housing in Essex & Herts
Contact via Chelmsford office

Wisbech

Nacro Educn & Emplt Services in E Anglia
1 Hill Street, Wisbech PE13 1BA
tel (01945) 467254 *fax (01945) 467855*
e-mail susan.gillies@nacro.org.uk

Woking

Nacro Surrey Probation Area Basic Skills & ETE Project
Woking Probation Centre
White Rose Court, Oriental Road
Woking GU22 7PJ
tel (01483) 776262 *fax (01483) 727244*
e-mail
andrew.humphreys@surrey.probation.gsx.gov.uk

Wolverhampton

Nacro Educn & Emplt Services in the Black Country
Devonshire House, Ettingshall Road
Wolverhampton WV2 2JT
tel (01902) 451055 *fax (01902) 451066*
e-mail karen.philips@nacro.org.uk

Workington

Nacro Educn & Emplt Services in Cumbria & Onside Football Project
Stanley Street, Workington CA14 2JG
tel (01900) 604488 *fax (01900) 608338*
e-mail rebeccakyra.wilson@virgin.net

Wrexham

Nacro Cymru Housing in N Wales
Contact via Llandudno housing office

Nacro Cymru DAWN
35 Chester Street, Wrexham LL13 8AH
tel/fax 01978 314313
e-mail deeyouthchoices@yahoo.co.uk

SACRO

National Office Services

1. **National Office**
    1 Broughton Market
    Edinburgh EH3 6NU
    info@national.sacro.org.uk
    tel 0131-624 7270 *fax 0131-624 7269*

    Publicity and Media Services
    Sacro Membership
    Service Development
    Research
    Administration
    Finance and Payroll
    Human Resources
    Operations Support
    IT Management and Support

    Criminal Justice Advisor
    Donald Dickie
    ddickie@cja.sacro.org.uk

2. **Community Mediation Consultancy
    & Training Service**
    21 Abercromby Place, Edinburgh EH3
    6QE
    info@cmconsultancy.sacro.org.uk
    tel 0131-624 9200 *fax 0131-557 2102*

3. **Learning and Development**
    109 Hope Street **Glasgow** G2 6LL
    info@staffdev.sacro.org.uk
    tel 0141-847 0738 *fax 0141-847 0736*

Aberdeen & Aberdeenshire

4. 110 Crown Street
    Aberdeen AB11 6HJ
    info@aberdeen.sacro.org.uk
    tel (01224) 560560 *fax (01224) 560 551*

    Intensive Support & Monitoring
    Supported Accommodation
    tel (01244) 560550

    Mediation & Reparation
    tel (01244) 560560

Youth Justice Services
tel (01244) 560560

Community Mediation
tel (01244) 560570

Groupwork Service (Domestic Abuse)
Street Mediation
Supported Tenancies
Youth Crime Strategy

Angus

5. 81 High Street **Monifieth** Angus
    DD5 4AA
    tel (01382) 537077/6 *fax (01382) 537019*
    hou_mediation1@angus.sol.co.uk

    Community Mediation in Arbroath,
    Brechin and Montrose

Argyll & Bute

6. **Helensburgh Youth Justice Service**
    Hermitage Academy, Campbell Drive
    Helensburgh G84 7TB
    tel (01436) 674049
    info@argyllbute.sacro.org.uk

Ayrshire

7. 60 Bank Street
    Kilmarnock KA1 1ER
    info@ayrshire.sacro.org.uk
    tel (01563) 525 815 *fax (01563) 525 328*

    Youth Justice Services
    Bail Service

8. **North Ayrshire Community Mediation**
    146 High Street **Irvine** KA12 8AH
    info@irvine.sacro.org.uk
    tel (01294) 314 020 *fax (01294) 314 021*

Clackmannanshire/Falkirk/Stirling

9. 22 Meeks Road
    Falkirk FK2 7ET
    info@groupworkservices.sacro.org.uk
    tel (01324) 627 824 *fax (01324) 622 006*

    Groupwork Service (Domestic Abuse)
    Groupwork Service (High Risk Offenders)
    Supported Accommodation
    info@falkirksas.sacro.org.uk

    Youth Justice Service
    info@falkirk.sacro.org.uk

Dumfries & Galloway

10. **Restorative Justice Service - East**
Children's Services, Council Offices,
Dryfe Road
Lockerbie DG11 2AP
SamL@dumgal.gov.uk
tel (01576) 205070 *fax (01576) 204411*

11. **Supporting People Service**
Unit 4, Castle Court
8 Castle Street **Stranraer** DG9 7RT
info@stranraer.sacro.org.uk
tel (01776) 706287 *fax (01776) 706287*

12. **Restorative Justice Service - West**
Youth Justice, Dunbae House,
Church Street **Stranraer** DG9 7JG
tel (01776) 702151 *fax (01776) 707282*
PaulineBa@dumgal.gov.uk

13. **Community Mediation**
75 Buccleuch Street, **Dumfries** DG1 2AB
tel (01387) 731270 *fax (01387) 731271*
info@dumfries.sacro.org.uk

14. Unit 4, Castle Court, 8 Castle Street
Stranraer DG9 7RT
tel (01776) 706683 *fax (01776) 706287*
info@stranraercm.sacro.org.uk

Tayside

15. **Dundee Community Mediation**
Suite E, Market Mews
Market Street, Dundee DD1 3LA
info@dundee.sacro.org.uk
tel (01382) 459252 *fax (01382) 459318*

16. **Dundee Youth Justice**
Suite F, Market Mews
Market Street, Dundee DD1 3LA
info@dundee.sacro.org.uk
tel (01382) 524758 *fax (01382) 524757*

East Dunbartonshire

17. **East Dunbartonshire Youth Justice**
c/o Social Work, 1 Balmuildy Road
Bishopbriggs G64 3BS
tel 0141-772 6384 *fax 0141-762 4677*

18. **East Dunbartonshire Community Mediation**
Broomhill Industrial Estate, Kilsyth Road
Kirkintilloch G66 1TF
tel 0141 574 5771 *fax 0141 574 5742*
Annabelle.mackie@eastdunbarton.gov.uk

East Renfrewshire

19. **Youth Justice**
Social Work Department
East Renfrewshire Council Buildings
211 Main Street **Barrhead**
East Renfrewshire G78 1SY
tel 0141-577 8332 *fax 0141-577 8342*
emma.short@eastrenfrewshire@gov.uk

20. **Community Mediation**
Thornliebank Depot CR, 190 Carnwadric Road
Thornliebank G46 8HR
tel 0141-577 3202 *fax 0141 577 8349*
angela.feherty@eastrenfrewshire.gov.uk

Edinburgh & Lothians

21. **East Lothian Community Mediation**
18 Bridge Street
Musselburgh EH21 6AG
info@eastlothian.sacro.org.uk
tel 0131-653 3421 *fax 0131-653 3071*

22. Epworth Halls
25 Nicolson Square
Edinburgh EH8 9BX
info@lothiancjs.sacro.org.uk
tel 0131-622 7500 *fax 0131-622 7525*

Criminal Justice Services
Throughcare
Supported Accommodation
Bail Supervision & Accommodation
Alcohol Education Probation Service
Intensive Support & Monitoring
Drug Arrest Referral Service
Travel Service

23. 21 Abercromby Place
Edinburgh EH3
6QEinfo@edincm.sacro.org.uk
tel 0131-557 2101 *fax 0131-557 2102*

Edinburgh Community Mediation
infor@lothianmedrep.sacro.org.uk
tel 0131 558 7759 *fax 0131 557 2102*
Edinburgh & Midlothian Mediation
& Reparation

24. **Edinburgh Youth Justice**
No Offence Project
57 North Castle Street
Edinburgh EH2 3LJ
Brenda.mcneill@edinburgh.gov.uk
tel 0131-220 3650 *fax 0131-220 5122*

25. **Pilton Community Mediation**
    73 Boswell Park Way
    Edinburgh EH5 2PW
    info@pilton.sacro.org.uk
    tel 0131-551 1753 *fax 0131-551 1677*

26. 4/3 Lothian Street
    Dalkeith Midlothian EH22 IDS
    info@midlothian.sacro.org.uk
    tel 0131-454 0841 *fax 0131-454 0982*

    Midlothian Youth Justice

Fife

27. 24 Hill Street
    Kirkcaldy **Fife** KY1 IHX
    info@fife.sacro.org.uk

    Supported Accommodation
    Supported Tenancies
    Youth Justice Servicestel
    (01592) 593100 *fax (01592) 593133*

    Community Mediation
    tel (01592) 597063 *fax (01592) 593133*

Glasgow

28. Central Chambers, 93 Hope Street
    Glasgow G2 6LD
    info@glasgow.sacro.org.uk
    tel 0141-248 1763 *fax 0141-248 1686*

    Supported Accommodation
    Bail Service
    Throughcare Service
    Intensive Support & Monitoring
    Travel Service

Highland

29. Ballantyne House, 84 Academy Street
    Inverness IV1 1LU
    info@highland.sacro.org.uk
    tel (01463) 716325 *fax (01463) 716326*

    Supported Accommodation
    Community Mediation
    Youth Justice

30. **Wick Youth Justice**
    Unit 5D, Airport Industrial Estate
    Wick KW1 4QS
    info@wick.sacro.org.uk
    tel (01955) 606873

31. **Fort William Youth Justice**
    Youth Action Team Office
    Lochaber High School
    Corpach, Fort William PH33 7NE

info@lochaber.sacro.org.uk
tel (01397) 704129

North & South Lanarkshire

32. 11 Merry Street
    Motherwell ML1 1JJ
    info@nslanarkshire.sacro.org.uk
    tel (01698) 230433 *fax (01698) 230410*

    Mediation & Reparation
    Family Group Conferencing
    Youth Justice Services
    Drug Arrest Referral
    Bail Service

Moray

33. **Moray Community Mediation**
    2/2 Ballantyne House, 84 Academy Street
    Inverness IV1 1LU
    tel (01463) 716325 fax (01463) 716326
    info@highland.sacro.org.uk

Orkney

34. 4b Laing Street
    Kirkwall Orkney KW15 1NW
    info@orkney.sacro.org.uk
    tel (01856) 875815 *fax (01856) 870481*

    Supported Accommodation
    Drink Drive Programme
    Streetwise Programme
    Community Mediation
    Adult Diversion
    Youth Justice Service
    Groupwork Service

Perth & Kinross

35. **Perth Community Mediation Service**
    Suite D, Moncrieff Business Centre
    Friarton Road
    Perth PH2 8DG
    tel (01738) 445753 *fax (01738) 627563*
    info@perthcm.sacro.org.uk

36. **Perth Youth Justice Service**
    Suite 3c, Kinnoull House
    Riverview Business Park
    Friarton Road **Perth** PH2 8DG
    tel (01738) 580582 *fax (01738) 622992*
    info@perth.sacro.org.uk

West Dunbartonshire

37. **West Dunbartonshire Youth Justice**
    c/o Leven Valley Enterprise
    Room 1.9, Castlehill Road

Dunbarton G82 5BN
tel (01389) 772032 *fax (01389) 772033*
info@dumbarton.sacro.org.uk

SOVA

Central Administration

1. **Sova Head Office**
   1st Floor Chichester House
   37 Brixton Road London SW9 6DZ
   tel 020-7793 0404 *fax 020-7735 4410*

   Gill Henson (chief exec)
   Janet Crowe (natnl dir opperations)
   Tarun Chotai (finance director)
   Haja Kallah-Kamara (financial controller)
   Jennie Spanton (finance mgr)
   Louise Castello (devpt director)
   Susan Cooper (director of training &
   learning)
   Martin McCabe (qa off)
   David Barlow (regional director)
   Godfrey Leak (progr/regional director)
   Diana Clough (head of personnel)
   Lauren Wheeler (personnel mgr)
   Nichola Forde (personnel off)
   Tony Savage (head of ict)
   Steve McPartland (ict off)
   Coral Evans (ict off)
   Sue Phillips (admin mgr)
   Michael Sojirin (support off)
   John James (support off)

2. **Regional Office (Sheffield)**
   St Silas House
   18 Moore Street, Sheffield S3 7UW
   tel 0114-270 3700 *fax 0114-270 3701*

   Pat Roach (dep chief exec)
   Dean Howson (regional director)
   Kathy Thomas (regional director)
   Julia Stanley (regional director)
   Gary Kernaghan (devpt director)
   Donna Ferguson (finance mgr)
   Keith Osborne (finance mgr)
   Stuart McQueen (financial controller)
   Lynne Spamer (financial off)
   Ann Naylor (financial asst)
   Heather Eyre (h&s mgr/office mgr)
   Tracey Smith (admin mgr
   Kerry Halsall (support off)
   Ruth Davis (support off)
   Linda Downs (admin asst)
   Menaz Younis (admin asst)

4. **SOVA Newtown Wales Office**
   2nd Floor, Ladywell House
   Newtown, Powys SY16 1JB
   tel (01686) 623873 *fax (01686) 623875*

   Chris Arnold (dir Wales)
   Martin Jones (admin mgr)

4. **Regional Office (Lincoln)**
   SOVA Volunteer Centre
   Lamb Gardens, Lincoln LN2 4EG
   fax (01522) 537490

   Sue Ford (regnl dir)
   tel (01522) 540251

   Amanda Marshall (supt off)
   tel 01522 540 251

Projects

5. **HIT Thorn Cross**
   HMP Thorn Cross
   Arley Road, Appleton Thorn
   Warrington WA4 4RL
   tel 01925 605115

   Karen Henry (proj mgr)
   Helen Griffin (supt off)
   Lynda Salt (supt off))

6. **Hull Befrienders & Independent
   Visitors**
   Stonefield House
   Young Peoples Support Service
   Stonefield House
   16/20 King Edward's Street
   Hull HU1 3SS
   tel 01482 331004 *fax 01482 318356*

   Louise Brown (proj mgr)
   Jill Smithson (co-ord - volunteers)
   Denise Pick (supt wrkr)

7. **Prison Service Plus
   Sheffield - Regional Office**
   St Silas House, 18 Moore Street
   Sheffield S3 7UW
   tel 0114 270 3700 *fax 0114 270 3701*

   Sibylle Batten (dir of ops (PS
   Plus/Prisons))
   Sarah Browne (admin/supt off)

8. **Prison Service Plus
   HMP Ashwell**
   Oakham, Rutland LE15 7LF
   tel 01572 884100 *fax 01572 884204*

   Dee Pandya (case mgr)
   Nicola Gowin (emplt supt wrkr)

9. **Prison Service Plus**
   HMP YOI Askham Grange
   Askham Richard, York YO2 3FT
   tel 01904 772000

   Adele Bilson (emplt supt wrkr)
   Helen Ramsay (case mgr)
   Robin Bradshaw (cover supt wrkr (PS Plus 2))

10. **Prison Service Plus**
    HMP Drake Hall
    SOVA-PS Plus 2
    Eccleshall, Nr Stafford ST21 6LQ
    tel 01785 774100 *fax 01785 774 280*

    Mick Allen (case mgr)
    Karen Foster (emplt supt wrkr)

11. **Prison Service Plus**
    HMP Featherstone
    PS Plus Office, New Road
    Wolverhampton,
    West Midlands WV10 7PU
    tel 01902 703000 *fax 01902 703266*

    Amanda Jones (case mgr)
    Anthony Whitehouse (cover supt wrkr (PS Plus 2))
    Anthony Whitehouse (supt wrkr)
    Karen Matthews (emplt supt wrkr)

12. **Prison Service Plus**
    HMP Highpoint
    Stradishall, Newmarket
    Suffolk CB8 9YG
    tel 01440 743100 *fax 01440 743059*

    Duncan Gibson (case mgr)
    Jane Smeeth (case mgr)
    Ruth Castles (case mgr)
    Gershom Donner (emplt supt wrkr)
    Jimmy McGavin (cover supt wrkr (PS Plus 2))

13. **Prison Service Plus**
    HMP Leicester
    Wellford Road, Leicester LE2 7AJ
    tel 0116 228 3000 *fax 0116 254 1289*

    Jayne Angrave (case mgr)
    Maxine Hough (case mgr)
    Sarah Williams (cover supt wrkr (PS Plus 2))
    Susan Longman (emplt supt wrkr)

14. **Prison Service Plus**
    HMP YOI New Hall
    Dial Wood, Flockton

Wakefield WF4 4XX
tel 01924 844200

Elizabeth Smith (case mgr)
Kelly Smalley (emplt supt wrkr)
Robin Bradshaw (cover supt wrkr (PS Plus 2))

15. **Prison Service Plus**
    HMP Ranby Near Retford
    Nottinghamshire DN22 8EU
    tel 01777 862000 *fax 01777 862294*

    Samantha Dumoulin (snr proj mgr)
    Elaine Nicholls (case mgr)
    Maureen Keddy (case mgr)

16. **Prison Service Plus**
    HMP Stafford 54 Gaol Road
    Stafford ST16 3AW
    tel 01785 773000 *fax 01785 773119*

    Pip Maddox (case mgr)
    Philip Bushe (emplt supt wrkr)

17. **Prison Service Plus**
    HMP Stocken
    Stocken Hall Road, Stretton
    Nr Oakham, Rutland LE15 7RD
    tel 01780 795100 *fax 01780 795190*

    Claire Suggett (case mgr)
    Melanie Dawson (cover supt wrkr (PS Plus 2))

18. **Prison Service Plus**
    HMP Stoke Heath
    Market Drayton, Shropshire TF9 2JL
    tel 01630 636000

    John Leach (snr proj mgr)
    Claire Banks (case mgr)
    Lynne Roberts (emplt supt wrkr)

19. **Prison Service Plus**
    HMP Sudbury Ashbourne
    Derbyshire DE6 5HW
    tel 01283 584000 *fax 01283 584001*

    Melanie Dawson (case mgr)
    Sarah Williams (cover supt wrkr (PS Plus 2))

20. **Prison Service Plus**
    HMP Wayland Griston
    Thetford, Norfolk IP25 6RL
    tel 01953 804100 *fax 01953 804210*

    Jean Guy (emplt supt wrkr)
    Jimmy McGavin (cover supt wrkr (PS Plus 2))

John Careford (case mgr)

21. **Prison Service Plus**
HMP Wellingborough
Millers Park, Doddington Road
Wellingborough, Northants NN8 2NH
tel 01933 232700 *fax 01933 232847*

Amy Smith (co-ord (ete))
Daina Molloy (case mgr)
Emma Shiells (case mgr)
Gloria Bates (emplt supt wrkr)
Kath Guest (emplt supt wrkr)
Melanie Dawson (cover supt wrkr (PS Plus 2))

22. **Prison Service Plus**
HMP Whatton
14 Cromwell Road
Whatton, Nottingham NG13 9FQ
tel 01949 859200 *fax 01949 859307*

Graham Whyborn (case mgr)
Gloria Bates (cover supt wrkr (PS Plus 2))

22. **Sheffield Millennium Volunteers**
1st Floor, Carver House
2 - 4 Carver Street, Sheffield S1 4FS
fax 0114 275 2357

Alice Blakey (proj mgr)
0114 273 9389/270 3740
Catherine Crompton (supt off)
Isadora Laurence (supt wrkr)

23. **SOVA Barnsley ETE**
2nd Floor, Central Chambers
74-75 Eldon Street, Barnsley S70 2JN
tel 01226 215257 *fax 01226 215262*

Joan Bradley (co-ord)
Lorna Szkliniarz (proj mgr)
Libby Wood (admin & monitoring off)
Andrea Chivers (supt off)
Bernard Makings (supt off)
John Gregory (supt off)
Racheal Rowe (supt wrkr)

24. **SOVA Barnsley Youth Justice**
1-3A Shambles Street, Barnsley S70 2SQ
tel 01226 773179 *fax 01226 773180*

Yvonne Winter (proj mgr)
Diane Rookledge (bail remand off)
Julie Sutton (bail remand off)
Stephanie Bradshaw (admin supt wrkr)

25. **SOVA Bexley**
c/o Leaving Care Team
Howbury Centre

Slade Green Road
Erith, Kent DA8 2HX
tel 0208 303 7777 *fax 0208 319 9602*

Chrissie Wild (co-ord (com supt))
Steve Hall (proj mgr)
Julie Clark (supt wrkr)
Henry Lawton (admin asst)
Jenny Hudson (admin asst)
Julie Clark (admin asst)

26. **SOVA Camden YOT Mentoring**
115 Wellesley Road
London NW5 4PA
tel 0207 974 6186 *fax 0207 974 4163*

Sarah Connor (supt off)

27. **SOVA CAST**
Leaving Care Team
92-98 Queen Street, Sheffield S1 1WU
fax 0114 275 2357

Thelma Whittaker (proj mgr)
Christian Dixon (supt wrkr)

28. **SOVA CJC Mentoring Liverpool**
Community Justice Centre
Boundary Street, Kirkdale
Liverpool L5 2QD
tel 0151 298 3610

Gary Jackson (co-ord)

29. **SOVA Connect**
Birmingham - Bissell Street
Unit 6 Saturn Facilities
Ephraim Phillips House
54-76 Bissell Street
Birmingham B5 7HP
tel 0121 666 6708 *fax 0121 666 6919*

Lynne Hughes (proj mgr)
Stephen Lally (proj mgr)
Mel Riley (co-ord (volunteers))
Debra McFarlane (supt off)
Marcia Dixon (supt off)
Sarah Roche (supt off)
Shirlene Morris (admin asst)

30. **SOVA Croydon Young People**
Cornerstone House, 14 Willis Road
Croydon CR0 2XX
tel 0208 665 5668 *fax 0208 665 1972*

Pauline McGrath (snr proj mgr)
Ali McKinlay (proj mgr)
Angela Pryce (supt off)
Joanne Freeman (supt off)
Vicki Barnett (supt off)

31. **SOVA Dearne Thurnscoe**
Unit 31, Thurnscoe Business Centre
Princess Drive, Thurnscoe
Rotherham S63 0BL
tel 01709 892068 *fax 01226 773180*

Yvonne Winter (proj mgr)

32. **SOVA Deerbolt**
HMP Deerbolt, Bowes Road
Barnard Castle, Co Durham DL12 9BG
tel 01833 633200 *fax 01833 633395*

Jacqueline Wilson (proj mgr)
Andrew Heron (supt off)
Susan Henley (admin asst)

33. **SOVA Derby City**
2nd Floor, St Peters House
Gower Street, Derby DE1 9BK
fax 01332 369297

Kelly Buswell (proj mgr)
01332 256 826
Alan Keeton (supt off)
01332 256 871
Jean Bailey (admin asst)
01322 256 829

34. **SOVA Ealing**
2 Cheltenham Place
Acton, Ealing, London W3 8JS
tel 0208 896 0042 *fax 0208 752 2179*

Jean-Michel Jordan (proj mgr)
Khurm Islam (co-ord)

35. **SOVA Essex/DAT Mentoring**
The Probation Office
4th Floor Ashby House
Brook Street, Chelmsford CM1 1UH
tel 01245 287154 *fax 01245 491321*

Peter Brown (proj mgr)
Alison Battersby (co-ord)

36. **SOVA Hampshire Probation Partnership**
Probation Office, 70 London Road
Southampton SO15 2AJ
tel 02380 635011 *fax 023 8023 1801*

Jayne Cookson (proj mgr)
Andy Rouillard (co-ord (volunteers))
Sîan James (supt off)

37. **SOVA Herts**
25d Alma Road
St Albans, Herts AL1 3AR
tel 01727 867 800 *fax 01727 811163*

Godfrey Leak (proj mgr)
Anne Regan (proj mgr)
Joanna McIntosh (supt wrkr)
Rachel Baker (admin asst)

38. **SOVA Impact (Thorn Cross)**
HMP Thorn Cross, Arley Road
Appleton Thorn, Warrington WA4 4RL
tel 01925 605115

Allison Green (snr proj mgr)
Joseph Hemington (acting proj mgr)
Sonia Holdsworth (acting proj mgr)
Patricia Fuller (co-ord (volunteers))
Alice Ranson (supt off)
Sonja Marsh (supt off)

39. **SOVA Lincolnshire Appropriate Adults**
SOVA Volunteer Centre
Lamb Gardens, Lincoln LN2 4EG
fax 01522 543 169

Susan Woolley (proj mgr)
Neil Phillips (supt wrkr)
01522 528 959

SOVA Lincolnshire Befriending & Mentoring
Diane Carchedi (proj mgr)
01522 575 692
Kenneth Yeates (co-ord (volunteers))
01522 575 692
Amanda Marshall (supt off)
01522 540 251
Davinia George (supt off)
01522 543 169
Judith Hibble (supt wrkr)
Kenneth Yeates (supt wrkr)
01522 575 692
Shelley Newton (supt wrkr)
01522 575 692

40. **SOVA Mentoring Lancaster Farms**
HMP/YOI Lancaster Farms
Far Moor Lane, Stone Row Head
off Quernmore Road, Lancaster LA1 3QZ
tel 01524 563 828 *fax 01524 563833*

Ruth Fielding (snr proj mgr)
Paula Harrison (co-ord (volunteers))
Laura Cole (admin asst)

41. **SOVA New Dawn**
137 High Street, Bangor LL57 1NT
tel 01248 352974 *fax 01248 364755*

Andy Esparon (supt off)
Maria Woolley (supt wrkr)
Kate Clancy (admin asst)

42. **SOVA New Dawn**
The Dawn Centre
35-37 Princes Drive
Colwyn Bay, Conway LL29 8PD
tel 01492 523695 *fax 01492 523691*

Catherine Fairley (proj mgr)
Melanie Newport (supt wrkr)
Chantelle Elie (admin asst)

43. **SOVA North Lincs**
55-57 Oswald Road
Scunthorpe DN15 7PE
tel 01724 853256 *fax 01724 851694*

Julie Lawson (snr proj mgr)
Lesley Sumner (co-ord)
Marilyn Lusby (co-ord)
Anne Cater (co-ord (volunteers))
Michele Briggs (supt off)
Nicola Rimmington (supt off)
Nicola Rimmington (supt wrkr)
Robin Tow (supt wrkr)
Marie Allcock (admin asst)

44. **SOVA North Notts**
Dukeries Complex
Whinney Lane, Ollerton
Notts NG22 9TD
tel 01623 860018 *fax 01623 860018*

Kerry Knowles (proj mgr)

45. **SOVA Rotherham**
Bank Courtyard, 2a Wellgate
Rotherham S60 2NN
tel 01709 839579 *fax 01709 515111*

Andrew Whitehead (proj mgr)
Wendy Baker (specialist mgr)
Aileen Housley (co-ord (ete))
Christopher Ruane (co-ord (volunteers))
Janette Walker (co-ord (appropriate adults))
Michelle Earp (co-ord (ete))
Graham Moule (supt off)
Jenny Mattrick (supt off)
Paula Martin (supt off)
Michelle Smith (admin/supt wrkr)

46. **SOVA Sheffield Youth Justice Project**
1st Floor, Carver House
2 - 4 Carver Street, Sheffield S1 4FS
fax 0114 275 2357

Darren Smith (proj mgr)
Rosie Chitty (proj mgr)
0114 2634291
Dennis Ward (supt wrkr)
0114 263 4291

Guy Long (supt wrkr)
Tasmen Stokes (supt wrkr)

47. **SOVA St Davids Centre**
Salvation Army Hall
Windsor Street, Rhyl LL18 1BW
tel 01745 362429 *fax 01745 362434*

Ruth Cole (proj mgr)
Brian Davies (supt off)
Jane Jenkins (supt wrkr)
Robert Hughes (supt wrkr)
Tami Russell (supt wrkr)

48. **SOVA Staffordshire**
Unit J, Ferranti Court, Gillette Close
Staffordshire Technology Park
Beaconside, Stafford ST18 0LQ
tel 01785 276984 *fax 01785 277710*

Becky Taylor (proj mgr)

49. **SOVA Wales Employment Pathfinder**
2nd Floor, 35 Chester Street
Wrexham, Clwyd LL13 8AH
tel 01978 262223 *fax 01978 263332*

Sheree Davies (supt off)

50. **SOVA Wales New Deal**
137 High Street, Bangor LL57 1NT
tel 01248 352974 *fax 01248 364755*

Andy Esparon (trainer)
Lesley Haggis (supt wrkr)

51. **SOVA Wales New Deal**
Marine House
23 Mount Stuart Square
Cardiff CF10 5DP
tel 02920 495281 *fax 02920 492148*

Sandra Taylor (snr proj mgr)
George Stephens (supt off (training))
Malcolm Evans (supt off)
Ruth Hawkins (supt off)

52. **SOVA Wales New Deal**
2nd Floor, Ladywell House
Newtown, Powys SY16 1JB
tel 01686 623873 *fax 01686 623875*

Martin Jones (admin & monitoring off)

53. **SOVA Wales New Deal**
33 Heathfield, Swansea SA1 6EJ
tel 01792 463597 *fax 01792 461884*

Elizabeth Beguin (proj mgr)
Christopher Collins (training mgr)
Lesley Evans (admin asst)

54. **SOVA Wales New Deal**
2nd Floor, 35 Chester Street
Wrexham, Clwyd LL13 8AH
tel 01978 262223 *fax 01978 263332*

Yvonne Reeves (supt off)
Angela Priest-Jones (admin asst)

55. **SOVA Wessex**
YOT Early Intervention Centre
Bolton Crescent, Basingstoke
tel 01256 854850 *fax 01256 840345*

Andrew Hood (supt off)
Anna Burchett (supt off)
Jason Weatherall (supt off)
Karen Salkeld (supt off)

56. **SOVA Wessex**
62 Crocker Street, Newport
Isle of Wight PO30 5DA
tel 01983 522799 *fax 01983 523175*

Margaret Martin (proj mgr)
Clare Fuller (admin supt off)

57. **SOVA Wessex**
Darby House, Skye Close
Cosham, Portsmouth PO6 3LU
tel 023 9232 7393

Alan Crisford (snr proj mgr)
Elaine Cameron (supt off)
Jan Howell (supt off)
Jane Baldacchino (supt off)
Sarah Pope (supt off)
Katherine Gunns (admin asst)

58. **SOVA Wessex**
Wheatsheaf House
24 Bernard Street
Southampton, Hants SO14 3AY
tel 023 8038 6837

Stephanie Braithwaite (snr proj mgr)
Emma Janowicz (reparation off (tupe))
Gail Dimmick (reparation off (tupe))
Kelly Sydenham (reparation off (tupe))
Emma Smith (supt off)

59. **SOVA Wessex**
2nd Floor, 85 High Street
Winchester, Hants SO23 9AE
tel 01962 876100 *fax 01962 876109*

Andy Rouillard (co-ord (volunteers))

60. **SOVA Yorkshire Prisons ETE**
HMP Everthorpe, Brough
East Yorkshire HU15 1RD

tel 01430 426500 *fax 01430 421351*

Craig Milner (monitoring off)
Gina Carter (prog mgr)
Philip Marsham (supt wrkr)

61. **SOVA Yorkshire Prisons ETE**
HMP Lindholme, Bawtry Road
Hatfield Woodhouse
Doncaster DN7 6EE
tel 01302 848891

Gina Carter (prog mgr)
Craig Milner (monitoring off)
Fiona Ross (co-ord (ete))
Michele Hilton (co-ord (ete))
Peter Wenyon (co-ord (ete))

62. **SOVA Yorkshire Prisons ETE**
HMP/YOI Moorland Closed
Bawtry Road, Hatfield Woodhouse
Doncaster DN7 6BW
tel 01302 523000 ext 3009
fax 01302 350896

Michele Hilton (co-ord (ete))
Peter Wenyon (co-ord (ete))

63. **SOVA Yorkshire Prisons ETE**
HMP/YOI Moorland Open
Thorne Road, Hatfield
Doncaster DN7 6EL
tel 01405 746705 *fax 01405 746702*

Gina Carter (prog mgr)
John Taylor-Jones (co-ord (ete))
Audra White (supt wrkr)
Craig Milner (monitoring off)
Laura Godley (supt wrkr)

64. **SOVA Yorkshire Prisons ETE**
HMP/YOI Northallerton
East Road, Northallerton DL6 1NW
tel 01609 780078

Gina Carter (prog mgr)
Anne Mableson (co-ord (ete))
Craig Milner (co-ord (ete)/monitoring off)
Philip Marsham (supt wrkr)

65. **SOVA Yorkshire Prisons ETE**
HMP Wealstun, Wetherby
West Yorkshire
tel 01937 844844 ext 3286
fax 01937 845862

Gina Carter (prog mgr)
Carol Wickow (co-ord (ete))
Claire Slack (co-ord (ete))
Mark Wilkinson (co-ord (ete))

Craig Milner (monitoring off)
Philip Marsham (supt wrkr)

66. **Swansea Refugee Mentoring Project**
Marine House, 23 Mount Stuart Square
Cardiff
tel 02920 495281 *fax 02920 492148*

Adil Shashaty (supt off)

67. **SYOP Skills Network**
St Silas House, 18 Moore Street
Sheffield S3 7UW
tel 0114 270 3700 *fax 0114 270 3701*

Gina Carter (prog director)
Sarah Hartley (prog director)
Jayne Fraser (specialist mgr - qual imp)
Mohammed Aklim (finance & monitoring mgr)
Kay Biggin (supt off)

68. **Women Into Work**
SOVA, St Silas House
18 Moore Street, Sheffield S3 7UW
tel 0114 270 3700 *fax 0114 270 3701*

Amy Christian (special progs mgr)
George Alexander (snr finance mgr)
Clare Bateman (finance mgr)
Joanne Tate (specialist mgr)
Julie Otter (prog director)

Women Building Futures
Maryann Quinn (specialist mgr)
Paul Rotherham (admin/supt off)
Kay Nixon (supt wrkr)

Women Moving On
Valerie Monti Holland (snr proj mgr)
Tanya Ferreyra (prog mgr)
Nichola Cadet (prog director)
Heidi March (finance mgr)
Jenny Douglas (supt wrkr)
Maryann Quinn (specialist mgr)
Claire Plant (admin/supt off)

69. **Women into Work**
Women Building Futures
SOVA, 1st Floor, Chichester House
37 Brixton Road, London SW9 6DZ
tel 0207 793 0404 *fax 0207 735 4410*

Ruthann Hughes (snr proj mgr)
Sîan Morgan (admin asst)

Women Moving On
Inoa Irving (prog director)
Anne Shomefun (prog mgr)
Aku Adjei (admin wrkr)
Julie Nguyen (admin/supt off)

RAINER

1. Rainer (Royal Philanthropic Society
incorporating The Rainer Foundation)
Rectory Lodge
High Street, Brasted
Nr Westerham, Kent TN16 1JF
tel (01959) 578200 *fax (01959) 561891*
e-mail mail@ raineronline.org
www.raineronline.org

Partnership projects providing education,
training and employment, housing and
support services for young people at risk.

**Projects in partnership with
Probation Services**

2. **Rainer Break Free**
Palm Tree Court
Unit 1, 4 Factory Lane
Bruce Grove, London N17 9LF
020-8885 5000

3. **Rainer Essex Motor Project**
Unit 9, Winstanley Way
Basildon, Essex SS14 3BP
(01268) 273380

4. **Rainer W Sussex Accommodation**
2nd Floor, 6 Liverpool Terrace
Worthing, W Sussex BN11 1TA
(01903) 219600

5. **Rainer Medway Motor Project**
Unit 28, Castle View Business Centre
Rochester, Kent ME1 1PH
(01634) 811466

6. **Rainer South Yorkshire**
4th Floor, 40 Castle Square
Sheffield, S Yorks S1 2GF
0114-275 9291

7. **Rainer West Mercia**
Camelot House, 60 Barbourne Road
Worcester WR1 1JA
(01905) 731831

8. **Rainer Humberside**
above 32-34 Wellowgate
Hainton Square, Grimsby
Humberside DN32 0RA
(01472) 358213

9. **Rainer London Housing**
Russell House, 84/90 Lordship Lane

East Dulwich, London SE22 8HF
020-8693 3311

10. **Rainer Wigan**
Coops Foyer
Chequer Street, Wigan WN1 1HN
tel (01942) 239871

11. **Rainer Lincolnshire**
76 South Park
Lincoln LN5 8ES
tel (01522) 523593

VICTIM SERVICES

NOMS Victim Helpline
NOMS Victim Helpline, Assisted Prison Visits
Unit, PO Box 4278, Birmingham B15 1SA

Telephone 08457 585112 - Monday to Friday
9am To 4pm (24 hour answer machine at other
times)

Part of the National Offender Management
Service in the Home Office

Head of Unit, A K Jones 0121 626 2208
Team leader 0121 626 3331
Information available at
www.hmprisonservice.gov.uk

Mediation UK
Alexander House, Telephone Avenue, Bristol
BS1 4BS
tel 0117 904 6661 *fax 0117 904 3331*
enquiry@mediationuk.org.uk

Tony Billinghurst (director)
Paul Crosland (head of restorative justice)

Mediation UK is the umbrella organisation for
victim-offender, community and schools
mediation work. It provides a link to existing
local mediation services and provides support
for the development of a comprehensive
provision of restorative approaches. The website provides information about finding a victim-
offender mediator as well as information about
publications, training, events etc. Anyone can
join Mediation UK to support the development
of the skills and processes underlying mediation
and reparation.

RJ Practitioner Network
c/o Mediation UK

The RJ Practitioners Network holds an annual
gathering (October) from which informal links
are developed to support restorative practice

working between victims, offenders and
community. Electronic discussion forums are on
the members section of the Mediation UK website. Contact Paul Crosland at Mediation UK for
further details.

Victim Support
National Office, Cranmer House, 39 Brixton
Road, London SW9 6DZ
020-7735 9166 *fax 020-7582 5712.*

Co-ordinates the work of local community-
based branches providing services to victims of
crime and their families, also co-ordinates the
Witness Service which supports witnesses in
every criminal court in England and Wales.

**SAMM (Support After Murder and
Manslaughter)**
Cranmer House, 39 Brixton Road, London SW9
6DZ
020-7735 3838

Offers understanding and support to families
and friends bereaved as a result of murder and
manslaughter, through the mutual support of
others who have suffered a similar tragedy.

Scotland
For information on restorative approaches in
the CJ system in Scotland
SACRO National Office
1 Broughton Market, Edinburgh EH3 6NU
info@national.sacro.org.uk
tel 0131-624 7270 *fax 0131-624 7269*

SACRO stands for Safeguarding Communities
Reducing Offending. Diversion from
prosecution services for adults are provided by
SACRO in a number of areas (see main SACRO
entry) taking referrals from the procurator
fiscal. Drawing on the principles of restorative
justice, these SACRO services offer victims of
crime and those accused the opportunity to
communicate safely and come to agreement on
how the crime and its affects can be resolved
without using the court process. Prosecution is
deferred pending the outcome of this type of
intervention.

ARTS FOR OFFENDERS

**Anne Peaker Centre for Arts in Criminal
Justice**
Neville House, 90/91 Northgate, Canterbury,
Kent CT1 1BA
tel (01227) 470629 *fax (01227) 379704*

e-mail info@apcentre.org.uk

The national umbrella organisation that promotes and supports the use of arts in criminal justice. Offering bespoke training, research, roundtables and an annual conference. The Centre promotes two online resources *www.joiningthedots.co.uk* (an interactive online resource providing details of experienced practitioners and workshop ideas) and *www.artsontheout.co.uk* (a web based resource for offenders and ex-offenders).

Professional membership of the **Arts in Criminal Justice Forum** offers networking, training, continuous professional development and other valuable support for creative professionals working in the arts in the criminal justice sector.

A comprehensive listing of arts projects can be found on the two web sites listed above. Below is a selection of directly relevant projects, including some that may not appear on the web sites.

Acting Out Company
The Roslyn Works, Uttoxeter Road, Longton, Stoke on Trent ST3 1PQ
tel (01782) 501504 e-mail: admin@rideout.co.uk

Develops and provides groupwork for young and adult offenders, as well as staff training in drama based groupwork techniques and conducting theatre based residential projects for prisons and probation.

Arts Alive Trust
55 Wellesley Road, Gospel Oak,
London NW5 4PN
tel 020-7482 2811

The central concern of the Trust is to encourage the creative ability of young offenders from ethnic minority backgrounds and give them a voice.

Burnbake Trust
29 North Street, Wilton, Wilts SP2 0HE
tel (01722) 743727.

Aims to aid the rehabilitation of offenders and ex-offenders through an active participation and enjoyment of the arts. It has three main areas of interest: arts & craft, music and poetry. The Trust provides art materials whether for cell hobbies or educational purposes.

Clean Break Theatre Company
2 Patshull Road London NW5 2LB
tel 020-7482 8600 *fax 020-7482 8611* e-mail general@cleanbreak.org.uk
www.cleanbreak.org.uk

Clean Break provides accredited and non-accredited education and training courses in theatre and the performing arts for women with experience of the criminal justice system or are at risk of offending due to drug/alcohol or mental health needs. The company produces an annual production on the theme of women and crime. It also runs vocational training and professional development courses nationally.

The Comedy School
15 Gloucester Gate, London NW1 4HG
tel 020-7486 1844
e-mail@thecomedyschool.com

Practical and realistic approaches to stand-up comedy in prisons nationally. Believes that comedy is a powerful tool that can be used to help people gain the motivation to learn.

Dance United
171 Glenarm Road, Hackney, London E5 0NR
tel 020-8533 0001 *fax 020-8985 4424* e-mail info@dance-united.com

Plays a part in helping marginalised or excluded people to transform the way they see themselves and the way they are viewed by society. Through the dance process offenders are able top research their identity as a community and as individuals.

Escape Artists Theatre Company
91 Cherry Hinton Road, Cambridge CB1 7BS
tel (01223) 245945 fax 01233 478140 e-mail info@escapeartists.co.uk
www.escapeartists.co.uk

Provides NOCN accredited arts based programmes and pre-employment training courses specifically designed for use within the criminal justice sector.

Fine Cell Work
38 Buckingham Palace Road,
London SW1W 0RE
tel 020-7931 9998 e-mail enquiries@finecellwork.co.uk
www.finecellwork.co.uk

A registered charity that teaches needlework to inmates, pays them for their work so they can accumulate a nestegg and sells their products.

The inmates are taught by volunteers from the Embroiderers Guild, the Royal School of Needlework and the world of professional design. The prisoners do the work in their cells and the earnings give them hope, skills and independence.

Geese Theatre Company
Midlands Arts Centre, Cannon Hill Park, Birmingham, B12 9QH
tel 0121-446 4370 *fax 0121-446 5806* e-mail mailbox@geese.co.uk www.geese.co.uk

Geese Theatre Company is a team of specialised theatre practitioners working within the criminal justice system. Geese design and deliver performances, workshops, groupwork programmes and creative residencies with offenders and young people at risk of offending both in a custodial and a community setting. Geese also provides staff training and consultancy with criminal justice system staff and bespoke performances at criminal justice conferences

Inside Job Theatre Projects
c/o PO Box 47058, London SW18 3YA.
e-mail inside.job@virgin.net www.InsideJob.org

Inside Job believes that the theatre's means of transformation can act as a powerful incentive to those who need to make changes to themselves if they are to emerge from custody as non-offenders. The work is led by Inside Job but carried out by inmates and the prisons themselves. Projects culminate in performances to a whole prison audience and invited guests.

Insight Arts
7-15 Greatorex Street, London E1 5NF
tel 020-7247 0778 *fax 020-7247 8077* e-mail info@insightarts.org

Insight Arts uses the arts as an imaginative territory to explore change and provides ground-breaking drama, multi arts and life skills projects for ex-offenders, probation clients, people in prison and young people at risk. The organisation offers social development, accreditation, progression and employment through courses, prison residencies, life-skills workshops, public performances and work placements.

Irene Taylor Trust
Music in Prisons, Unit 114, Bon Marche Centre, 241 Ferndale Road, London SW9 8BJ
tel 020-7733 3222 *fax 020-7733 3310* e-mail

info@musicinprisons.org.uk
www.musicinprisons.org.uk

'Music in Prisons' is committed to encouraging and establishing the use of music as part of the rehabilitation process. By working directly with men, women and young offenders the Trust is helping to raise the profile of music and arts in prisons through the evaluation and dissemination of its working practices

Koestler Trust
Koestler Arts Centre, 168a Du Cane Road, London W12 0TX
tel 020-8740 0333 e-mail info@koestlertrust.org.uk

A prison arts charity, founded by Arthur Koestler in 1962. Through its annual competition and exhibition, it promotes and encourages the arts and creativity in UK prisons, YOIs, high security hospitals, secure units and probation. In addition, the projects conducted under its Learning to Learn through the Arts scheme are designed to help prisoners gain new skills and self confidence required to engage in education, training and subsequently employment.

London Shakespeare Workout (LSW) Prison Project
181a Faunce House, Doddington Grove, Kennington, London SE17 3TB
tel 020-7793 9755 fax 0207-735 5911 e-mail londonswo@hotmail.com

Acts as a service organisation for the professional theatre community and in turn, one that reaches out in terms of modified workouts. It aims to unveil creative abilities where perceived disabilities previously prevailed and offer arts access that may not have been an easy option in the past.

Safe Ground Productions
PO Box 11525, London SW11 5ZW
tel 020-7228 3831 *fax 020-7228 3885* e-mail safeground@aol.com

Produces projects and programmes of education using drama, design and film. Also focuses on peer education and parenting projects, and mapping key skills.

Soft Touch Community Arts
120a Hartopp Road, Leicester LE2 1WF
tel 0116-270 2706 e-mail sally@soft-touch.org.uk

An experienced community arts organisation that works across a wide range of art forms (music, video, graphics, digital media, drama and street art). They aim to encourage and achieve participation in the arts, particularly in sections of the community experiencing disadvantage or discrimination.

Synergy Theatre Project
Hyde Park House, 5 Manfred Road, London SW15 2RS
tel 020-8870 2112
e-mail synergytheatreproject@hotmail.com

Runs theatre based projects in prisons and creates drama opportunities for ex-offenders on their release.

The Theatre in Prison and Probation Centre (TIPP)
c/o Drama Department, Manchester University, Oxford Road, Manchester M13 9PL
tel 0161-275 3047 *fax 0161-275 3877*
e-mail tipp@man.ac.uk

Uses theatre to explore issues (drugs, anger management, employment, etc) with socially excluded groups; particularly within the criminal justice system. Also provides specialist training.

The Writers in Prisons Network
PO Box 71, Welshpool SY21 0WB
tel (01938) 811355 e-mail wipn@btinternet.com

Supports a wide range of prison-based projects (and in the wider Criminal Justice system) that use creative writing, oral storytelling, publishing, video, radio, theatre, reading and music to address issues such as adult literacy, parenting, journalism and personal development. Writers in residence are placed in prisons to work for 2.5 days a week for up to three years. The scheme is jointly funded by Arts Council England, the Learning & Skills Council and individual establishments. Lord Longford Prize Winner 2004.

EDUCATION FOR PRISONERS

Prisoners' Education Trust
Wandle House, Riverside Drive, Mitcham, Surrey CR4 4BU
tel 020-8648 7760 *fax 020-8648 7762*
e-mail info@prisonerseducation.org.uk

A national charity that aims to extend and

enrich educational opportunities available to prisoners. It offers grants to prisoners with at least six months to serve (or a good chance of completing the course before release) to enable them to study by distance learning. Courses that have been studied range from GCSEs, A levels, Open University Degrees to subjects such as fitness, counselling, computing, navigating and horticulture. Prisoners are advised to discuss their plans with their prison's education department, complete an application form (the education department has copies), and write a short letter to the Trust outlining their aims and stating how the course they have chosen will help meet them. Applications are normally processed within 6 to 8 weeks.

Forum on Prisoner Education
Room 207, 2 Abbot Street, London E8 3DP
tel 0870 75 65 795 *fax 0870 75 65 796*
e-mail info@fpe.org.uk

A national charity to advance the quality, availability and consistency of education and training within the criminal justice system. It organises a range of events and seminars to widen and further the debate on the benefits of education. Members include probation officers and other criminal justice professionals. It publishes The Directory of Offender Education.

RELIGIOUS ORGANISATIONS OFFERING SERVICES TO PRISONERS

Organisations marked with an asterisk have failed to respond to a request for information for 2006, but are listed for the sake of completeness. If they continue to fail to respond they will be deleted from the next edition.

Chaplain General of the Prison Service, William Noblett, Chaplaincy, HQ NOMS, Room 620, Horseferry House, Dean Ryle Street, London SW1P 2AW. 020-7217 8201 (admin) *fax 020-7217 8980*

*Angulimala, The Buddhist Prison Chaplaincy Organisation, The Forest Hermitage, Lower Fulbrook, Nr Sherbourne, Warwickshire CV35 8AS. phone (01926) 624385. e-mail prakhem@foresthermitage.org.uk The Buddhist Religious Consultative Service to HM Prisons and provides visiting Buddhist chaplains for prisons and advises the Prison Service on Buddhist matters.

The Baptist Union of Great Britain, Baptist House, PO Box 44, 129 Broadway, Didcot, Oxon OX11 8RT (01235) 517705. Contact The Ministry Support Administrator, Ministry Department.

Churches Criminal Justice Forum, 39 Eccleston Square, London SW1V 1BX 020-7901 4878 *fax 020-7901 4874* info@ccjf.org.uk A national, ecumenical group that seeks to raise awareness of criminal justice concerns among people of faith. It encourages people to get involved in the criminal justice system in ways that will improve it, and also urges politicians to address those aspects of social disadvantage that lie behind crime.

The Church of Jesus Christ of Latter Day Saints, Office of Area Presidency, 751 Warwick Road, Solihull, West Midlands B91 3DQ. 0121-712 1200. Members of the church are sometimes known as 'Mormons' or 'Latter Day Saints'.

*IQRA Trust Prisoners' Welfare, 3rd Floor, 16 Grosvenor Crescent, London SW1X 7EP 020-7838 7987 *fax 020-7245 6386*. www.iqraprisonerswelfare.org Promotes better understanding of Islam in Britain. It supports prisoners through its Prisoners' Welfare Directorate by providing books, religious clothing and special foods. It can also train people who are working with Muslim inmates. For their publications phone 020-7838 7987 or e-mail info@iqratrust.org

*The National Council for the Welfare of Muslim Prisoners, 3rd Floor, 16 Grosvenor Crescent, London SW1X 7EP 020-7838 7987. Gen Secretary Salah El Hassan

The Jewish Prison Chaplaincy, Rev Michael Binstock, United Synagogue, 8/10 Forty Avenue, Wembley, Middx HA9 8JW 020-8385 1855 *fax 020-8385 1856*

The Methodist and Free Churches Prison Ministry. Contact Rev Alan Ogier, Superintendent Methodist Chaplain, NOMS, Horseferry House, Dean Ryle Street, London SW1P 2AW 020 7217 8048 *fax 020 7217 8980* e-mail alan.ogier@hmps.gsi.gov.uk In collaboration with the Prison Service Chaplaincy, is responsible for appointing, training and giving pastoral support to Methodist/Free Church chaplains in every prison in England and Wales.

The Pagan Federation, c/o Suzanne White, National Manager for Visiting Pagan Ministers, BM Box 7097, London WC1N 3XX. e-mail suzanne@prisonministry.org.uk Covers all areas of Paganism including Wicca, Druidry and the Northern Tradition. Can supply information and reading lists for inmates as well as providing visiting Ministers

Prison Fellowship *England & Wales*, PO Box 945, Maldon, Essex CM9 4EW. (01621) 843232 *fax 01621 843303* e-mail enquiries@prisonfellowship.org.uk Web www.prisonfellowship.org.uk *Northern Ireland*, 39 University Street, Belfast BT7 1FY tel/fax 028-9024 3691, e-mail info@pfni.org *Scotland*, 110 St James Street, Glasgow G4 0PS tel/fax 0141-552 1288 e-mail prisonfellowship@lineone.net A Christian ministry providing practical and spiritual support to prisoners and ex-offender's families. Volunteer based organisation with local groups throughout UK that work closely with prison chaplaincy teams and local churches.

The Prison Phoenix Trust, PO Box 328, Oxford OX2 7HF. www.prisonphoenixtrust.org.uk Supports prisoners of any faith or none in their spiritual lives by teaching the disciplines of meditation and yoga, working with silence and the breath. It sends out free books *We're All Doing Time, Freeing the Spirit* and *Becoming Free Through Meditation and Yoga* and supports prisoners by regular correspondence, newsletters and by establishing weekly prison yoga classes. The trust also works with prison officers.

Religious Society of Friends (Quakers), Quaker Prison Ministry Group, QPSW, Friends House, 173 Euston Road, London NW1 2BJ. 020-7663 1035 *fax 020-7663 1001*. e-mail qpsw@quaker.org.uk The group supports about 100 Quaker prison ministers throughout Britain.

Seventh-day Adventist Church, Search Prison Ministries, 25 St John's Road, Watford, Herts WD17 1PZ (01923) 232728 fax (01923) 250582.
North England Conference of Seventh-day Adventists, 22 Zulla Road, Mapperley Park, Nottingham NG3 5DB
Welsh Mission, Ty Capel, Twyn Road, Ystrad Mynach, Caerphilly CF82 7EU
Scottish Mission, Gwydyr Road, Crieff, Perthshire PH7 4BS

Irish Mission Office, 9 Newry Road, Bambridge, Co Down, N Ireland BT32 3HF Provides spiritual help and counselling to oprisoners and their families. Teams of volunteers in London and other large cities.

HIGH SECURITY HOSPITALS

1. **Ashworth Hospital**
   Mersey Care NHS Trust
   Parkbourn, Maghull, Liverpool L31 1HW
   tel 0151-473 0303 *fax 0151-526 6603*

   Social Care
   tel 0151-471 2312/473 2713
   fax 0151- 437 2720
   e-mail name@merseyside.nhs.uk

   McLean, Robert (head of forensic social care)
   Murray, Michelle (pa)
   0151-473 2808

   Anson, Sue (forensic social care mgr)
   Hicks, Douglas (forensic social care mgr)

   Appleton, Phil (ssw)
   Caffrey, Karen (ssw)
   Carroll, Jane (ssw)
   Elliott, Phillip (ssw)
   Goodridge, Liz (ssw)
   Heywood, Lynne (ssw)
   Hughes, Dennis (ssw)
   McBride, Amanda (ssw)
   Miles, Tim (ssw)
   Mounsey, Martin (ssw)
   O'Mara, Joyce (ssw)
   Shea, Nicholas (ssw)
   Sheard, Claire (ssw)
   White, Lesley (ssw)
   Whittred, Stephanie (ssw)
   Blything, Sue (forensic mgr, safeguarding children)
   Warwick, Anne (child protection liaison mgr)
   Tunstall, Neil (vol sector liaison mgr)
   Francis, Irene (snr admin mgr)

2. **Broadmoor Hospital**
   Crowthorne, Berks RG45 7EG
   tel (01344) 773111 *fax (01344) 754625*

   Social Work Services
   tel (01344) 754522 *fax (01344) 754421*

   Frost, Carol (sw mgr)
   Townsend, Ruth (acting asst mgr)
   Ackerman, Joanne
   Barker, Dennis

   Blower, Mike
   Casey, Geoff
   Chalk, Pat
   Croome, Anne
   Davies, Helen
   Hames, Carol
   Hefferman, Susan
   Hulin, Gillian
   Kelly, Gareth
   Kenworthy, Frances (locum)
   Phillips, David
   Rogers, Evangeline

3. **Rampton Hospital**
   (Nottinghamshire Healthcare NHS Trust)
   Retford, Notts DN22 0PD
   tel (01777) 248321 *fax (01777) 248442*

   Forensic Social Care Service
   11/12 Galen Avenue, Rampton Hospital,
   Retford, Notts DN22 0PD
   tel (01777) 247354 *fax (01777) 247259*

   Parkinson, John (acting hd of social care/ nominated officer child protection)
   Brown, Jane (pa)
   Vacancy (children's safeguarding mgr)
   Cove, Wendy (admin mgr)

   sfswp snr forensic social wk practitioner

   Learning Disability Directorate
   Parkinson, John (sw mgr)
   Clayton, Amanda (sfswp)
   Cowling, Steve (sfswp)
   McNeil, Kevin (sfswp)

   Mental Health Directorate
   Cochrane, Sarah (sw mgr)
   Greenaway, Clare (sfswp)
   Head, Paul (sfswp)
   Hodgson, Karen (sfswp)
   Johnson, Lynn (sfswp)
   Singh, Janga (sfswp)
   Wray, Corrina (sfswp)
   Vacancy (sw asst, natnl deaf service)

   Peaks Unit
   Corcoran, Lynne (sw mgr)
   Cochrane, David (sfswp)
   Leitch, Bob (sfswp)
   Robertson, Kim (sfswp)

   Personality Disorder Directorate
   Corcoran, Lynne (sw mgr)
   Hahn, Gill (sfswp)
   Humphries, Gail (sfswp)
   Odunze, Rachel (sfswp)
   Oliver, Sonia (sfswp)

Women Services Directorate
Cochrane, Sarah (sw mgr)
Briggs, Myra (sfswp)
Garrib, Aasra (sfswp)
Vacancy (sfswp)

Family Support/Volunteer Co-ordination
Phillips, Janet (mgr)
Christian, Carmel (family supt wrkr)
Bridge, Karen (family supt wrkr)
Strawson, Val (vol co-ord)

NATIONAL SPECIALIST COMMISSIONING ADVISORY GROUP

Department of Health, Ground Floor North, Wellington House, 133-135 Waterloo Road, London SE1 8UG
tel 020-7972 4654
"The Personality Disorder Service is a national service funded centrally by the National Specialist Commissioning Advisory Group (NSCAG). The service provides for clients who cannot easily be contained within local personality disorder and mental health services, and is based on the Therapeutic Community model. It is delivered at The Henderson Hospital, (London), and two more recently opened centres, Webb House (Crewe), and Main House (Birmingham).

The three therapeutic communities treat adults suffering from personality disorder characterised by emotional and behavioural difficulties.

Since 2004 all three units have been drawing up service development plans to improve access and affordability. As a result, Webb House is developing community based services and has closed the residential service. At the time of writing therefore, Henderson Hospital and Main House provide in-patient treatment (including pre-admission preparation and post discharge follow-up); and Webb House (in partnership with local services) provides intensive day treatment, initially in Leeds, Liverpool and Manchester (opening Autumn 2004). It is planned to extend this service across several towns in the North West."

Residents of the in-patient services are encouraged to stay for a maximum of one year, and during their stay they will take on responsibility for the running of the community.

All residents are free to discharge themselves at any time.

Treatment at each of the communities is entirely voluntary. Residents can be on probation orders, a supervision register, a suspended sentence or parole, but treatment at any one of the therapeutic communities cannot be made as a condition of any such order.

Referrals are accepted from anywhere in the UK, but those from outside England and Scotland do require identified funding. Henderson Hospital referrals are generally from London and the South East Regions. Webb House has referrals from the Northern, North West Regions and Scotland. The Birmingham based therapeutic community accepts referrals from West Midlands and South West Regions, referrals should be directed to Bridger House.

A wide variety of leaflets and videos are available from all three units. Further information on the service can be found on www.swistg-tr.nhs.uk Further information on NSCAG can be found on www.advisorybodiesdoh.gov.uk/NCSAG/.

The services will become the commissioning responsibility of local NHS organisations (PCTs) through specialised commissioning arrangements from April 2006.

Henderson Hospital
2 Homeland Drive, Brighton Road, Sutton, Surrey SM2 5LT
tel 020-8661 1611 *fax 020-8770 3676*

A free book 'Perspectives on Henderson Hospital', a referrer's guide and a prospective resident's guide can be obtained from Sue Garner (Admin).

Henderson Hospital also provides consultation, advice and supervision for professionals working with people with personality disorder and education and training for multi-professional staff.

Webb House
Victoria Avenue, Crewe, Cheshire CW2 7SQ
tel (01270) 614400 fax (01270) 614401
e-mail info@webbhouse.bstmht.nhs.uk

Webb House is developing a range of non-residential services across the North of England. At present these include day services, in Liverpool, Leeds and Manchester, provided in partnership with local services. Webb House also provides an assessment and consultation service and offer training to other agencies to

develop their skills in working with people who have personality disorder.

For more information on current services and service developments contact Webb House or see website www.webbhouse.org

Personality Disorder Service

Main House and Bridger House come under the Personality Disorder Service. In the first instance, requests for further information or referrals should be addressed to the Outreach Team at Bridger House (contact details below).

"The service treats individuals with severe and enduring emotional, behavioural, relationship and/or interpersonal difficulties. Many will have a diagnosis of 'severe personality disorder' and many will have engaged in law breaking activities. The Personality Disorder Service covers the West Midlands and South West regions as well as parts of Leicestershire, Northamptonshire and Rutland, and Oxfordshire.

The service accepts referrals of men and women aged from of 18 upwards. The service welcomes referrals of people from diverse ethnic backgrounds and has facilities for disabled access. As an NSCAG funded service there has been no direct cost to referrers for the treatment of their patients during this year. Additional funding is only required for referrals outside England. This arrangement is under review and likely to change, updated information can be requested from the outreach team.

The central philosophy of the service model is that patients are empowered to be active participants in their own and others treatment, all therapy is provided in groups and is based on psychosocial principles. "

Main House
Hollymoor Way, Northfield,
Birmingham B31 5HE
tel 0121-678 3630 *fax 0121-678 3635*

Main House is the 27-bedded residential unit that provides therapeutic community treatment for individuals for up to one year. Treatment at Main House is entirely voluntary. Residents can be probation orders, a supervision register, suspended sentence or parole, but treatment at Main House cannot be as a condition of any such order.

Bridger House
22 Summer Road, Acocks Green,
Birmingham B27 7UT
tel 0121-678 3244 *fax 0121-678 3245*

Bridger House is the base of the Outreach Service. This provides a group based Day Treatment Service, liaison with referrers or potential referrers, training and consultation

SPECIALIST ACCOMMODATION FOR OFFENDERS

Basford House
in partnership with NACRO
40-42 Isandula Road, Basford, Nottinghamshire
NG7 7ES. 0115-978 5851

6 bed (in single rooms) high support housing for male offenders 25+, with supported move on accommodation in 5 properties nearby also 2 self contained one bedroom flats. Established contact with Nottinghamshire Probation Service essential.

Carr-Gomm Society
North London Region, 270-272 Camden Road,
London NW1 9AE. 020-7482 2048
South London Region, Telegraph Hill Centre,
Kitto Road, London SE14 5TY. 020-7277 6060

A charitable housing association that provides supportive environments for single people with a range of needs, including physical and mental health, ex-alcohol, drug users, ex offenders and those who cannot live on their own without support, referred by social services or housing departments

Heantun Housing Association
3 Wellington Road, Bilston, Wolverhampton
WV14 6AA. (01902) 571100

Shared housing for male ex-offenders in Wolverhampton, Willenhall, Dudley and Cannock (17 places). Also outreach support in Wolverhampton and Walsall (6 places male or female). Maximum stay 12 months.

Iris House
68 Bath Road, Worcester WR5 3EW (01905) 353884 *fax (01905) 763574*

13 bed, specialist hostel for difficult to place offenders including parolees and bail assessment. 24 hour staff cover, keyworking and support. Nationwide catchment area. Close

links with West Mercia Probation Service via
LPO. Part of Stonham Housing Association. 'We
have a proven track record of successful work
with serious long term offenders.' Outreach
support offered to successful tenants who move
into their own tenancies. Also at Clarendon
House, 18 London Road, Worcester (14 bed
hostel, day time support).

Langley House Trust
Head Office: PO Box 181, Witney, Oxfordshire
OX28 6WD. (01993) 774075 *fax (01993) 772425*
e-mail info@langleyhousetrust.org

A national Christian charity and Registered
Social landlord providing specialist resettlement
accommodation for those who are hard to place
(ex-offenders and those at risk of offending). 16
projects and associated move-on provision.

Referrals direct to the chosen project or via
Witney office

Drug Rehabilitation Centres
(Registered Care Homes)
Chatterton Hey, Edenfield, Ramsbottom,
Lancashire BL0 0QH. (01706) 829895 *fax
(01706) 828761*
Chatterton@langleyhousetrust.org
Murray Lodge, 1 Whitley Village, Coventry
CV3 4AJ. 024-7650 1585 *fax 024-7650 5759*
Murray@langleyhousetrust.org

Fresh Start Projects
Ashdene, 29 Peterson Road, Wakefield, West
Yorkshire WF1 4DU. (01924) 291088 *fax
(01924) 366529*
Ashdene@langleyhousetrust.org
Box Tree Cottage, 110 Allerton Road, Bradford,
West Yorkshire BD8 0AQ. (01274) 487626 *fax
(01274) 543612*
BoxTree@langleyhousetrust.org
The Chalet, 9 Downshire Square, Reading,
Berkshire RG1 6NJ. 0118 957 2457 *fax 0118 956
8536* Chalet@langleyhousetrust.org
Langdon House, 66 Langdon Road, Parkstone,
Dorset BH14 9EH. (01202) 747423 *fax (01202)
256718* Langdon@langleyhousetrust.org
The Shrubbery, 35 Frindsbury Road, Strood,
Rochester, Kent ME2 4TD. (01634) 717085 *fax
(01634) 291049*
Shrubbery@langleyhousetrust.org

Residential Training Centres
Elderfield, Main Road, Otterbourne,
Winchester, Hampshire SO21 2EQ.
(01962) 712163 *fax (01962) 711174*
Elderfield@langleyhousetrust.org
House of St. Martin, 1 Langford Lane, Norton

Fitzwarren, Taunton, Somerset TA2 6NU.
(01823) 275662 *fax (01823) 352455*
StMartin@langleyhousetrust.org
Wing Grange, Preston Road, Wing, Oakham,
Rutland LE15 8SB. (01572) 737246 *fax (01572)
737510*
WingGrange@langleyhousetrust.org

Resettlement Projects
Bedford Project, PO Box 395, Bedford MK40
2NN (01234) 356081 *fax (01234) 364349*
Bedford@langleyhousetrust.org
Rothera Project, PO Box 977, Bradford BD5 9YJ
(women only) (01274) 603664 *fax (01274)
605677*
Rothera@langleyhousetrust.org
Kent Resettlement Project, PO Box 409,
Chatham, Kent ME4 4XF (accepts men and
women, housed seperately) (01634) 880070 *fax
901634) 830485*
Kentproject@langleyhousetrust.org

Homeless Project
The Torbay Project, Northaven, 6 Factory Row,
Castle Circus, Torquay TQ2 5QQ (some direct
access places) tel (01803) 212234 *fax (01803)
213525* torbay@langleyhousetrust.org

Registered Care Homes
The Knole, 23 Griffiths Avenue, Cheltenham,
Gloucestershire GL51 7BE. (01242) 526978
fax (01242) 237504
Knole@langleyhousetrust.org
Longcroft, 58 Westbourne Road, Lancaster
LA1 5EF. (01524) 64950 *fax (01524) 844082*
Longcroft@langleyhousetrust.org

Nacro
Nacro has a number of specialist housing
projects. These are listed in the NACRO
Section.

Stonham-Norman House
15 Aberdeen Park, Islington, London N5 2AN
020-7704 2857 *fax 020-7704 2171*

A residential high support hostel for men
(25-65yrs) who wish to challenge their past
offending and establish new patterns of
behaviour. On arrival, tenants are allocated a
key worker who will work in partnership with
the tenant to develop an individually tailored
support package designed to assist him in his
progression towards independent living.
Support packages are regularly reviewed and
support is delivered through one to one key
working sessions.

Penrose Housing Association
Head Office: 356 Holloway Road, London, N7 6PA. 020-7700 0100 *fax 020-7700 8133*
Chief Executive: Janice Horsman

Specialist housing association providing supported housing and resettlement service for homeless male and female offenders in the London area. All housing is shared ranging from 2 bedroomed flats to 14 bed hostel. Assured short hold tenancies are issued. Move-on for most tenants through public and private sector accommodation with resettlement support.

Women: women only housing provided in small shared flats and self-contained flats using high care and floating support.

Priority: lifers and other long term prisoners
Exclusions: Penrose operates no blanket exclusions

All enquiries to head office or the relevant project. Applications can only be accepted from probation officers in the London Area or other approved referral soources.

Penrose also operates separate accommodation for mentally disordered offenders.

The Progress Project
22 Winchester Road, Worthing.
West Sussex. BN11 4DH.
tel/fax 01903 233390 email:
progressproject@btconnect.com
Manager: Kenny Brady RMN Assistant
Manager: Ian Genner

The Progress Project is an 8 bed (extending to 15 in 2006) specialist rehabilitation unit for men aged 18 - 65 with enduring mental health problems together with complex needs (offending history linked to mental illness, alcohol / substance misuse, dual diagnosis and other complex needs) 24 hour cover, keyworking, support and a comprehensive package of theraupeutic interventions. Referrals accepted from community mental health teams, probation services and prisons.

Stepping Stones Trust
Referrals to: Suffolk House, George Street, Croydon CR0 1PE
e-mail stepsto@tiscali.co.uk
Park View, 51 Clapham Common West Side, London SW4 9AS. phone & fax 020-7228 0863
Hope House, 14a St Augustine's Ave, South Croydon CR2 6BS phone & fax 020 8680 1474

Supported housing for ex-prisoners or referrals from probation services. No local connection necessary. Our focus is on helping residents find employment and move-on accommodation and providing spiritual support (from a Christian perspective) for people who feel this would help them stay clear of crime. Residents must be clean of drugs, accept a curfew (11 pm to 7 am) and want support.

Bridge House, PO Box 3209, London SW8. 020-7720 6421 *fax 020 7622 1864*

Accomodation and care for Christian male sex offenders. For the unemployed, rent covered by DSS and Housing Benefit. Residents will usually stay for up to two years and can receive psychiatric assessment and treatment through the NHS. NOTE: before making any referral please contact SPO, 217a Balham High Road, London SW17 020 8767 5905

Stonham
Head Office, Octavia House, 50 Banner Street, London EC1Y 8TX. 020-7549 0000
www.stonham.org.uk
Stonham, a division of the Home Group, is England's largest specialist provider of housing with support for socially excluded people. It runs 578 directly managed services, working in partnership with local authorities, health care providers, probation services and others, delivering services to 13,000 people each year. Stonham works with ex-offenders, including those with mental health problems, drug and/or alcohol addiction and basic skills needs. There are over 100 Stonham projects for ex-offenders around England

Regional offices:
From January 2006, Stonham's five current regions are being reduced to three administrative units: North, West and East.
North Administrative Unit
Key contact: Derek Caren (Operations Director)
Meridian House, Artist Street, Armley, Leeds LS12 2EW
tel 0113-246 8660 *fax 0113-246 8665*
e-mail derek.caren@homegroup.org.uk

West Administrative Unit
Key contact: John Buttery (Operations Director)
2nd Floor, High Point, Thomas Street, Taunton, Somerset TA2 6HB
tel (01823) 327388 *fax (01823) 327390*
e-mail john.buttery@homegroup.org.uk

West Administrative Unit
Key contact: Molly Newton (Operations Director)
Octavia House, 50 Banner Street,
London EC1Y 8TX.
tel 020-7549 0000
e-mail molly.newton@homegroup.org.uk

Gordon House Association
see section on services for problem gamblers

SERVICES FOR DRUG & ALCOHOL USERS

The following list is not comprehensive. Further information on local treatment services is contained in two directories from the Standing Conference on Drug Abuse 020-7928 9500

Drug Problems: where to get help lists contact details for 700 residential and community services in England and Wales

Residential drug services: a comprehensive guide to rehabilitation in England and Wales provides information on 100 residential services. Price £20.00 (£16.00 to SCODA members)

Directory of Specialist Drug Services in Scotland lists contact details of over 160 agencies, available from Scottish Drugs Forum.

Frank (national drugs helpline)
0800 77 66 00 www.talktofrank.com

Drinkline
helpline 0800 917 8282

National Organisations and Head Offices

1. **DrugScope**
    32/36 Loman Street, London SE1 0EE
    tel 020-7928 1211 *fax 020-7928 1771*
    library enquiry line 0870 774 3862
    e-mail info@drugscope.org.uk
    web site www.drugscope.org.uk

    DrugScope is the UK's leading centre of expertise on drugs. Its aim is to inform policy and reduce drug related risk. Provides information, promotes effective responses to drug taking, undertakes research at local, national and international levels, advises on policy making, encourages informed debate and speaks for member bodies working on the ground. (Formerly SCODA and ISDD)

2. **Alcohol Concern**
    Waterbridge House, 32-36 Loman Street,
    London SE1 0EE
    tel 020-7928 7377 *fax 020-7928 4644*
    e-mail contact@alcoholconcern.org.uk
    http://www.alcoholconcern.org.uk

    Library, information service, can refer caller to local agencies, produces a variety of literature and directory of local services.

3. **ADFAM**
    Waterbridge House, 32-36 Loman Street,
    London SE1 0EH
    tel 020-7928 8988 *fax 020-7928 8923*

    The national charity for the friends and families of drug users. Specialist support for prisoners' families. A 'ringback' service on 020-7202 9446 Mon-Fri 10am-5pm. More information at www.adfam.org.uk

4. **Release**
    388 Old Street, London EC1V 9LT
    tel 020-7729 9904 (office) *fax 020-7729 2599*
    helpline 0845 450 0215

    Advice on legal drug related problems. Office staffed Mon-Fri 10am-5.30pm

5. **Re Solv**
    30a High Street, Stone, Staffs ST15 8AW
    tel (01785) 817885 *fax (01785) 813205*

    free national helpline 0808 800 2345 (9am-5pm, Mon-Fri)
    e-mail helpline@re-solv.org

    National charity dealing with all aspects of solvent and volatile substance abuse (that currently kills an average of 6 young people a month). Research, dissemination of educational materials, training and community projects

6. **Cranstoun Drug Services**
    4th Floor, Broadway House, 112-134 The Broadway, London SW19 1RL
    tel 020-8543 8333 *fax 020-8543 4348*
    www.cranstoun.org

    Major NGO provider of a range of services for substance misusers in the UK. Encompasses high care residential services, supported housing, combination day services.

7. **Mainliners**
    195 New Kent Road, London SE1 4AG

tel 020-7378 5840 *fax 020-7378 5489*
www.mainliners.org.uk

Working with people affected by, or at risk of HIV, Hepatitis and other blood borne viruses. Offers a range of services both locally and nationally. All frontline services can provide sterile injecting equipment and condoms.

SMART Services, 9 Mitcham Lane, London SW16 6LQ
tel 020 8677 9541 *fax 020 8664 6017*
e-mail smart@mainliners.org.uk

SMART is Mainliners street drugs agency working with people with drug issues in Streatham Hill, Herne Hill, Tulse Hill and surrounding areas of Lambeth. Can help in addressing the effects of drug use and withdrawal, treatment choices and referrals in relation to stabilisation, maintenance/reduction prescribing or stopping use of drugs. Can also advise around safer drug use, safer sexual practices, HIV/AIDS, Hepatitis and other issues.

8. **Turning Point**
    New Loom House, 101 Back Church Lane, London E1 1LU
    tel 020-7702 2300
    e-mail info@turning-point.co.uk

    Turning Point is a leading social care organisation. It provides services for people with complex needs, including those affected by drug and alcohol abuse, mental health problems and those with a learning disability

9. **Phoenix House**
    3rd Floor, Asra House, 1 Long Lane, London SE1 4PG
    tel 020-7234 9740
    e-mail info@phoenixhouse.org.uk

    National referral number for adult & family residential rehab services: 0845 600 7227
    e-mail intake@phoenixhouse.org.uk

    Offers structured rehabilitation services, designed around the needs of substance misusers. Largest UK provider of residential rehabilitation services for single adults and families and structured community day services. Extensively involved in resettlement, aftercare, supported housing, tenancy sustainment

services and education and retraining services. Work in partnership with probation and prison services in England and Scotland delivering a full range of intervention services

10. **Aquarius Action Projects**
    6th Floor, The White House
    111 New Street, Birmingham B2 4EU
    tel 0121-632 4727 *fax 0121-633 0539*
    e-mail whitehouse@aquarius.org.uk
    www.aquarius.or.uk

    Drug and alcohol projects in the Midlands, providing information, training, counselling, residential and day services. Also delivers the Alcohol and Offending Programme in partnership with W Midlands Probation Area in Solihull, Wolverhampton, Walsall, Sandwell and Dudley; and alcohol arrest referral programmes in Dudley and Sandwell.

11. **Langley House Trust**
    The Langley House Trust has two dry rehabs. See their entry under the Specialist Accommodation for Offenders Section

Drugs And Criminal Justice Organisations

12. **RAPt (Rehabilitation for Addicted Prisoners Trust)**
    Riverside House, 27-29 Vauxhall Grove, London SW8 1SY
    tel 020 7582 4677 *fax 020 7820 3716*
    e-mail info@rapt.org.uk www.rapt.org.uk

    National charity with full accreditation from the joint Prisons and Probation Accreditation Board. Provides intensive abstinence based treatment and supportive counselling services to substance users in the cj system. Services include prison based 12 step treatment and CARAT services , community based CARAT and 12 step treatment services, and rehab services.

13. **Compass - Services to tackle problem drug use**
    Langton House, 5 Priory Street, York YO1 6ET
    tel (01904) 636374 *fax (01904) 632490*
    www.compass-uk.org

    Provides a range of community services in York and North Yorkshire, Hull and East Riding, Nottingham and the East Midlands,

and Milton Keynes. Services include structured day programmes, young people's services, throughcare after care and resettlement, arrest referral, progress2work, substitute prescribing services, and tier 2 and 3 adult services.

Self Help Organisations

14. **Narcotics Anonymous**
UK Service Office, 202 City Road, London EC1V 2PH
tel 020 7251 4007 *fax 020 7251 4006*
e-mail ukso@ukna.org

   helpline 020 7730 0009
   e-mail: helpline@ukna.org

   Public Information e-mail pi@ukna.org

   Clean Times
   c/o UK Service Office
   e-mail cleantimes@ukna.org

15. **Alcoholics Anonymous**
PO Box 1, Stonebow House, Stonebow, York YO1 7NJ
tel (01904) 644026 helpline 0845 7697 555
www.alcoholics-anonymous.org.uk

16. **Al-Anon Family Groups**
61 Great Dover Street, London SE1 4YF
tel 020-7403 0888 (10am-10pm daily confidential helpline) *fax 020-7378 9910*
e-mail alanonuk@aol.com website www.al-anonuk.org.uk

   Al-anon is worldwide and offers understanding and support for families and friends of problem drinkers, whether the alcoholic is still drinking or not. Alateen, a part of Al-Anon, is for young people aged 12-20 who have been affected by somone else's drinking, usually that of a parent. For details of meetings throughout UK and Eire, please contact the helpline.

17. **Families Anonymous**
Doddington & Rollo Community Association
Charlotte Despard Avenue, Battersea, London SW11 5HD
tel 0207-498 4680 help line 0845 1200 660 (lo-call)
e-mail office@famanon.org.uk
www.famanon.org.uk

   Advice and support groups for families and friends of drug users (inc. alcohol). Office staffed Mon–Fri 1pm to 4.00pm. Outside

these hours, telephone numbers of volunteer contacts are given by recorded message.

18. **PADA (Parents Against Drug Abuse)**
12-14 Church Parade, Ellesmere Port, Cheshire CH65 2ER
admin & fax 0151-356 1996
helpline 08457 023 867
e-mail admin@pada.org.uk
www.pada.org.uk

   A national network of local support groups offering help and support to parents and families of drug users. Helpline (confidential) staffed 24hrs 365 days a year, calls charged at local rate.

Campaigns

19. **Transform Drug Policy Foundation**
Easton Business Centre, Felix Road, Easton, Bristol BS5 0HE
tel 0117-941 5810 *fax 0117-941 5809*
e-mail info@tdpf.org.uk www.tdpf.org.uk

   The leading drug policy reform charity in the UK aiming to create a just humane and effective drug policy. It campaigns for an effective system of regulation and control to replace the failed policy of prohibition through advocating reform at national and international levels.

SERVICES FOR PROBLEM GAMBLERS

The following information has been supplied by GamCare

National Organisations

GamCare Units 2&3, Baden Place, London SE1 1YW 020 7378 5200 *fax 020 7378 5233*, helpline 0845 6000 133 (8am to 12 midnight Mon-Sun). The national centre for information, advice, and practical help regarding the social impact of gambling, providing: a national helpline, telephone and face-to-face counselling, network of (and referral to) local organisations, training, literature, and advice on gambling dependency issues for the probation service.

Gamblers Anonymous PO Box 88, London SW10 0EU. National helpline

number 020-7384 3040. GA is a self help fellowship of men and women who have joined together to do something about their own gambling problem and to help other compulsive gamblers to do the same. Over 200 groups throughout the UK and in many prisons.

Gam-Anon address as GA above. 'Sister' organisation to GA, providing advice and support to the spouses and parents of compulsive gamblers.

Residential/Rehabilitation

Gordon House Association 186 Mackenzie Road, Beckenham, Kent BR3 4SF 020-8778 3331. (13 bed unit) and Somerset Mews, 43/47 Maughan Street, Dudley, W Mids DY1 2BA (01384) 241292 (21 bed unit, + 4 bed women's project) National catchment area providing residential facility for men & women 18+, including offenders on court orders or ex-prison. Therapeutic environment, individual and group counselling and support whilst at hostel and after. Contact houses direct.

Groups & Organisations with Local Projects

England

Cumbria Alcohol & Drug Advisory Service (CADAS) 1 Fisher Street, Carlisle, Cumbria CA3 8RR (01228) 544140. Provides a telephone and one-to-one counselling service to problem gamblers and their relatives/friends.

Off The Record 250 Fratton Road, Portsmouth PO1 5HH & Threeways, 138 Purbrook Way, Leigh Park, Hampshire PO9 3SU. (02392) 785111. Client Line (02392) 815322. Freephone 0808 801 0724 Point of contact for young people, 11-25, who wish to receive counselling support and information in Hampshire regarding problem gambling.

North East Council on Addiction (NECA) Philipson House, 5 Philipson Street, Walker, Newcastle upon Tyne (head office) 0191-288 3544. 0191-234 3486 *fax 0191-263 9908*. e-mail headoffice@neca.co.uk Centres in Newcastle, South Tyne, Gatehead,

Durham, Consett, Peterlee, Hartlepool, Washington, Stanley, Mid Tyne, Chester le Street, Sunderland, Bishop Auckland, Seaham, Sedgefield, Darlington. All centres provide telephone and one-to-one counselling to problem gamblers and their relatives/friends. Addresses and phone numbers from Philipson House.

Alcohol Problems Advisory Service (APAS) 36 Park Row, Nottingham NG1 6GR 0115-941 4747 or Lo-call 0845 7626 316. Provides advice, information and counselling service to problem gamblers, drinkers and drug takers and for people affected by someone else's dependency on alcohol, drugs and gambling

The Matthew Project 24 Pottergate, Norwich, Norfolk NR2 1DX (01603) 626123. 24hr helpline (01603) 764754. www.matthewproject.co.uk Provides an advice, training and counselling service to young gamblers who make contact or who are referred.

Aquarius 20 Homer Road, Solihull B91 3QG. 0121-711 3732. Well established alcohol and drug agency with trained GamCare appointed counsellor based in Solihull. offering counselling and guidance for problem gamblers, their families and friends who are affected by gambling dependency.

Options (Southampton) 147 Shirley Road, Southampton SO15 3FH 02380 630219. Well established agency on the South coast provides one-to-one counselling, information and guidance for problem gamblers, their families and friends who are affected by gambling dependency.

Wales

Islwyn Drug & Alcohol Project Markham Miners Welfare Society, Bryn Road, Markham, Nr Blackwood, Gwent. (01495) 229299. Provides information, advice and one-to-one counselling to problem gamblers and their relatives/friends who are affected by a gambling dependancy as part of a community project within South Wales and surrounding districts.

Scotland

Renfrew Council on Alcohol Mirren House, Back Sneddon Street, Paisley PA3 2AF. 0141-887 0880. In conjunction with other services, also offers information, advice, and one-to-one counselling to problem gamblers, their relatives and friends affected by gambling dependency as a part of a community project.

Northern Ireland

Parents Advice Centre Franklin House, 12 Brunswick Street, Belfast, Northern Ireland BT2 7GE. 028-9023 8800. www.pachelp.org e-mail belfast@pachelp.org Centres in Belfast, Derry, Dungannon & Ballymena. provides telephone and one-to-one counselling and advice to parents and family members who are affected by gambling dependency as part of the help and support they provide to parents

VOLUNTARY WORK

CSV (Community Service Volunteers)
237 Pentonville Road, London N1 9NJ.
tel 020-7278 6601 *fax 020-7833 0149*
e-mail volunteer@csv.org.uk

CSV provides opportunities for people to volunteer in the community. CSV's non-rejection policy ensures that anyone aged 16-35 can volunteer full time, away from home at one of hundreds of social care and community projects throughout Britain. Volunteers receive a weekly allowance plus free accommodation and food. CSV also works through service and contract agreements (e.g. with the probation services) to involve volunteers as mentors to young offenders and also places as volunteers in their local area young people at risk of offending.

Volunteering with CSV gives young people greater self-confidence and provides them with a range of workplace skills such as team working and decision making.

Of special interest to probation officers based in YOIs and Cat C prisons is CSVs partnership with HM Prison Service. CSV offers, as part of an effective resettlement process, one month full time away from home volunteering opportunities to young people usually in their last month prior to release.

In 2005, CSV launched Cleartrack, a 'virtual young offenders institution' in Sunderland to provide training, accommodation and 24 hour supervision to young offenders funded by HM Treasury (contact cwilson@csv.org.uk

Voluntary Service Overseas
317 Putney Bridge Road, London SW15 2PN
tel 020-8780 7200 *fax 020-8780 7300*
www.vso.org.uk

The World Youth Programme, part of VSO . An international youth exchange programme aimed at building active global citizens. Nine young adults from the UK are paired with nine from an African/Asian country (all aged 18-25) to carry out voluntary work, three months in the UK and three months in the exchange country.

INSURANCE SERVICES FOR EX-OFFENDERS

When obtaining insurance, non-disclosure, or giving false information about any criminal convictions, will almost certainly mean that the policy will be declared void in the case of a claim. It must be remembered that a criminal conviction is a *material fact* and must be declared. By giving false information another crime is being committed. When disclosing their convictions the majority of ex-offenders will find getting insurance for home, building and contents, motor and business cover, practically impossible.

N.B. The editor accepts no responsibility for any of the statements below. They have been supplied by the companies listed.

Specialist insurance for ex-offenders is available through:

Fresh Start
Vinpenta House, 4 High Causeway, Whittlesey, Peterborough PE7 1AE
tel (01733) 208278 *fax (01733) 204668*
e-mail mail@culpeck.co.uk

Fresh Start is supported and recommended by Nacro, the Probation Service, CABs, Banks, Building Societies, Insurance and Mortgage Brokers throughout the UK. Fresh Start believes it is well placed to offer a comprehensive choice of cover (in particular providing cover for those people seeking buildings and contents insurance when looking for a mortgage) along with premium instalment

facilities for buildings, home contents and business insurance packages. A fully comprehensive, supportive and confidential service is provided by experienced staff offering the best service and cover at the most competitive premiums. Regulated by the Financial Services Authority.

Fairplay Insurance Services
Charter House, 43 St Leonards Road, Bexhill-on-Sea, East Sussex TN40 1JA tel (01424) 220110 *fax (01424) 731781* e-mail cover@fairplayhelp.com www.fairplayhelp.com

Fairplay Insurance Services, part of the Bureau Insurance services Group, authorised and regulated by the FSA, was established solely to promote Household and Motor Insurance for proposers with criminal convictions. Fairplay guarantees that each applicant will be dealt with in a sensitive, non-judgmental and helpful way. Every proposer will be treated with respect and in total confidence, regardless of previous convictions. Fairplay has been in existence for several years and is confident in its ability to provide household and motor insurance for ex-offenders.
Fairplay Home Insurance
(01424) 220110 Terry, Browning
Fairplay Motor Insurance
08700 774466 Gerry Buck

MISCELLANEOUS ADDRESSES

Descriptions of the organisations are those provided by themselves; the publisher takes no responsibility for these statements. Organisations marked with an asterisk have failed to respond to a request for information, but are listed for the sake of completeness. Any information about other organisations that might usefully be included will be welcomed. Please send it to Owen Wells, 23 Eaton Road, Ilkley LS29 9PU (01943) 602270 *fax (01943) 816732* e-mail o.r.wells@gmail.com

Prisoners' Families Helpline 0808 808 2003
free confidential, national helpline that provides information and support for prisoners' families and friends

Action for Prisoners' Families (formerly Federation of Prisoners' Families Support Groups), Unit 21, Carlson Court, 116 Putney Bridge Road, London SW15 2NQ 020-8812 3600 *fax 020-8871 0473.* www.prisonersfamilies.org.uk info@actionpf.org.uk National umbrella organisation acting as the voice for, and encouraging the development of organisations that provide assistance for the families of people in prison. Provides details of local support services, publishes a National Directory and other resource material.

Adult Dyslexia Organisation, Ground Floor, Secker House, Menit Road, Loughborough Estate, London SW9 7TP. 020-7737 7646, (admin) *fax 020-7207 7796* helpline 020-7924 9559 e-mail dyslexia.hq@dial.pipex.com www.adult-dyslexia.org

Advisory Service for Squatters, Angel Alley, 84b Whitechapel High Street, London E1 7QX. 020-3216 0099 (phone first, Mon-Fri 2-6pm) 0845 644 5814 (local rate) *fax 020-3216 0098.* e-mail advice@squatter.org .uk www.squatter.org.uk Legal and practical advice for squatters and homeless people.

The Aldo Trust, c/o NACRO, 169 Clapham Road, London SW9 0PU. 020-7582 6500 *fax 020-7735 4666.* Charitable small grants to prisoners in England and Wales only, no applications direct from prisoners.

Alternatives to Violence Project, contact AVP London, Grayston Centre, 28 Charles Square, London N1 6HT. 0207-324 4757 or 0845 458 2692 e-mail info@avpbritain.org.uk Offers workshops on alternatives to violence in prisons and the community. Also trains AVP workshop facilitators including serving and ex-prisoners and people on probation. During a workshop a sense of community is built up, based on trust, confidentiality, co-operation and respect for self and others.

Apex Trust, Head Office, St Alphage House, Wingate Annexe, 2 Fore Street, London EC2Y 5DA 0870 608 4567 *fax 020-7638 5977.* e-mail jobcheck@apextrust.com www.apextrust.com Helps people with a criminal record obtain appropriate jobs, self employment, training or further education through its 22 projects in England and Wales providing direct advice and guidance to ex-offenders. Provides employers with information about the best ways of recruiting and retraining preople with a criminal record. Operates a national telephone helpline called Jobcheck; it offers

confidential information on issues relating to employment and having a criminal record: 0870 608 4567.

ARC (Antenatal Results & Choices), 73 Charlotte Street, London W1T 4PN phone & fax 020-7631 0280. Offers non-directive, specialised support to parents who discover that their unborn baby may have an abnormality, gives support to parents making a decision about ante-natal testing and offers support regardless of the future of the pregnancy.

ARX (Advocacy Resource Exchange) , Unit 162 Lee Valley Technopark, Ashley Road, Tottenham Hale, London N17 9LN. 020-8880 4545 *fax 020-8880 4546*. e-mail info@advocacyresource.net www.advocacyresource.net Maintains a national database of independent advocacy schemes and provides information, training & publications on advocacy.

Asian Family Counselling Service, Suite 51, Windmill Place, 2-4 Windmill Lane, Southall UB2 4NJ Offers family, marital and individual counselling to the Asian community.

Assist: Assistance Support and Self Help In Surviving Trauma, 11 Albert Street, Rugby CV21 2RX (01788) 551919 *fax (01788) 553726*. Provides therapeutic support and counselling to probationers, prisoners and all those involved in the prison system, who have been affected by trauma, including their friends and families. Specialist treatment for those suffering from Post Traumatic Stress and Post Traumatic Stress Disorder. Nationwide helpline, Mon-Fri 10am-4pm, (01788) 560800.

*Association for Shared Parenting, PO Box 2000, Dudley, West Midlands DY1 1YZ. (01789) 751157. helpline 01789 750891 (evenings) www.sharedparenting.org.uk Seeks to promote the rights and needs of children following separation or divorce, through promoting view that children have the right to receive love and nurture from both parents. Offers support workshops for parents and a child contact centre for families.

Brook, 421 Highgate Studios, 53-79 Highgate Road, London NW5 1TL. 020-7284 6040 *fax 020-7284 6050* helpline 0800 0185 023 (9-5 Mon-Fri). Offers young people free confidential advice on health and contraception. For immediate information about contraception (inc emergency), pregnancy testing, abortion, sexually transmitted infections - helpline 0800 0185 023 or 'Ask Brook' at www.brook.org.uk for a confidential response to an enquiry. Contact publications@brookcentres.org.uk for info on Brook publications.

Cambridge Family Mediation Service, 3rd Floor, Essex House, 7 Regent Street, Cambridge CB2 1AB (01223) 576308 (info & answerphone) *fax (01223) 576309*. Specialist family mediation service for divorcing or separating couples. Has free counselling service for under 19s (see below 'The Children's Service').

Centre for Crime & Justice Studies (ISTD), King's College London, 26-29 Dury Lane, London WC2B 5RL. 020-7848 1688 *fax 020-7848 1689*. e-mail ccjs.enq@kcl.ac.uk www.kcl.ac.uk/ccjs An independent educational charity, offering membership, courses, conferences, seminars, lectures, study visits, research and publications to all with an interest in criminal justice.

The Child Bereavement Trust, Aston House, High Street, West Wycombe, High Wycombe, Bucks HP14 3AG. (01494) 446648 *fax (01494) 440057*. Cares for bereaved families by offering specialised training and support to the professional carer, also offers resources for families and professionals (e.g. videos and books).

ChildLine, 45 Folgate Street, London E1 6GL. address for children Freepost NATN1111, London E1 6BR. admin 020 7650 3200 *fax 020 7650 3201* helpline 0800 1111 24 hr national telephone helpline for children and young people in trouble or danger. Specialist helpline for children living away from home 0800 884444 (mon-fri 3.30pm-9.30pm, sat & sun 2pm-8pm) 0800 400222 minicom (mon-fri 9.30am-9.30pm, sat & sun 9.30am-8pm) The service is free and confidential. e-mail info@childline.org.uk (cannot answer problems or offer counselling online).

Child Poverty Action Group, 94 White Lion Street, London N1 9PF. 020-7837 7979 *fax 020-7837 6414* www.cpag.org.uk. For details of CPAG and training courses and membership schemes contact above address. Welfare rights enquiries (advisors only): Citizen's Rights Office 020-7833 4627, 2-4pm Mon-Fri e-mail info@cpag.org.uk Promotes action for relief, directly or

indirectly, of poverty among children and families with children. Works to ensure that those on low incomes get their full entitlement to welfare benefits. Aims to eradicate the injustice of poverty.

Children's Legal Centre, University of Essex, Wivenhoe Park, Colchester, Essex CO4 3SQ (01206) 872466 (admin and publications) *fax (01206) 874026.* e-mail clc@essex.ac.uk Free and confidential advice and information service covering all aspects of law and policy affecting young people in England and Wales. Publishes 'Childright' and other publications. Education law helpline 0845 456 6811.

The Children's Service, Cambridge Family Mediation Service, Essex House, 71 Regent Street, Cambridge CB2 1AB (01223) 576308 (info & answerphone) *fax (01223) 576309.* Counselling for children and young people aged 4-19 experiencing difficulty as a result of a current or past parental divorce or separation. Offers support rather than therapy.

Citizens Advice, Myddleton House, 115-123 Pentonville Road, London N1 9LZ. 020-7833 2181 (admin) *fax 020-7833 4371 (admin)* www.citizensadvice.org.uk The independent national organisation for Citizens Advice Bureaux. CABs provide free, confidential, and impartial advice to anyone on all subjects. Citizens Advice monitors the problems that CAB clients are experiencing and reports these findings to show where services and policies are failing both locally and nationally. The address and telephone number of local offices can be found in the telephone directory or on the website. For CAB information on-line see www.adviceguide.org.uk

CLAPA, Cleft Lip & Palate Association, 1st Floor, Green Man Tower, 332B Goswell Road, London EC1V 7LQ 020-7833 4883 *fax 020-7833 5999* e-mail info@clapa.com www.clapa.com Offers information and support to all people affected by cleft lip or palate. bottles and teats available by mail order.

CoDA (Co-dependents Anonymous), CoDA UK, PO Box 2365, Bristol BS6 9XJ 07000 263645 e-mail coda_uk@hotmail.com www.coda-uk.org An informal Twelve Step fellowship of men and women, whose common problem is an inability to maintain functional

relationships with self and others as a result of co-dependancy in their lives. CoDA uses the Twelve Steps, as a part of its suggested programme of recovery and for building healthy relationships, in a safe and confidential environment.

The Commission for Racial Equality, St Dunstan's House, 201-211 Borough High Street, London SE1 1GZ. 020 7939 0000 e-mail info@cre.gov.uk www.cre.gov.uk CRE has three main duties: (1) to work towards the elimination of racial discrimination and to promote equality of opportunity (2) to encourage good relations between people from different racial backgrounds (3) to monitor the way the Race Relations Act is working and recommend ways in which it can be improved. It is the only government appointed body with statutory power to enforce the Race Relations Act. It has a reference library that is open to the public (by appointment).

The Compassionate Friends, 53 North Street, Bristol BS3 1EN. office 0117-966 5202 (helpline 0845 123 2304 9.30am-10.30pm every day). An organisation of and for bereaved parents and their families.

Criminal Cases Review Commission, Alpha Tower, Suffolk Street Queensway, Birmingham B1 1TT. 0121-633 1800 *fax 0121-633 1823* e-mail ccrc@gtnet.gov.uk An independent public body reviewing alleged miscarriages of justice with power to refer convictions and sentences to the appeal courts.

Criminal Injuries Compensation Authority, Tay House, 300 Bath Street, Glasgow G2 4LN. 0141-331 2726 *fax 0141-331 2287.* Administers the government funded scheme to provide compensation to innocent victims of violent crime in Great Britain.

Cruse Bereavement Care, Cruse House, 126 Sheen Road, Richmond, Surrey TW9 1UR. 0870 167 1677 *fax 020-8940 7638.* e-mail info@cruse.org.uk. The UKs largest and only national organisation that helps and supports anyone who has been bereaved by death. Since 1959 it has been providing advice, bereavement support and information on practical matters for bereaved people entirely free of charge. Cruse's bereavement support is delivered through a network of 180 branches across the UK. It also offers training, support,

information and publications to those working to care for bereaved people. Cruse aims to increase public awareness of the needs of bereaved people through education and information services.

Down's Syndrome Association, Langdon Down Centre, 2a Langdon Park, Teddington TW11 9PS. 0845 230 0372 *fax 0845 230 0373*. e-mail info@downs-syndrome.org.uk www.downs-syndrome.org.uk Exists to support parents and carers of people with Down's Syndrome and to improve the lives of those with the condition.

Dyspel, Office G5, James House, 22-24 Corshan Street, London N1 6DR 020-7251 6770 *fax 020-7251 9181* A project that helps dyslexic offenders and offers training in the screening of dyslexia to probation officers and partnership staff. Dyspel opperates in NE, SW and Central London boroughs

Eating Disorders Association, 1st Floor, Wensum House, 103 Prince of Wales Road, Norwich, Norfolk NR1 1DW morning 0870 770 3256 *fax (01603) 664915*. helpline 0845 634 1414 (weekdays 8.30am-8.30pm, sat 1pm-4.30pm), youth helpline 0845 634 7650 (up to 18yrs, weekdays 4pm-6.30pm, sat 1pm-4.30pm), recorded information service 0906 302 0012 (calls cost 50p a minute). e-mail info@edauk.com. www.edauk.com. Provides information, help and support for people affected by eating disorders and, in particular, anorexia and bulimia nervosa.

Epilepsy Action, New Anstey House, Gate Way Drive, Leeds LS19 7XY. 0113 210 8800 *fax 0113 391 0300* helpline 0808 800 5050 e-mail epilepsy@epilepsy.org.uk www.epilepsy.org.uk Advice and information on all aspects of living with epilepsy.

The Equal Opportunities Commission, Arndale House, Arndale Centre, Manchester M4 3EQ. helpline 0845 601 5901 *fax 0161-838 8303*. e-mail info@eoc.org.uk website www.eoc.org.uk helpline 0845 601 5901 (interpreting service available) typetalk service 18001 0845 601 5901 An independent statutory body that works towards the elimination of discrimination on the grounds of sex or marriage; to promote equality of opportunity for women and men; to provide legal advice and assistance to individuals who have been discriminated against.

Fairbridge, 207 Waterloo Road, London SE1 8XD 020-7928 1704 *fax 020-7928 6016*. e-mail info@fairbridge.org.uk www.fairbridge.org.uk National youth charity working with people aged 13-25 in 15 disadvantaged areas of UK. Many are ex-offenders or are at risk of offending. Using a combination of challenging activities and long term support, young people are encouraged to re-engage with mainstream opportunities in education training and employment.

Families Need Fathers, 134 Curtain Road, London EC2A 3AR 08707 607111. helpline 08707 607496 mon-fri 6-10pm. www.fnf.org.uk National network of voluntary contacts. Keeping children and parents in contact after separation or divorce. Regular meetings are held around the country.

Family Planning Association, 2-12 Pentonville Road, London N1 9FP 020-7837 5432. Helpline 0845 310 1334 (mon-fri 9am-6pm) providing information and advice on contraception, sexual health, planning a pregnancy and pregnancy choices, and family planning and sexual services.

Family Rights Group, The Print House, 18 Ashwin Street, London E8 3DL. 020-7923 2628 *fax 020-7923 2683*. Telephone advice service: mon-fri 10am-12pm & 1.30-3.30pm, freephone 0800 731 1696. e-mail info@frg.org.uk www.frg.org.uk Provides a phone and written advice service for parents, relatives and carers who have children in care, on the child protection register, or who are receiving services from social services departments.

Family Welfare Association, 501-505 Kingsland Road, London E8 4AU. 020-7254 6251 *fax 020-7249 5443*. www.fwa.org.uk Provides a range of social care services including community mental health services, activity based resource centres, family centres, grants to people in need, and grants advice for students undertaking vocational courses.

Fellowship of Depressives Anonymous, Box FDA, Self Help Nottingham, Ormiston House, 36-36 Pelham Street, Nottingham NG1 2EG 0870 774 4320 *fax 0870 774 4319* e-mail fdainfo@hotmail.com Self help organisation for people with depression (and relatives). Members receive six newsletters

a year, can join penfriend/phonefriend schemes. Some local self help groups. Information line open to anyone at anytime, including weekends, answered personally four hours a day. Messages left at other times resopnded to as soon as possible.

Female Prisoners' Welfare Project/Hibiscus, 18 Borough High Street, London SE1 9QG. 020 7357 6543 *fax 020 7407 5646*. e-mail fpwphibiscus@aol.com Charity providing advice and support to women in prison, their children and families. Visits and supports British and foreign national women also group sessions for foreign nationals including Spanish speaking women. Provides Home Circumstance Reports for the Courts via an office in Jamaica. Staff speak a wide range of languages.

FSU (Family Service Units), 207 Old Marylebone Road, London NW1 5QP 020-7402 5175 *fax 020-7724 1829* e-mail centraloffice@fsu.org.uk   www.fsu.org.uk Provides holistic family and children's support services for families experiencing serious problems, through a network of family centres and projects.

Gingerbread (the association of one parent families in England and Wales, 300 local self-help groups), 1st Floor, 7 Sovereign Close, Sovereign Court, London E1W 3HW. 020-7488 9300 *fax 020-7488 9333*. advice line & membership 0800 018 4318. e-mail office@gingerbread.org.uk

Headway – the brain injury association, 4 King Edward Court, King Edward Street, Nottingham NG1 1EW 0115 924 0800 *fax 0115 958 4446* helpline 0808 800 2244 www.headway.org.uk e-mail enquiries@headway.org.uk Exists to promote the understanding of all aspects of brain injury and to provide information, support and services to people with brain injury, their family and carers.

Homeless Link, 1st Floor, 10-13 Rushworth Street, London SE1 0RB 020-7960 3010 www.homeless.org.uk Membership body for local organisations and individuals providing services and support to homeless people. Also runs the Homeless Services Unit which brings together front line workers in the resettlement and emergency accommodation fields.

Howard League, 1 Ardleigh Road, London N1

4HS. 020-7249 7373 *fax 020-7249 7788*. e-mail info@howardleague.org www.howardleague.org A charity working for humane and effective reform of the penal system

Institute of Criminology, University of Cambridge, Sidgwick Avenue, Cambridge CB3 9DT (01223) 335360. *fax (01223) 335356*. e-mail enquiries@crim.cam.ac.uk A centre for teaching and research in criminology and criminal justice matters, a biennial senior course for practitioners in the criminal justice system, and a part-time masters degree course for senior corrections officials and police officers.

Irish Commission for Prisoners Overseas. **Dublin Office:** Columba Centre, Maynooth, Co Kildare, Ireland (00353) (1) 5053156 *fax (00353) (1) 6016401*. e-mail icpo@iecon.ie **London Office:** 50-52 Camden Square, London NW1 9XB 020-7482 4148 *fax 020-7482 4815*. e-mail icpolondon@hotmail.com Fr Gerry McFlynn. ICPO is a subsection of the Bishops' Commission for Emigrants. It cares for all Irish prisoners abroad, regardless of faith, offence or prison status, and their families when requested. ICPO works at an international level to ensure that minimum levels of human rights for Irish migrants, refugees and prisoners abroad are respected and enforced. As an NGO, ICPO operates on a not for profit basis to represent the needs of Irish individuals imprisoned overseas and to improve standards of rights enforcement and service provision.

Joint Council for the Welfare of Immigrants, 115 Old Street, London EC1V 9JR. 020-7251 8708 (admin) *fax 020-7251 8707*. www.jcwi.org.uk An independent national organisation that exists to campaign for justice in immigration, nationality and refugee law and policy. It undertakes strategic casework and acts as an expert training resource for others who work in this field.

Justice, 59 Carter Lane, London EC4V 5AQ 020-7329 5100 *fax 020-7329 5055* e-mail admin@justice.org.uk Justice is a law reform and human rights group. It cannot deal with individual cases, but has produced 'How to Appeal' a simple guide to the criminal appeal process. The guide is free to prisoners (send sae 9"x6" with 34p stamp). It is available to others at £2.50 inc p&p.

KIDSCAPE, 2 Grosvenor Gardens, London SW1W 0DH. 020-7730 3300. Provides books, posters, videos, teaching materials and training about prevention of child sexual abuse and school bullying. Send sae (A4 60p) for information and leaflets. Helpline 08451 205 204 for parents of children bullied at school, Mon-Fri 10am-4pm.

Law Society, 113 Chancery Lane, London WC2A 020-7242 1222. www.lawsociety.org.uk The representative body and regulator of solicitors in England & Wales

Lincolnshire Action Trust, Beech House, Witham Park, Waterside South, Lincoln LN5 7JH (01522) 806611 fax (01522) 806610 www.lincolnshire-action-trust.org.uk Employment, training and education advice and guidance, etc for offenders in community and prison Lincolnshire and surrounding area. Also provides assistance to employers considering recuitment of people with a criminal record.

MESSAGE HOME helpline 0800 700 740 a 24 hr national freecall confidential helpline for adults aged 18+ who have left home, or run away, to send a message to someone and get confidential help and advice.

MENCAP (Royal Mencap Society), 117-123 Golden Lane, London EC1Y 0RT. 020-7454 0454 fax 020-7696 5540. e-mail information@mencap.org.uk www. mencap.org.uk The largest charity for people with learning difficulties.

Mind (Nat Assn for Mental Health), Granta House, 15/19 Broadway, Stratford, London E15 4BQ 020- 8519 2122 fax 020-8522 1725 Mindinfoline (0845) 7660163. Mind is the leading mental health charity in England and Wales and works for a better life for everyone with experience of mental distress. There are over 220 local Mind associations. Call 020-8215 2225 or log on to www.mind.org.uk to find the nearest one.

Missing Persons Helpline (National), PO Box 28908, London SW14 7JU 020-8392 4545 fax 020-8878 7752 national helpline 0500 700 700 e-mail admin@missingpersons.org www.missingpersons.org The charity is dedicated to helping missing people, their families and those who care for them.

Muslim Youth Helpline, 4th Floor, Barkat House, 116-118 Finchley Road, London NW3 5HT tel (admin) 0870 774 3518 fax 0870 774 3519 helpline (freephone) 0808 808 2008 or 020-8795 5321 (mon-fri 6pm-12am sat/sun 12pm-12am) e-mail (admin) info@myh.org.uk (helpline) help@myh.org.uk A free confidential counselling and befriending service for young Muslims in need.

National Association of Child Contact Centres, Minerva House, Spaniel Row, Nottingham NG1 6EP. tel 0845 4500 280 fax 0845 4500 420 e-mail contact@naccc.org.uk www.naccc.org.uk Promotes safe child contact within a national framework of child contact centres. These exist to provide neutral meeting places where children of a separated family can enjoy contact with one or both parents, and sometimes other family members, in a comfortable and safe environment where there is no viable alternative.

National Association of Official Prison Visitors, 32 Newham Avenue, Bedford MK41 9PT tel/fax (01234) 359763 e-mail info@napov.com www.napov.org.uk

National Children's Bureau, 8 Wakley Street, London EC1V 7QE. 020-7843 6000 fax 020-7278 9512. www.ncb.org.uk Identifies and promotes the interests of children and young people through policy, research and practice development. The Bureau is multi disciplinary, working with professional across all sectors.

NORCAP – supporting adults affected by adoption, 112 Church Road, Wheatley, Oxon OX33 1LU (01865) 875000. e-mail enquiries@norcap.org www.norcap.org.uk Provides support, guidance and sympathetic understanding to adult adopted people and their birth and adoptive relatives. Contact Register. For members – telephone helpline, intermediary role for those seeking renewed contact, advice on searching and research service, comprehensive research pack.

NSPCC, Weston House, 42 Curtain Road, London EC2A 3NH. 020-7825 2500 fax 020-7825 2525. 24hr child protection helpline 0808 800 5000 e-mail infounit@nspcc.org.uk The NSPCC is the UK's leading charity specialising in child protection and prevention of cruelty to children. It exists to prevent children from suffering significant harm as a result of ill treatment; to help protect children who are at risk from such harm; to

help children who have suffered abuse overcome the effects of such harm; and to work to protect children from further harm.

National Youth Agency, Eastgate House, 19-23 Humberstone Road, Leicester LE1 6GD. 0116-242 7350 *fax 0116-242 7444* www.nya.org.uk Information, advice and support for those working with young people. Validates qualifying training for youth and community work

New Bridge, 27a Medway Street, London SW1P 2BD. 020-7976 0779. *fax 020-7976 0767* e-mail info@newbridgefoundation.org.uk www.newbridgefoundation.org.uk New Bridge is one of only 20 national charities in Britain providing resettlement support to prisoners. For nearly 50 years it has been committed to supporting prisoners through its network of voluntary associates and the provision of professional resettlement services. Provides family matters courses in a number of establishments and publishes 'Inside Time' the national newspaper for prisoners.

New Bridge Prison Liaison Project, 4 & 5 Laurel Business Centre, 15 Laurel Road, Liverpool L7 0LJ 0151-254 2558 *fax 0151-254 2559* e-mail info@prisonlisaisonproject.co.uk www.prisonliaisonproject.co.uk Provides services and information working with offenders who will be settling in Liverpool.

Nurses Welfare Service, 32 Buckingham Palace Road, London SW1W 0RE. 020-7233 5500 *fax 020-7976 6770* e-mail info@nurseswelfareservice.co.uk www.nurseswelfareservice.co.uk Help for nurses, midwives and health visitors whose right or fitness to practise is being investigated by their regulatory body.

One Parent Families, 255 Kentish Town Road, London NW5 2LX. 020-7428 5400 *fax 020-7482 4851*. Helpline for lone parents 0800 018 5062 www.oneparentfamilies.org.uk Information service for lone parents, other organisations, local authorities and the media. Providing consultancy on employment initiatives for lone parents and rights based training for professionals working with lone parents. Campaigning and lobbying to change the law and improve provision for lone parents and their children.

Out-Side-In, PO Box 119, Orpington, Kent BR6 9ZZ. helpline (01689) 835566 Support group

for gay/lesbian/transgendered prisoners their partners, families and friends

Parentline Plus, 520 Highgate Studios, 53-79 Highgate Road, Kentish Town, London NW5 1TL. 020-7284 5500 *fax 020-7284 5501* Helpline 0808 800 2222, Textphone 0800 783 6783 e-mail parentsupport@parentlineplus.org.uk (for parents, not general enquiries) www.parentlineplus.org.uk National charity offering help and information for parents and families via a range of services including a free 24 hour confidential helpline, workshops, courses, leaflets and website. Works to recognise and to value the different types of families that exist and expand services available to them; understands that children's needs cannot be separated from the needs of parents/carers, believes that it is normal for all parents to have difficulties from time to time.

Partners of Prisoners Families Support Group, Valentine House, 1079 Rochdale Road, Blackley, Manchester M9 8AJ. tel/fax 0161-702 1000. e-mail mail@partnersofprisoners.co.uk www.partnersofprisoners.co.uk Offers a wide range of services to anyone who has a loved one in prison. Advice, information, moral support is available to families from arrest to release. Manchester based, but telephone calls taken from all areas as acts as a referral agency to support groups nationally. Manages the Black Prisoner Support Project that provides groupwork to black men in prison.

The POW Trust, 295a Queenstown Road, Battersea, London SW8 3NP 020-7720 9767 *fax 020-7498 0477*. Devoted to helping the socially excluded, especially assisting inmates and ex-offenders, to fit back into society with a 'second chance'.

The Prince's Trust, 18 Park Square East, London NW1 4LH. 020-7543 1234 *fax 020-7543 1200* General enquiries freephone 0800-842842 or visit website www.princes-trust.org.uk Helps 14-30 year olds to develop confidence, learn new skills, move into work and start businesses. It offers training, personal development opportunities, business start up support, mentoring and advice. The Trust has four priority target groups - unemployed, educational under achievers, offenders/ex-offenders, and those leaving care.

Prison Advice & Care Trust (PACT), Suite C5, 196 Old Street, London EC1V 9FR 020-7490 3139 e-mail info@pact.uk.net Provides services for families including information, advice and support. Visits Centres in London, South West and at HMP Woodhill. First night in custody schemes at HMP Holoway and HMP Exeter.

Prison Dialogue, PO Box 44, Chipping Campden, Glos GL55 6YN (01386) 849186 *fax (01386) 840449*. e-mail enquiries@prisondialogue.org.uk www.prisondialogue.org.uk Relationship based approach to organisational and therapeutic issues in the criminal justice system. Work is targeted across the criminal justice continuum from high security to local prisons and into the community.

Prison Link, 29 Trinity Road, Aston, Birmingham B6 6AJ 0121-551 1207 *fax 0121-554 4894* www.ueponline.co.uk A black and Asian prisoner support scheme providing services to offenders and their families.

POA, The Professional Trades Union for Prison, Correctional and Secure Psychiatric Workers, Cronin House, 245 Church Street, London N9 9HW. 020-8803 0255 Trade Union and professional staff association for workers in penal institutions and secure psychiatric units in England, Wales, Scotland and Northern Ireland.

Prison Reform Trust, 15 Northburgh Street, London EC1V 0JR. 020-7251 5070 *fax 020-7251 5076*. e-mail prt@prisonreformtrust.org.uk www.prisonreformtrust.org.uk Runs a research and publishing programme, and offers advice and information on all aspects of penal policy, publishes a quarterly magazine 'Prison Report'. Jointly (with HM Prison Service) publishes "Prisoners' Information Book"

Prisoners Abroad, 89-93 Fonthill Road, Finsbury Park, London N4 3JH. 020-7561 6820 *fax 020-7561 6821*. e-mail info@prisonersabroad.org.uk www.prisonersabroad.org.uk The only UK charity providing information, advice and support to Britons detained overseas, to their families and friends, and to released prisoners trying to re-establish themselves in society. Prisoners Abroad makes no moral judgement about its clients: it helps

convicted and unconvicted, guilty or innocent, solely on the basis of need.

Prisoners Advice and Care Trust (PACT), Family Support Service, Suite C5, City Cloisters, 196 Old Street, London EC1V 9FR 020 7490 3139 *fax 020 7490 0755* Formed by the merger of the Bourne Trust and the Prisoner's Wives and Families Society. Services for families include information, advice and other support. Overnight accommodation for families visiting relatives in London prisons.

Prisoners' Advice Service, PO Box 46199, London EC1M 4XA. 020-7253 3323 *fax 020-7253 8067* freephone 0800 018 2156 The PAS is an independent charity that offers free confidential advice and information to prisoners in England & Wales, particulary concerning prisoners' rights and the application of Prison Rules. Publishes a quarterly bulletin "Prisoners' Rights".

Prisoners' Families and Friends Service, 20 Trinity Street, London SE1 1DB. 020-7403 4091 *fax 020-7403 9359*. free helpline for families 0808 808 3444 e-mail info@prisonersfamiliesandfriends.org.uk Advice and information service for prisoner's families. Other facilities available in the London area.

Prisoners' Families Helpline 0808 808 2003 free confidential, national helpline that provides information and support for prisoners' families and friends e-mail info@prisonersfamilieshelpline.org.uk

Probation Managers Association, Hayes Court, West Common Road, Bromley, Kent BR2 7AU. 020-8462 7755 *fax 020-8315 8234* e-mail david.w.thomas@ntworld.com

Repetitive Strain Injury Association, c/o Keytools Ltd. PO Box 700. Southampton. SO17 1LQ 023 8058 4314 *fax 023 8055 6902* e-mail rsia@keytools.com www.rsi.org.uk

Rethink (formerly National Schizophrenia Fellowship), 28 Castle Street, Kingston-upon-Thames KT1 1SS, advice service 020-8974 6814 (mon-fri 10am-3pm) *fax 020-8547 3862*. A national voluntary organisation that helps people with a severe mental illness, their families and carers and provides training for professionals.

The Rights Shop (Bethnal Green), 296 Bethnal Green Road, London E2 0AG, 020-7739 4173 *fax 020-7033 9184;* open Mon & Wed

9am-2.00pm (drop-in service), Tues & Thurs 9am-2pm (appt only). Drop-in welfare rights/housing advice/money advice.

Royal National Institute of the Blind (RNIB), 105 Judd Street, London WC1H 9NE. 020-7388 1266 *fax 020-7388 2034*. Helpline 0845 766 9999 General enquiries: RNIB Resource Centre, London; benefit rights; education; employment and leisure enquiries; services for local societies; health, social and environmental services; reference library; advice on wills and legacies; enquiries on multiple disability; physiotherapy support.

RNID - for deaf and hard of hearing people, 19-23 Featherstone Street, London EC1Y 8SL. 0808 808 0123 (voice), 0808 808 9000 (text), *helpline fax 020-7296 8199*. e-mail informationline@rnid.org.uk www.rnid.org.uk The RNID is the largest charity representing the 9 million deaf and hard of hearing people in the UK. As a membership charity it aims to achieve a radically better life for deaf and hard of hearing people. It does this by campaigning and lobbying, by raising awareness, by providing services and through social, medical and technical research

SANDS (Stillbirth And Neonatal Death Society), 28 Portland Place, London W1B 1LY. Admin 020-7436 7940, *fax 020-7436 3715*, helpline 020-7436 5881 e-mail helpline@uk-sands.org www.sands-uk.org Support and advice for parents and families whose baby dies before, during or after birth

SANE, 1st floor, Cityside House, 40 Adler Street, London E1 1EE 020-7375 1002 *fax 020-7375 2162* Saneline (helpline) 0845 767 8000 (12 noon-11pm Mon-Fri, 12noon -6pm Sat/Sun). A national mental health helpline for anyone with a mental health problem, their friends, families, carers and interested professionals. Can offer emotional support and information on local and national services, illnesses, medications, therapies and mental health law.

Schizophrenia Association of Great Britain, The Crescent, Bangor, Gwynedd LL57 2AG. (01248) 354048 *fax (01248) 353659*. Special leaflets available for probation officers and magistrates. Free information pack for all enquirers.

*Sex Addicts Anonymous, BCM Box 1457, London WC1N 3XX. 020-8946 2436 www.saa.recovery.org12 step fellowship

based on model pioneered by AA, meetings (in London & elsewhere) open to anyone who feels their sexual behaviour is causing problems either to themselves or others. Newcomers meeting each Monday (inc bank holidays) 6pm, at The Church Hall of St Mary-the-Virgin, Eversholt Street, London NW1, nearest tube Euston

Shelter (National campaign for homeless), 88 Old Street, London EC1V 9HU. 020-7505 2000 *fax 020-7505 2169*. www.shelter.org.uk Freephone emergency 24hr advice 0808 800 4444. Runs a network of housing aid centres providing advice and advocacy to people who are, or are threatened with, homelessness, and campaigns on their behalf.

SITRA, 3rd Floor, 55 Bondway, London SW8 1SJ 020-7793 4711 *fax 020-7793 4714* e-mail post@sitra.org www.sitra.org.uk Training, advice, policy information and consultancy on all supported housing and supporting people matters. Monthly journal 'SITRA Bulletin' goes to all SITRA members.

Survivors UK, 2 Leathermarket Street, London SE1 3HN office 020 7357 6222 (mon-fri 9.30am-5.30pm) *fax 020-8357 7766* helpline (Tues & Thurs 7-10pm) 0845 122 1201 e-mail info@survivors.org.uk www.survivors.org Provides information, support and counselling to men who have experienced any form of sexual abuse, and to advance public education about all matters relating to the sexual abuse of men.

Together, 1st Floor, 296-302 High Holborn, London WC1V 7JH 020-7061 3400 *fax 020-7061 3401* e-mail contactus@together-uk.org www.together-uk.org A national charity providing a wide range of high quality community and hospital based services for people with mental health needs and their carers; including advocacy, assertive outreach schemes, community support, employment schemes, forensic services, helplines/information, respite for carers, social clubs, supported accommodation including 24 hour care.

Women in Prison, 3b Aberdeen Studios, 22 Highbury Grove, London N5 2EA. 020-7226 5879 *fax 020-7354 8005*. www.womeninprison.org.uk Established as a support and campaigning group for women prisoners, visits women prisoners and offers practical advice on a range of welfare issues, particularly accommodation referrals. Also

the Education & Training Connection that provides bursaries for distance learning courses for women prisoners, and links women with education/ training centres on release.

Women's Aid Federation of England Ltd, PO Box 391, Bristol BS99 7WS. national co-ordinating office telephone 0117-944 4411 e-mail info@womensaid.org.uk www.womensaid.org.uk Freephone 24hr National domestic violence helpline 0808 2000 247 (run in partnership between Women's Aid and Refuge. Public information, publications and training on domestic violence. National helpline for women and children experiencing domestic violence. Co-ordinates work of women's refuges in England.

Workaholics Anonymous, PO Box 11466, London SW1V 2ZQ 12 step self help programme for compulsive workers. Free literature in return for an s.a.e. www.workaholics-anonymous.org

Zito Trust, 16 Castle Street, Hay on Wye, Hereford HR3 5DF. 01497 820011. A registered mental health charity that seeks to provide advice and support for victims of community care breakdown and to carry out research into services for the severely mentally ill and disordered.

PRISON SERVICE ESTABLISHMENTS ENGLAND & WALES

HMP ACKLINGTON
MORPETH, Northumberland NE65 9XF
tel (01670) 762300 *fax (01670) 762301*

HMP ALBANY
NEWPORT, Isle of Wight PO30 5RS
tel (01983) 556300 *fax (01983) 556301*

HMP ALTCOURSE
Higher Lane, Fazakerley, LIVERPOOL L9 7LH
tel (0151) 522 2000 *fax (0151) 522 2121*

HMYOI ASHFIELD
Shortwood Road, Pucklechurch, BRISTOL BS16 9QJ
tel (0117) 303 8000 *fax (0117) 303 8001*

HMP ASHWELL
OAKHAM, Rutland LE15 7LF
tel (01572) 884100 *fax (01572) 884101*

HMP/YOI ASKHAM GRANGE
Askham Richard, YORK YO23 3FT
tel (01904) 772000 *fax (01904) 772001*

HMYOI AYLESBURY
Bierton Road, AYLESBURY, Bucks HP20 1EH
tel (01296) 444000 *fax (01296) 444001*

HMP BEDFORD
St. Loyes Street, BEDFORD MK40 1HG
tel (01234) 373000 *fax (01234) 273568*

HMP BELMARSH
Western Way, Thamesmead, LONDON SE28 0EB
tel (020) 8331 4400 *fax (020) 8331 4401*

HMP BIRMINGHAM
Winson Green Road, BIRMINGHAM B18 4AS
tel (0121) 345 2500 *fax (0121) 345 2501*

HMP BLAKENHURST
Hewell Lane, REDDITCH, Worcs B97 6QS
tel (01527) 400500 *fax (01527) 400501*

HMP BLANTYRE HOUSE
Goudhurst, CRANBROOK, Kent TN17 2NH
tel (01580) 213200 *fax (01580) 213201*

HMP BLUNDESTON
LOWESTOFT, Suffolk NR32 5BG
tel (01502) 734500 *fax (01502) 734501*

HMYOI & RC BRINSFORD
New Road, Featherstone, WOLVERHAMPTON WV10 7PY
tel (01902) 532450 *fax (01902) 532451*

HMP BRISTOL
19 Cambridge Road, Horfield, BRISTOL BS7 8PS
tel (0117) 372 3100 *fax (0117) 372 3013*

HMP BRIXTON
P O Box 369, Jebb Avenue, LONDON SW2 5XF
tel (020) 8588 6000 *fax (020) 8588 6283*

HMP BROCKHILL
REDDITCH, Worcs B97 6RD
tel (01527) 552650 *fax (01527) 552651*

HMP BRONZEFIELD
Woodthorpe Road, Ashford, Middx TW15 3JZ
tel (01784) 425690 *fax (01784) 425691*

HMP BUCKLEY HALL
Buckley Road, ROCHDALE, Lancs OL12 9DP

tel (01706) 514300 *fax (01706) 514399*

HMP BULLINGDON
P O Box 50, BICESTER, Oxon OX25 1WD
tel (01869) 353100 *fax (01869) 353101*

HMP/YOI BULLWOOD HALL
High Road, HOCKLEY, Essex SS5 4TE
tel (01702) 562800 *fax (01702) 562801*

HMP CAMP HILL
NEWPORT, Isle of Wight PO30 5PB
tel (01983) 554600 *fax (01983) 554799*

HMP CANTERBURY
46 Longport, CANTERBURY, Kent CT1 1PJ
tel (01227) 862800 *fax (01227) 862801*

HMP & RC CARDIFF
Knox Road, CARDIFF CF24 0UG
tel (02920) 923100 *fax (02920) 923318*

HMYOI CASTINGTON
MORPETH, Northumberland NE65 9XG
tel (01670) 382100 *fax (01670) 382101*

HMP CHANNINGS WOOD
Denbury, NEWTON ABBOTT, Devon TQ12 6DW
tel (01803) 814600 *fax (01803) 814601*

HMP/YOI CHELMSFORD
200 Springfield Road, CHELMSFORD, Essex CM2 6LQ
tel (01245) 272000 *fax (01245) 272001*

HMP COLDINGLEY
Bisley, WOKING, Surrey GU24 9EX
tel (01483) 804300 *fax (01483) 804427*

HMP COOKHAM WOOD
ROCHESTER, Kent ME1 3LU
tel (01634) 202500 *fax (01634) 202501*

HMP DARTMOOR
Princetown, YELVERTON, Devon PL20 6RR
tel (01822) 892000 *fax (01822) 892001*

HMYOI DEERBOLT
Bowes Road, BARNARD CASTLE, Co Durham DL12 9BG
tel (01833) 633200 *fax (01833) 633201*

HMP/YOI DONCASTER
off North Bridge, Marshgate, DONCASTER, S Yorks, DN5 8UX
tel (01302) 760870 *fax (01302) 760851*

HMP DORCHESTER
North Square, DORCHESTER, Dorset DT1 1JD
tel (01305) 214500 *fax (01305) 214501*

HMP DOVEGATE
Uttoxeter, Staffordshire ST14 8XR
tel (01283) 829400 *fax (01283) 820066*

IRC DOVER
The Citadel, Western Heights, DOVER, Kent CT17 9DR
tel (01304) 246400 *fax (01304) 246401*

HMP DOWNVIEW
Sutton Lane, SUTTON, Surrey SM2 5PD
tel (020) 8929 3300 *fax (020) 8929 3301*

HMP/YOI DRAKE HALL
ECCLESHALL, Staffordshire ST21 6LQ
tel (01785) 774100 *fax (01785) 774010*

HMP DURHAM
Old Elvet, DURHAM DH1 3HU
tel (0191) 332 3400 *fax (0191) 332 3401*

HMP/YOI EAST SUTTON PARK
Sutton Valence, MAIDSTONE, Kent ME17 3DF
tel (01622) 845000 *fax (01622) 845001*

HMP EASTWOOD PARK
Falfield, WOTTON-UNDER-EDGE, Glos GL12 8DB
tel (01454) 382100 *fax (01454) 382101*

HMP EDMUNDS HILL
(previously HMP Highpoint North & HMP North Ridge)
Stradishall, Newmarket, Suffolk CB8 9YN
tel (01440) 743500 *fax (01440) 743560*

HMP ELMLEY
Church Road, EASTCHURCH, Sheerness, Kent ME12 4AY
tel (01795) 882000 *fax (01795) 882101*

HMP ERLESTOKE
DEVIZES, Wiltshire SN10 5TU
tel (01380) 814250 *fax (01380) 814273*

HMP EVERTHORPE
BROUGH, E Yorks HU15 1RB
tel (01430) 426500 *fax (01430) 426501*

HMP/YOI EXETER
New North Road, EXETER, Devon EX4 4EX
tel (01392) 415650 *fax (01392) 415691*

HMP FEATHERSTONE
New Road, Wolverhampton, Staffs WV10 7PU
tel (01902) 703000 *fax (01902) 703001*

HMYOI & RC FELTHAM
Bedfont Road, FELTHAM, Middx TW13 4ND
tel (020) 8844 5000 *fax (020) 8844 5001*

HMP FORD
ARUNDEL, West Sussex BN18 0BX
tel (01903) 663000 *fax (01903) 663001*

HMP/YOI FOREST BANK
Agecroft Road, Pendlebury,
MANCHESTER M27 8FB
tel (0161) 925 7000 *fax (0161) 925 7001*

HMP FOSTON HALL
Foston, DERBY,Derbyshire DE65 5DN
tel (01283) 584300 *fax (01283) 584301*

HMP FRANKLAND
Brasside, DURHAM DH1 5YD
tel (0191) 332 3000 *fax (0191) 332 3001*

HMP FULL SUTTON
Full Sutton, YORK YO41 1PS
tel (01759) 475100 *fax (01759) 371206*

HMP GARTH
Ulnes Walton Lane, Leyland,
PRESTON, Lancs PR26 8NE
tel (01772) 443300 *fax (01772) 443301*

HMP GARTREE
Gallow Field Road, MARKET
HARBOROUGH,
Leics LE16 7RP
tel (01858) 436600 *fax (01858) 436601*

HMYOI & RC GLEN PARVA
Tigers Road, Wigston, LEICESTER LE8
4TN
tel (0116) 228 4100 *fax (0116) 228 4000*

HMP/YOI GLOUCESTER
Barrack Square, GLOUCESTER GL1 2JN
tel (01452) 453000 *fax (01452) 453001*

HMP GRENDON
Grendon Underwood, AYLESBURY,
Bucks HP18 0TL
tel (01296) 443000 *fax (01296) 443001*

HMP/YOI GUYS MARSH
SHAFTESBURY, Dorset SP7 0AH
tel (01747) 856400 *fax (01747) 856401*

IRC HASLAR
2 Dolphin Way, GOSPORT, Hants PO12
2AW
tel (02392) 604000 *fax (02392) 604001*

HMP HAVERIGG
MILLOM, Cumbria LA18 4NA
tel (01229) 713000 *fax (01229) 713001*

HMP HEWELL GRANGE
REDDITCH, Worcs B97 6QQ
tel (01527) 552000 *fax (01527) 552001*

HMP HIGH DOWN
Sutton Lane, SUTTON, Surrey SM2 5PJ
tel (020) 8722 6300 *fax (020) 8722 6301*

HMP HIGHPOINT
Stradishall, NEWMARKET,
Suffolk CB8 9YG
tel (01440) 743100 *fax (01440) 743092*

HMP/YOI HINDLEY
Gibson Street, Bickershaw, WIGAN,
Lancs WN2 5TH
tel (01942) 855000 *fax (01942) 855001*

HMP/YOI HOLLESLEY BAY
WOODBRIDGE, Suffolk IP12 3JW
tel (01394) 412400 *fax (01394) 410115*

HMP/YOI HOLLOWAY
Parkhurst Road, LONDON N7 0NU
tel (020) 7979 4400 *fax (020) 7979 4401*

HMP HOLME HOUSE
Holme House Road, STOCKTON-ON-
TEES,
Cleveland TS18 2QU
tel (01642) 744000 *fax (01642) 744001*

HMP HULL
Hedon Road, HULL HU9 5LS
tel (01482) 282200 *fax (01482) 282400*

HMYOI HUNTERCOMBE
Huntercombe Place, Nuffield,
HENLEY-ON-THAMES, Oxon RG9 5SB
tel (01491) 643100 *fax (01491) 643101*

HMP KINGSTON
122 Milton Road, PORTSMOUTH,
Hants PO3 6AS
tel (023) 9295 3100 *tel (023) 9295 3181*

HMP KIRKHAM
Freckleton Road, PRESTON,
Lancs PR4 2RN
tel (01772) 675400 *fax (01772) 675401*

HMP KIRKLEVINGTON GRANGE
YARM, Cleveland TS15 9PA
tel (01642) 792600 *fax (01642) 792601*

HMP LANCASTER
The Castle, LANCASTER,
Lancs LA1 1YL
tel (01524) 385100 *fax (01524) 385101*

HMYOI & RC LANCASTER FARMS
Far Moor Lane, Stone Row Head,
off Quernmore Road, LANCASTER LA1
3QZ
tel (01524) 563450 *fax (01524) 563451*

HMP LATCHMERE HOUSE
Church Road, Ham Common,

RICHMOND, Surrey TW10 5HH
tel (020) 8588 6650 *fax (020) 8588 6698*

HMP LEEDS
Armley, LEEDS, W Yorks, LS12 2TJ
tel (0113) 203 2600 *fax (0113) 203 2601*

HMP LEICESTER
Welford Road, LEICESTER LE2 7AJ
tel (0116) 228 3000 *fax (0116) 228 3001*

HMP LEWES
Brighton Road, LEWES, E Sussex BN7
1EA
tel (01273) 405100 *fax (01273) 405101*

HMP LEYHILL
WOTTON-UNDER-EDGE, Glos GL12
8HL
tel (01454) 264000 *fax (01454) 264001*

HMP LINCOLN
Greetwell Road, LINCOLN LN2 4BD
tel (01522) 663000 *fax (01522) 663001*

HMP LINDHOLME
Bawtry Road, Hatfield Woodhouse,
DONCASTER DN7 6EE
tel (01302) 524700 *fax (01302) 524750*

HMP LITTLEHEY
Perry, HUNTINGDON, Cambridgeshire
PE28 0SR
tel (01480) 333000 *fax (01480) 333070*

HMP LIVERPOOL
68 Hornby Road, LIVERPOOL L9 3DF
tel (0151) 530 4000 *fax (0151) 530 4001*

HMP LONG LARTIN
South Littleton, EVESHAM, WorcsWR11
5TZ
tel (01386) 835100 *fax (01386) 835101*

HMP LOWDHAM GRANGE
LOWDHAM Nottinghamshire NG14 7DA
tel (0115) 966 9200 *fax (0115) 966 9220*

HMYOI LOW NEWTON
Brasside, DURHAM DH1 3YA
tel (0191) 376 4000 *fax (0191) 376 4001*

HMP MAIDSTONE
36 County Road, MAIDSTONE,
Kent ME14 1UZ
tel (01622) 775300 *fax (01622) 775301*

HMP MANCHESTER
Southall Street, MANCHESTER M60 9AH
tel (0161) 8175600 *fax (0161) 8175601*

HMYOI MOORLAND OPEN
Thorne Road, Hatfield, DONCASTER,
S Yorks DN7 6EL
tel (01405) 746500 *fax (01405) 746501*

HMP MOORLAND CLOSED
Bawtry Road, Hatfield Woodhouse,
DONCASTER, S Yorks DN7 6BW
tel (01302) 523000 *fax (01302) 523001*

HMP MORTON HALL
Swinderby, LINCOLN LN6 9PT
tel (01522) 666700 *fax (01522) 666750*

HMP THE MOUNT
Molyneaux Avenue, Bovingdon,
HEMEL HEMPSTEAD, Herts HP3 0NZ
tel (01442) 836300 *fax (01442) 836301*

HMP/YOI NEW HALL
Dial Wood, Flockton, WAKEFIELD,
W Yorks WF4 4XX
tel (01924) 844200 *fax (01924) 844201*

HMYOI NORTHALLERTON
15A East Road, NORTHALLERTON,
N Yorks DL6 1NW
tel (01609) 785100 *fax (01609) 785101*

HMP NORTH SEA CAMP
Freiston, BOSTON, Lincs PE22 0QX
tel (01205) 769300 *fax (01205) 769301*

HMP/YOI NORWICH
Knox Road, NORWICH, Norfolk NR1 4LU
tel (01603) 708600 *fax (01603) 708601*

HMP NOTTINGHAM
Perry Road, Sherwood,
NOTTINGHAM NG5 3AG
tel (0115) 872 3000 fax (0115) 872 3001

HMP/YOI ONLEY
Willoughby, RUGBY, Warwickshire CV23
8AP
tel (01788) 523400 fax (01788) 523401

HMP/YOI PARC
Heol Hopcyn John, BRIDGEND,
Mid-Glam CF35 6AP
tel (01656) 300200 fax (01656) 300201

HMP PARKHURST
NEWPORT, Isle of Wight PO30 5NX
tel (01983) 554000 fax (01983) 554001

HMP PENTONVILLE
Caledonian Road, LONDON N7 8TT
tel (020) 7023 7000 fax (020) 7023 7001

HMP PETERBOROUGH
Saville Road, Westfield, Peterborough PE3
7PD
tel (01733) 217500 *fax (01733) 217501*

HMYOI PORTLAND
The Grove, PORTLAND, Dorset DT5 1DL
tel (01305) 825600 *fax (01305) 825601*

HMYOI PRESCOED
Coed-y-Paen, Pontypool,
Gwent NP14 0TD
tel (01291) 675000 *fax (01291) 675158*

HMP PRESTON
2 Ribbleton Lane, PRESTON,
Lancs PR1 5AB
tel (01772) 444550 *fax (01772) 444551*

HMP RANBY
RETFORD, Nottinghamshire DN22 8EU
tel (01777) 862000 *fax (01777) 862001*

HMP/YOI READING
Forbury Road, READING, Berks RG1 3HY
tel (0118) 9085000 *fax (0118) 9085001*

HMP RISLEY
Risley, WARRINGTON,
Cheshire WA3 6BP
tel (01925) 733000 *fax (01925) 733001*

HMP & RC ROCHESTER
1 Fort Road, ROCHESTER, Kent ME1 3QS
tel (01634) 803100 *fax (01634) 803101*

HMP RYE HILL
Willoughby, RUGBY Warcs CV23 8AM
tel (01788) 523300 *fax (01788) 523311*

HMP SEND
Ripley Road, Send, WOKING,
Surrey GU23 7LJ
tel (01483) 471000 *fax (01483) 471001*

HMP SHEPTON MALLET
Cornhill, SHEPTON MALLET,
Somerset BA4 5LU
tel (01749) 823300 *fax (01749) 823301*

HMP SHREWSBURY
The Dana, SHREWSBURY,
Shropshire SY1 2HR
tel (01743) 273000 *fax (01743) 273001*

HMP SPRING HILL
Grendon Underwood, AYLESBURY,
Bucks HP18 0TH
tel (01296) 443000 *fax (01296) 443001*

HMP STAFFORD
54 Gaol Road, STAFFORD ST16 3AW
tel (01785) 773000 *fax (01785) 773001*

HMP STANDFORD HILL
Church Road, EASTCHURCH,
Sheerness, Kent ME12 4AA
tel (01795) 884500 *fax (01795) 884638*

HMP STOCKEN
Stocken Hall Road, STRETTON,
Nr Oakham, Rutland LE15 7RD

tel (01780) 795100 *fax (01780) 410767*

HMYOI STOKE HEATH
Stoke Heath, MARKET DRAYTON,
Shropshire TF9 2JL
tel (01630) 636000 *fax (01630) 636001*

HMP/YOI STYAL
Styal, WILMSLOW, Cheshire, SK9 4HR
tel (01625) 553000 *fax (01625) 553001*

HMP SUDBURY
Ashbourne, DERBYSHIRE DE6 5HW
tel (01283) 584000 *fax (01283) 584001*

HMP SWALESIDE
Brabazon Road, EASTCHURCH,
Isle of Sheppey, Kent ME12 4AX
tel (01795) 884100 *fax (01795) 884200*

HMP SWANSEA
200 Oystermouth Road, SWANSEA,
W Glam SA1 3SR
tel (01792) 485300 *fax (01792) 485301*

HMYOI SWINFEN HALL
Swinfen, LICHFIELD, Staffs WS14 9QS
tel (01543) 484000 *fax (01543) 484001*

HMYOI THORN CROSS
Arley Road, Appleton Thorn,
WARRINGTON, Cheshire WA4 4RL
tel (01925) 805100 *fax (01925) 805101*

HMP USK
47 Maryport Street, USK, Gwent NP15 1XP
tel (01291) 671600 *fax (01291) 671752*

HMP THE VERNE
The Verne, PORTLAND, Dorset DT5 1EQ
tel (01305) 825000 *fax (01305) 825001*

HMP WAKEFIELD
5 Love Lane, WAKEFIELD,
W Yorks WF2 9AG
tel (01924) 246000 *fax (01924) 246001*

HMP WANDSWORTH
PO Box 757, Heathfield Road,
LONDON SW18 3HS
tel (020) 8588 4000 *fax (020) 8588 4001*

HMYOI WARREN HILL
WOODBRIDGE, Suffolk IP12 3JW
tel (01394) 412400 *fax (01394) 412767*

HMP WAYLAND
Griston, THETFORD, Norfolk IP25 6RL
tel (01953) 804100 *fax (01953) 804220*

HMP WEALSTUN
WETHERBY, W Yorks LS23 7AZ
tel (01937) 848500 *fax (01937) 848501*

HMP WELLINGBOROUGH
Millers Park, Doddington Road,

WELLINGBOROUGH Northants, NN8 2NH
tel (01933) 232700 *fax (01933) 232701*

HMYOI WERRINGTON
Werrington, STOKE-ON-TRENT, Staffs ST9 0DX
tel (01782) 463300 *fax (01782) 463301*

HMYOI WETHERBY
York Road, WETHERBY, W Yorks LS22 5ED
tel (01937) 544200 *fax (01937) 544201*

HMP WHATTON
14 Cromwell Road, NOTTINGHAM NG13 9FQ
tel (01949) 859200 *fax (01949) 859201*

HMP WHITEMOOR
Longhill Road, MARCH, Cambs PE15 0PR
tel (01354) 602350 *fax (01354) 602351*

HMP WINCHESTER
Romsey Road, WINCHESTER, Hampshire SO22 5DF
tel (01962) 723000 *fax (01962) 723001*

HMP WOLDS
Everthorpe, BROUGH, E Yorks HU15 2JZ
tel (01430) 421588 *fax (01430) 421589*

HMP WOODHILL
Tattenhoe Street, MILTON KEYNES, Bucks MK4 4DA
tel (01908) 722000 *fax (01908) 722001*

HMP WORMWOOD SCRUBS
PO Box 757, Du Cane Road, LONDON W12 0AE
tel (020) 8588 3200 *fax (020) 8588 3201*

HMP WYMOTT
Ulnes Walton Lane, Leyland, PRESTON PR26 8LW
tel (01772) 444000 *fax (01772) 444001*

SCOTTISH PRISON SERVICE ESTABLISHMENTS

HMP ABERDEEN
Craiginches, 4 Grampian Place ABERDEEN, Aberdeenshire AB11 8FN
tel (01224) 238300 *fax (01224) 896209*

HMP BARLINNIE
Barlinnie, GLASGOW G33 2QX
tel 0141-770 2000 *fax 0141-770 2060*

HMP CASTLE HUNTLY
Castle Huntly, LONGFORGAN, Near Dundee, Angus DD2 5HL
tel (01382) 319333 *fax (01382) 360510*

HMP/YOI CORNTON VALE
Cornton Road, STIRLING, Stirlingshire FK9 5NU
tel (01786) 832591 *fax (01786) 833597*

HMP DUMFRIES
Terregles Street, DUMFRIES, Dumfriesshire DG2 9AX
tel (01387) 261218 *fax (01387) 264144*

HMP EDINBURGH
33 Stenhouse Road EDINBURGH EH11 3LN
tel 0131-444 3000 *fax 0131-444 3045*

HMP GLENOCHIL
King O'Muir Road, TULLIBODY, Clackmannanshire FK10 3AD
tel (01259) 760471 *fax (01259) 762003*

HMP GREENOCK
Gateside, GREENOCK, Renfrewshire PA16 9AH
tel (01475) 787801 *fax (01475) 783154*

HMP INVERNESS
Porterfield, Duffy Drive INVERNESS, Invernessshire IV2 3HH
tel (01463) 229000 *fax (01463) 229010*

HMP KILMARNOCK
Bowhouse, Mauchline Road KILMARNOCK KA1 5AA
tel (01563) 548800 *fax (01563) 548845*

HMP LOW MOSS
Crosshill Road, Bishopbriggs GLASGOW G64 2QB
tel 0141-762 4848 *fax 0141-772 6903*

HMP NORANSIDE
Fern, By Forfar, Angus DD8 3QY
tel (01356) 319333 *fax (01356) 650245*

HMP PERTH
3 Edinburgh Road, PERTH Perthshire PH2 8AT
tel (01738) 622293 *fax (01738) 630545*

HMP PETERHEAD
PETERHEAD Aberdeenshire AB42 2YY
tel (01779) 479101 *fax (01779) 470529*

HMYOI POLMONT
BRIGHTONS, Near Falkirk, Stirlingshire FK2 0AB
tel (01324) 711558 *fax (01324) 714919*

HMP SHOTTS
SHOTTS, Lanarkshire ML7 4LE
tel (01501) 824000 *fax (01501) 824001*

SCOTTISH PRISON SERVICE COLLEGE
Newlands Road, BRIGHTONS,
Near Falkirk, Stirlingshire FK2 0DE
tel (01324) 710400 *fax (01324) 710401*

SCOTTISH PRISON SERVICE HQ
Calton House, 5 Redheughs Rigg
EDINBURGH EH12 9HW
tel 0131-244 8745 *fax 0131-244 8774*

STATE HOSPITAL
State Hospital, Carstairs Junction,
Lanark ML11 8RP
tel (01555) 840293 *fax (01555) 840100*

NORTHERN IRELAND PRISON SERVICE ESTABLISHMENTS

HMP/YO CENTRE HYDEBANK WOOD
Hospital Road, BELFAST BT8 8NA
tel 028-9025 3666 *fax 028-9025 3668*

HMP MAGHABERRY
Old Road, Upper Ballinderry
LISBURN, Co Antrim BT28 2PT
tel 028-9261 1888 *fax 028-9261 9516*

HMP MAGILLIGAN
Point Road, MAGILLIGAN
Co Londonderry BT49 0LR
tel 028-7776 3311 *fax 028-7772 0307*

HMP MAZE
Halftown Road, Maze
Lisburn, Co Antrim BT27 5RF
tel 028-9268 3111 *fax 028-9268 3603*

HM PRISON SERVICE COLLEGE
Woburn House, MILLISLE,
Co Down BT22 2HS
tel 028-9186 3000 *fax 028-9186 3022*

NORTHERN IRELAND PRISON SERVICE HQ
Dundonald House
Upper Newtownards Road
BELFAST BT4 3SU
tel 028-9052 2922 *fax 028-9052 5100*
public enquiries 028-9052 5265
e-mail info@niprisonservice.gov.uk

ISLE OF MAN, JERSEY, GUERNSEY

ISLE OF MAN PRISON
99 Victoria Road, Douglas,
Isle of Man IM2 4RD
tel (01624) 621306 *fax (01624) 628119*
special visits (01624) 663813

HMP LA MOYE, JERSEY
La Moye, St Brelade, Jersey,
Channel Islands JE3 8HQ
tel (01534) 497200 *fax (01534) 497280*

STATES PRISON GUERNSEY
Les Nicolles, Baubigny, St Sampson
Guernsey, Channel Islands GY2 4YF
tel (01481) 248376 *fax (01481) 247837*
admin fax (01481) 200949

INDEX OF OFFICE NAMES

Offices are indexed by Area Name and
reference number, not page numbers
i.e to find Andover, look up Hampshire
office number 4

Late entry

The following entry was received too late for inclusion in the Probation Service Organisations section:

National Disabled Staff Support Network

The national organisation set up to support staff with disabilities in the Probation Service and CAFCASS and to provide information about, and campaign for, Disability Equality

Chair: David Quarmby (07736) 087019
Vice Chair: Gilly Hagen (07921) 094861
Secretary: Desiree Leete (01392) 861538
Treasurer: Phil Hill

Regional Coordinators
North West: Karen Lavelle (07790) 552253
North East: Barbara Randall (01670) 520121
Midlands: Carol Buckley (01743) 231525
South West and Wales: Lucy van Waterschoot (01752) 827507
East and South East:
Elaine Ford (01268) 412241
and Nick Alderson-Rice (01474) 569546
London: Aidan Linton-Smith 020-7222 0331

Published for Napo by
Shaw & Sons Limited
Shaway House
21 Bourne Park
Bourne Road
Crayford
Kent DA1 4BZ

tel 01322 621100
fax 01322 550553

www.shaws.co.uk

© 2006 Shaw & Sons Limited

Published January 2006

ISBN 0 7219 1558 2
ISSN 0142-1328

Page make-up by Groundwork, Skipton
Printed and bound in Great Britain by
William Clowes Limited, Beccles, Suffolk

The Editor

The Napo Probation Directory is compiled by a probation officer, Owen Wells. If you have any suggestions or questions about the directory, please contact him on:

(01943) 602270
07951 436126 (mobile)
fax (01943) 816732
e-mail o.r.wells@gmail.com

Introduction

The Napo Probation Directory is compiled each October. Wherever possible, changes that occur after October are included in the text up to 20th December. The very short time between compilation and publication means that the Napo Probation Directory is probably the most up-to-date book of its kind published anywhere. Errors will, of course, occur; any that are notified to the publisher will normally be corrected in the *Probation Bulletin*.

Acknowledgement

Without the help of the Chief Probation Officers and their administrative staff, the NPD and Prison Department, and many others this directory could not have been produced. The publisher wishes to thank them all.

Abbreviations

aco	Assistant Chief Officer
cclo	Crown Court Liaison Officer
co	Chief Officer
csa	Community Service Assistant
cso	Community Services Officer
dco	Deputy Chief Officer
js	Job-sharing
mclo	Magistrates' Court Liaison Officer
p	Part-time
pao	Principal Administrative Officer
psco	Probation Service Court Officer
psa	Probation Service Assistant
pso	Probation Service Officer
qa mgr	Quality Assurance Manager
spo	Senior Probation Officer
ssw	Senior Social Worker
sw	Social Worker
vlo	victim liaison officer

PROBATION DIRECTORY
2006

Compiled by Owen Wells

Shaw & Sons Limited